Related books of interest

Introduction to Competence-Based Social Work: The Profession of Caring, Knowing and Serving
Michael E. Sherr and Johnny M. Jones

Interviewing for the Helping Professions: A Relational Approach
Fred McKenzie

New Perspectives on Poverty: Policies, Programs, and Practice
Elissa D. Giffords and Karen R. Garber

Modern Social Work Theory, Fourth Edition
Malcolm Payne

Straight Talk about Professional Ethics, Second Edition
Kim Strom-Gottfried

Spirituality, Religion, and Faith in Psychotherapy: Evidence-Based Expressive Methods for Mind, Brain, and Body
Helen Land

Cross-Cultural Practice: Social Work with Diverse Populations
Karen V. Harper and Jim Lantz

Social Work Practice with Latinos: Key Issues and Emerging Themes
Rich Furman and Nalini Negi

Getting Your MSW: How to Survive and Thrive in a Social Work Program, Second Edition
Karen M. Sowers and Bruce A. Thyer

CULTURALLY GROUNDED SOCIAL WORK

SECOND EDITION

Diversity, OPPRESSION & CHANGE

FLAVIO FRANCISCO MARSIGLIA

STEPHEN KULIS

Arizona State University

OXFORD
UNIVERSITY PRESS

OXFORD
UNIVERSITY PRESS

Oxford University Press is a department of the University of Oxford.
It furthers the University's objective of excellence in research, scholarship,
and education by publishing worldwide.

Oxford   New York
Auckland   Cape Town   Dar es Salaam   Hong Kong   Karachi
Kuala Lumpur   Madrid   Melbourne   Mexico City   Nairobi
New Delhi   Shanghai   Taipei   Toronto

With offices in
Argentina   Austria   Brazil   Chile   Czech Republic   France   Greece
Guatemala   Hungary   Italy   Japan   Poland   Portugal   Singapore
South Korea   Switzerland   Thailand   Turkey   Ukraine   Vietnam

Oxford is a registered trade mark of Oxford University Press
in the UK and certain other countries.

Published in the United States of America by
Oxford University Press
198 Madison Avenue, New York, NY 10016

The painting on the cover is a watercolor by Richard Hull.

Library of Congress Cataloging-in-Publication Data

Marsiglia, Flavio Francisco.
    Diversity, oppression, and change: culturally grounded social work / Flavio Francisco
Marsiglia and Stephen Kulis, Arizona State University.—Second Edition.
        pages   cm
    Includes bibliographical references and index.
    ISBN 978-0-19-061551-2
    1. Social service and race relations.   2. Social work with minorities.   3. Social work
with indigenous peoples.   I. Kulis, Stephen Stanley, 1953–   II. Title.
HV41.M282   2015
361.3—dc23
                                                            2014002305

*This book is dedicated
to the memory of our mothers—
Lucia and Dottie—
who taught us so much
about cultural diversity and resiliency.*

Contents

PART IV
The Profession of Social Work Grounded in Culture

Figures, Tables, and Notes from the Field

Figures

Tables

Notes from the Field

Preface to the Second Edition

This book is the result of a concerted effort to advance the theoretical and applied underpinnings of a culturally grounded approach to social work practice. It explores cultural diversity and its relationship to oppression and transformative action in the context of social work education at both the undergraduate and graduate levels. This book was born in part out of the need for a text that explicitly addresses the dynamic intersectionalities among identities based on race or ethnicity, gender, sexual orientation, social class, religion, and ability status. The culturally grounded perspective presented here aims at making accessible culturally specific ways of helping that are not generally part of mainstream social work practice methods. In these pages, the social worker is seen as a learner and as an advocate capable of integrating community assets as the foundation for any intervention.

Most social work programs infuse cultural diversity content throughout their courses, and many require students to take courses that specifically examine cultural diversity, oppression, and race and ethnicity. We have participated in the design of diversity-specific courses and currently teach a course entitled Diversity and Oppression in the Social Work Context. This book emerged out of these teaching experiences, the burgeoning literature on the subject, findings from our own culturally grounded professional practice and research, and the shared perspectives gained from dialogue with students, community members, and colleagues. The book attempts to improve social work practice by breaking through the compartmentalized methods that are currently used to teach social work practice.

Because many readers are members or allies of cultural minorities who often travel across real or imaginary cultural boundaries, these materials are presented not out of a postcolonial need to explain identity groups to the uninformed, but rather as a means of viewing cultural diversity as a strength within current social work practice. We have purposely attempted to avoid the laundry-list approach of reviewing one by one all cultural groups and identities. That method runs the risk of omitting, underemphasizing, or overemphasizing certain groups. Instead, we stress concepts that can be applied in a variety of social contexts and with different cultural communities while at the same time reviewing core cultural norms of selected groups as illustrations or examples of those concepts.

For some time in social work circles and allied professions, culturally grounded social work practice has been understood as a form of practice deliberately embedded in the culture of the client. Over time, this approach has emerged as an indigenous alternative response to Eurocentric approaches to social work that rely on an implicit Westernized belief that there can and should be a mainstream, standardized, and culturally neutral form of practice and that focus on the materialistic and individual aspects of human beings (Schiele, 1997). Culturally grounded social work is firmly rooted in the rich soil of culture. This book facilitates a process of gaining awareness about the nutrients present in that fertile ground and suggests attitudes and behaviors for culturally grounded social work practice.

Although the point of departure and key focus of this book is ethnicity and race, throughout the text there is an infusion of content on gender, sexual orientation, ability status, and social class. The main purpose of this integration is to advance the concept of intersectionality—that is, the belief that humans form identities that are culturally multidimensional and beautifully complex. For example, at an intake interview, a European American social worker forms initial impressions of Sharon as a middle-class African American heterosexual woman, but learns that she identifies herself as Afro-Caribbean lesbian. Sharon's presenting problem may be related to the pressure she feels to define herself according to society's rigid classifications of race, gender, and sexual orientation. By listening to her stories, the social worker starts to understand who Sharon is and honestly question, revise, or dismiss any preconceived ideas or labels she imposed on her.

This book is as much about social workers as it is about the people they work with, but the clients are the focus of the inquiry. It is the social worker rather than the consumer or client who is presented as the other—not to induce guilt, but as an exercise in awareness. This personal awareness enables social workers to overcome obstacles that may arise when there are differences between them and those they work with. Professionals may or may not share the norms and values of the individuals and communities they encounter, but they are ethically mandated to avoid imposing their own values on them and are called on to work with all oppressed and vulnerable populations.

Regardless of one's cultural roots, as products and members of academe, all practitioners are subject to the acculturative effects of higher education. This influence can lead to the adoption of white-, heterosexual-, male-, and middle class–oriented attitudes that can set up boundaries that become obstacles between practitioners, their communities of origin, and the people they serve. This book provides social workers and other practitioners with an understanding of the complex intersectionalities of cultural and other group identities through the introduction of culturally grounded social work practice, which aims at helping social workers to work effectively in collaboration with individuals and communities from different cultural backgrounds.

Throughout the text, the reader is prompted to ask him- or herself the existential question, "Who am I?" Answering this question entails an ongoing examination of perceptions of self vis-à-vis one's clients. Through this journey, social workers are invited to ask themselves how they are perceived by the individuals, families, groups, and communities with whom they work. Whom, and what, do they represent through their professional interactions? Issues of race, ethnicity, social class, gender, sexual orientation, and ability status—both their own status and those of their clients—are key factors that influence how they answer these questions. This self-awareness helps workers maintain their honesty and professional competency.

This text invites readers to see themselves as agents of change in partnership with individuals, groups, and communities. In order to help readers embrace such a role completely and competently, the text delves into the history and contemporary experiences of selected communities. Oppression and inequality are addressed as the essential context in which culturally grounded social work practice takes place. Social work is presented as a means to help individuals and communities move toward liberation in the manner advocated by the Brazilian philosopher Paulo Freire—that is, by recognizing both the roots of their oppression and their collective and individual resources for social action and lasting change.

Culture is approached as a means of individual and community strength and as a source of identity that nurtures humans on their individual and collective journeys. Culture is a lens through which people understand their lives, needs, and possibilities, and is a framework through which they construct their dreams and gain the support necessary to make them a reality. Culture may also contain restrictions, constraints, and negative messages that can become the basis for differentiation, scapegoating, and oppression. Practitioners can approach the cultural views and beliefs of their clients with honest curiosity and see their cultural differences, but not as a barrier to be overcome, bypassed, altered, or finessed. Instead, culture can be approached as a needed resource to be tapped by the professional in order to achieve effective social work practice. In situations where cultural narratives are perpetuating oppressive norms and values, the social worker's role is to respectfully challenge the client to examine more deeply the foundation or genesis of their cultural assumptions.

The word "culture" is commonly associated with tangible objects: artifacts such as an impressionist painting or a classical opera are considered high culture, while reality television shows and popular music are seen as examples of low culture. This book, however, views culture in a more expansive way, as a very dynamic and collective process. Culture inspires and connects people. It is spoken and unspoken; it is often maintained and preserved through symbols and symbolism. It needs boundaries to survive and to be identifiable. The boundaries are dynamic and constantly shifting, always producing new sets of insiders and outsiders. Culture requires interpretation and a context for those interpretations; it needs a community in order to exist and transform itself. Culture is so pervasive that it is a constant factor in the social worker–client relationship.

In these postmodern times, culture can be appreciated as a multidimensional and multilayered phenomenon—as the sum of many levels of meaning. An individual's culture is the result of the intersection of factors such as ethnicity, gender, sexual orientation, ability status, acculturation status, immigration status, religion, and social class. Cultures also have a history and carry a narrative about their origins and how they came to be what they are today. For that reason, it is important to examine the oppression of cultural minority groups from historical and sociological perspectives. An outsider seeking basic information about an individual's cultural background may perceive intersectionality as a confusing web of meanings that do not always align. The outsider may ask, "What are you?" The question presumes that there is a simple unidimensional label that fits the person's identity, but intersectionality requires a different type of question: "Who are you?" This question goes beyond old labels and honors the ways in which people explain and make sense of their lives, identity, and intersectionality. Every individual is a complex collection of identities that draw from many different types of heritages and from membership in different social groups, and the individual plays a role in how these identities are brought together. The pronoun "who" is a reminder that individuals are not objects and that it is through culture and their narratives that they become fully human.

An anti-oppressive social work stance also challenges us to ask ourselves, "For what purpose?" Too often social work interventions merely address the symptoms of a much larger structural issue. To address oppression, social workers need to look past its observable consequences (e.g., depression, unemployment, domestic violence) to address larger structural elements that maintain inequality. By identifying oppressive conditions in partnership with communities, culturally grounded social work facilitates real and lasting social change that will result in a more just society. Culturally grounded social work shares much with the anti-oppressive practice (AOP) model, which has been widely used in Australia, Canada, England, and other countries of the Commonwealth since the 1970s (Dominelli, 1998) as well as more recently in the United States (Hines, 2012). AOP aims at the "eradication of oppression through institutional and societal changes" (Sakamoto & Pitner, 2005, p. 436). Our proposed approach shares with AOP an emphasis on the unique cultural and historical experiences of communities and individuals in the conceptualization of social work practice and research (Graham, Shier, & Brownlee, 2012).

Cultural identity formation is a process or journey through which individuals integrate their contextual experiences within their communities of origin and communities of choice. Social work practice is presented as having a liberating role when it operates in partnership with oppressed cultural communities at the micro, mezzo, and macro ecological levels. This book highlights the multiple layers of meaning and the ever-changing nature of culture. It rejects static definitions of culture based on labels and outsiders' perspectives of "what" the other is.

Instead, it proposes a narrative approach where the professional learns how to listen and comes to understand step by step "who" the client is.

Traditional ways of labeling or describing a person's culture, such as referring to an individual's race, ethnicity, gender, sexual orientation, or social class, are reflections or products of a social structure that produces privilege and oppression. At the same time, race, ethnicity, gender, sexual orientation, and social class are sources of identity, peoplehood, and support. Social work and other allied professions are called through these pages to embrace the "who" paradigm and, in partnership with communities, overcome the "what" paradigm that deters change and perpetuates oppression. Labels can be a source of oppression, while the embrace of identities can be a source of strength and can carry the promise of liberation.

Information about selected communities and identity groups is presented as part of a framework for examining attitudes toward difference, and to suggest culturally specific professional attitudes and behaviors. The text provides both theoretical foundations and specific approaches for a humanistic social work practice that recognizes the strengths and resiliency inherent in the cultures of individuals, groups, and communities.

The overall aims of this book are (1) to provide a foundation for culturally grounded social work practice; (2) to explain how the intersectionality of social factors affects the client; (3) to foster an understanding of how the intersectionality of factors affects the social worker; (4) to strengthen critical thinking skills in analyzing oneself, other individuals, community, and society; and (5) to provide readers with the knowledge and skills needed to move beyond cultural awareness into social action and change.

The content of this book is organized into four main areas: an introduction to the culturally grounded approach, a review of the key theories on which the approach rests, an exploration of key identity factors, and an application of the culturally grounded approach to the social work profession.

Examples and illustrations of key concepts are presented throughout the text. The purpose of these case studies is to promote critical thinking and integration of knowledge. These case studies can be used to conduct small-group class exercises or for individual reflection. This is a possible discussion guide:

1. Summarize the content. What does it say?
2. Share your reactions, both intellectual (e.g., vis-à-vis new or old knowledge, confusion, stimulation) and emotional (e.g., anger, sadness, happiness, validation), to the material.
3. Universalize the content. What are the broad implications of this content for society?
4. Personalize the content. What are the applications and implications for you as an individual and as a professional?
5. Discuss other social work practice, policy, and research implications.

We encourage readers to integrate the content of this book by asking themselves throughout, "How do the concepts and issues presented here apply to the communities I am working with?" Further, we encourage you to use your own personal experiences and the narratives you collect from your work with diverse communities as the compass that guides your efforts to become a culturally grounded practitioner. We wish you a fruitful journey.

Acknowledgments

We would like to acknowledge the students and community partners of Arizona State University; our ongoing dialogue with them has informed and motivated us in writing this book. We thank our publisher David Follmer for his kindness and support throughout this process. Many colleagues and graduate assistants have also provided ongoing support. We especially wish to thank our dedicated graduate student Jaime Booth and colleague Monica Parsai for their support with this second edition. Other reviewers and supporters during the first edition were David Becerra, Myriam Hillin, Jennifer Jacobson, Julieann Nagoshi, Veronica Peña, Jason Castillo, Kathryn Shahan, Evelyn Hawkins, Robert Leighninger, Ben Robinson, Ellie Yepez, and Paz Zorita. We also acknowledge our gratitude to Howard Goldstein and Eugene Litwak, whose mentorship early in our careers expanded our lens, appreciation, and toolkit for studying cultural diversity.

Part I

Cultural Diversity and Social Work

1

Culture

CULTURE AND CULTURAL DIFFERENCES HAVE HISTORICALLY HAD A MAJOR influence on the development of modern nations. Current international issues such as immigration, globalization, violence and wars sparked by ethnic and religious conflict, and fast-developing economies have influenced the social work profession and present a new set of opportunities and challenges for those in this field. As ideas about cultural diversity broaden in scope, social work as a profession is asking itself anew how culture affects the way people think and behave. Through their practice, social workers recognize culture as a source of strength for individuals and communities, and at the same time often identify differences in culture that can create cultural boundaries, leading to discrimination, isolation, and a lack of access to resources for ethnic minority clients. These cultural differences may also create a barrier between the social worker and the client. If the social work professional does not acknowledge the differences in class and culture between the social worker and the client, then she or he will not be able to work effectively with the client. Social workers need to develop cultural competency not only to understand how culture affects the client, but also to move beyond simple cultural labels and develop a sense of the cultural identity of the client. Although social workers can never be fully knowledgeable about all other cultures, which would be challenging if not impossible, they can have "cultural competence," or the awareness of difference and a genuine acknowledgment of not knowing. A culturally competent social work practice creates space for dialogue and the exploration of each individual's realities, which are often shaped by multiple intersecting identities. This chapter provides social work students with an understanding of culture, how it affects individual behavior, and how social workers can acknowledge cultural differences and acquire the skills necessary to work with members of different cultural backgrounds.

When asked to describe their culture, social work students offer an array of revealing responses. They are likely to mention personal qualities or personality characteristics, such as distinctive ways of communicating and expressing emotion (e.g., "We are comfortable with loud disagreements," "We all hug a lot"). Some refer to their professional culture and shared social work values, such as the value they place on helping others. Still others connect culture to family but cast it in terms of the roles they play as daughters, sons, or parents (e.g., "We are always there for each other"). Other students are puzzled by the question and wonder if they belong to a distinctive culture at all. The students who respond by explicitly connecting their own culture to race, ethnicity, gender, social class, or sexual orientation tend to come from groups that are not always considered part of the mainstream culture. For example, students are more likely to describe their culture as Japanese American, Jewish, African American, or gay than as upper-middle class, heterosexual, or white. As the class discussion progresses, it often becomes clear that some students feel uncomfortable identifying any cultural differences that set them apart from others, as if such differences need to be deemphasized because they are irrelevant to the professional role of the social worker or are obstacles to understanding one another.

The discomfort and avoidance surrounding the topic of culture have many sources: lack of the right vocabulary, a fear of creating distance, or reluctance to acknowledge the cultural differences and power differentials that exist between social workers and their clients. Although it may be difficult to identify some aspects of culture, or individuals may feel uncomfortable sharing those aspects, conversations about culture are necessary rehearsals for negotiating the cultural differences between the social worker and the client that are an essential part of social work practice.

Recognizing the influence of culture is a necessary first step to the application of a culturally grounded approach. Culture and cultural differences are elusive topics in part because culture is both an outcome and a process that arises from the meaningful interaction of people. Culture is often defined as a group's distinctive way of life as reflected in its language, values, and norms of behavior. Although cultural background influences the way people think and act, many take these cultural influences for granted and often are unaware of their profound impact on their lives and the lives of others. Members of cultural minorities, however, do not have the privilege of forgetting about their cultural background. Their minority status is always present, affecting their daily thoughts, conversations, and interactions, and often reminding them that others view and treat them as different.

Still, culture is much more than a way of distinguishing groups according to their differences. Culture not only is a distinctive set of prescriptions about how to act and what to expect in the world, but also is a source of strength and inspiration that helps people cope with the daily stressors they face. When social workers welcome culture into the client-worker relationship, they allow for the utilization of the full range of resources that the clients bring with them and a more accurate interpretation of behavior.

Culture often needs to be interpreted and understood in its social context because behaviors become meaningful in a community when they are repeated and encoded and eventually take on symbolic value. Codes are the identifiable categories of behaviors or practices repeated over time. For example, in Iranian culture, as in many other non-Western cultures, male friends and family members greet each other with two kisses, signifying familiarity, friendship, and trust in their culture. In many countries people wear black as a sign of mourning. In Egyptian culture, people use their right hand to interact with others; for anyone to use the left would be offensive. These codes become the backbone of culture. Once certain behaviors and their corresponding norms and values become familiar to a cultural group, its members develop expectations about what practices are appropriate in given situations. Some of these expectations can become resources and strengths that nurture, protect, and inspire individuals and community members toward social participation and well-being. Although those codes or behaviors are easily recognizable among members of a cultural group (insiders), they can easily go unrecognized by members of another cultural group (outsiders). Even to insiders these codes may be so commonplace that they are not identified as aspects of culture that can present a challenge when these norms and values are perpetuating oppressive narratives. Social workers' cultural awareness guides them as they navigate the uncharted waters of unfamiliar cultures and helps them recognize and decipher cultural codes in order to maintain high levels of professional competence and effectiveness.

Culture provides the filters through which women and men look at their lives and the lives of those in their social environments. Through culture, people find connections and solidarity as they view and interpret the world around them (Takaki, 1993). Cultures are identifiable constellations of shared ideas and values, a guide to how people are expected to think and behave in their community. Culture allows people to share their interpretations of the past as well as the future. These shared ideas and beliefs change over time and are connected to a particular geographic place and a particular time in history. Culture is dynamic and is constantly evolving in its social and political context. In addition, not all members of a cultural group respond in the same way to their common culture: individuals vary in their level of adherence to the collective norms and often may have their own unique interpretations of the cultural worlds they inhabit. It is therefore important for social workers to understand the value of culture and its influence on individuals, but it is also important for social workers to be aware of these potential individual differences within a cultural group so they do not perpetuate cultural or group stereotypes.

CULTURAL IDENTITY AND CULTURAL BOUNDARIES

Cultural identity refers to the set of values held by a community and its corresponding worldview. The two combine to form a referential framework that in turn influences both the relationship among individuals within that society and their collective sense of identity. Although a community has a shared cultural

identity, individuals within that community have unique expressions of that collective identity. Social class, race, ethnicity, religion, and language make important contributions to an individual's cultural identity. Cultural identity is present
in the institutions, the habits and traditions, and the knowledge that define any
society. Virtually all societies have more than one culture, each marked by its own
language or languages, diet, manners, and other characteristics. The coexistence
of multiple cultures creates a system of social stratification, where differences of
social class, power, and prestige can emerge among groups. Those differences are
enforced through boundaries that groups develop and enforce over time. Through
boundaries, people learn what is permissible and what is not permissible. Individual cultural identities are shaped and are affected by those boundaries. For example, some identity choices may be encouraged, while others may not be available
to members of a group. Some members may have access to—and be expected to
pursue or take advantage of—certain resources such as higher education, while
other members may not perceive that they have access to such resources.

In contemporary society, most people find themselves crossing cultural
boundaries on a regular basis in their daily lives. Our world has become much
more interdependent as a result of the development of technology and the afford-
ability of modes of transportation that facilitate traveling. Social workers often
work with immigrants and refugees, and/or are called to assist in humanitarian
efforts (Estes, 2009). Historically, countries around the world have had a variety
of responses to the movement of people across borders, with some attempting to
restrict movement and others taking a more welcoming stance. Regardless of
formal immigration policies, people cross both real and virtual cultural boundaries daily. Some may say that interacting with people who look, speak, dress, or
think in ways that are different from what is perceived as the norm is a form of
daily cultural boundary crossing. Most cultural groups are constantly exposed to
a great variety of outside cultural influences, resulting in an ongoing cultural
transaction where individuals adopt aspects of other cultures. Although culture is
dynamic and changing, the mixture of cultural influences does not result in a
simple blend where all cultures add equally to an evolving recipe. For those who
are outside what is considered the cultural mainstream, cultural change occurs
through a variety of processes that can involve assimilation, acculturation, and
enculturation.

ASSIMILATION

Assimilation is the process of letting go of one's culture of origin while incorporating norms and behaviors of the majority or dominant culture. The unidirectional nature of this process cannot be solely explained by numbers or the relative
size of the cultural groups. A dominant culture can be a numerical minority but

have the most power and the ability to enforce its supremacy over a larger cultural group. For example, in some cities in the southwestern United States, Latino students are in the numerical majority, but laws forbid schools to teach in Spanish. Many Latino students are forced in elementary school to speak exclusively in English and later find that in high school they need to enroll in Spanish classes to relearn the language and fulfill the foreign language requirement. Assimilation describes a unidirectional process shaped by power differentials and assumptions about difference that are often illogical or simply false.

Assimilation involves activities by which a minority group abandons the unique features of its culture of origin and adapts to the values and behaviors of the dominant culture. Often the dominant group accepts some limited aspects of the minority group's cultural or social life, and both groups become integrated into a common social structure. Assimilation can be both cultural and structural. Cultural assimilation occurs when two or more groups develop a common culture that is based on the dominant group's culture, into which minor aspects of the minority group culture are incorporated. Structural assimilation occurs when two or more groups participate in the same social institutions, organizations, and interpersonal networks—for example, through intermarriage, workplace integration, and overlapping friendships (friendships between members of majority and minority ethnic and racial groups that require the members of minority groups to adjust to the norms and behaviors of the friend representing the dominant group)—and when they hold equal positions in these social structures (Healey, 2011). The barriers to cultural and structural integration may include the prejudice and discrimination that differences in phenotype (racial or ethnic appearance), language, and surnames may breed (Ayers, Kulis, & Marsiglia, 2013).

ACCULTURATION AND ENCULTURATION

Because culture is a dynamic process, culture of origin is just one ingredient in the formation of cultural identity. The acculturation process allows individuals to integrate elements of other cultures as they develop their new identities. Acculturation is a form of cultural synthesis that takes place when the original norms, values, and behaviors are mixed and changed by new influences. The process is influenced by differences in public policy, social class, power, and prestige. Although minority cultures generally experience stronger pressure to change than do mainstream cultures, the majority culture often voluntarily absorbs desired aspects of the minority culture. Thus acculturation is not a unidirectional process but is instead multidirectional and multidimensional. White middle-class teenagers may incorporate the dress and mode of speech of their Mexican American or African American classmates. They have a choice whether or not to incorporate these behaviors, while their minority classmates may feel that they need to speak and dress like their white classmates in order to advance academically and professionally.

Acculturation is the process of adapting to a non-native culture that occurs when individuals from different cultures come into contact with each other. Acculturation occurs in two distinct dimensions. Behavioral acculturation relates to the adoption of external aspects of the dominant culture, such as language and social skills that allow the individual to fit in. Psychological acculturation relates to an individual's degree of concordance with the ideologies of the dominant culture or its way of thinking and seeing the world (cosmology). These two forms of acculturation run along parallel paths but do not necessarily occur at the same pace (Van Oudenhoven, Judd, & Ward, 2008).

Acculturation models were developed during the first half of the twentieth century to explain the experiences of different groups of European migrants who entered the United States in successive waves, and who initially faced much discrimination and had to make difficult adjustments. These groups became accepted and assimilated into U.S. educational, economic, political, and social institutions within three generations, during which time there was widespread intermarriage across ethnic group lines. These original assimilationist models proposed a linear and progressive process of acculturation into the mainstream culture; these models are less applicable to today's immigrants. Among the key differences between the early twentieth-century European immigrants and many twenty-first century immigrants from Latin America, the Caribbean, Asia, and Africa is the intensity and duration of the experience of discrimination and the greater ease of maintaining contact with the culture of origin fostered by less expensive and more convenient communication and transportation options. A century ago, first-generation European immigrants faced opposition from native-born Americans who questioned their loyalties and feared they would compete for the same jobs. Today, however, the second and third generations of immigrant families often confront these same obstacles. The self-identification of the children, grandchildren, and even great-grandchildren of Mexican immigrants as just as Mexican as American may be a reflection of discrimination and a reaction to their perception of unequal treatment and less-than-full acceptance by mainstream U.S. culture, rather than of their unwillingness to acculturate.

For instance, a study of children of Latin American background born in the United States who experienced discrimination showed that they were less likely to self-identify as Americans than their classmates. This was true even among some third-generation Latinos, but the effects of discrimination were less apparent for Latino children who phenotypically look white (Golash-Boza, 2006). Waters (1994), in her study of second-generation West Indian and Haitian American adolescents in New York City, found three types of identities: a black American identity, a hyphenated ethnic or national origin identity (e.g., Jamaican-American), and an immigrant identity. The different identities reflected the youths' different perceptions of the impact of race on their social and economic opportunities in the United States. The youths who identified with a black American identity tended to experience more racial discrimination than those who identified with a West Indian identity.

Similar trends have been found in international comparisons. The process of acculturation is influenced by the political and economic climate in the receiving country at the time of immigration. This varies from country to country and at different points in history. For example, immigrants' ability to obtain documented status, a process that varies greatly from country to country, has a significant influence on their opportunities for fuller integration into the receiving country (Warfa et al., 2012). In a comparison of Somali refugees' immigration experiences in London and Minneapolis, employment status was the strongest predictor of well-being, with individuals in Minneapolis reporting higher rates of employment (Warfa et al., 2012). When considering employment and contextual factors such as integration services, the economic climate and discriminatory hiring processes within countries could have a significant impact on the desire and ability to acculturate to the dominant culture. An immigrant's experience of discrimination, which is a reflection of an overall national attitude toward immigration, also determines an individual's decision to acculturate (Berry, Phinney, Sam, & Vedder, 2006). Immigrants who feel accepted and comfortable in the receiving country are more likely to adopt norms and values of that country. If they are frustrated with their ability to meet their basic needs, or if feel they like an outsider, they are more likely to actively seek to maintain strong ties to their culture of origin. For Russian and Ukrainian Jewish adolescents migrating to Israel, experiences of discrimination diminished their initial intention to acculturate over and above a variety of other individual factors including psychological resources (Tartakovsky, 2012). Similar to trends observed in the United States, the political, economic, and social context of the receiving country influences the process of acculturation for recent immigrants.

The cultural adaptation of the children of immigrants is often described as problematic or troubled. Andall (2002) speaks of a second-generation decline, a second-generation revolt, and a second-generation attitude. Second-generation decline describes unwillingness among children of immigrants to accept low-paying and low-status jobs that leave them stranded outside the mainstream economy. Second-generation revolt refers to rejection among children of immigrants of elements of mainstream culture and its opportunities for social mobility, such as the value of education as the pathway to success. Second-generation attitude refers to the greater assertiveness of the children of immigrants compared to their parents, and the resulting intergenerational conflicts. The heightened awareness of children of immigrants of their status as both insiders and outsiders shapes the way they construct and navigate their hyphenated identities, as well as the paths that they pursue in their social, economic, and political lives.

One classic typology describes four possible outcomes for those undergoing the acculturation process: assimilation, which replaces the culture of origin with the host culture; integration of elements of the culture of origin with those of the host culture; separation through the strict maintenance of the culture of origin; and marginalization through a rejection of both the host and origin cultures (Sam & Berry, 2010). Related studies have found that members of cultural minority groups with greater differences from the mainstream culture are not well accepted by the host society. They have limited opportunities to choose among these different pathways of acculturation, and many either feel pressure to assimilate, or become marginalized socially and economically (Loch, 2009). The experience of male Caribbean immigrants exemplifies this situation. The pressure to replace the more polarized attitudes and behaviors regarding gender roles of Caribbean culture with a more gender-neutral and egalitarian perspective can heighten acculturation stress; this pressure contributes to their relationship problems, addictive behavior, and mental illness (Kosberg, 2002). When working with clients of different cultures, social workers use culturally competent assessment methods to understand their acculturation status. For example, ethnographic interviewing is a method that may be used to understand the experiences and worldviews of individuals and families from cultural minorities (Center for Advanced Studies in Child Welfare [CASCW], 2001). This type of assessment helps workers uncover possible acculturation stress and identify how the ethnic community may be a source of strength and assistance for those community members to cope with stress.

Enculturation is the process of connecting back to the culture of origin or to a renewed and recreated version of it. Rather than simply maintaining the elements of a culture of origin, enculturation involves recapturing that culture by learning about it, identifying with it, and reinforcing its basic norms and values. For researchers and practitioners who work with ethnic minority communities, the concept of enculturation redirects attention toward the strengths of minority cultures and their inherent cultural resiliencies. Through enculturation, individuals can become anchored in their cultures of origin by practicing aspects of the traditional culture and by identifying with that culture (DryWater-Whitekiller, 2006; HeavyRunner & Marshall, 2003). Enculturation takes into account the cultural strengths of ethnic minority communities, helps people reinforce or reclaim their cultural heritage, and renews their sense of community belongingness, all of which lead to increases in overall subjective well-being (Yoon, Hacker, Hewitt, Abrams, & Cleary, 2012).

Enculturation is especially relevant to First Nations or Native Americans, African Americans, and Chicanos because of the many historical efforts there have been to destroy and disconnect them from their original cultures, and to force them to assimilate into the white mainstream without fully accepting them. The rites of passage developed by African American communities in the United States and by other peoples of the African diaspora that aim at connecting youths to ancestral African rituals as a source of resiliency are a form of enculturation. Urban First Nations or Native American communities and some tribal communities have promoted enculturation through traditional community-based support systems for their members. Prevention interventions sometimes use an enculturation approach to connect to culture of origin as a ritualistic or cultural source of resiliency. The Chicano movement has used enculturation as a means to reconnect with the Native American cultural aspects of Chicano precolonial identity of Mexican heritage communities in the Southwestern United States.

Assimilation, acculturation, and enculturation tend to stress culture over other factors in the formation of cultural identity. Cultural identity and cultural processes are often shaped by ideas about race and the existence of racial groups.

RACE

The United States is a race-conscious society, and racial lines of demarcation still influence people's access to social and economic opportunities, as well as how individuals interact with one another in everyday life and how they are treated by the justice system. For example, 85 percent of the individuals stopped and frisked as part of a citywide law-enforcement policy implemented in New York City from 2002 to 2012 were people of color, 90 percent of whom were released without ever being charged with a crime (el-Ghobashy & Saul, 2013). The fact that racism has persisted in the United States is remarkable in light of the codification of laws requiring equal treatment regardless of race. The persistence of racial distinctions in social life is also remarkable given the fact that race, as a biological concept, has not survived the test of scientific scrutiny. Humans cannot be categorized reliably based on phenotypical characteristics, such as those aspects of physical appearance like skin color, hair texture, and bone structure that are often thought to be markers of one's racial background. Such categorization is a discredited idea that is a vestige of nineteenth-century phrenology, the study of the human skull based on the belief that mental faculties and personality could be determined from its shape (Staum, 2003).

Advancements in DNA analysis have allowed scientists to trace historical patterns of migration across the globe through genetic similarities and differences among people living in different regions of the world. Even as these efforts uncover evidence of distinctive genetic markers among those who can be traced to common ancestors, this research has added to the evidence that pure races have never existed because humans cannot reliably be distinguished genetically from one another along racial lines. Indeed, genetic research has shown that humans who are labeled as belonging to distinct racial groups are, in fact, virtually indistinguishable genetically. This inability to find systematic genetic or biological variations that can reliably classify individuals by race has led researchers to conclude that the concept of race has no basis in genetics or biology. Rather, externally observable differences like skin color and facial features are influenced by evolutionary natural selection. For example, degree of skin pigmentation is explained as an adaptation to strong or weak sunlight. However, individuals who have similar skin color as a result of such adaptation may be genetically very different, whereas individuals who do not have similar skin color because of different selective forces may be genetically quite similar (Bamshad & Olson, 2003). Nonetheless, racial categorizations continue to influence people's perception of differences among individuals in skin color, hair texture, eye shape, height, and other physical characteristics. Highlighting the fact that meanings associated with race are socially constructed, these differences are matters of perception, not genetics, and the meaning assigned to these differences varies across societies and even within societies. In the United States there is a growing consensus among anthropologists and historians that approaching race as a biological phenomenon is inaccurate (see Smedley & Smedley, 2005).

There is also consensus around the idea that race should be viewed as a socially constructed concept rather than as a biological fact. That is, race has taken on such importance because of the cultural and social meanings that people learn to attach to it. These meanings develop through a social and historical process of racial formation, in which racial categories are created, altered, and sometimes discarded (Massey, 2009; Omi & Winant, 1998). The prime purpose of racial formation is to establish a hierarchy and target certain groups for discrimination. People are taught to believe that there are racial groups with distinctive characteristics, and that some races are innately superior or inferior to others, thereby justifying the dominance of one over the other. The history of slavery in the United States epitomizes such dominance. Even Abraham Lincoln, the president who issued the Emancipation Proclamation, echoed the prejudicial sentiments of his time in the years just before he assumed the presidency:

> I will say then that I am not, nor ever have been in favor of bringing about in any way the social and political equality of the white and black races, [applause]—that I am not nor ever have been in favor of making voters or jurors of negroes, nor of qualifying them to hold office, nor to intermarry with white people, and I will say in addition to this that there is a *physical difference* between the white and black races which I believe will forever forbid the two races living together on terms of social and political equality. And inasmuch as they cannot so live, while they do remain together, *there must be the position of superior and inferior,* and I as much as any other man am in favor of having the superior position assigned to the white race. (Lincoln quoted in Angle, 1991, p. 235, emphasis added)

Racism—the subordination of any person or group because of some physically distinctive characteristic—has been a central element in the foundation of the United States and its economic, political, social, and cultural development

(Feagin, Johnson, & Rush, 2000). Although science has provided sufficient evidence to demonstrate that humans share a common biological and genetic heritage across racial lines, the social experience of race needs to be recognized and integrated into a culturally grounded approach to social work. Because the client's perception of the race of the social worker can influence the dynamics of the working relationship, it is necessary for the social worker to understand how race is experienced by clients, as well as to understand negative preconceptions the clients may have toward the social worker. This understanding can be achieved only through open dialogue that allows for the exploration of different experiences of race in America. Other societies have dealt with race and racism differently. For example, Canada follows a multicultural approach that deemphasizes race and in theory reduces racism; some contemporary Canadian scholars, however, have created controversy by saying that Canada is still racist after all these years (Marcellin, Bauer, & Schein, 2013). Cultivating such awareness helps social workers to foster collaboration and achieve positive outcomes.

ETHNICITY AND RACE

Despite the constantly evolving notions of what race is, what it signifies, and how prominent it is in the lives of communities, the enduring legacy of racism is one reason that race and racial identity cannot be ignored in efforts to understand cultural diversity. This book approaches race as one of several important dimensions of culture, with which it often overlaps. In the United States, as in other race-conscious societies, it is difficult to ignore the belief that race exists. As helping professionals, social workers walk the fine line of recognizing and acknowledging the impact of racism while reducing the human experience to narrow racial terms.

Ethnicity is another construct that can be applied to the human experience of cultural distinctiveness, and one where the boundary lines separating people into groups sometimes—but not always—run parallel with racial differences. In the 1970s the Reverend Jesse Jackson advocated the use of the ethnically based term "African American" instead of the racially based term "black." He shifted attention from reductionist phenotypical characteristics to cultural traits that unify and empower a community.

In addition, ethnicity and race intersect with other key social characteristics, such as gender, sexual orientation, ability status, social class, acculturation, and immigration status. For example, any assessment of a client who is a Haitian immigrant and works as a doctor in a clinic for refugees and immigrants must recognize that her higher socioeconomic status (SES) and educational advantages most likely will allow her to navigate acculturation obstacles more efficiently and effectively than her patients. Because of her physical appearance, she may experience racial discrimination in ways that mirror the experiences of African Americans whose families have lived in the United States for many generations, but her cultural upbringing in Haiti provides her with a distinctive ethnic identity and a different cultural heritage. Recognizing this intersectionality helps prevent simplistic generalizations and allows for an examination of within-group as well as between-group differences. If appropriately tapped, culture as a multilayered and intersecting phenomenon can be a source of resiliency, motivation, and inspiration for individuals and communities.

Structures of oppression such as racism, sexism, ageism, nationalism, ableism, and heterosexism are not independent of each other, but rather are interrelated (Knudsen, Heckman, Cameron, & Shonkoff, 2006). These mechanisms of inclusion and exclusion result in an imbalance between the privileged and the underprivileged that is perpetuated by the media, religion, politics, schools, and institutional rules and policies.

These structures reside within culture and function in complex ways. A person may be privileged in some contexts and underprivileged in others. For example, a professional white gay male can be respected and successful in his career, and yet may feel the need to be closeted about his sexual orientation. In low SES neighborhoods, in which most residents share low income, lack opportunities for education, often lack the benefit of health insurance, and suffer many other perils, there is a gradient of oppression, with some community members being more or less oppressed based on their own personal circumstances or demographics.

In addition to intersecting identities, both construction of the meanings of race and ethnicity and the oppression that is related to being a member of a nondominant group occurs on multiple layers of the ecological system. Socially constructed meanings surrounding race, ethnicity, oppression, and privilege take place on personal, cultural, and structural levels (Mullaly, 2002). On a personal level, oppression can be internalized. Internalization happens when oppressed groups accept and perpetuate disempowering narratives about themselves. These narratives can be constructed within the group in reaction to experiencing barriers to upward mobility, or from outside the group as a tool to maintaining power structures. Internalized oppression can also result in social policing in which individuals in the subordinate group react negatively to others within the group who adapt norms and values of the dominant culture or in the form of horizontal violence. Horizontal violence refers to inappropriate ways that oppressed people may release built-up tension when they are unable to redress their oppression directly. It is a form of intergroup conflict that is manifested in overt and covert hostile behaviors, such as criticism, bickering, sabotage, undermining, infighting, scapegoating, or finger pointing (Duffy, 1995; Freire, 1970). It is associated with oppressed groups who are subject to unequal power relations that limit their self-expression and autonomy, and it may reflect internalized self-hatred and low self-esteem that result from being part of an oppressed group.

On a cultural level, oppression is apparent when a society's cultural norms and values are based exclusively on the dominant culture. This can be seen in the meaning that the headscarf (*hijab*) worn by Muslim women has assumed in Western societies. By the standards ascribed by the cultural norms of the dominant culture, *hijabs* are seen as a symbol of oppression; many women who wear the *hijab*, however, interpret the symbol as an expression of their devotion to God or as a political act of defiance (Golnaraghi & Mills, 2013; Mohanty, 1988). Like all other aspects of culture and race, there are no universal interpretations. Instead, there are wide variations in the way people interpret the same behavior or practice based on political and historical contexts. Structural oppression also occurs on an institutional level and is observed in policies that result in unequal access to resources and overrepresentation in the social service (i.e., child welfare) and criminal justice systems.

ETHNICITY AND CULTURAL IDENTITY FORMATION

Max Weber (1928/1968), in *Economy and Society*, his pioneering work on ethnic groups in Germany and the United States, used the terms *ethnische Gruppen* (ethnic group) and *ethnische Gemeinschaften* (ethnic communities) to describe ethnicity as a collective phenomenon. The collective dimension of ethnicity affects not only how people see themselves as members of an ethnic group, but also how they are seen by others. As a result, ethnic identity requires each person to behave in ethnically consistent ways so others can identify that person with an ethnic group. In a sense, for an individual to have an ethnic identity, it is just as important for others to identify the individual as a member of an ethnic group as it is for the individual to identify personally with that ethnic group.

Minority ethnic groups are differentiated from the dominant group through cultural differences based on their language, religion, attitudes toward marriage and parenting, dress, and foods. An individual cannot choose to be a member of an ethnic group without having any tangible connection to that group. Someone may follow the prescribed dress code, eat the same foods, and listen to the same music but not be recognized by the members of the group as one of them. In other words, one does not automatically gain membership in the ethnic group by mimicking ethnic customs; in fact, such actions can be seen as irreverent, even offensive. For example, crossover singers like the white rapper Eminem have been criticized as inauthentic wannabes who appropriate a culture and musical genre that is not theirs. This view represents a bipolar model of cultural identification in which ethnic group membership boundaries are sharply drawn and not readily crossed. A less discrete, more flowing multidimensional model allows for the possibility that human beings can identify simultaneously with more than one culture, and that identification with any culture can have positive implications for an individual's personal health and social well-being.

Just as an ethnic identity cannot be chosen at will, neither can it be lived in isolation. Ethnic identity requires a connection to a community and a set of shared norms and behaviors. It is with others that culture is defined, learned, celebrated, and preserved. It is also with others that members of cultural minorities change conditions of oppression. The collective nature of ethnic identity can be harnessed to spur social action that results in social change.

Anthropologists speak of ethnicity as an identity that is embraced under certain conditions. That is, people do not choose any ethnicity but do have a choice to learn about, accept, identify, and acknowledge their ethnicity. Acquiring an ethnic identity involves an individual act of affirmation of that identity and the adoption of various values and behaviors within a restricted range of possibilities (Phinney, 2003). For example, research with Asian American children shows how preadolescents assess their choices based on anticipated outcomes (Tse, 1999). The choice of embracing an Asian American identity or the choice of not embracing it brings rewards or negative consequences, and the choices children make reflect the social context in which they live. A Japanese American student attending a school that is predominantly European American may choose not to accentuate her ethnic identity or her parents' culture of origin due to the lack of acceptance of diversity or fear of rejection and discrimination. At other times, children may not be aware that their ethnicity is perceived as being different from that of the majority, particularly if they live in ethnically homogenous neighborhood enclaves. However, once they start school they may go through a stage of ambivalence, confusion, and perhaps vacillation before they identify with, reject, or selectively adopt elements of their ethnic heritage. An Asian American student may encounter racism at school, something not under her or his control. Racism, although an external force, may have a negative impact on the student's well-being and functioning as well as on her or his identity development.

There is an ongoing debate about how parents should prepare their children as they enter potentially racist environments. One point of view is that it is better not to predispose children to the idea that they will be victims of racism. Another view is that the negative effects of racism can be mitigated when parents have such conversations with their children and teach them coping strategies (Brooks & Hampton, 2005). Still others advocate collective social action that recognizes and addresses the oppressive effect of racist social structures on children. This is not an either/or conversation; these concerns highlight the need to minimize the effects of a negative environment on individuals while working toward changing the root causes of racist behaviors.

Being connected to one's ethnicity or race does not mean a separation from the larger society and its opportunities for social and economic advancement. Nonetheless, some societies convey the message that to achieve social and economic advancement, individuals must discard certain norms connected to their ethnicity or culture of origin. Making such a choice may result in a form of cultural deprivation. The ideal situation is to be able to keep what is of value in one's culture—what inspires and moves the individual—while at the same time being integrated enough into the larger society to benefit socially and economically from the full range of opportunities that are available to others. This pragmatic approach does not negate the importance of engaging in social action to change oppressive structures. The acceptance of the structures that perpetuate oppression is rewarded by providing economic and social benefits to individuals who assimilate into the dominant culture without challenging it. Individuals who do not assimilate are often denied those rewards. Social workers and other professionals have an ethical responsibility to support efforts to increase communities' access to resources and to achieve economic and social equality at the same time that oppressive structures are identified and changed. It is possible to advocate for a successful navigation of the existing system while supporting the conscientization and empowerment of oppressed groups; such advocacy ultimately results in social action that challenges and transforms the oppressive systems (Freire, 1970).

SOCIAL WORK AND CULTURAL DIVERSITY

Social workers play an important role in supporting communities to maintain the balance between social advancement and cultural preservation while engaging in social action to change oppressive social structures. Achieving this balance is the goal of culturally grounded social work. Ideally, the social worker enters the community's world in dialogue with its members and aware of any preconceived ideas she or he has about what the community's needs are or who the community members are. Identifying preconceived ideas requires an examination of one's own positionality in the existing social structure and an attitude of curiosity and acceptance about our lack of knowledge of other cultures. This level of awareness can be achieved through open dialogue with colleagues and communities about oppression and their interactions with members of the social work profession. For example, when conducting an evaluation project with a community, a social worker introduced the terms "program" and "training" into documents outlining the evaluation plan. In a meeting with the community partner, the social worker was informed that these terms had a negative connotation and that they reflected a history of paternalistic social service delivery in the community. The terms were removed and replaced with more empowering language such as "initiative" and "development." The open dialogue between the social worker and the community partner ensured cultural competence by creating the space for the conversation to occur.

Because cultural identity formation is a subjective and evolving process that involves personal choice, as well as a personal journey within the boundaries and recognition of the community, it is the task of the social worker to inquire about the client's ethnicity, gender, religion, ability status, nationality, or sexual orientation and the meaning that this identity holds for the individual. Two individuals or groups with very similar backgrounds and appearances may relate differently to these social constructions.

There is a tendency for practitioners and researchers to make ethnicity, gender, ability status, and sexual orientation fixed and sometimes mutually exclusive characteristics—the client *is* Latino or the client *is* gay—instead of understanding how ethnic and cultural differences intersect and change over time. It is at the intersection of identities that the social worker engages with the client (James & Gilliland, 2008; Tsang, 2001).

Listening to community-based narratives allows social workers to move beyond labels and to assess the client's true cultural identity. Through these stories, they learn *who* the client is instead of *what* the client is. The client becomes a subject, not an object of the work; the client plays the leading role in the story, not a supporting role. Additionally, by engaging in dialogue with clients, social workers are able to begin to identify their cultural biases and how their behavior in practice may be unconsciously perpetuating oppression. In other words, a narrative and dialogical approach facilitates culturally grounded practice, which in turn provides the opportunity for empowerment.

Historically, the social work profession has been committed to working with different ethnic and racial communities and has defined its purpose as working with the oppressed. The preamble to the Revised Version of the Code of Ethics of the National Association of Social Workers (2008) calls on social workers to be "sensitive to cultural and ethnic diversity and strive to end discrimination, oppression, poverty, and other forms of social injustice" (p. 9). As a result, social work has directed considerable attention toward issues of social reform and civil rights. Thousands of practitioners join the profession primarily because of social work's abiding concern about values germane to human rights, welfare rights, equality, and the prevention of discrimination and oppression (Reamer, 2006). Because cultural minorities are overrepresented among oppressed populations, a culturally grounded approach to practice is both natural and necessary. A culturally specific approach, however, can easily be critiqued as an exercise in divisiveness. These issues are hotly debated by social work and its allied professions.

Culturally grounded social work emerged in response to the awareness of the need for social work practice to take root in the culture of the client. Social work and its allied disciplines have developed two pathways toward a more culturally grounded approach. The first pathway stresses cultural sensitivity, and the other focuses on cultural competency. The cultural sensitivity stance calls attention to the diversity among clients and communities, focusing on the cultural gap that exists between the service delivery system and the clients it serves. Simply increasing awareness of cultural diversity, however, may or may not result in the delivery of culturally relevant services. One can be aware of or sensitive to existing differences but still be unable or unwilling to reach out effectively to specific constituencies (Gutierrez, Ortega, & Yeakley, 2000).

The cultural competency stance moves the profession a step closer to the goal of culturally grounded service delivery by emphasizing the knowledge, values, and skills needed for workers to make services culturally relevant, thereby increasing their effectiveness. In addition, this approach calls on social workers to understand the dynamics of oppression and to promote social justice by increasing their awareness of their own positionality and partnering with communities to enhance their capacity to exercise collective power within existing social structures. To engage in authentic culturally grounded practice, members of the helping professions develop both cultural sensitivity and cultural competency.

As figure 1.1 illustrates, the progression from unawareness to culturally grounded practice is not unidirectional. Rather, the steps illustrate the possibility that one can take steps back to a lower level of awareness and competency at any time. This is not a progressive and linear process; instead the journey into culturally grounded social work can be curvilinear and can take us back and forth until we reach the desired stage of awareness and culturally competent practice. When dealing with clients from various cultures, a practitioner can be operating simultaneously at different stages of the continuum.

For example, a European American practitioner who is very well versed with Mexican American culture might be located at the culturally grounded stage. She

Figure 1.1. The Culturally Grounded Practice Continuum

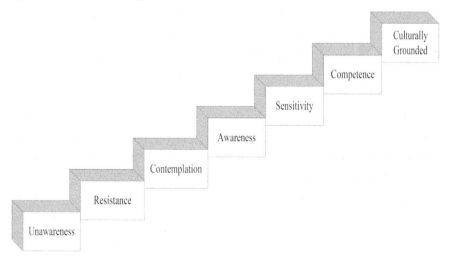

is able to access her clients' culture as a resource and to develop immediate empathy. However, she may be at the stage of unawareness when working with Filipino clients; for example, she may have no knowledge of the norms regarding gay identity within Filipino culture, which are more flexible than those within Mexican culture. She may assume that because of their common colonial experience with Spain, she can transfer her knowledge and experience working with Mexican Americans to her work with Filipino families without modifying her approach. As a result, her lack of knowledge and awareness of Filipino culture could make her ineffectual as she proposes a family intervention that she has found effective with Mexican families when one of the children shares that he is gay.

The cultural competence stance has been challenged by claims that it is unrealistic (Schiele, 2007; Yan & Wong, 2005). Critics argue that due to its very nature as a socially constructed phenomenon, culture is a moving target because, like the language that reflects it, it is an ever-evolving, emergent phenomenon. At the same time, those outside the culture produce stereotypes and biases that are very difficult to change. This point of view proposes the acceptance of the lack of competence in cross-cultural matters as an inevitable fixture of social work practice. Although this analysis provides important insights, accepting the status quo is too fatalistic a response because it does not lead to change. A more useful approach, one that is developed in partnership with communities, promotes an ongoing process of developing cultural competency and awareness of the strengths of different cultures.

CULTURALLY GROUNDED KNOWLEDGE, ATTITUDES, AND BEHAVIORS IN SOCIAL WORK

Culturally grounded social work practice is realized through the acquisition of specific *knowledge*, the development of a set of *attitudes*, and the mastery and practice of certain *behaviors* (KAB). The KAB approach was originally developed and tested in the public health field and is commonly used in research related to health issues as a model for promoting the client's involvement in health outcomes (e.g., de-Graft Aikins, Boynton, & Atanga, 2010). This approach can be expanded to include the practitioner. In the culturally grounded approach, KAB is examined in terms not only of the client's willingness and ability to change, but also of the practitioner's ability to learn and change along with the client. A culturally grounded approach to social work practice requires that practitioners identify both their strengths and their shortcomings as they integrate the different stages of the culturally grounded continuum.

The KAB framework can also be applied to the analysis of structural barriers. Structural barriers can include a lack of access to healthy foods or safe recreational spaces that limit healthy lifestyle choices, lower-quality education, or lack of employment opportunities in areas where access to transportation is limited, which may significantly stifle upward mobility. In the face of structural barriers, social workers can partner with clients to identify and assess (knowledge) the barriers, develop a sense of efficacy (attitudes), and take steps to effect social change (behavior).

In developing and strengthening these KAB dimensions, social workers use their own personal life stories as a starting point. As might be expected, social workers from backgrounds similar to their clients' do appear to have certain advantages. Among other things, they can more easily decode and interpret cultural messages than can workers from other cultures. Indeed, some researchers have argued that a cultural match between providers and clients is the only way to achieve cultural competence, while other social work researchers have labeled such a stance a form of cultural chauvinism (e.g., Taylor-Brown, Garcia, & Kingson, 2001). There is little evidence that cultural matching produces better and more-lasting results. Thus, to segregate individuals within service delivery systems seems too extreme a response to the need for cultural competency. There is certainly evidence that social service providers working with culturally similar clients do not always have an adequate understanding of their clients (Yan, 2008). Viewed from the perspective of the complexities of intersecting identities, this finding is not surprising: although practitioners and clients may have had similar experiences due to their gender or ethnicity, it is less likely that their lives overlap in their experience of social class.

Nonetheless, skillful social workers from different backgrounds can indeed learn how to competently decode and respond to culturally specific messages and behaviors. It is the culturally grounded attitudes of service providers—not simply their cultural background—that yield higher levels of client service satisfaction (Walker, 2001). The personal biography or demographic profile of a worker is no guarantee of cultural competence. An individual is not born culturally competent; rather, an individual becomes culturally competent by acquiring the necessary awareness, knowledge, and relevant skills, and developing a welcoming and affirming attitude.

The philosophy underlying a culturally grounded approach places the cultural identity of the client or consumer at the center of the social work intervention. Cultural identity that is not connected to the misuse of power or the perpetuation of privilege or oppression can be a source of resiliency. Indeed, according to the Afrocentric perspective—a perspective that places African and African American ideas and cosmology at the center of any analysis of African and African American cultures and behaviors (Asante, 2000)—cultural identity can be viewed as a source of identity, inspiration, and pride that can be used to overcome challenges and difficulties. The culturally grounded approach values what minority cultures have to offer and incorporates the community-based ways of helping into the professional interventions. Notes from the field 1.1 provides an example

---

NOTES FROM THE FIELD 1.1

The Long Bus Ride to School

Joe, an 11-year-old Apache student, is referred to Christine, the school social worker, because he is not participating in class. Mr. Andrews, his teacher, is concerned about Joe's poor performance and suspects he may be depressed.

Scenario A

Christine attempts to engage Joe in conversation without success. She asks Joe questions that touch on his relationships with his parents, siblings, and friends. Joe feels uncomfortable talking to Christine, an authority figure and someone he doesn't know. He looks withdrawn and distant and gives short and vague or evasive answers, sometimes falling into long silences. Christine also starts to feel uncomfortable and decides to refer Joe to a mental health clinic for an assessment. Her session with Joe lasts five minutes.

Scenario B

Christine attempts to engage Joe in conversation without success. She realizes that her direct questions will not help her establish rapport with Joe but instead are becoming an obstacle. After a few minutes, she suggests that they play a game. Joe is rather reticent at first but very quickly becomes involved in the game. He is having a good time and soon starts to talk about the fact that he lives far away from school. He gets up very early and often has to run out without eating breakfast. He is often hungry and sleepy until lunchtime. He does not eat breakfast at school because the county bus gets in a bit too late for him to make it before they close the cafeteria. Christine arranges to enroll Joe in the school's breakfast program and makes sure his food will be kept warm until his arrival. A week later, Mr. Andrews reports that Joe's class participation has improved significantly since his visit with the social worker.

---

of how a practitioner checked her ethnocentrism. She did not utilize very specialized skills, just some common sense and cultural awareness. She knew that in some Native American cultures direct questioning is not the norm, and that it might make some Native American clients uncomfortable. Practitioners can be more effective in developing rapport with clients by using icebreakers before asking direct questions. Quick reactions and faulty first impressions are common. When the client's communication is slower than expected, before labeling or clinically diagnosing the client, the practitioner may need to ask not only why the client is not communicating as expected, but also why the practitioner expected a different type of interaction in the first place. Although it was not addressed in the field notes, this social worker could also handle this presenting problem on a more structural level by examining why this student has to travel so far to school or why he does not have access to food in the home. By examining the larger barriers to receiving breakfast before school, the social worker has the opportunity to consider larger forms of oppression that may be affecting this case.

PRIVILEGE AND EMPATHY

Privilege is the sum of the unearned advantages of special group membership. A social worker from a developed country working for a year in a war- and poverty-stricken developing country is privileged compared to the refugee families on her caseload. When social work professionals are working across social, economic, and cultural boundaries, their worldviews, beliefs, and values strongly influence the type of relationship and comfort level they experience with their clients, as well as their ability to empathize (Yan, 2008). If unchecked, the social worker's privilege can be a barrier to empathy and an obstacle to culturally grounded practice. Privilege makes professionals assume—consciously or unconsciously—certain things about their clients. For example, the practitioner may assume that the client has what she or he has, such as a car or a comfortable home, or that the client was able to eat a hot breakfast before coming to the session. It is important to be aware of one's privilege and the client's lack of privilege in order to build rapport and accurately assess and interpret the client's behaviors.

In 1990 Peggy McIntosh published the now-classic "White Privilege: Unpacking the Invisible Knapsack," in which she documented some of the daily effects of privilege that she experienced and generally took for granted as a white middle-class person in the United States. The checklist (which is available online) can be edited and updated in many ways to accommodate the experiences of different cultural groups, but the original checklist remains provocative and insightful. It focuses on what the author does not need to do or think about. In other words, it is a catalog of situations in which white Americans experience the absence of discomfort, barriers, and oppression. Oppressed clients are aware of their social workers' privilege due to the practitioners' race; ethnicity; higher economic, professional, and educational status; and the practitioners' differential power. A client learns quickly that the practitioner often controls the resources that the client needs. If left unaddressed, this perceived privilege can become an obstacle to effective communication and rapport building, as clients may assume that the professional cannot understand what they are going through due to the professional's lack of experience with certain oppressive situations. Social workers, including those from minority groups, may be in denial about the privileges they enjoy that their clients do not. Self-awareness about privilege increases social workers' effectiveness and, in the end, enhances their professional and personal growth. Ignoring privilege or minimizing its impact on the client-worker relationship may compromise rapport and trust, leading to ineffective practice.

Like other aspects of identity, privilege is not a binary concept. The multiple intersecting identities held by each individual carry more or less privilege. For instance, a gay white man may have more power in the corporate world than does a heterosexual woman of color. It is helpful for a social worker to consider the multiple identities that an individual holds when assessing a client's experience of privilege and oppression. It is also quite possible, given the disproportionally high number of women in the profession, that the social worker inhabits a position of less privilege than his or her clients. This dynamic may create barriers in the client relationship in different ways. Rather than failing to empathize, oppressive dynamics of domination may be reproduced within the relationship where the client is not receptive to the social worker's suggestion because of his or her subordinate position in the larger social structure. Regardless of who in the relationship experiences more privilege based on the norms and values in the dominant culture, these power dynamics have the potential to significantly influence the social worker's interactions if they are not discussed openly.

HIGHER EDUCATION AND THE RISK OF CLASSISM

Higher education is a great cultural equalizer, as it provides very effective means for social mobility. Often, one is not possible without the other. Although the need for multiculturalism and inclusion has been extensively demonstrated, higher education and its structures are not yet sufficiently inclusive and representative in terms of cultural diversity. Social work as a profession has done better than many other disciplines in recruiting and retaining a diverse workforce. However, higher numbers of women and ethnic minorities joining the profession do not automatically translate into higher levels of cultural competence.

Higher education can also act as a cultural homogenizer, prompting students and faculty to conform to majority culture norms and behaviors regardless of their ethnic and social class backgrounds. The professional credentials imparted to them by higher education can make graduates operate from an implicitly classist and patriarchal standpoint. Consciously or unconsciously, they can adopt the perspective that because they have a college degree, they now know more about social problems and their solutions than do the poor and oppressed people who experience them.

Classism provides justification for the oppression of the poor and the working poor by those who control the economic and social resources of society. Classism is based on the belief that working-class people and poor people in general are inarticulate, lack education, and need the leadership and guidance of the educated classes. Social work practice can be classist, as it may recognize only one source of valid knowledge—the knowledge generated in institutions of higher learning, which typically exclude the poor and the oppressed and their accumulated knowledge and wisdom. In social services systems (i.e., child welfare, Department of Economic Security) social workers are put in a position to enforce cultural and class norms. When given the power to decide who gets what services and under what circumstances, class and cultural norms are imposed in tangible ways that create barriers and mistrust between the social work profession and disadvantaged communities.

To keep their classism in check, practitioners can use cultural experts and alternative sources of knowledge and conduct community-based participatory research (CBPR; see chapter 15) with communities. Social work research can be an important source of new knowledge that can bridge the gap between communities and higher education. Schools of social work can take advantage of their affiliation with universities and their close partnerships with communities to produce the best science in partnership with the communities they serve. As a profession, social work has the unique advantage of living in both worlds—communities and higher education—and can serve as a link between them to produce the best possible applied social science. Culturally competent social workers recognize that regardless of their social class and cultural background, their training can give them a middle-class, male, and Eurocentric perspective on life. Higher education has an acculturative effect that, if left unaddressed, can create cultural distance and mistrust between practitioners and clients. An individual can be born into privilege or access privilege through social mobility. Notes from the field 1.2

NOTES FROM THE FIELD 1.2
Starting Out on the Wrong Foot

Cindy, a 23-year-old Mexican American MSW student, is doing her internship at a women's shelter. One of her roles is to cofacilitate the young women's support group. The group members are all Mexican American and close to her age. She starts the session by giving a mini-lecture on gender roles and the negative consequences of machismo (the traditional male gender role) in Latino cultures. The second part of her presentation centers on the implications of feminism and women's rights for Latinas. She invites the group members to share their opinions on the subject. No one speaks; two group members get up and go to the restroom, and another asks permission to go to the nurse's office. Cindy asks the remaining women to share examples of machismo in their families, starting with their fathers. No one speaks. The session ends quickly.

illustrates how a social work intern was perceived as distant from or alien to her clients' world when she shared important information from her graduate student perspective; as a result, she did not effectively reach her audience. She assumed that the idea of sisterhood would immediately connect her with the group members and that they would freely share their experiences. In reality, their loyalty to their families and the academic framework Cindy used were real barriers to group discussion. Cindy shared some demographic characteristics with the group members, but in fact her presentation made her an outsider. She was lacking a link or connection; the content and goals of the group session were not grounded in the culture and worldview of the group members.

Connecting with clients and reaching the desired level of effectiveness are often achieved through partnerships and coalitions. When social workers become aware of the distance between them and their clients, they can work with others who are culturally close to the target population and who can help them bridge a psychological or cultural distance. Notes from the field 1.3 illustrates how a youth outreach worker developed a partnership that allowed him to reach out to a community and use outreach strategies with which he was already familiar to work with a cultural group he had not worked with before. Some commonly used strategies work across groups, but some do not. Often, it is not simply a matter of choosing the right strategy. In James's case, the chance of success was higher from the start because his efforts were cosponsored by the Office of the Cambodian Liaison, which was well regarded in the community. This is an example of

---

NOTES FROM THE FIELD 1.3
Reaching out to Cambodian Youths

James is a youth outreach worker at an HIV/AIDS services agency. He is African American and English monolingual. One of the goals of his agency is to increase its outreach among local Cambodian American youths. His first strategy is to create posters in English and Cambodian inviting young men and women to come to the agency for an ice cream social and to initiate a conversation about safe sex. James collaborates with Sovann, the representative from the Office of the Cambodian Liaison, which is highly regarded in the Cambodian community. Together, James and Sovann design and post announcements at stores located in the neighborhood where many Cambodian families live. The evening of the planned workshop, he is introduced to the large audience by Sovann, who has also agreed to interpret James's remarks for a large number of Cambodian monolingual parents at a later event.

coalition building, and of effective language and cultural adaptation of outreach strategies.

Awareness of one's privilege, status as an outsider, or lack of understanding of a particular culture can lead practitioners to develop a sense of discomfort, which in turn may lead them to avoid certain individuals and communities. In such cases, self-reflection can help practitioners assess for privilege and ethnocentrism and, in partnership with others, develop effective strategies to reach out to the target community. The notion of intersectionality helps workers to identify shared sources of identity with the clients and to bridge distance while developing effective rapport. For example, an intake worker refers a Native Hawaiian grandfather to a 25-year-old African American social worker who has no previous experience working with Native Hawaiian clients. As an icebreaker, the worker shares a story about his own grandfather, which allows them to begin to develop a sense of connection and comfort. These feelings serve as the foundation for the development of effective interventions.

At times, workers' values, communication styles, and expectations are different from the clients' because the workers come from different worlds and have different worldviews. For example, if a client does not come on time to an appointment, the social worker cannot automatically assume that it is due to resistance. Instead, it would be appropriate to inquire about transportation. Does the client own a car in working condition and have money for gas? If not, does she have money for bus fare? It is only natural to think that clients have access to the basic resources most people possess and take for granted. The social worker's privilege—that is, her or his higher status and relative wealth—may lead her or him to overlook important aspects of the client's life. More importantly, even though the more privileged are often not consciously aware of their higher status, the less privileged can quickly identify a difference in social class.

Cultural background often intersects with SES in interesting ways. For example, some clients may feel uncomfortable informing the social worker that they do not have money for the bus fare. They may feel that sharing such information makes them lose face or is an assault to their personal dignity. An unchecked sense of privilege may become a barrier to understanding such behavior. That is why cultural awareness is a key component in the repertoire of all culturally grounded social workers regardless of their ethnicity, gender, or social class.

RECOGNIZING AND CROSSING BOUNDARIES

Social workers move beyond the demographic or identity characteristics of their clients when applying the profession's standards of cultural competency. Most social workers interact with people from more than one culture every day; therefore, they honor difference as a first step toward adopting a culturally grounded paradigm. The recognition of cultural differences ensures that, in any intervention, different worldviews are recognized and cultural boundaries are taken into consideration in their practice.

Differences in worldviews occur as a result of the individualistic views of the world that are encouraged by many postindustrial cultures and the more collectivistic view of the world that is common among traditional cultures. These divergent cosmologies can present challenges to effective social work practice because the most commonly used interventions may operate at the individual level, whereas the client's natural support systems operate mostly at the collective level. Cultural boundaries act as imaginary lines that establish comfort zones for members of different cultures and can become no-crossing zones for outsiders. Cultural minority groups, as a result of their lack of power, need to establish boundaries between themselves and the majority culture, and between themselves and other minority groups with more power. The dominant culture, in turn, has the power to enforce its boundaries on minority groups and overlook cultural differences.

Boundaries help groups preserve inequality by protecting the cultural capital (the social and material fruits of privilege) of the dominant group, thereby safeguarding its dominance (Schwalbe et al., 2000). Social workers and the institutions they represent are often confronted by these boundaries and have the choice of perpetuating or overcoming them in partnership with their clients. Practitioners who come from the majority culture often lack experience with the conditions that members of the oppressed group face on a daily basis. Such lack of experience and awareness often prevents representatives of the dominant culture from developing the appropriate attitude and language for effective communication.

Because cultural boundaries are a constant feature in the daily life of practitioners, recognizing and honoring boundaries and finding effective ways to cross them is a lifelong journey. Particularly important is the fact that, in certain social settings, boundaries make social workers the outsiders as they work with families, groups, and communities. Research has demonstrated that outsiders are not very tolerant of or open to certain practices and beliefs held by minority cultures. However, the outsider's acceptance level significantly increases when minority practices are similar to the practices of majority cultures (Shaw & Wainryb, 1999). Therefore, tolerance appears to be correlated with comfort level. In other words, the more a given cultural practice deviates from what is familiar to members of the dominant culture, the less tolerant they become. A practitioner using a culturally grounded approach addresses these issues by assessing indigenous helping practices and recognizing their inherent value and benefits to the well-being of community members.

Through their engagement in dialogue with a community, social workers learn the rituals necessary to cross the boundaries that separate them from their clients. For example, practitioners working with Latino clients must understand that the figurative traditional casa (house or home) of the Latino family is similar to a circular temple with thick walls. Inside the walls, there is a courtyard surrounding the casa. Inside the casa, wonderful things happen, and many stories are shared around an altar called the dining room table. There is, however, only one gate into the courtyard. The social worker is often on the outside knocking on that gate, and those inside may not willingly open the gate. The social worker's role is to learn the right ritual to unlock the gate and gain entrance into the courtyard and eventually into the casa. Once they have learned the rituals, social workers are welcomed into the courtyard, and later into the casa as if they are family. If the social worker does not invest time in learning and practicing the appropriate rituals, communication with the family will only happen through a closed gate and a thick wall, which inevitably leads to misunderstandings. Admittedly, such cultural rituals are sometimes straightforward and driven by common sense and basic courtesy. For example, while working with Latino families, social workers may be expected to ask about the children first, remember the names of the children, and remember to use honorifics (e.g., Mrs. or Señora) until invited to use first names. However, at other times rituals can be much more complicated to decipher (i.e., taboo beliefs and practices), and learning them may require much time, patience, and a willingness to be taught.

Ignoring the boundaries that result from cultural and social class differences or pretending they do not exist only detracts from efforts to develop rapport and empathize with clients. Boundaries must be crossed not only when a client is of a different ethnicity, race, or social class, but also when she or he is differently abled or when there are issues regarding immigration status. Social workers are more effective border crossers when they are aware and when they know who they are and who they are not. Awareness of differences fosters honesty. Social workers in their community-based practice face situations where they are reminded of their own privilege and the challenges they face in establishing meaningful rapport with a particular client, group, family, or community. A quick assessment may give the worker only an outsider's view, and a lack of client engagement may lead to misunderstandings. A rushed assessment and the lack of knowledge of cultural rituals may give the worker only a distant and impersonal view from outside the courtyard walls. On the other hand, spending an additional session to develop rapport will certainly lead to a more effective assessment and a more effective intervention plan that incorporates family assets.

In a cultural sense, boundary crossing requires practice and patience, but most importantly it requires honest dialogue. Notes from the field 1.4 illustrates a case of heterosexual privilege in which the worker is unaware of the unique disadvantages that gay and lesbian couples face when their relationships are not legally recognized. The social worker in this example has never before encountered two people who love each other and are not able to live together in the same

---

NOTES FROM THE FIELD 1.4
Same-Sex Love and Immigration

Alison works at the Refugee and Immigrant Families Services Center. When two professional-looking young men enter her office, she thinks they are in the wrong place. Most of her clients are families with children. One of the young men, Tom, is an American citizen; the other, Paulo, is Brazilian. They have lived together as a committed couple for five years. However, Paulo's student visa is expiring soon, and the couple's relationship is not legally recognized by the U.S. Citizenship and Immigration Services (formerly the Immigration and Naturalization Service) as a factor in whether he qualifies as a permanent resident. They have explored many alternatives, and they are running out of time. Alison realizes that she has never worked with a gay couple before. She starts by recognizing that fact and, together with Paulo and Tom, reviews their short-term and long-term strategies, as well as the community and legal resources available to help them.

---

country. She suddenly recognizes that she has worked exclusively within the realm of heterosexual love. Meeting this gay couple challenges her to see beyond heterosexual privilege and consider the experiences of many other couples. The case of Tom and Paulo illustrates how the privilege status that U.S.-born citizens take for granted does not automatically extend to documented and undocumented immigrants.

Language can be another cultural boundary that workers and their clients must cross. Being able to communicate using the spoken word is often taken for granted, except within the hearing-impaired community. In the fields of social work, counseling, and psychology, talking is a fundamental tool for practice. Clients whose first language is not English may be the target of harassment and rejection, which may lead them to feign a level of comprehension they do not possess. Consciously tuning in to such experiences can be of great value to the worker when she or he is entering a new social and cultural environment.

Working across social and cultural boundaries can be very rewarding; at the same time, however, it can be challenging. Therefore, it is understandable and even predictable that social workers may feel unprepared or uncomfortable working with certain cultural groups. In these cases, it is important to identify and closely examine the sources of those feelings, and to look for ways in which to grow professionally and personally to meet the clients' needs. It is a journey that never ends, but one that needs to start right away.

In summary, being a culturally grounded practitioner means moving beyond awareness by acquiring new knowledge and developing new attitudes and behaviors. In other words, culturally grounded social work requires transformative practice or action. Change does not happen in big increments but is the result of small steps that the social worker assesses from a client-centered perspective. This process, termed "praxis" by Paulo Freire (1970), can be explained as learning by doing. Praxis leads to personal and professional growth and takes place in dialogue with colleagues and clients. It is a collective process incorporating the following components:

1. Being aware of a need or issue
2. Identifying a practical step to start addressing that need or issue
3. Taking a first small step
4. Assessing the outcome and the process with others
5. Celebrating the progress made and identifying the next step

These five action steps can be applied at field units, in social service agencies, or even with a group of social work classmates. Regardless of the setting, praxis requires awareness, the ability to engage in dialogue with others, and the courage to engage in transformative action as well as reflect on those actions. Culturally grounded social work integrates praxis as a natural component of practice.

Key Concepts

Culture: An identifiable grouping of shared values, traditions, norms, and customs that guide how people think and behave in a community

Cultural codes: The identifiable categories of behaviors or practices repeated over time.

Assimilation: Unidirectional process of letting go of the culture of origin while incorporating fundamental aspects of the majority culture

Acculturation: The behavioral and psychological process of adjusting to a nonnative culture when two or more cultures come into contact with each other

Enculturation: The process of connecting back to the culture of origin or to a renewed and recreated version of it

Cultural sensitivity: Understanding the diversity among clients and communities, and focusing on the cultural gap that exists between the service delivery system and the clients it serves

Cultural competency: Possession of the knowledge, values, and skills necessary to make services culturally relevant, thereby increasing their effectiveness

Culturally grounded social work practice: The combination and utilization of cultural sensitivity and cultural competency in social work practice

Praxis: The transformative cyclical process of action, reflection, and action.

2

Cultural Diversity, Oppression, and Action: A Culturally Grounded Paradigm

THE OPPRESSION OF NONMAJORITY GROUPS HAS OCCURRED THROUGH-
out the world for hundreds of years, including in the United States. Because the
United States is a highly race-conscious society, members of racial and ethnic
minorities experience prejudice and discrimination and are often underserved or
poorly served by multiple systems. Becoming familiar with the strengths of
minority communities allows social workers to partner more effectively with their
clients and to use those assets to achieve common goals and change oppressive
conditions. This chapter provides information on the effects of oppression on
members of different cultural groups and how social workers can use a culturally
grounded approach to support oppressed communities as those communities
empower themselves and achieve positive social change.

Cultural diversity is not an easy concept to define, in part because there is no
consensus about which groups should be considered to be contributing diversity
to a community or society. For instance, does someone need to belong to a recognizable minority group to be considered a member of a minority cultural community? The use of the term "minority" is controversial as well, in both its accuracy
and its implications for power relations. The ethnic diversity of the United States
is increasing such that whites of European ancestry will soon be in the numerical
minority (Lichter, 2013). Moreover, applying the term "minority" to a group can
perpetuate the unequal power structure by implying that the group is the exception and out of the mainstream. However, should we view each cultural group
that differs in some way from the mainstream as a cultural minority? One could
argue that definitions of cultural diversity need to be broad enough to accommodate the wide variations and intersecting identities of those within the majority
culture.

Because of the lack of consensus, there is a risk of approaching cultural diversity from an overly narrow or an overly broad perspective. For example, by stressing cultural diversity as opposed to racial or ethnic diversity in a more specific

sense, society runs the risk of overlooking crucial issues related to inequality and unequal treatment of ethnic and racial minority groups. On the other hand, if diversity is approached as being based exclusively on traditional racial and ethnic paradigms, there is a risk of excluding many of the expressions of social and cultural diversity that are present in contemporary society. When defined too broadly, cultural diversity can be seen as a superficial pluralistic celebration of variety that overlooks the oppression of cultural minority groups and its consequences. The danger here is that the idea of cultural diversity is reduced to a potpourri of different ethnic group festivals and weekend parades, or is watered down to describe groups that share some cultural characteristic or taste, like body piercers or Grateful Dead fans. Such an approach can be seen as throwing the net too widely and grouping too many different people with varied experiences into the cultural minority category. On the other hand, basing our definitions of cultural minorities exclusively on racial and ethnic differences may exclude other truly oppressed or disenfranchised groups, such as Appalachians, or gays and lesbians.

Different approaches to cultural diversity have real consequences for members of minority groups because they influence policy, equity, and access to services and benefits. When difference is defined broadly to encompass every imaginable factor that distinguishes one person from another, there is a risk of diluting key differences, overlooking their societal implications, and overemphasizing less critical factors. For example, Americans of Irish, Polish, and Italian heritage can maintain different elements of their cultural origins through the intergenerational transmission of many cultural practices, such as the use of ancestral language and traditional foods, celebrations, and ceremonies. Historically, these European American groups have experienced different degrees of prejudice and discrimination, but they are no longer seen as minority groups due to their successful integration and assimilation into the white middle class.

The various sources of cultural identity may also differ in the degree to which they are on display and easily identifiable in social settings. An African American heterosexual professional whom we will call Ralph illustrated this point with the comment, "I cannot hang my blackness in the closet." Ralph's point is that racial oppression and oppression based on sexual orientation are experienced differently. Ralph recognizes the oppression that the gay community has encountered and continues to encounter, but does not feel comfortable equating that experience with the relentless social stress most African American men and women experience in their daily lives. Ralph explains that his race is always apparent when he interacts with others. In contrast, white gay men and white lesbians who do not make their sexual orientation known may be assumed to be from the majority culture. Most African Americans and many Latinos, Native Americans, and Asian Americans seldom experience the default presumption that they are part of the mainstream. The same can be said for women in many situations. How they look, dress, and speak and even their job titles and promotions are often scrutinized. A good criterion to use in identifying these differences is the intensity and frequency with which individuals are targeted for prejudice and discrimination. The more respites an individual can take from prejudice and discrimination, the more privileged she or he is.

Cultural diversity can be viewed as both a source of oppression and a springboard for liberation. The cultural orientation and the oppression or power-based paradigms have significantly increased society's awareness of the experiences of members of different cultural groups.

THE CULTURAL ORIENTATION PARADIGM

The cultural orientation paradigm is based on the premise that cultural differences exist and that becoming familiar with those differences is the solution to any intergroup misunderstandings. Problems emerge when different sets of cultural rules and norms regarding appropriate behavior get in the way of effective communication. In other words, communication is assumed not to be working either because people do not possess sufficient information about a group's norms and expectations, or because they operate from an ethnocentric point of view and see their perceptions and behaviors as the natural or right ones.

The cultural orientation paradigm views a lack of cultural knowledge as the source of misunderstanding, embarrassment, and anger that occur when others are perceived as acting in ways that are disrespectful, rude, or offensive. The barriers created between majority and minority groups by ethnocentric superiority and privilege often lead to the development of prejudice against groups of people or cultures that are perceived as being different. These prejudices result from the difference between the behavior of the minority group, and the cultural rules and norms imposed and regulated by the majority or mainstream cultural group. As a result, those differences are believed to be the consequence of misunderstanding or lack of affinity, and are not necessarily a form of intentional mistreatment, discrimination, or oppression.

The cultural orientation paradigm assumes that prejudice disappears once everyone understands that the problems are merely a misunderstanding. According to this framework, the solution to these problems is relatively simple: (1) become aware of the different sets of norms governing various cultural, ethnic, and racial groups; (2) set aside ethnocentric ideas; and then (3) learn each other's cultural rules and standards. These steps provide those participating in cross-cultural interactions with the tools to interpret each other's behavior correctly (Naylor, 1997). From a cultural orientation perspective, knowing each other's rules and standards is the key to eliminating misunderstanding, embarrassment, and anger, and the way to establish clear communication in any interactions.

In recent years, so-called diversity training has become part of corporate America's lexicon. Cultural diversity training seminars aimed at improving communication between people of different cultural backgrounds are frequently offered in settings traditionally recognized as bastions of white male dominance, such as corporations, universities, and government institutions. These seminars are based on the cultural orientation paradigm, which tends to assume that cultural rules exist at an intellectual level that is easily accessible to both those who live by those rules and to outsiders. Diversity training often requires representatives of minority groups to share their experiences and help with this process. In a classroom, for example, the only African American student may be asked to speak for all African Americans and explain to the class what it is like to be black in America. Notes from the field 2.1 illustrates how the burden of improving communications and making cultural adjustments can be placed on an ethnic minority organization. The practices carried out by the foundation in this example are

NOTES FROM THE FIELD 2.1
We Told You So

A charitable foundation has decided not to fund a grant proposal submitted by a local Latino agency because the foundation deems that the agency does not have a good board of directors or strategic plan. The foundation's program officer decides to hire a consultant to help the agency recruit new board members, improve its organizational structure, and engage in a long-range strategic plan. The ultimate goal is for the agency to become more competitive and to make itself more attractive to potential funding sources. The consultant is not Latino and has to be educated by the board members about the community's cultural norms and values, and about the agency's history and culture. After three months and after several long meetings and interviews, the consultant feels very good about the cultural training he has received from the agency. During this time, the consultant has been well paid for the time he has spent learning, while the agency representatives have not been compensated for the training they have provided. At the end of the training, the board members decide not to apply again to the foundation. They feel frustrated, have a sense that they have been used by the consultant, and are tired of having to explain themselves to the foundation. The foundation has never in its long history given a grant to a Latino agency, and it now views the failure of its strategy to improve the agency as evidence of the agency's problematic operations.

perceived by the community-based agency as expressions of cultural colonialism rather than of cultural diversity. At the end of the process, not only are the agency's board members tired, frustrated, and angry, but they are also unable to access badly needed resources. This example illustrates how cultural knowledge is an asset, whereas cultural ignorance is a shortcoming or deficit. The majority culture and its institutions often do not see the knowledge and expertise of minority communities as a resource or strength. On the contrary, different approaches to acquiring knowledge, expertise, and management and leadership are frequently seen as deficits to be fixed by the imposition of so-called neutral or mainstream knowledge. For example, knowledge transmitted by way of oral tradition often is not accepted by academics as true or scientific knowledge. In reality, ethnic-specific nongovernmental organizations often have alternative ways of running a board of directors that can be as effective as more-traditional white middle-class approaches to governance. If the foundation's program officer in notes from the field 2.1 had been truly concerned with helping the agency build its capacity, she would have hired a consultant who was knowledgeable about Latino agencies, and not an uninitiated consultant in need of training.

Overall, the cultural orientation paradigm runs the risk of not accounting for social and historical oppression. In other words, the paradigm does not put the experience of difference into its social, historical, and political context. It does not account for the experiences of those labeled as different and fails to acknowledge the historical roots of existing differences. For example, someone could study cultural diversity from a naive perspective and admire cultural products without considering the living conditions of those who created them. In contrast, as notes from the field 2.2 illustrates, adopting a culturally grounded approach can counteract such cultural ignorance. Concerns such as those raised in notes from the field 2.2 can surface in many settings of social work practice. In this case, the appropriate community expert was invited to provide guidance in order to lead the integration of culturally specific rituals and helping techniques. Non-Native practitioners who attempt to lead traditional rituals such as talking circles or sweats outside their cultural context can engage in a form of cultural colonialism. However, a non-Native practitioner such as Debbie can partner or collaborate with the appropriate community shaman or holy man or woman. Attempts to integrate culturally specific approaches are commendable, but there is a time and a place to do so. Culture and its products are never content or context free. Rather, as practitioners become exposed to other cultures, their interactions, presence, and privilege become part of the cultural diversity experience and the potential for oppression or liberation.

THE OPPRESSION OR POWER-BASED PARADIGM

The oppression or power-based paradigm sees difference as a political phenomenon with power as its central factor. This perspective recognizes that the

NOTES FROM THE FIELD 2.2
An Integrated Healing System

Debbie is a medical social worker at the health center of a Native American reservation. The clinic is staffed by two physicians, four nurses, and Debbie, the one social worker. The entire professional staff is non-Native, while the great majority of the patients are Native. Debbie learns from some of the elders in a group she facilitates that they would like traditional healing approaches to be integrated with the work being conducted by the staff. The elders invite Mr. Thomas—the shaman in the community—to a group session at the clinic. Debbie realizes that Mr. Thomas has been a patient at the clinic for many years but no one in the professional team has known about his role in the community. In response to an invitation he receives from the clinic director, Mr. Thomas visits with the professional team. After brief introductions, Mr. Thomas suggests that a room that once served as the cafeteria be used as a place where family members can gather to pray and conduct healing ceremonies. The elders have volunteered to participate in decorating the old cafeteria with the help of some of their grandchildren, and Mr. Thomas agrees to lead prayers at the community room with families from remote areas of the reservation who accompany relatives for doctor's visits. Debbie suggests that they explore the possibility of designing a dual referral system and hiring Mr. Thomas as a member of the treatment team. She explains that Mr. Thomas meets many people in need of medical care as he visits community members throughout the reservation, while she as well as the clinic's doctors and nurses often encounter patients who need more than medical care. They conclude the meeting by deciding that the former cafeteria will be transformed into a community room, and Mr. Thomas agrees to attend the next staff meeting in order to brainstorm ideas for the dual referral system.

experience of oppression shapes people's lives. Historically, race and to some extent gender have been the most visible and dramatic sources of difference, inequality, and oppression in the United States. Indeed, not only was "the problem of the color line" (Du Bois, 1903/1969, p. 15) the quintessential problem of the twentieth century, but also some have argued that the color line and racism continue to be a major social issue in the twenty-first century (Bonilla-Silva, 2006). Although the United States is often hailed as a diverse society, it has struggled and continues to struggle with oppression and inequality, in ways that are both evident and subtle. As a product of the hierarchical organization of society, oppression constitutes a complex web of dynamics that generate and maintain inequitable conditions (Bishop, 2002). Racial and gender inequities in the United States and in other countries continue to generate a great deal of oppression and unjust conditions, but they intersect in complex combinations with other dimensions of privilege and oppression such as social class, sexual orientation, ageism, ability status, religion, and migration status. The oppression paradigm recognizes these forces and offers a critique of current tendencies to make diversity a broad concept that obscures the centrality of race and ethnicity in the social construction of difference.

Cultural diversity does not exist in a vacuum; it is part of a social and political context in which individuals may experience prejudice and discrimination as a result of their cultural minority status. The oppression paradigm approaches cultural diversity as an issue of politics and justice and recognizes differences as a resource in an increasingly global economy. For example, the sociologist Orlando Patterson (2003) has argued that when addressing issues of diversity, we should emphasize ethnic and racial categorization instead of using all-encompassing cultural diversity categories. For example, he recommends that affirmative action should be targeted to avoid an overly broad and all-inclusive cultural diversity approach and remain faithful to its original goal of racial integration in all areas of public and private life.

A counterargument to Patterson's (Patterson, 2003) thought-provoking stance is that American society has radically changed since affirmative action was originally instituted nearly four decades ago (Girves, Zepeda, & Gwathmey, 2005). While the original race-based focus of affirmative action continues to be needed today, there are other cultural diversity factors that need to be addressed at the same time. An alternative example of the social construction of difference is the belief that men provide the social norm to which women should adjust. Although it is important from an oppression perspective to recognize that not all minority identities encounter the same kind or amount of oppression, there is a need for a broader representation of gender identities around the cultural diversity table. This breadth is especially important in dealing with dichotomies like white/black, male/female, heterosexual/lesbian, gay, bisexual, transgender, and queer or questioning (LGBTQ), and mainstream/other. Placing those viewed as the "other" in inferior positions leads to their experience of oppression. It is for this reason that identifying oppressive conditions and working with the oppressed toward change have historically been priorities for social work. The social construction of difference can be illustrated through a metaphor of an orchard with many types of fruit trees, where the fruitful branches of different cultures become interconnected.

The social and cultural context in which communities live is represented in the orchard metaphor by the soil in which the trees are planted. The resources of society are represented by the irrigation system that does not reach each group of trees equally. Lack of water weakens some trees and prevents them from bearing fruit. The keeper of the orchard (society and its institutions) may attempt to correct these wrongs by identifying whole groups of trees that have been consistently deprived of the water they need to bear fruit, and to work to guarantee that all trees have an equal opportunity to access water. The keeper may also favor some trees, believing that they bear better fruit and therefore intentionally may divert scarce resources from one type of tree to another. In a healthy ecosystem, there may be no need for a keeper with the seasonal rains providing enough water for all of the plants equally.

For some cultural groups, lack of water is akin to challenging social conditions that impede advancement, such as lack of jobs, good schools, or decent housing, all of which fall under the broad definition of oppression. The cultural diversity approach recognizes oppression as a key factor in understanding and addressing inequality between groups. Leaving oppression out of the diversity equation may lead to a romantic or superficial view of difference that cannot address the real needs of individuals, groups, and communities.

OPPRESSION

Paulo Freire (1970) defined oppression as human beings' perverse tendency to deprive others of freedom and happiness. In a capitalist society, oppression often manifests itself as the deprivation among certain groups of needed material resources. However, oppression is not limited to excluding people from resources, but also refers to excluding people from other opportunities. Those who oppress others have power, and power is needed to enact anti-oppression policies (Thompson, 2006). Empowerment involves addressing the imbalance of power between groups which can come in the form of capacity building for social action (Gil, 1998). This is not to say that power and money are not intimately connected in the political systems in the United States and other countries, but rather that money is only one aspect of the complex systems that maintain the power imbalance between the oppressed and the oppressor (Bishop, 2002). For example, because empowerment is the primary issue underlying female poverty, micro approaches to dealing with the problem have produced only limited improvements. The well-publicized micro loans program developed in Bangladesh provides women and some men with very small loans to establish home- and village-based businesses that make and sell textiles, crafts, and agricultural products. Micro loans have encountered some criticism because in some instances they provide funding but do not address the other resources that some women in emerging economies need in order to overcome their oppression. Other critics claim that these programs also do not address the failure of the system to monetarily value women's work in the home or the uneven distribution of household duties when women decide to pursue entrepreneurial activities that are rewarded in the current system. Critics recommend that to adequately address the problem and produce lasting changes, issues of patriarchy, abuse, and discrimination against women and macrolevel reforms need to be considered (Rice, 2001).

For oppression to exist, two basic ingredients are needed: a group that is being oppressed, and an oppressor who benefits from such oppression. In the process of oppression, the oppressors externalize their fears by projecting them onto those people who most seem to fit the category of the other (Moraga, 2004, p. 33). The oppressed are perceived as socially and morally deficient or as a pathology afflicting an otherwise healthy society (Freire, 1994). The Jewish Holocaust—an extreme example of oppression—was preceded by a two-year extermination program of about 50,000 mostly non-Jewish psychiatric patients, who were granted a "mercy death" under the Nationalist Socialist "euthanasia program" (Szasz, 1970, p. 314). Hitler also contemplated adopting health regulations under which physically ill people, especially those with diseased hearts and lungs, would no longer be allowed to reproduce or circulate freely in public. Such oppression has been described as the experience of "being caged in: all avenues, in every direction, are blocked or booby trapped" (Frye, 2003, p. 49). The ultimate outcome of oppression, as was amply demonstrated in Nazi Germany, is the dehumanization of both the oppressed and the oppressor.

Although the Nazi regime is an extreme example of oppression, the tendency of seemingly ordinary people in positions of power to act in barbarous ways toward subordinates has been well documented in social psychology experiments. For example, the classic mock prison experiment at Stanford University in which students were assigned at random to prisoner and guard roles had to be halted prematurely when guards began to treat their prisoners in an increasingly dehumanizing and violent manner (Zimbardo, 1971). Revelations that U.S. military guards subjected Iraqi detainees to sexual degradation and torture at the Abu Ghraib prison in Baghdad provide a more recent reminder that people are more likely to treat others in an inhumane fashion (and to enjoy doing so), and that this behavior is more likely to be tolerated by others, when those being subjected to such treatment are labeled as the despised other. Methods of torture and coercion that are utilized in an attempt to maintain total psychological and physical control of humans in systems of oppression include isolation, induced debility and exhaustion, threats, degradation, enforcing trivial demands, and occasional indulgences (Poole & Galpin, 2011). These methods of oppression can be found in various forms and intensities during political conflicts, as well as in oppressive intergroup and interpersonal relationships.

In times of war and political upheaval this perception of the despised other is especially strong. The other is also frequently targeted with more intensity when a political system is experiencing a crisis or economic contraction (King, Massoglia, & Uggen, 2012). This pattern can be seen in the long and ambivalent history of immigration policy in the United States. During the economic recession that began in 2008, there was a sharp increase in the general public's support of deportations. The growing anti-immigrant sentiment could be attributed to an increase in perceived ethnic competition and prejudice; these sentiments cut across political party lines (Cosby, Aanstoos, Matta, Porter, & James, 2013).

The placement of groups into the category of other, however, is relative. Some oppressed groups may have more power than another group and may become that group's oppressor. For example, in schools with many immigrant students, those who already speak English fluently may ridicule more-recent immigrants who do not. This can occur as a result of deculturalization, or denial of one's culture or identity, and can threaten the healthy development of the individual and the community (Fisher & Sonn, 2003). This sometimes happens when oppressed individuals fall into what Freire (1994) calls internalized oppression or a state of self-hate. At the personal level, internalized oppression can be experienced as stress, guilt, stigma, and shame. Notes from the field 2.3 provides an example of a gay man who has suffered the consequences of homophobia. Art appears to have internalized the homophobia he encountered while growing up; he still perceives that oppression. He tries to enforce a form of strict behavioral heterosexism on himself and others, a form of constant role-playing. He pretends to be heterosexual in his most meaningful relationships and is looking for a same-sex partner who is willing to do the same. He is appropriating attitudes and behaviors that oppress him, and in turn he is using those attitudes and behaviors to avoid getting close to other gay men.

NOTES FROM THE FIELD 2.3
Why Can't I Find Mr. Right?

Art is a 29-year-old African American gay man who comes to a counseling session to discuss his difficulties finding the right partner. He has not dated since he graduated from college seven years ago. He states that all the available men he meets at social gatherings and clubs are "very out" or "too flamboyant" for him. He does not like to go out with men who might be recognized as gay or who are active in gay organizations. He is looking for a "straight-acting" and "straight-looking" partner like himself. Art believes that his parents, siblings, and coworkers do not know he is gay, and he would like to keep it that way. He states, "It is none of their business; they don't tell me who they go to bed with." He has tried online personal ads and dating services without success. He feels lonely and is concerned about turning thirty and not having a partner. He expresses repeatedly his frustration about not being able to find Mr. Right. He is having problems sleeping and often feels irritable.

Internalized oppression can also be experienced by members of ethnic or racial minority groups. An individual who experiences racism and internalizes such oppression can in turn discriminate against other people based on their ethnic background. For example, Dolores, a Puerto Rican homemaker, does not like to send her children to a Puerto Rican dentist whose office is around the corner from her apartment building and instead drives them to see Dr. Cook, a European American dentist. She says that Anglo dentists are better than Puerto Rican dentists. She has internalized the prejudice she has experienced as a Puerto Rican woman. Instead of challenging the stereotype, she internalizes the message and perpetuates it. Within immigrant communities it is not rare to find internal hierarchies based on income, religious affiliation, education, generational status, skin color, and language abilities.

What role can a social worker play in these cases? Helping the client understand why this way of thinking is important to her or him is a necessary first step. Internalized oppression and deculturalization can have negative effects on the person experiencing them. Internal oppression can result in the rejection of oneself as well as the rejection of others. It is stressful for Art to not accept himself and to try to fit the heterosexual mold every hour of the day, as evidenced by his irritability and trouble sleeping. His lack of self-acceptance can create distance between himself and those who love him. Moreover, how can an intimate gay relationship be formed when the identity that brings together the two men is denied, rejected, or repressed?

The process of partnering with clients to address internalized oppression can be challenging and may require the social worker to take on several different roles. The first is to help clients identify the oppressive forces that may be at the root of their presenting problems, through the process of nonjudgmental and unbiased inquiry. Through this one-on-one or group dialogue, both the community members and the social workers start to disentangle internalized oppression and identify the systemic forces that may be affecting the presenting problem, effectively taking the fault away from the individual when the individual does not deserve it (Mullaly, 2007). Once the sources of oppression are identified, the social worker can shift roles from educator to facilitator or advocate. At this stage the social worker partners with the individuals, ideally in a group setting, to consider possible actions that could be taken to address the source of oppression.

ACTION AS LIBERATION

The groups and individuals who experience the widespread negative effects of oppression can use different mechanisms to resist oppression. Freire (1970) argued that an oppressed individual cannot liberate himself in isolation. Oppressed individuals can liberate themselves only with others, as a group or as a community. Oppressed individuals, groups, and communities can reach empowerment through a collective process of freeing themselves from the conditions that dehumanize them. This process of liberation must occur both for those who are deprived of opportunities to advance socially and for those obstructing that advancement. In his classic book *Pedagogy of the Oppressed*, Freire (1970) proposed education as the path to permanent liberation: first individuals must become aware (conscious) of their own oppression, and then through praxis (which encompasses self-determination, creativity, and rationality) they can change that state of oppression. For instance, the gay liberation movement could become a significant social force only when individuals who had historically been isolated as a result of their sexual orientation came together. They formed communities where they could experience a sense of belonging and could interact without the threat of persecution and discrimination, and then went on to organize to change attitudes and policies.

Social work as a field has a historical commitment to supporting communities in their move toward liberation. However, as social work becomes more professionalized and depends more on state and private funding, its allegiance to the oppressed may become less clear. Social workers are called on to be vigilant about their allegiance and commitment to the poor and the oppressed. Social workers practice in partnership with people who have been silenced and isolated, helping them regain a voice in the decisions that affect their lives. However, some social work theorists have argued that change will not occur until social workers are able to connect the problems of clients who are members of oppressed groups to the roots of their oppression (Vodde & Gallant, 2002).

Liberating social work practice uses policy challenge as a tool for change. Social workers are called on to move beyond social service delivery and to be involved at the macro level collaborating with communities to design and attain funding for social services that meet their needs. Engaging only in micro-level practice limits the profession's ability to effect systemic change. On the other hand, ignoring microlevel practice would neglect the individual and family needs of communities. A culturally grounded approach to social work aims at achieving a balance between the micro and macro levels of practice in partnership with oppressed communities. In other words, in the tradition of the anti-oppressive practice, culturally grounded social work is informed by the opinions and experiences of social service users in families and communities, by means of user-led and user-controlled research (Rush & Keenan, 2013).

When working with oppressed communities, social workers constantly assess their own values, norms, power, and privilege in relationship to the client; they also assess the extent to which they are imposing these values due to their potential position of power. Social workers and social agencies need to be aware of and avoid falling into the commonly held stereotype of "poverty pimp." That pejorative term has arisen in oppressed communities based on the perception that social work agencies move into their community and benefit unduly—through financial and career opportunities for agency workers—by acting as intermediaries for poor and disadvantaged communities, suggesting that the agencies are not primarily motivated to eliminate the root causes of the community's societal problems because they profit from the continuation of those problems (Brophy-Baermann & Bloeser, 2006; Diversi & Finley, 2010). These community reactions also occur when social workers practice in areas in which they do not have much expertise, intending to "save" people who don't need saving, and when agencies fail to consider the community's assets and strengths, and take a paternalistic stance that does not leave room for the community to solve its own problems.

In order to address oppression, social workers partner with oppressed communities and work to facilitate change. The process of change does not ignore the need for services, but instead engages the community in identifying needs and providing services that are relevant in the social context. Despite their importance, social workers interested in addressing oppression cannot stop with delivering social services. Addressing oppression also means creating spaces and facilitating discussion that identify sources of oppression, and creating strategies to address these root causes collectively.

CHALLENGES TO ACTION: STEREOTYPES, PREJUDICE, AND DISCRIMINATION

Stereotypes

Change and the creation of a more just society can be challenged by oppressive policies, which are often based on stereotypes. Stereotypes are beliefs that individuals hold about members of a group based on generalizations about the characteristics of all members of that group. Although it is common to think that only bigoted people use stereotypes, the truth is that everyone uses them, often without being aware they are doing so. Humans have the need to belong to a group, and the tendency to see the members of their group as individuals, and the members of out-groups as undifferentiated. Thus, stereotypes emerge from in-group/out-group dynamics. Group identification can exaggerate the social distance between members of different groups and can affect individuals' perceptions of others as well as of their own psychological well-being (Sharlin & Moin, 2001; Whitley & Kite, 2006).

Once individuals are exposed to the societal stereotypes attached to a particular group, they tend to perceive individual members of that group according to those generalizations, focusing on aspects of the person that fit the stereotype and deemphasizing aspects of the person that do not fit the stereotype. They see themselves and those like them as unique and as individual personalities, while seeing members of the stereotyped out-group as undifferentiated from each other—as if they share all the same traits (Hilton & von Hippel, 1996). The insider-outsider divide makes one's own group behavior and beliefs seem natural, normal, appropriate, or morally correct, and the other group's behaviors seem unusual, unnatural, peculiar, deviant, or even immoral. Stereotypes often attach negative traits to members of the out-group. Once they are learned, they become part of society's cosmology and permeate most social interactions.

Besides being overly simplistic and often highly exaggerated, ethnic and gender stereotypes are usually learned secondhand—through a process of labeling and social learning—in our interactions with agents of socialization like family and school. Negative racial and ethnic stereotypes held by teachers and students have been shown to disrupt the academic functioning of African American and Latino students, both by leading ethnic minority students to question the value of academic achievement and by undermining their academic self-confidence (Rousseau & Tate, 2003). This is a reciprocal process: low academic achievement among some ethnic minority students has been linked to stereotypes (Crocker & Knight, 2005), and stereotypes feed prejudice and provide an explanation or rationale for students' low achievement and the schools' failure to address it.

Exaggerated stereotypes have long been used in television commercials and print ads to get attention, increase recall, and foster identification with products and services. One of the most effective methods is to portray the stereotype humorously, which not only uses entertainment to hold the viewer's attention, but also softens the message by seeming to suggest that the stereotype is not meant to be taken seriously. Stereotypes in advertising abound, and it might be said that they make fun of all groups—even white heterosexual males. For example, straight white men are sometimes portrayed as obsessed with sports and inept at household tasks. To get by in life, they need the forbearance and common sense of their more knowledgeable and skillful spouses and children.

Stereotypes of African Americans have come a long way from the subservient Aunt Jemima and Uncle Ben. In contemporary commercials, media watchers have noted the emergence of a new stereotype: the heavy black woman who is verbally assertive, impatient with annoyances, and controlling—even someone who is aggressive or physically intimidating in interactions with family members and strangers (Givens & Monahan, 2005). Although the African American women in these commercials are presented humorously, critics contend that the stereotypes reflect the views of their white creators on Madison Avenue, and that people laugh at the stereotypes for different reasons (Creedon & Cramer, 2006). White viewers may laugh at the outrageousness of the portrayal, in part because they know that their own cultural group is not like that. African Americans may also laugh because they can identify with aspects of the portrayal. Although openly negative racial stereotypes are rare in today's advertising, the question remains how much these subtle messages continue to influence how cultural minority groups are perceived.

Prejudice

Prejudice is an irrational and unsubstantiated negative feeling toward members of different cultural groups, such as racial and ethnic groups, women, gays and lesbians, people with disabilities, and certain religious groups, that generates stereotypes about those groups.

According to contemporary theories of prejudice, people are reluctant to voice prejudicial attitudes unless they can do so in ways so that their views or criticisms cannot be attributed to race, thereby keeping intact the perception that they are fair and unprejudiced. For example, an undocumented Mexican immigrant in the United States has by definition engaged in illegal activity and may therefore face discrimination that is justified as being anticrime rather than anti-Mexican." This rhetoric persists, despite the fact that the presence of undocumented immigrants in the United States is not a violation of the U.S. Criminal Code but rather a violation of Civil Immigration Laws; the offender cannot be sent to prison for being in the country without authorization (U.S. Criminal Code, 2012). However, ethnic prejudice that surrounds the issue of undocumented immigration is illustrated by the round-up campaigns conducted by agents of the U.S. Citizenship and Immigration Services that often target "Mexican-looking" permanent residents and American citizens. Ethnic profiling has been identified as one of the main explanations for the overrepresentation of racial and ethnic minorities among drivers stopped by traffic police around the nation (Birzer & Birzer, 2006). Because African American drivers have historically experienced disproportional rates of harassment from the police, many parents in that community coach their children who drive on how to deal with police harassment (Warren, 2011).

Scapegoating and projection are two processes that lead to prejudice. Scapegoating occurs when a group or individual blames others for a problem for which they are not responsible. The group or individual takes out feelings of frustration on someone other than the true source of the frustration; this someone is often a member of the out-group. Those looking for a scapegoat believe that they are society's victims and as such are being abused, whereas the scapegoat is usually incapable of offering resistance to such accusations. The most likely targets of scapegoating are people with no power, such as immigrants who have not been naturalized and cannot vote (Magana & Short, 2002; Sowards & Pineda, 2013). Scapegoating can occur at all levels of the power continuum; for example, women may become the scapegoat within a marginalized ethnic group, and girls may become the scapegoat among the women. Frequently even groups with little power in the larger social structure find a segment of society within their own group or other oppressed groups to use as a scapegoat in their narratives and social constructions of problems.

Projection is a process through which people minimize or deny undesirable characteristics that they possess by exaggerating the same characteristics in someone from the out-group. In general, individuals have a tendency to empha-size the positive when describing themselves and those close to them. The differ-entiation hypothesis assumes that people look for differences between themselves and others and then balance their need for uniqueness and similarities by project-ing positively onto the in-group and negatively onto the out-group (Clement & Krueger, 2002). Projection is an attempt to secure one's identity by excluding, avoiding, or eliminating the other. The deficiencies of the individual or group doing the projecting do not have to be acknowledged because these deficiencies are transferred to members of an out-group; in this way projection is used to perpetuate racism, sexism, homophobia, and other prejudices.

Social workers are bound by the *Code of Ethics* to help reduce racial and ethnic prejudice through its involvement in policy change at the macro level and through different strategies at the micro level, including persuasive communica-tion, education, intergroup contact, simulation and experiential exercises, and therapy (National Association of Social Workers, 2008). Persuasive communica-tion is a direct attempt to influence beliefs and behaviors. In order to persuade, social workers can present evidence and clear logical argument that challenge the assumption underling prejudicial beliefs. Through education, social workers can share information to break down incorrect stereotypes. Intergroup contact shows people that the stereotypes they hold about out-groups are unfounded. Inner-group contact in dialogue and/or conversation can be used as an experiential exer-cise to unpack assumptions and prejudice. Prejudices are addressed within the context of a conversation when the participants are encouraged to consider oppos-ing ideas (Baker, Jensen, & Kolb, 2005). In the contexts of the conversation, the role of the facilitator is to guide the exploration of all perspectives and to draw awareness to the emerging contradictions, rather than to create a consensus. The facilitator asks participants to sit with alternative constructions of reality rather than to discard or deny perceptions that do not align with what they already accept to be true (Baker et al., 2005). In a series of intergroup dialogues among individuals from different religious organizations, participants were able to explore their biases and similarities and eventually move toward a discussion of social change efforts (Dessel, Rogge, & Garlington, 2006). Intergroup dialogues have also been used to facilitate discussions between Arab and Israeli students, with results suggesting that these dialogues lead to an increased understanding of multiple perspectives and action to address the conflict (Alatar, Smith, & Umbreit, 2004). Simulation and experiential exercises also allow members of the majority group to experience discrimination and the feelings associated with it. For exam-ple, in an experiential learning activity designed to help the participants under-stand sexism, individuals were divided into groups, then were guided through a simulation. To help generate empathy for individuals experiencing sexism, groups took turns picking gender-specific cards that described typical workplace scenar-ios in which men and women were treated differently; the groups then assigned a value to the experience. The activity was designed so that during the course of the game it became clear that the women were at a disadvantage and could not win the game, simulating the experience of discrimination for the participants. Participating in this activity was shown to decrease sexist attitudes by increasing knowledge and empathy (Zawadzki, Shields, Danube, & Swim, 2013). Therapy is recommended only when prejudice is rooted in deep personality needs—in other words, when prejudice consumes the thoughts and emotions of an individual.

Discrimination

Discrimination is the unequal treatment of individuals based on their group membership rather than on their individual qualities. Discrimination is not an individual behavior that occurs in isolation, but rather is the expression of a system of social relations and beliefs. Discrimination involves actions by a dominant group that are harmful to the members of the subordinate group.

Discriminatory actions can vary in severity from minor forms, to more serious forms that carry greater risk of injury and involve exclusion from the economic, social, and political realms of society. Discrimination can range from the use of derogatory labels and pejorative ethnic references; to the denial of access to housing, health, education, and justice; to the use of violence against individuals or groups. An overt act of hatred perpetrated by one person toward another person due to the latter's group membership is individual discrimination. Institutional discrimination is less overt and occurs when institutions are organized in a manner that allows some privileged people to maintain an advantage over others based on group membership. Employers may rely on racist and ethnic stereotypes about the work aptitude and motivation of ethnic minorities to deny them jobs or promotions without fully considering their individual merits and qualifications. Institutional discrimination can also be an inherent part of organizational structures, such as the elaborate personnel systems and complex hierarchies of job titles that keep women from advancing in the workplace and from being fairly compensated for their work (England, 2010). For example, although men and women graduate from law school at similar rates, men still significantly outnumber women in law firms and judiciary positions around the country, a disparity that may be perpetuated by persistent gender biases (Levinson & Young, 2010).

Group distinctiveness is sometimes achieved when the opportunities of groups and their members are protected in ways that exclude outsiders. For example, before laws were passed to outlaw this practice, there were social and recreational clubs in the United States that did not permit African Americans or Jews to join. People who belonged to these clubs often saw this exclusion as a symbol of the clubs' respectability and social prominence, and saw their own membership as ensuring their own respectability and social prominence.

A Culturally Grounded Paradigm

A culturally grounded approach to social work practice calls for the acquired knowledge of the roots of stereotypes, prejudice, and discrimination to be applied in context. The social worker must assess the context, or environment, for prejudice and discrimination and develop an action plan accordingly. A practitioner using a culturally grounded approach addresses oppressive conditions effectively by moving beyond the levels of practice debate and recognizing the importance of micro-, mezzo-, and macro practice as multilayered and interconnected approaches to empowerment. Inherent in this framework are several important tenets for praxis.

1. First, the choice of intervention type is not determined by the worker's level of comfort, but instead by what feels most natural to clients from their cultural perspective and by what will yield the best outcomes while using the fewest resources. Therefore, the choice of any practice intervention is driven by concerns about good fit and effectiveness.
2. Second, interventions are chosen because the change they produce is sustainable once the social worker is no longer engaged with the individual, family, group, or community. Interventions that feel strange or uncomfortable to clients will most likely not survive the test of time and will not be conducive to empowerment.
3. Third, interventions are selected according to evidence-based research, and their implementation is closely evaluated for applicability, fidelity, and effectiveness. Formal research and innovation by the social worker together facilitate the constant retooling needed for practice in an ever-changing society.

The culturally grounded approach views clients as experts and partners of theorists and helping professionals. Their joint efforts facilitate effective and ethical social work practice and result in the highest levels of client satisfaction. Notes from the field 2.4 illustrates the need for practitioners to assess their own behavior and its impact on their clients, and how a lack of cultural attunement may be interpreted as prejudice. Arlene reached out to a cultural expert for help and was able to develop a culturally grounded explanation for the behavior she noticed among some of her clients. Arlene developed a skill that all social workers could benefit from: a graceful acceptance that there is always much to be learned about individuals and communities. Social workers often need help in understanding cultural gaps and in identifying effective strategies to apply to those gaps. In supervision and through other confirmatory sources, Arlene can test the explanation she received from Ms. Martinez and implement the appropriate corrective action.

Cultural misunderstandings and actual discriminatory practices affect the client's access to quality services. The ongoing delivery of equitable and effective

---

NOTES FROM THE FIELD 2.4
Don't You Like My Kids?

Arlene is in the first semester of her social work practicum. She has been assigned to a prenatal clinic. She enjoys working with the mothers and children the nurses and doctors refer to her. Her role is to conduct psychosocial assessments of new patients and assess for assets and possible barriers to compliance with the regime of prenatal and postpartum visits. She has noticed that some of the Mexican mothers appear to be a bit distant with her. She decides to ask one of her clients, Ms. Martinez, about her perception. Ms. Martinez explains that some of the mothers are concerned by the fact that Arlene never touches their children, even when greeting them, which they interpret as meaning that their children are not worthy of warmth and affection or that Arlene thinks they are dirty. Ms. Martinez explains that some of the mothers expect her to touch their children's heads as if in a *bendición* (blessing).

---

services is at the core of continuous professional self-assessment, which examines attitudes and behaviors in addition to awareness. This process requires a constant examination of the professional and personal self and perceptions of and interactions with clients. This form of professional praxis greatly benefits from group and individual professional supervision and from ongoing dialogue with clients.

Key Concepts

Oppression: The denial of an individual's or group of people's freedom, happiness, and access to resources by another

Deculturalization: The denial of one's culture or identity resulting from the internalization of oppression

Stereotypes: The beliefs that individuals hold about members of a group, based on overgeneralizations about the characteristics of all members of that group

Prejudice: The irrational sense of dislike that individuals or groups experience toward members of different cultural groups

Scapegoating: Blaming and taking out feelings of frustration on someone other than the true source of one's frustration

Projection: The processes through which people minimize or deny undesirable characteristics that they possess by exaggerating the same characteristics in someone from a different cultural group

Discrimination: The unequal treatment of individuals based on their membership in a particular cultural group, rather than on their individual qualities

Culturally grounded paradigm: An approach to social work practice that recognizes the client as the expert; partners with clients to explore the roots of discrimination, oppression, and stereotypes; and works to address both the presenting problem and the root cause on multiple layers of the ecological system by building on strengths and empowering communities

3

The Intersectionality of Race and Ethnicity with Other Factors

INDIVIDUAL IDENTITY DEVELOPS BASED ON NUMEROUS WAYS IN WHICH people differ, such as along the lines of gender, race, ethnicity, sexual orientation, religion, ability status, and social class. The way in which these factors are weighted and the way they intersect in a person's life may create disadvantages or privileges for her or him. It is important for social work professionals to understand that an individual's identity cannot be easily defined by just one factor. In most cases, a variety of factors contribute to an individual's sense of identity. This chapter provides general information on intersectionality and its effects on individuals in society and how social workers can use this knowledge about intersectionality to work effectively with members of various cultural groups.

INTERSECTIONALITY

The term "intersectionality" refers to the multidimensionality and complexity of the human cultural experience and describes the place where multiple identities come together, or intersect. Individuals hold positions within multiple systems of inequality based on race, ethnicity, gender, social class, sexual orientation, age, and ability status; particular sets of identities carry important social implications. For example, issues of race and gender oppression cut across social class lines. Women experience sexism—stereotyping, male dominance, and discrimination—regardless of their education and abilities and how well they are paid for their work, while men from racial minority groups retain privileges afforded to them in a sexist society. Such intersections of race and gender lead to a variety of experiences and opportunities for different individuals, producing outcomes that may reflect an accumulation of social advantages or disadvantages. P. Collins (1998) described the intersection of race, gender, and social class as constituting a "matrix of domination" (p. 18). Within this matrix, individuals may experience disadvantage or privilege as a result of their combination of identities. Ethnic minority women may face double jeopardy due to the combined disadvantages of their gender and their ethnic background, and may be relegated to the most devalued occupations and jobs. Ethnic minority and poor immigrant women make up the vast majority of household domestic workers, who rank as the lowest-paid occupational group in the United States. In contrast, white women are much more likely to attain white-collar positions and typically are the middle- or upper-class employers of ethnic minority and poor immigrant women (Hondagneu-Sotelo, 2001).

Increasing recognition of the intersectionality of identities has prompted extensive research on its social implications. The existence of multiple systems of inequality suggests that the social world cannot be easily divided into oppressors and the oppressed. For example, white males, who exemplify privilege in U.S. society, are quite diverse as a group, with their own within-group variations in terms of privilege. Substantial numbers of white males live out their lives in the working class, suffering economic exploitation and bearing greater occupational risks to their health than do white men in higher social classes. White gay men and those with disabilities are often denied the full range of benefits that white heterosexual and able-male privilege brings to other men.

Research on intersectionality has demonstrated that different systems of inequality are interconnected (Anderson & Collins, 2004). For example, African American lesbians face triple jeopardy because they simultaneously occupy disadvantaged positions in social hierarchies based on gender, race, and sexual orientation. Despite the identities they share with other oppressed groups like white lesbians and heterosexual African American women, African American lesbians have struggled to gain visibility and influence within the feminist, gay, and black liberation movements (Diamond & Savin-Williams, 2000). All too often these groups strive for liberation in isolation or at cross-purposes from one another, without recognizing areas where they may enjoy privilege that other groups do not. Moreover, conflict and dissension among oppressed groups can be instigated by the majority groups in power, which diverts attention from the underlying systems of privilege.

In the history of the United States, successive immigrant ethnic groups have been blamed for the economic ills plaguing the U.S.-born working class and have become the targets of officially sanctioned discrimination. During an economic depression in 1893, strong opposition emerged against the admittance of immigrants from Italy, and Italians were suddenly regarded as paupers. Similarly, Chinese immigrants, who were originally welcomed as "honest," "peaceful," and "industrious," came to be perceived as "dangerous," "vicious," and "deceitful" when jobs became scarce and the Chinese started to seek work in mines and in factories, and on farms (Levin & Levin, 1982, p. 152). During the late nineteenth century, when cotton prices declined in the South, there was an increase in the number of lynchings of African Americans (Behrens, Uggen, & Manza, 2003). More recently, in the 1980s, an anti-immigrant movement in California was renewed and consolidated during an economic slowdown. Disempowered Mexican immigrants working predominantly in minimum-wage jobs that few U.S.-born individuals would accept were viewed by some as responsible for the economic ills of the entire state of California.

The social implications of intersectionality, like the systems of inequality those implications are based on, are constantly changing. The civil rights and women's movements have produced important changes in racial and gender relations, but these successes have also helped to alter the issues in contention. The history of affirmative action is a case in point. Established in the late 1960s and early 1970s to take steps beyond the elimination of open discrimination, affirmative action actively promoted racial and gender equity in employment, government contracting, and educational access. In recent years, societal debates and legal action concerning affirmative action have been focused on the use of race and ethnicity in the criteria for admission to colleges and universities. The ensuing controversies have revealed a growing awareness of multiple systems of inequality, particularly the intersections of race, ethnicity, and social class.

Arguments against affirmative action have frequently centered on its alleged failure to provide protection and assistance to those most in need and the alleged harm inflicted on others through reverse discrimination. Some critics of affirmative action have portrayed its beneficiaries as mostly ethnic minorities from middle- and upper-class families who do not need help as much as lower-class African Americans and Latinos or equally needy low-income whites. Debate has also arisen over differences in levels of need and the application of affirmative action to ethnic minority groups, such as the exclusion of Asian Americans from affirmative action and the higher educational achievement of Afro-Caribbean students than of African American students. This issue highlights the significant within-group diversity that exists within large racial categories. Notes from the field 3.1 provides an example of multiethnic and multiracial identities. Manuel's story highlights the complexity of intersecting identities and illustrates how discreet ethnic and racial categories may not apply to some individuals.

SOCIAL CLASS

Societies throughout history have organized themselves into social classes. Although there are differences among societies in the degree of opportunity for upward mobility, such social stratification is ubiquitous. Even societies that undergo bloody revolutions to effect a rapid change in social structure often merely substitute one social class system for another. For example, under the official egalitarian ideology of Communist countries like the former Soviet Union, China, and Cuba, de facto social classes existed, allowing the small elite to enjoy privileges derived from their membership in the ruling party or close association with its members rather than from inheritance.

NOTES FROM THE FIELD 3.1

Who Is Manuel?

When asked about his race, Manuel Silva self-identifies as a black man and honors his African ancestry, but culturally he also recognizes his Puerto Rican–Latino background, his Roman Catholic faith, and his Taíno (indigenous) roots. Manuel's identity and social experiences emerge from the intersection of all those identities. Depending on his environment, he may stress a certain identity more than others. On the U.S. mainland, Manuel is often defined racially by others based on his physical appearance rather than on his multiple cultural roots. Others' definitions of who he is often overlook Manuel's intersectionalities and multiple sources of identity. When Manuel applies for a job with the city government, he asks his social worker which race/ethnicity category he should mark on the application form. The form allows for only one choice under race/ethnicity. Because he would like to recognize all his cultural heritages, he is thinking about choosing "other."

Class is a powerful force in U.S. society, although it is not always as well recognized as many other forms of oppression and discrimination. Dividing lines between social classes in the United States are fluid, somewhat flexible, and often hidden. Rather than a rigid class hierarchy, the U.S. social class system is rooted in a triad of interconnected socioeconomic differences in income, education, and occupational status. These differences determine an individual's position in the social hierarchy (and its associated privileges or disadvantages) and have wide-ranging implications for cultural identities, because they are systematically associated with gender, race, ethnicity, ability status, and other cultural identities.

People do not choose their social class. Members of the poor and working classes are limited by the opportunities afforded or denied by capitalism and its controlling profit motive. Political elites, the mass media, and the education system frequently promote the idea that U.S. society is a meritocracy, where rewards are allocated based on individual merit alone. However, the uneven playing field of social class gives crucial advantages to those from privileged backgrounds. Our education system is, in fact, a prime example of class-based inequities. School districts, and even the schools within them, vary enormously in terms of the adequacy of building facilities and equipment, teacher preparation and pay, class sizes, range of academic offerings, and quality of instruction. School financing through local property taxes and the residential segregation of the poor ensure that families from higher social classes are able to transfer their wealth directly into better schools for their children. These children also benefit from cultural capital, such as their parents' better educational preparation, high educational aspirations, knowledge of educational options and purchasing power, and more-extensive social networks that help them locate the best schools. Cultural capital also includes the implicit transmission of norms, values, and behaviors expected when socializing in higher social classes that enable individuals to fit in with fraternities or sororities, when they are out to lunch with colleagues, and in board rooms. Meanwhile, families from low-income neighborhoods struggle to afford even basic education, and their modest incomes and property values limit the taxable resources that are available to support their local public schools.

Overall, social class governs many of the life chances that determine opportunities for a long life and decent quality of living. The impact of social class on life chances was exemplified quite literally in 1912 when the *Titanic* sank. Only 25 percent of the third-class passengers survived. Most of the passengers in first class were American or upper class British, while most of the third-class passengers who perished were immigrating from Great Britain or other countries in Europe to the United States (Hanley, Turner, Bellera, & Telsch, 2003).

In the United States, there is a persisting gap between the upper and lower classes' access to a college education. Statistics from the National Student Loan Program comparing families in the top income quartile to those in the bottom income quartile (that is, the quarter of the population earning the most vs. the quarter earning the least) show that whereas around 90 percent of children from the most affluent families attend college, barely half of those from the least affluent families do so, and this gap shows signs of widening rather than closing (Price, 2004). Students from families in the top income quartile are five times more likely to complete a college degree than are those from families at the bottom income quartile (Bailey & Dynarski, 2011). Moreover, contrary to the ethos of the meritocracy, a student's socioeconomic background has been found to be a more important factor in whether she or he attends college than the student's educational ability (Berliner, 2006). Only 8 percent of high-achieving low-income high school students apply to a wide spectrum of colleges that includes very selective schools, compared to 68 percent of their high-income counterparts, a disparity that helps account for the underrepresentation of low-income students at the most selective colleges and universities (Hoxby & Avery, 2013). In states that have begun to dismantle affirmative action policies governing college admissions, ethnic minority student enrollments did not decrease overall but their admissions shifted away from selective colleges to less-selective institutions (Hinrichs, 2010). This shift has significant implications for the eventual earning power of those students.

Although it is a common perception that the United States is a classless society, recent trends in the income distribution suggest that wealth and influence are becoming more concentrated in the hands of a small elite. Economic analyses have demonstrated that the top 1 percent of income earners in 2010 reaped more than 93 percent of all of the nation's total gains in income, with an average income gain of $4.2 million for individuals in the top .01 percent and $105,637 for those in the top 1 percent. On the other hand, the average person in the remaining 99 percent of the population had earnings gains of only .02 percent in that same year, with an average gain of only $80 annually (Piketty & Saez, 2012). The belief that well-educated people are making major advances socioeconomically (a characteristic of a meritocracy) is also challenged by the data. For example, U.S. census data show that real incomes for college graduates declined from 2009 to 2010 (U.S. Census Bureau, 2013).

These sharp socioeconomic differences are powerful evidence of the importance of social class in the perpetuation of inequalities in the United States. For many cultural groups whose opportunities for social and economic mobility have historically been blocked or thwarted, problems of socioeconomic inequality remain an acute challenge to their well-being.

GENDER

The United States as a society was profoundly shaped by eighteenth-century European American men who resisted or gave little thought to empowering others. Women continue to be a group that struggles to gain a place at the table of equality. Although they constitute a slight numerical majority, women remain a sociological minority in the United States, as they do in most societies. Indeed, gender equality has yet to be achieved in many important ways. For instance, women are paid less than men for doing the same jobs. Women who are the head of their households are more likely to live below poverty levels, and they are still primarily responsible for child care even when they have a partner and are employed full-time (McKernan & Ratcliffe, 2005). In a comparison of eighteen affluent democratic countries, the United States had the highest rate of single mothers living in poverty, followed in this order by the United Kingdom, the Netherlands, Canada, and Australia. Differences in rates of poverty among single mothers were explained by individual characteristics such as education, as well as by national policies that included universal wage replacement programs (Brady & Burroway, 2012).

Many women dwell on the periphery of society, on the lower rungs of social and institutional hierarchies, and in positions where they face oppression. This oppression is maintained in part by cultural norms that specify appropriate roles for men and women. These gender norms are socially constructed; violations of the norms can result in marginalization, discrimination, and violence. Men are socialized to be family providers and leaders and are provided with relatively clear guidelines about how to combine occupational and family roles, while women receive mixed messages about these same roles. Male roles are associated with highly valued characteristics like authority, strength, and decisiveness, while women's roles emphasize nurturance and caring, which are judged as having lesser value (O'Brien et al., 2000).

The persisting gender gap in wages makes it difficult for many women to manage financially as heads of households. This gender-wage gap is perpetuated by employers' beliefs that women need to devote more of their energy to child care and family demands than men do; as a result, employers often do not consider women to be viable candidates for certain leadership positions. This perception then decreases women's chances of securing jobs that have the most responsibility, authority, and remuneration. In 2011, even among the highly educated, women earned on average $27,677 less annually than their male counterparts with the same level of education (U.S. Census Bureau, 2013). Among some minority ethnic and religious groups, education for women is still considered inappropriate, and to be a waste of precious family resources best reserved for males. In many contemporary societies, women remain financially dependent on men because social taboos prevent them from accessing education and employment outside the home.

In societies like the United States, where women are highly involved in the labor force, they generally are relegated to less-lucrative occupations and professions. As organizational management emerged as a distinct professional field in the early twentieth century, many of its defining characteristics were imbued with a masculine ethic. Men established their privileged status by describing rationality and reason, a tough-minded approach to problems, and the analytic capability to abstract and plan (all of which were viewed as male characteristics) and the ability to set aside distinctly "feminine" personal, sentimental, and emotional considerations as the essential traits of the effective manager (Gartzia, 2011; Kanter, 1977).

Some feminists argue that the traditional Western family, with its authoritarian adult male rule, is the training ground that initially conditions individuals to accept group oppression as the natural order (hooks, 1984; Kuhn, 2013). Patriarchy has taken different shapes in different cultural subgroups and social classes, but has mostly survived, if not been strengthened, over time. Violence against women is one manifestation of patriarchal structures that perpetuate oppression (Hunnicutt, 2009). Although women are less likely to be victims of homicide, robbery, or assault, they are seven to fourteen times more likely to be victims of domestic violence (Tjaden & Thoennes, 2000) and they account for 90 percent of all incidents of reported rapes (Catalano, 2005). In a World Health Organization international survey of violence against women, lifetime rates of physical and sexual violence ranged from 15 percent to 71 percent, depending on the country (Garcia-Moreno, Jansen, Ellsberg, Heise, & Watts, 2006). In resource-poor countries and countries that had recently experienced war, women reported a much higher incidence of violence (Kaya & Cook, 2010); in Ethiopia, for example, 54 percent of the women reported experiencing sexual and physical violence (Garcia-Moreno et al., 2006), and in Pakistan 56 percent reported sexual violence and 52 percent reported physical violence (Ali, Asad, Mogren, & Krantz, 2011). In addition to these explicit expressions of oppression, the United Nations compiled statistics highlighting the wide variety of oppression that women face globally: women comprise 50 percent of the world's population, but they do three-fourths of the world's work, receive one-tenth of the world's salary, own one one-hundredth of the world's land, form two-thirds of all illiterate adults, and together with their dependent children are three-fourths of the world's starving people.

One source of the power of systems of gender privilege and inequality is the idea that gender divides people in a fundamental and innate way into two clearly distinct groups. Although this idea is still largely taken for granted, there is growing evidence and recognition that gender is not a dichotomous characteristic. This fact is amply demonstrated by the existence of a transgender community, which, although traditionally grouped with lesbians, gays, and bisexuals, does not constitute a sexual orientation group but rather a gender group. Although definitions are evolving, the term "gender queer" is used increasingly to refer to a spectrum of gender identities that include transgender (those who have gone through or plan to undergo sexual reassignment) and a growing population of people who identify as intersex or as not fitting any traditional notions of gender, people who sometimes are referred to as nongendered or gender fluid.

SEXUAL ORIENTATION

The privilege accorded to a heterosexual orientation is based on heteronormativity, a belief system that views heterosexual attraction as superior to and more natural than same-sex or bisexual attraction. Heterosexism is a form of discrimination that reinforces systems that place nonheterosexuals in marginalized social and political positions. Heterosexism is a means of exerting social control through intimidation and exclusion. It is a way for heterosexuals to retain social positions that are widely agreed to be superior to those held by lesbians, gay men, bisexuals, and other queers. Heterosexual privilege is based on the unexamined assumption that heterosexuality is the norm and all other sexual orientations are deviations from that norm. Heterosexuals do not have to make public their sexual identity or come out. In contrast, lesbians, gays, bisexuals, and transgender people are part of a minority group. As a result, they are sometimes the target of homophobia (irrational fear of and aversion to sexual minorities), which is often expressed through discrimination and violence. Although the repression experienced by sexual minorities makes it difficult to obtain representative samples of them, studies of hate crimes and violent victimization suggest that a very large percentage of the lesbian, gay, bisexual, and transgender (LGBT) community is victimized by assault, vandalism, and theft. Unlike most violent crime in general, most of the crime prompted by homophobia is perpetrated by strangers rather than by acquaintances (Herek, Cogan, & Gillis, 2002). Not only does homophobia manifest itself in acts of aggression and discrimination against the LGBT community, but it also can be internalized by members of the community who have unconsciously accepted heteronormative norms and derogatory cultural messages about themselves.

In addition, members of the LGBT community experience many legal disadvantages. In the United States same-sex couples have only recently been awarded equal rights in the areas of immigration, adoption, marriage, and inheritance at the federal level but not by many states. In older age they may face unequal treatment under Social Security (e.g., no rights to share a partner's benefits), housing discrimination, and discriminatory practices in health care and long-term care. The U.S. Supreme Court in June 2013 ruled that married same-sex couples were entitled to federal benefits and, by declining to decide a case from California, effectively reinstated same-sex marriages there. The ruling did not affect the ban on gay marriage that exists in many states but had important consequences for married lesbian and gay couples in terms of benefits and other rights. For example, if a gay man is hospitalized, hospitals in many states may bar his partner from visiting because he is not considered a family member. Moreover, same-sex partners in some states may not make legally binding decisions about treatment or care for their partners when their partners are unable to do so for themselves. The federal protections for same-sex couples in the United States increased significantly after the Supreme Court struck down the federal Defense of Marriage Act in 2013, but the levels of protection continue to vary greatly from state to state and from municipality to municipality.

Historically, policies and laws have been used more often to oppress sexual minorities than to protect them. For example, in 1951 the U.S. Civil Service Commission, in a document entitled "Employment of Homosexuals and Other Sex Perverts in Government," forbade the employment of LGBT people in government. One year later, the McCarran Act's categorization of same-sex sexual attraction as a psychopathic personality trait barred them from entering the United States. The act also allowed for the deportation of alien (noncitizen) homosexuals, even those who had been living in the country for several years. Throughout most of the twentieth century, many forms of same-sex sexual behavior were explicitly outlawed in state constitutions, usually in the form of antisodomy laws. It was not until 1974 that the American Psychiatric Association removed the term "homosexuality" from its list of pathological diagnoses, and not until the U.S. Supreme Court's 2003 ruling in *Lawrence & Garner v. State of Texas* that remaining statutes outlawing specifically same-sex sexual conduct were ruled unconstitutional.

These government statutes were generally a rejection of same-sex sexual conduct among men. The process of gay liberation has also often emphasized a male gay culture while silencing or deemphasizing lesbian feminism and many other forms of gay life and identity. It is not surprising, then, that many ideas and assumptions about the LGBT community are based on the experiences and writings of white, middle-class gay men.

Oppression based on sexual orientation can intersect in complex ways with many other identities (see notes from the field 3.2). Social workers may be unprepared if called upon to work with clients who do not fit the stereotype of the white, well-off gay man. An occupationally successful lesbian client may be entangled in a relationship with a physically abusive female partner. An African American man might be referred for the stressful and health-threatening consequences of the double life that he leads as a heterosexual married man who has anonymous sex with other men. A working-class lesbian mother may be struggling to avoid losing custody of her children to an ex-husband who says her sexual orientation makes her an unfit parent. In each of these examples, in order to intervene in a culturally competent manner, the social worker must recognize the different ways in which the client expresses her or his sexual orientation.

NOTES FROM THE FIELD 3.2
Discussing Female Sexuality

Rachel has been blind since birth. She was actively involved in the blind community in high school and worked on campaigns to address stigma and promote Braille education, a crucial skill for employment success. She came out as a lesbian her sophomore year of college but continued to identify more with her blind identity than with her sexual orientation. Rachel attributed this to the fact that her blindness is the first thing that people notice about her in any interaction. Incorporating some of the new feminist ideas that she has been recently exposed to in college, Rachel has become increasingly involved with feminist issues in the blind community. She is very interested in addressing the stereotypical images of women with disabilities as nongendered, nonsexual, and dependent. To begin a dialogue among women with disabilities about these issues Rachel has started an informal group where a small but growing number of young women with disabilities meet once a week to talk about sexuality, gender identity, and their experiences with dating. Creating this space for discussion and support has enabled Rachel to continue her advocacy work with the blind community and reaffirm her gender identity. In a future session, she plans to introduce the topic of sexual orientation and is considering coming out to the group, but she is not yet sure whether she will do so.

RELIGION

Religion can be an important source of identity and an instrument for positive social change, but at the same time it has been used throughout history to justify social inequities and promote discrimination against individuals and communities. For example, passages of the Bible equate blackness with punishment by God: "The punishment of my people is worse than the penalty of Sodom" (Lamentations 4:6, King James Version). "Her crowned princes were once purer than snow, whiter than milk. But their faces turned blacker than soot, and no one knew them in the street" (Lamentations 4:7–8, King James Version). As early as the first century CE, Christian warnings about Satan such as the Epistle of Saint Barnabas drew on the same imagery: "The Way of the Black One is crooked and full of cursing, for it is the way of death eternal with punishment, and in it are the things that destroy their soul: idolatry, forwardness, arrogance of power, hypocrisy, double-heartedness, adultery, murder, robbery, pride, transgressions, fraud, malice, self-sufficiency, enchantments magic, covetousness" (Barnabas, quoted in Owens, 1976).

Because religion provides the core beliefs that lay the foundation for its group members' shared perceptions of social reality, religion can play an important role in a person's identity. Not only are religious organizations important in the lives of many, but also even those who do not claim religious beliefs feel the influence of religious values on social life and politics. Religious texts need to be interpreted, and it is often in the interpretation that biased people are able to insert their prejudice. Christian texts, for example, are often used by some fringe groups to justify racism, anti-Semitism, sexism, and homophobia. For example, according to some Christian interpretations, the city of Sodom was destroyed because of its citizens' same-sex sexual behavior.

Sometimes religion serves as a unifier of people and an agent of social control, while at other times it contributes to social conflict. The French sociologist Emile Durkheim (1912/1965) argued that the function of religion is to preserve social order by discouraging deviant behavior and giving moral authority to the established social system. Karl Marx (1843/1970) had originally adopted a more critical view of religion as a form of what he named "false consciousness," that helps the ruling class perpetuate its domination by encouraging the poor and struggling to bear their suffering in the hope that they will be rewarded in the afterlife. Religion often plays a central role in defining political divisions, the distribution of power, and social inequalities. In medieval Europe, the Roman Catholic Church promoted the idea that kings ruled by divine right, thereby sustaining the feudal system. Similarly, throughout Indian history Hinduism helped preserve the hereditary caste system that restricted certain groups to particular occupations and social circles and institutionalized segregation and oppression. Even though the caste system was legally abolished in the 1960s, it had become so entrenched over the two thousand years of India's history that it still pervades most social transactions today.

The Spanish conquest of Mexico, as in the rest of Latin America, utilized both the sword and the cross. Following their military successes, the colonizers instituted a systematic campaign to eradicate indigenous religious belief systems and replace them with Christianity. Christianity was used to justify the exploitation and oppression of the Native populations. The suffering endured by the original inhabitants of Mesoamerica was viewed by their conquerors as a form of redemption and salvation. In the United States, enslaved Africans and Native Americans were also forced to adopt Christianity. More recently, China's Falon Gong movement, a loosely organized group promoting spiritual development that meets in public places to practice its rituals, has become the target of repressive actions, including harassment and the imprisonment of the movement's leaders, by the Chinese government.

Religion, whether expressed through violence, activism, or pacifism, can be employed as a force for political and social change. The Protestant majority and the Roman Catholic minority in Northern Ireland have been in conflict for several centuries. In the decades since 1968, outbreaks of sectarian violence between those groups have claimed over three thousand lives. When armed conflict in the disintegrating former Yugoslavia broke out in the 1990s, the most violent rifts were along the religious lines that separated Croatian Catholic, Serbian Orthodox, and Bosnian Muslim ethnic communities, resulting in systematic ethnic cleansing and the loss of tens of thousands of lives. Conflict in the Middle East provides almost daily examples of how religious differences can be used to ignite simmering political and economic grievances into waves of violence and retribution. Although it is virtually impossible to separate ethnic, political, economic, and historical motivations for conflict, religious narratives fuel clashes between the Sunni and Shia in Iraq, between Muslims and Buddhists in Burma, and between Muslims and Christians in Egypt.

Despite the use of religion to incite and justify acts of violence, religion can also be a vehicle for positive social change through nonviolence. Religious leaders came together at the Southern Christian Leadership Conference to launch and sustain the U.S. civil rights movement of the 1950s and 1960s, providing moral authority to their drive to end racial segregation and discrimination. In the 1970s a liberation theology movement in Latin America developed both the religious ideas and the social organization needed to focus attention on redressing massive economic inequities within society.

In the United States, religion has been used to promote social change, defend the status quo, justify inequities, and agitate for the redress of injustices. Among Westernized democracies, the United States stands out as an unusually religious nation. Over 90 percent of the population says they believe in God, the majority claim to belong to a religious denomination and report that religion is very important in their lives, and nearly half say they attend weekly religious services (Wald & Calhoun-Brown, 2006). Stances on controversial issues like legalized abortion, gay and lesbian marriage, and the death penalty vary not only across religions, but also within religions. Many religious organizations sponsor their own social service networks, and social workers may encounter conflicts between the profession's code of ethics and the policies of their employers. For example, a social worker working with adolescent boys in a group home setting run by a Roman Catholic charity organization may be told that she cannot talk to the youths about birth control. Although there is no consensus in Islam about abortion, a Muslim social worker employed in a health clinic that provides abortions may feel that offering these services as an option to the patients is a violation of her personal ethics. In these situations, the social worker has a responsibility to adhere to the policies of the organization as long as they are in place and serve the best interest and well-being of the client. This may require the social worker to make referrals to other agencies or seriously consider if remaining employed at the agency is in her own best interest or in the best interest of the individuals that she serves. The social worker also has the option of challenging agency policies that he or she feels are unjust or unethical. Religious faith can be a source of inspiration and commitment for social workers, but religious commitment and loyalty to a doctrine emanating from organized religion are very personal and private choices. While performing a professional role, if any conflicts emerge between the expectations of the religious group and the profession, social workers adhere to the profession's code of ethics.

ABILITY STATUS

The stigma attached to mental and physical disability frequently results in discrimination, and sometimes oppression, against the people who bear those labels. Since the early twentieth century, researchers have argued that individuals who are labeled mentally ill are often those who simply do not conform to the prevailing cultural definition of normality (Koh, 2006). Because normality is culturally defined, people labeled mentally ill in one culture may be able to function well in another. A respected mystic, visionary, or healer with extraordinary powers in a traditional society may be considered psychotic in many postindustrial societies. Additionally, a client's reactions to trauma, poverty, abuse, and neglect, such as depression, anxiety, and PTSD, are often pathologized and labeled as mental illness. Unlike other intersecting identities that have been identified, ability status may be temporary or fixed, with an individual having the potential to become disabled at any time. This is illustrated in notes from the field 3.3.

NOTES FROM THE FIELD 3.3

Addressing Unseen Wounds

Michael's convoy had been hit by an IED when it was conducting a regular patrol in Afghanistan. Michael lost a leg in the explosion and was sent to an army hospital in the United States to recover. In addition to coping with his new disability, Michael was grieving the loss of two friends in the explosion. He had conflicting emotions: he was grateful that his life had been spared, but also felt extreme grief and a desire to take the place of his buddies that died. His wife had been with him every day as he went through physical therapy and was his biggest fan, but he felt isolated from her and was not able to explain what he had experienced and to share his profound sadness. He put on a strong face for her but inside he was devastated. He was healing well physically, and after four months of intense physical therapy he was released home. Once he got home he started having dreams about the explosion that would not allow him to sleep through the night. He was dealing well with his physical disability, which is what people saw, but the emotional difficulties he was experiencing, or the invisible disability, was paralyzing him. When he was fully mobile with his prosthetic leg, his wife began to encourage him to do some work outside of the house, hoping that the activity would pull him out of the depression; instead, the extreme anxiety that he felt in crowded public places kept him from going out. After having a panic attack at a local shopping mall, Michael began attending support groups at the VA for veterans of the recent conflicts. In the groups he found out that what he was going through was the normal signs and symptoms of PTSD. He was able to talk about the guilt he felt leaving his fellow soldiers behind, his fear, his anxiety, and his grief. Although talking about it did not immediately take away the symptoms, it did make him feel like he was not alone and that he had a place he could go where he was understood. Additionally, his wife started attending groups for spouses and, like her husband, found support from other people who had been living with the nightmares, the mood swings, and the anxiety. She was able to develop strategies to take care of herself and help her husband heal.

Society's views of mental illness reflect a social construction of the notion of mental illness rather than the reality, and can result in feelings of distrust, embarrassment, and fear for people who carry the burden of a diagnosis of mental illness. This is important in social work, as the mistaken and hurtful views and beliefs perpetuated by society's construction of mental illness affect many clients and their relatives. As part of the assessment of the social context, social workers can serve clients by investigating the role that cultural beliefs play in shaping community responses to mental illness. The negative attitudes held by much of society toward mental illness and the stigmatization of mentally ill individuals have eased significantly since the 1990s, but the desire that many people have to maintain their distance from people who have been diagnosed with a mental illness persists, particularly in ethnic minority communities and around the globe (Aromaa, Tolvanen, Tuulari, & Wahlbeck, 2011; Ouellette-Kuntz, Burge, Brown, & Arsenault, 2010). This stigmatization makes many people in need of psychological help reluctant to seek that help for fear that they will be labeled mentally ill.

Such responses to the label of mental illness parallel society's attitudes toward the concept of disability; disability, like mental illness, is in many ways often a matter of perception, and is not just a physical or bodily state. Many of the problems of the mentally ill and physically disabled arise primarily from an ideology of ableism that discriminates against and stigmatizes them. A key factor in society's treatment of people with physical disabilities is the process of social labeling, by which the disability becomes their defining or master status. The stigma imposed by society on people with disabilities erects social obstacles for them that may be more difficult to manage than the disability itself. People may respond to this stigma by treating people with disabilities like helpless and dependent children in need of guidance, avoiding or condescending to them, reacting to them with fear, or being reluctant to view them as having an equal claim to society's resources. Shawn responds to this stigma in notes from the field 3.4.

More than two decades after passage of the Americans with Disabilities Act in 1990, people with disabilities are at higher risk than the nondisabled of being unemployed, living on very low incomes, lacking health insurance, and being unsatisfied with life (Centers for Disease Control and Prevention[CDC], 2007). Despite the perception that they are a small minority consisting mostly of the elderly, over one in five Americans—54.4 million people—is disabled, and 37.8 percent of these are under sixty-five years of age (Brault, 2012). Ethnic minorities are disproportionally represented among the disabled as a result of motor vehicle–related injuries and the HIV pandemic, in part as a result of a lack of awareness of and access to services (McKenna, Michaud, Murray, & Marks, 2005).

Invisible disabilities refer to symptoms that are not obvious to the onlooker but that can limit daily activities. About 10 percent of the U.S. population has invisible disabilities that can include debilitating pain, fatigue, dizziness, weakness, cognitive dysfunctions, learning differences, mental disorders, and hearing and vision impairments (Brault, 2012).

AGE

Some cultures associate youth with health and beauty, and associate age with weakened health and loss of beauty (Calasanti, 2005). Age-related discrimination

NOTES FROM THE FIELD 3.4

"Don't Talk about Me As If I Am Not in the Room"

Shawn began hearing voices when he was twenty. He was living with a roommate in college when the noise became overwhelming and he was not able to distinguish what was real from what was imaginary. Unable to focus in class or sleep, he had to drop out and move home with his parents. When living at home, his parents noticed that he was talking to himself and insisted that he see a psychiatrist. He was diagnosed with schizophrenia and put on medication. After his diagnosis, his parents and friends started to treat him as if he were a child. They would constantly ask him if he was okay, and if he needed anything. They stopped bugging him about getting a job or what he was going to do in the future. That was nice at first, but then Shawn started to feel they were patronizing him. The medication that he was prescribed was working; it quieted the voices and took the edge off the anxiety, but he did not feel like himself. It dulled his emotions and took away his sense of humor; he was not able to banter with his friends because everything seemed to be slowed down. During their meetings, his psychiatrist rushed him through a series of questions, nodded, and then wrote another prescription for the same medication. His parents attended these meeting with him and frequently spoke for him when the doctor asked the questions. Shawn became very frustrated and decided that at the next meeting he was going to talk for himself and ask for a different medication. The meeting started out the way it usually did, with Shawn's parents and the doctor talking about him as if he were not in the room. Halfway through the appointment, Shawn said, "I don't like the medication that I am on and I would like to be prescribed something else." Shocked, the doctor and his parents turned and looked at him as if they were surprised to find him sitting there. They did not respond to him and simply continued talking. A couple of seconds later Shawn said again, "I don't like the medication I am on and I would like to try something different." This time the doctor responded asking him what he did not like about the medication. He explained how the medication made him feel. The thought of changing the medication made his parent feel very uncomfortable. What if the voices come back? They chimed in and said, "But you are so much better. We don't want to go back to how things were." Shawn was not deterred. He was tired of being treated like a sick child. He said, "Look, I am a grown man with a mental illness. I am the only one who knows how it feels to be me, and I am capable of making my own decisions. I don't like what I am on and I want to try something else. Yes, the voices are gone, but I don't feel happy because I am not able to be myself. I need something that will quiet my voices and my anxiety but not the rest of me." Finally hearing, the doctor nodded his head, waited a minute, and then said, "I understand. I will prescribe you something else. Also, while I want to continue to include your parents in your treatment plan, I think you and I should start meeting without them every other week." Pleased that the doctor recognized his need for independence and control over his treatment, Shawn agreed.

is often called ageism; it occurs when someone is treated less favorably than another person just because of his or her age. Ageism and age discrimination can affect anyone throughout life, from children to elders. In some countries, including many Latin American countries, the United States, and others, there is a lack of legal protection against discrimination by age. For example, in many countries the law protects adults from corporal punishment, but does not protect children in the same way. In the United States, even the Age Discrimination clause in the Americans with Disabilities Employment Act (ADEA) forbids age discrimination only against people who are age forty or older.

Researchers have consistently found that older adults are perceived more negatively than younger individuals in terms of attractiveness, competence, and behavior (Kite, Stockdale, Whitley, & Johnson, 2005). From advertising to television, youth is the standard by which people are judged (Bayer, 2005; Hatch, 2005). Age is viewed as taking a greater toll on the physical appearance and social worth of women than of men. This attitude is based on the notion that women's power is based on temporary values such as beauty and sexual attraction, whereas men's power is embedded in more-durable values such as status and wealth (Calasanti & Slevin, 2001). Age-discrimination in employment is worse for women in professions that place an emphasis on an individual's appearance, such as modeling, acting, and advertisement/media (Clarke, 2002). While the U.S. Equal Employment Opportunity Commission reported a 17 percent jump in the number of age-discrimination complaints filed since 2007, the number of unemployed older workers has increased by 330 percent from 2003 to 2013 (Neumark & Button, 2013). This tendency to favor youthfulness transcends life. A recent study of obituaries suggested that the age-inaccurate photographs chosen to remember the deceased were another indication of the preference for youth (Ogletree, Figueroa, & Pena, 2005).

INTERSECTIONALITIES: JEWS AND ARABS

This review of the key factors of gender, ethnicity, religion, social class, sexual orientation, and ability status provides the foundation for the rest of this book. Intersectionality will be presented as the unifying concept that allows for an integration of these factors into the lives of real people living in real social and historical contexts. The intersectionality of cultural identities is a very dynamic phenomenon and reflects changes in time and place; it is, in other words, contextual. But the full significance and meaning of intersectionality cannot be limited to a short list of its possible axes. For example, age and ageism, immigration and acculturation status, and place of residence (urban or rural) are all critical factors to consider in social work practice. Jews and Arabs provide interesting examples of the complexity of intersectionality.

There is disagreement as to whether Judaism is a religion, an ethnicity, or both. Many Jews who are not religious think of themselves as being part of an ethnic group or a culture that is connected to their Jewish heritage. Social workers may encounter clients who are culturally Jewish but who self-identify as secular (not religious), or clients who were not born Jewish, and thus cannot be considered ethnically Jewish, but who have converted and are very observant. According to those who believe that Judaism is a religion, not an ethnicity, most American and European Jews can be divided into two ethnic groups: Ashkenazi Jews, whose ancestry can be traced to Central or Eastern Europe; and Sephardic Jews, descendants of Jews who were expelled from Spain and Portugal in 1492 during the Spanish Inquisition. However, there are other sects of Judaism that do not fall into these categories, such as the Bene Israel of India and the Jews of Ethiopia, often called Falasha. Many of the Bene Israel and the Falasha now live in Israel.

Although the great majority of American Jews are Ashkenazi, the original twenty-three Jews who landed in New Amsterdam (New York) in 1654 were Sephardim who first immigrated to Recife, Brazil, but who then left when the Portuguese recaptured Brazil from the Dutch (Karp, 1976). There are families in New Mexico and in other areas of the Southwest that trace their ancestry to the crypto-Jews, Jews who were forced to convert to Christianity during the Spanish Inquisition but who secretly continued to practice the Jewish faith. Although these families do not consider themselves Jewish, many of them continue to practice aspects of the Jewish faith that their families kept alive and passed on from one generation to the next.

There are several aspects of Judaism with which practitioners working with Jewish clients must be aware: Ashkenazi Judaism consists of religious branches or movements (e.g., orthodox, conservative, reform) with corresponding sets of norms and beliefs and their own synagogues. For example, gender roles and the level of equality between women and men can vary greatly across Jewish communities. These and other variables such as migration history, level of assimilation, intermarriage, posttraumatic stress related to anti-Jewish prejudice and discrimination, and the family's history related to the Holocaust need to be considered.

Arabs and Arab Americans are also very diverse groups. To be an Arab is to be a member of an ethnic group, but many people think of Arab culture as synonymous with Islam. Although most Arabs are Muslim, many Arabs are Christian, and some belong to religions other than Islam or Christianity (for example, some Arabs are Jewish) or do not belong to any religion. In the United States there are about 6 million Arabs, about one-third of whom are Muslim (Dwairy, 2006). On the other hand, millions of the world's Muslims, including those in Indonesia, the nation with the largest Muslim population in the world, are not Arabs. There are many Muslims who do not speak Arabic as their vernacular language; all Muslims read the Qur'an and conduct Islam's five daily prayers in Arabic, however.

The tragic attacks against the World Trade Center and the Pentagon on September 11, 2001, exacerbated anti-Muslim and anti-Arab sentiments and fostered distrust toward Muslim communities across the nation. Many social service agencies serving these communities are attempting to convey the message that their agencies are safety zones and that they are committed to providing high-quality culturally relevant services. Muslim clients might not self-identify to the social worker as Muslim for fear of being rejected or judged (Dwairy, 2006). Because of the centrality of the faith in many Muslim families, religious affiliation is a core identity that can be integrated effectively into the biopsychosocial-spiritual assessment.

Key Concepts

Intersectionality: The meeting point of multiple identities such as race, ethnicity, gender, social class, sexual orientation, age, and ability status

Double jeopardy: The compounding of disadvantages based on the intersection of two individual characteristics, such as ethnicity and gender

Affirmative action: Legal regulations that promote racial and gender equality in employment, government contracting, and educational access

Meritocracy: A system in which rewards are allocated based on individual merit alone

Part II

Theories and Perspectives on Oppression

4

Evolutionary and Structural Functionalist Theories

THEORIES ARE THE LENSES THROUGH WHICH SOCIAL SCIENTISTS EXAM-
ine, evaluate, organize, and interpret social phenomena. Theories are often used
to justify privileges for some members of society and the oppression of others.
Theories are also used to explain the causes of inequality and oppression within
society. This chapter reviews various theories that have been used over time to
explain how different cultures interact when they come in contact, to justify
oppression, or to explain injustice.

This chapter embarks on a theoretical exploration of diversity in its social and
cultural context by approaching cultural diversity in relation to the social and
political forces that shape it, with an emphasis on oppression and inequality. This
overview of theories will act as a foundation for the following chapters, which will
introduce theories that are more applied, and connected to the culturally
grounded approach to social work.

This review sorts through traditional theories to identify the elements most
relevant to the culturally grounded approach. This exercise is necessary because
without an understanding of these theoretical perspectives we would be unable to
practice within the realm of science and would be unable to conduct professional
practice. Theory provides the compass for social work practice and research with
different cultural communities. Some perspectives discussed in the next pages
may already be familiar to readers, but they will be reviewed with an emphasis on
diversity, inequality, and oppression. Some theories have blind spots regarding
diversity, while others will help readers understand how cultural differences can
be recognized and addressed as assets in social work practice. Because most of the
theories presented here are interrelated, some will be given more emphasis than
others. Our review of each theory will be guided by three questions: How are
cultural diversity and its role in the life of the community recognized? What are
the root causes of social inequality and oppression, and how is the system of
inequality perpetuated? and, What are the theory's implications for social work
practice and research?

Oppression is not an inherent characteristic of human organization (Gil,
1998). Although some have argued that oppression and violence are a part of

human nature, others have claimed that they are simply potential human reactions to the environment, reactions that are possible but not inevitable. Gil (1998) points to preagrarian society as an example of humans living without systems of oppression embedded in social structures. He goes on to claim that oppression arose as a result of the development of agriculture as one of the primary means of production. The agrarian lifestyle allowed some individuals to become landowners and others to become laborers. This fundamental social stratification led to increasingly complex cultural, political, economic, and religious structures designed to maintain this division of labor. Theories about the development and the role of oppression in society are addressed in this chapter.

The theoretical perspectives are grouped into families of theories according to the commonalities they share. These groupings do not necessarily follow traditional theoretical frameworks because they integrate classical theories and metatheories with more applied social work theories. The first set of perspectives, the evolutionary and conflict theories, provide a macro perspective that has at its core ideas about sources of oppression and inequality. The second set of perspectives, the structural functionalist theories, recognize inequality and offer various explanations for it, often with an emphasis on the achievement of balance and stability at the expense of conflict and change. Chapter 5 will review the inclusive, constructivist, and postmodern theories, which are concerned with intergroup relations, and will look at diversity from a micro and subjective perspective, respectively.

EVOLUTIONARY AND CONFLICT THEORIES: EXAGGERATING AND MINIMIZING DIFFERENCE AND INEQUALITY

As stated earlier in the text, it is generally accepted by anthropologists that ideas about racial groups are socially constructed rather than biologically given. Much effort, however, has gone into theorizing about the existence of race as a real and scientific phenomenon. Such conjecture is often a thinly disguised means of justifying the privilege of some members of society and the oppression of others. Social Darwinism is a good example of an evolutionary theory.

Social Darwinism

Social Darwinism is based on the premise that Darwin's theory of the evolution of biological traits by natural selection can be applied to societies or groups within a society. Although Darwin never intended for his research on animals and plants to be applied to the study of differences between humans, social Darwinism became popular in the latter part of the nineteenth century and maintained its popularity until the end of World War II. Xenophobic fringe groups (such as anti-immigrant groups) and xenophobic politicians use these tenets today. According to social Darwinists, success in life occurs because of an individual's biological superiority over others. Social Darwinists argue that since humans are a product of nature, and conflict and struggle are laws of nature, the strongest humans take the top prizes (e.g., in employment, housing, health care, and education) (Dorling, 2011). Social Darwinists believe that evolution rewards people who are strong, intelligent, and attractive (based on an ethnocentric idea of beauty) and who have a good work ethic, and that it punishes those lacking these characteristics. This theory supports the categorization of people based on their racial and ethnic backgrounds. According to this theory, those who are successful are destined by their ethnic and racial heritage to succeed, while those who are unsuccessful are simply destined to fail. Social Darwinism provided its proponents in Victorian England and elsewhere with a convenient academic justification for colonialism, slavery, genocide, and other forms of exploitation and oppression.

The legacy of social Darwinism has continued to hold sway through the twentieth and twenty-first centuries. For example, the laws of apartheid in South Africa were inspired in part by social Darwinist ideas. Apartheid (meaning "separate") was a system of legislation in South Africa that enshrined political, economic, and social rule by a white numerical minority and the oppression of its black numerical majority. Under apartheid, whites in South Africa were considered the best race. This product of colonialism and racism was based partly on social Darwinian ideology. Although apartheid rule ended in 1994, its legacy of officially imposed poverty and discrimination continues to be felt by black and mixed-race South Africans today. The New National Party, the South African party that designed and enforced apartheid, was dissolved only in 2004. At that time, nine out of every ten acres of commercial farmland remained in the hands of 50,000 white farmers, while most of the 40 million nonwhites remained landless (Louw, 2004).

The ideology behind social Darwinism contradicts all the basic principles of the social work profession; it is important to understand its tenets, however, because they are based on ideas about difference that promote oppression and may still be held by some individuals and communities. Notes from the field 4.1 illustrate how ideas based on social Darwinism may be observed in social work practice today. This theory provides the ideological roots of many contemporary policies and practices that dehumanize others by defining them as different, inherently inferior, and less deserving. Sometimes social policies and social services are inadvertently influenced by social Darwinist ideas about different individuals' and communities' abilities and potential for change. For example, a social service agency may want to enforce a family planning policy that calls for any woman labeled mentally incompetent to be sterilized. Some aspects of social Darwinism have survived through seemingly benign theories, such as Murray Bowen's family theory and the theory of the culture of poverty, both of which argue

---

NOTES FROM THE FIELD 4.1

Only the Strong Survive

Marcus, a medical social worker at the local county hospital, is advocating for housing services for a homeless man, but has not been successful in generating much support from the rest of the medical staff. He is not sure why he is getting resistance to what he considers to be an essential service. While eating lunch in the cafeteria he overhears two members of the treatment team discussing the case. One said, "I don't understand why we would waste a house on such a hopeless case." The other said, "I know. I think we should save the money and spend it on someone who is healthier and will be able to use it." How can the social worker interpret from a social Darwinist perspective the resistance to offer services to the patient? What is the role of the social worker in this case?

---

that people from certain backgrounds are prone to dysfunction due to their learned heritage (Gurman & Fraenkel, 2002; Lewis, 1966). Ideas advanced by social Darwinism can be seen in modern policies built on the argument that individuals are responsible for their own fate; that is, if an individual is not being successful in the current economic system it is due to a deficiency in skills, attitudes, or abilities that are inherent in the individual. This belief is frequently accompanied with the belief that social stratification is an inevitable part of society that cannot or should not be changed.

Marxist and Neo-Marxist Theories

Marxist and neo-Marxist theorists focus on social inequality, often deemphasizing racial, ethnic, and gender differences. Marxist thought proposes that social class, rather than other social variables like ethnicity, race, and gender, is the key factor explaining social inequality. Marxist theory explains that the accumulation of wealth by one social class results in and is dependent on the deprivation of wealth among the other classes. The central belief is that the distribution of economic resources shapes social life, values, beliefs, culture, and other aspects of society. The main theoretical contribution of Marxism is the idea that people in similar economic positions share interests and become grouped together, while divergent interests between classes result in class struggle. That is one of the reasons why Marxist theories are also known as conflict theories. Groups in power may echo social Darwinist ideas—for example, by claiming that they are smarter, harder working, more entrepreneurial, or better strategic decision makers than

those who are excluded from power. The groups in power develop their own explanations to justify their monopoly of power and the exclusion and oppression of
other groups. Marxist theory dismisses the relevance and importance of cultural
differences while stressing the importance of class differences.

Communist party rule in China and Cuba provides two examples of the political applications of Marxist theory. After the 1949 Communist revolution in China,
the state promoted the identity of all citizens as workers; such identity supported
the goal of equality between men and women. However, the Communist government also used its power to repress many ethnic minority groups and downplay
their possession of separate linguistic and cultural identities. In Cuba, citizens of
African ancestry benefited from the 1959 revolution, attaining equal status with
nonblacks for the first time, as well as increased access to employment, health
care, and education. The Communist regimes in both China and Cuba have
worked to minimize the role of racism and ethnocentrism in the distribution of
resources and citizens' access to social opportunities. Nevertheless, they, like the
former Soviet regime, have been unable to prevent racial and ethnic social identities from persisting as a major source of identity and as an important variable in
people's social and political lives.

Marxism continues to be considered a viable theory and ideology by groups
in some developing societies, especially those experiencing dramatic levels of
inequality in the distribution of resources and political power and those seeking
to organize for radical social and political transformation. Examples include
Nepal, where Marxist rebels instigated revolts against direct rule by the country's
king; and Chiapas in southern Mexico, where Marxist-inspired organizers have
mobilized disenfranchised peasants to protect their lands from exploitation by
multinational mining and agricultural interests. At the same time, as economically developed societies have moved from an industrial to a postindustrial and
now to a globalization phase, traditional Marxist thought has been revisited and
adapted to contemporary society by theorists known as neo-Marxists.

Some neo-Marxists believe that cultural factors play an independent role in
maintaining inequalities, while others argue that ethnic identities that persist for
a very long time after immigration or annexation are the result of discrimination
and social rejection rather than an effort to preserve something of cultural value
(Steinberg, 1981). The choice of maintaining or embracing an ethnic identity is
thus seen as a way of coping with the experience of rejection by the majority
culture. Therefore, in prejudiced environments cultural segregation becomes a
form of survival for ethnic minorities while at the same time it reflects their
forced exclusion from society.

Neo-Marxist thought is evolving as it strives to integrate cultural variables
with social class as key factors in explaining inequality. For example, some neo-
Marxist theorists have argued that if people have contact across ethnic and cultural lines, they will relate differently and as a result, prejudice will decrease,

which will open up opportunities for social advancement (McCollom, 1996). New critical theorists, in the tradition of Marxist thought, have emerged, arguing that it is not just class but the intersection of race and class that has perpetuated inequality; in some cases both class and race have been used to create internal divisions among the poor by distracting them from addressing the true sources of inequality (Harris, 2012). Some aspects of Marxist theory can be applied in the construction of a culturally grounded approach. The socialist principle of working to achieve equal access to resources for all segments of society, an outgrowth of Marxist analysis, has influenced social work in different ways. First, it has led social work to define social problems as having social and structural rather than individual causes. The social work profession views individual relationships as the product of social relations in a capitalist society. In fact, social work came into existence partly in order to identify and address social inequalities, especially those resulting from social class differences. From a Marxist perspective, radical social workers in the 1930s during the creation of the New Deal legislation in the United States argued that social work, when defined simply as the provision of services, could be used by groups in power to keep the underclass at a minimum level of comfort that would prevent them from challenging the dominant capitalistic system (Ferguson & Woodward, 2009). Although Marxism theory does not recognize ethnic culture as central to the human experience, its emphasis on inequality can be helpful for understanding oppression and change.

World Systems Theory

World systems theory is connected to neo-Marxist thought and focuses on economic and social differences at a global level. According to world systems theory, the current world capitalist system is organized into a center, or core, in which the wealthy countries monopolize the production of research and technology, and a periphery, in which poor countries that provide raw materials, cheap labor, and transportation to the core are located (Wallerstein, 1974). This view is no different from the traditional colonial structure for which the terms "metropolis" (the center) and "colonies" (the periphery) were used (Ashcroft, Griffiths, & Tiffin, 2013). In both cases, the center benefits from the exploitation and suffering of the periphery. This is the reason the antiglobalization movement often uses the term "neocolonialism" in its critique of the economic world system.

This thesis is taken a step farther by claims of the world systems theorists that capitalism inevitably leads to world integration and interdependency, thereby producing a system in which the core dominates the periphery. Globalization creates an integrated economic and financial system that, some have argued, influences not only the economic life of societies, but their educational and cultural systems as well. Starbucks, McDonalds, and Pizza Hut can be found in cities all over the world and have become emblematic of how economic globalization is affecting local tastes and customs.

Guided by classic economic rationalism and liberalism, economic globalization determines the value of individuals solely according to their contribution to the economy. Globalization has influenced social policy in the United States and other countries under U.S. economic and political influence with the consequence that market forces are allowed to structure social relations. In response, millions of citizens across the world have demonstrated against the institutions and policies of corporate globalization. While corporate globalists see globalization as spreading democracy and generating vibrant market economies, world systems theory and many citizen movements are concerned by what they see as the power to govern shifting to corporations and slipping away from people and communities. Critics charge that globalization replaces democracies of people with democracies of money—that is, political, economic, and social policies that are dictated by the flow of economic capital. Traditional self-organizing local markets are destroyed by globalization and replaced by centrally planned corporate economies. World systems theorists also contend that the actual beneficiaries of globalization have become all too obvious: top corporate executives of the largest global companies make salaries five hundred times those of bottom-level production workers, and that gap is increasing annually. As for claims that globalization aids the global poor, world systems theorists argue that the gap between the wealthy and the poor within and among countries of the world is getting steadily larger (International Forum on Globalization, 2002).

Influenced by economic rationalism, many social workers must deliver services in an environment that seems to exacerbate inequalities and does little to advance social justice. In the face of these realities, new organizing structures have been created, such as the rapid growth of cooperatives and the rise of large citizen movements orchestrated by social media. This fact was highlighted when the World Health Organization designated 2012 as the year of the cooperative, and in 2011 *Time* magazine selected a protester as the person of the year. Despite these advances, the following questions raised by globalization remain unanswered: Who is benefiting from globalization and who is not? Is the role of social work to facilitate the incorporation of individuals and communities into the market economy? Are there social and economic cores and corresponding peripheries within the United States? If so, are ethnic minorities and women overrepresented in the peripheries?

STRUCTURAL FUNCTIONALIST THEORIES: MANAGING CONFLICT, INTEGRATION, AND SOCIAL STABILITY

Structural Functionalism

Structural functionalism, not to be confused with the structural approach to social work practice advanced by Mullaly (2007), has its roots in the mid-nineteenth-century works of Auguste Comte, often called the father of sociology, as well as in the works of others who compared societies to living organisms, social classes and castes to bodily tissues, cities and communities to the body's organs, and families to biological cells. Comte understood all these components as forming a functional interconnected social body. Twentieth-century theorists used these concepts to develop structural functionalism, which emphasizes the importance of social consensus in maintaining social balance and identifies some aspects of society as dysfunctional because they threaten to disrupt social stability. Within this framework, social differentiation, rather than social conflict and struggle, is seen as the key to the evolution of social systems. Differences based on gender, ethnicity, and social class are seen largely outside their political context.

Specifically, social stratification is viewed as a desirable and necessary stage of development in the evolution of complex industrial societies, with social inequalities serving larger societal needs. For example, Emile Durkheim (1933/2004) explained the social forces that assign people to different occupations—the primary basis for contemporary social class systems—as part of a larger social system that creates a rational division of labor in society. Talcott Parsons (1961) described gender roles as complementary and operating in tandem, allowing homemakers to accomplish important family and societal goals like child socialization, and breadwinners to concentrate on maximizing families' chances of upward social mobility.

Structural functionalism came under strong attack in the 1960s for its inability to explain social change, inequality, conflict, and the power of the wealthy. Feminist scholars criticized functionalist thought as a justification for male privilege that largely ignores women's contributions to society. Feminists have also criticized functionalist theory because it implicitly accepts a system of inequality within the male-dominated structure of the family. According to feminist critics, this system of inequality is often a cause of abuse and domestic violence, especially when men view the struggles of women to expand their options as a threat to male control. These power dynamics presume that women's central role and responsibility are as wives and mothers, which take precedence over their personal needs, goals, and rights. In the same vein, by focusing on shared values and the role of core societal institutions, functionalist theorists tended to treat ethnic minorities as outsiders or the other, while placing white heterosexual males in a privileged position at the center (Farley, 2000). Far less of their effort went into understanding minority cultures than into explaining how minority cultures were different from the dominant culture.

Structural functionalism continues to influence social thought and policies in contemporary society. In fact, similar to the critique of social work found in Marxist theory, it could be argued that social work can be used as a tool for maintaining the equilibrium of society and attempting to remedy what is labeled dysfunctional or unbalanced before it disturbs the social equilibrium. A major component of the person-in-environment (PIE) framework posits that individuals experience distress when there is disequilibrium between their needs and the resources found in the environment. Operating from this framework, the goal of the social worker is to re-achieve equilibrium either by leveraging resources or by changing the individuals' demands on their environment. Although this framework can also be used to identify structures in the environment that may need to be modified, this is not typically how PIE is approached in social work practice. Such an approach has important consequences for the way social workers relate to clients who come from different cultures. Therefore, some aspects of the concepts of social cohesion, balance, and stability will be useful to the culturally grounded approach, but these concepts must be integrated with the recognition of the importance of cultural diversity, equality, and empowerment. Several theories that are rooted in the structural functionalist perspective explore specific ways that this perspective has been used to understand how different cultural groups relate to society as a whole.

Assimilation Theory

Assimilation is a strategy for achieving the societal balance to which functionalists aspire by ultimately eliminating differences. The United States was transformed into a great world economy in part because of the benefits society reaped from the oppression of ethnic minority groups born out of slavery, colonialism, and annexation. As the country accumulated wealth and inequality persisted, assimilation was looked upon as a means to complete the absorption of various cultural groups into American mainstream society with the least disruption to the nation's social and economic fabric.

In the early twentieth century, Park (1930) defined social assimilation as "the process or processes by which peoples of diverse racial origins and different cultural heritages, occupying a common territory, achieve a cultural solidarity sufficient at least to sustain a national existence" (p. 281). Assimilation is often associated with a complete abandonment of the culture of origin and an unconditional embrace of the host culture. Park, however, used terms suggesting a mixture, like "amalgamation" and "fusion," interchangeably with "assimilation," and did not view assimilation as a complete and unconditional surrender of all aspects of the culture of origin. In later years other sociologists such as Milton Gordon (1964) further contributed to the development of classical assimilation theory by separating the process of acculturation from what he called "structural assimilation." Structural assimilation resulted from primary group relationships between members of the ethnic minority group and members of the majority group—for example, through intermarriage. Acculturation, which was perceived to be inevitable and a first step leading to structural assimilation, was defined as the minority group's adoption of the cultural patterns of the host society (Gordon, 1964). In other words, immigrants must acculturate in order to acquire a common cultural code for interaction with the majority culture.

Although Gordon and other assimilation theorists have been cited as proponents of what has been referred to as Anglo-conformity (Paxton & Mughan, 2006), assimilation continues to be an important theoretical concept in the consideration of contemporary society. Social workers have traditionally been described as agents of assimilation. If assimilation is a one-way train, the natural question that emerges is, Where is the train going? For most of the twentieth century, the dominant or mainstream U.S. culture—a culture based on values and norms representing white European middle-class males—was the assumed destination. However, being of European ancestry has not always been enough to facilitate assimilation: early Irish, Polish, and Italian immigrants, most of whom were Roman Catholic, were not originally welcomed by mainstream culture. For example, Ignatiev (1995) argues that the Irish were originally identified not with the WASP rulers of the nation, but rather with free blacks, with whom they shared many economic and social conditions, but that over time they gained economic and social acceptance, and eventually these groups also "became white."

The implicit message of classic or straight-line assimilation theory—which has roots in structural functionalism and posits that the absorption of immigrant cultures into the mainstream is inevitable—is that nonmainstream cultures are maladaptive, deficient, or not as good as mainstream culture. Therefore, to advance socially and economically, people who come from nonmainstream cultures need to detach themselves from their cultures of origin and fully embrace mainstream culture. This paradigm, however, fails to account for the rejection and active suppression of certain groups by mainstream culture that have taken place throughout history as mainstream culture has forced these groups to assimilate.

Since its formulation, scholars have continued to examine and reformulate the assimilation theory and its application to the study of the assimilation experiences of contemporary non-European ethnic groups. Some contemporary researchers have proposed that immigrants do acculturate into other minority groups (Alba & Hee, 1997). Others have provided alternative models; for example, Rumbaut and Portes (2001) have proposed the theory of segmented assimilation, which describes three possible paths for immigrants to America: (1) assimilation and upward mobility by immigrants who possess plentiful human capital; (2) downward assimilation by immigrants with limited resources, which confines them to poor neighborhoods, where they join a permanent lower class; and (3) selective acculturation, or biculturalism, where some aspects of the host culture are adopted and some aspects of the culture of origin are preserved. Researchers have identified numerous barriers to assimilation. In addition to a lack of human capital in the form of education and job skills, commonly cited barriers to assimilation include prejudices and discrimination based on ethnic or racial appearance, native languages other than English, and religion. The closer the group is to the norm established by the dominant mainstream culture in these three areas, the easier the path to assimilation is (Golash-Boza, 2006).

Critics of the belief that assimilation is a desirable societal goal not only argue that the cost of assimilation outweighs the benefits, but also question the assumption that assimilation is inevitable and advantageous (Shrake & Rhee, 2004; Smokowski & Bacallao, 2007). They point out that members of a community suffer psychological harm and serious socioeconomic setbacks when their traditions are not honored or are disrupted through forced assimilation into another pattern of life. In general, when individuals share a common social identification, the sense of group belonging contributes to the development of a positive self-concept. However, when an individual is a member of a devalued social group—especially when that group is unable to assimilate into the mainstream—her or his personal identity and emotional adjustment suffer (Huo, Molina, Binning, & Funge, 2010).

Language can create various types of barriers to assimilation. Mainstream social institutions such as schools are used today as tools of assimilation, just as they were at the beginning of the twentieth century. The recent success of English-only movements and the suppression of native languages in the name of assimilation in some areas of the country show that individuals and institutions still approve of forced assimilation. By blocking access to bilingual education, mainstream society tells members of language minority groups that they need to let go of a central pillar of their cultural identity. The policies that perpetuate this message can be a great source of stress for those who are affected, who are pushed toward assimilation and at the same time not fully welcomed by mainstream society. This dynamic can be seen in notes from the field 4.2.

Three examples serve to illustrate this issue: First, one of the main purposes of the forced placement of Native American children in boarding schools in the early to mid-twentieth century was the imposition of English and the decimation of Native languages. Second, during and following the Great Depression of the 1930s, the U.S. government forced a million Mexican and Mexican American individuals to migrate to Mexico. They are known as the *repatriados,* or the repatriated ones. Some of these families eventually returned to the United States and encouraged their children not to speak Spanish because language had served as a way for the government to identify them for forced repatriation. Finally, the institution of slavery forbade enslaved people from speaking their ancestral African languages and seriously weakened their connection to their cultures and religions of origin (Begard, 2007).

Meanwhile, the low priority given to mastery of languages other than English has become a major liability for the United States (Welch, Welch, & Piekkari, 2005). The lack of Arabic-speaking staff in the military, the CIA, and the State Department has been well documented as a liability in the Iraqi conflict as well as in antiterrorist efforts in general. Closer to the domestic front, in social services

---

NOTES FROM THE FIELD 4.2

Growing Pains

Concerned with maintaining the prominence of English as the national language, the state legislature outlawed the use of Spanish in public school classrooms, except for foreign language classes. Ernesto, a second grader, is new to the country and is confused as he enters a world where he cannot understand what teachers or fellow students are saying. He finds a couple of other students that speak Spanish but becomes increasingly frustrated in the classroom. He tells his mom that he does not like school and does not want to go any more. Concerned, Ernesto's mom decides to go to the school to discuss his frustration with his teacher. She is told that he is in America now and will only be successful in this country if he speaks English; not speaking Spanish in the classroom is for his own good. Ernesto's mom is confused. Should she advocate for her son to speak Spanish in the classroom so that he retains his love for school, or is the teacher right: should she just allow him to struggle through it?

---

the need for bilingual social workers and agency staff is greater than ever (Ferguson, Lavalette, & Whitmore, 2005).

Internalized oppression and stigma often influence identity choices made by members of devalued groups, which in turn has a detrimental effect on their emotional well-being. Despite these risks, different private and public institutions continue to strongly support assimilation.

The concept of straight-line assimilation is not part of the culturally grounded approach, but assimilation and its related concepts provide important insights into the lives of immigrant groups and the conflict that they may face as they negotiate their identity.

The Melting Pot

According to the melting pot theory, ethnic and racial groups develop relationships in successive stages that ultimately lead to cultural and social fusion, or amalgamation (Newman, 1973). Past generations of immigrants in America, it is argued, became successful by shedding their historical identities and adopting the ways of their new country, which allowed them to achieve upward social mobility. As a metaphor for the process through which homogenous societies develop, the melting pot describes how the combination of different identities meld into a single identity. Just as when cooks mix ingredients in a pot, each identity (or ingredient) loses its distinctiveness, yielding a uniform composite identity in which the original ingredients can no longer be identified.

In the United States, the melting pot is often associated with the idea of the model minority (Choi & Lahey, 2006). Many consider Asian immigrants a model minority group in the United States due to the widespread belief that all Asian immigrants came to America with little or nothing and through hard study and work become successful and assimilated into mainstream culture despite the initial disadvantages and discrimination they faced. However, this view fails to account for the fact that different people's experiences of integration vary widely—even when those people belong to the same ethnic or racial group. For example, some Asian immigrant subgroups tend to be highly educated at the time of migration; thus, they get a completely different start in life in the United States than other minorities. And while many people imagine that most Asian immigrants came to the United States as boat people escaping the ravages of war and Communism, this image describes only Southeast Asians, who actually have one of the slowest social mobility rates of all Asian immigrant groups (Akresh, 2006). And although many people of Asian ancestry achieve high levels of social mobility in the United States, Asian Americans still bump into the glass ceiling, receive lower pay even with the same qualifications, and have high poverty rates (Sakamoto & Woo, 2007). They may also experience discrimination or pressure based on the stereotypes surrounding model minority status such as assumptions that they are high achieving (Lee, Wong, & Alvarez, 2008).

The melting pot approach underestimates the unidirectional forces at work as members of minority cultures are pressured to melt, or assimilate, into mainstream culture. One of the shortcomings of the metaphor of the melting pot is that is assumes that all people—immigrant groups and those who were born in the United States—are playing on a level playing field. However, in a capitalist society like the United States, economic resources are related to political power, and oppressed communities tend to have less economic power and as a consequence less political and cultural power. Therefore, the melting pot theory is applicable to the culturally grounded approach only in terms of its recognition of acculturation and assimilation as two different processes rather than as a basis for understanding differences between ethnic groups.

Structural Role Theory

While the melting pot theory argues that there are forces encouraging social equilibrium at a macro level as the cultures of different ethnic groups merge and are amalgamated, structural role theory addresses the production of social cohesion at a more micro level. Structural role theory views interactions among individuals as governed by the positions or statuses that they occupy in social structures. Each of these positions has corresponding roles that shape its individual identity and guide how the individual occupying the position acts. Some positions—like gender, ethnicity, and national origin—are ascribed to individuals, often at birth, and are beyond the individual's control. Others—like occupational and marital status—are achieved statuses, which reflect the social opportunities that are open to them. Each position an individual holds has an associated role; therefore, one person can have many roles, each with particular behavioral expectations.

Although many theorists, including George Mead, Robert Park, Georg Simmel, Ralph Linton, and Robert Merton, have contributed to role theory, no single theorist can be considered its author, and there are important differences among theorists in how roles are conceived. Social roles can be viewed as more or less rigid, guided by social norms that are clear, ambiguous, or shifting, depending on the social context. At one extreme, roles are like parts in a play for which every word and move of the actors is scripted. At the other extreme, roles are like the positions in an improvised game in which individuals are free to adjust their tactics in response to the moves of other players.

As a key status, or position, in social life, gender roles provide an excellent example of the various ways in which social roles are adopted and enacted. Gender socialization begins early as girls and boys are encouraged to act in different ways, play with different toys, and perform different chores around the house (like washing dishes rather than cutting the grass) and sends a powerful early message about the gendered division of labor in the family. Parents have been shown to communicate different expectations about academic performance and appropriate academic interests to their female and male children (Probert, 2005). Gender role development is the lifelong process of acquiring the attitudes and developing behaviors that are culturally defined as appropriate for members of one's sex; the beliefs that one acquires regarding how appropriate various attitudes and behaviors are to one's sex are reinforced in school, at work, and through language and the media (Constantinople, 2005). Although female and male roles are not universal even across the most traditional societies, because different cultures shape gender roles in distinctive ways, similar patterns of gender socialization have been noted around the world (Macionis & Gerber, 2010).

In most societies, women are socialized into submissive roles and taught not to question the privilege of their male counterparts. Gender roles in patriarchal societies tend to perpetuate these roles. However, it is important to remember that women's submission is mediated by privilege. Women in positions of privilege (because they have more education, money, higher social class, etc.) have more of an opportunity and have more frequently in history challenged gender norms. From the perspective of role theory, it is not because they are female that women adopt certain roles, but because the societies in which they live prescribe their behavior (role).

Recognizing the multiplicity of roles individuals play and the complexity of the behavioral expectations attached to each role, role theory has identified the problems of role strain and role conflict. Role strain is the stress that occurs when contradictory expectations are attached to the same role, while role conflict causes distress when two or more different roles place incompatible expectations on an individual. Many applications of role theory in social work practice and research grew out of the concepts of role strain and role conflict. One example of role strain is the situation commonly faced by low-income single mothers who turn to state assistance programs like Temporary Assistance to Needy Families (TANF) to help provide for their children's needs. Program eligibility requirements often force mothers receiving aid from TANF to leave their children in day care to attend job training or mandated job placements, which in turn may earn them criticism as poor or neglectful mothers. In their roles as mothers, they face the strain of being expected to care for their children around the clock while also being full-time breadwinners, but with inadequate outside support to do both well. Role strain may also occur within families when family members become unhappy with the conflicting demands of their assigned gender roles, as when, contrary to the expectations of her traditional parents, a young woman does not see herself as a future wife and mother (Perrone, Wright, & Jackson, 2009). Women also face contradictory role expectations as they enter the world of work. The importance of masculine traits, such as dominance, aggressiveness, and competition, are internalized and acted out by women occupying management positions. Although these are universally accepted as necessary traits of leaders, women are also frequently judged negatively for embodying them. Additionally, when women choose to perform traditional gender roles, such as being providers of nurturant work, they are not rewarded financially in the current economic system. This creates a no-win situation and is a source of role strain. Role conflict also causes distress from incompatible role expectations, but those expectations come from different roles, such as when an adult child's obligations to care for an elderly parent conflict with her or his job responsibilities. In notes from the field 4.3, the social worker utilizes structural role theory to gain better insight into her clients' presenting problems.

Role theory is helpful for identifying contradictions and tensions that emerge from rigid gender roles, the multiplicity of statuses that all individuals occupy, the complex ways that roles may be combined or the ways in which roles intersect, and the many conflicting role expectations individuals face in their daily lives. However, role theory, like structural functionalist theory, falls short in specifying how roles come to be established and which expectations prevail when there are conflicting norms or a clash of cultures. Nor does it address role inequalities from a moral or judicial standpoint. Role theory fails to recognize culture as a force that shapes people's roles and expectations. However, an awareness of the conflicts that emerge in the lives of clients as a result of the multiple roles they play is

---

NOTES FROM THE FIELD 4.3

Mothers Supporting Mothers

A social worker, working at a family counseling center in an urban area providing services to the local Puerto Rican community, has noticed a pattern among her clients. Preteens are being referred to the agency by probation officers after a single incident of underage drinking or breaking curfew. After discussing the incidents with the children and their parents, typically a single mom, the social workers discovers that the mothers are being forced to leave their child at home for long periods in the evening. Many of the mothers live far from the extended family members that would typically watch the children when they are working. The mothers must work evening shifts or second jobs to support the family and feel they are left with little choice other than to leave the children at home unsupervised. Aware of the multiple roles that the mothers are being required to fill and the stress that this puts on them and their family, the social worker decides to implement an intervention that addresses the mothers' role strain rather than the children's behavior. The social worker invites the mothers to participate in a group where they are able to build supportive relationships and problem-solve the issue of supervision. The mothers' understanding of each other's situation leads them to develop a system of support and supervision where every individual contributes their time once a week and their children have a place to go where a responsible adult will provide a meal and supervision every night. Over the next few weeks the social worker notices a marked improvement in the parent-child relationships and less reoffending among the preteens.

---

crucial to competent social work practice. One's opportunities and choices are often influenced by expectations and boundaries set by one's culture. Identifying those boundaries and learning how to negotiate them is an important aspect of many social work interventions.

Human Capital Theory

Human capital theory focuses on the type and amount of knowledge and experience that individuals acquire through education and job training and bring to the labor market (Becker & Woessmann, 2009; Olaniyan & Okemakinde, 2008). Differences in human capital are produced by variations in the level, type, and quality of educational credentials, job training, and work experience that people have. Therefore, the income that individuals earn is a direct result of the choices available to them regarding the amount and kind of education they receive—as well as their training, work experience, and job commitment in the workplace—and how well these choices mesh with the needs of the labor market. This theory attributes the gender-wage gap to the fact that women make different choices—different human capital investments—than men do about schooling and job preparation in anticipation of demands they will face as spouses and mothers. As a result, women accumulate less work experience and become overrepresented in occupations that require less education and training, as well as those that allow for more-flexible work schedules and career interruptions. Furthermore, if a woman leaves the labor force to become involved in child bearing and child rearing, her level of human capital deteriorates due to nonuse, and her accumulated skills could become obsolete (Gray, Stone, & Stockard, 2006).

All the tenets of human capital have been fiercely contested, and the evidence puts most of its principles in doubt. Studies of educational and occupational choices have shown that human capital factors account for only a small portion of the gender gap in pay and promotions, that female-dominated occupations do not carry lower penalties for career interruptions, and that men are actually more likely than women to have flexible work schedules (Menéndez, Benach, Muntaner, Amable, & O'Campo, 2007). In addition, the theory overlooks the impact of men's unequal sharing of child-raising responsibilities with their partners, which could significantly decrease women's human capital. Moreover, economic imbalance can be due to demographic differences such as women choosing to have children on their own without a male partner. Such imbalances exist even in industrialized nations with long traditions of gender equality. For example, even though Scandinavian societies have enacted proactive work-life balance policies supporting the role of fathers among heterosexual couples with young children, Scandinavian men are still much less likely to take paternity leave than women are to take maternity leave (Aybars, 2007).

Overall, it is the roles that societies assign to different groups that influence the manner in which resources are allocated, making more or fewer opportunities available to its members. For these differences to be addressed, a redefinition of roles is needed at the personal level, and systemic changes are needed at the policy level. Such redefinition requires a reexamination of how society defines human capital. Existing patriarchal norms, for example, place no human capital value on raising children or being a homemaker. The care of children and others is devalued, not only at home, but also at work. Studies of the gender-wage gap suggest that jobs that require nurturing skills, and in which women are heavily represented, such as nursing, social work, child care, and elementary school teaching, carry a steep net wage penalty, even when human capital differences are adjusted for. The salaries paid for these jobs do not adequately reflect the accumulated educational skills and work experience of those who perform them (Zigler, Marsland, & Lord, 2009).

Studies have shown the extent to which differences in education, training, and job experience account for ethnic, racial, and gender differences in occupational and economic attainment. However, they also reveal the extent of other sources of these inequalities, such as prejudice and discrimination. Studies of human capital have highlighted the fact that certain assumptions regarding such ethnic, racial, and gender differences—such as the idea that women select more-flexible and low-paying jobs—are unfounded and lack economic viability. Human capital approaches add an economic dimension to the overarching culturally grounded theoretical approach.

Human capital theory and the other theories reviewed in this chapter serve as the roots or the foundation for some of the theories presented in the following chapters. The theories presented in this chapter have influenced the thinking of powerful groups in society and are an expression of worldviews that influence contemporary political, economic, and social science analyses about cultural diversity, oppression, and social change.

Key Concepts

Social Darwinism: The premise that Darwin's theory of evolution of biological traits by natural selection can be applied to human beings

Apartheid: A system of legislation in South Africa that guaranteed political, economic, and social rule to a white numerical minority and institutionalized the oppression of the black numerical majority

Marxist theory: A theory whose major tenet is that class conflict is created because the accumulation of wealth by one social class depends on and results in the deprivation of wealth among a lower social class

World systems theory: The theory that wealthy countries (the core) monopolize the production of research and technology, while poor countries (the periphery) provide raw materials, cheap labor, and transportation to the core

Structural functionalism: The theory that social stratification is a necessary and even desirable stage of development in the evolution of a complex industrial society that supports the system of interdependent and complementary social roles and structures

Melting pot theory: The theory that different ethnic and racial groups in a society develop relationships in successive stages that ultimately lead to cultural and social fusion in which the cultures of origin can no longer be recognized

Structural role theory: The theory that interactions among individuals are governed by role expectations associated with the multiple positions or statuses they occupy in a social structure

Human capital theory: The theory that individuals acquire knowledge and experience through education and job training that later can be brought to the job market

5

Theoretical Perspectives on Diversity

AS THE UNITED STATES BECOMES A MORE DIVERSE NATION, IT IS IMPOR-
tant for social work practitioners to understand how interactions between people
and cultures affect behavior. While chapter 4 provided a review of selected classical perspectives on difference and oppression, chapter 5 focuses on theoretical
perspectives on cultural diversity and intergroup relations. These perspectives are
smaller in scope and have been developed to different degrees, but they all recognize and appreciate the differences that exist among and between cultures and
they all share a focus on inclusiveness, at least implicitly.

PERSPECTIVES ON INCLUSIVENESS: RECOGNIZING
AND PROMOTING DIVERSITY

Contact Theory

Gordon Allport's contact theory questioned the viability of functionalism as a
means of understanding intergroup relations and the origins of prejudice. According to Allport (1954), "prejudice is an antipathy based upon a faulty and inflexible
generalization. It may be directed toward an entire group, or toward an individual
because he is a member of that group" (p. 9). Prejudice can be expressed through
interpersonal discrimination that exists on a continuum ranging from what Allport calls antilocution (remarks made against, but not directly to, a person, group,
or community), avoidance, exclusion, and physical attack, to extermination. Prejudiced attitudes and behaviors are an expression of the social distance and antipathy that exist between people. Therefore, prejudice is an expression of people's
unfamiliarity with each other and the inhumanity they carry within from an early
age. Studies of children's playground behaviors have confirmed that prejudice is
socially learned as children segregate themselves by ethnicity, race, and gender
after a certain age. The evidence shows that by age four, children prefer playmates
who engage in activities that are gender typical, and that between the ages of
three and five, children develop biases in favor of their own ethnic or racial groups
(Kowalski, 2003).

The contact theory of intergroup relations does not propose that individuals and groups can reduce their prejudice and get along with each other simply by sharing a common space. On the contrary, this perspective proposes that prejudice can be reduced only if certain necessary conditions are in place:

1. There must be sustained contact between people who are different from one another.
2. Individuals interacting with each other must be of equal status.
3. Individuals need to be working toward common goals.
4. There must be sufficient resources to prevent competition for these resources.
5. There must be institutional support to implement the other four conditions. (Hewstone, 2003)

These conditions are often difficult to achieve because of power and resource differentials between dominant and minority groups. For example, based in part on an application of contact theory, school busing was court ordered to integrate schools racially in many cities around the nation because residential and school segregation along social class and ethnic lines presented major barriers to meaningful social contact. As a response to the racial segregation of neighborhoods, children from one neighborhood were bused to a school in another neighborhood, in another part of the city so that children of different ethnic and racial backgrounds could learn in the same classrooms and play together on the same playgrounds. In response, many families with the most resources took their children out of the public schools or moved to areas without busing, which resulted in schools consisting predominantly of ethnic minority children (Caldas, Bankston, & Cain, 2007). As a result, this seemingly simple solution to segregation actually increased segregation in some school districts.

One difficulty in applying contact theory is that it assumes that people want to spend time with people they perceive to be different from themselves. In reality, individuals generally follow a principle of homophily; that is, they prefer to develop social bonds with people who look and act like themselves (Lazarsfeld & Merton, 1954; McPherson, Smith-Lovin, & Cook, 2001; Yuan & Gay, 2006). For example, such de facto segregation is all too common in the cafeterias of the nations' high schools as students share their unplanned time with classmates they perceive to be like themselves (Davis, 2007).

The positive impact of contact between different groups has been well documented, but the logistics of achieving contact remain unclear. For example, further theory development could address how to make voluntary social contact possible and conducive to people's acceptance of differences and the production of lasting social harmony. Nonetheless, contact theory, particularly its principles and the conditions it sees as necessary for reducing prejudice and segregation, contributes important insights to the culturally grounded approach.

Cosmopolitanism

The concept and theory of cosmopolitanism has a long history dating back to the Sophists and the Stoics (Baubôck, 2002). This discussion will concentrate on the work of Feher (1994), as it is based more directly in an application of cosmopolitanism in the United States. However, Vertovec and Cohen (2002) provide a very good additional reference for those interested in further theoretical and contextual considerations. Cosmopolitanism (from the Greek *cosmo polis*, a cosmos within a city) constitutes a notable expansion of contact theory, and it is relevant to cultural diversity within the context of globalization. Cosmopolitanism challenges individuals to come closer to the other; it takes a step beyond contact theory by suggesting curiosity about difference and the other, and encourages proximity to and interaction with those who are different (Gilroy, 2005).

From the cosmopolitan perspective, differences are not meant to define a strictly separate territory, nor should they be reduced to an insignificant variation on a theme. Rather, differences are understood as a source of attraction. A cosmopolitan paradigm is an invitation for mutual transformation through dynamic engagement with those who are different, and not just an invitation for polite or intellectual respect for others or a general affirmation of all humanity (Feher, 1994). It recognizes that there are different ways of thinking that create meaning and that all the resulting interpretations of reality are valid and worth knowing. Cosmopolitanism is the antithesis of totalitarian thinking, ignorance, provincialism, and prejudice.

"Cosmopolitan" was the word frequently used by the mainstream media to characterize life in Sarajevo before the onset of the war in Bosnia-Herzegovina that led to its separation from the former Yugoslavia during the 1990s (Skrbis, Kendall, & Woodward, 2004). Before the war, the city's different ethnic and religious groups enjoyed sustained contact with each other, similar status, sufficient resources, and government support. Partly as a result of its cosmopolitan character, the city of Sarajevo became a powerful symbol of unity across cultural boundaries during a cruel national war fought along bitter ethnic and religious divides (Tazi, 2007). Its experience of devastating conflict, loss of human life, and physical destruction does not negate the cosmopolitan vision but rather cautions against idealism in favor of realistic alertness to negative manifestations of differences and prejudice. In the United States, the word "cosmopolitan" has been used to describe the alliance between the African American and Jewish American communities exemplified by some aspects of the civil rights movement (Sundquist, 2005).

Prewar Sarajevo and the African American–Jewish alliance are strong testimonies that different groups can coexist in harmony and develop effective coalitions across cultural boundaries even within insular social and historical contexts. In both cases, the ability of different communities to be cosmopolitan has been challenged, creating tension within the communities themselves and also within institutions. There are parallel issues to consider within the social work profession. Are social workers cosmopolitan? Are they comfortable with the unfamiliar? Do they enjoy learning about different cultures, values, and lifestyles? Are they aware of cultural boundaries and are they willing to learn the rituals necessary to cross those boundaries effectively? Curiosity, not as a casual tourist but as an interested and caring person, is a valuable trait in the culturally grounded approach. Indeed, cosmopolitanism in general is a vital component in the development of the theoretical approach to culturally grounded social work, but its treatment of prejudice could be further advanced. Certain questions remain to be addressed. What are the limits of tolerance? How can democratic societies defend and nurture tolerance and prevent prejudice and discrimination?

Naturally, of the many things that happen in a city—good, bad, and neutral—not all are admirable, but many need to be tolerated. When tolerance is not part of the equation, extremism and intolerance emerge, as is evidenced in the contemporary culture wars that reflect sharp ideological divides between liberal and conservative groups over issues like evolution, gay marriage, and women's reproductive rights.

Pluralism and Multiculturalism

The pluralistic perspective maintains that people should be able to advance socially and economically without having to sacrifice their values and cultural heritage unwillingly. Pluralism emerged in part because of the lack of success of the so-called melting pot (Brammer, 2004). Pluralism provided the salad bowl metaphor as an alternative to the melting pot (Pope, 1995). Each vegetable (cultural group) preserves its unique taste and texture (cultural identity), while the dressing provides unity and contributes a common flavor (national identity) to the salad (the nation or the community).

Thus, pluralism is an alternative to assimilation that entails respect among different cultural groups and encourages the retention of each group's cultural values as they incorporate the values of the host or majority culture. Different groups' cultural traits and expressions have persisted mostly because of the advocacy for cultural pluralism by ethnic, religious, and racial minorities. Cultural pluralism leads to a policy of multiculturalism, in which different cultures are encouraged to share their knowledge, experiences, and creative expressions.

In Canada, the salad bowl metaphor is commonly known as the cultural mosaic (Kalman, 2009), an idea that was first introduced by John M. Gibbon in 1938 as immigrants started to increase in numbers and became more diverse ethnically and racially. Canadian residents identified themselves as belonging to over 200 ethnic groups in the 2006 Census, a dramatic increase from the 1901 Census when only twenty-five different ethnic groups were recorded (Qadeer, Agrawal, & Lovell, 2010). Early European interactions with First Nations and

Inuit populations in Canada were relatively peaceful compared to the experiences of American Indians in the United States (Seed, 2011). First Nations have had a lasting influence on Canada's national culture and have in great part preserved their own identity (Macklem, 2001). Canada has followed a multicultural approach in recognizing its bilingual and bicultural (English/French) historical national identities, recognizing the rights and cultural distinctiveness of the First Nations communities, and welcoming large numbers of immigrants from many different countries, though not without difficulties and controversies (Winter, 2007). The province of Quebec, for example, has advocated and gained through its Quiet Revolution recognition as a distinct society with its unique language and culture (see Dickinson & Young, 2003).

Spain is another country with autonomous regions (i.e., Catalonia, the Basque Country, Galicia, etc.) that have their own distinct languages and cultures while maintaining a connection to the Spanish state. Canada and Spain, like many other countries, have within their geographic and political boundaries a variety of cultures and identities that sometimes are labeled nations within a state. These countries can be located at the progressive end of the multicultural continuum. In the United States, some sectors of society, such as the English-only and anti-immigrant movements, have grown preoccupied by what they perceive to be the negative consequences of radical multiculturalism and actively advocate more homogeneity and the repression of distinctive cultural expressions such as the use of the Spanish language or learning about the Chicano movement in school (Olneck, 2009).

Multiculturalism has become a main organizing concept in social work education. The influence of pluralism on social work and its affirmation of diversity are obvious in the National Association of Social Workers' cultural competence standards, which are endorsed by the Council on Social Work Education. Since 1968 the Council on Social Work Education has required accredited social work programs to reflect the diversity of a pluralist society in the composition of their faculty and student body, and has mandated that the social work curriculum include content on cultural competence. Thus the principles of multiculturalism are encouraged through the representation and inclusion of multiple cultural groups in the curriculum, the student body, and the faculty. The principles encourage the development of awareness among social work academics and students of the importance of celebrating and nourishing the coexistence of multiple cultural identities within their communities.

Ensuring diversity is the first step in creating multicultural environments; oppressive norms and values perpetuated in the larger society still influence the dynamic in social work departments, however. Multiculturalism starts with inclusion and contact but must also work to ensure equality, which may require addressing systems outside the institution. For example, even when efforts are made to increase the number of Native Americans in social work departments,

Native students report feeling isolated by the academic culture and a lack of respect for the indigenous world view (Weaver, 2000). Effective recruitment efforts are often not followed by effective retention efforts.

Although the multicultural paradigm can be the basis for promoting tolerance as a means of transcending differences between people, it also constitutes an implicit critique of mainstream society. Influenced in part by critical theory, which emanated from the Frankfurt school and various French poststructuralist philosophers, multiculturalists have questioned the hegemony (the preponderant authority or influence of one group over another group or groups) of Western humanism. Multiculturalism rejects the idea that Western society is superior to other traditions. Pluralism has embraced a relativist analysis that reinterprets history by recognizing and adopting the perspectives of a broad array of social groups. With more or less success, this reinterpretation attempts to bring back, resurface, and value the contributions of different groups and traditions to the economic development of societies, knowledge, science, literature, and the arts.

Pluralism questions dogmas from structural functionalist theory about the legitimacy of systems of inequality, male dominance, and the supremacy of anything European. Nonetheless, it is notable that even though the multicultural paradigm rejects Eurocentrism, multiculturalism has been developed almost exclusively from theoretical models within the European tradition. As a result, multiculturalism has been criticized for lacking a vision of how to address differences in power among different cultural groups because the very tools multiculturalism uses to analyze difference are culturally specific, patriarchal, and rooted in a European and European American perspective. Multiculturalism as a theoretical approach has some limitations in its understanding of those who have been oppressed and excluded due to the cultural and social privilege of its leading theorists. At its most extreme, some oppressed groups view multiculturalism as perpetuating inequality by focusing attention on the heterogeneity of cultural groups but deemphasizing their differences in status and power (McKerl, 2007).

Multiculturalism is a limited perspective that may be unable to recognize its own constraints. For example, multiculturalism often fails to acknowledge that cultural symbols vary in legitimacy, authority, and power, and thus risks considering all such symbols equally valid. In Western societies there is a tendency to accept Christian symbols as universal while treating symbols coming from other traditions as foreign. The constraints of multiculturalism are illustrated by controversies in contemporary democratic societies over the display of religious symbols in public life. In France, young Muslim women have been forbidden to wear the *hijab* or traditional veils prescribed by their religious customs in public schools; crucifixes often hang on classroom walls and other students are allowed to wear discreet crosses or stars of David around their necks, however (Thomas, 2005). In the United States, Muslim women have reported being harassed for expressing their religious and cultural identities by wearing a *hijab* (headscarf) in public places (Droogsma, 2007). Do these situations reflect the failure of the multicultural paradigm to suffuse adequately into the societal consciousness? Are they evidence of a political and social backlash against multiculturalism, an attempt to set limits on its expression? Alternatively, do these situations demonstrate that, despite the growing recognition of different cultural groups in society, some are still viewed as inherently inferior? One needs to wonder if these limitations are due to multiculturalism's impotence, its failure to gain wider acceptance, or fundamental flaws in the multicultural approach.

The multicultural perspective often supports the expression and celebration of differences in the private sphere, but it fails to consider how tensions arising from these differences can be managed in the public space. President Bill Clinton's "Don't ask, don't tell" policy for gay men and lesbians in the military extends the ideal of private multiculturalism to its limits by promoting the message, "You will be tolerated as long as you remain in the closet." This bare tolerance falls far short of acceptance of diversity in sexual orientation.

Multiculturalism has come under attack in some circles. The outcomes it achieves—both intended and unintended—have been questioned, and its rhetoric of tolerance has faced outright rejection. By recognizing the heterogeneity of cultural groups and the many ways in which these groups intersect, multiculturalism provides a starting point for the introduction of tolerance in democratic societies. However, the pluralist discourse that emphasizes the expression of cultural differences may not always result in the diminishment of prejudice. Therefore, if the primary purpose of multicultural efforts is to delineate and heighten boundaries and allow for the expression of a wide range of cultural differences, then it can probably be interpreted more as an antithesis of Allport's contact theory than as a perspective that complements or furthers the scope of contact theory.

Nonetheless, pluralism is an essential component of the culturally grounded approach because it assists communities in delineating boundaries and marking the lines within which minority cultures can express themselves freely. Yet sexism, racism, and homophobia continue to be barriers to pluralism. In addition, because not all cultural artifacts and cultural products are inherently good, multiculturalism can be misused to promote tolerance of oppressive behaviors such as child abuse, domestic violence, and female genital cutting. The fact that certain practices are common among members of a particular group does not mean that their consequences can be justified in the name of culture.

CONSTRUCTIVISM AND POSTMODERNISM: WORDS CREATE WORLDS

Constructivism

Constructivism—the idea that learners are able to build their own knowledge—grew out of Friedrich A. Hayek's (1963) Nobel Prize–winning treatise *The*

Sensory Order, which showed that what humans believe they know about the external world is actually knowledge of themselves. Instead of seeing knowledge as existing in an objective external "real" world, social constructivism stresses that social processes generate knowledge and ideas about reality. That is, humans do not just passively receive knowledge, but rather actively build knowledge as creative beings. Therefore, constructivism emphasizes that knowledge is actively constructed rather than discovered and transmitted, while social constructivism suggests that the knowledge is constructed through collaborative social interaction. In relationships with others, individuals can tell someone else about their lives. Social workers, for example, help their clients acknowledge their perceptions of themselves and their perceptions of their own lives and stories as they constructed them.

Postmodernism

Postmodernism, which has been described as an alternative and collective interpretation of society, is defined as an interpretive device that questions traditional forms of knowledge construction and its distribution (Hassan, 2003). Postmodernism does not accept the typical or normative ways of describing reality. In other words, it questions existing meta-narratives. "Meta-narrative" is a term used by postmodernists to refer to a larger story that justifies smaller stories. A meta-narrative determines which stories are central and acceptable to society, and which stories are marginal or unimportant to the understanding of society and to the way it is organized, its norms, and its practices (Foucault, 1980). A meta-narrative is often seen as synonymous with an ideology and a worldview. A meta-narrative is like a universal truth or a story about a story (Middleton, Anderson, & Banning, 2009). Western society's acceptance of the idea that men are aggressive and women are nurturing as a fact influences the way men and women see themselves and each other. The meta-narrative that may accompany this belief is the story of the cave and how men were hunters and women were gatherers and caretakers. This story aims at providing an evolutionary rationale for a widely accepted gender stereotype. Postmodernism questions the story as well as the stereotype by not accepting the universal nature of its premise. A contemporary example of such a story is the demonization of so-called welfare mothers in the 1980s and early 1990s, which emerged as an irrational and unscientific reaction to a financial crisis but became part of the meta-narrative that resulted in the federal legislation enacting sweeping U.S. welfare reform, including the withdrawal of guarantees of assistance to mothers with dependent children and stringent work requirements for recipients.

In a now-famous 1968 speech at Johns Hopkins University, the philosopher Jacques Derrida (1982) proclaimed the end of modernism and the beginning of a postmodern era. Since that year postmodernists have argued that what people call knowledge is a special kind of story, a discourse that puts together words and images in ways that seem pleasing or useful to a particular culture or to those with the most power in that culture. While modernism tends to present its fragmented view of human subjectivity as something tragic, postmodernism probes, analyzes, and celebrates fragmentation and contradictions (Kawai, 2006).

Postmodernism, however, can present some challenges for a culturally grounded approach to social work. Despite seeming to be based on the universal value of individuality and difference, it lacks a collective dimension to its understanding of the experience of ethnic minority individuals and other cultural minority communities. In many of these communities, the group—not the individual—is the primary social unit. A sense of belonging to the group and being accepted by it is a primary social goal that overrides individual needs, goals, and viewpoints. Another cultural bias that is often inherited by postmodernism is its strong reliance on the transformative power of the spoken word. Due to postmodernism's reliance on stories, the spoken word is needed to construct the personal narratives that question existing meta-narratives. Traditional cultures—for example, many Native American and Asian American cultures use various means of communication and may rely less than European-based cultures on the spoken word. Despite these limitations, postmodernism provides important insights into different perspectives on diversity in its rebuke of ethnocentrism of any kind.

Postmodernism has much in common with social work theory, as social workers are challenged to be open to different—sometimes marginal—viewpoints, to accept alternative understandings of society, and to be alert to the messages presented by meta-narratives (Howe, 2005).

Symbolic Interactionism

Postmodernism shares several key insights with an earlier theoretical approach from the first half of the twentieth century that recognized how social meaning is socially created rather than a universal given. Symbolic interactionism maintains that humans develop their social identities and formulate ideas about the social world through interactions with people and communities by using symbols like language. Following the philosopher and sociologist George Mead's insights, symbolic interactionists hold that human behavior is based on the meanings they attach to these symbols, which include words, actions, or objects that communicate meaning. For example, extending a hand when being introduced to someone is a nearly universal symbol of goodwill in Western societies but the acceptable strength and length of the handshake as well as the meanings associated with these actions vary by country. Some religious groups forbid women from shaking hands with any men outside the family, while in other societies a kiss or two kisses on the cheek are expected instead of a handshake. Eye contact is another factor that varies greatly, with direct eye contact communicating respect and attention in some cultures and disrespect in others. As they emerge through interactions between people, these meanings are modified through a subjective and interpretative process, becoming a vehicle for how people learn the values and norms of society.

Even though symbols like language facilitate the process of interacting with others, for these interactions to be effective both parties must understand the symbols. Humans become social beings and develop a sense of self through their interactions with others. This process may involve what Charles Hooten Cooley (1918) called the looking-glass self, the notion that individuals' ideas about themselves are formed by how they imagine that other people see their behavior. The term "significant others," coined by George Mead (1934), emphasizes the role that interactions with key members of primary groups such as parents play in the development of the young self. In other words, attitudes and behaviors are shaped by others and by the perceptions the individual develops about her- or himself.

Symbolic interactionism views people as actors performing for those around them but also taking on the role of those around them. While people may sometimes imitate others to gain their approval, symbolic interaction is usually much more nuanced. It is a process of reacting to others by anticipating how they will react and imagining their point of view. This process is complex because it takes place in different social contexts involving different audiences. Developmental issues and specific social contexts, for example, strongly influence the degree to which individuals react and how they react to outside social influences. In addition, there is disagreement among symbolic interactionists regarding the extent to which individuals improvise and actively create meanings in each interaction rather than following a predictable script as they develop a stable core self-identity.

Sandstrom, Martin, and Fine (2001) provide the following useful and succinct description of the importance of symbols in interactions between humans, which serves as an introduction to the application of symbolic interactionism in social work from a culturally grounded perspective.

- People are unique creatures because of their ability to use symbols.
- People become distinctively human through their interactions.
- People are conscious and self-reflexive beings, who actively shape their own behavior.
- People are purposeful creatures who act in and toward situations.
- Human society consists of people engaging in social interaction.
- To understand people's social acts, we need to use methods that enable us to discern the meaning they attribute to their acts. (pp. 218–219)

In the case of minority cultural groups, interactions might be heavily influenced by a core sense of identity, one of allegiance to the group and conformity to certain symbols, meanings, and group norms that may not be shared or easily transferred to the outside community. Members of an ethnic group may have their own meanings and rules about how they should act or dress in a given situation that are different from those of other groups. Thus members of ethnic groups actively define their own reality rather than passively reacting to mainstream definitions of reality.

In notes from the field 5.1, factors such as age and race create symbolic distance between Phyllis Johnson and Claire Atkins. In addition, the worker uses a very informal approach to address an elder who is accustomed to more formal and respectful treatment from younger people. The use of a symbolic interaction perspective to evaluate this situation would probably yield alternative approaches for establishing rapport, such as acknowledging some of the differences and addressing individuals from a variety of communities in a formal manner.

In an extreme situation such as imprisonment, symbolic interaction is useful for identifying how the emotional resources of inmates are grounded individually, contextually, and culturally. For example, Greer (2002) used interactionist perspective to interpret the strategies women in prison use to develop and maintain social relationships in a very controlled and oppressive setting in which expressions of emotion are closely regulated by the prison system as well as by informal subcultures. Prison gangs provide protection and demand allegiance that often needs to be demonstrated through the adoption of symbols.

Understanding the power of symbols as expressions of culture is crucial for social workers who follow a culturally grounded approach. Symbolic interactionism emphasizes the dynamic way that interactions can socialize both parties. For example, while interacting with clients, social work practitioners are open to the

---

NOTES FROM THE FIELD 5.1
R-E-S-P-E-C-T

Mrs. Marjorie King, an 81-year-old African American woman, has been referred to the community mental health center by the senior center's social worker because she appears to exhibit signs of depression. She has been arriving at the senior center later than usual and does not wish to participate in any group activities. The intake at the mental health center is conducted by Claire Atkins, a 32-year-old European American. The worker introduces herself as Claire and addresses Mrs. King on a first-name basis. Mrs. King says little during their meeting. Once she completes all the forms, she excuses herself and leaves. She tells the social worker at the senior center that the social worker at the mental health clinic was not respectful or professional. She did not like the way she was treated and is not willing to go back.

subjective meanings communicated to them by their clients. Workers must learn how to take the role of the other and remain open to the fact that the socialization process is affecting them as well as their clients.

Symbols are rooted in culture and are expressed through behaviors. Social workers are exposed to many different symbols and codes throughout the day, sometimes without noticing them. Practitioners search for meaning and should openly ask clients for help when the meaning of certain symbols or behavior is not clear. Symbolic interactionist approaches are sensitive to the ways individuals interpret their lives and how they make sense of them. The theory is not deterministic like Marxism or functionalism; it leaves open the range of possibilities for how any two individuals interpret and react to the same situation. Symbolic interactionism provides guideposts for social workers and cautions against generalizing behaviors based solely on the group membership (culture) of their clients. The key to understanding behavior is to understand how individuals define and organize the social situation, a process in which culture appears to play a key role.

Extensions of symbolic interactionist theory have explored in detail the question of how everyday reality is socially constructed. In other words, how is it possible that subjective meanings become objective fact? Theorists have studied the process people go through as they transform their subjective interpretations of their own experiences into something real and factual that can be seen by others, and how they challenge the assumption that the world is shared or sharable (Berger & Luckmann, 1966). The assumption interactionists make is that a different person—whether a social worker or a family member—looking at the same experience will interpret it differently. The observer's interpretations build structures of plausibility—that is, accounts of how the social world operates and consequently what can be changed. Symbolic interactionism is relevant to the development of a culturally grounded approach because—as notes from the field 5.2 illustrates—it supports the principle that objectivity is elusive in the human experience. What is Sarah's role in this case? From a symbolic interactionist perspective, her question and Ann's answer reflect different perceptions of the same

---

NOTES FROM THE FIELD 5.2
Choosing to Live Outside

Sarah, an MSW student, interviews Ann, a homeless woman, as part of an assignment for one of her courses. After Ann gives her consent to participate, Sarah starts her interview by asking her, "What is it like to be a homeless woman?" Ann appears to be very upset by the question and responds, "I am not a homeless woman. I have chosen to live outside." From a symbolic interactionist perspective, how should Sarah interpret Ann's response?

reality. What is the practitioner's role in situations where the client's symbology does not match the worker's?

Social Identity Theory

Human beings have the need for inclusion and belonging to some social groups while maintaining distinction from other groups (Padilla & Perez, 2003). Social identity theory (Tajfel & Turner, 2004) explains these needs of belonging and differentiation and their significance. Tajfel's personal experiences as a Polish Jew in Europe during the rise of the Nazis, World War II, and the Holocaust fueled his examination of identity and his desire to understand intergroup conflict, oppression, and discrimination (Hogg, 2006). Identity is a function of an individual's membership in various social groups and is formed and performed in different contexts (Hogg, 2006). In such social contexts, a person may choose to act and think as the member of one or the other group to which he or she belongs (for example, one may choose to act as a parent at home or as an American citizen in the voting polls).

Social identity theory provides insights into how and why people choose to be part of one or another group and what being a part of that group means to them. The theory elaborates on a key element of symbolic interactionism—the idea that individuals form a sense of self and formulate identities through interactions with others in varied social contexts. Individuals are continuously comparing their beliefs about themselves to how they believe others perceive them, to the social norms that they perceive to be in operation, and to how their environment reacts to the image that they project. In that process a person self-categorizes and in some situations changes or adapts his or her behavior or perception (Stets, 2006). This process of self-categorizing and self-verification is in constant motion. Burke (2006) proposes that the individual's self-perception changes to align to the feedback he receives during self-categorization. During that comparison individuals tend to gravitate toward people who affirm their self-identity. Thus, a sense of belonging may develop when the individual finds a group that shares his or her beliefs and values (Stryker & Burke, 2000). Consider, for example, a member of a church. He identifies himself as belonging to a church (not just a religion, but to a certain mosque, parish, synagogue, etc.). He will most likely join special groups at his church, such as a men's group, a sports team, a youth group, or a service-oriented group; people in these various groups share not only a religious belief, but also an interest and/or value. Once a person joins a group, he will take roles and adjust his personal standards to the feedback he receives from other members of the group (Stets, 2005). This sense of belonging to a group activates a sense of self-worth (Stets, 2006), at the same time accentuating the process of differentiating people who do not belong to the group (the out-group people). In the cases in which the group identity is very strong, members develop an "us" versus "them" attitude (Smith, Terry, & Hogg, 2006). Sometimes people enhance the status of the group to which they belong because that also increases their own self-image. For example, a U.S. citizen may say, "America is the best country in the world!" The opposite dynamic may also operate, where a person feels the United States is not the best place for her or him. Sometimes the self-image is increased by discriminating against the out-group (the group we do not belong to). An example might be claiming, "The French [Latinos, those people from a different neighborhood, people of a different religion, people of a different political party, that neighborhood, etc.] are a bunch of losers!" Central to social identity theory is that members of a group will seek to find negative aspects of out-group individuals, thus enhancing their self-image. Social identity theory also explains the mechanics of competition, prejudice, and discrimination. The preference for in-group members is called the "loyal member" effect (Castelli, DeAmicis, & Sherman, 2007), while prejudice is the negative feeling toward individuals based on their group membership (Allport, 1954). Stets and Burke (2000) argued that the need to evaluate in-groups more positively than out-groups forms the basis for social competition that is motivated by a need for self-esteem, rather than just fulfilling one's personal interests.

The loyal member effect is very strong, even in childhood. Experiments conducted with children as young as four to seven years of age showed favoritism for the in-group over the out-group. Castelli et al. (2007) showed two drawings to a group of young, white children. In the first drawing both children were white; in the second drawing one child was black and one was white. The young participants were told that in both scenarios the children were playing happily. Then, they were asked to pick which child in the drawing would be their playmate, and to rate all of the white kids in the drawings using either positive traits or negative traits. The results indicated a stronger preference for the white child in the drawing that played with another white child rather than a white child who played with a black child (74% vs. 26%). Even very young children preferred to interact with in-group members; they evaluated their peers who interacted with in-group members more favorably than those who interacted with out-group members, indicating the loyal member effect.

Narrative Theory

Some postmodernist philosophers have argued that humans organize knowledge as novelists rather than as scientists. People think, perceive their lives, experience happiness and sadness, imagine, and make choices according to narrative structures, or the stories they have created about themselves and others around them (Gonçalves, Matos, & Santos, 2009; Sarbin, 1986). It is as storytellers that individuals get to know themselves and others, interpret their pasts, imagine their futures, make decisions, and justify their lives to themselves and to others. Individuals constantly narrate their experiences from their own point of view, assigning roles very much as a novelist or a screenwriter would. One of these roles is their own.

Narrative theory focuses on the stories that help individuals interpret and give meaning to their life experiences. Narratives also connect different generations by allowing people to link their lives with those of their ancestors. Narrative theory sees storytelling as a mode of communication that is pervasive and transcultural. Narratives are guideposts for the moral choices people make and provide organizing principles for thought and behavior. More than basic thought, narratives are a meaningful communicative tool through which individuals express themselves while creating images of the past and the present and images of their own future actions. Thus, individuals are not simply storytellers but rather are story dwellers; they are constantly creating and modifying their stories (Fasching, 1992, p. 25). People's options and choices, including those for coping with crises and challenges and those that enable them to persist in their efforts to change oppressive conditions, are embedded in stories. As a result, storytelling can be a tool of liberation. Storytelling can be liberating personally and collectively. When individuals gather to share their stories, they are able to identify commonalities among them. As discussed in previous chapters, Freire (1970) calls this a dialogical process of conscientization that starts when individuals share their personal narratives and begin to construct a collective narrative that identifies sources of oppression and avenues for positive change.

The culturally grounded approach shares the postmodern understanding that words create worlds, or that humans construct their own reality by naming it and forming it into a story. As social workers listen to their clients' narratives, they often identify recurring patterns in the way clients portray themselves and other significant people in their lives. Narrative theory proposes that the social world cannot be treated as an objective system and that the stories told are essentially subjective. From this perspective, social work practitioners must become aware and respectful of the way in which reality is linguistically constructed by individuals, groups, and communities. The stories people tell are not just individually invented worlds that guide their day-to-day social relationships and negotiations; they are also the product of their social contexts.

People do not live in isolation, and conversely their stories are not constructed in isolation. Rather, individual stories inscribe themselves in larger narratives that create shared vocabularies (namely, life as it is perceived and interpreted by community members), delineate the structure of what was and what is (reality), and define what is possible (opportunities, followed by dreams, plans, goals, and action). These narratives define the forbidden and determine to whom prohibitions apply.

Stories are also ideological structures permeated by political and contextual realities that establish nonnegotiable privileges and boundaries of freedom, and supported by meta-narratives (Gregg, 1991; Haidt, Graham, & Joseph, 2009). Power relations are a strong external reality that individuals confront in their everyday lives. The ability to overcome obstacles and live full lives depends in great measure on an individual's interactions with master narratives—the stories that have been constructed from the point of view of dominant groups about social reality. These stories tell individuals who they are, who they are not, and what they can and cannot do or become. For example, the master narrative may tell girls in junior high that they are not as good in algebra as their male classmates. Some girls believe that message and opt out of or underperform in advanced math. These encompassing master narratives supply a ready-made template for the cultural minority individual to fit into. They furnish socializing mechanisms and justify power relations and interactions, often protecting the privilege of a few.

From colonial times, whites in what is today the United States crafted master narratives to define African Americans in ways that justified their enslavement, their denial of the full benefits of citizenship, and denigration of their culture. Master narratives were used in the twentieth century to portray all black families as dysfunctional, inevitably consigned to poverty, economically marginalized, dependent on social welfare programs, and plagued by high rates of deviant and criminal behavior and cultural decay (Williams & Peterson, 1998). Such narratives have been instrumental in halting and often reversing the progress of government poverty programs and in the dismantling of federal entitlement programs.

The culturally grounded approach shares the postmodern understanding that words create worlds, or that humans construct their own reality by naming it and forming it into a story. Narrative theory, as a direct derivative of postmodern thought, challenges social workers, educators, and other agents of socialization to support clients in their efforts to become storytellers. A storyteller is able to integrate resiliency into the story and to verbalize needs and paths to address those needs. Once the story is told, the client, in partnership with the worker, can examine the roles played by the different characters and the strengths and the weaknesses of her or his interpretation of the story. The social worker may perceive the influence of a powerful meta-narrative that sets limits and perpetuates oppressive relationships. Working together, the client and worker identify the strengths that have been overlooked and assess the potential for change and empowerment. The objective is to allow the client to construct a more liberating narrative that can be translated into real life, one that eventually leads to lasting change. The new narratives generated by the client allow for the emergence of new roles and a reinterpretation of stories that perpetuate oppression. In the new narratives, the assets of the client are highlighted and oppressive conditions are targeted for reflection and action. Daily life is the social context in which change will take place. The particular place and time in which narratives are constructed influence the stories that are told. Social workers may want their clients to adopt what they consider the language of aspirations and success, encouraging clients to create new stories of change and success. At times, clients say what they think is expected and what satisfies the criteria established by a naive social worker. However, a situation in which the client mimics the social worker until she or he sounds like the social worker can hardly be described as an empowering or transforming process of change. Assessing progress over time based on how much the client adopts the practitioner's language, insights, point of view, and values would be the antithesis of a culturally grounded approach to practice, as it perpetuates oppressive relationships. It is through action in addition to stories (praxis) that individuals make concrete plans and plan actions toward change and create sustainable structures of plausibility.

Because most of social work practice takes places around the telling of stories, the narrative approach is central to the culturally grounded approach. Social work as a profession, in its attempts to respond to the unique needs and opportunities it faces as an applied field, has integrated many postmodernist concepts and approaches and has adopted related theories that guide social work practice and research. Narratives are a vital component of transformative social work practice.

Indigenous Theories

Indigenous theories suggest that theoretical perspectives on culture that originate in Western philosophy and scientific tradition cannot adequately describe minority groups' experiences and therefore cannot truly inform culturally grounded social work practice (Alatas, 1993). This orientation does not discard Western philosophy and scientific traditions, but argues for the integration of indigenous knowledge and worldviews in the development of social work research and the development of interventions. This theoretical perspective argues that the superiority of science over all other forms of knowledge perpetuates colonialism by imposing dominant cultural values. This viewpoint does not put forward any uniform theoretical perspective but argues that indigenous worldviews should shape theory formation that informs a culturally grounded social work perspective. Narrative theory provides a method for working toward the articulation of indigenous theories, the incorporation of which will lead to culturally grounded interventions (Duran & Walters, 2004).

RELEVANCE OF THEORIES TO CULTURALLY GROUNDED SOCIAL WORK

Table 5.1, which summarizes the level of fit of the different approaches reviewed, is offered as a thinking tool more than as a definitive way of organizing

Table 5.1   Level of Fit between Theories and the Culturally Grounded Approach

Theory	None	Low	Medium	High
	Level of fit			
Social Darwinism	X			
Structural functionalism		X		
Assimilation		X		
Melting pot		X		
Marxist/neo-Marxist theory			X	
Contact theory				X
Pluralism				X
Cosmopolitanism				X
Structural role theory				X
Human capital theory				X
Postmodernism				X
Symbolic interactionism				X
Narrative theory				X

the theories reviewed thus far. The search for an appropriate theoretical foundation for social work is an ongoing process. Social work as a discipline has developed approaches based on many of these theories. At the same time, it has
embraced broader theoretical approaches and added its own applied flavor to
them. Some of these efforts at theoretical synthesis are described in the next
chapter.

Key Concepts

Principles of homophily: The theory that individuals prefer to develop social
bonds with people who look and act like themselves

Pluralist perspective: The belief that people should be able to advance socially
and economically without having to sacrifice values and cultural heritage
unwillingly

Multiculturalism: The spreading of knowledge, experiences, and creative expressions of different cultures

Social constructivism: The theory that individuals actively construct knowledge
and ideas about reality and themselves through social processes and
experiences

Postmodernism: An alternative and collective interpretation of society that questions traditional forms of knowledge construction and distribution

Symbolic interactionism: Interactions through which people learn the values and norms of society and learn to attach meanings to symbols, images, and ideas

Narrative theory: The theory that the human experience is conveyed through stories or through storytelling and that changes in behavior and attitudes can be initiated through a rewriting of these stories

6

Intersecting Social and Cultural Determinants of Health and Well-Being

THE CLOSE CONNECTION BETWEEN HEALTH AND SES, RECOGNIZED throughout history and richly explored in literature, is also well established in research on health disparities. The concept of health disparities refers to diseases, disorders, and health conditions that disproportionately affect individuals who are members of racial and ethnic minority groups and certain other groups, such as the poor (National Institutes of Health, 2002). Studies have consistently shown that people on the lower end of the SES spectrum have significantly higher rates of mortality (death) and morbidity (disease), and are exposed to more risk factors for poor health than others within their racial/ethnic group with higher SES, even controlling for differences in access to and utilization of health care (National Center for Health Statistics, 2012). These findings have led to a wide-ranging search for other determinants beyond medical factors that may help explain disparities in health outcomes. Thus, the social determinants of health perspective have emerged as a means to understand disparities related to SES and other non-medical factors.

Social determinants influence health through a variety of mechanisms, including money, knowledge, power, prestige, social connections, physical environment, and social policies (Koh et al., 2010; Koh & Nowinski, 2010; Link & Phelan, 1995). Social determinants include behaviors such as parenting, substance use, and nutrition, as well as structural factors such as unemployment, work stress, discrimination, and socioeconomic opportunities and resources. Efforts to ameliorate health disparities require that the social determinants of health are addressed at both the individual and community levels (Koh et al., 2010). These determinants directly affect the ability of individuals and communities to avoid disease. Examining social determinants of health as fundamental causes of disease is a useful approach for understanding the existing vast socioeconomic and racial disparities in health and is also a guide for improving the health of communities (Phelan & Link, 2005) (see figure 6.1).

Figure 6.1   Percent of Population Whose Self-Reported Health Status Is Not Excellent or Good

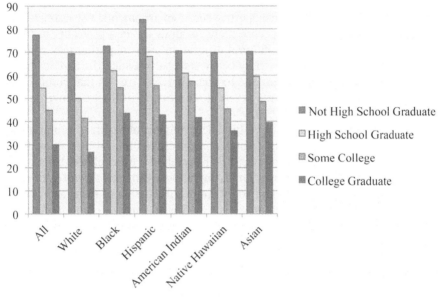

Source: Braveman et al. (2010).

Medical care is not excluded from the social determinants approach, but rather is considered in a much larger context. Some social determinants are described as upstream or major causal factors (i.e., poverty), while others are considered downstream or the result of the major causal factor (i.e., poor nutrition). Upstream and downstream determinants are illustrated in the following river metaphor: People in a village are getting sick because the river, their main source of drinking water, has been contaminated. In a downstream approach a person would distribute filters or teach the people to boil their water before consumption. In an upstream approach a person would work to shut down the chemical plant that is dumping pollutants into the water (Braveman, Egerter, & Williams, 2011). There are several key upstream and downstream social determinants of health: stress, early life, social exclusion, employment, social support and cohesion, addiction, food, transportation and neighborhoods (Marmot & Wilkinson, 2006; Wilkinson & Marmot, 2003). These social determinants do not occur in isolation but are interrelated, each affecting the other.

The social determinants of health perspective emphasize the social stressors and structural barriers that communities need to overcome in order to improve their well-being. The concept of social determinants as fundamental causes of disease can be expanded to address the role of other social statuses besides SES in the creation and elimination of health disparities. Cultural background, ethnicity, immigration status, age/generation, gender, sexual orientation, and ability status may serve as sociocultural determinants that promote health but may also threaten health in risky or unsupportive social environments. For example, cultural values promoting strong connections to family can be a protective factor for poor immigrant families, but cultural dislocation after migration may result in children being exposed to new risky behaviors against which the parents can no longer effectively protect them due to acculturative stresses that compromise effective family functioning and parental monitoring in the new environment (Szapocznik & Coatsworth, 1999).

This chapter introduces the cultural determinants of health as a complementary concept from a culturally grounded perspective. Cultural determinants are the assets present in communities that help prevent the onset of health disparities and that are a valuable resource for changing upstream and downstream social conditions. This chapter attempts to integrate a discussion of social and cultural determinants of health around previously discussed concepts of intersectionality and the need to consider all of the social positions and cultural identities that together play crucial roles in health and well-being.

HEALTH DISPARITIES, HEALTH EQUITY, AND THE SOCIAL GRADIENT

A first step in advancing this integration of social and cultural determinants of health is to further define and distinguish health disparities and health equity. Health disparities have historically been defined as documented differences in mortality and morbidity between social groups, a lack of equality in opportunity, treatment or status, and an inequality that is unfair, unjust, unnecessary, and avoidable (Frieden, 2011). Disparities in health and well-being occur by SES, race/ethnicity, gender, sexual orientation, ability status, immigration status, geography/environment, and age. More often they occur at the intersection of two or more statuses. For example, children (age) from low-income families (SES) of ethnic/racial minority (ethnicity) backgrounds living in rural (geography) communities are more susceptible to infectious diseases and injuries from accidents in unsafe environments (Cohen, Tiesman, Bossarte, & Furbee, 2009). Sustained poverty and racial inequality in rural America has been linked to multiple co-occurring physical and/or mental health problems within families (Burton, Lichter, Baker, & Eason, 2013; Sano & Richards, 2011). Child health is a very important concern in rural America; a large number (81%) of the counties with persistent child poverty are located in rural areas (Mattingly, Johnson, & Schaefer, 2011). As in many other instances where health disparities are pronounced, it is not possible to isolate one social determinant of health as the root cause of a single health disparity affecting poor rural children. Social determinants and related disparities seem to be grouped in clusters.

The term "health inequality" refers to the differences in health outcomes between populations and can be seen in operation both between countries and within countries. Although some have argued that health inequalities and inequities are synonymous terms that can be used interchangeably, others argue that there are important differences in meaning that have a potentially large impact (Braveman & Gruskin, 2003). From this perspective, not all inequalities are inequities. Some health inequalities are caused by biological variations. For example, Latinos, Native Americans, and Filipinos are more vulnerable to Valley Fever—a disease commonly found in the desert areas of the Southwest—than are people of other ethnic backgrounds (CDC, 2012a). Other health disparities are attributable to the external environment and conditions mainly outside the control of the individuals concerned. For example, the high rates of cancer found among people living in neighborhoods with highly contaminated soil and water are manifestations of externally caused health inequities (Liu-Mares et al., 2013). In the first case it may be impossible or unethical to change the health determinants and so the health inequalities are unavoidable. In the second, the uneven distribution of people across residential areas and housing segregation may be unnecessary, unjust, and unfair, making the health inequality also an inequity.

Until the middle of the twentieth century, health inequalities among some ethnic and socioeconomic groups were often assumed to be genetic and therefore not modifiable. Certain groups were thought to be inherently at higher risk of diseases and death. Subsequent research has shown that this is not the case in all but a very few circumstances (Cooper, Kaufman, & Ward, 2003; Krieger, 1987). There is, however, some debate about which determinants of health can be attributed to the unfair distribution of resources and which are inherent and therefore not modifiable. At what point does a health inequality become an inequity? For instance, cigarette smoking is a choice that people make that has a significant impact on their health. Some would argue that this is health inequality and not a health inequity because individuals are making a choice about their behavior. Others may argue that smoking is not entirely a free choice but is instead directly linked to the number of chronic stressors in a person's environment, the amount of advertising that takes place in their neighborhood, and the number of outlets that are willing to sell cigarettes to children under the legal age, which starts the tobacco addiction process. From the latter perspective, cigarette smoking is a health inequity, the result of social determinants that lead to an uneven distribution of risk factors for smoking.

Variations in health are considered health inequities when there is a pattern of differences that is systematic, socially produced, unfair, and unavoidable by reasonable action (Blas & Kurup, 2010). A large body of evidence has accumulated that suggests that disparities in health outcomes are not biological but are rather a result of environmental, behavioral, and psychosocial factors that are influenced by SES. This perspective advocates for a preventive approach that addresses the underlying social determinants of health inequality (Marmot & Wilkinson, 2006). A consideration of cultural determinants can be added to this approach as a means to include cultural assets in any prevention effort.

The counterpart of health disparities is health equity or equal opportunities to achieve and maintain well-being and equal access to quality care (including behavioral health) for all. Achieving health equity has been the World Health Organization's primary goal since its inception, in 1946. In its constitution, the World Health Organization stated that "the highest standards of health should be within reach of all, without distinction of race, religion, political belief, economic or social condition," outlining for the first time on an international scale the goal that everyone regardless of SES, nationality, and/or ethnicity should have a fair opportunity to be healthy (World Health Organization quoted in Whitehead & Dahlgren, 2006, p. 5).

Although the World Health Organization goals for health equity have not yet been achieved, significant progress has been made in some areas during the half century since the World Health Organization was founded. A consistent inverse relationship, however, continues to exist between SES and life expectancy such that the more income an individual has the longer he or she is expected to live (see figure 6.2). This trend is seen nationally and internationally and has been constant over time. For example, in the United States the gap in life expectancy between men living in Washington, DC, and men living in Maryland, a contiguous state, is seventeen years; the poverty rate in Washington is more than double the rate in Maryland (Banks, Marmot, Oldfield, & Smith, 2006). In Estonia the gap in life expectancy between groups with different levels of education is as high as thirteen years (Leinsalu, Vågerö, & Kunst, 2003). The gap in life expectancies is also observed between countries. In Sierra Leone the average life expectancy is forty-seven years of age, compared to Japan where it is nearly double, eighty-three years (World Health Organization, 2013).

The more economic inequality observed within a country, the greater the disparities in health outcomes (Wilkinson, 1992; Wilkinson & Pickett, 2006). In the United States, the income differences between the rich and poor have been widening since 1975, with two major spikes in the widening gap during economic recession in the administrations of George Bush senior and George Bush junior (Wilkinson & Pickett, 2009). In 1979 annual incomes for the top five percent of income earners were eleven times larger than the bottom twenty-five percent of income earners, but by 2005 this ratio nearly doubled to twenty-one times more (Mishel, Bernstein, & Allegretto, 2007).

Despite being one of the richest nations in the world, considering average per capita income, the United Sates displays the largest gaps in SES and the largest disparities in health outcomes in the developed world (Organisation for Economic

Figure 6.2   Life Expectancy at Age Twenty-Five, by Sex and Education Level: United States 2006

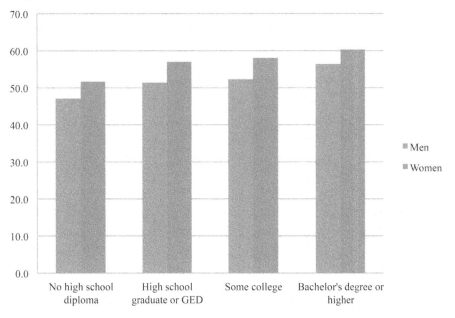

Source: National Center for Health Statistics (2012).

Co-operation and Development [OECD], 2011; Wilkinson & Pickett, 2009). Health is not the only social problem that is exacerbated with growing inequality: income inequality within a country is also linked to higher rates of violence, homicide, imprisonment, poor education outcomes, teenage birth, mental illness, drug abuse, child violence, racism, drug overdose mortality, and low levels of social trust, social capital, and social mobility (Kaplan, Pamuk, Lynch, Cohen, & Balfour, 1996; Wilkinson & Pickett, 2007, 2009).

It was long thought that the relationship between income and health (and mental health) was simple and direct: those at the bottom fare worse than those at the top. However, recent evidence suggests that the relationship between income and health is gradual (see figures 6.1, 6.2, and 6.3). For example, 33 percent of adults who live below the poverty line have two or more chronic health conditions, compared to 30 percent of individuals with incomes just above the poverty line, 21 percent of those earning between 200 percent and 399 percent above the poverty line, and 16 percent of individuals who earn more than 400 percent above the poverty line (National Center for Health Statistics, 2012). This social gradient, where there is a gradual decline in health as levels of income, education, prestige, and status decrease, is consistently observed across countries

Figure 6.3 Mortality Ratio by Individuals and Household Income

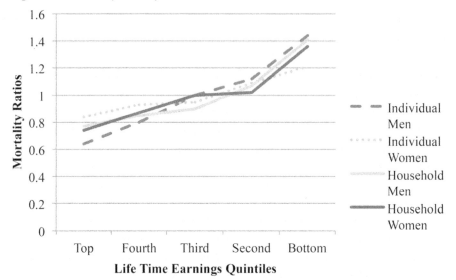

Source: Cristia (2009).

and health outcomes (Krieger et al., 2008; Mackenbach et al., 2008; Mirowsky & Ross, 2003; Schnittker, 2004).

Variations in outcomes by SES are one of the clearest patterns in health inequality. However, intersecting statuses complicate the picture. In the United States health inequalities are also seen across races, even among those at the same rungs of the socioeconomic ladder. Life expectancy for white females is eighty-one years, for black females is seventy-seven years, for white males is seventy-six years, and for black males is seventy years (National Center for Health Statistics, 2012). Not only are African Americans more likely to be in the lowest SES brackets, but they also experience the social gradient in health outcomes (Williams, Mohammed, Leavell, & Collins, 2010). A black man with an income in the lowest quartile has on average a lower life expectancy than does a white person in the same income group (Lin, Rogot, Johnson, Sorlie, & Arias, 2003). Life expectancy for a black man in the highest quintile of the SES distribution is higher than it is for a black man in the lower SES bracket but is still lower than it is for a white man in the same group. Pronounced racial disparities in health appear even among people with very high SES. African American physicians have earlier onset and higher rates of cardiovascular disease than do white physicians, and infant mortality and poor maternal health outcomes are much more common among highly educated African American women than among their white counterparts (Thomas, Thomas, Pearson, Klag, & Mead, 1997).

Although African Americans have lower life expectancy than whites, Latinos have the highest among all three racial groups: eighty-three years for females and seventy-eight years for males (National Center for Health Statistics, 2012). Despite higher rates of life expectancy, the social gradient is still observed among Hispanics for some health outcomes such as self-reported health (see figure 6.4) and the number of activities that are limited due to chronic disease (Braveman, Cubbin, Egerter, Williams, & Pamuk, 2010). Because of immigration and circular migration (repeated movement between host and origin countries), the Latino case needs to be considered with care; several explanations can account for the relatively higher life expectancy of Latinos. The "healthy migrant" or "migrant selection" hypothesis suggests that healthier individuals migrate due to the demands connected with the process; in effect, migration selects or favors healthier people. The Latino lifestyle hypothesis focuses on Hispanics' strong social ties and better health behaviors, which can be attributed to cultural factors. The reverse migration argument suggests that the Latino morbidity profile in the United States is affected by the fact that many older Latinos return to their country of birth when they are ill or after retirement, before their health declines (Crimmins, Soldo, Kim, & Alley, 2005; Vega, Rodrigues, & Gruskin, 2009). The many factors that contribute to the relatively high life expectancy of Latinos in the United States are an excellent example of intersecting social and cultural determinants of health.

Figure 6.4   Social Determinants of Health

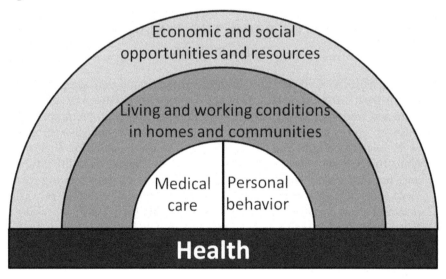

Source: Braveman et al. (2011).

ACCESS TO HEALTH CARE AND THE MEDICAL
POVERTY TRAP

Historically, many efforts to eradicate health inequities were focused on improving access to health care (Adler & Stewart, 2010). And indeed access to health care seems to follow the social gradient and can be influenced by location, cost, and cultural barriers (Larson & Halfon, 2010). About 20 percent of the U.S. population is affected by barriers to health-care utilization related to the distance they must travel to health-care facilities. The sparse distribution of hospitals in rural counties can be blamed for large disparities in health (U.S. Department of Health and Human Services [DHHS], 2004). In Canada, this problem is similar to that in the United States: people requiring specialized health services sometimes travel two hundred kilometers to the nearest hospital; in the northern Canadian regions, harsh weather conditions make road and air travel dangerous and sometimes impossible for days at a time (Grzybowski, Stoll, & Kornelsen, 2011).

Often health care is available within a reasonable distance but many patients in the United States are not able to access it because the cost is prohibitive. In the absence of universal health-care coverage, people with lower incomes and/or jobs that do not provide insurance are less likely to have health insurance. Notes from the field 6.1 illustrates a family's struggle to afford treatment and day care for their son. Due to the rising cost of health care, uninsured individuals frequently delay seeking both preventive and urgent medical care because they cannot afford it (Ayanian, Weissman, Schneider, Ginsburg, & Zaslavsky, 2000). When people use

---

NOTES FROM THE FIELD 6.1
Finding the Funds

The Chens, a second-generation Chinese American family, are struggling to pay for their autistic son's treatment and day care. They own a small grocery store and work long hours but are not able to pay the high premiums for their son's preexisting condition. Because they make more than 200 percent of the poverty level, they do not qualify for state health insurance. They are going through the process of having their son assessed for disability insurance but have encountered several barriers that have delayed receiving services. The added financial stress of paying for specialized child care is putting a strain on the family. They are considering having their other son take a year off from high school so that he can help his father in the store and his mother can stay home with his brother. The son is willing to do it for his family, but is concerned that once he quits he will not go back to complete his education.

health care and are not able to afford it, they run the risk of going into debt. This is demonstrated in notes from the field 6.2. Impoverishment caused by paying for medical care is referred to as the "medical poverty trap" (Whitehead, Dahlgren, & Evans, 2001). In both the developing and developed worlds the medical poverty trap is prevalent. An appreciable proportion of households in fifty-nine countries face catastrophic out-of-pocket health expenses: 5 percent of households in Ukraine, 6 percent in Argentina, 10 percent in Brazil, and 11 percent in Vietnam are in substantial debt due to unpaid medical bills (Xu et al., 2003). In the United States 62 percent of all bankruptcies in 2007 were caused by inability to pay medical bills, and, in a revelation of the limits of health insurance, 78 percent of the individuals whose illness led to bankruptcy had health insurance at the onset of the illness (Himmelstein, Thorne, Warren, & Woolhandler, 2009).

NOTES FROM THE FIELD 6.2

Hard Choices

Maria was diagnosed with breast cancer last May. She was terrified. Her grandmother had passed away from breast cancer when she was only fifty-eight, and Maria was fifty-two at her diagnosis. She knew that treatment options have progressed since that time and, depending on the type and stage of cancer, the prognoses are getting better, but she also knew that it was expensive and she did not have insurance. Maria's husband was employed and making enough money to disqualify him and his wife from the state health insurance program. He was given the option of adding his wife to his insurance, but the $500-a-month price tag was beyond his reach. Before the diagnosis they had both been healthy. Raul was fifty-six, and although relatively young, they felt their age from time to time, but they had not had any serious illnesses. After a discussion with her doctor Maria decided that she wanted to take the most aggressive course of action, a double mastectomy. Maria has young grandchildren and wanted to do everything that she could to ensure that she would be around for their marriages and graduations. The medical bills for a double mastectomy could reach as high as $50,000, a bill that they could not afford to pay. After days of discussion about possible solutions, Maria and her husband decided that the only way to get her the insurance that she would need to cover this expensive but potentially life-saving treatment was to divorce her husband and have Maria apply for Medicaid. The thought of divorcing her husband of thirty years broke her heart, but the thought of leaving her family was even more painful. In order to have a fighting chance at survival, she would need to legally divorce her husband.

In the United States there are disparities in access to health insurance by race and SES. Although Medicaid is designed to provide insurance to individuals living in poverty, 61 percent of Hispanics who live below the poverty line do not have insurance, a rate that is substantially higher than whites (35%) and African Americans (37%) (National Center for Health Statistics, 2012). Some of this disparity can be attributed to undocumented or recent immigrant status, a lack of knowledge about the health-care system, and lack of language and cultural competence to navigate successfully within the system (Derose, Escarce, & Lurie, 2007; Ku & Matani, 2001). Many Americans believe that immigrants' use of health services strains the health-care system, when in fact average per capita health expenditures for immigrants are half of those born in the United States (Ku, 2009). Despite evidence to the contrary, these beliefs have led to increased restrictions on state-provided health insurance for low income-families. Undocumented immigrants have never had access to Medicaid but aggressive federal laws passed in 1996 also prohibited documented immigrants from obtaining state health insurance during their first five years of legal residency in the United States (Espenshade, Baraka, & Huber, 1997). Among Latinos, even those who are eligible for state health insurance face significant barriers when applying for benefits. Barriers include the complexity of application, misunderstanding of eligibility rules and verification, administrative errors, transportation and logistics, and climates of fear and mistrust perpetuated by anti-immigrant legislation (Perreira et al., 2012). As a result of these barriers, many eligible Latinos go without coverage. A lack of insurance translates directly to unmet medical needs in this population. Uninsured immigrants were four times more likely to have unmet medical needs and seventeen times more likely to not have a primary care physician (Siddiqi, Zuberi, & Nguyen, 2009). The likelihood of having unmet medical needs was much greater for both uninsured and insured immigrants living in the United States when compared to immigrants living in Canada, where immigrants are covered under that country's universal health-care system (Siddiqi et al., 2009).

There are also cultural barriers to accessing health services (Whitehead et al., 2001). Access to culturally relevant health services requires not only linguistically appropriate services, but also culturally appropriate services. Providers who receive federal funds in the United States are mandated to adhere to fourteen standards for culturally and linguistically appropriate services. These standards, among other things, require providers to hire culturally diverse staff, attend training in culturally and linguistically appropriate services, ensure the language competence of translators, and provide reading materials in the language of the patients (Office of Minority Health, 2013). Despite these regulations, in focus groups ethnic minority patients commonly reported negative experiences with health-care providers (Barr & Wanat, 2005). African Americans reported that they felt that doctors did not have an understanding of the discrimination they regularly faced and that they experienced rude and unhelpful office staff. Native Americans reported feeling offended by their doctors' stereotypes and therefore ignored prevention messages about diet, obesity, alcohol, and drugs. Native American elders also conveyed that they had been cut off by health-care providers when they were describing symptoms or asked questions of the providers, which they interpreted as a sign of disrespect. Latinos reported experiencing major language barriers and perceived doctors as rude and insensitive. Pacific Islanders stated that they experienced long waits, followed by rushed encounters with their doctors, difficulty understanding the physicians, and poor translation services (Barr & Wanat, 2005). Cultural barriers to access can be overcome by utilizing relatively simple and cost-effective interventions that increase the medical staff's competence in working with the client and increases the client's ability to insist on quality care (Alegría et al., 2008; Marsiglia, Bermudez-Parsai, & Coonrod, 2010). Notes from the field 6.3 demonstrate how cultural barriers to health care may affect health outcomes.

Although a lack of access to culturally competent care may explain unattended medical needs and therefore some of the social gradient observed in mortality, morbidity, and life expectancy, it does not explain the disproportionality in the occurrence of health issues or the Latino health paradox. The Latino health paradox is used to explain trends in Latino health that do not follow the social

---

NOTES FROM THE FIELD 6.3
Revolving Door

Vlad, a recent Russian immigrant living in a rural community, has had to take his son Sasha into the emergency room (ER) five times in the past two months for breathing problems. The ER doctor prescribed a rescue inhaler for Sasha for emergencies but does nothing to address the frequency of his attacks. Vlad is told that he needs to take his son to a primary care physician for preventative care but Vlad is not able to understand the doctor's reasoning, is unfamiliar with the American health-care system, and is concerned about the cost. Finally understanding that part of the frequent readmittance is lack of understanding of the nature of the medical problem and the American health-care system, the medical center assigns Vlad a case manager that is fluent in Russian. While discussing the possible reason for Sasha's frequent attacks, she discovers that Vlad lives two blocks away from a chemical plant that releases large amounts of toxic fumes, a by-product of their manufacturing. In addition to helping Sasha get an appointment with a primary care physician, she also is able to help Vlad obtain an air purifying system for his home and puts him in touch with a group of parents who are working with a lawyer to address the problem of chemical fumes in the area.

gradient; first-generation Latinos consistently display superior health outcomes than do their second- and third-generation counterparts despite the latter having higher SES (Acevedo-Garcia & Bates, 2007; Braveman et al., 2010). This trend exists despite the fact that Latinos in the United States are the least insured ethnic group (DeNavas-Walt, Proctor, & Smith, 2013). Cultural determinants and social explanations for the Latino health paradox may suggest possible protective factors in the relationship between SES and health outcomes; these explanations include high levels of social support, strong family orientation, a healthy diet, and fewer risk behaviors such as substance use (Hayes-Bautista, 2002). The paradox observed among Latinos in some health outcomes lends support to the importance of cultural determinants of health as the communities' cultural assets counteract or compensate for barriers to health-care access and utilization. This is not to say that Latinos do not need to have access to quality health care: on the contrary, the cultural determinants perspective calls attention to the need for culturally grounded resources on which to build strategies to close the access gap.

SOCIAL DETERMINANTS OF HEALTH: SOCIETAL RISKS AND PROTECTIVE FACTORS

Stress

The idea that psychosocial factors work through chronic stress to affect health is one of the most important findings advancing our knowledge of social determinants of health (Brunner & Marmot, 2005). Stress is the subjective state that occurs when individuals experience a threat that they believe exceeds their ability to cope (Lazarus & Folkman, 1984). Stress can be positive in situations where a person is able to address the sources of the stress, resulting in a feeling of mastery and success, as when an effective head administrator of a hospital is under great stress during a natural disaster in the community and is able to mobilize the hospital staff to meet the crisis. In situations where an individual is not able to modify the source of stress but has substantial social support, the stress may not be toxic or affect health. But in situations where the stress is chronic, where the individual feels powerless and lacks resources to modify the source of stress, and where the individual has inadequate social support, stress may become toxic and damaging to a person's health (Adler & Stewart, 2010).

The distinction between chronic and acute stressors is important when talking about the link between stress and health inequality. Chronic stressors can be defined as stress that continues abnormally and lasts for a significant amount of time because it is continuous, episodic, or poses a threat that cannot be easily changed (Baum, Garofalo, & Yali, 1999). Baum and colleagues (1999) suggest that these are the stressors that exist in the background and are "embedded in the living or working environments" (p. 132). Acute stressors, including a one-time stressful event such as a car accident or burglary, seldom result in negative health outcomes or long-term psychological distress (Aneshensel, 1992; Thoits, 1983). However, chronic stressors are linked to negative health outcomes (Grippo et al., 2007; Williams & Jackson, 2005).

Experiencing chronic stress influences health physiologically. The physical stress response that releases cortisol, cytokines, and other substances can damage immune responses, increase inflammation, and damage organs, which can lead to chronic illness and may accelerate aging (McEwen, 2008; McEwen & Gianaros, 2010; Steptoe & Marmot, 2002). The chronicity and severity of a stressor are strong predictors of its eventual impact on health (Segerstrom & Miller, 2004). The stress response diverts energy away from the body's normal functions. When the stress event and response are short or acute, a person is able to reestablish equilibrium quickly, but when stress hormones are elevated for more than an hour, immunity is affected. When stress is experienced for weeks, months, or years, the damage that results puts a person at risk for poor health (Wilkinson & Pickett, 2009). Chronic levels of stress have been found to predict high blood pressure, susceptibility to infection, fat build-up in the blood vessels and in the abdomen, and atrophy of brain cells (Bobak & Marmot, 1996; Epel et al., 2004; Ferrie, Shipley, Stansfeld, & Marmot, 2002; Gianaros et al., 2007; Larsson et al., 1989).

Several biological studies have firmly established the relationship between psychosocial factors, stress, and biological processes. In an experiment with non-human primates, low social status caused higher stress hormones and more-rapid build-up of fatty material in arteries, a process that reversed when social statuses were changed or switched (Shively & Clarkson, 1994). Additionally, two biological markers have been associated with both stress and SES: allostatic load and telomere length (Adler & Stewart, 2010). Allostasis is the process that healthy bodies go through when they have experienced a stressful situation in order to maintain balance or homeostasis. Allostatic load is a marker of how quickly a person's physiology, cardiovascular, metabolic, nervous, hormonal, and immune systems are able to regain normal functioning after a stress response has been triggered (McEwen, 1998). When individuals experience chronic or frequent stressors, their stress response process is strained and their body takes longer to recover from stressful experiences, resulting in higher allosteric loads. Individuals with low SES are more likely to have high allostatic loads, which have been associated with higher rates of cardiovascular disease and mortality (Seeman et al., 2004). Telomeres, another biological marker, are found at the end of DNA strands in cells. Shorter telomeres are associated with aging and mortality (Blackburn, Greider, & Szostak, 2006; Cawthon, Smith, O'Brien, Sivatchenko, & Kerber, 2003). Objective and subjective stress and income levels have been associated with shorter telomeres, providing a biological explanation for the relationship among SES, stress, and health outcomes (Cherkas et al., 2006; Epel et al., 2004). This research has created a strong link between stress and health, potentially explaining much of the social gradient observed in health outcomes.

Early Life

An argument has been made for taking a life-course approach to social determinants of health. A life-course approach proposes that circumstances, both social and physical, in early life affect health across the life course. From the time of conception, the mother's experiences and decisions during the pregnancy will have an impact on the health of the child she carries (Braveman & Barclay, 2009). Lack of nutrition during prenatal growth and low birth weight increase the risk of adult cardiovascular disease, type 2 diabetes, stroke, and hypertension (Al Salmi et al., 2008; Barker, 2003; Barker, Eriksson, Forsen, & Osmond, 2002; Rich-Edwards et al., 2005).

Early childhood is also a crucial developmental period in the life course when discussing health outcomes. Early experiences affect children's cognitive, behavioral, and physical development (Bradley & Corwyn, 2002; Cohen, Janicki-Deverts, Chen, & Matthews, 2010; Hertzman, 1999). Slow physical growth and a lack of emotional support in childhood leads to disrupted cognitive and emotional functioning in adulthood (Wilkinson & Marmot, 2003). Exposure to high levels of stressors in early childhood can also alter biological structures and psychosocial functioning, increasing the risk of disease in adulthood (Shonkoff, Boyce, & McEwen, 2009). When children are raised in environments with high levels of conflict and low levels of warmth, they show greater physical reactivity to stress, elevated blood pressure, and activation of the sympathetic nervous system (Repetti, Taylor, & Seeman, 2002; Taylor, Lerner, Sage, Lehman, & Seeman, 2004). Extreme stress in childhood also puts adults at risk for negative health outcomes by increasing their likelihood of using negative coping strategies that harm health. Childhood trauma and abuse are linked to poor mental health outcomes and behavioral risk factors such as substance abuse and sexual risk behaviors (Anda et al., 1999).

However, most life-course approaches to health disparities do not focus on individual factors but rather on the accumulation of circumstances as a result of disadvantaged social status that either cluster or trigger a sequence of events. For example, prenatal nutritional deficits have been shown to combine with early childhood exposure to stress to change gene expressions that contribute to elevated cardiovascular disease risk in adult African Americans (Kuzawa & Sweet, 2009). Growing up in poverty increases the likelihood of experiencing a cluster of risk factors for poor health in adulthood, including stress, poor nutrition, and inadequate early childhood education. The prevalence of poverty among children in the United States is staggering: nearly one in four U.S. children lives in poverty. The poverty rate for children living in the United States ranks as thirty-second highest out of thirty-three developed countries (see figure 6.5). Childhood poverty disproportionally affects minority children, with 35 percent of Hispanic children

Figure 6.5   Child Poverty Rates in High-Income Countries, around 2008

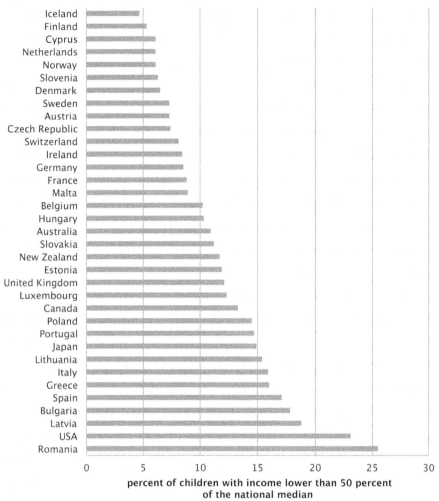

percent of children with income lower than 50 percent
of the national median

Source: Bradshaw et al. (2012).

and 39 percent of African American children living below the poverty line; this is drastically more than white (12%) and Asian American (14%) children (National Center for Health Statistics, 2012). Not only is childhood poverty experienced at high rates among black and Latino youths, but they are also exposed to environmental stressors at a higher rate. In 100 of the nation's metropolitan cities, 76 percent of African American and 69 percent of Latino children live in worse neighborhood environmental conditions than the most disadvantaged whites (Acevedo-Garcia, Ospuk, McArdle, & Williams, 2008).

Like other health issues, childhood health challenges occur on a social gradient with those at the bottom being most affected. Developmental differences have been linked to differences in engagement and stimulation from caregivers, both of which are parenting behaviors that follow the social gradient (Evans, 2004; Guo & Harris, 2000; Votruba-Drzal, 2003). In a study examining mother-child communication, the number and length of utterances that mothers made to their two-year-old children varied by SES, and had a significant impact on the child's language development. In interviews with the higher and lower SES groups, the mothers had the same goals for their children but differed in how important they thought it was to talk to a child and the amount of leisure time they were able to spend doing so (Hoff, 2003). There is a significant gap in low-and middle-income children's readiness for school when they enter kindergarten, a gap that persists through elementary and secondary education and beyond (Ryan, Fauth, & Brooks-Gunn, 2006). Delayed cognitive development can have dramatic effects on income potential across the life course by influencing educational outcomes, which in turn have a significant impact on adult SES and health (Garces, Thomas, & Currie, 2002). Children living in poverty are also exposed to more environmental stressors: in a study of high school students, low SES and high SES high school students interpreted potential threats in the same way, but low SES students were much more likely to interpret ambiguous situations as threatening, which resulted in higher diastolic blood pressure (Chen, Langer, Raphaelson, & Matthews, 2004).

These social factors that occur on the social gradient affect health outcomes in childhood and later in adulthood. A higher percentage of children living in poverty across all racial groups have asthma when compared to children living in households with income just above the poverty level (National Center for Health Statistics, 2012). A social gradient is also observed for diagnoses of ADHD and obesity (National Center for Health Statistics, 2012). Additionally, childhood SES conditions are related to the following health conditions in adulthood: alcoholic cirrhosis, smoking-related cancer, stomach cancer, cardiovascular disease, diabetes, depression, functional limitations, and respiratory disease (Braveman & Barclay, 2009).

Poverty has an intergenerational impact on health. Women who grew up in poverty are more likely to give birth to a child with low birth weight (Astone, Misra, & Lynch, 2007). The intergenerational transmission of poor health outcomes could also occur through lower educational attainment. In the United States, fifteen-year-olds whose parents had low educational achievement had worse math scores than those whose parents were highly educated, a gap that was larger than any other country included in the study (OECD, 2008). However, parental upward mobility may have differential impacts on the outcomes of their children, depending on race. For example, for women who grew up in households whose income fell below the poverty line, upward mobility was related to healthier birth outcomes for white women but not for black women (Colen, Geronimus, Bound, & James, 2006). This relationship may be due to the disproportionate amount of chronic stressors, both economic and racial, that African American women experience in their childhood (Braveman et al., 2005), to continuing experiences of discrimination regardless of their SES, and increased sensitivity to stress later in life due to exposure to early childhood stressors (Ellen, Cutler, & Dickens, 2000; Rich-Edwards et al., 2001; Foster, Wu, Bracken, Semenya, & Thomas, 2000). All of these processes influence the amount of stress hormones that are released during pregnancy, which influences poor birth outcomes like low birth weight and premature birth by increasing inflammation during pregnancy and decreasing the mother's and child's immune system (Dominguez, 2008; Holzman, Jetton, Siler-Khodr, Fisher, & Rip, 2001; McEwen, 1998).

Social Exclusion

Absolute poverty, relative poverty, and social exclusion limit a person's access to resources and full participation in social life, with major impacts on health. Homeless people, one of the most socially excluded groups in the United States, have the highest rates of premature death (Wilkinson & Marmot, 2003). In India there are large disparities between different castes in both health outcomes and access to care, which can be attributed to widespread social exclusion based on social status (Nayar, 2007). Rather than absolute poverty, it is relative poverty— earning less than 60 percent of the median income—that significantly reduces a person's access to housing, education, transportation, food, and health care, and increases their social exclusion (Wilkinson & Marmot, 2003). An individual may also be excluded from society based on race, gender, age, or religion (Nayar, 2007). In addition to the economic disadvantages that occur with relative poverty, social exclusion can also take the form of residential segregation, racial discrimination, and a lack of political power or influence. All forms of social exclusion contribute to an individual's overall stress burden.

The experience of racial discrimination in the United States has been linked to a wide variety of risk factors for negative health outcomes, including violence, poor-quality sleep, abdominal fat, high blood sugar, artery calcification, breast cancer, and smoking (Landrine & Klonoff, 2000; Williams, Neighbors, & Jackson, 2003). The perception or appraisal of discrimination experiences as stressful is a better predictor of smoking than education, gender, income, and age (Landrine & Klonoff, 2000). Not only does the experience of discrimination negatively affect health, but also the anticipation of discrimination experiences is related to health outcomes (Kessler, Mickelson, & Williams, 1999). Some have argued that social exclusion, or discrimination, accounts for continued health disparities between African American and white Americans (Mays, Cochran, & Barnes, 2007). These findings are consistent internationally. In New Zealand, perceived discrimination accounted for disparities in self-reported health between individuals of Maori and European descent (Harris et al., 2006). Similarly, discrimination explained disparities in Aboriginal and non-Aboriginal health and mental health in Australia (Larson, Gillies, Howard, & Coffin, 2007).

Discrimination can take many forms and may affect individuals in multiple ways. Discrimination may prevent someone from being hired for a job or considered for a promotion, may result in rude treatment in restaurants, or may be internalized by the recipient. Internalized discrimination occurs when racial groups accept the negative narratives that are present in the culture as being true (Ahmed, Mohammed, & Williams, 2007). Internalized discrimination is one of the most subtle forms of social exclusion and has been linked to increases in blood pressure, alcohol consumption, psychological distress, overweight, and negative cardiovascular outcomes (Williams & Mohammed, 2009).

The effects of discrimination and marginalization on mental health also disproportionally affect Latinos. Rates of mental health issues increase substantially the longer that immigrants live in the United States, and with each succeeding generation (Alegría et al., 2007). Some have attributed this to increased experiences of barriers to upward mobility and discrimination among second- and third-generation Latinos (Finch, Frank, & Vega, 2004), while others have argued that it is driven by the adoption of negative health behaviors such as substance use. The reception of immigrants in the United States, or the degree of social inclusion that they experience when they arrive, is related to stress and distress. In California in 2001, a time of increased anti-immigrant sentiment, native-born Mexican Americans reported less distress than did their immigrant counterparts (Williams & Mohammed, 2008).

Neighborhoods

The concentration of poverty and environmental risks in neighborhoods is another aspect of social exclusion that contributes to health inequality. Individuals who live in neighborhoods with lower aggregate SES have poorer health outcomes regardless of their individual income, indicating that processes within the neighborhood may be influencing health (Diez-Roux et al., 1997; Yen & Syme, 1999). Neighborhoods with high rates of disadvantage are typically spaces that also have high rates of other mutually reinforcing social problems. The neighborhood that a person lives in may limit upward mobility by reducing access to quality jobs and education, which ultimately increases economic hardship and stress (Fernandez, 2004; Pastor, 2001; Williams & Collins, 2001). It may also decrease access to healthy food and increase access to harmful substances, including drugs, alcohol, and cigarettes (Chuang, Cubbin, Ahn, & Winkleby, 2005; Morland, Diez-Roux, & Wing, 2006). Concentration of poverty in neighborhoods often results in higher rates of crime due to a lack of access to legal means of income generation and attention from law enforcement, which can erode social cohesion, trust, and ultimately social support (Morenoff, Sampson, & Raudenbush, 2001). Additionally, neighborhoods with high rates of poverty are often the site of industry facilities that produce environmental toxins and of poor-quality housing that poses health threats, such as elevated risk of childhood asthma (Evans & Kantrowitz, 2002; Northridge, Ramirez, & Stingone, 2010). Finally, communities with concentrated poverty are less likely to have sufficient quality health care and social service agencies (Deichmann, 1999).

All of these factors work together to create an environment in which there is a high concentration of chronic stressors and a deprivation of resources to cope, affecting health outcomes (Boardman, 2004; Massey, 2004; Roberts, 1997). Residential segregation is linked to increased risk for illness, death, preterm births, and the presence of risk factors for cardiovascular disease (Acevedo-Garcia, Lochner, Osypuk, & Subramanian, 2003; Matthews et al., 2005; Osypuk & Aceveo-Garcia, 2008; Williams & Collins, 2001). Living in disadvantaged neighborhoods is also related to poor mental health outcomes (Mair, Roux, & Galea, 2008). Women exposed to community violence are twice as likely to report depression and anxiety (Clark et al., 2008). Children are particularly vulnerable to stressful neighborhood environments and show higher rates of teen pregnancy, substance abuse, obesity, smoking, limited exercise, and poor dietary habits, all of which are risk factors for poor health in adulthood (Mather & Rivers, 2006). For children in poor neighborhoods, community violence interacts with environmental risks, like pollution, to affect rates of asthma (Williams, Sternthal, & Wright, 2009).

One important way that neighborhood segregation influences health is through access to affordable and healthy food and safe spaces to exercise. Economic growth and increased sanitation in the United States has created an epidemiological shift in the primary causes of death, moving from infectious diseases at the turn of the twentieth century, to the chronic diseases of today that account for most deaths, such as diabetes and cardiovascular disease (Mathers & Loncar, 2006; World Health Organization, 2012). The growing incidence of diabetes and cardiovascular disease is related to the growing obesity trend and can be at least partially attributed to poor diet and a lack of exercise (Mokdad, Marks, Stroup, & Gerberding, 2004).

A social gradient is observed in rates of childhood obesity, healthy eating, and sedentary behavior, which may be linked to access to health services (Braveman et al., 2010; Braveman & Barclay, 2009). Disadvantaged neighborhoods typically have few grocery stores with a variety of fruits and vegetables and more convenience stores (Morland, Wing, & Roux, 2002). These conditions have led to neighborhoods being labeled as "food deserts" (Cummins & Macintyre, 2002). Between 1970 and 1990, when large segments of the population were moving out of city centers and into the suburbs, one half of city grocery stores in the major U.S. cities closed in response to a decreasing median income (Nayga & Weinberg,

1999). The disparity in access to food is stark in cities such as Philadelphia, where the highest-income neighborhood had 156 percent more supermarkets than the lowest-income neighborhood in the city (Walker, Keane, & Burke, 2010). The decline in supermarkets has resulted in an increased consumption of calorie-dense inexpensive food sold at convenience stores and fast food restaurants (Drewnowski & Specter, 2004). When residents living in food deserts do not have access to a vehicle, live in an environment where it is unsafe to walk, or work long hours leaving little time to grocery shop or prepare food, this dynamic can have detrimental impacts on their diet and on their overall well-being (Lake & Townshend, 2006).

In consumer markets in urban areas, both the price of healthy foods and the quality of fresh fruits and vegetables are also deterrents to healthy eating behavior (Powell, Slater, Mirtcheva, Bao, & Chaloupka, 2007). Living in a food desert is related to diabetes, heart disease, and cancer (Cotterill & Frankin, 1995). In addition to having less access to healthy foods, lower SES blocks also have fewer recreational facilities, which in turn is associated with higher rates of overweight residents and lower rates of exercising at least five times a week (Gordon-Larsen, Nelson, Page, & Popkin, 2006). Reported incidents of serious crime also decreased adolescents' likelihood of engaging in vigorous exercise (Popkin, Duffey, & Gordon-Larsen, 2005). Although many of the driving forces behind obesity are believed to be behavioral, the built environment and access to healthy food can seriously restrict attempts to change behavior.

Although not always the case, there is often overlap between neighborhood racial segregation, the proportion of ethnic minority residents, and concentrated poverty, when more than 40 percent of the neighborhood residents live below the poverty line (Massey, 2004). Living in these neighborhoods is related to multiple risk factors for poor health in both the United States and internationally (World Health Organization, 2010). Income and racial segregation typically have an inverse relationship for most ethnic groups: the more one earns, the less likely it is that one will live in racially segregated neighborhoods. This is not, however, the case for African Americans; regardless of an individual's SES, African Americans are more likely to live in racially segregated neighborhoods (Massey, 2004). Living in a racially segregated neighborhood and having higher income levels may not decrease the potential health risk that upwardly mobile African Americans experience. When comparing two primarily African American communities, one with a median income below the poverty level and one with a median income slightly above it, the neighborhood with the higher median income had similar health outcomes on nine of thirteen indicators (Diez-Roux et al., 2001). The risk posed by racial segregation is not the impact of living with members of similar ethnicity per se, but rather the overlap with concentrated poverty, a dynamic that is the result of America's history of racial inequality (Williams et al., 2010).

Employment and Unemployment

In general, having a job is better for health than not having a job, but the type of work and the organizational structure can negatively affect health (Wilkinson & Marmot, 2003). Employment has the potential to improve health by providing income, increasing access to insurance, providing contact with coworkers that could increase social support, and providing opportunities for feeling a sense of accomplishment or control. On the other hand, employment can expose people to physical and emotional strain that may negatively influence their health. The physical nature of work makes occupations a clear pathway to health. Jobs that require repetitive movement or heavy lifting put individuals at risk for musculo-skeletal injuries (O'Neil, Forsythe, & Stanish, 2001), and sedentary jobs put people at risk for obesity, diabetes, and heart disease (Warburton, Nicol, & Bredin, 2006). Compared to whites, ethnic minorities have higher levels of exposure to occupational hazards and are at greater risk of injury or death on the job (Murray, 2003). The relationship between work and health is not limited to employment in hazardous conditions, but also applies to professionals. Significant stress that affects health occurs when professionals feel a low sense of control or inadequately rewarded, given the effort required by their jobs (De Jonge, Bosma, Peter, & Siegrist, 2000; Marmot, Bosma, Hemingway, Brunner, & Stansfeld, 1997). As one ages, transitioning into jobs that reflect one's interest is related to increased job satisfaction and better health outcomes (Padavic & Reskin, 2002).

Over the past century, women have entered the labor market in record numbers. In general, employed women have better health outcomes compared to their unemployed counterparts (Klumb & Lampert, 2004). For women, however, role strain can contribute to work overload, which may have a negative impact on health (Presser, 2000; Repetti, Matthews, & Waldron, 1989). For working mothers who reported both parenting stress and work stress, morning cortisol levels, a biological marker for stress, were significantly higher on work days when compared to nonwork days (Hibel, Mercado, & Trumbell, 2012). Overall, black women had a less positive perception of their overall employment trajectory when compared to white women. For black women, perceived control was a significant predictor of perceiving a positive work trajectory, which in turn was associated with lower mortality (Shippee, Rinaldo, & Ferraro, 2012). Employment status also has an effect on birth outcomes. For pregnant women, low job control is linked to low birth weight and premature delivery (Meyer, Warren, & Reisine, 2008). The combination of work and family responsibilities seems to influence how employment affects health. However, control at work is consistently shown to have a positive impact on the health of women.

Employment also affects access to health insurance. Although the number of individuals who obtain health insurance through their employer is decreasing and the number covered under government health insurances is on the rise, more than half (56%) of Americans still rely on their employer for health insurance (DeNavas-Walt et al., 2013). Employment is no guarantee of insurance coverage. The majority of educated professional women have health insurance, but women who work in the service sector frequently do not (Montez, Angel, & Angel, 2009). Compared to whites, Mexican Americans and African Americans are more likely to work at jobs that do not offer insurance (Montez et al., 2009). Prior to the extension of universal health care through the Affordable Care Act under the Obama administration, the presence of preexisting conditions kept 25 percent of workers at a job they would prefer to leave because their medical benefits may be jeopardized if they were to seek employment elsewhere (Madrian, 1994). Losing employer-based health insurance is also a barrier to entrepreneurship (Fairlie, Kapur, & Gates, 2011). Self-employment puts the heavy cost of insurance on the individual, often resulting in no coverage. This is especially important for immigrants who frequently strive to become upwardly mobile by owning their own business (Kesler & Hout, 2010). For women, health insurance coverage is dependent on their own employment or the employment of their spouse (Moen & Roehling, 2005). Depending on her spouse for insurance can increase a woman's dependence on her mate, especially for stay-at-home mothers (Pascall & Lewis, 2004).

Unemployment has negative impacts on health (Bartley & Plewis, 2002). Both the financial and psychological consequences of unemployment pose a substantial health risk. Mortality more than doubles for men who have been unemployed for five consecutive years (Morris, Cook, & Shaper, 1994). Mental health worsens after a job loss and improves after reemployment (Paul & Moser, 2009). Unemployment has also been associated with a high risk of suicide (Li, Page, Martin, & Taylor, 2011; Yoshimasu, Kiyohara, & Miyashita, 2008). The impact of unemployment on health starts before individuals actually lose their job, when they begin to sense that they will be let go. The anxiety and insecurity that people feel when they might lose their job are related to increased mental health problems, self-reported general ill physical health, and heart disease specifically (Marmot & Wilkinson, 2006). Compared to permanent employees, temporary workers have higher rates of psychological distress, and poor physical and global health, further reinforcing the effect of job insecurity on distress and health (Virtanen et al., 2005).

Substance Use

Tobacco is the leading cause of preventable death in the United States, responsible for over 400,000 deaths annually (Koh & Sebelius, 2012). Tobacco is a contributing factor in morbidity and mortality from cancer, heart disease, stroke, complications during pregnancy, and respiratory illness (CDC, 2008). Parents who smoke also put their children at risk for asthma and other respiratory problems in the short run and a higher chance of smoking as adults in the long run (Barnoya & Glantz, 2005; Cook & Strachan, 1997). In fact 49,400 deaths annually are attributed to second-hand smoke (CDC, 2008). Poor housing, low income, single parenting, and unemployment are all associated with high rates of smoking, a major risk factor for heart disease and cancer (Marmot & Wilkinson, 2006).

Substance abuse is both a reaction to inequality and, in the cases of alcohol and illicit drug abuse, the cause of a decline in SES. Rates of alcohol dependence, illicit drug use, and cigarette smoking all occur on the social gradient. For example, in 2011, 45 percent of adults with a GED, 35 percent of adults who attended between nine and eleven years of school, 24 percent of adults with a high school diploma, 9 percent of adults with an undergraduate college degree, and 5 percent of adults with a postgraduate degree smoked (CDC, 2012c). This disparity in rates of smoking does not necessarily translate into racial disparities. African Americans and Latinos smoke less than their white counterparts, surpassed only by Native Americans (Fagan, Moolchan, Lawrence, Fernander, & Ponder, 2007). However, African American males are diagnosed and die from lung cancer at higher rates than any other racial group (Fagan et al., 2007).

Very similar trends are found in the estimated 80,000 preventable deaths in the United States annually due to alcohol use and abuse, making it the third-most frequent lifestyle-related cause of death. Excessive alcohol use has short-term and long-term impacts on health. In the short term, alcohol abuse is related to unintentional injuries, violence, sexual risk behaviors, miscarriages, and alcohol poisoning (CDC, 2012b). Excessive use over an extend period of time is related to dementia, stoke, hypertension, depression, anxiety, suicide, unemployment, family conflict, cirrhosis of the liver, and gastritis (CDC, 2012b). In the United States alcohol use disorder and dependence fall on the social gradient but alcohol abuse does not (Lee et al., 2010). As with cigarette use, compared to white Americans, Hispanic, African American, and Asian Americans report less alcohol use and heavy episodic (or binge) drinking; only Native Americans surpass the rates for whites (Chartier & Caetano, 2010). However, once alcohol dependency occurs, Hispanics and African Americans have a higher prevalence of recurrent or persistent dependence and mortality (Dawson et al., 2005). Despite the relatively low rates of use, Hispanics and blacks are also at greater risk of developing cirrhosis (Flores et al., 2008); Hispanic men have the highest rate of mortality due to the disease (Yoon & Yi, 2012). Some of these disparities in recurrence and mortality may be due to an unmet need for alcohol abuse treatment among ethnic minorities and lower rates of treatment completion (Bluthenthal, Jacobson, & Robinson, 2007). Studies have shown that when treatment is completed, success rates are the same as whites (Tonigan, 2003). Additionally, American Indian, African American, and Hispanic people reported higher rates of concurrent substance use (alcohol and another drug) compared to whites (Office of Applied Studies, 2008). Despite higher rates of co-occurrence, there has been a dramatic decrease in the use of injection drugs in ethnic minority groups (Substance Abuse and Mental Health Services Administration, Center for Behavioral Health Statistics and Quality, 2011).

Tobacco and alcohol are aggressively marketed in low-income neighborhoods (Koh, Massin-Short, & Elqura, 2009). Alcohol outlets are more densely located in disadvantaged neighborhoods (Romley, Cohen, Ringel, & Sturm, 2007) and their concentration is related to increased rates of alcohol-related violence and morbidity, including intimate-partner violence, violent assaults, sexually transmitted infections, and liver problems (Gruenewald, Freisthler, Remer, LaSala, & Treno, 2006; McKinney, Caetano, Harris, & Ebama, 2009). The CDC has taken a comprehensive social determinants approach to smoking, which includes media, policies, and price increases; this approach has had an impact on some populations. However, people on the lower socioeconomic rungs of society continue to smoke at rates well above the norm (CDC, 2014). Although historically rates of lung cancer did not follow a social gradient, in recent years a gradient has emerged (Adler & Stewart, 2010).

Social Networks and Support

Social networks shape health outcomes by influencing health behaviors (positive or negative); providing social support, including emotional and instrumental support, social engagement, and attachment; and providing access to material resources (Berkman & Glass, 2000). Social support has the potential to interrupt the relationship between poverty and stress and to help prevent negative health outcomes (Link & Phelan, 1995). There is substantial evidence that social support decreases blood pressure and hypertension and increases self-rated health (Strogatz et al., 1997; Uchino, 2006; Uchino, Cacioppo, & Kiecolt-Glaser, 1996; Zunzunegui, Alvarado, Del Ser, & Otero, 2003). Social support has been shown to decrease stress in a variety of settings. Among African Americans, religious involvement has been shown to mitigate the effects of discrimination (Ellison, Musick, & Henderson, 2008). Social support in work settings is linked with health and may buffer against the negative effects of physical and mental stressors (Kuper, Singh-Manoux, Siegrist, & Marmot, 2002). Social support also buffers the effect of neighborhood disadvantage on distress (Rios, Aiken, & Zautra, 2012). For elderly people living in the high-poverty neighborhood of Little Havana, a primarily Cuban community in Miami, having a front porch increased feelings of social support and buffered against stress (Brown et al., 2009).

However, individuals living below the poverty line report smaller social networks, less social support, and less integration (Gecková, Van Dijk, Stewart, Groothoff, & Post, 2003; House & Williams, 2000). For example, social support has been found to prevent stress for individuals living in high-income neighborhoods, but not those living in low-income neighborhoods (Elliott, 2000). Similarly, informal ties are more beneficial in high-income white neighborhoods where they are coupled with more-formal institutions, but negatively affect well-being in disadvantaged neighborhoods (Caughy, O'Campo, & Muntaner, 2003; Latkin & Curry, 2003; Wen, Cagney, & Christakis, 2005). Individual social integration predicted higher hypertension for individuals with less than a high school diploma, but began to have a protective effect for high school graduates (Gorman & Sivaganesan, 2007). Wilkinson (2006) provided a possible explanation for these dynamics through the historical influence of social inequality on social cohesion. Historically, when the gap in income inequality was narrower, there was more social cohesion and a sense of solidarity in society; as income inequality grew, so did social mistrust and conflict and consequently poorer health. The idea that social support and social cohesion positively impact health is known, but what is not known is if those factors can potentially inhibit the impact of SES on negative health outcomes.

CULTURAL DETERMINANTS OF HEALTH

As our understanding of the social determinants of health, well-being, and health disparities has advanced, evidence is accumulating that the determinants of health-related resources such as money, knowledge, power, prestige, social connections, physical environment, and social policies (Koh & Nowinski, 2010; Koh et al., 2010; Link & Phelan, 1995) are also shaped by cultural processes (Phelan, Link, Diez-Roux, Kawachi, & Levin, 2004). The cultural mechanisms that are associated with social determinants expand our understanding of ethnic minorities' health vulnerabilities and manifestations of risk and resilience behaviors, and help to identify effective prevention and treatment approaches that would curtail the negative effects of minority status on health while strengthening protective elements of cultural backgrounds. Approaching health disparities as being directly or indirectly influenced by cultural processes is a holistic approach to understanding social determinants of health. Culture is a multidimensional and multilevel system that extends beyond beliefs and values to include biopsychosocial and ecological systems (Kagawa-Singer, Dadia, Yu, & Surbone, 2010). Culture encompasses the social, historical, political, and geographical lived experience of people, allowing them to create meaning, share experiences, and construct behaviors (Kagawa-Singer et al., 2010). Yet, little attention in the health disparities research has been given to culture as a contextual factor in health disparities (Adler, Boyce, Chesney, Cohen, & Folkman, 1994). Fluid, dynamic, and enveloping, culture is active long before a person gets sick or needs care.

Culture influences the pathways leading to illness and thereby patterns the need for and entry into health care where disparities emerge. Cultural norms, for instance, dictate which health and risk behaviors are acceptable, and these behaviors have consequences for health and the emergence of health disparities (Cockerham, 2000). Culture also influences how people cope with everyday problems and adverse events, and how families are structured to support their members (DHHS, 2001). Cultural processes, such as immigration, acculturation, maintenance of cultural heritage, and development of ethnic and gender identity, all relate to people's integration into society, their sense of self and belonging, and their access to and utilization of various resources, including health care and social services. For example, an immigrant's limited English proficiency or inability to understand mainstream American forms of interaction may cause stress, and this stress may translate into negative health outcomes through various pathways. At the same time, the ability to speak one's native language can promote feelings of connectedness and facilitate social integration with one's cultural group, both serving as a source of strength and resilience in times of stress. They may also facilitate ties to coethnic sources of social and material support, leading to positive health outcomes. Viewed in this light, culture is more than a collection of beliefs and values; it is also a responsive and adaptive system that serves a function (Kagawa-Singer et al., 2010). Knowledge of the function of culture as well as cultural processes influencing health and health disparities is vital for designing and implementing prevention and treatment interventions at the population level and eliminating health disparities (Dreher & MacNaughton, 2002).

Cultural processes can directly influence health in a number of ways. Cultural norms for Mexican immigrants, for example, may permit or tolerate heavy episodic alcohol consumption by males but not females, thus resulting in different levels of risk by gender (Caetano & Medina-Mora, 1988; Kulis, Marsiglia, & Hurdle, 2003; Loury & Kulbok, 2007). Culture influences how people experience and cope with everyday problems and adverse events (DHHS, 2001) and how families are structured to support their members. Stress resulting from the ethnic minority experience and the acculturation process can produce ill effects and disease (Clark, Anderson, Clark, & Williams, 1999), but an individual's social support system, which is closely related to culture or protective cultural processes, can buffer the effects of stress.

Culture also influences how families interact and deal with health disparities. For example, different types of family interactions predicted schizophrenia relapse in Mexican American and white families: in Mexican American families whose interactions featured distance or lack of warmth, but in white families whose interactions featured criticism (Lopez et al., 1998). Latino cultural norms, such as closely interdependent intergenerational families, religious values, strong commitment to family, and respect for adults, all serve to protect poor adolescents from teen parenthood (Denner, Kirby, Coyle, & Brindis, 2001).

The process of acculturation—adaptation to another culture—and its outcomes are associated with health. As acculturation progresses, the risk of greater substance use generally grows (Marsiglia, Kulis, Wagstaff, Elek, & Dran, 2005; Marsiglia & Waller, 2002). Greater acculturation has been associated with lower HIV risk due to greater condom use, but also to higher HIV risk due to earlier and more frequent sexual activity (Marsiglia & Navarro, 1999). Very rapid acculturation processes have been associated with poorer mental health and greater substance use among youths and young adults (Castro, 2005).

Like acculturation, the cultural process of developing a strong ethnic identity as a member of an ethnic minority group is dynamic and associated with health. People who identify strongly with their cultural group, for example, have been found to report less substance abuse (Marsiglia, Kulis, Hecht, & Sills, 2004). Cultural orientation and traditionalism are key variables to consider in prevention for Native Americans (Kulis, Napoli, & Marsiglia, 2002; Stiffman et al., 2006). Research with Native Americans youths suggests that those in more traditional families have later ages of sexual initiation and higher rates of condom use (Mitchell, Kaufman, & the Pathways of Choice and Healthy Ways Project Team, 2002). Yet the effects of strong ethnic identity are not always protective (Marsiglia, Kulis, & Hecht, 2001): the effect of strong ethnic identity on mental health, for example, may vary by acculturation level, and in some cases may have a negative effect (Gamst et al., 2002).

Closely intertwined with acculturation and ethnic identity are associated stressors experienced by ethnic minority groups: acculturation stress, family acculturation gaps, and ethnic discrimination. These experiences of cultural dislocation and conflict can create stressors for Latino and Asian immigrants and their children that lead to deleterious health outcomes (Ayers et al., 2013; Kulis, Marsiglia, & Nieri, 2009; Kulis, Marsiglia, Yabiku, & Kopak, 2010). Ethnic discrimination affects mental health, self-esteem, and ethnic identity (Ayón, Marsiglia, & Parsai, 2010; Umaña-Taylor & Guimond, 2010; Umaña-Taylor & Updegraff, 2007). Parent-adolescent acculturation gaps may lead to externalizing and internalizing problem behaviors (Delgado, Updegraff, Roosa, & Umaña-Taylor, 2011; Marsiglia, Kulis, Fitzharris, & Becerra, 2010).

PRACTICE AND POLICY IMPLICATIONS

The evidence of social determinants of health that result in unequal outcomes in mortality and morbidity along a social gradient has implications for social work practice and significant policy implications. The social gradient itself is not fixed and can be changed by political, social, and economic shifts that make gaps in inequality more narrow (Marmot & Bell, 2009). In the United States the social gradient for life expectancy for both men and women has become steeper since 1980, reflecting the growing inequality in society as a whole (Woolf, Johnson, Fryer, Rust, & Satcher, 2004). It is easy to quickly assess the social gradient in health outcomes as a function of access to quality health care, but health care accounts for only 10 percent of the variation in health statuses (McGinnis, Williams-Russo, & Knickman, 2002). Although access to quality health care is certainly essential to addressing health inequality, addressing social determinants of health that disproportionately affect individuals at the lower end of the socio-economic spectrum may be essential to achieving health equality.

Social workers are ideally positioned to follow the recommendations that health disparities be addressed through a multilevel approach focusing on individual behaviors as well as on social conditions (Koh et al., 2010). This multilevel approach links the health of individuals and the health of the community (Koh, Nowinski, & Piotrowski, 2011). Thus, focusing only on single risk factors and proximal causes of disease will fail to explain and address the underlying causes of poor health outcomes. If health disparities are to be eliminated, interventions seeking to change individual risk factors need to integrate social determinants as fundamental causes of health and well-being (Koh et al., 2010; Link & Phelan, 1995). Interventions that effectively account for underlying causes of disease that affect multiple health outcomes, rather than single diseases, will have wider-reaching effects. Interventions should not incorporate only social determinants, poor health behaviors, and health outcomes to reduce health disparities effectively (Ansari, Carson, Ackland, Vaughan, & Serraglio, 2003), but should also account for the intersection of social statuses, geography, risk factors, and diseases that create and maintain health disparities (Koh et al., 2010). Interventions that account for these intersections and incorporate multiple levels of influence will be the ideal strategies for reducing and eliminating health disparities in socially vulnerable groups, such as racial/ethnic minorities (Koh et al., 2010). In turn, framing health disparities in this way will lead to interventions that empower ethnic minority communities because the multiple levels of their world are being integrated and incorporated to produce change (Koh et al., 2010).

Social determinants of health are complex and interconnected. Individuals are affected by stress in their job and in their neighborhood, and as a result of social exclusion. Children who are born into poverty and as a result have a lack of access to nutritious food, quality education, and early childhood medical care are more likely to remain poor and experience negative health outcomes in adult-hood. The experiences of stress in childhood may make a person more sensitive to stressful experiences in adulthood. The complexity and interconnectedness of social determinants of health and their impact on health behaviors makes them more difficult to address (Braveman et al., 2011). Despite the complexity, as we discover more about what is driving health inequalities, examples of how social workers can partner with community to address social determinants of health proliferate. Here are a few.

In an effort to addresses conditions in the home that may determine a child's educational trajectory even before he or she enters school, a program called Baby

College was developed as part of the cradle-to-college wrap-around services provided by the Harlem Children Zone. In Baby College, parents with infants attend classes on topics ranging from brain development and the importance of reading to a child, to immunizations. Baby College's goal is to give children in the Harlem neighborhood a fair start on the pathway to college, knowing that by addressing early childhood education they are addressing educational attainment and a variety of health outcomes.

A residential neighborhood outside the port city of Oakland, California, used science to advocate for a healthier living environment. East Oakland was the main route for diesel trucks carrying goods out of the port, which subjected the neighborhood residents to excessive toxic exhaust and noise. The neighborhood was also experiencing childhood hospitalization for asthma twice as high as the entire county. To address this health inequality, the neighborhood partnered with a local university to develop a device so that residents could collect air quality samples. The result of the test showed that the neighborhood had extremely high levels of a particulate matter. These data were used to advocate that the truck route be diverted out of the neighborhood (Communities for a Better Environment, 2010).

In his neighborhood in South Central Los Angeles, Ron Finley decided to address the lack of access to healthy food by starting an organization; LA Green Grounds converts vacant lots and city spaces into gardens full of fresh fruits and vegetables. Engaging the community in gardening projects not only increased their access to healthy foods in a food desert, but also educated participants about nutrition and risk factors for diabetes.

By definition, health inequities are an injustice. Social workers have a critical role to play in reducing health inequity in both micro and macro social work practice. To reduce health disparities, social workers may need to shift their thinking when approaching community-wide health issues (such as from treatment to prevention) and from immediate health behaviors (such as substance abuse and exercise), to more distal factors (such as access to healthy foods, employment, and chronic stressors) (Braveman et al., 2011). Social workers in direct practice frequently work with clients to increase coping mechanisms to decrease stress. Working to minimize the impact of stress on individuals is crucial to reducing health inequality, but social workers may also want to address the underlying sources of stress and reduce the number and severity of stressors that clients need to cope with on a daily basis. Addressing stressors at the source, and early in life, may take a more macro or upstream approach. By working to create less-stressful work, school, and institutional environments, and by providing safety-net services that reduce financial stress, social workers are addressing health inequality.

The Commission on Social Determinants of Health (2008) recommends three action steps:

1. Improve the living conditions in which people are born, grow, work, live, and age.

2. Improve the inequitable distribution of resources and power, which is the structural driver of daily living conditions.
3. Expand the knowledge base by measuring the problem and evaluating the impact of action.

Social workers can address these action steps by working with individual clients in direct practice to identify aspects of their social environment that may be compromising their health. Social workers can help clients recognize, draw from, and build up protective factors in health such as social support. They can partner with communities to identify neighborhood conditions that may be undermining health and work to actively address them by challenging policymakers to consider the impact of legislation on social determinants of health.

7

Social Work Perspectives: Social Context, Consciousness, and Resiliency

THIS CHAPTER PROVIDES AN OVERVIEW OF CONTEMPORARY SOCIAL WORK theories and perspectives that are based on or have been derived from the more established theories reviewed in previous chapters. These are applied theories and are commonly used to guide social work practice, research, and policy development. In their role as practitioner-researchers, social workers draw from and contribute to theory development. Through cultural grounding, they can work to operationalize notions of cultural strengths and resiliencies based on the knowledge acquired from practice within different cultural communities. Social work theory describes in applied terms how resiliency can be expressed and how change can be produced in different communities and in different social environments. The culturally grounded perspective is presented at the end of the chapter as a synthesis of many theories that help workers understand the cultural assets of clients and their role in transformation and change.

The perspectives discussed in this chapter help practitioners capitalize on the resiliency of their clients, as well as on the assets of different oppressed communities, and help them counterbalance the so-called medical or deficiency model that is a common approach in many fields of practice. Social work and its allied fields function within environments and institutions that identify presenting problems as symptoms and interventions as treatment, often without much regard for clients' assets or strengths. This deficiency approach tends to follow the following steps:

1. Intervene when there is a problem (illness).
2. Diagnose the problem (assessment).
3. Prescribe medication to alleviate the symptoms (intervention).

The approach focuses on what is not working and runs the risk of pathologizing individuals, families, groups, and communities because they are different from the providers. These differences often lead to misunderstandings and unnecessary labeling, which can result in social services, policy, and research that perpetuate and contribute to oppression. A deficiency approach is oppressive because it inevitably exaggerates the client's shortcomings and overlooks assets. For example, phrases like "culture of poverty" and "at-risk youths" set the stage for a deficiency approach to practice with members of communities labeled in such a manner.

Practitioners can fall into the trap of assessing what the client lacks instead of trying to understand who the client is and what she or he has to offer in overcoming the presenting problem, and identifying the underlying social causes of that problem. There is also a risk of assuming that statistical descriptions of elevated risks for a social or cultural group apply equally to all its members. For example, health disparities among different groups are statistically well documented, but little is known about the members of disadvantaged communities who live healthy and productive lives against all odds. Different theoretical perspectives have—with different levels of success—been developed and tested through empirical research in an attempt to provide a more balanced approach to social work practice. The perspectives presented here were selected based on their relevance for social work practice with different cultural communities that have faced or continue to face oppression.

STRENGTHS OR RESILIENCY PERSPECTIVE

The strengths perspective, also known as the resiliency perspective, focuses on understanding the personal and social processes that help individuals maintain a positive level of functioning (i.e., productive and healthy lives) despite the environmental challenges they face. The strengths perspective is based on the belief that human beings have the inherent capacity to grow and change, even under adverse conditions.

Resiliency is the ability to cope with and bounce back from challenging and difficult experiences. For example, resilient young people can be described as having strong relationships—with their friends, family, school personnel, and classmates; and within their community. Saewyc, Wang, Chittenden, and Murphy (2006) have identified a number of protective factors that are present in the families, schools, and communities of successful youths. When at least some of these protective factors are present, children develop resiliency—that is, the ability to cope with adversity. There are at least four common attributes of resilient children: they possess social competence, problem-solving skills, autonomy, and a sense of purpose and future (Benard, 2002). The strengths or resiliency perspective proposes that these are some of the attributes that are present to some degree in most people of all ages. Whether they are strong enough to help an individual cope with adversity, however, depends on the presence of protective factors during the individual's childhood. From a culturally grounded perspective, there is a concern about how to identify and define protective factors, as they may be expressed in various ways by people of different cultures.

Like individuals, families can be resilient in the way they cope with stress and respond to challenging situations (Patterson, 2002). The family resiliency perspective emphasizes family strengths and resources rather than family deficits and pathology, with particular attention to positive mental health and good functioning. The family resiliency literature provides a useful collective approach to understanding resiliency and introduces a level of complexity to understanding the source of resiliency. Culture plays an important role in family resiliency. In some cultures family resiliency can be interpreted as the sum of the individual family members' resiliency, while in other cultures family resiliency may be seen as independent from the resiliency of its individual members. In work with cultures that are more collectivistic, family resiliency needs to be considered an important resource, in addition to individual resiliency.

Some of the criticism of resiliency theory focuses on its lack of an empirical basis. However, important culturally specific resiliency research has been conducted with children and families. For example, a longitudinal study (over a forty-year period) was conducted with seven hundred Hawaiian residents born under adverse circumstances such as chronic poverty (Werner, 2005). The sample was composed of children whose parents and grandparents had immigrated to Hawaii from Asia or Europe. Approximately two-thirds of the sample had one or more various diagnosable conditions during childhood, while one-third had none. By the time the study participants reached their mid-thirties, almost all (including many who had experienced problems) had become positively motivated and were productive and well-adjusted adults. A distinguishing factor shared by the individuals who showed resiliency was a close long-term childhood relationship with a caring, responsible parent or other adult. Only about thirty of the original group of seven hundred individuals did not bounce back from the adverse circumstances in which they grew up. Interestingly, the researchers found that socioeconomic and ethnic background did not have explanatory power for the experiences of the non-resilient study participants.

Other resiliency-focused studies have used data from the National Education Longitudinal Study to examine family influences on children's achievement, paying special attention to ethnic variables. For example, immigrant families generally have lower SES, which places them at risk for lower educational attainment. However, immigrant students from Mexico have one strong advantage: their parents expect that they will graduate from college, which is a strong predictor of better academic outcomes (Bohon, Johnson, & Gorman, 2006; Glick & White, 2004). Proficiency in both Spanish and English is also related to social and emotional well-being, leading some to label bilingual youths "translation artists," again highlighting a strength that might contribute to academic resilience (Collins, Toppelberg, Suárez-Orozco, O'Connor, & Nieto-Castañon, 2011; Portes & Rivas, 2011).

In a study with Latino youths in an urban school, the principal difference between socially and academically resilient and nonresilient students was that the resilient youths had more confidence in their cognitive abilities (Gordon, 1996). Students excelled academically because they believed that they could understand the material and information presented in class and that they could do well on homework and tests. Where did these perceptions come from? How were those positive messages conveyed to the children, and by whom? Research in the fields of child and human development, schools, and communities reveals that successful development in any human system relates directly to the quality of relationships in the system and opportunities for participation in those relationships (Sameroff, 2010). Three key characteristics support productive development: (1) caring relationships, (2) communication of high expectations, and (3) positive beliefs and opportunities for participation. The most important of these protective factors is a caring relationship with someone, regardless of whether that person is a parent, teacher, or community mentor (Werner, 2005).

In sum, the literature on resiliency identifies five key protective factors of families, schools, and communities: (1) supportive relationships, particularly encouragement from school personnel and other adults; (2) individual characteristics such as self-esteem, motivation, and accepting responsibility; (3) family cohesion factors such as parental support/concern and school involvement; (4) community cohesion factors, such as the availability of community youth programs (e.g., sports, clubs); and (5) school support for prosocial activities and academic success (Feinberg, Rindenour, & Greenberg, 2007) and prosocial skills training. Social work plays a key role in strengthening or restoring the social contexts and the social processes identified in this research.

Table 7.1 provides a summary of selected protective factors identified by the resiliency literature on children. If a child does not have positive relationships within her or his immediate or extended family, social workers can help connect the child and the family with resources that can provide those relationships; such relationships might be found through organized religion, Boys and Girls Clubs, or a community center, for example. Although there is agreement about these factors, some concerns remain regarding their cross-cultural generalizability and how they are measured or assessed (Torres Stone & Meyler, 2007). A white middle-class American expression of parental care may be very different from a Tongan expression of parental care. The main role of the social worker is to identify—in partnership with the clients—the existing strengths and resources and to apply them from a culturally relevant perspective to achieve their goals in interpersonal interaction as well as in the larger community (Saleebey, 2002).

In the strengths-based approach, social workers support the client's engagement in behaviors that respect the needs of other community members and that promote personal gratification and a sense of accomplishment (Kisthardt, 2002). Clients transform themselves by getting in touch with their own natural resources

Table 7.1   Psychosocial Protective Factors for Children

Characteristics of the child	Family characteristics	Social support from outside the family
Is positive, has easy temperament	Child lives at home with parents.	The child has an adult mentor outside the immediate family.
Shows autonomy and independence as a toddler	There is a secure mother-infant attachment.	The family caretaker has help.
Has high hopes and expectations for the future	Child has warm relationship with a parent.	The child has support from friends.
Has internal locus of control as a teenager	Parents practice consistent discipline.	The child receives support from a mentor at school.
Is interpersonally engaging, likable	Child perceives that parents care.	The family receives support from a religious congregation.
Has a sense of humor	There are established routines in the home.	The family receives support from the workplace.

that equip them with the power and tools to become effective agents of change. They use their strengths to advocate for social systems that facilitate empowerment and healthy development. The strengths perspective follows the philosophies of contact theory, cosmopolitanism, and pluralism because it proposes that a caring community is one that affirms diversity through egalitarian relationships that give each person (or group) an opportunity to be who she or he (or it) is and contribute her or his (its) share toward change and social advancement.

Although the bulk of research on resiliency has focused on individual response to adversity and crises, the concept can also be applied to larger social systems like families and communities, as well as to the broader social context of human behavior and development. The ecosystemic resiliency perspective suggests that protective influences (e.g., personal attributes, family strengths, culture, social policies promoting education) can be introduced into an individual's life through any relationship in any part of the ecosystem and that this positive change can have reverberating positive effects throughout the individual's ecosystem that enhance the possibility of desirable outcomes (Schwartz, Pantin, Coatsworth, & Szapocznik, 2007).

The resiliency perspective recognizes that all cultural groups have unique strengths that can be used to empower their members. When applying the strengths perspective and empowerment models, practitioners build an awareness of their own culture, are open to cultures different from their own, and become committed to a client-oriented and horizontal way of relating that suggests constant learning.

The strengths perspective recognizes culture as a source of resiliency; it approaches culture as a potential protective factor against adversity. For example, the ecological risk and resiliency approach proposes to understand and integrate the cultural and contextual processes that make interventions effective, and to understand and integrate the cultural circumstances under which these interventions fail to work (Bogenschneider, 1996). This perspective assumes that effective interventions are those that focus on learning or relearning (through enculturation) the attitudes, behaviors, and strategies that foster strengths rather than those that undermine social competencies. Culture of origin plays a key role in this process, as it often provides a connection to the collective strengths and traditional helping and support systems that are rooted in and nurtured by culture. The strengths perspective occupies a central place in the culturally grounded approach: it informs the client-worker relationship and capitalizes on the client's culture as a source of strength to be tapped.

Resiliency theory can guide practitioners as they work with families from different cultures. The following guidelines for practice are resiliency based and illustrate the connection between resiliency theory and social work practice:

- Listen to the story.
- Acknowledge the pain.
- Look for strengths.
- Ask questions about survival, support, positive times, interests, dreams, goals, and sources of pride.
- Point out strengths.
- Link strengths to the client's goals and dreams.
- Link the client to resources to achieve goals and dreams.
- Find opportunities for the client to be a teacher (Benard, 2002).

Some of these guidelines are particularly relevant in work with cultural minority clients. For example, cultural pride can be a very useful counterbalance to the acculturation stress that clients may be experiencing.

PERSON-IN-ENVIRONMENT PERSPECTIVE

The person-in-environment (PIE) perspective is a social work adaptation of an ecological approach to integrating individuals, families, and communities within their unique social contexts. The influences from the different ecosystemic levels can be strengths or sometimes barriers to change and self-realization. Additionally, an imbalance between needs and resources in the ecosystem can cause stress or distress. Following a PIE perspective, social work practice aims at enhancing the psychosocial functioning of individuals and supporting them in their efforts to obtain needed resources or change the oppressive social conditions that have a negative effect on the interactions between individuals and their environments (Longres, 2000). The social worker views clients as possessing untapped reserves of mental, physical, and emotional resources that the clients can draw from to help them develop, grow, and overcome the different challenges they face as they interact in different social environments. The PIE perspective provides a broad ecological perspective that guides social workers in identifying naturally occurring support systems and resources at the disposal of the client, as well as aspects of the environment that can be changed to better meet the client's needs.

The PIE perspective also provides social workers with a common classification system for communicating about challenges their clients face. It offers four dimensions for describing, classifying, and approaching possible client stressors: (1) social-role stressors, (2) environmental stressors, (3) disturbing psychological processes, and (4) physical disorders (Ashford, LeCroy, & Lortie, 2006). Each of these dimensions can appear in different communities, social environments, and contexts, which in turn provide resources that can be used to overcome or cope with the identified stressors. Culture is a key component of the environment or social context. Key concepts related to a culturally grounded approach are found in the cultural context of the client.

For example, organized religion plays a very important role as a source of cultural identity in many African American communities. The Taylors, an African American family, reside in a suburban neighborhood and face the decision of whether to attend services at a historical African American church an hour from their home where the children's grandparents worship, or to attend a predominantly white church of the same denomination located only two blocks away from their home. What are the pros and cons of each decision? What are the advantages or disadvantages for the parents and children? The PIE perspective provides a much-needed emphasis on the environment or social context. Attending the grandparents' church offers the family an opportunity to strengthen their bond with family, community, and culture. On the other hand, because the Taylors' children attend school and live in a white neighborhood that is not near that church, they may be seen as outsiders and may not be readily accepted by other African American children living in the neighborhood surrounding the grandparents' church. Social workers applying a PIE perspective can help families and individual clients manage the tension that can emerge between cultural maintenance and ethnic identity as they navigate other environments.

FEMINIST THEORY

Social work has been at the vanguard in the development of feminist theories and its application to professional practice. Contemporary social work methods are firmly grounded in feminist and postfeminist theory. It can be argued that feminism has existed for a long time: women have struggled for centuries for their rights. Since the late nineteenth century, a defined set of principles has emerged and evolved into a relatively unified theoretical body of work examining the subordinate position of women and their struggles to overcome their oppression. Feminist theorists like Dorothy Smith have explored the everyday lives of women and their subordinate positions. Smith (1988), a sociologist, has attempted to interpret the structures of male domination experienced by women and to identify how women think and feel about these experiences. The study of the gendered nature of all relationships is generally at the center of most feminist theory, which aims at understanding how gender is related to social inequalities and oppression. Thus, these gendered relationships are interpreted as social creations that can and should be changed.

Some branches of feminism incorporate elements of micro-social theories related to constructivism and postmodernism, but that also look at the macro-social variables affecting the lives of women. For example, neo-Marxist feminism views hierarchical social class relations as the source of coercive power and oppression, and gender oppression as a dimension of class power. According to this perspective, gender inequality emerges from the unequal economic base of society, one that first created private wealth in a class system while treating women as a form of property. The economically based devaluation of women in contemporary society can be seen in what has been called the feminization of poverty, the sharply higher risk of living in poverty that women, especially minority women, and their children face compared to men. The division of labor between the sexes also contributes to women's unequal status. Traditionally, women have carried out a variety of domestic duties that are unpaid, and they continue today to shoulder most of those tasks. In the workplace they are still hired disproportionately to occupy administrative positions (i.e., secretary, receptionist) while men retain a disproportionate share of the management ranks. By hindering women's access to institutional power, this system perpetuates gender inequality and oppression.

One theme of feminist theory that is often adopted by social work is feminism's celebration of differences. In addition, feminism is congruent with the PIE perspective, as it emphasizes social context. Feminist social work is influenced by the relational model of women's development, which emphasizes connection and mutual empathy in the development of a woman's sense of self. In this model, the client-worker relationship is egalitarian and characterized by reciprocity as an alternative to patriarchal models.

Social work as a profession is overwhelmingly female, and the majority of the people it serves are women (Stewart, 2005). It is only natural that the profession has engaged in an effort to integrate feminist thought into social work practice and research. Furthermore, a feminist perspective occupies a central place in the development of a culturally grounded approach. This perspective can be useful in assessing specific client needs. In a study of homeless women receiving treatment in a hospital, researchers found that feminist frameworks allowed social workers to approach women's needs on a personal level and within their social and political context (Boes & Van Wormer, 1997). Feminist theory places great importance on the helping relationship, in which the capacity to produce change (power) is understood to take different forms and have different implications (Hill & Ballou, 2013). Within a relational model of women's development drawn from feminist theory, change is used in social work practice to empower people and promote the client's goals. Feminism calls on social workers to identify, acknowledge, and struggle against the macrolevel forces that oppress women, including inadequate funding sources, accrediting bodies, and agency bureaucracies.

INTERSECTIONALITY THEORY

The intersectionality of gender, ethnicity, social class, and sexual orientation has become an important area of research and concern among feminists. An evolving body of theory on the intersection of race/ethnicity and gender addresses concerns that early feminist theory represented the experience and cosmology of white middle-class women. Within that framework, women's experience was made synonymous with what it was like to be a white woman. In exploring the structures of domination, women from ethnic minority groups may see their own experiences and opportunities as being very different from those of their white middle-class sisters. bell hooks (1981), among others, questioned the analysis of the oppression of women and blacks as separate and discrete phenomena. Such practice, she explains, undermines the experiences of black women because it implies that all women are white and all African Americans are male. The intersectionality perspective addresses this problem by following the premise that race is "gendered" and gender is "raced," and by considering the simultaneous and interacting effects of categories of difference such as race and gender (Hancock, 2007b). These explorations have led to calls for intersectionality and a form of multiracial feminism that recognizes that because of their racial and ethnic backgrounds, there are important differences in the types and levels of inequality experienced by women of color.

Contemporary Chicana and African American feminists, among others, are addressing these intersectionalities and shining some light on how women of different ethnic backgrounds experience social class, and their potentially divided loyalties. Women are often put in the unfortunate position of having to favor one identity over another: Am I a woman who happens to be African American or am I an African American who happens to be a woman? White privilege may lead feminists to overemphasize gender oppression by treating it as a discrete phenomenon separate from racial and ethnic oppression. Many feminists and other commentators have come to realize that the advances many white women have made in their professional careers were possible only because of the low-wage positions minority women assumed as their families' housekeepers, nannies, and day-care providers (Baker, 2005).

Important theoretical developments have been made in understanding and addressing the unique experiences of lesbians, who may experience double (as women and lesbians) or triple jeopardy (as women, lesbians, and people of color). African American lesbians are a group that has faced a triple dosage of silence and marginality because of homophobia within some African American communities and churches, the relative invisibility of lesbians in black feminist thought, and the fact that less attention is paid to lesbians than to gay men in studies of sexuality (James, 2001; Purdie-Vaughns & Eibach, 2008).

Intersectionality theory is an alternative to approaches that are solely gender based or race based. It recognizes the unique experiences that result from the intersection (i.e., meeting point) of gender, race, and other categories, and how the coexistence of multiple oppressions affects the individual. Although the term "intersectionality" and its related contemporary body of literature has become better known since the 1980s, intersectionality theory has deeper roots. W. E. B. Du Bois, for example, has been identified as one of the forefathers of intersectionality due to his pioneering recognition of the roles of race conjoined with class, and race conjoined with gender (Hancock, 2005).

Intersectionality provides a compass for gaining a better understanding and promoting recognition of the unique experiences that emerge from the possession of multiple subordinate statuses as opposed to a dominant or master narrative (McCall, 2005). The concept of intersectionality provides a culturally grounded lens through which to look at the complex identities women and men form through their multiple experiences of race, gender, social class, sexual orientation, national origin, and other categories of difference (Hancock, 2007a). Intersectionality theory offers an alternative perspective to the one-size-fits-all approach to addressing multiple sources of discrimination, and provides a counterpoint to the assumption of sameness or equivalence of social categories connected to inequalities and the mechanisms and processes that create and perpetuate them (Verloo, 2006).

Practitioners, policymakers, and researchers interested in quantifying the oppression of African American women may fall into the trap of combining the results of studies of gender focused on white women with those of studies of race focused on black men. This strategy perpetuates the view of race and gender as separate, parallel phenomena. The intersectionality approach avoids falling into this trap by adding categories and their possible equal explanatory power. It proposes an interactive, mutually constitutive relationship between identity categories in shaping the experience of oppression of women and men and their related behaviors (Hancock, 2005). Intersectionality theory aims at integrating interconnected categories from the start and avoids approaching them as discrete or separate variables. Intersectionality theory approaches phenomena as the merging of conditions—rather than viewing the conditions as separate entities. Such an approach allows for the recognition and the inclusion of intergroup diversity as well as the identification of the implications of intersectionality for policy, practice, and research.

The intersectionality perspective is also useful for examining privilege. Those who enjoy normative or nonmarginalized statuses such as whiteness, masculinity, heterosexuality, and upper-class status do not simply experience the absence of oppression, but also enjoy direct social and material benefits resulting from the intersection of those statuses (Van Herk, Smith, & Andrew, 2011). Because hierarchies of power intersect, it is likely that a person will be simultaneously advantaged by particular identities and disadvantaged by others (Steinbugler, Press, & Johnson Dias, 2006). For example, a gay Asian American man may experience privilege as a result of his gender, but may experience marginalization because of his race and sexual orientation. These hierarchies intersect at all levels of social life, in both social structures and social interactions (Symington, 2004). Individuals differ in terms of which identities they share with others and how their identities are expressed differently across different social contexts. Individuals who possess multiple marginalized identities have experiences that are probably different from the experiences of individuals who have a combination of marginalized and privileged identities (Hancock, 2005). For example, the income gap between lesbian and gay men working couples can be explained in part by the privilege experienced by two male income earners in gay men couples compared with the two female income earners in lesbian couples (Leppel, 2007).

The concept of structural intersectionality is useful for understanding how inequalities and their intersections are directly relevant to the experiences of real people in a given social context (Mason, 2011). Structural intersectionality can explain why a Mexican American woman may not be considered for one job because she is Latina, since the norm employee is an Anglo woman, while also not being considered for other jobs since the jobs available to Mexican Americans are generally given to men. Structural intersectionality highlights the fact that heteronormativity (the traditional gender expectations of men and women in a given society) is also part and parcel of gender inequality, which means that the position of lesbians is very different from the position of heterosexual women. Key questions to ask in analyzing structural intersectionality are, How and when does racism amplify sexism? How and when does class exploitation reinforce homophobia? How and when does homophobia amplify racism?

Researchers have advocated the development of a battery of survey items that measure how race is gendered and how gender is "raced" across a number of gender/racial categories (Steinbugler et al., 2006). They suggest, for example, that researchers consider developing scales on Asian masculinity, white femininity, Chicana femininity, and so forth. Such a project would require resources and effort to construct and refine intersectional stereotype measures, but such investments are necessary if scholars hope to use social surveys to understand the complicated relationship among intersecting prejudices, public policy, and social work practice.

Finally, the intersectionality paradigm can provide clients and practitioners with common ground as well as a realistic view of their social and cultural boundaries. For example, their common ground can be a shared gender identity, and ethnicity can be a border to be crossed and negotiated. On the other hand, the client and the practitioner may share the same ethnic background and gender but come from different social classes or have different sexual orientations. Intersectionality theory provides a useful framework for sorting similarities and differences and discovering the common ground needed to develop a strong therapeutic alliance.

LIBERATION PEDAGOGY

The term "social pedagogy" came into general usage in Germany in the nineteenth century when Friedrich Diesterweg used the term to argue for a social pedagogy, or educational action, to help the disadvantaged, believing that people were capable of respecting others and working for the good of the community. The linking of pedagogy to community and democracy was later adopted by Paulo Freire (1994), whose original interest was primarily in addressing the needs of the illiterate and oppressed unskilled workers of Brazil. Extending the traditional definition of pedagogy, Freire integrated elements of different perspectives such as Marxist and neo-Marxist thought, symbolic interactionism, and other constructivist and postmodern philosophies to develop liberation pedagogy, the comprehensive cultural transformation of the learner. He understood that human relations are influenced by power and wealth and that the oppressed, as a first step toward changing their conditions, need to become conscious of their oppression. For example, the working poor must become aware of the forces that prevent them from accessing the educational system as a means of ensuring the continuous supply of cheap labor before they can attempt to change it. Liberation pedagogy strives to help the oppressed take a step back from their daily existence and see how they are affected by interrelated societal factors, ultimately becoming aware of the barriers they need to overcome to change their lives and the lives of other members of their communities.

This awareness can be achieved only through challenging what Freire (1994) referred to as the "banking approach to teaching" (p. 208), where classrooms are organized like banks. The teacher, who has a monopoly on knowledge, stands in the front of the room, while treating the students like empty vessels. The teacher's role is to deposit knowledge into the empty vessels. The students' positioning facing the teacher, and not facing each other, gives students the implicit message that they have nothing to share with each other and nothing of value to contribute because the teacher possesses all the real knowledge. Such an unequal relationship gives all the power to the teacher and ensures that the students remain disempowered. Freire proposed that students should be allowed to recognize the knowledge and experience that other students bring with them to the classroom. Thus the role of the teacher is to facilitate the dialogue from which critical consciousness will emerge. Critical consciousness is attained through dialogue as part of a collective process that cannot be achieved in isolation. Awareness is possible only through the collective nature of the exchanges, and the sharing of ideas and knowledge that emerges from individual and collective life experiences.

Freire's core concept of critical consciousness has been applied in social work as a means for individuals and communities to identify, examine, and act on the root causes of their oppression (Hegar, 2012). This process involves a gradual and cyclical action-reflection-action chain of behaviors, or praxis. A culturally grounded approach to social work practice incorporates praxis by using the narratives of community members as the means for raising their consciousness and inspiring them to engage in transformative action by using their resources and validating what they already know to be true from their experiences. To them, poverty is not an abstract concept; they know what it is like to be poor and to lack the resources to pay the electric bill.

Although praxis was developed and tested in South America and later in Africa, it has been found to be a useful approach in the United States, Canada, and Mexico in the creation of social structures that are more just and communities that are more caring (Abram, Slosar, & Walls, 2005). Praxis advances the social justice–social diversity mission that is central to the social work profession. Freire's work occupies a central place in the culturally grounded approach: it directly addresses both oppression and action and advances the notions of critical consciousness and empowerment, both of which are critical to culturally grounded social work.

SYNTHESIS: AN ECLECTIC THEORETICAL APPROACH TO CULTURALLY GROUNDED SOCIAL WORK

The theories discussed in this chapter offer a number of valuable concepts for a culturally grounded approach to social work. The key elements of the culturally grounded approach derived from these theories can be conceptualized as three main theoretical components: (1) honoring narratives, (2) integrating those narratives in their appropriate social and political contexts, and (3) developing critical consciousness and liberation. These three components are interrelated and complement each other through a web of theoretical connections and practice applications.

Honoring Narratives

Culturally grounded social work begins with stories based on the client's life, stories that honor both the individual and her or his collective experiences (shared experiences she or he had at the family, group, or community level). Because social workers may be unaware of what it is like to be a member of a particular cultural group, they may start by recognizing their own lack of knowledge and engage in dialogue with the client simply to find out what the client is experiencing and what she or he is doing about it. The way that the client tells her or his story provides important information about how she or he interprets the presenting problem and about the resources within the client's culture that are available to help her or him overcome challenges. Social workers honor the client's expertise, strengths, and abilities to cope with and overcome distress. At the same time, social workers start to identify their professional helping role in partnership with the individual, family, group, or community. In this way, the client's stories become a pivotal starting point, as they provide the social worker with information about the client's culture, which checks the social worker's ethnocentric views and attitudes. Social work aims at helping clients dream of a better future. The stories clients share are based on their interpretation of their daily experiences and pave the way for change. The subjectivity of the social worker is as important as her or his objective knowledge. A thorough understanding of one's background, beliefs, and position in the larger social structure allows social workers to differentiate between their own subjective experience and that of their clients, and brings awareness of how those differences may be affecting their interpretation of the clients' narratives. Strong rapport and an open mind are necessary to prevent unnecessary editing of clients' stories. The social worker avoids making any kind of biased judgment such as, "That's very unusual behavior," as such comments will only deter clients from telling the story as they perceive it. The culturally grounded social worker is more than anything else a good active listener.

Social workers play an important role as partners of cultural minority clients in their efforts to enter mainstream society and to access its benefits. Integration, however, is understood as a process through which the stories of the cultural minority client transform the dominant ideology. These stories are rooted in clients' collective memories, or the way in which the community has interpreted certain events, statuses, and choices. For example, a recent immigrant community approach to housing is to rent residences from landlords from their country of origin that are located close to relatives of friends from home, which limits their choices and can lead to lost employment and educational opportunities. Once the stories and explanations for this choice of housing emerge, the narratives can be used as springboards from which clients engage in praxis (Freire, 1994). The narrative approach creates cognitive, emotional, and behavioral links between cultural minority clients and their efforts at change and advancement (Vygotsky, 1979). The process can be summarized in four questions that can be posed to the client: What is the presenting problem? How do you feel about the situation? What is the underlying cause of the problem? How can you produce change? These questions are connected, and community or culturally based explanations and community experiences help workers understand the behavior. For example, housing discrimination could be the main reason why community members do not live outside their enclaves.

When clients perceive a connection between their cultural norms, values, and experiences and the social work intervention, they are able to make effective links among the different dimensions of their lives. These connections make it easier for them to respond favorably to the intervention and to become engaged in the process. On the other hand, if the intervention feels strange or alien and the cultural link is missing, clients will feel uncomfortable and will probably stop participating fully or even drop out.

Linkages are created in two ways: (1) through the exploration of the network of clients' stories (the client's stories as well as the stories of members of the family and community, the messages of which are repeated over and over and become accepted as truth), and (2) through the inquiry into how the dominant narrative of the majority society affects the client. As clients share their narratives, their network of stories is strengthened, expanded, and enriched. For instance, when Latino clients use words such as *casa*—meaning both house (a place) and home (an emotion)—the practitioner may discover that the word has a different connotation than when non-Latino clients use the word "home." Latinos often feel a devotion and loyalty to *la casa* that is difficult to explain to others. This understanding can be integrated into the assessment and valued as knowledge by the social worker.

The culturally grounded approach maximizes the potential of clients' linguistic and narrative legacies as it supports their cognitive development. Narrative traditions (proverbs; stories, both fiction and nonfiction; songs; biographies) that are familiar to the client act as a cognitive bridge (the cognitive link) for the acquisition of new and unfamiliar knowledge. Through the use of accessible and familiar types of narratives, clients can venture into the unfamiliar and become committed (the emotional link) to their own change process (the behavioral link). Clients' narrative networks are further enriched and validated by the use of short stories, metaphors, and parables common to their communities of origin, stories that often provide insight into the experiences the clients are living out every day.

Narratives related by the client to the practitioner or shared in group sessions can be enriched by the examination of stereotypes about minority communities. For example, while discussing professional choices in a teen support group, Trisha says that she wants to be an electrical engineer. The other group members—male and female—make fun of her and say that her choice is not appropriate for a girl. Trisha does not respond and remains quiet. The group facilitator questions the group and helps them examine their reactions to Trisha's comment. In this process the group worker attempts to honor Trisha's narrative by providing the group with new knowledge and helping the group reexamine her wishes in light of that knowledge. For example, the group worker introduces a statistic on the percent of female electrical engineers in the nation and their ethnic breakdown; this information expands the group's perception of the realm of possibilities open to women. The incident strengthens the group members' analytical abilities. This process starts with the language or terminology used by the clients. The narratives are then enriched by the awareness or consciousness process. Notes from the field 7.1 provides an illustration of how a client's concerns can be reframed in this way. In this example, the dominant narrative of society can be subjected to scrutiny through the facilitation of the social worker. For example, Jane may blame herself for not being awarded a promotion, question her motivation or her

---

NOTES FROM THE FIELD 7.1

What's the Matter with Jane?

Jane is referred to a social worker by her doctor because he suspects she is depressed. As Jane's story unfolds, the social worker notices that Jane is focused on having been denied a promotion at work. Jane knows she was the best-qualified candidate and the only woman ever to have applied for such a high management position in her company. She tells of her middle-class background and of the support she received from her father for her educational achievement and career advancement, as well as the more mixed signals she received from her mother. Jane wonders if she should be so focused on career objectives or if she should perhaps redirect her energy to her parenting responsibilities. The social worker explores her depressive symptoms not in isolation, but in the context of the sexism and discrimination that may exist in her company, and Jane begins to relate what she has seen and heard of the company's unfair treatment of other women. By encouraging Jane to tell her story and by placing it in its proper organizational and societal context, the social worker helps Jane reframe her difficulties and to see them as much more than a personal failure, an individual inability to cope, or misplaced priorities.

abilities, or react passively to a situation that she feels is beyond her control. The social worker must not act in a condescending or dismissive manner but must lead the conversation toward a discussion of oppression in the workplace.

A culturally grounded approach would validate Jane's experience and perspective while also suggesting alternative ways to reframe her story and understand the institutional reasons why she may have been denied the promotion. Validating the feelings of the client—even if they appear counterproductive—is the first step to developing an effective and honest cross-cultural relationship.

Integrating Narratives in Social and Political Contexts

The culturally grounded approach is not just a celebration of diversity and multiculturalism, but also is a process of action and transformation. An important part of culturally grounded social work practice is its contextual approach, or the assessment of social conditions and their ability to nurture change and quality of life, and the determination of whether they need to be transformed because they deprive individuals and communities of opportunities and limit their quality of life.

The contextual approach in the health-care field, for example, focuses on the fundamental causes of illness as a way of balancing biological and medical conceptions of risk with those from the social and behavioral sciences (Link & Phelan, 2000). In past decades, epidemiological research has focused attention on risk factors like diet, cholesterol level, and exercise as the proximal causes of disease. Researchers have argued that greater attention needs to be paid to basic social, or contextual, conditions. For example, to craft effective interventions that improve the nation's health, individually based risk factors need to be contextualized; this involves asking probing questions about what puts people at risk. Social factors such as SES, access to health information and health care, and social support within family and friendship networks are relevant to disease prevention and treatment because they affect the outcomes of multiple diseases, including diabetes and asthma, as well as drug abuse and HIV/AIDS, and influence whether people have the resources to remain healthy

Many cultural minorities do not have access to culturally competent social services. Although efforts have been made to increase their availability, the political context of the nation limits availability and accessibility, particularly in certain regions. For example, in "English only" states, making language-specific social services available to clients could be more difficult than in other states where workers' need to communicate with clients in a language they comprehend is not questioned (Ortíz Hendricks, 2005).

Ethnicity and culture are important social contexts that influence SES and shape social support. Although membership in a particular ethnic or cultural community is not itself a social risk factor (even though membership in some racial and ethnic groups may be inherent risks for stressors such as discrimination stress), it may influence an individual's access to prevention resources and effective service delivery systems. It is important for practitioners to maintain an ecosystemic perspective that attends not only to the relationship between the individual and the stressor (discrimination), but also to the context in which this relationship takes place. Conversely, culture also produces indigenous resiliencies. Considering the relational and ecosystemic contexts of clients' life stressors enhances practitioners' understanding of why some individuals live healthier lives than others.

Developing Critical Consciousness and Liberation

Culturally grounded interventions promoting social justice start at the cultural awareness level or with conscientization efforts. Conscientization is a process of learning to become aware of social, political, and economic conditions in order to take action against the oppressive elements present in one's social and political context (Freire, 1970). It is from this perspective that a culturally grounded approach to social work emerges as a means to resist oppression and promote social justice through praxis. For example, in notes from the field 7.1, the social worker, in addition to listening and validating Jane's experience, can also empower her to take action to address the sexism in the company. Ethically the social worker is responsible for working with Jane to examine the possible consequences of pursuing change, such as the possibility of losing her job. If Jane would like to work to address the injustice, with full knowledge of possible repercussions, the social worker might suggest that she create a group with the other women in her workplace who have experienced similar treatment. The group could meet to discuss strategies to change the discriminatory practices and atmosphere at the company.

As social workers attempt to decode narratives, stories, and symbols in partnership with their clients, they become aware of the master narrative that frames those stories. That is, the narrative process is embedded in the social, political, and cultural contexts of clients' communities. In the process of understanding these narratives, a liberating cultural transformation emerges and the client is able to question larger narratives and work toward personal affirmation and liberation. Larger narratives, often produced without the input of minority communities, are connected to policies that can either facilitate or block social advancement. When these policies block social advancement, communities' narratives can eventually lead to policy advocacy as a means to create better conditions for all.

Cultural identity and social advancement are woven into one comprehensive approach; this single approach facilitates the cultural grounding of policies and services. If transformative processes focus only on equalizing opportunities but fail to encourage individuals to retain and nurture the aspects of their culture that make their lives worthwhile and give them meaning, cultural deprivation may result. On the other hand, if cultural maintenance is supported to the detriment of social advancement, the result may be oppression. In other words, completely assimilating into mainstream culture and taking advantage of the opportunities it provides may leave members of ethnic minority groups feeling empty inside. However, if they decide to maintain their ethnic identity by not participating at all in society, they risk not being able to access the benefits, resources, and services to which they are entitled as members of society and as taxpayers.

APPLYING A CULTURALLY GROUNDED APPROACH TO SOCIAL WORK PRACTICE

The theoretical synthesis provides guidelines for a culturally grounded approach to social work practice. The starting assumption is that the possession of relevant information about a particular ethnic group or culture alone is not enough for social workers to practice in a culturally responsive manner. The methods a social worker acquires through professional education need to be examined for cultural bias. Those methods may reflect an ethnocentric cosmology and culturally specific understandings of how people seek and give help.

The universal applicability of social work methods has been questioned by empowerment scholars. They note that social work methods are not culturally neutral and that more than surface adaptations are needed to apply them across cultural groups (Lee, 2001). There is growing consensus, however, that social work methods are the product of their social and economic context and as such they cannot be applied in different contexts without in-depth adaptations or fundamental changes (Reamer, 2006). The universality of social work methods versus the need to adapt them to unique environments is an important and complex issue that requires careful examination.

The traditional way to describe classic social work methods is to group them according to the type, or level, of intervention—micro, mezzo, or macro. Most schools of social work embrace a generalist approach, educating social workers to function effectively in different settings by utilizing a variety of interventions. The interventions most commonly used by practicing social workers are micro, or one-on-one, interventions. Yet one-on-one helping may not be the preferred approach or most natural way of helping for members of many cultural groups. On the other hand, individuals belonging to predominantly collectivistic (as opposed to individualistic) communities may welcome the opportunity to meet alone with the social worker without their relatives' presence and scrutiny. Notes from the field 7.2 provides an example of such a situation and shows that applying

---

NOTES FROM THE FIELD 7.2

Individual or Family Sessions?

Cheryl is an African American teenager who feels very close to her extended family and has an active social life. Cheryl requests a private session with the school social worker—without any members of her family present—in order to address concerns about her family relationships. Eventually, the social worker may invite the parents to join in, but initially one-on-one sessions address Cheryl's needs and allow Cheryl and the worker to build rapport. The social worker is aware of the interdependence between Cheryl and her family but involves the parents based on the needs of the client. The family members may not be physically present at the first few sessions, but they are included through stories and narratives because the social worker is aware that they are the client's key social support system, as families are for most school-age children and youths regardless of their ethnicity.

---

a culturally grounded social work generalist approach usually entails a consideration of timing—when to use different methods—more than a decision about which level to use.

SHIFTING FROM A "CULTURALLY NEUTRAL" TO A CULTURALLY GROUNDED PARADIGM

Social work methods cannot be completely culturally neutral because they are the product of certain worldviews and reflect particular social contexts. As a result, they tend to perpetuate specific cultural paradigms and reflect existing power relationships in the larger society. From a culturally grounded approach, social workers are most effective when they are wary of assimilationist tendencies that are embedded in so-called standardized interventions. These are practices that may implicitly encourage clients to let go of their cultural norms and values and adopt the majority culture's norms and values. For example, the insistence of some workers on personal autonomy in family relationships undervalues many minority clients' experiences of interdependence—for example, children living in extended family households well into adulthood, or the very close relationships that often exist between parents and children. Interdependence, which is healthy and provides a means of emotional and financial support for family members, can sometimes be mistaken for codependence. Being interconnected, basing family relationships on interdependence, supporting one's family, and being supported by family are all strengths, not weaknesses.

Imposing external values and using culturally inappropriate approaches to helping may underutilize the wealth of naturally occurring resources within communities that are already effective. Some of these natural ways of helping have been perfected over millennia (Werbner, 2005). However, a social worker who is a cultural parachuter—an individual who drops into the community without any awareness or knowledge of the community—could easily overlook, misunderstand, or underutilize such rich resources. Outsiders often make assumptions based on their previous experiences and are unaware of what the community has long been doing successfully. In contrast, workers grounded in the culture of the community naturally embrace what already works as they contribute their professional expertise and support. Another risk is that communities may lose their own abilities to help themselves and become dependent on professionalized service systems. For example, it has been demonstrated that the enormous growth of the death-and-dying field has weakened traditional ways of assisting the dying in the United States and in China (Pressman & Bonanno, 2007). Heightened cultural awareness and vigilance can help ensure that effective natural or culturally grounded approaches are supported, not just supplanted by the professionalized service delivery system. An informed and well-researched integration of both systems (the traditional and the professional) is the ideal outcome.

Culturally grounded social work avoids simplistic overgeneralizations by validating community-based narratives and integrating community-based practices into the helping process. This approach increases the effectiveness of social work interventions by recognizing existing natural helping and informal social networks as valuable resources to be tapped by professional interventions. Culturally grounded social work is a form of quality control that improves the effectiveness of the services provided to cultural minority clients. It is based on a theoretical framework that advances social justice and as such is guided by the common good. Instead of merely adapting existing models, this approach questions the assumptions behind the models and starts with the client's worldview and strengths.

Culturally grounded interventions integrate community-based perspectives and resources into services that promote equity, access, and effectiveness. Clients who find their culture reflected and recognized in the substance and the format of interventions and services are more likely to participate in and benefit from the experience. Prevention programs for youths—whether targeting substance use, unsafe sex, or suicide—have long recognized that it is important to represent the culture of the targeted youths in the prevention message in authentic ways. Programs and services for particular cultural groups need to incorporate central cultural values, styles of learning, and ways of interacting. It may be important to include examples or representations of the culture in the design of the program or service. For example, the illustrations and pictures on a program's Web page or brochure need to celebrate the heritage and the identity of the targeted youths and their subcultures. A graphic designer needs to think of this form of cultural branding not just as Vietnamese cultural branding, but as Vietnamese American youth cultural branding. This level of specificity gives the target audience a sense of connection with the characters conveying the message. However, a symbolic representation of a culture that goes beyond the culturally appropriate visual images or language may be needed. For example, youths may use certain terms that are not entirely English or Vietnamese but rather a fusion of the two. Key terms that are used in focus groups conducted with youths can add depth and specificity to the message, which can increase its effectiveness. The same can be said about social work interventions in general. Awareness of specific cultural products is essential. In addition, project design teams applying a culturally grounded approach must constantly check themselves for stereotypes that may unintentionally emerge as a result of these efforts.

Culture is best approached as the platform from which social work practice is launched. When treated as an addendum to the services planning and design process, culture becomes an afterthought rather than an integral part of the intervention. The culturally grounded approach honors and integrates culture from the start of the planning process and delivers services through social workers whose practice modalities are grounded in the culture of the clients they serve. As social workers work in partnership with cultural minority communities, they must honor and negotiate cultural and social boundaries. Members of the targeted population can be engaged through focus groups or other methods in the service design process. Such a practice ensures representation and helps the design team check for biases.

As agents of change, social workers must engage in their own transformation by scrutinizing their own narratives and heightening their own consciousness. To facilitate this exploration, social workers can be encouraged to form inquiry teams not only as a professional development and support mechanism, but also as a tool for gaining personal awareness and professional retooling. Inquiry teams can function as sounding boards for workers to examine and challenge each other's knowledge, attitudes, and practices. Members of these teams can discuss their own reality frames, biases, preconceived ideas, and fears about change. In this way, the social worker begins to experience some of the same conflicts with hospitals, social service agencies, schools, and other institutions that some of their clients may experience. As a result, the institutional culture of social service agencies (the guiding values and norms that give the agency its identity) is questioned, and clients and social workers can come together to advocate changes that anchor the agency more firmly in cultural groundedness. These change processes are particularly important in agencies that are not culturally aware and have not incorporated the assets of minority clients or responded to their unique needs in a culturally competent manner.

To uncover individuals' biases and cultural frames, social workers may need to engage in self-examination in isolation, supervision or a group. The following questions may be helpful to start this process:

a. What am I assuming about my client's situation?
b. Where do my assumptions come from?
c. Am I making judgments about my client's actions, attitudes, or beliefs?
d. What norms are these judgments based on?
e. Could these norms be different from the client's cultural perspective?

When implemented in practice, these questions can help guide an honest assessment of how one's own culture is affecting interaction with clients. For example, Shelia utilized these questions when she was working with Marisol, a mother of four who was contemplating having another child. In her intake assessment, Marisol reported that she was overwhelmed by stress and feeling unfulfilled. Based on this report, Sheila suggested alternatives such as pursuing a career outside of the home, and presented this to Marisol as one more choice to consider in their clinical interactions. Afterward, using these questions to examine her own cultural frame, Sheila realized that she assumed that Marisol's children were the source of her stress and that her lack of employment was why she was not feeling fulfilled. Upon further inquiry, she identified that these assumptions were based on the norms and values of her own culture. Once she realized the source of the assumption, she was able to more fully examine the underlying cause of Marisol's feelings. Through discussion she discovered that Marisol's children were a source of joy and that she had no desire to work outside of the home. She also heard that Marisol had not been able to attend church since her recent relocation and was feeling disconnected from her spirituality and her supportive spiritual community. This was an underlying cause that led to a very different social work intervention than would have resulted if Sheila had acted on her assumptions. By examining her own biases, Sheila was able to move past her subjective judgments and hear the clients' perspective, leading to more culturally grounded and effective social work practice.

When the culturally grounded approach is incorporated into social work practice, clients encounter social workers who are engaged in a process of inquiry about themselves and their positions in the social service delivery system. Such inquiry can correct erroneous perceptions that they may have of themselves as gatekeepers guarding resources and services from ethnic minority clients or as agents of the assimilation of ethnic minority clients.

REVISITING PRAXIS

An understanding of social and cultural identities, social representations, and shared power is crucial for constructing a social psychology of participation

(Campbell & Jovchelovitch, 2000). Communities cannot, however, preserve and integrate their unique social identities, worldviews, and natural helping practices if they are not aware of them. As a result of assimilation, younger generations may have lost a connection to their cultural roots. This is why culturally grounded interventions start with cultural awareness, or what Freire called conscientization efforts. Although awareness as a collective phenomenon is the product of a group or community, the social worker plays a key role in facilitating its emergence and channeling its use. Individuals and communities who have been alienated from their culture can be encouraged to identify, examine, and act on the root causes of their oppression. Such critical consciousness involves a gradual and cyclical action-reflection-action chain of group behaviors, also known as praxis (Freire, 1970).

Praxis implies that clients identify issues and look for solutions. The role of the social worker is to help clients become aware of their power to act and to transform their social environment. In becoming a transforming force, clients initially decide on small action steps, then develop plans to implement them. Once the course of action is implemented, they reflect on and evaluate their accomplishments and their plans' shortcomings. In doing so, they link the outcome to the larger social phenomena that concern them and start planning the next action step. This process empowers cultural minority clients to challenge and reject the messages they receive from society that say nothing can be changed. As notes from the field 7.3 illustrates, they relate personal problems to political issues by

---

NOTES FROM THE FIELD 7.3
Don't Rock the Boat!

A neighborhood committee is concerned about the lack of appropriate street lighting on local streets. Individually, the members of the committee have already attempted to deal with city hall, but without success. As a committee, they assess the situation, including the ways in which the city hall representatives perceive them and their neighborhood. They conclude that the fact that many of the families are recent immigrants and not yet eligible to vote in municipal elections has disempowered them, and politicians do not take them seriously. The message they have heard is "Be happy with what you have. Do not rock the boat." As they plan and implement small and larger steps to overcome their oppression, they become more ambitious dreamers and formulate larger goals such as promoting equal treatment; they realize that they are tax-paying residents regardless of their citizenship status. They begin to frame their situation as a social justice issue, not as a favor they are asking of those who are supposed to be serving them.

connecting their personal and group-defined issues to larger societal issues such as racism, xenophobia, sexism, and heterosexism.

Social workers cannot define for the community what social justice is or suggest the right steps to bring it about, but neither is it their role to remain neutral. Freire (1994) stated that "claiming neutrality does not constitute neutrality; quite the contrary, it helps maintain the status quo" (p. 141). Social workers become openly political as clients become political by starting to take a position on human rights and social justice, and weighing conceptual, cultural, and political aspects of their lives and their communities' lives. Social workers can explore social justice issues with community members and look for solutions with them.

In this way, praxis becomes a compass not only for clients, but also for social workers. It helps workers find a balance between the needs of the individual, family, group, or community on one hand, and their worldviews and the profession's code of ethics on the other hand. As notes from the field 7.4 shows, social work methods that are grounded in the client's culture can contribute to the neutralization of the power differential and oppression exercised or perpetuated by the worker. As in Andrea's case, many clients may be experiencing oppressive situations that are part of a larger context. Praxis helps the worker and the client integrate the presenting problem into that larger context and recognize their strengths and resources as tools for achieving lasting change.

Key Concepts

Strengths or resiliency perspective: The belief that human beings have an inherent capacity to grow and change, even under adverse conditions

Praxis: The transformative cyclical process of action, reflection, and action

Person-in-environment (PIE) perspective: A perspective that integrates the individual, family, and community within their unique social contexts

Feminist theories: Cultural and group theories that generally incorporate elements from micro-social theories and macro-social variables affecting the lives of women

Culturally grounded social work: An approach to social work practice, policy, and research that incorporates culturally specific ways of helping and community-based tools promoting social change

NOTES FROM THE FIELD 7.4

Immigrant Labor Rights

One of Francis's clients is Andrea, a mother of three who is pregnant with her fourth child and is very distressed. Her family immigrated to the United States four years earlier, and both she and her husband have been working for minimum wage, which makes it very hard for them to meet the family's needs. When Francis asked Andrea at intake what was troubling her, she first said that she had lost her job but did not elaborate. After Francis offered her a cup of tea, Andrea became more comfortable and began to explain that she had worked for the same company for three years. The company paid her for eight hours of work a day, but her supervisor forced her to work up to ten hours a day, and six to seven days a week. She was told that if she did not do this, they would terminate her. During those three years, she had no vacation days and no sick days, and she worked on every holiday. Some years she was not allowed to go home to her children and husband until midnight on Christmas Eve. When it became obvious that she was pregnant, her supervisor started to harass her and tell crude sexual jokes. She was told that she was lazy and that nobody would hire her because of her limited English proficiency. Her life at work became intolerable, and she often went home crying. Seven months into her pregnancy, exhausted and frustrated, Andrea dared to request a day off. Her boss told her, "Sure, but don't bother to come back because someone else will be doing your job." She was worried about the upcoming birth of her fourth child and the fact that the family did not have enough money to meet their basic needs, so she continued working. At the next payday, however, she was told that she was being laid off, and her paycheck was half what was due her.

As Francis explored the situation with her, Andrea mentioned that other employees suffered similar treatment. They were all immigrants who spoke very little English and did not know what resources were available to them. Francis told her about the options available to her and encouraged her to think of ways she could contribute to making changes so other people would not suffer the same treatment to which she and her coworkers had been subjected. Eventually, Andrea contacted the U.S. Labor Department and asked to speak with a Spanish-speaking employee to make her complaint, and she encouraged a couple of other former employees to do the same. The Labor Department was able to act on the complaints and made the company pay back wages on all overtime to the three former employees. In addition, the Labor Department is now monitoring the company's labor practices closely. Andrea's situation, while still economically challenging, is better. The former coworkers have developed a strong friendship and support system. They take turns babysitting for their children and attend evening ESL classes.

Part III

Cultural Identities

8

The Formation and Legacies of Racial and Ethnic Minorities

THE PREVIOUS CHAPTERS HAVE ARGUED THAT MANY SOCIAL DIFFER-
ences between individuals and groups are socially constructed rather than a
reflection of intrinsic biological differences, and that these constructed ideas
about difference are often used to justify or perpetuate oppression. Ethnic and
racial distinctions, for example, are routinely taken for granted and assumed to
represent fundamental differences between groups of people. Whether true or fic-
titious, these ideas about racial and ethnic differences have been used throughout
history to categorize people. At the same time, identification with ethnic and
racial groups, and the sense of belonging those groups foster, is often a source of
pride, resistance, and resiliency. Ethnic and racial groups are a vital part of the
fabric of society, and we will review some of the historical and social processes
that led to the emergence of the minority status assigned to several ethnic and
racial groups in the United States and explore how the minority status of several
different ethnic and racial groups is rooted in a legacy of oppression and discrimination and a rich history of resistance and resiliency. Minority status will be
explained in its social and historical contexts. The minority status assigned to
some groups is not a natural given but the product of particular historical contexts and events (Preece, 2006). For example, being black in Nigeria does not
make a person part of a racial minority group; being black in the United States or
in Brazil makes a person part of a minority group, however. It is the history of
slavery and its legacy of oppression in Brazil and in the United States that gave
this group its minority status. The term "minority" is not used in this chapter in
a numerical sense but instead is used in a sociological sense to describe the
group's lesser power and status compared to other groups, particularly vis-à-vis
the white majority. Likewise, when the term "majority" is used, it is not used in
a numerical sense but reflects the concentration of power with that group.

COLONIALISM AND GENOCIDE: NATIVE AMERICANS

Colonialism is a system of organizing society that concentrates all the power
over the local population in the hands of an invading outsider group. The process

of colonization not only targets land, but also aims at colonizing the minds, the emotions, the bodies, and the labor of those residing on the occupied land (Bodei, 2002). The process of colonization is justified by the oppressor or dominant group's definition of the conquered group as inferior. Conversely, from a social Darwinist viewpoint, the dominant group views itself as superior and better equipped to rule.

Colonialism has been part of the human experience since the beginning of civilization: examples of empires that have practiced colonialism are the Roman, Portuguese, Spanish, British, and Japanese empires. Although Rome, Lisbon, Madrid, London, and Tokyo were very different colonial metropolises that reached their zenith of power and expansion at different times in history, these empires shared much in terms of goals, organizational styles, and outcomes. In all cases, the top authority of the colonial power (the caesar, king, queen, or emperor) never resided on the colonized lands. The empires not only imposed their culture on the colonized populations, but also extracted raw materials from the colonies and made them buy back the manufactured goods they produced using the raw materials. The original residents of the colonized lands were viewed by their conquerors as lacking the social and intellectual capacity to govern their own affairs.

During the nineteenth and early twentieth centuries, Africa underwent an intensive process of colonization. With only two exceptions, by the beginning of World War II Africa had become a fully colonized continent. The colonial political map of Africa shows how European powers carved out pieces of the continent and its wealth to benefit themselves. The colonial ambition of rulers such as King Leopold of Belgium has been well documented in books such as *King Leopold's Ghost* (Hochschild, 1998). The resurgence and expansion of slavery is intimately related to the colonial experience of Africa from the sixteenth to the nineteenth centuries. Slavery on such a large scale and with such a high level of organization would not have been possible without colonialism as its economic and political engine. The legacy of colonialism continues to cast its shadow over Africa. For example, artificial national borders created by European powers and favoritism toward one indigenous group over another during colonial rule led to ethnic group conflict and genocide in Rwanda in the mid-1990s. Colonial administrations deliberately suppressed or stunted the development of strong educational and health institutions. Since political independence was won in the second half of the twentieth century, African nations struggled in a global economy dominated by the West, subject to rich nations' manipulation of the raw materials and commodities that are Africa's chief revenue source. Beleaguered by the demands of rapid population growth, the HIV/AIDS pandemic, interethnic strife and civil war, falling agricultural production, and poor industrial and technology capacities, even very resource-rich countries, including the Democratic Republic of the Congo (formerly Zaire), have seen their average incomes cut in half in recent decades.

Colonialism is closely related to the concept of internal colonialism, which was first introduced by Robert Blauner (1972) to show how African Americans faced social conditions in the United States, such as lack of political and economic power, that were similar to those faced by developing nations as a result of European colonialism. Internal colonialism does not require incursions across international borders. The oppressive power relations take place within national borders, although the relationship and its results are similar to the classic forms of colonialism. The United States followed a colonial path, subjugating African Americans, Native Americans, Native Hawaiians, Mexicans, Filipinos, and Puerto Ricans to colonialism when their land or labor became attractive economic and political targets. Internal colonialism continues to be a means for the dominant racial group to perpetuate social inequalities for its own benefit. The shadow of internal colonialism is reflected in contemporary society's perception that some groups are racially inferior as well as in the persistence of racially segregated ghettos and neighborhoods. The extreme social isolation and economic marginalization of some African American and Latino urban communities has been attributed to their lack of economic, administrative, and political control, which is typically held by white outsiders. In the 1960s, for example, young black militants interpreted their racial oppression as a form of internal colonialism and aligned themselves with developing countries and groups struggling for liberation from the legacy of colonialism in Africa (Takaki, 1993). Despite these important struggles, the legacy of internal colonialism persists, as evidenced by the fact that one in every four black men comes under the control of the criminal justice system at some point in his life, the majority for nonviolent offenses (Brown-Dean, 2007). This has very damaging consequences not only for these men, but also for their families and their communities.

The concept of internal colonialism explains how racial inequality in the United States has been perpetuated over time, but it does not explain the changing conditions of African Americans and members of other ethnic minority groups, such as the gains that have been achieved in educational and occupational opportunities and in earnings, which have increased upward mobility for some. Although the concept of internal colonialism needs to be updated to maintain its relevance in a rapidly changing world, it continues to provide important insights into the ongoing oppression of ethnic and racial communities in the United States and around the world.

Genocide is often connected to colonialism, but it can occur autonomously within nations without outside intervention. Genocide is the organized effort to eliminate an entire group of people. The United Nations (1951) defines genocide as "actions committed with intent to destroy in whole or in part a national, ethnic, racial, or religion group as such" (p. 10). Some argue that this definition is too narrow because it limits genocide to the killing of a group and does not consider policies of cultural, social, political, and economic destruction. It also leaves out classes and groups that are not necessarily ethnic or communal, such as lesbians, gays, and transgender groups (Gellately & Kiernan, 2003). These groups were targeted by the Nazi party and continue to be vulnerable to the threat of genocide in many societies (Abed, 2006). Another definition of genocide—as organized state murder—highlights the role of the state as a key component of modern premeditated genocide (Fein, 2002).

Genocide has devastating consequences not only for those who perish, but also for those who survive. Native American scholars have argued that some contemporary ills experienced by Native American communities in the United States can be traced to their ancestors' experience of genocide. That is, the posttraumatic stress disorder experienced by survivors of genocide can be passed on to later generations, as shown by research on descendants of Holocaust survivors and Bosnian survivors of so-called ethnic cleansing (Field, Om, Kim, & Vorn, 2011; Wiseman, Metzl, & Barber, 2006). These studies all demonstrate that the posttraumatic stress disorder associated with survival of genocide is as much of a collective phenomenon as the phenomenon of genocide itself. Genocide that is connected to colonialism and internal colonialism is part of the legacy of many ethnic and racial communities in the United States and other countries. For example, the legacy of colonialism and genocide affects many Vietnamese, Cambodian, and Laotian refugee communities that have settled in the United States. It is often through narratives that those legacies surface, which allows the refugees to honor their collective stories so that together community members can address the related trauma.

The experience with both colonialism and genocide and their legacy resulted in the present minority status of the descendants of the original inhabitants of what is today the United States and Canada. Native Americans, also called American Indians and First Nations people, were the only inhabitants of North America for many centuries before the arrival of Europeans. These groups developed a variety of cultures (identities) and political organizations. When the Europeans invaded the Americas in the late 1400s, Native Americans were a numerical majority, but over time and due to colonialism and genocide, they were decimated; in addition to becoming a sociological minority (that is, they had less power than those in control), they also eventually became a numerical minority.

Genocide commenced almost immediately after the arrival of European explorers in the so-called New World, beginning in 1493 with Christopher Columbus's enslavement and mass extermination of the Taíno population of the Caribbean. Within three years, 5 million Taíno had perished, and a Spanish census from fifty years later records only two hundred left alive. Columbus's contemporary, the historian Father Bartolomé de las Casas (1552/1992), reported numerous atrocities perpetrated on indigenous people, including mass hangings, the roasting of people on spits, and the hacking of children to pieces for use as dog food.

Later European colonists and subsequently the United States government resorted to various means for removing Native Americans, including the extermination of whole villages, bounties on the scalps of Natives, and bacterial warfare. In one of the first reported uses of bacterial warfare, British agents murdered more than 100,000 members of the Mingo, Delaware, Shawnee, and other Ohio River tribes by distributing blankets purposely contaminated with smallpox, an Old World disease to which the Native population of the Americas had virtually no resistance. The same measure was used against the Ottawa and Lenape tribes, and the U.S. Army later successfully duplicated the practice on Plains tribal populations (Friedberg, 2000). The colonial governments offered large sums of money to whites for the scalps of Native Americans. The state of California spent approximately $1 million each year in 1851 and 1852 from Gold Rush revenue to finance campaigns whose purpose was exterminating the Native people. Whites received between fifty cents and five dollars for each severed head (Chatterjee, 1998). In addition to this intentional slaughter, Native Americans were forced by whites to give up their traditional occupations, which resulted in poverty, hunger, illness, and death (Berkhofer, 1978).

The enormity of what David Stannard (1993) has called an American holocaust parallels the unfathomable and more recent human losses suffered during the Nazi Holocaust. The systematic murder of European Jews under the Nazi regime is estimated at around 65 percent of the prewar population, while the rate of attrition of indigenous populations in the United States is calculated at around 98 to 99 percent, meaning that only about 1 to 2 percent of the original indigenous population survived genocide (Friedberg, 2000). White attitudes to the slaughter are exemplified by an editorial by L. Frank Baum (the author of *The Wonderful Wizard of Oz*) that was printed in the *Aberdeen Saturday Pioneer*, a weekly South Dakota newspaper, in 1890: "Our only safety depends upon the total extermination of the Native Americans. Having wronged them for centuries we had better, in order to protect our civilization, follow it up by one more wrong and wipe these untamed and untamable creatures from the face of the earth. In this lies safety for our settlers and the soldiers. . . . Otherwise, we may expect future years to be as full of trouble with the redskins as those have been in the past" (quoted in Ritter, 1997, p. 21). In addition, cultural misperceptions and stereotypes contributed to the cultural demise of Native American communities. European and European American failure to appreciate the cultures and tribal identities of the Native American nations led to a history of confusion, myths, stereotypes, and misunderstanding that has been particularly destructive to Native communities. Native Americans were viewed as savages and as scalp hunters. The Europeans' lack of appreciation for and understanding of the Native American cultures, as well as other indigenous cultures in colonies such as Australia, allowed them to label the Native people they encountered as less than human and to target them for elimination (Fenzsch, 2005).

Although Europeans had engaged in a nearly continuous history of warfare before coming to the Americas and continued fighting among themselves for control of the New World, in order to justify their genocide of Native people they constructed an image of the Native Americans as fierce and savage fighters (Bellamy, 2012; Mihesuah, 1996). Even the U.S. Declaration of Independence refers to Native populations as "merciless Indian Savages." This helped disguise the reality that many armed conflicts with the Native communities occurred because the Europeans wanted to expropriate Indian land and enslave Indians to serve as laborers for mines and farms. More often than not, Native Americans were merely defending their territories, families, way of life, and sovereignty from the intruders.

Through government decrees and policies, surviving Native people lost not only their lands, but also their parental rights. This practice started as early as the 1540s, when Franciscan friars took the children of the leaders of tribal communities in the Yucatan in Mexico away from their families to be educated in Franciscan schools (Pagden, 1975). In 1898 the U.S. Indian Peace Commission recommended that Native children be educated in the ways of European Americans so their cultural differences would disappear (Adams, 1995). The mission boarding schools created in light of this recommendation, largely under the control of the Federal Bureau of Indian Affairs, took Native children from their parents, homes, and communities—often forcibly—to distant institutions (Cross, Earle, & Simmons, 2000). Forbidden to speak their own language, and given European-style clothes and Christian names, the Native American children who would become tribal leaders once they returned to their communities were systematically stripped of their cultural heritage. These boarding schools took generations of Native Americans away from their homes, and since their way of learning was different from that of European Americans (traditional Native American learning often took place through observation, listening, and hands-on activities rather than through passive lectures and readings), these children struggled in school (DeVoe, Darling-Churchill, & Snyder, 2008). Torn between their own culture and the one they were supposed to embrace, Native students were often made to feel inferior, and many ultimately lost their connection to Native American culture and never became accustomed to European American ways (Larsen & Jesch, 1980). It was not until 1978 that the Indian Child Welfare Act was created to protect Native American children in need of homes from being placed in non-Native adoptive and foster homes, although today there are still a disproportionate number of out-of-home placements of Native children (Hand, 2006).

Reservations are another legacy of colonialism. As a result of treaties and forced relocation, the number of Native Americans living on reservations had reached 300,000 by 1880 and continued to grow (Thorton, 2000). In 2010, 22 percent of the native population in the United States (1.14 million people) were living on reservations or tribal land (Norris, Vines, & Hoeffel, 2012). Although it was not easy to leave their lands and lifestyles behind, Native Americans demonstrated their resiliency by adapting to reservation life. In Oregon, the Native Americans of Grand Ronde demonstrated creativity, flexibility, and initiative during the transition from their vast ancestral lands to the much more limited reservation by developing an agricultural life but continuing to use tribal doctors and methods of healing (Leavelle, 1998). Native Americans viewed their lives on the reservation as different from their lives "outside." They struggled to maintain their traditions and cultural knowledge, and many started to view reservations as safe places where they were able to preserve and nurture their cultural identity (Doble & Yarrow, 2007; Lone-Knapp, 2000).

Native American youths who attend school on reservations may develop stronger connections to their cultural heritage because they are not exposed to prejudice from the dominant culture. However, families who decide to stay on the reservation often face inequalities, as they do not have access to the resources and opportunities available in cities. The social problems those inequalities engender, such as unemployment, poverty, and alcoholism, have a negative impact on the well-being of the whole family. Urban tribal members in need often go back to their reservation of origin because the reservation is home. This can present challenges to limited reservation resources and infrastructure, as those returning for help may have multiple and acute needs. In addition, the Community Policing Consortium (2004) reports that returnees often "bring with them attitudes and values that conflict with traditional ways[,] causing disorder and crime" (p. 11).

During the 1950s, in yet another attempt to promote assimilation into the dominant culture, the Bureau of Indian Affairs coordinated efforts for relocation that would lead more than 160,000 Native Americans to leave their reservations by promising them jobs and housing in cities across the nation. Since then, the number of Native Americans leaving the reservations has continued to rise, and currently more than 60 percent live outside Native American communities and reservations (Duran, 2005).

For most of its history, the Bureau of Indian Affairs was paternalistic and authoritarian in nature, and it was regarded with justifiable suspicion by Native American communities. By the 1960s U.S. federal policy began to shift toward a goal of self-determination, meaning that Native American nations would have the power to govern themselves and in turn preserve their culture. The core components of self-determination were the preservation of treaty rights, consultation on policy making, and economic self-sufficiency (Riggs, 2000). New approaches to furthering the Native American cause appeared in 1972, when the American Indian Movement staged the Trail of Broken Treaties, a cross-country protest that brought attention to the mistreatment of Native Americans and the drastic effects of colonization and genocide. Although nothing ever came of the movement's twenty-point paper advocating the restoration of Native governments (American Indian Movement, 1972), the Self-Determination Act of 1975 granted all tribes the right to manage services and programs formerly administered by the Bureau of Indian Affairs. Notes from the field 8.1 describe one tribe's response to New York State's attempt to undermine those rights.

The history of colonialist exploitation of indigenous peoples is not unique to the United States. In Australia, for instance, a system of reserves, missions, and other institutions was also established in the nineteenth century with the purpose of segregating the Aboriginal Australian communities from the European Australian population. Much has been written about the ruthless way in which the Aboriginal people of Australia were treated, such as the forced removal of children from Aboriginal families and their placement with white families (Human Rights and Equal Opportunity Commission, 1997). Indigenous reserves continue to be created today in countries including Australia, Brazil, and Peru. Modern reservations are often created with the stated purpose of protecting the rights, the culture, and the lands of the indigenous inhabitants, but the actual outcomes are mixed. The Brazilian case is impressive in scope and illustrates the continuing

---

NOTES FROM THE FIELD 8.1
This Is Our Land

In the late 1990s, pressured by the state's gas distributors, the state of New York passed a law requiring the Native American tribes within state boundaries to collect a tax on gas sold on tribal land. This tax was deemed lawful based on a Supreme Court ruling that determined the state could require businesses to charge a tax when selling to nontribal members. Many tribes felt that this law violated their nations' sovereignty granted to them by treaty. Two tribes, the Mohawk and the Seneca, refused to sign the law and implement the new tax. To further pressure the tribes to comply, the state of New York enforced an embargo on all gasoline, including home heating oil. Gasoline trucks were confiscated and anyone who transported gasoline to the reservations was charged with a felony. The Seneca tribe responded by conducting protests along the interstate and disrupted traffic. State troops were sent in to control the situation and many Seneca tribal members were arrested. After months of protesting, the tribe was invited to negotiations with the governor, but talks were cut short when the governor did not participate in person and backed out of a deal the day after it had been negotiated. Despite a lack of progress in negotiations, the court ruled that the seizure of gasoline trucks was illegal; less than one year after the beginning of the action, the governor repealed the state law. His reasoning for the repeal was that it was in the state's best interest to avoid further disruptions on the state's highways. (Based on Weaver, 2000).

struggles of indigenous peoples to preserve their culture, health, and well-being in the face of exploitation. Approved expansions of reserves in Brazil in the second decade of the twenty-first century have enlarged its protected indigenous lands to more than 674 reserves covering 107.6 million hectares, an area twice the size of Spain. However, the morbidity and mortality rates of indigenous communities continue to be much higher than the rates for the general Brazilian population (Coimbra et al., 2013).

Despite the organized attempts by European colonial powers and later by the U.S. government to exterminate the original inhabitants of the land, and subsequent policies designed to destroy their cultures and forcibly assimilate them into the dominant society, the number of Native Americans has increased by at least 30 percent in each of the last five decennial censuses (Norris et al., 2012). The census for the year 2010 reported a 39 percent increase in the Native American population over the prior ten years, with over 5.2 million individuals claiming heritage as a Native American or Alaska Native, over half of whom (56%) claimed only their native heritage rather than a combination of racial backgrounds (Norris et al., 2012; U.S. Census Bureau, 2010). Nonetheless, this group still constitutes less than 2 percent of the total U.S. population and only a small fraction of the estimated 15 million Native people residing in the territory that is now the United States during the 1500s (Wissler, 2005).

In their struggle for survival, Native Americans have made use of a range of strategies for dealing with oppression while maintaining or renewing their connections to their cultural heritage. One way of accommodating the outside pressures involved not calling attention to themselves or to their cultural differences. Those who adapted in this way may sometimes be seen by other tribal members as not being Native American enough (Ring, 2001). Despite these strategies for survival, the dominant culture's failure to validate Native American pain has resulted in unresolved historical trauma and a myriad of social problems connected to generational posttraumatic stress and its symptoms of alcoholism, rage, depression, and anxiety (Cohen, Mannarino, & Deblinger, 2006; Cohen, Mannarino, & Knudsen, 2004; Heart, 2003).

Recently, a shift from tribal or clan identity to a broader umbrella Native American identity that has variously been called a pan-Indian, pan-tribal, and pan-traditions identity has taken place. Pan-Indianism offers Native Americans the opportunity to practice Native traditions and retain or regain (through enculturation) a Native cultural identity when away from tribe of origin and even while living among a dominant culture that rejects their culture of origin. Instead of clustering in neighborhood enclaves, Native Americans living in cities—who now constitute the majority of all Native Americans in the United States—tend to live in the midst of other ethnic groups (Powers, 2006). In contrast to reservation identities tied to a specific place and tribal enrollment, membership in urban Native American communities is defined by various criteria that can include

Native American ancestry, cultural or tribal knowledge, and active participation in Native American community activities. Native Americans living in urban areas face challenges in forming supportive communities because of differences in tribal backgrounds, connections to reservations, and intermarriage across tribes and nonnative ethnic groups (Moran, Fleming, Somervall, & Manson, 1999). These differences produce variations in the complexity and diffuseness of their identities as Native people, but also present opportunities to recognize and sustain cultural heritages based on common values. For example, urban Native Americans often have shared experiences due to their ethnic minority status, such as similar acculturation-related stresses, family legacies of forced migration, encounters with discrimination, and reactions from nonnatives who do not differentiate across tribes. Their relatively small proportional representation in urban neighborhoods and schools may encourage formation of heterogeneous Native social networks that cross tribal lines, and promote sharing and mixing of cultures. They also share the experience of crossing regularly between cultural worlds, operating daily in social settings where Native cultural traditions may not be practiced regularly and where social interaction with nonnatives is pervasive (Moran et al., 1999).

Urban Native Americans are often described as "invisible" to non–Native Americans, mainly as a result of their wide geographic dispersion (Lobo, 2002). Urban Native American communities are also very fluid because of frequent movement back and forth between the city and reservations for educational and employment reasons as well as return visits for ceremonies and family responsibilities (Howard-Bobiwash & Krouse, 2009). As a result, not only are Native Americans frequently underserved by the health and mental health service systems, but in addition misunderstandings and disagreements about who is eligible for social services can result in an inability to access services mandated by federal law to be available to all Native Americans through the Indian Health Service (Frith-Smith & Singleton, 2000).

Some tribal nations have been able to develop their own sources of revenue through mining, farming, fishing, industry, and gambling and are using generated revenue to improve the educational, health, and social services infrastructures of their communities. For the first time since colonization started, many individuals are meeting their basic needs and advancing economically and socially without having to let go of their cultural traditions. The use of culturally grounded social work can support a community's efforts to achieve self-determination and improve its quality of life.

SLAVERY: AFRICAN AMERICANS, EMANCIPATION, RECONSTRUCTION, JIM CROW, AND THE CIVIL RIGHTS MOVEMENT

Slavery, which many consider a tragic but distant chapter in U.S. and world history, actually continues to be a major problem in contemporary societies. It encompasses a variety of widespread human rights violations, including the traditional slave trade, the selling of children, sexual exploitation of children and women, the use of children in armed conflicts, debt bondage, and the selling of human organs. Often referred to as human trafficking, it is estimated that 12.3 million people are forced into labor annually; these numbers may drastically underestimate the scope of modern slavery (Koettl, 2009).

Slavery dehumanized those who were enslaved as well as the enslavers who benefited from this form of oppression. Prior to the Civil War, there were approximately 4 million enslaved African Americans in the United States, numbering more than ten times the number of African Americans living as free men and women (Franklin & Moss, 1994). In order to justify slavery, and very much in alignment with the social Darwinist principles reviewed previously, the ruling elite established an elaborate theory of biological inferiority based on skin color to support the idea that slavery was the proper state of the "inferior" race (Guelzo, 2006). Because people who were enslaved were brought to the American colonies involuntarily, racial inequality had existed from the start (Farley, 2000). Africans who were enslaved as well as free blacks were the victims of discrimination, segregation, violence, and negative racial images that contributed to their racial degradation and poverty, which in turn reinforced prejudice (Takaki, 1993). Slavery provided economic rewards for those involved at every level of the slave trade except for those who were enslaved and their descendants. Slavery benefited slave traders, plantation owners, exporters, and merchants. These dynamics played a large role in the pervasive acceptance of a slavery system that today is universally condemned.

Unlike most of the instances of slavery around the world today, the slave trade in the Americas was part of a system of exploitation that was officially sanctioned by major societal institutions, from politics and law to education, the family, and religion. The slave system in the New World started in the sixteenth century as a way to provide free labor to European colonies in Central and South America and the Caribbean; it was spurred in part by the colonists' inability to turn many of the indigenous peoples of the Americas into readily exploitable slave labor due to cultural resistance, susceptibility to Western diseases, and genocide (Eltis, 2000).

During the seventeenth century, the first generations of Africans were brought involuntarily to what is now the United States. The first to arrive in the English colony in Jamestown, Virginia, were indentured African servants from the West Indies who were sold by a Dutch ship captain in exchange for supplies (Rawley & Behrendt, 2005). Initially, indentured Africans in British North America had a legal status somewhat comparable to that of English indentured servants, which meant that they were servants for a limited period of time, after which they were released to live a free life and given land of their own. All indentured servants at that time, both white and black, were considered personal property. Soon, however, a legal precedent for racially based discrimination was set. In a 1640 case involving the capture of three runaway indentured servants, the two white run-aways were given thirty lashes and an extra four years of servitude, but the black servant was sentenced to servitude for life (Catterall, 1968). By the 1660s it was understood in the English colonies that black slaves were property with few or no legal rights (Farley, 2000).

Upon their arrival on American soil—after a perilous ocean voyage in inhu-mane conditions that claimed many lives—enslaved African people confronted a painful period of adjustment and disorientation and then had to face illnesses, a life of hard work, and often an early death. Africans captured and forced into slavery were considered expendable, and many slaves died at the hands of their masters through beatings, lynchings, and burnings. In the New World, they lived mostly on plantations, growing cash crops such as cotton, sugar, and tobacco, in dilapidated dwellings and cramped quarters, with substandard food and clothing. Spouses, parents, and children could be separated at the slave owner's whim and sold to different masters because African slaves lacked legal sanction for their marriages. Sexual assaults of women of color by their owners and other white males were common; because slavery was defined as a racial and hereditary condi-tion, children born of an enslaved mother and her white owner were considered slaves and were sometimes sold by their own biological fathers for a profit (Camp-bell, Miers, & Miller, 2006). Interracial marriage was outlawed in 1662 throughout the English colonies.

People who were enslaved were considered objects with no legal rights and could not act in their own defense. They could be convicted by the testimony of only one white accuser (Outwin, 1996). The only right that most slaves retained was the right to profess their religious beliefs: in 1670 the colonial government of Carolina declared that religion alters only people's souls, not their civil state or rights; therefore, all people, slaves included, were free to follow their own reli-gious beliefs. However, even that prerogative was limited. Although the open prac-tice of their ancestral African religions was suppressed, many aspects of these religions came to be integrated in the enslaved people's expression of Christianity (Griffith & Savage, 2006). Even before Emancipation, African Americans devel-oped their own religions institutions. Richard Allen, a free black who was an ordained Methodist minister, founded the African Methodist Episcopal Church in Philadelphia in 1794. Organized religion became a crucial part of African Ameri-can culture, providing the cohesive force that helped Africans resist slavery (Keithly & Rombough, 2007).

During and in the years following the U.S. Civil War, African Americans even-tually gained their freedom through the passage of several Constitutional amend-ments, but Emancipation did not mean equality. Segregation and discrimination continued to be practiced and were reinstated through laws that provided a legal framework for racial discrimination, exclusion, and the denial of access to eco-nomic and educational opportunities and social advancement (what are known today as Jim Crow laws) in the South, and informal practices that had much the same result in the North. In 1896, with the U.S. Supreme Court's decision in *Plessy v. Ferguson*, a doctrine of "separate but equal" helped to entrench the system of legal and social resegregation in the South. Under *Plessy,* African Americans were disenfranchised at the voting booth and relegated to second-class status in the public school, transportation, housing, health-care, and economic systems.

Throughout history, violence against African Americans often has increased as they have gained more social and political power. For a century after the Civil War, African Americans were routinely victims of violence at the hands of white individuals and mobs (Watson, 2006). Lynchings were used regularly by whites to instill fear, to intimidate African Americans, and to enforce economic exploitation and residential and educational segregation. According to civil rights activists, lynching continues to be practiced in contemporary U.S. society, but under the guise of self-defense or punishment. For example, according to the Stolen Lives Project, 90 percent of unarmed civilians who are suspected of no crime and are shot or killed by police in the United States are black (Lawson, 2003). This reality was brought to the forefront nationally in 2013 when Trayvon Martin, an unarmed African American teenager, was shot and killed by a neighborhood watchman who thought Martin's behavior was suspicious. The shooter was found not guilty of second-degree murder on the grounds that he had acted in self-defense. This incident ignited a national conversation about the continuing role of race in judgments about who is suspicious, threatening, or out of place (Alverez & Buckley, 2013). Notes from the field 8.2 describe one African American family's response to these types of events.

During the 1950s and 1960s, two distinct versions of black resistance gained national visibility: one a nonviolent movement inspired by Gandhi, and the other

---

NOTES FROM THE FIELD 8.2

Walking to Avoid Suspicion

After Ray heard about an unarmed African American teenager being shot by police in their neighborhood, he felt like he needed to talk to his young son Rodney about how to behave in public to avoid suspicion. He hated that he had to have the conversation and make his son worry about his safety, but felt it was necessary. Ray told Rodney to avoid alleys and stay in well-lit areas, to walk at a relaxed pace, if approached to be respectful, and to keep his hands where they can be seen. Ray also asked Rodney to think about the way he dresses and to avoid wearing hoodies. Rodney said that he understood, but Ray continues to worry about him when he is out in the neighborhood by himself.

embracing more-direct confrontation as the means to produce change. Malcolm X, the leader of the latter group, disagreed with the nonviolent approach of Dr. Martin Luther King Jr. (Blumberg, 1984). Before both were assassinated in the 1960s, both Dr. King and Malcolm X worked at improving the life conditions of African Americans, but through different means. These two traditions continue to be used today to analyze current events in African American communities across the nation. To some degree, they have influenced the design and implementation of many community-based organizations where social workers are employed (Sherr, 2006).

As an outgrowth of the civil rights movements and the related passage of civil rights legislation, African Americans slowly gained political power from the dismantling of state laws that had disenfranchised them for centuries, and they experienced an increase in electoral participation and coalition building. During the administration of President Bill Clinton, six African Americans served as secretaries of commerce, agriculture, energy, labor, transportation, and veterans' affairs. Unfortunately, these positions did not entail broad policymaking powers providing opportunities to change the distribution of economic and political resources. Nonetheless, these appointments did reflect an increased representation of African Americans in high government positions. The administration of President George W. Bush continued this trend to some degree by appointing African Americans to selected top posts, including two successive African American secretaries of state. These appointments have been interpreted by some as a form of tokenism rather than a reflection of true equality or representation, but they are also indications of ongoing changes in the national boundaries of political participation. The election in 2008 and reelection in 2012 of Barak Obama, the first African American president, were seen as historical moments and viewed by some as evidence that the United States had arrived as a postracial society. Although these events provided a visible symbol of racial equality, they did not signal that U.S. society had adequately addressed the social stratification that still disproportionally affects people of color (Dawkins, 2010). The legacy of slavery and oppression of African Americans can still be seen in persisting racial disparities in education, economic advancement, and health care (Bertocchi & Dimico, 2012).

Slavery has been identified as a cultural marker that continues to influence the identity formation of African Americans today (Eyerman, 2002). Slavery left a legacy of both collective memory and collective trauma and is being reinterpreted by African American communities around the nation. As part of the reconceptualization of slavery, the postcolonial interpretation of the institution of slavery that takes into account the slaves' experiences of oppression and perspective of the institution and at the same time calls attention to the bountiful benefits that slavery produced for the slaveholders in black Atlantic America is being questioned, and a more accurate and complete story is being developed in its place (Sweeney, 2006). This analysis aims at recognizing the resiliency and the cultural contribution of enslaved African Americans, and at the same time advocates the recognition of the enormous economic contributions they were forced to make as slaves. Slavery, for example, has been described as a key institution that allowed the United States to develop into the economic superpower that it is today (Wright, 2006). Inhumane free labor provided the basis for the accumulation of extensive sums of capital that made possible the enormous economic development of the country. A national campaign seeking reparations is under way to persuade the federal government and local governments to approve some kind of compensation for the descendants of the victims of American slavery and the century of de jure racial discrimination that succeeded it.

There is a continuing generational legacy of mistrust toward people outside the African American community as well as a style of communication that has been passed down within families. In her book *Yearning,* the African American feminist writer bell hooks (1990) tells of how her grandmother taught her grandchildren to keep their distance from white outsiders in order to be safe and to protect their otherness. The federally funded Tuskegee experiment provides an example of the mistreatment African Americans received at the hands of outsiders, in this case the scientific establishment. This study, which began in 1932 and ended only in 1972, tricked impoverished black sharecroppers who had syphilis but were told they had "bad blood" into taking part in a "treatment plan" that, unknown to them, offered no medical care, even after penicillin became the standard treatment for syphilis. Scientists documented the men's declining health but did nothing to cure the disease, which over time can cause tumors, paralysis, blindness, insanity, and death. In addition, because the men were not told that they had syphilis, many passed the disease on to their wives and children. In 1997 President Bill Clinton offered an apology to the eight remaining survivors of the Tuskegee syphilis experiment.

Culturally grounded social workers can honor this legacy by designing and implementing interventions that take into account the African American community's history and traditions. Honoring the struggles of African Americans throughout history is a key component of culturally grounded interventions with this community.

ANNEXATION: MEXICAN AMERICANS

"The border crossed us before we ever crossed the border" is a common saying among older Mexican Americans residing in the borderlands of the Southwest that refers to the annexation of Mexican territories by the United States. Annexation occurs when a group expands its territory by taking control of an area occupied by another group through military action or when residents of the area request annexation (Edelstein, 2004). Although similar to colonialism in its impact on the local population, annexation occurs when the territory that is con-quered is contiguous or next to the expanding territory. For example, the Anglo leaders of the Republic of Texas—then a part of Mexico—requested annexation by the United States in 1837. The U.S. government originally refused the request out of fear that Mexico would be offended. The "voluntary" annexation of Texas into the United States occurred because of agitation for independence by Anglo settlers in Texas and the subsequent war between the United States and Mexico that it triggered.

In the United States, the idea of Manifest Destiny gave rise to the annexation of vast territories and, during James Madison's presidency, the belief that the United States' mission was to spread democracy, the only fair way of government. Advocates of Manifest Destiny believed that expansion was necessary, good, obvi-ous ("manifest"), inevitable ("destiny"), and ordained by God. Originally a politi-cal catchphrase of the nineteenth century, Manifest Destiny has served as a historical metaphor for the territorial expansion of the United States across North America toward the Pacific Ocean, which displaced both the previous colonial rulers and indigenous populations. Manifest Destiny has racist overtones, as it suggests that white European Americans should lead the expansion over territory already occupied by other peoples without any regard for them, their rights, or their cultures.

Annexation may occur in peaceful or violent ways; for example, the United States' acquisition of Louisiana from France in 1803 (the Louisiana Purchase) was a peaceful annexation, in contrast to the vast territorial annexation of what is now the Southwest United States, which was accomplished through an expansionist war with Mexico in 1846. This war and its consequences have in many ways shaped the history and current status of the Mexican American community. Through forced purchase of land and armed conquest, Mexican territories originally located in the northern territories of New Spain's colonies and later the independent nation of Mexico, and the people residing in them, became part of a new country, and Mexican Americans became a subordinate ethnic group (Bacal, 1994). This experience and its consequences have shaped the history and current status of the Mexican American community.

During the centuries when the Southwest and California were under the political control of Spain and later Mexico, vast regions of the present-day states of California, Texas, Colorado, Utah, New Mexico, Nevada, and Arizona were sparsely populated by Mexican settlers. Thus, when English-speaking Americans started to move into these regions in the 1800s to farm and look for gold, they were usually welcomed by the Mexican inhabitants, and marriages between members of the two groups were common. During the Gold Rush, the Anglos' efforts to displace Mexicans, Spaniards, and Native Americans intensified and the efforts toward independence deepened as a means to secure control over the resource-rich lands (Truett, 2006).

In 1846 the United States invaded Mexico and its northern territories. A final military attack on Mexico City gave the Mexican government no choice but to agree to a peace treaty, which took place at Guadalupe Hidalgo in 1848 and forced Mexico to relinquish approximately a third of its national territory to the United States (Hernández, 2012). Under the Treaty of Guadalupe Hidalgo, Mexicans who remained in what became U.S. territory were nominally guaranteed all the rights of citizenship, protection of their property, and the right to maintain religious and cultural integrity, including the use of the Spanish language for all government transactions (Rosales, 2000). However, only the state of New Mexico has honored these provisions. Soon after the treaty was signed, the other territories and states began ignoring the provisions that protected the cultural, political, and economic integrity of Mexican American families and communities (Chanbonpin, 2005; Weber, 1973). A classic example of a violation of the treaty was the lack of recognition of the property titles (land grants) of Mexican families, as a result of which great extensions of land were taken away from their lawful owners. These families appealed to the courts of their new country without success, and many cases reached the Supreme Court (Soltero, 2006). As a result, even though they had been guaranteed citizenship, Mexicans in the U.S. territory became a disenfranchised minority, foreigners in their own land. At best, Mexican Americans were treated as second-class citizens; at worst, they were victims of overt discrimination (Haney-Lopez, 2006). Mexican Americans were divested of their properties through legal and political ploys by Anglo farmers, who coveted the land and used claims that the new Americans were not industrious and used the land inefficiently to justify their seizure (Rosales, 1996). This process was facilitated by two conflicting legal systems: the Napoleonic Code of Spain and Mexico, and the new U.S. legal system. The latter often refused to recognize the property rights established by the Napoleonic Code, including property rights for communally or collectively owned agricultural lots (*ejidos*), which U.S. law treated as land without ownership (Taylor, 1972). As a result, many families of Mexican and Spanish heritage lost their ranches and found themselves reduced to day laborers on land that was theirs. Overt discrimination, including the loss of property and status in society, forced others, many of whom had never been to old Mexico before, to cross the newly drawn border to return to a shrunken Mexico (Weber, 1973).

At times during the early and mid-twentieth century when their labor was needed, Mexicans were encouraged to cross the border to become temporary workers through the Bracero Program (discussed below), but were not truly welcomed. Mexicans were excluded from mainstream society and isolated by ethnic segregation. Discrimination was rampant even in schools, where children of Mexican descent were trained to become obedient workers and discouraged from pursuing white-collar careers (Rodriguez, 2005). In California and throughout the Southwest, there were elementary schools for Mexican Americans only, leading to unequal educational opportunities for Mexican American children. The Mexican

American community again went to the courts and in 1946 won the first significant legal case against school segregation with *Mendez v. Westminster*, which served as a springboard for the later case of *Brown v. Board of Education* (Valencia, 2005).

Over time, a Chicano identity developed in reaction to the history of oppression experienced by U.S. Mexican communities. Originally meant as an insult implying a lack of sophistication, the term "Chicano" was appropriated during the 1960s by youthful political militants to signify Mexican Americans' growing awareness of their special ethnic and cultural heritage (Rinderle, 2005). Chicanos saw themselves as an exploited and conquered people suffering from the deculturalization carried out in schools. *Chicanismo* emphasized the ideology of *la raza* (the people), which favored collective versus individual achievement of goals. Some of the main goals of the Chicano movement were to strengthen the ethnic identity and pride of Mexican Americans and to advance a civil rights agenda aimed at ending discrimination and promoting equality in jobs, housing, and education (Chávez, 2002). Although in some communities the word Chicano has lost its connection to the Chicano movement and is often used as a synonym for Mexican American, the term Chicano continues to signify a more defiant approach to ethnic pride and identity.

Even before the height of the Chicano movement, Mexican Americans had displayed a great deal of strength in the face of oppression. By 1933, Mexican fieldworkers' protests against their degrading living conditions and poor wages were taking the form of strikes (Takaki, 1993). During the 1950s and 1960s, a Chicano organization called the GI Forum fought discrimination and conducted voter registration drives throughout the Southwest and California (Farley, 2000). It also focused on system reform to improve the educational attainment of Mexican Americans by challenging school segregation. It was during the 1960s that Mexican Americans turned away from assimilation and started emphasizing a self-defense ideology that promoted the preservation of the Spanish language and Mexican American culture and heritage (Torres-Saillant, 2006).

In order to ease the shortage of workers produced by World War II, the U.S. government established the Bracero Program, which brought 5 million Mexican-born farmworkers to the United States between 1942 and 1964 (Borjas & Katz, 2007). The Bracero Program was abruptly discontinued as the need for imported workers decreased, but migrant workers (both documented and undocumented) continue to be hired to work in the fields, and continue to come to the United States in great numbers. Today Mexicans account for approximately 77 percent of the total number of migrant workers and continue to endure the most oppressive working and living conditions. César Chávez was raised under such conditions and in 1962 started the National Farm Workers Association, a crusade he called *el movimiento*. Chávez used Gandhi's nonviolent methods to unionize farmworkers and improve their working conditions and overall quality of life. He dedicated his life to the struggles of migrant workers and fought for basic amenities and decent wages, as well as protection against occupational hazards like exposure to pesticide spraying. At this time, farmworkers' exploitation and misery resulted from the fact that corporate farm owners were either too far away or too indifferent to notice their workers' suffering, even when conditions were so bad that children were dying of malnutrition. Although Chávez was successful and saw changes in many areas, migrant farmworkers continue to face oppressive conditions such as lack of medical insurance and decent housing.

After more than a century of domination, exploitation, and oppression, Mexican Americans continue to be targets of stereotypes and prejudice. Mexican immigrants who have arrived recently regularly find their choices in jobs, housing, and political participation are restricted (Gutierrez et al., 2000). Despite all the challenges Mexican Americans have faced as a subordinate group, their experiences with discrimination have produced an ethnic consciousness that in turn has helped them develop a strong ethnic identity (Gutiérrez, 2013). In many Mexican American communities, murals are a display of community strength, providing a canvas on which to demonstrate pride in a common cultural heritage and articulate struggles against historical and current oppression (Arreola, 2012). Notes from the field 8.3 illustrate one Mexican American community's response to continued marginalization.

Mexican and Mexican American culture has been identified by some as a source of strength that has given rise to the so-called Mexican paradox: despite the fact that Mexican-born mothers (as well as other foreign-born Latina mothers) tend to have lower incomes and less access to health care and begin prenatal care later than other groups, they give birth to healthy babies at rates higher than other ethnic minority groups and non-Latino whites (Buekens, Notzon, Kotelchuck, & Wilcox, 2000). Infant mortality rates are lower for Mexican-born mothers than they are for whites and African Americans, and even lower than for Mexican American mothers born in the United States. Similar patterns of low infant mortality have been found for mothers from many other parts of Latin America. Immigrant Latina mothers, especially those from Mexico, appear to possess some protective factors related to pregnancy and childbirth that outweigh other risks they face. However, those advantages appear to weaken over time as Mexican mothers become more acculturated. Culturally grounded social work aims at identifying protective factors that lead to positive outcomes so that interventions that capitalize on the strengths of families navigating the acculturation process can be designed and implemented.

An example of such an intervention is Keepin' It REAL, a culturally grounded intervention that utilizes the protective factors that inhere in the culture of origin to help participants retain healthy behaviors and attitudes. Keepin' It REAL is a substance abuse prevention program designed for and tested with predominantly Mexican and Mexican American middle school students in the Southwest United States. It draws on the values and communication styles of Mexican American

---

NOTES FROM THE FIELD 8.3

Fighting for Infrastructure

La colonias are communities, usually close to but just outside of border towns in Texas, New Mexico, California, and Arizona. These neighborhoods typically lack basic services and infrastructure such as water, sewerage, and paved roads. In one community in Texas, migrant workers were sold inexpensive housing with the promise that electricity and running water would be brought to them shortly after they purchased their home. Despite the guarantee, many of the homes in the community are still without running water and electricity years later. The lack of infrastructure creates hazardous living conditions. The residents of the community would like to partner with the nearest town to obtain water and electricity lines but are not able to tap into the town's existing infrastructure unless they are incorporated into the town. The residents of this community do not want to be legally under the jurisdiction of the town because they are worried that doing so will undermine their *colonia*'s cultural identity. Using the *promotoras* model, a local community organization decides to train indigenous leaders to mobilize the community to advocate for policies that would increase the communities' access to resources. The community pursued state legislation that would give them access to the town utility lines without having to become part of the town. The bill passed, much to the surprise of the organization's staff, empowering residents to seek further action.

(Based on Arizmendi & Ortiz, 2004).

---

culture to teach youths strategies for resisting drugs—refuse, explain, avoid, and leave, or REAL—in ways that are appropriate for the social situations that the youths encounter in daily life. Results from the randomized trial conducted to evaluate the effectiveness of the program showed that recent Mexican immigrant students who spoke predominantly Spanish had a significantly lower drug use rate and significantly stronger antidrug attitudes than their more acculturated Mexican and Mexican American classmates. The lower levels of acculturation found among students who still used Spanish at home and with friends appeared to offer a protective effect against alcohol and other drug use. This protective effect weakened over time as students began to use English as their primary language. Ironically, the intervention was particularly effective among the more acculturated students, mostly because they were more at risk for substance use than their less acculturated counterparts (Marsiglia et al., 2005).

Anti-immigration narratives that surfaced in recent years can be linked to strong anti-immigration legislation passed in several states. Such narratives perpetuated a rationale for discriminatory attitudes and in some cases violence against Latinos. In California, the state with the largest population of people with Mexican heritage, the number of reports of anti-Latino hate crimes has increased sharply since 2003. In Shenandoah, Pennsylvania, an undocumented Mexican immigrant, Luis Ramirez, was beaten to death in 2008 by several young men who were heard yelling racial epithets. In 2010, a Mexican, Rodolfo Olmedo, was beaten by a group of teens shouting anti-immigrant sentiments in front of his home in Staten Island (Azpurua & Long, 2010). The attack on Olmedo was one of eleven anti-Hispanic reported assaults that were attributed to a renewed tension between ethnic groups living in that borough of New York City. Some residents of the community believed the attacks were due to the immigration debate that had increased suspicions of "outsiders," while others attributed the tension to an effort to maintain the culture in a neighborhood quickly changing due to immigration. The neighborhood responded to the rise in violence by increasing the police presence and having numerous town hall meetings where residents could discuss their concerns.

At the same time that anti-immigrant tensions have risen in many neighborhoods and communities, federal deportations of undocumented immigrants rose to 400,000 in 2010, a 25 percent increase from 2007. The Obama administration argued that the deportations were targeting criminals and that their goal was to make existing federal laws work (Slevin, 2010). In order to make those laws work, they shifted their immigration enforcement tactics away from workplace raids and increased deportations that originated in the criminal justice system.

Despite the strength that comes from their cultures of origin, in many parts of the country Mexican Americans are at risk of poverty and poor physical and mental health. They are overrepresented in the criminal justice system and typically have low levels of education, alarming school dropout rates, and high unemployment rates. Anti-immigrant attitudes have caused these community members to be fearful of using social services (Paris, Añez, Bedregal, Andrés-Hyman, & Davidson, 2005). Therefore, culturally grounded social work with Mexicans and Mexican Americans starts with the recognition and validation of the civil and human rights of all clients.

MIGRATION, EXPLOITATION, REJECTION, AND THE MODEL MINORITY: ASIAN AMERICANS

Migration has played a central role in the formation of most major American ethnic groups, including Asian Americans. Migration has been part of the human experience for millennia. It can be defined as the movement of people from one geographic location to another; it can take place within a country or across international borders. Migration can be voluntary (e.g., migration of Europeans in the nineteenth century) or involuntary (e.g., slavery and human trafficking). Migration is a complex process entailing the need to let go of a familiar environment and adjust to an unfamiliar environment. Migration processes are very diverse because they can be triggered by different factors at the sending point and are influenced by different sets of conditions at the receiving point. For example, the migration experience of a wealthy English-speaking family from Hong Kong relocating to Vancouver, Canada, is very different from the experience of a Sudanese refugee family from Darfur relocating to Minneapolis, Minnesota. These differences are often captured by terms used to describe migrants: "immigrant," "undocumented immigrant," "refugee," "asylum seeker," "permanent resident," and "naturalized citizen." These terms are imposed from the outside to describe different journeys in legal but not necessarily psychosocial terms.

In 1882 the United States passed a law that banned Asians from immigrating to the country. Although ethnic prejudice might have played a role in such an exclusionary policy, economic competition between whites and Asian Americans was more likely the major cause (Farley, 2000). Asians had been coming to the United States in debt as a result of the large amounts of money they had to pay to immigrate and were willing to work for lower wages than whites. Thus negative stereotypes of Chinese and Japanese immigrants stemmed primarily from their roles as laborers and their impact on the job market, allegedly one that drove down wages for native-born workers. The term "coolie labor" (denoting undignified work) dates from this period. The perception that Asian immigrants were taking jobs away from whites or lowering their wages created tension and fed the xenophobia of working-class whites who felt threatened by the influx of Asian immigrants. In some areas with larger Asian communities, intergroup tensions resulted in widespread violence against Asian immigrants (Anbinder, 2006).

In addition, prejudice was fueled by myths that racial mixing through intermarriage between whites and minorities resulted in the contamination of white racial purity and was therefore dangerous (Kenney, 2002). In 1880 California and other states and territories passed antimiscegenation laws prohibiting marriages between whites and individuals of other races; this was the first such law to outlaw marriages between whites and Asians (Kennedy, 2003). (The first antimiscegenation law had been passed in the colony of Maryland in 1661, but it applied only to marriages between blacks and whites.) These laws not only served to maintain group boundaries and the power and privilege of the dominant group, but also created other problems owing to exclusionary laws that made it difficult for Chinese immigrants' wives to migrate to the United States and resulted in serious gender imbalances within the Chinese community in America (Chin & Karthikeyan, 2002).

Another devastating aspect of the so-called yellow peril was the widespread fear that Chinese and Japanese immigrants were loyal only to their countries of origin and, if not stopped, would take over the United States. This social hysteria reached its height after the bombing of Pearl Harbor, when much of the Japanese American population, most of whom were American born and therefore denied the fundamental civil rights guaranteed by the U.S. Constitution, was interned. The internment experience meant that Japanese Americans had to liquidate their businesses; they lost their life savings, homes, and possessions, and lived with the knowledge that American democracy had failed to provide protection for all its citizens. (The belief that immigrants constitute a foreign peril has resurfaced recently in response to newcomers from Mexico and other countries in Latin America.)

Anti-Chinese laws, economic exploitation, and racial antagonism set up an effective exclusionary system that ensured that Chinese immigrants remained strangers in their adopted land (Takaki, 1998). Even today, certain Asian groups are victims of antagonism and are perceived to be foreigners regardless of their immigrant status or history. For example, a customer at a local store may express her surprise when the third-generation Asian American cashier responds to her in unaccented English. Seemingly innocent questions about their origins that imply that they do not belong (e.g., "And where are you from?") constantly remind Asian Americans whose families have lived in the United States for many generations that the majority culture sees them as outsiders. Those who are immigrants continue to experience hardships related to migration. Asians of lower SES often face mistreatment as they attempt to immigrate to the United States and are employed by individuals and companies that exploit their precarious financial situations. During the 1990s federal investigators found seventy-two Thai immigrants indentured illegally in Californian sweatshops—living in virtual slavery behind barbed-wire fences—while their salaries were confiscated to pay the costs of their trip to the United States (Finnigan, 1995). As recently as July 2012, temporary guest workers in a seafood processing plant were forced to work 24-hour shifts, eighty hours a week; they were barricaded behind blocked exits, and threatened with beatings or reprisals against relatives to work faster. Wal-Mart, a client to the crawfish supplier, located in Louisiana, eventually stopped using the seafood plant's products due to wage and labor violations (Greenhouse, 2012).

Recent changes in the way Asian Americans are viewed in our society demonstrate that their status is determined not only by their behaviors and achievements, but also by the dominant group's openness to and approval of them. Asian Americans are no longer perceived to be inassimilable and exotic but are now viewed as industrious and smart. Today, Asian Americans often need to cope with the stereotype of the model minority. The image of Asian Americans as a monolithic group characterized by supportive and self-reliant family ties, high educational aspirations, and personal discipline was created by a changing racial climate rather than by the inherent characteristics of this very heterogeneous group. Attitudes started to change in the 1960s as the term "Asian American" started to be used instead of "Oriental," and Asian Americans' incomes and educational attainment began to resemble those of whites (Zhou, 2004). The model minority stereotype has been exploited by political conservatives and used by policymakers who believe that nongovernmental assistance (i.e., help provided by nongovernmental organizations) is the key to helping ethnic minorities get ahead. Unfortunately, this stereotype of Asian American self-sufficiency, enterprise, and success leaves many Asians at the mercy of underfunded community assistance programs (Thrupkaew, 2002). A comprehensive review of published social work research on Chinese Americans concluded that they continue to be essentialized, otherized, and viewed in a negative light (Tsang, 2001). The stereotype not only promotes antagonism between ethnic minority groups, but also overlooks the real needs many Asian American have and makes them vulnerable to being underserved.

THE END OF RACISM?

Since the civil rights movement and the rights legislation it triggered, public opinion polls have revealed that an increasing number of people think that racism has weakened or even disappeared from U.S. society (Bonilla-Silva, 2006). When people think of racism, many think only of public expressions of extremist racist attitudes and behaviors (like the white students who hung a noose from a tree at a Louisiana high school in 2006), which have become increasingly rare; they do not think about the more subtle expressions of racism and discrimination that are still prevalent in our society. In 2009, 61 percent of whites reported that racial equality had been achieved in America, in stark comparison to the 17 percent of African Americans who endorsed the same sentiment (Bobo, 2011). The struggle led by African Americans and their allies during the second half of the twentieth century has produced significant results. In fact, society has witnessed an important reduction in personal racism (i.e., individuals overtly espousing racist and bigoted views and subscribing to stereotypes). There is, however, ample evidence that racism and the problems it engenders have not faded away. The National Opinion Research Center's General Social Survey shows that about one in six white adults still holds the opinion that laws should prohibit marriage between whites and African Americans and that whites should have the right to keep African Americans from living in their neighborhoods (Paradies, 2006). Racially prejudiced attitudes have also been shown to be a source of the opposition of a substantial number of whites to school busing (a measure implemented to create schools that are more racially integrated), bilingual education, affirmative action, government assistance to ethnic minorities, and residential integration; it also influences their views of how crime should be fought (see Bobo & Fox, 2003). Institutional racism continues to be present in the workplace and in politics, often in subtle, symbolic, and indirect ways that are transmitted during early childhood socialization (see Feagin, 2000). Even though institutional racism may be subtle, unintentional, nearly invisible, and virtually undetectable, it can be measured more by its impact than by the intentions behind it (Keleher & Johnson, 2001). One way to see institutional racism is as a barrier within organizations that prevents ethnic minority employees from reaching higher positions in the system. Within the health-care system, racism has even been found in patterns of organ donation and organ transplants. Even though African Americans are more often in need of kidney transplants, they are much less likely than whites to be referred for or receive a transplant, and they wait twice as long on waiting lists before receiving transplants (National Institutes of Health, 2006). Racial bias has been found at every step in the criminal justice decision-making process, resulting in higher rates of incarceration among ethnic and racial minority groups. One in four African American men and one in six Latino men can be expected to be incarcerated in their lifetime (Mauer, 2011). Racial bias through ethnic profiling was demonstrated in New York City's "stop and frisk" program, which gave the police wide discretion to interview and search anyone they thought was acting suspiciously. Under this policy, declared unconstitutional in 2013, more than 80 percent of individuals who were stopped and frisked were people of color (Buettner & Glaberson, 2012).

Despite the scientific evidence developed over the past century showing that race is a socially constructed concept, racism continues to pervade contemporary society, and socially constructed categories of race are still used to set up social hierarchies that affect millions of individuals' experiences and opportunities (Esposito & Murphy, 2000). Regardless of its roots, racism continues to limit the independence and freedom of America's racial and ethnic minorities, reduce their empowerment, and deny their dignity and inherent worth. Racism—whether conscious or unconscious, deliberate or unintentional—continues to be present in society. Racial and ethnic appearance has historically constituted an important line of demarcation in U.S. social, cultural, economic, and political life, and it continues to do so. Although judging people based on color lines seems like a remnant of the nation's repudiated past, contemporary studies show that African Americans and Latinos with darker skin tone face more challenges and disadvantages than those with a lighter complexion and more European facial features. Skin tone and facial features continue to predict objective quality-of-life indicators such as educational and occupational advancement, even after differences in educational and socioeconomic backgrounds are adjusted for (Herring, Keith, & Horton, 2004; Murguia & Telles, 1996; Telles & Murguia, 1990). Studies have also found that relatively darker skin tone has negative effects on self-esteem, perceived attractiveness, life satisfaction, and depression (Brown, Ward, Lightbourn, & Jackson, 1999; Klonoff & Landrine, 2000). Rather than reflecting some inherent racial quality, these disparities arise from an individual's awareness and internalization of the dominant culture's norms and beliefs, which continue to give preference to light complexions and European features (Perry, Stevens-Watkins, & Oser, 2013; Pyke, 2010).

Border vigilante movements (e.g., the Minutemen) are contemporary forms of racism that target groups whose often-imagined differences in appearance are perceived to signify much more fundamental cultural differences. For example, Mexican American families in Arizona border towns who can trace their ancestry many generations back have reported repeated incidents of harassment by the Minutemen militia (Rosas, 2006). Many members of the Minutemen and related fringe anti-immigrant organizations harass anyone around the border who "looks Mexican." The Minutemen mentality was taken farther in 2010 with the passage of Arizona state law SB-1070, whose core components the U.S. Supreme Court would later find unconstitutional. Despite the unconstitutionality of this law, the sentiment that it generated and the copycat laws that it inspired in other states, including Alabama, created tension and serious health consequences in Latino communities. By increasing fear among Latino residents, adding to their mistrust of officials, and restricting their mobility, anti-immigrant laws create barriers to health and well-being: they alter help-seeking behaviors, limit access to care, and decrease perceptions of neighborhood safety (Hardy et al., 2012).

It is important to be familiar with the history of different ethnic and racial groups: this history can often help explain status differentials that exist among individuals and groups. Social workers can become better practitioners by becoming aware of the long struggle that members of those communities have led and of their ability to endure and overcome difficult situations, both individually and collectively. Culturally grounded social work honors those struggles and encourages practitioners to partner with ethnic and racial minority communities as they overcome oppression and work toward creating a more just society.

Key Concepts

Colonialism: A system of oppression of and domination over the local population imposed by an invading outside group

Internal colonialism: Oppressive power that is exerted by the majority culture over minority groups within national borders

Genocide: The organized effort to eliminate an entire group of people

Jim Crow laws: Post–Civil War laws that provided the "separate-but-equal" legal framework for the racial discrimination against, segregation of, and denial of political, economic, educational, and social opportunities to African Americans

Annexation: The taking of an area already occupied by another group, either through military action or the invitation of residents living there

Treaty of Guadalupe Hidalgo: The treaty that ended the war between the United States and Mexico and forced Mexico to cede the territories of what is now most of the states of New Mexico, Arizona, California, Colorado, Nevada, and Utah to the United States

Chicano (Chicana): A Mexican American (male or female); a term that came out of, and often continues to signify solidarity with, the Chicano movement

Migration: The movement of people from one geographic location to another either within a country or across international borders

9
Gender

DIFFERENT SOCIETIES HAVE DIFFERENT GENDER ROLE EXPECTATIONS. Although children are taught that their genes decree whether they will grow into men or women, people are not born socially or culturally female or male. Like race and ethnicity, gender can be thought of as socially constructed. Cultures have different ways of teaching children how to be male or female based on shared norms and values. These consciously or unconsciously agreed-upon patterns of expected behavior often reinforce a dichotomous view of gender and the relative power of men and women. The belief that all individuals fall into distinct and complementary genders with natural roles (man and woman) is termed "heteronormativity," and is the dominant paradigm (Lovaas & Jenkins, 2007). The growing transgender community—a diverse group that may include the intersexed, transsexuals, gender-non-conformists, as well as certain lesbian and gay subgroups, depending on the definition to which one subscribes—is a reminder of the oppressive nature of these restrictive gender labels, yet the influence of gender roles extends to everyone. Because gender role expectations are contextual, there are great differences concerning these expectations not only between cultural groups, but also within groups. Intersectionality plays an important role in explaining some of these differences. Religion, ethnicity, and social class—among other factors—strongly influence how an individual perceives her or his identity and gender roles.

Social work and allied professionals work with individuals of different gender identities and individuals who grew up with different gender role expectations. It is important for these professionals to understand how these gender role expectations interact with other factors to influence an individual's overall identity and behavior. This chapter explores some of these issues and provides some suggestions for gender-aware social work practice.

GENDER, GENDER ROLES, AND GENDER IDENTITY

The term "gender" refers to the social and cultural patterns associated with women and men; in other words, gender defines what behaviors are expected from men and women and which behaviors are considered atypical or out of bounds. Like race, gender is not a biological category but rather a socially constructed one. In fact, one's biological sex does not have to be consistent with one's gender identity. The binary conception of gender reflects a taken-for-granted view of humans as inherently male or female by virtue of their genetic or biological makeup, despite the reality that an appreciable portion of the population has ambiguous primary or secondary sex characteristics (Ahmed, Morrison, & Hughes, 2004; Fausto-Sterling, 1993).[1] In actuality, it is primarily through social learning that individuals organize information in gendered terms (Bandura & Bussey, 2002). Ideas about distinctively feminine and masculine behavior have varied widely across cultures and throughout history.

Gender identity is learned at an early age and is institutionally enforced by family, religion, the media, and politics. Those individuals who internalize a gender identity incongruent with their genital configuration typically are subjected to severe sanctions because they do not enact gender in socially prescribed ways. The earliest emergence of gender identity is membership knowledge ("Are you a boy or a girl?"), whereas gender constancy (the idea that sex does not change over time) is achieved later. Studies of gender development provide considerable evidence that young children manifest gender preferences and gendered behavior before they develop an intrinsic sense of their gender identity, and that these preferences reflect social influences rather than an innate impulse to adopt a self-concept consistent with gender stereotypes (Bandura & Bussey, 2002). The problems and lack of acceptance encountered by girls who are labeled tomboys and boys who are labeled sissies illustrate the social sources of gender identity. Sanctions against gender nonconformity start early in a child's life. By the age of three, membership knowledge sets in motion intergroup processes that prompt children to interact mainly within same-sex groups; these interactions trigger other dynamics, including preferential treatment of the gender in-group and devaluation of the out-group (Carver, Yunger, & Perry, 2003). In many cultures, including mainstream American culture, female roles are believed to encompass nurturance and emotional expression, while male roles emphasize achievement, dominance, and self-reliance (Levant, 2011; Manion, 2003).

Both females and males develop a gender strategy, or a "plan of action through which a person tries to solve problems at hand, given cultural notions of gender at play" (Hochschild & Machung, 1989, p. 15). The kind of strategy that a

---

[1] The term "intersex" is used to refer to individuals whose sex assignment is ambiguous because they possess a mixture of male and female gonads and/or genitalia. Fausto-Sterling (1993) identifies three main types that nonetheless overlook many variations within each group: true intersex, who have both an ovary and a testis; male pseudo-intersex, who have only testes but also some female genitalia; and female pseudo-intersex, who have only ovaries but some male genitalia as well. Infants and children were frequently referred for surgery to make their sex less ambiguous from the 1960s through the 1980s, but this practice became increasingly controversial in the 1990s (Diamond, 1999; Kessler, 1997).

person chooses depends on her or his learned beliefs about womanhood and manhood. Gender ideology is rooted in early experiences and is the result of internalized messages received at home from one's family. Gender is an ongoing social creation that can go through radical changes throughout the life span (see notes from the field 9.1). Because our society views gender differences as natural, individuals rarely question the extent of these differences. In fact, males and females tend to accept such stereotypes even when their own behavior differs from them, and learn to see their behavior as anomalous if it is not congruent with the stereotypes created by society. As society's ideas about gender identity are systematically reinforced through socialization, gender can become associated with many different attributes and qualities; for example, leadership is often confused with masculinity. Such stereotypes often have a prominent role in shaping reality: the belief that men are more assertive than women results in men occupying leadership positions more often than women. Research shows that the social construction of gender reinforces power differentials between men and women and perpetuates the oppression of women (Kanter, 1977; Kidder, 2002). Traditional female roles support the norm that men are the primary breadwinners and women the caretakers. Even when women work in full-time jobs, they are often expected to care for the children, do all of the housework, coordinate social gatherings and holidays,

---

NOTES FROM THE FIELD 9.1

Life after Death

Susan, an African American woman, has recently lost her husband and is struggling to adjust to her new identity as a single woman. Born in 1938, Susan was raised with traditional gender roles and continues to adhere to those roles. She was a housewife and felt fulfilled in her role for many years. Although she is close to her three children, they live in other states. Since her husband's death, Susan finds herself wandering around the empty house unsure of how to spend her time. The social worker in the local Area Agency on Aging is working with Susan to explore her interests and talents. Susan is connected to her church and is intrigued one morning when the pastor announces that they are looking for someone to manage the development of the community garden and to be engaged in mentoring the youths in the process. Susan remembered her early years working in the fields with her parents and realized she had the knowledge and skills to make this venture a success. Susan decides to take on this leadership role and was surprised by her ability to connect with the youths and manage every aspect of the project. Susan is now embracing her shifting identity and is exploring her dormant talents and skills.

and care for their male partner. This double shift of multiple roles that women fulfill has been documented worldwide (Goñi-Legaz, Ollo-López, & Bayo-Moriones, 2010).

In many societies even the forms of language that are used deny women's importance and represent men's experiences as the norm. It is often argued by traditionalists that male generic language (such as businessman, chairman, and mankind, or the use of the word "he" to mean "he or she") is gender neutral, but researchers have demonstrated that this type of language is related to sexist attitudes (Wasserman & Weseley, 2009). One illustration is the inverse relationship between the extent that a country's language is gendered and the degree of gender equality, measured by parity for women and men in economic involvement, educational attainment, political involvement, health, and survival. Countries where the primary language is highly gendered tend to have less gender equality in these other realms, lending support to efforts like those in Norway to remove gendered language from the national lexicon (Prewitt-Freilino, Caswell, & Laakso, 2012). Thus the gender patterns of dominance and subordination that characterize sexism may be reinforced in communication. The gender power imbalance is manifested as well in conversations. Despite the stereotype that women are the talkative ones, communication researchers have shown both in experimental and real-life settings that in mixed-sex groups, men tend to initiate more conversations, monopolize conversations, and talk for the longest time (Edelsky, 1981; West & Zimmerman, 1983). Conversely, women tend to speak in a more tentative manner, adding qualifiers and other words to make their statements sound less direct and authoritative, thus conforming to gender norms (Leaper & Robnett, 2011).

SEXISM

Sexism involves the negative evaluation of an individual or group of individuals based merely on the individual's or group's membership in a particular sexual category. Sexism is the product of norms and expectations that exist in religious dogma, kinship relations, and the laws that assign women a subordinate place in society. Due to the unequal treatment of women in most societies, sexism is usually associated with the oppression of women. Both women and men, however, may be the victims of sexism. Men's organizations such as the National Organization for Changing Men and the National Congress for Men argue that the stereotypes that men are tough, unemotional, and aggressive can subject men to unfair treatment in several arenas, such as in evaluations for certain jobs, and in divorce and child custody proceedings.

Sexism is commonly defined as the subordination of a woman or group of women and the assumption of the superiority of a man or group of men based only on sex. This view of sexism attributes the oppression of women to patriarchy, which is a whole system of gender inequality that operates throughout society. Such sexism can be encountered at both an interpersonal level and an institutional level. At the interpersonal level, sexism may first be experienced within the home when children witness a gendered division of labor in the tasks performed by mothers and daughters versus fathers and sons, such as assumptions that mothers have sole responsibility for cooking, cleaning, and caring for children while husbands have ultimate authority and control over important decisions. Male chauvinist beliefs, such as the stereotype that women are less competent than men, are also expressions of sexism. Rather than regarding women as the targets of discrimination, chauvinist beliefs support the view that women actually enjoy unearned or undeserved privileges that are denied to men, such as preferential treatment in hiring practices and promotions. Such beliefs may account for the indifference or outright opposition to policies designed to improve women's status in society. Institutionalized sexism is present in all spheres of society and can be more subtle than interpersonally expressed forms of sexism. In the classroom, it exists in the form of stereotypical images in textbooks; lack of recognition of female authors, female historical figures, and women's point of view in standard curricula; teachers' tolerance for sexist remarks; and sexual harassment (Wood, 1994). Despite postfeminist narratives and attitudes that regard gender discrimination as a thing of the past, female students continue to report incidents of differential treatment in the classroom but without labeling these experiences as manifestations of sexism (Pomerantz, Ruby, & Stefanik, 2013). These types of postfeminist beliefs that communicate to women that they can be, do, and have whatever they want may leave girls without the awareness or the vocabulary to discuss sexist behavior when they do encounter it.

At work, institutionalized sexism may be either hostile or benevolent: hostile sexism is manifested through dominant paternalism and the idea that women are inferior and unable to do the same work as men, while benevolent sexism reflects the belief that women are better suited to nurturing occupations like nursing or are in need of the protection of male mentors. In addition, many organizations have a masculine culture in place, which means that power is asymmetrically distributed among men while female employees hold lower-status jobs (Bonvillain, 2001). Institutional sexism can also manifest itself in the differential treatment of men and women that results from institutional policies. Those involved in institutional sexism do not need to be prejudiced against women or even intend to be engaging in discrimination, but the effect is the same as if there were blatant discrimination (Gorman, 2005).

There are many different forms of institutionalized sexism in the workplace. They encompass a wide array of ways that men benefit from occupational and organizational privileges. These benefits are built into the system so that men reap rewards denied to women without having to actively or consciously discriminate against women (Gorman, 2005; Tomaskovic-Devey & Skaggs, 2002). These privileges become codified within workplace norms, recruitment procedures, the division of labor, and informal networks of information and decision making (Cohen, 2004; Gorman, 2005; Ortiz & Roscigno, 2009). The norms in place at the office may pressure women to seek advancement by moving into positions in which they supervise other women in clerical jobs rather than those in which they would have to supervise men who are uncomfortable with a female boss. Women who try to ascend the organizational hierarchy face elaborate screening, not just to guarantee that they meet requirements and have the right credentials, but also to determine if they are have social backgrounds and outlooks similar to those of the men already in dominant positions (Moreau, Osgood, & Halsall, 2007). Men can control the highest organizational positions by spreading word of openings and seeking nominations of promising job candidates through informal male-dominated channels and activities, such as golf games with fellow employees. This kind of gender discrimination, found world-wide (Charles & Grusky, 2004), allows men to maintain their privileges by keeping jobs requiring the highest levels of skill and offering the greatest authority, status, and remuneration among men.

The magnitude of continuing gender discrimination is suggested by the almost complete exclusion of women from the upper reaches of the workplace pyramid, among top management (Kimmel, 2000; Roth, 2006; Thompson & Sekaquaptewa, 2002). In 2013 women accounted for less than 5 percent of the CEOs in Fortune 1000 corporations, 8 percent of top earners, and 14 percent of all senior executives, despite comprising 47 percent of the total workforce (Catalyst, 2013). Even in professions dominated by female workers, like social work, men appear to have advantages over women in authority and pay. Although women make up an overwhelming proportion of the students who receive MSW degrees and are active social work practitioners, they are much less well represented among social work faculty, and men are still more likely than women to occupy the top rung of positions in social work programs as dean, directors, and chairs (Di Palma & Topper, 2001; McPhail, 2004). Salary studies have shown repeatedly that men in social work tend to make more money than their female counterparts; this is true among social work faculty, social workers employed outside academia, and even social workers in private practice (Koeske & Krowinski, 2004; McPhail, 2004). For example, despite holding 82 percent of social work positions nationally, women in the field earn 88 percent of their male counterparts' salaries (Bureau of Labor Statistics, 2013). This may be due in part to the overrepresentation of males in managerial and higher-status positions in social service agencies (Gray & Heinsch, 2009, 2010). However, these gender gaps in salary are not completely explained away when gender differences in educational degrees or academic rank or differences in setting, auspices, function, experience, and geography are taken into account (Whitaker, Weismiller, & Clark, 2006). Notes from the field 9.2 demonstrates how structures within the work place can disadvantage women and affect their earning potential.

Some people believe that the gender gap in pay has been erased as women have entered the labor force over the past few decades in rates nearing those of men. In fact, although the gap has narrowed somewhat, women's pay continues to lag behind that of men doing the same type of work (Farrell, 2005). In 2009 wages for women workers in the United States were still only 80 percent of their male counterparts (Bureau of Labor Statistics, 2010). Another myth is that barriers to women's participation in politics have been breached. The reality is that women make up 51 percent of the U.S. population but in the 113th Congress held only 20 percent of the seats in the Senate and 18 percent in the House of Representatives (Center for American Women in Politics, 2013). Although the numbers of female representatives in the U.S. Congress have been steadily increasing, they still do not mirror the demographic composition of the country.

Much of the workplace gender inequality in pay, authority, and opportunity for advancement persists as a result of gender segregation of occupations and jobs (Charles & Grusky, 2004; Huffman & Cohen, 2004). A large part of the gender gap in pay is due simply to the fact that so many women are concentrated in low-wage jobs that men rarely occupy and that offer fewer opportunities for advancement.

NOTES FROM THE FIELD 9.2

While You Were Away

Sabrina has been working for Dannica Mental Health Services for three years as an intake specialist. She just completed her MSW and is hoping to be promoted to intake coordinator when the position becomes available. Sabrina and her husband just got the exciting news that they would be expecting their first child in May. Three weeks before her due date she is told that the current intake coordinator is leaving the agency for another position. Sabrina is so excited; this is her chance to move into management. She asks the clinic's director when they will be interviewing for the position and makes it clear that she is interested in applying. She is told that they are planning on leaving the position vacant for a couple of months and will reevaluate the job description at that time, but that they will let her know when they start the job search. Sabrina has her baby and is enjoying her maternity leave. She starts to wonder about the position and why she had not been notified of its opening. She decides to call the director to ask about it and is told that the position has been filled. Sabrina is so angry and is finding it hard to be motivated to go back to work after what happened.

Some of the lowest-paying jobs in the United States are occupied almost exclusively by women; for example, women make up over 96 percent of secretaries, 92 percent of receptionists, and 98 percent of dental hygienists (Bureau of Labor Statistics, 2013). Although the divergent occupational paths of men and women reflect gender socialization that starts in childhood and continues through the school years, it also reflects our society's evaluations of work that is done by men and women. For example, jobs within companies and agencies are structured—through an elaborate system of job titles and job ladders called an internal labor market—to segregate men and women even more acutely than might result from their preexisting differences in educational and occupational choices. In the 1980s it was established that men and women are so segregated into different jobs within firms that over 80 percent of men and women in U.S. firms would have to switch job titles to make the gender composition consistent across all jobs (Bielby & Baron, 1984, 1986). There are pockets of the occupational and organizational structure where this is changing to some extent. In firms that have more female managers, there is more gender parity in lower-level positions, a dynamic that is promising given the growing number and proportion (over one-third) of female managers in the workforce (Bureau of Labor Statistics, 2013; Huffman, Cohen, & Pearlman, 2010). Nevertheless, the gender segregation of jobs at the top of the organizational hierarchy remains acute.

Occupations in which gender composition changes over time also show traces of institutionalized sexism. For example, in its early stages, computer programming was thought to be an occupation suitable for women because it resembled the relatively low-skilled and modestly paid keypunch operations that women generally performed. Only when it was recognized as a highly valuable, marketable, and financially rewarding skill did society begin to see computer programming as a job more appropriate for men. Bakers, on the other hand, have gone from being predominantly male to female, but that transition has witnessed relative declines in wages, as baking increasingly uses semi-automated or routine methods in supermarkets. Labor market studies have also shown that women pay a salary penalty for doing nurturing work that involves caretaking (e.g., nursing, elementary school teaching, and social work), work that is not highly valued by society, and that work that becomes female dominated over time loses the ability to command high status and wages (England, 1992). Similarly, even in fields once dominated by men where women have gained a stronger presence, like law and medicine, their pay still lags significantly behind that of men doing the same work (Theurl & Winner, 2011).

Such extreme gender disparities are clearly inconsistent with the widely held view that gender equality of opportunity has been achieved. Researchers have explained this as a form of modern sexism, one that is replacing the "old-fashioned" sexism that defended traditional gender roles and the unequal treatment of women and men based on gender stereotypes about competence and intelligence. Modern sexism is characterized by a denial that women are still targets of sexism; exaggeration of the extent to which women have achieved economic, political, and social equality with men; rejection of policies that aim to help women advance in the workplace and in education; and general antagonism toward women's demands for equality (Pomerantz et al., 2013; Swim, Aikin, Hall, & Hunter, 1995). People—both men and women—who hold this view perceive greater gender equality than really exists and tend to blame individual women for segregation in the workforce and in politics. Women may minimize the impact of sexism on their lives by using as their reference group women in situations similar to their own, rather than men, a strategy that may be a coping mechanism to deal with discrimination.

Women and their lower economic status are affected by sexism outside the workplace as well. For example, reforms in divorce and child custody laws are commonly thought to benefit divorced women and their children. However, research has shown that after divorce, women and their children typically suffer a serious drop in their standard of living, whereas men see an improvement even after paying alimony and child support (Feijten & Mulder, 2010; McKeever & Wolfinger, 2006; McManus & DiPrete, 2001).

Although most people believe that there is widespread support for women's rights in the United States, the fact is that the Equal Rights Amendment, which was proposed by Congress in 1972 to prohibit discrimination based on sex, was passed by only thirty-five state legislatures, three short of the required two-thirds of all the states. Sexism continues to affect women's family lives, educational and career plans, and success in the workplace and in politics (Hyde & Kling, 2001). As recently as 2012, Ellen Pao, a 43-year-old junior partner at Kleiner Perkins Caufield and Byers, filed a sex discrimination law suit alleging that she had been excluded from male-dominated social functions, had been sexually harassed by a senior partner, and was denied a performance evaluation three months before and after taking maternity leave in retaliation for reporting that she had been harassed (Kim, 2013). This high-profile case made headlines, exposing the male-dominated mentality of Silicon Valley venture capital firms; it was followed by several other sex discrimination suits filed against lower-stature firms in the industry (McBride, 2013). In 2013 the Justice Department resolved allegations that the Griffith (Indiana) Police Department had discriminated against the only female in the department, a 22-year veteran, when they passed her over and promoted to shift commander a male with less experience and lower rank. As part of the settlement she was given the position and financial compensation; in addition, the town was asked to revise their equal opportunity employment policies (U.S. Department of Justice, 2013). In the same year, in Pennsylvania, a former administrator in the state Department of Environmental Protection filed a discrimination law suit stating that she was consistently paid less than her male counterparts and was unlawfully terminated in retaliation for advocating for a higher wage and replaced by a less qualified male (Miller, 2013). Sexist discrimination has been associated with changes in adult identity and identity crises among women and can negatively affect women's physical and mental health (Anthis, 2002; Landrine, Klonoff, Gibbs, Manning, & Lund, 1995; Swim, Hyers, Cohen, & Fergusen, 2001). It may be important for social workers to consider how sexism affects a female client's sense of self and help her to reexamine her identity.

Perhaps the most extreme manifestations of sexist beliefs and patriarchal norms are domestic violence and sexual violence. Violence against woman is both a human rights issue and a public health issue. Women who have experienced violence have increased rates of mood disorders, suicide attempts, and life years lost due to disability (Rees et al., 2011). In the United States one in four women (26%) reports having experienced sexual and/or physical intimate-partner violence in her lifetime (Breiding, Black, & Ryan, 2008). Rates of intimate-partner violence in the United States are lower than in many countries. In a cross-national study, lifetime rates of intimate-partner violence ranged from 15 percent to 71 percent, with nine out of the fourteen countries studied reporting rates over 40 percent (Garcia-Moreno et al., 2006). In addition to intimate-partner violence, 11 percent, or 1.7 million women, report having been forced to have sex in their lifetime. Of these women, 60 percent reported that they were under eighteen the first time they were forced to have sex, most commonly by a nonintimate family member (Basile, Chen, Black, & Saltzman, 2007). Violence against women is a key aspect of women's gendered experience that may be important for social workers to consider in practice. Social workers can partner with women to not only help them heal from these traumatic experiences, but also to empower them to identify and address the patriarchal norms that may be undergirding these experiences.

THE WOMEN'S MOVEMENT AND FEMINISM

Feminism is the result of the various ways that women have struggled collectively in response to their specific forms of subordination. All versions or strands of feminism are grounded in the premise that differences in women's and men's positions in society are the result of social factors, and that women's experiences, ideas, and concerns are as valuable as men's and deserve the same respect. A central feature of feminism is the differences in female access to power, a power differential that is related to class, race, ethnicity, religion, sexual orientation, and ability status (Moane, 1999; Ostrove, Cole, & Olivia, 2009). In the United States, the first wave of the women's movement started in 1848 with the efforts of Elizabeth Cady Stanton and Susan B. Anthony, among others, to gain political equality for women through suffrage during their involvement in the movement to abolish slavery. Anthony focused on economic independence for women while Stanton explored the sexual emancipation of women (DuBois, 1999). During what is referred to as the first feminist wave, the domestic roles assigned to women were not challenged directly, but organizations such as the Women's Christian Temperance Union were formed to fight for child labor laws and female prisoners' rights (Wood, 1994). First-wave feminists were concerned with securing women's access to education and certain occupations such as clerical work (Cohn, 1985). First-wave feminists also worked to secure protections for women in the areas of marital property rights and child custody laws. These feminists were mainly responding to injustices that they themselves had experienced as middle-class white Christian women.

By 1960 a second feminist wave was under way, propelled in large part by developments within the civil rights and antiwar movements that revealed the need to address persisting inequities affecting women. Through her activism and now classic book, *The Feminine Mystique*, Betty Friedan (1963/2001) exercised a pivotal leadership role in shaping the modern feminist movement. Her description of the oppression of the "happy housewife" ignited a revolution that radically altered the consciousness and lives of women as well as the culture of society as a whole.

Several branches that emerged from this second wave of feminism have advanced different solutions to discrimination against women while promoting women's rights and identities within the spheres of reproduction, sexuality, living arrangements, and the larger culture. One branch, liberal feminism, has concentrated on reforms that would better integrate women into existing social, economic, and political institutions rather than working to change these institutions fundamentally. Organizations like NOW (the National Organization for Women) have pursued this agenda through antidiscrimination lawsuits, political lobbying, and educational campaigns to increase public awareness of issues affecting women, such as domestic violence. Another branch, radical feminism, in contrast, focuses on achieving fundamental change through the rejection of patriarchal institutions like marriage and emphasizes ways for women to support one another in resisting oppression in their personal lives. Radical feminists have explored female-centered redefinitions of the notion of family and new ways to conceptualize the division of labor at home and at work. Another branch, Marxist or socialist feminism, emphasizes the harmful role of capitalism in the lives of both women and men, and the way that sexism undermines the ability of the working class to address their economic exploitation. Second-wave feminism also championed issues surrounding reproductive rights, including birth control options and abortion, arguing for a woman's right to control her body (Outshoorn, 2012). The different branches of feminism have increased awareness of women's issues in general and have created new ways for women to explore the roots of oppression in their personal lives, allowing them to pursue new avenues for effecting change and to enlist new allies, including men who support the feminist movement

(Wood, 1994). Amid the successes of second-wave feminists, divisions also emerged among the different branches of feminism, and the voices of black feminists, Chicana feminists, and lesbian feminists came to the fore.

In the 1990s, amid questions about the identification of younger women with earlier feminist ideals and the cooptation and depoliticization of feminist issues, a third wave of the feminist movement emerged, one emphasizing individual rights and empowerment and focused mostly on women between the ages of fifteen and thirty. This wave emphasizes intersectionality and has sought to connect women who continue to strive for self-determination in their personal lives and local communities, raise awareness of human rights issues, and increase appreciation for the impact of race, ethnicity, religion, and class in women's lives. Despite the advances made by the three waves of feminism to date, women in the United States retain their lower status in almost all aspects of life.

According to public opinion polls, the majority of U.S. women support feminist ideas like equal pay for equal work; greater opportunities for all women regardless of race, class, or sexual orientation; and prevention of violence against women (Jennings, 2006). However, feminism is often equated erroneously with a hatred of men or estrangement from them, lesbianism, and political extremism. Some women reject feminist ideas because they hold these misconceptions and wish to avoid being associated with them, while others may think that feminism is passé or no longer necessary. In addition, it is commonly (and erroneously) assumed that all heterosexual men who support gender equality or take courses on feminism must be gay (see White, 2006). Being a gay man does not, of course, mean that one is aware or supportive of the women's movement; it appears that men who adopt less-stereotyped gender roles, however, regardless of their sexual orientation, are often strong supporters of the feminist movement (Suter & Toller, 2006).

Despite all the differing perceptions of what it means, feminism offers a much-needed perspective. One important goal of feminism is to make information available to women so they can make choices. Social work plays a key role in this regard and as a profession has embraced a feminist agenda, recognizing the unique perspectives of women and their abilities to overcome oppressive conditions. Yet much of the oppression that exists goes unidentified because it constitutes part of women's daily lives, what Slattery (2004) describes as "walking with two-pound ankle weights, impediments that are overlooked until removed" (p. 67).

SEXISM AND INTERSECTIONALITIES

One of the most important contributions of third-wave feminism has been its acknowledgement that gender cannot be considered in isolation; women experience their gender status as it intersects with their social class, race, ethnicity, nationality, immigration status, religion, and sexual orientation. Women from lower socioeconomic backgrounds, for example, face compounded disadvantages in health, education, and employment due to gender and social class inequities in society. Women in Western societies tend to live longer than men but experience more chronic illness, in part because of their longevity. However, lower-class women—those with lower education, income, and occupational status—have much higher rates of morbidity and mortality than women from the middle and upper classes, and certain groups of poor women are at especially high risk (Marmot, 2003). Some working poor women earn too much income to qualify for Medicaid and earn too little to purchase private health insurance. Therefore, these women and their children are more likely to receive care in hospital emergency rooms (because they do not have a personal physician) and often do not seek care because they lack transportation or child care. As a result, poor women give birth to more babies with health problems, and infant mortality is higher among this population. In the United States there is a nexus connecting gender, poverty, marital status, and infant and maternal health because single mothers and divorced mothers are more likely than married women and men to live in poverty (National Center for Health Statistics, 2006; Stewart, Dean, & Gregorich, 2007).

Feminist ideas and feminist organizations have helped to awaken our society to the plague of domestic violence, and third-wave feminists have pointed to ways that a woman's intersecting identities can elevate the risk that she will experience such violence. Intimate-partner violence occurs at unacceptably high rates among all ethnic and racial groups, but the risk of domestic violence is magnified for women whose ethnicity or race places them at an increased disadvantage. African Americans are three times more likely to experience mutual partner violence and Latino women are nine times more likely to experience male to female violence compared to white women (Field & Caetano, 2005). Ethnic minority women experience multiple layers of oppression and may not report intimate-partner violence in order to protect their families and their communities from stereotyping, and as a result of their distrust of the police (Sokoloff & Dupont, 2005).

Immigrant women often face a similar set of compounded disadvantages due to their cultural backgrounds, the isolation they experience following migration, and restrictions imposed by their immigrant status—a form of triple jeopardy. These disadvantages have been described as contributing to an epidemic of intimate-partner violence among immigrant women in the United States that affects from 30 to 50 percent of women immigrants from Latin America, South Asia, and Korea (Raj & Silverman, 2002). A number of factors converge to place immigrant women at special risk of domestic violence. They and their partners often have been socialized into traditional gender roles that assign men ultimate authority and power within the relationship and within the family. There may be cultural norms that approve of or tolerate men's use of physical discipline when women stray beyond the limits of their prescribed spousal and family roles. These norms, along with rejection of marital separation and divorce, are sometimes supported by male perpetrators, female victims, and their immigrant communities (Kulwicki & Miller, 1999; Morash, Bui, & Santiago, 2000). Some members of immigrant communities may not be aware that intimate-partner violence is a criminal offense in their adopted country; even if they are aware, though, they may not accept that it is a crime (Tran & Des Jardins, 2000). Not all countries offer equal legal protection from physical and sexual assault. In 127 countries, for example, marital rape is not a criminal offense (Turquet, Seck, & Azcona, 2011). Immigrant women are more vulnerable to domestic violence when they are cut off from family and friendship networks of social support, which increases their dependence on male partners and the in-laws with whom they may be living (Morash et al., 2000). When women are subjected to violence, their options for seeking information and help can be further limited by their English proficiency, immigration status and insecure economic position (Vidales, 2010). The legal status of documented immigrant women may be tied to their husbands' status, which would limit the women's options for obtaining employment. Undocumented immigrant women may justifiably fear deportation if they seek help from authorities. In 2012 this fear became a topic of wider public discussion when the U.S. House of Representatives bill reauthorizing the Violence Against Women's Act included provisions that limited protections for undocumented individuals leaving abusive relationships and pursuing prosecution (Pear, 2012). The protections that were removed in the passage of the bill were later reinstated, when the House approved the Senate's version of the bill, but the issue brought attention to the vulnerable position of immigrant victims of domestic violence.

Prompted by a feminist approach that explores how women may face oppression on many levels, practitioners are increasingly recognizing that it is necessary to move away from a culturally neutral approach to intimate-partner violence. Social workers, who often encounter clients and families ravaged by violence at home, have begun to acknowledge the importance of racial and social class awareness in the prevention and treatment of intimate-partner violence, thus confirming the need for a culturally grounded approach to social work practice (Richie, 2000).

MEN AND MASCULINITY

Robert Connell (1987) introduced the concept of hegemonic masculinity to describe the kind of masculine character that is idealized in Western cultures, an ideal that associates manhood with power and dominance, condones violence, and marginalizes many men. The notion of hegemonic masculinity recognizes the very dynamic nature of cultural ideas about gender, and the fact that gender is socially constructed in everyday life for men just as it is for women. Studies of hegemonic masculinity have emphasized the ways that economic and institutional structures affect the prevailing conception of masculinity and have recognized important variations among groups of men who adopt different forms of masculinity. The concept of hegemonic masculinity is a reminder that it is more accurate to speak of plural masculinities than of a singular masculinity.

The concept of hegemonic masculinity operates at many levels. When applied to individual men, it describes each man's quest to accumulate and display accepted cultural symbols of manhood. Looking at differences among men based on race and ethnicity, social class, ability status, and sexual orientation, hegemonic masculinity points out that not all men have equal claims to the privileges of manhood. The concept also aims to clarify the roots of gender inequalities in society by describing an overarching cultural system that gives a privileged group of men the power to maintain dominance over all women and many other men (Connell & Messerschmidt, 2005).

In the United States and many other societies, the defining cultural image of hegemonic masculinity is of men who hold power. Their manhood has been tested in a figurative or literal field of battle—the marketplace, politics, war, or sports—in which they have demonstrated the supposedly necessary masculine traits of aggression, competitiveness, strength, toughness, and success. Their predominant position is reflected in power relations, giving them the upper hand when their interests conflict with those of women and other men. Masculinity is a critical part of the system of gender politics: men who are viewed as economically successful, racially or ethnically superior, and visibly heterosexual sit at the top of a pyramid of privileges. Masculinity is thus not defined in isolation but is constructed in relation to ideas about femininities and marginalized masculinities. In this way, hegemonic masculinity is linked to all the major stratification systems of Western societies, whether economic (rich vs. poor), racial/ethnic (white vs. nonwhite), religious (Christian vs. non-Christian), gender (male vs. female), or sexual orientation (opposite sex vs. same sex). The characteristics of hegemonic masculinity can evolve over time and differ from one culture to another, and they actually describe only a small proportion of all men. Nonetheless, all men have to confront and adapt to the hegemonic version of masculinity that governs their particular society.

The cultural ideals of masculinity that men in the United States and other postindustrial societies strive to meet have been aptly summarized by Robert Brannon (1976):

◆ "No Sissy Stuff": Men do not display feminine traits like vulnerability.
◆ "Be a Big Wheel": Men become successful by acquiring power, wealth, and status.
◆ "Be a Sturdy Oak": Men control their emotions, are tough and self-reliant, and never cry.
◆ "Give 'Em Hell": Men are aggressive and enjoy taking risks.

The social implications of these rules are wide ranging. The repudiation of "sissy stuff" does not simply mean that men have to avoid acting in effeminate ways; rather, men can bolster their manhood by denigrating marginalized groups that our culture places most clearly outside the hegemonic masculine realm, in particular, all women, and men who have sex with men (MSM). Men can achieve masculinity by not being or appearing feminine or gay, and by expressing approval of homophobic and sexist ideas and behaviors, either implicitly or openly. The second rule effectively weakens the claims of most men to full-fledged masculinity, including those from the working class and men of color, who are less likely to be a "big wheel"— that is, less likely to ascend to the top ranks of organizational and political hierarchies. These groups could be seen as being consigned to pursue a form of failed masculinity. The last two rules pose difficult dilemmas for all the men who try to follow them. They urge men to lead a constricted emotional life and fear the intimacy that would provide them with needed social support while encouraging them to engage in risky behaviors that threaten their mental and physical health.

Could masculinity be hazardous to men's health? The danger lies in the health risks that are associated with aggressive and risky behaviors like drug and alcohol consumption, hazardous occupations, stress-related illnesses, and reluctance to seek preventive medical care (Hasin, Stinson, Ogburn, & Grant, 2007; Nolen-Hoeksema, 2004). Rates of accidental deaths (often alcohol related), vehicular accidents, suicides, and homicides for men are at least double those for women. Among those under age thirty, the rate of death by homicide is eight times higher for men than for women. Mortality rates due to disease are higher for males than females at every age, from conception on. In the United States, men are more likely than women to die from nine of the ten leading causes of death (diabetes is the exception). Men are almost twice as likely as women to die of heart failure, the number one killer, because they smoke more and engage in more Type A (competitive, impatient, ambitious, aggressive) and Type D (strong, silent, unemotional) behaviors (Heron, 2007). Approximately 356,598 men die of heart disease each year in the United States, and approximately 5.8 million men alive today have suffered a heart attack or chest pain (Barnett, Braham, Casper, Elmes, & Halverson, 2007). The role they are expected to perform as providers can lead men to not take time off for health care unless illness is critical and overt. Men are also more likely than women to be the perpetrators and victims of violent crimes, perpetrating 76 percent of family violence and 80 percent of nonfamily violence (Durose et al., 2005). There is some evidence, however, that the rate of male victimization in the home is underreported due to stigma and embarrassment (Drijber, Reijnders, & Ceelen, 2013). When men are victims of assault in scenarios outside of the home, they are far more likely to be assaulted by other males (Frederick, McCarthy, & Hagan, 2013). Male bodies are expected to be tough, to endure pain and abuse, and to be under the owner's complete control at all times.

Being masculine is also increasingly associated with having a very muscular body (McCreary, Saucier, & Courtenay, 2005). The belief that bigger is better—that muscular males are taken more seriously—may account for the new male syndrome of muscle dysmorphia. This disorder is characterized by excessive exercise and consumption of proteins, great attention to diet, dissatisfaction with body image, and an almost compulsive tendency to check one's body in mirrors (Clark, 2004). Adolescent boys are at particular risk because of anxiety about their stage of physical development relative to that of their peers. The cultural expectations that contribute to their feelings of dissatisfaction and inferiority are reflected in the tremendous increase in the size of male action figures over the past three decades. The 1964 original GI Joe, converted to life size, would have been a 5'10" male with a 32" waist, 44" chest, and 12" biceps, close to average proportions for American males of that time. The more recent GI Joe Extreme dolls have the equivalent of a 30" waist, 57" chest, and 27" biceps—bodily dimensions that are far larger than those of any bodybuilder in history. It may not be surprising, then, that although about 90 percent of all teenagers treated for eating disorders are female, the occurrence of eating disorders in males appears to be increasing (Cassin & von Ranson, 2005).

Cultural ideals about masculinity can also complicate intimate relationships across gender lines. Strict adherence to the rules of masculinity may undermine men's abilities to form strong and supportive ties with significant others. Notes from the field 9.3 demonstrate how a man's idea about masculinity may affect his relationship. Men's emotional lives may be stifled by socialization that tells them always to keep their emotions hidden under a shield of calmness, strength, and rationality. They may think that only women explore their inner emotional lives, and that for them to do so would be unmanly. They may approach dialogues with their spouses or romantic partners as another way to establish and protect their superior status, rather than as an opportunity to create rapport and connection. Researchers who observed couples therapy found that men commonly rely on emotionally skilled girlfriends, wives, or partners to help them sense what they are feeling and then name and interpret the feeling (Chodorow, 1978). Men may resist women's desires for more intimacy in committed relationships because they are taught to be independent and are ambivalent about taking emotional refuge or receiving comfort from another. Male emotional inexpressiveness may also be a way for men to maintain power in relationships with women by demonstrating that they are acting rationally (not emotionally). It also protects men from the exposure, shame, and loss of status that may result should they reveal their vulnerabilities.

MASCULINITIES AND INTERSECTIONALITIES

Several decades before the concept of hegemonic masculinity appeared in scholarly explorations of gender, the sociologist Erving Goffman (1963) captured

---

NOTES FROM THE FIELD 9.3

Examining the Past to Change the Future

Tom was raised believing that men should be the breadwinners and make decisions in the household, and that they were better at negotiating in business transactions. Women are delicate, sensitive, make decisions based on their emotions, and need to be protected. Tom had never really thought much about these assumptions. It was just how he believed the world worked. In June, Tom and his wife Alice decided they were going to remodel their house. Tom assumed that Alice would not be interested in selecting the contractor or negotiating the contracts. Tom was surprised and kind of irritated when Alice insisted on being present at the meetings but he let her come along. In the meeting when Alice made a comment about the price of the job Tom made eye contact with the male contractor and shook his head signaling that he should not pay attention to what his wife was saying and mentioned that they would discuss it later. Alice noticed the gesture and stopped talking. Her feelings were obviously hurt. After the meeting Tom started to think about his behavior and his frustration with his wife. He loved his wife and respected her as an intelligent and strong woman. Why would he feel the need to undermine her perspective in a meeting with another man or be irritated with her interest? He began to think about his father and how he treated his mother in similar situations. He realized that he was behaving in the same way and felt ashamed he had silenced his wife. When the time came to pick a contractor Tom asked his wife to take the lead in the negotiations over the price of the bid. This made him feel very uncomfortable but rather than silencing Alice he used the experience to examine his own beliefs about gender roles.

---

an essential aspect of the idea: "There is only one complete unblushing male in America: a young, married, White, urban, northern, heterosexual Protestant father of college education, fully employed, of good complexion, weight and height, and a recent record in sports. . . . Any male who fails to qualify in any of these ways is likely to view himself . . . as unworthy, incomplete, and inferior" (p. 128).

Hegemonic masculinity creates whole categories of marginalized men whose membership in the masculinity club is denied or who are relegated to a second-class membership; these groups include members of racial and ethnic minorities, gay and bisexual men, the elderly, the working class and the poor, and the disabled. These out-groups are seen as feminine or nonconformist, or as "failed" masculinities. Poor and working-class men may fail to live up to expectations that they be successful providers. Yet white working-class men seldom blame more-privileged upper-class white men for their plight, perhaps because they think that they deserve these privileges simply because they are men. Asian American men face stereotypes that serve to emasculate them. They are perceived as physically inferior and less attractive than men of European heritage; more polite, nurturing, and exotic; better educated; and better family men (Lu & Wong, 2013; Wong, Owen, Tran, Collins, & Higgins, 2012). Interestingly, these stereotypical views of Asian men have been found to be held by college-age women of all ethnic and racial backgrounds—including Asian American women (Espiritu, 1996). For many other men of color, economic marginalization compounds their problems of "failed" masculinity. Among Latino and African American men, the social expectations and the ethnic/cultural requirements for men may conflict. Men are "supposed" to be competitive, aggressive, and successful, but in African American and Latino cultures men must also promote the survival of the group through cooperation and place the welfare of the extended family and community above individual desires for achievement. These Latino gender roles are demonstrated in notes from the field 9.4.

Gender politics—the interpersonal power dynamics between the genders—have an added cultural dimension in relationships between men and women of color. African American men and women have been described as approaching relationships with noncomplementary gender role expectations. Because of the legacy of racial discrimination and economic marginalization of African Americans, and the resulting emasculation of African American men, African American women often have relatively high economic power compared to their male counterparts. These women may embrace stereotypical roles of expressivity, nurturance, and warmth, but reject the idea that they should be emotionally or economically dependent on men. African American men receive conflicting messages regarding their race and their gender. They may struggle with a sense of emasculation in the face of a history of racial subordination, feelings of powerlessness, and the messages they receive from society that tell them they are inferior. With fewer opportunities than white men to display a successful masculinity through dominance at work or career success, they may express their masculinity in relationships with women through sexual dominance and physical aggressiveness (DiPiero, 2002). Similar dynamics have been described in heterosexual Latino couples; these dynamics are attributed to the hypermasculinity known as machismo. However, there is disagreement about the source of the conflicts introduced by machismo. Working-class Latino males may adopt domineering and patriarchal attitudes and behaviors within their families not only or even principally for cultural reasons, but rather, like African American men, in reaction to their loss of economic status in mainstream U.S. society (Saucedo & Morales, 2010).

NOTES FROM THE FIELD 9.4

The Mothers of East Los Angeles

Lucia, a 25-year-old second-generation Mexican American, joined a group called the Mothers of East Los Angeles last summer when she heard that they were attending city council meetings to fight against the placement of a garbage dumping station in their neighborhood. Although she did not yet have children, as a woman she felt that she had a responsibility to the children in her community to make sure they have a healthy place to grow up. She loves participating because she feels like she is a part of a community and finds the women's passion infectious. However, she is struggling to understand some of the organization's decisions about its leadership structure. Despite the fact that the women are clearly the ones moving the organization's mission forward, all of the top leadership positions were occupied by men. Being from this neighborhood she understood that in the past men have been the symbolic head of the households and of many organizations, but she knows that the community and the larger society has changed. Lucia decided to talk to Maria, one of the elders in the group, about her concerns. Maria explained that the women wanted the men to be involved in the movement because they are members of their family and their community and the women knew that giving them leadership positions would engage them in the organization's activities and would make them feel respected and recognized. Maria explained that the roles that each gender plays maintain balance and makes everyone feel comfortable. She said that when deciding on the structure, the women had their eyes on the goal of creating a healthy community for the children to grow up in and that this seemed like a minor compromise that needed to be made to create a strong functioning organization that could achieve their goals. After the conversation Lucia had a renewed respect for the women in her community and her cultural heritage but still believed that her generation might be able to do it differently. (Based on Pardo, 1998).

The myriad ways that cultural ideals about gender are translated into real people's lives suggest that men are at least as diverse as women. One can argue that the concept of hegemonic masculinity fails to capture the experience even of most white men in the middle class. Hasn't popular culture become increasingly comfortable with the ideal of the sensitive man? Perhaps, but Robert Bly (1990), a leading representative of the men's movement that seeks to liberate men from oppressive socialization, has pointed out that even the expectations society has of the sensitive man can be a burden. Because of the stereotype that men are unable to express their feelings as articulately as women can, these expectations can become a source of shame for the sensitive man, another way to manifest a "failed" masculinity. Some men's movements, called mythopoetic movements, seek ways for men to (re)discover a more primeval sense of deep masculinity allegedly lost in the face of industrial society's insistence that men be competitive. The appeal of these movements, which are popular mostly among middle-class men, has been attributed to their vague suggestion that men and women are essentially different and that men are not brutish and domineering but the actual victims of hegemonic masculinity (Silliman, 2011).

THE TRANSGENDER COMMUNITY

A person's identification as male or female is established very early in life and is highly resistant to change. Most people who are born with female bodies have a female gender identity, and most individuals born with male bodies have a male gender identity. Sometimes, however, there is a conflict between physical sex and gender identity. The word "transgender" describes a growing array of people whose gender identity does not fit into a simple binary system in which genitalia dictate a clear turn down one of only two identity paths. Traditionally, the transgender community has been mistakenly grouped with the lesbian, gay, and bisexual (LGB) community. However, in reality a transgender person can be heterosexual or attracted to people of the same sex. The word "transgender" was often used early on to distinguish between gender nonconformists and lesbians or gay men, or between cross-dressers and surgically affirmed transsexuals (Wilchins, 2004). However, a much broader definition of transgenderism has since gained acceptance; this definition encompasses the experiences of all people who live outside normative sex and gender relationships, among them transsexuals, bigenders, gender radicals, cross-dressing married men, masculinized women, butch lesbians, effeminate gay men, drag queens and drag kings, gender-blenders, gender queers, two spirits, he-she's, multigendered, androgynous, and intersexual (Burdge, 2007). The terminology used by individuals in this community to self-identify are fluid and quickly evolving. One individual may prefer the term transgender while another seemingly similar person may prefer gender queer. According to this broad definition, the transgendered can include those who engage in same-sex relationships, have sex with both males and females, prefer clothes and adornments used by people of the opposite sex, or seek a new identity as members of the biologically opposite sex through surgery. Many members of the transgender community share the experiences and challenges of gay men and lesbians because they face society's negative reactions to those who have same-sex relationships. Nevertheless, these individuals may not identify themselves as gay men or lesbians, preferring an identity focused on their sense of gender identity rather than their sexual orientation. This is also the case for many members of the transgender community who have only opposite-sex relationships.

Regardless of their sexual behavior, transgender individuals often face rejection, as indicated even by the terms often used to define them: "Tellingly there is not a single word for people who don't fit gender norms that is positive, affirming, and complimentary. . . . Because all our language affords are strings of insults, it is impossible to talk about someone who is brave enough to rebel against gender stereotypes without ridiculing or humiliating them at the same time" (Wilchins, 2004, p. 38). Historically, many societies, including the United States, have considered transgenderism an aberrant form of gender confusion. From this perspective, transgenderism might be viewed technically as a problematic medical and mental health condition. The addition of "gender identity disorders" to the Diagnostic and Statistical Manual (DSM) in the 1980s codified and blatantly enforced this perception. The American Psychiatric Association removed "gender identity disorders" from the fifth edition of the DSM and added "gender dysphoria," defined as distress that arises when experiencing incongruence between gender identity and biological sex (American Psychiatric Association, 2013). Transgender advocates saw this as a large step in addressing the stigma associated with the transgender identity. Rather than pathologizing transgender individuals, the new diagnosis recognizes the alternative viewpoint that Western society considers transgenderism deviant or disordered primarily because it does not conform to the dominant culture's expectations that gender and sex be congruent and in line with prevailing gender role norms. Despite some movement toward acceptance, strongly held beliefs about gender binaries persist and implicitly denigrate individuals who deviate from these categories. Individuals whose gender is not seen as matching their sex may live in communities that provide little social, organizational, or institutional space in which to live comfortably with themselves and without fear of psychological and physical assault. As a result, some transgender individuals undergo hormone therapy and sexual reassignment surgery to change their physical sex and alleviate the emotional conflict and pain they experience owing to their unmatched anatomical sex and gender identity. Other gender nonconformists who in the past felt pressured to align themselves with conventional gender expectations are coming forward in increasing numbers in a transgender rights movement to claim their right to enact a gender identity that feels authentic to them. About one in seven cases filed with the federal Equal Employment Opportunity Commission now involves men claiming harassment by other men, mostly for perceived gender nonconformity such as transgender identities (Clair, Beatty, & MacLean, 2005). These claims are challenging society's thinking about gender-based discrimination.

Transgender identity has been approached differently in other cultures throughout history. In contrast to the dominant U.S. culture, many Native American cultures hold transgender individuals in high regard. For example, the Lakota

Winkte (from *Winyanktehca,* meaning "two-souls person") is believed to possess a special spirituality and have unique abilities to fulfill community needs. The source of these special capacities is thought to be their ability to adopt the perspective and draw on the insight of both sexes. In both Zuni and Diné (Navajo) culture there are two-spirited deities who are revered for their ability to help make peace and ensure the survival of the tribe. The Europeans who first encountered two-spirited people in the Americas recoiled at what they interpreted to be simply same-sex sexual behavior and reacted with cruel brutality. During the Spanish Conquest, two-spirited people were sometimes burned to death. The societies that embraced two-spiritism were viewed as meriting enslavement under religious law because they were assumed to demonstrate the irrationality and immorality of the people.

In contemporary society the emerging transgender community has found important allies among feminist, gay, and lesbian movements but has also raised some uneasy questions. Some feminists may be uncertain how to interpret the role of patriarchy in a female-to-male sex reassignment surgery or may question how much gender solidarity a male-to-female transsexual shares with other women (Stryker & Whittle, 2006). In the gay and lesbian activist community, the B (bisexual) and T (transgender) have been incorporated into the mission of most LGBT organizations. However, there continues to be discussion and dissension about how to prioritize and align the interests and special forms of discrimination that the many different types of transgender people face relative to each other and to gay men, lesbians, and bisexuals. For example, should the transgender movement champion the rights of the large silent majority of cross-dressers (men, often heterosexual, who dress as women but do not consider sexual reassignment) who lead lives that are more conventional? Should it focus its energy on what is probably a much smaller number of transsexuals (those who have gone through sexual reassignment or are in the process of doing so)? One interesting development that has emerged from the alliances among these movements is that as gay and lesbian organizations are increasingly emphasizing that a same-sex orientation does not dictate gender identity, the transgender movement is making the case that gender identity does not necessarily dictate sexual orientation.

As the meaning of transgenderism evolves and acceptance of transgender individuals in our society—along with the number of groups claiming an identity under that umbrella—grows, it is likely that people will increasingly identify as having a transgender identity. The number of transgender people cannot be gauged precisely and varies greatly according to different definitions. Some rough estimates place the number of transsexuals at 0.3 percent of the total U.S. population, or 697,529 individuals (Gates, 2011). In addition, even though intersexed individuals—those whose gonads, genitalia, and hormonal development are neither unambiguously male nor female—may not adopt a transgender identity, they may account for as many as 4 percent of the population, or one in every twenty-five individuals (Gough, Weyman, Alderson, Butler, & Stoner, 2008).[2] Because of the surgical difficulty of reconstructing male genitals, 90 percent of intersexed individuals undergoing surgical reassignment in infancy have been assigned female genitalia, a procedure that they may or may not be aware of as they age (Cooper, 2009). Another group that may claim membership in the U.S. transgender community—cross-dressers—has been estimated to number several million (Wilchins, 2004).

As societal and self-awareness of transgender identity grows, social workers are increasingly likely to encounter transgender clients who bring with them unique narratives and life challenges. Personal narratives and reports from therapists indicate that many, and perhaps most, transgender individuals sense some inconsistency between their bodies and their gender identity from an early age, well before puberty. They feel intense pressure from their parents, families, playmates, and teachers to conform to stereotypical gender expectations. Many develop—at least for a time—ways to pass as normatively gendered but continue to feel that they do not really fit in; at some level they may secretly hope to outgrow their nonconforming gender identity. To the extent that their gender nonconformity is on display in their behavior or personality, transgender individuals—especially effeminate boys and masculine girls—are targets for bullying and violence. The onset of puberty is often especially traumatic for transgender teens, who may feel acute anxiety or disgust at the emerging signs of their sexualized bodies (Morrow, 2004). In navigating typical adolescent development and identity struggles, transgender youths are likely to experience especially acute uncertainty and confusion about who they are. They may be unaware of the range of transgender people in society and may not understand the concept of a transgender gender identity or even have words to describe it. Contacts with physicians, counselors, therapists, and social workers may represent their first encounters with the notion of transgenderism. Unfortunately, until recently the medical profession subscribed to a highly stigmatizing disease model of transgender identity. Despite changing policies of psychiatric and psychological associations, some psychiatrists continue to view transgender youths and adults as suffering from a gender identity disorder or cross-dresser fetishism, for which they sometimes claim they can

---

[2] The rates of different forms of intersexuality vary greatly across different ethnic, racial, and geographic groupings. Roughgarden's (2004) review of the various studies concluded that true intersexes, who have both an ovary and a testis, are rare—only one in every 85,000 people worldwide. The chromosomally intersexed, individuals with chromosome configurations other than the typical XX or XY pairings, are far more common (approximately one in 1,000 people). Even more common are people who have typical sex chromosomes but other genetic variations that influence sex hormones, such as those with congenital adrenal hyperplasia or androgen insensitivity syndrome.

provide therapy (Winters, 2005). The persistence of these views within professional circles is a sobering reminder of the power of our society's negative stereotypes about transgender people.

Because their transgressions of gender role stereotypes are often quite evident, transgender individuals are especially vulnerable to blatant social rejection, public ridicule and harassment, and physical and sexual assault. As many as 60 percent of participants in studies of transgender individuals have reported physical assaults, 66 percent have reported sexual assaults, and 23 percent have reported having been victims of or witnessed sexual violence five times or more (Stotzer, 2009). More sexual assaults were reported by male-to-female individuals than by female-to-male, 69 percent versus 30 percent (Kenagy, 2005), potentially reflecting the perceived threat that male-to-female identity poses to the social construction of the hegemonic male.

The term "transphobia" has been coined to describe prejudice and discrimination against transgender individuals. Transphobia is an emotional fear of, aversion to, or sense of revulsion toward people who express an internal gender identity that does not conform to society's expectations (Hill &Willoughby, 2005). Many hate crimes commonly categorized as antigay violence actually involve transgender prejudice. As many as 62 percent of transgendered individuals have experienced gender discrimination and 83 percent have experienced verbal gender victimization (Clements-Nolle, Marx, & Katz, 2006). Brandon Teena, whose life, rape, and murder were recounted in the movie *Boys Don't Cry,* was sometimes portrayed by the media as a cross-dressing lesbian but actually had the gender expression of a male (Halberstam, 2005). The persecution and violence directed against Teena were prompted by extreme reactions to perceived transgressions of gender boundaries. Similarly, Barry Winchell, an Army private murdered on an Army base in 1999 by another soldier for allegedly being gay, was actually dating a transgender woman whom the media misidentified as a gay man (Belkin & Bateman, 2003). Incidents of gender discrimination and victimization are strongly associated with suicide attempts, an issue that is very prevalent in the transgender population (Clements-Nolle et al., 2006). While public sentiment has at times been effectively mobilized to publicize and condemn antigay violence, as in the case of the 1998 murder of Wyoming college student Matthew Shepard, violence against transgender individuals has yet to evoke similar high levels of widespread public outrage.

In addition to being aware of the extreme prejudice that transgender individuals confront daily, as well as their vulnerability to harassment and violence, social workers with transgender clients need to consider how lives that do not strictly follow polarized gender roles can be made healthy and fulfilling. The ever-present possibility of rejection for a life led openly and the need to maintain a separate secret life both create stress that may lead to depression, coping through substance use, and risk of suicide. Like some gay men and lesbians, transgender people are likely to have to navigate a coming-out process that begins with denial and ends with acceptance, a process that has been described as similar to grieving (Bockting & Coleman, 2007). A policy statement on transgender/gender identity issues put forward by the National Association of Social Workers states that social workers can support and empower transgender individuals in coming out; dealing with family, friends, and coworkers; and finding ways to face societal stigma (Lev & Moore, 2000). Although similar in some ways, the coming-out process for transgender individuals may differ from LGB experiences. When coming out, both transgender individuals and their family members must renegotiate roles based on the individual's new gender identity, which can include the use of different names and pronouns (Biblarz & Savci, 2010). Because familial relationships are often defined by gender, this process can be very challenging. Families are frequently not prepared to embrace an individual's transgender identity and often perpetuate oppression in the home (Kane, 2006).

Historically, research, assessment, and treatment in social work and allied professions have tended to pathologize transgender individuals, transsexuals, cross-dressers, and transqueers (lesbians and gay men who openly defy gender conventions) by attempting to place them in one of the two defined gender categories. Working competently with transgender individuals requires the social worker to confront socially constructed gender binaries and become more comfortable with gender ambiguity. By acknowledging gender identities outside of the dominant paradigm, social workers allow clients to be who they are without having to choose; that choice can cause a considerable amount of stress (Cooper, 2009). In line with this approach, transgender advocates are actively working to end sexual reassignment surgery for intersex infants, arguing that they should have the right to choose their gender when they are able. Social workers can acquire knowledge about the differences between sex, gender, and sexuality, which will give them more familiarity with the issues concerning transgender, queer, and intersex populations. Practitioners can learn much by simply adopting the attitude that people are who they say they are, and by accepting the identity that the client presents.

Social workers potentially play a variety of roles in the lives of transgender individuals. Social workers may provide services for transgender youths in the child welfare systems, work with families to foster a safe and supportive environment for a transitioning member, assist schools to create safe spaces for transgender youths on campus, support transgender individuals in the medical field as they go through affirmation surgery, and provide victim services for transgender individuals who have been assaulted (Burdge, 2007). Social workers are sometimes placed in the role of gatekeeper for sexual affirmation surgery, a medical procedure that may require a psychological evaluation before individuals are allowed to undergo the procedure. This role of gatekeeper places social workers in a prime position to advocate for the dignity and empowerment of transgender individuals. Social workers can also partner with the transgender community to advocate for policies that are inclusive. For example, in 2013 when a bill was introduced to the Arizona state legislature making it a crime for transgender individuals to use a bathroom other than the one designated for their sex at birth, advocates won significant modification to the bill and the eventual tabling of the issue. Social workers can also actively work to raise their awareness of transgender issues and assist transgender individuals to find supportive transgender communities.

A useful approach for social workers is to view gender overall as a multilevel system: at the individual level, it consists of identities and roles; at the mezzo level, it involves the ways in which people interact with one another and the influence of the gender composition of groups; and at the macro level, it is an influential component of cultural beliefs and societal institutions for distributing power and resources. A working understanding of the intersection of gender with race, ethnicity, sexual orientation, and social class is at the core of a culturally grounded approach to social work practice. Not only do issues of gender affect social workers' understanding of and interaction with clients, but they also affect how social workers relate to colleagues and structures within the profession. Social work is becoming increasingly female, a shift that some attribute to professional roles that align more with the traditional gender roles attributed to females (Pease, 2011). Despite the predominance of females in the field, masculine organizational structures and a technorational approach to practice remain the dominant approach, leading some to argue that men are in control of the profession. Although feminist approaches to social work practice have been advanced to curb this dynamic, a feminist-oriented curriculum needs to be cognizant of male social workers' potential feelings that they are being demonized as the so-called oppressor, creating barriers to their professional development and understanding of oppression (Hyde & Deal, 2003). The deconstruction of traditional male identities and the recognition of the inherent power associated with them may provide a path forward. Examining the restrictive effects of sexism on both women and men may limit defensive reactions to feminist inspired ideas, creating a climate where men can partner with women to address male-dominated practices within the profession. Addressing the impact of gender identity and its social construction on clients and the profession is central to culturally grounded social work practice.

Key Concepts

Gender: The culturally and socially constructed expectations of behaviors for male, female, and transgender individuals

Sexism: The subordination and oppression of women based on the assumption of the superiority of men, an assumption based solely on their biological sex

Hegemonic masculinity: The type of masculinity idealized by a particular culture—for example, the stereotypical view in the West of men as domineering, unemotional, and violent

Transgender: A spectrum of gender identities that include pre- and postoperative transgender individuals and heterosexual cross-dressers, and a growing population of people who identify as intersex or as not fitting any traditional notions of gender.

10

Sexual Orientation

TODAY, "SEXUAL ORIENTATION" IS THE WIDELY PREFERRED TERM FOR describing how people classify themselves—and others—sexually. Sexual orientation involves feelings of attraction to other people, the gender categories of the objects of people's romantic as well as erotic desires, and the models of socially prescribed sexual behaviors that individuals follow. Like ethnic and gender cultures, sexual orientation has an effect on an individual's attitudes, values, and behaviors, as well as on how that person is viewed and treated by others. It is important for social work practitioners to understand how sexual orientation can affect not only the behavior of the individual, but also how that person is treated by others, and how beliefs concerning sexual orientation can lead to prejudice, discrimination, and oppression.

DIFFERING VIEWS ON SEXUAL ORIENTATION

The categories used to describe different sexual orientations vary across cultures and across time. In the United States and other Western societies, people typically identify as being attracted to the opposite sex or the same sex and divide others into the same two categories. In other cultures, people may not make such definite or clear distinctions, approaching sexuality more as a continuum than as a dichotomy. For example, historians have documented the widespread practice of same-sex sexual behavior in classical Greece. The ancient Greeks celebrated love between men, and sex between men was often a part of men's socialization into sexuality, just as it continues to be in some contemporary Mediterranean and Latin American societies (Dode, 2004). Some, but definitely not all, of these manifestations of sexuality were rooted in what would be thought of today as romantic or erotic desire. However, ancient Greek society, and the men themselves, did not categorize individuals based on the biological sex of their sexual partners; thus same-sex sexual relations between men in ancient Greece were not thought to signify a homosexual sexual identity. Foucault (1978) argued that the notion of fundamentally different sexual orientations—marked by the appearance of the homosexual versus heterosexual dichotomy—emerged only in recent centuries.

This categorization—today referred to as sexual orientation—is, like most identity factors, socially constructed. Modern Western conceptions of sexual orientation have been shaped by political and religious ideas that enshrine heterosexuality as the preferred default option and deem all departures from that norm undesirable and deviant (Foucault, 1978; Kimmel, 1996; Naphy, 2006). Among some Native Americans, it was once acceptable for people they called two-spirited to engage in same-sex sexual relations, and at times they were expected to do so; in these cultures, religious or spiritual power often was assigned to those not following the heterosexual norm (Wald & Calhoun-Brown, 2006). However, because of colonialism and other forms of oppression such as the imposition of Christianity on Native peoples, many cultures that once embraced different manifestations of sexuality now condemn same-sex attraction (Aldrich, 2003). Nonetheless, there are signs of growing acceptance and increased understanding of same-sex attraction and bisexuality in many societies, including in the United States. The evolution of attitudes is also reflected in the rapid succession of terms that have emerged as sexual minorities have increasingly shaped the labels used to describe and define themselves. Rejecting words with negative connotations that were common in the 1950s, such as "sexual invert" or "homosexual," more recently preferred terms have attempted to reconcile the diversity and commonality of expressions of same-sex attraction and embrace all individuals who do not fit the heteronormative paradigm of the dominant society (see Wilcox, 2014, for a review of changing terminology). Wilcox points out that, although more-generic and more-encompassing terms like "queer" persist, the most commonly used and preferred labels—particularly among the younger Generation X and Millennial generations—are LGBT or LGBTQ, preserving the distinctiveness of lesbians, gay, bisexual, transgender and queer/questionning individuals but uniting them under the umbrella of their common struggles. Although it is important to remember that these terms include some transgender individuals who are sexually attracted to the opposite sex, the remainder of this chapter uses an encompassing term—LGB—to refer to people attracted to those of the same sex.

EXPLAINING SAME-SEX SEXUALITY: ESSENTIALISM AND CONSTRUCTIVISM

Western science and medicine have demonstrated an intense interest in explaining same-sex attraction that has at times bordered on obsession. Nearly a century after Freud introduced the idea that same-sex attraction results from disorders in the natural process of psychosexual development, researchers have still not arrived at a consensus regarding the nature of same-sex attraction. Although it could be argued that there is as much need for an explanation of heterosexual orientations as there is for an explanation of LGB orientations, the origins of heterosexuality have received far less attention. The Heterosexual Questionnaire (figure 10.1) was developed to make the point that heterosexual desire and behavior tend to be regarded as a norm that does not require any explanation, the assumption of heteronormativity. In contrast, the voluminous research on the origins of same-sex attraction can be divided into two main types: studies emphasizing biological factors, and those emphasizing social and contextual factors. A common theme in these studies, and their counterparts in both social science theory and popular thinking, is the debate regarding the role of choice in sexual orientation. Do people have a choice to be or not to be gay, lesbian, or bisexual? Similarly, do people make a choice to be heterosexual?

Various biological explanations for sexual orientation make an argument for an essentialist view of sexuality; that is, they approach sexuality as a product of fundamental biological and/or psychological drives that are hardwired within an individual, perhaps genetically. According to this view, same-sex attraction is the result of an unknown factor that all LGB individuals share, regardless of race, ethnicity, religion, or class. The biological approach was originally concerned with the study of hormonal levels and their influence on sexual orientation. Although some studies of hormone levels in the 1970s found differences between lesbian and heterosexual women, research that is more recent has failed to find significant hormonal differences on multiple measures (Barinaga, 1991; Berendaum & Beltz, 2011; Dancey, 1990; Downey, Ehrhardt, Schiffman, Dyrenfurth, & Becker, 1987).

Studies of twins in the early 1990s provided evidence for a possible biological basis for sexual orientation but failed to settle the matter. These studies typically estimated the rate of concordance in same-sex sexual orientations by asking gay individuals with a twin if their twins were also gay. They found that the concordance rate for identical twins, which ranged from about 25 to 50 percent, was double or more that of the rates found for fraternal twins (Bailey & Pillard, 1991; Bailey, Pillard, Neale, & Agyei, 1993; Whitam, Diamond, & Martin, 1993). A Swedish study that drew a representative population-based sample of twins from a national registry rather than by recruiting convenience samples of gay twins through gay-oriented media, as prior studies had done, also found a higher concordance rate in identical twins than in fraternal twins, although the highest rate of concordance—for male identical twins—was only 39 percent (Långström, Rahman, Carlström, & Lichtenstein, 2010). Because identical twins share the exact same genetic makeup, while fraternal twins do not, these results point to a genetic predisposition to same-sex attraction. However, while some interpret these findings as showing that genes account for as much as half of the variation in sexual orientation, it can also be argued that the social environment may be 61 percent responsible for determining sexual orientation. In recent years there has been a growing emphasis on the role of genetics in the determination of an individual's sexual orientation. The media have devoted much attention to scientists' quest to

Figure 10.1   The Heterosexual Questionnaire

This questionnaire is for self-avowed heterosexuals only. If you are not openly heterosexual, pass it on to a friend who is. Please try to answer the questions as candidly as possible.

1. What do you think caused your heterosexuality?
2. When and how did you first decide you were a heterosexual?
3. Is it possible your heterosexuality is just a phase you may grow out of?
4. Could it be that your heterosexuality stems from a neurotic fear of others of the same sex?
5. If you've never slept with a person of the same sex, how can you be sure you wouldn't prefer that?
6. To whom have you disclosed your heterosexual tendencies? How did they react?
7. Why do heterosexuals feel compelled to seduce others into their lifestyle?
8. Why do you insist on flaunting your heterosexuality? Can't you just be what you are and keep it quiet?
9. Would you want your children to be heterosexual, knowing the problems they'd face?
10. A disproportionate majority of child molesters are heterosexual men. Do you consider it safe to expose children to heterosexual male teachers, pediatricians, priests, or scoutmasters?
11. Even with all the societal support for marriage, the divorce rate is spiraling. Why are there so few stable relationships among heterosexuals?
12. Why do heterosexuals place so much emphasis on sex?
13. Considering the menace of overpopulation, how could the human race survive if everyone were heterosexual?
14. Could you trust a heterosexual therapist to be objective? Don't you fear she or he might be inclined to influence you in the direction of her or his own leanings?
15. Heterosexuals are notorious for assigning themselves and one another rigid stereotyped sex roles. Why must you cling to such unhealthy role-playing?
16. With the sexually segregated living conditions of military life, isn't heterosexuality incompatible with military service?
17. How can you enjoy an emotionally fulfilling experience with a person of the other sex when there are such vast differences between you? How can a man know what pleases a woman sexually or vice versa?
18. Shouldn't you ask your far-out straight cohorts, like skinheads and born-agains, to keep quiet? Wouldn't that improve your image?
19. Why are heterosexuals so promiscuous?

Figure 10.1 (Continued)

20. Why do you mistakenly claim that so many famous lesbian and gay people are in fact heterosexual? Is it to justify your own heterosexuality?
21. How can you hope to actualize your God-given homosexual potential if you limit yourself to exclusive, compulsive heterosexuality?
22. There seem to be very few happy heterosexuals. Techniques have been developed that might enable you to change if you really want to. After all, you never deliberately chose to be a heterosexual, did you? Have you considered aversion therapy or Heterosexuals Anonymous?

Source: Adapted from Rochlin (1992, pp. 203–204).

identify the so-called gay gene (O'Riordan, 2012). Despite the mixed nature of the evidence, some researchers now conceptualize sexual orientation as a polygenetic trait, one that is influenced by a number of genes (Brookey, 2002; Hyde, 2005).

On the other side of the debate are social environmental explanations such as social constructivist perspectives, which argue that sexual orientation is shaped by the social environment and individual choice. For example, the psychological literature about the etiology of same-sex sexual orientations once associated male same-sex attraction with emotionally absent or weak fathers. Darwinist economists have explained the rise of modern same-sex attraction in industrial societies as a product of affluence and its resultant low mortality and low fertility, which lowers social pressure to procreate. Sociologists and historians have argued that as workers moved from farms to factory jobs in the city and work life became separated from home life, men could gather more often in groups away from home, which offered opportunities for sex away from the strictures of the men's families and home towns (Giddens, 2006). It has also been theorized that newly acquired wealth in industrialized societies allowed more people to forgo marriage and having children, which permitted greater freedom for individual sexual choices (Jandt & Hundley, 2007). This sort of argument has also been used to explain the emergence of a counter reaction in the form of the strongly enforced dichotomy between heterosexuality and homosexuality that has emerged in Western societies over the past few centuries (Foucault, 1978; Levy, 2009).

An essentialist explanation for sexual orientation supports the argument for LGB normalcy—that same-sex attractions are expressions of naturally produced, innate, and immutable forces. Essentialists view a same-sex sexual orientation as a biologically driven phenomenon, rather than a choice made by the individual. At the same time, this argument could be used to support policies that would allow doctors to "prevent" same-sex attraction by altering biological or genetic processes. For example, if genetic screening could identify a fetus's future sexual orientation, expecting parents might decide to end pregnancies if they learned that their offspring were destined to be LGB or might try to modify the genetic base of the fetus's sexual orientation to satisfy their aspirations for their offspring. These and other dilemmas generated by genetic and biological research findings will continue to arise if scientists find that there is a definitive genetic basis for sexual orientation.

Research findings that provide evidence for a social or behavioral basis for same-sex attraction can be misused to argue for the sexual preference position, which maintains that same-sex attraction is a choice made by the individual. If same-sex attraction is a choice, then widespread homophobia could motivate society to implement interventions to change the sexual orientation of individuals. This position has been promoted by fringe groups that are often sponsored by religious organizations that aim at "converting" gays and lesbians to heterosexuality. Variously called conversion, reparative, and sexual reorientation therapy, these methods attempt to change gay and lesbian sexual orientations by suppressing or extinguishing same-sex desires and behaviors through the use of such techniques as behavior modification, aversion therapy, psychoanalysis, prayer, and religious counseling. These interventions have shown little evidence of lasting success (Glassgold, 2009; Maccio, 2011). Whereas no sound evidence shows that any so-called therapies to cure same-sex attraction have ever changed anyone's sexual orientation, it is clear that failed treatments like aversion therapy and even electroconvulsive shock treatment have inflicted unnecessary pain on thousands of individuals and increased their risk of anxiety, depression, and self-destructive behaviors (Glassgold, 2009).

Because of the persistence of the belief that LGB orientations are an abnormal condition that needs to be fixed or cured, it was only relatively recently that the professional community abandoned both its attempts to cure same-sex attraction and gender-nonconforming identities, discarding the disease model that underlies such efforts. It was not until 1998 that the American Psychoanalytic Association acknowledged its own history of homophobia and brought its official position on LGB orientations in line with that of the American Psychiatric Association, which had removed the term "homosexuality" from its list of diagnosable mental disorders twenty-six years earlier. The major psychiatric and psychological professional associations in the United States have also concluded that conversion therapies targeting gays and lesbians are not only ineffective, but also harmful. Same-sex attraction cannot be "cured," because it is not a disease.

THE NUMBERS GAME: SAME-SEX SEXUAL BEHAVIOR, ATTRACTION, AND IDENTITY

Alfred Kinsey's classic studies on sexuality and sexual orientation in the 1940s and 1950s were the first to muster data—rather than anecdotes—contradicting the essentialist view that sexuality is binary. Kinsey, Pomeroy, and Martin (1949) found that sexual experiences between people of the same sex varied widely in frequency and intensity, and that it was not uncommon for individuals to alternate between heterosexual and same-sex behavior. Kinsey's studies made many methodological breakthroughs by asking people direct questions and requesting detailed information about their sexual behaviors at different times over the life course. The results showed that substantial proportions of men engaged in same-sex sexual behavior for at least some part of their lives, and that the sex lives of an appreciable subgroup of these could be classified as mostly or exclusively attracted to people of the same sex. However, Kinsey's larger contributions have been overshadowed in some ways by estimates based on his work of the prevalence of same-sex attraction in the United States. Because Kinsey did not select random probability samples for his studies and relied on respondents' recall of past sexual behavior, which can be inaccurate, it now appears that he substantially overestimated the prevalence of same-sex sexual behavior (Fay, Turner, Klassen, & Gagnon, 1989). His widely cited 10 percent estimate of LGB prevalence actually reflected the proportion of men—overwhelmingly white men—who were exclusively engaging with men in their sex lives for at least a three-year period, while only 4 percent were exclusively engaging in sex with only men throughout their lives. Kinsey's figures regarding the extent of same-sex sexual behavior are considerably higher than those shown in several more-recent national population surveys, which find the proportion of the population that is mostly or exclusively engaging in same-sex sexual behavior to be something more in the range of 1 to 2.5 percent, of whom there are more gay men than lesbians (Chandra, Mosher, Copen, & Sionean, 2011; Michael, Gagnon, Laumann, & Kolata, 1994). Surveys generally find that in addition to gay men and lesbians, there are as many or even more people who are bisexual, with bisexual women outnumbering bisexual men (Gates, 2011). Together, the LGB population in the United States in 2012 was estimated to account for 3.5 percent of adults (Gates & Newport, 2013), or around 8 million individuals.

It is important to remember that Kinsey—as well as other researchers after him—investigated sexual behaviors, and not sexual orientation specifically. Nonetheless, Kinsey's studies made important contributions by showing that same-sex sexual behavior, attraction, and identity do not always go together. That is, some sexual fantasies are never acted on, and sources of sexual pleasure, desire, and excitement, upset, and guilt can change or may remain the same over a lifetime. Moreover, sexual behaviors may or may not affect whether an individual self-identifies as heterosexual, gay, lesbian, or bisexual. An individual can engage in same-sex sexual behavior without same-sex desire, as in prison (by volition or by force) and in strict traditional societies in which young men have limited sexual access to women (Bejel, 2001; Van Wormer, 1984). The evidence indicates that an even more common behavior is hidden same-sex sexual behavior among individuals who do not self-identify as LGB, which is reported frequently both by gay people who later come out and by youths who experiment with different types of sex before becoming exclusively LGB. Estimates from national surveys (National Survey of Family Growth, National Health and Nutrition Examination Surveys, National Survey of Sexual Health and Behavior, General Social Survey) of the prevalence among men of having same-sex sexual contact at some point in their lifetimes have remained very consistent for two decades at 5 to 6 percent (Chandra et al., 2011; Laumann, Gagnon, Michael, & Michaels, 1994). The comparable figures for women have ranged much more widely—from 4 to 12 percent reporting lifetime same-sex sexual contact—with the highest figures reported in more-recent surveys (Chandra et al., 2011).

A national probability sample of U.S. adults and older teens (ages fifteen to forty-four) showed that there are sizeable discrepancies in the prevalence of reports of same-sex sexual behavior, attraction, and identity, and that these vary according to gender, ethnicity, and age (Chandra et al., 2011; see figure 10.2). Both women and men were more likely to report having experienced same-sex attraction than having engaged in same-sex sexual behavior, and even smaller proportions identified themselves as "homosexual" or "bisexual." Among men, same-sex sexual behavior, same-sex attraction, and LGB identity were all more

Figure 10.2   Prevalence of Same-Sex Sexual Behavior, Desire, and Identity among U.S. Adults

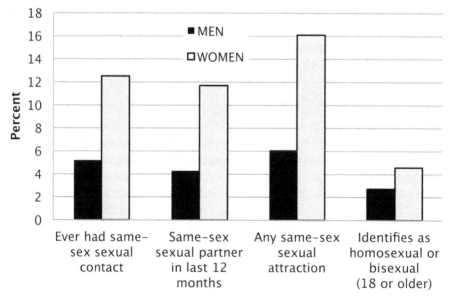

Source: Mosher, Copen, & Sionean (2011).

commonly reported by college-educated whites forty and older than by African Americans, less-educated men, and younger men. Some of these patterns were reversed for women, who were more likely to report same-sex sexual behavior if they were less educated, under thirty-five, and white rather than Latina. The differences between men and women, however, were even more striking than the differences in age, education, and ethnicity. In this survey, from 2006 to 2008, same-sex sexual behavior, attraction, and identity were more commonly reported by women than by men, reversing the direction of gender differences that were found in a representative national survey two decades earlier when men reported higher rates in all three areas (Laumann et al., 1994). To some degree the reversal can be attributed to broader definitions of same-sex sexual conduct for women in the questions that have appeared in more-recent surveys. But the trend for growing proportions of younger women to report same-sex attraction, behavior, and identity suggests that a generational change in society is under way. Another notable gender difference in the more-recent study is that discrepancies between same-sex attraction and identity were more pronounced for women than for men. Among those who said they had felt any attraction to people of the same sex, more women than men identified their sexual orientation as heterosexual (27.2% of women vs. 13.2% of men) or as bisexual (42.1% of women vs. 20.8% of men). Only 19.7 percent of the women with same-sex attraction identified as LGB, compared to almost half (47.5%) of the men (Chandra et al., 2011). These recent trends suggest that U.S. society is moving toward greater awareness and acceptance of different forms of sexual expression and more flexible categories of sexual identity.

One consistency in national surveys of sexuality over the past two decades is that nearly all those men and women who self-identify as LGB also report same-sex attraction and behavior. Although they are only a minority of all the individuals who have sex with others of the same sex at some point in their lifetimes, they are clearly the group most likely to fit widely held definitions of who is considered LGB. This core group of people who identify themselves as lesbian, gay, or bisexual, have same-sex sexual partners, and experience same-sex attraction constitutes around 3.5 percent of adult men and women in the United States. Although they comprise a somewhat larger proportion of some states (over 4% of the populations of West Coast and New England states) and smaller proportions of others (less than 3% of most Upper Plains states), the range in their representation is narrow (from 1.7% of North Dakota to 5.1% of Hawaii) (Gates & Newport, 2013). Thus, the LGB population is present throughout the nation and is less highly concentrated in particular areas than may be widely perceived. Also contrary to some stereotypes is that non-Hispanic whites, men under thirty, and those with college degrees are less likely to identify as LGB than are nonwhites, women under thirty, and the less well educated (Gates & Newport, 2012). Among the LGB population is another notable subgroup that is growing in size, and gaining increasing visibility and recognition within U.S. society and worldwide—same-sex couples and their children.

Increasingly reliable estimates of the number of households in the United States with same-sex partners have become available from the U.S. Census Bureau, including the last two decennial censuses and the annual American Community Surveys of large national samples. Pinpointing the exact number of same-sex couples is complicated due to their evolving legal status and differences among the fifty states in the available legal options, from no recognition, to domestic partnerships, civil unions, and full marriage equality. Some same-sex couples report themselves to be currently married even when they are not legally married, especially those who are older, those who have been together for many years, and those with children at home (Lofquist, 2012). What is clear from the census data, however, is that the number of same-sex couples is increasing, they are about equally divided between two-male and two-female partners, and they are concentrated in different regions and states. In 2011 the American Community Survey estimated that there were about 605,000 gay and lesbian households in the United States, which accounts for less than 1 percent (0.5%) of all households and reflected slow but steady growth from 2008 (U.S. Census Bureau, 2011). The 2010 decennial census—an enumeration of everyone living in the United States—found roughly the same number of same-sex households (about 646,000) after adjusting for probable errors in the gender of household partners (O'Connell & Feliz, 2011). The 2010 census was the first to collect data on same-sex marriage; it found that 41 percent of all same-sex couples living in states where gay marriage was legal (five states at the time the data were collected) reported being married. In contrast, 21 percent of same-sex couples living in states that did not legally recognize same-sex marriage reported being married (Lofquist, 2012). The geographic concentration of same-sex couples, whether married or unmarried partners—is displayed in figure 10.3, which shows these couples comprise a higher percentage of all households in states that have legally recognized same-sex marriages (as of 2013 the New England states, New York, Maryland, Delaware, Minnesota, Iowa, California, and Washington, as well as the District of Columbia), in addition to a number of states in the extreme southeast and west. In addition to living in a state where same-sex marriage was legal, same-sex couples were more likely to report being currently married in 2010 if they were older, if neither partner had a college degree, if they were Asian or Hispanic, and if there was a child under eighteen in their household (Lofquist, 2012).

Notably for social workers, LGB people are frequently heading families with children and facing special challenges. Over a third of LGB individuals are raising children under eighteen, including nearly half of LGB women under fifty, over a fourth of female same-sex couples, a fifth of LGB men under fifty, and over a tenth of male same-sex couples (Gates, 2013). It is estimated that as many as 6 million

Figure 10.3 Percent of U.S. Households Comprised of Same-Sex Couples in 2010

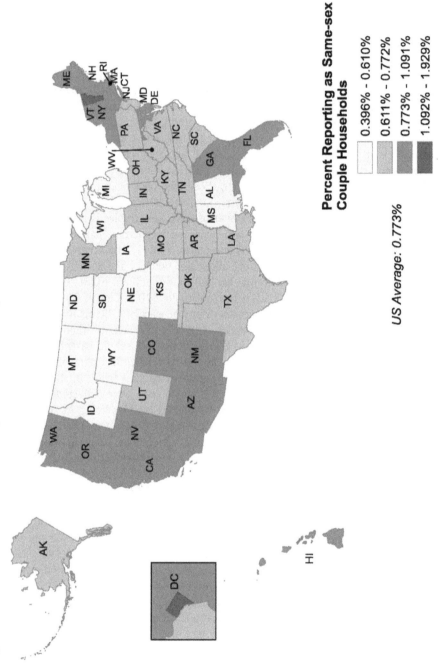

Percent Reporting as Same-sex Couple Households

0.396% - 0.610%
0.611% - 0.772%
0.773% - 1.091%
1.092% - 1.929%

US Average: 0.773%

Source: O'Connell & Feliz (2011).

people in the United States have a parent who identifies as gay, lesbian, or bisexual and that 220,000 children are being raised in households with same-sex parents (Gates, 2013). In addition to the typical challenges of parenting, many LGB families with children are often contending with social and economic disadvantages. Whether they are headed by single parents or same-sex partners, LGB households are two to three times as likely to report incomes near the poverty threshold as are non-LGB households with children. In addition, same-sex couples with children are more likely than opposite sex couples to have a nonbiological child: four times more likely to have an adopted child, and six times more likely to have a foster child (Gates, 2013). Notes from the field 10.1 illustrate one couple's decision to adopt.

As the stigma attached to any nonheterosexual sexual expression has diminished, our categories for describing sexuality are undergoing scrutiny and expanding. Scholars who are interested in how gender and sexuality are fused into identities are beginning to recognize individuals who resist sexual identity labels. Ritch Savin-Williams (2005) describes many contemporary gay teenagers as "post-gay," meaning that they have moved beyond the developmental trajectories and

---

NOTES FROM THE FIELD 10.1
Who Says We Cannot Do It?

Dominic and Jay just got married last September and were thinking about expanding their family. They have both dreamed about being parents when they were younger but had later dismissed the idea. Dominic has since seen many gay couples adopt and decided that this was something that he wanted to pursue, but Jay was not as sure. Jay wanted to be a father but was still caught in the idea that children needed to have a dad and a mom in their life to be raised "right." He knew that this was the heteronormative paradigm of dominant society but he could not shake the feeling that their child would not have a normal life by having two daddies. After extensive discussion Dominic and Jay decided they wanted to bring a child into their family and that they would be great dads. During the adoption process they encountered a lot of the same heteronormative beliefs that Jay had internalized. With the support of Dominic, every time they were questioned and forced to articulate why they would make good parents, Jay felt himself become stronger in his belief that their home and their family would be an excellent place to raise a child. The papers just went through for the adoption of a little girl and they are so excited. They have prepared the nursery and their families are throwing them a baby shower. Although it will still be three months before their daughter is born, they already feel like a family.

identity struggles that characterized the coming-out process in the latter part of the twentieth century. In the absence of the intense stigma that once surrounded identifying as LGB, these youths have greater freedom to feel, explore, describe, and act on their same-sex attractions without the need to conform to stereotypical LGB identities.

In considering the increasingly diverse ways in which people think of and describe themselves as sexual beings, practitioners need to be mindful that same-sex couples and those individuals who identify themselves as gay or lesbian represent only a portion of those who may be engaging in same-sex sexual behavior or navigating complex or conflicting sexual desires. Discrepancies in reports of same-sex sexual behavior, desire, and identity underscore the need to recognize that sexual orientation requires an understanding of oneself and the choices one perceives as being available for expressing one's sexuality. Individuals who engage in same-sex sexual behaviors may not think of themselves as being gay, lesbian, or bisexual. They may even reject all sexual identity labels as irrelevant or too constraining. The social context and the norms and values present in the environment also have a strong influence on this kind of self-identification.

Stigma theory suggests that sexual minorities are likely to avoid disclosure of their sexual identity when they expect to be viewed unfavorably by it. It is more than a matter of social embarrassment and gossip. When sexual minorities disclose their sexual orientation, they are at appreciable risk of becoming the victims of hate crimes, which tend to be underreported and often result in prolonged psychological distress (Herek, 2009a; Herek et al., 2002). In certain workplaces, gays and lesbians live in constant fear of being outed and losing their jobs as a result. Because discrimination based on sexual orientation is not specifically prohibited in many states and localities, such fears are realistic and can be a constant source of stress.

INTERSECTIONALITIES: GAY MEN OF COLOR

Sexual minorities experience proportionally more negative life events than heterosexuals because they often have to cope with many stressors, such as sexism, racism, homophobia, and heterosexism, simultaneously. African American gay and bisexual males, for example, face the challenges of managing a dual minority status (Crawford, Allison, Zamboni, & Soto, 2002). Facing the prospect of disapproval or condemnation, some African American gay and bisexual men feel compelled to conceal their sexual orientation in order to gain acceptance, both within the African American community and in the larger society. Always aware of the possible negative reaction if they reveal their sexual orientation or behavior to their own communities, they often feel they must live a dual existence, presenting an image as exclusively heterosexual men to the outside world. These challenges confront gay and lesbian people from all ethnic communities because homophobia exists in all ethnic groups. However, there is a distinctive set of pressures faced by gay and bisexual men from African American communities. The legacy of slavery and continuing oppression of African Americans may be experienced by African American men as a form of emasculation that needs to be countered with strong expressions of heterosexual masculinity, or hypermasculinity (Crichlow, 2004). When it is associated with effeminacy, a same-sex sexual orientation may be seen as contributing to African American men's relative lack of power and status in society (Lemelle & Battle, 2004). Black nationalist ideology at times has promoted hypermasculinity and rejection of male same-sex attraction as a way to protect the African American community from racism and exploitation (Ward, 2005). Another potent force is the highly influential role of black churches in the African American community, many of which subscribe to conservative religious ideas that condemn same-sex sexual activity as sinful and unnatural (Griffin, 2000; Hill, 2013).

These converging cultural and institutional homophobic pressures present difficult choices for African Americans who are gay and bisexual and restrict their ability to live open and authentic lives. Some of them seek European American gay communities in which to explore and express their sexual identities, but they do not always find complete acceptance. Gay and lesbian African Americans have reported encountering racial discrimination in gay and lesbian bars and clubs and at social gatherings (McKeown, Nelson, Anderson, Low, & Elford, 2010). The lack of a sense of belonging and of a sense of recognition and support from within the community of origin or the larger gay community can affect the well-being of African American gay and lesbian individuals, as well as the larger communities to which they belong.

Considerable media attention has been given to a so-called down low subculture rooted at the intersection of sexual orientation and ethnic identity. The phrase "on the down low" is used to describe African American men who have sex with other men but lead lives as heterosexuals in public. Their need to hide their attraction to men is shaped by cultural forces in their communities that contribute to internalized homophobia, the acceptance of homophobia by a lesbian or a gay man, and its incorporation into her or his self-concept. Internalized homophobia has been linked to substance abuse, self-destructive behavior, and feelings of powerlessness (Igartua, Gill, & Montoro, 2003). The challenge is not one of simply emerging from a figurative closet: some of these men are torn between their true feelings and desires and cultural ideals of masculinity—their roles as procreators and responsible fathers—and the denigration of same-sex sexuality as a perversion that belongs to white culture and has no place in African American communities. The secrecy embraced by these men may create serious health risks for them and their sexual partners—both male and female. Their closeted existence and the stigmatization of same-sex behavior in their communities tend to block these men's access to HIV/AIDS-related information and services that are more widely available to white middle-class gay men. In addition, cultural attitudes sometimes discourage condom use. The down low phenomenon is suspected of contributing to the developing crisis of HIV infection among African Americans, who now make up half of all new HIV cases in the United States. But it is likely that the very rapid increases in HIV infection rates among African American women are largely due to having sex with heterosexual black men who have multiple sex partners—not the very much smaller number of bisexual black men on the down low (Watkins-Hayes, Pittman-Gay, & Beaman, 2012).

The precise role of the down low phenomenon in the spread of HIV is unknown due to the stigma surrounding men who have sex with men. It is important to remember that the down low phenomenon occurs in all ethnic and racial groups, not just among African Americans (Boykin, 2005). Some women do become infected by bisexual men, but the inherent difficulty of identifying men who are on the down low means that little is known with certainty about their relative HIV risk level, tendency to engage in risky sexual behavior, and role in HIV transmission. There is evidence that openly gay African American men are more likely to practice safe sex than African American men on the down low (CDC, 2003), and recent studies suggest that the down low identity is not always associated with more risky sex behaviors (Bond et al., 2009). Mixed and uncertain findings point to the need to avoid stereotypes and conduct more research while also approaching HIV as a public health and social issue in the African American community. Effective community-level HIV/STI prevention programs should be targeted toward all black men and women, rather than singling out a specific group.

The down low phenomenon has been reported to be as common among Latino men as among African American men (Boykin, 2005). Latino men who are sexually attracted to men must contend with similar cultural and religious pressures to deny or hide their sexual identities. They face not only the church's refusal to accept gay and bisexual identities, but also beliefs in Latino cultures that men's identity is closely tied to their privilege of giving life to many children (Abalos, 2002; Heatherington & Lavner, 2008). The concept of machismo refers to the ideal of what it means to be a man in Latino culture: that is, chivalrous and protective of kin, but also controlling, possessive, sexist, and domineering, at times. Its female counterpart, *marianismo,* describes the virtuous, self-sacrificing image (associated with the Virgin Mary) of Latinas, as well as a sense of powerlessness and resignation in the face of sexist oppression. Latino gays and lesbians may experience conflict between these gender roles and their sexual identities. Because machismo focuses men's behaviors on penetrative sexual practices, sex without penetration is not considered to be sex by large sectors of Latino communities (Diaz, 1997; Lo, Reisen, Poppen, Bianchi, & Zea, 2011). Some Latino men may thus engage in same-sex sexual behavior without feeling that such behavior conflicts with their heterosexual identity. At the same time, cultural perceptions and internalized stereotypes about low sexual control among gays can result in unprotected sex and an increased risk of HIV infection among this population (Jarama, Kennamer, Poppen, Hendricks, & Bradford, 2005). Because of the shame they often feel, Latino gay men may tend not to make an effort to learn about prevention strategies and delay seeking medical help as the HIV/AIDS epidemic within their communities spreads (Ramirez-Valles, Fergus, Reisen, Poppen, & Zea, 2005).

A recurring theme in the narratives told by gay men and lesbians from ethnic minority communities is that the intersection of their ethnic identities and their sexual orientations often makes their experiences quite different from those of white gays and lesbians. Social movements advocating recognition of the rights of gays and lesbians have rapidly spread from community to community and from nation to nation. The result is that the idea of a distinctive gay identity and gay community is rapidly being adopted around the globe (Grewal & Kaplan, 2001). The identity that is often believed to represent and be embraced by all gays and lesbians is that of a white middle-class male gay culture. For example, because the much-emphasized coming-out process—which may be less common among ethnic minorities than among whites—implies both an acceptance and an assertion of one's sexual identity, for some it may create conflicts over the priorities given to their intersecting identities. For members of ethnic minority communities, asserting a gay identity can be especially stressful if it carries the risk of rejection by the ethnic group, the place in which they have found refuge from the racism or ethnocentrism of the uncomprehending or hostile mainstream.

These examples of incompatible cultural pressures on African American and Latino gay men show how historical prejudices toward gays and lesbians can be perpetuated by a culture. Sometimes these pressures are deeply rooted in polarized ideas about gender roles or a culture's historical alignment with religions that condemn homosexuality. Rather than coming out in a dramatic way to friends and family, gay men and lesbians may find acceptance by some cultures in a more tacit manner. For example, cultural notions of family may be flexible enough to include gay and lesbian members and their partners around the table while maintaining taboos against speaking of gay identities, a family version of "Don't ask, don't tell." Cultures may even lack adequate or appropriate language for describing gay life and identity. That is, members of ethnic minority cultures—both gay and lesbian individuals and their families and friends—may be reluctant to use their own culture's derogatory vocabulary for gays and lesbians but also feel uncomfortable with the language of identity preferred by the white gay and lesbian community. This kind of communication blockage leads to frustrations and misunderstandings.

Therefore, it is important for social workers working with gays and lesbians from ethnic minority communities to respect the ways that these individuals decide to handle their intersecting identities. It would be hasty to assume that those who choose to give priority to ethnic identity and community solidarity over the full disclosure of their sexual orientation are in denial of their gay or lesbian identity or are showing symptoms of emotional dysfunction. Some families may employ a dual approach to relating to a gay or lesbian child, disclosing more and showing greater acceptance or tolerance at home than in public. Although these differences in treatment may be stressful and seem glaringly inconsistent, what appears to be denial in front of the community and more extended family may reflect a desire to protect a lesbian or gay family member from rejection rather than a conscious attempt to oppress her or him.

HETEROSEXISM, HOMOPHOBIA, AND SEXUAL PREJUDICE

The term "homophobia" was coined by George Weinberg in the early 1970s. Defined as both an attitude and a disease (Victoroff, 2006), homophobia is the "fear, disgust, anger, discomfort, and aversion that individuals experience in dealing with gay people" (Hudson & Ricketts, 1980, p. 358). Such prejudice against LGBs is generally expressed more openly and is seen as more acceptable than other kinds of prejudice, such as racist attitudes (Farley, 2000). Rather than focus on homophobia as an individual expression, Gregory Herek (2009a) has advocated for the use of the term "sexual prejudice," linking it to the pervasive and multilayered social stigma that is directed toward sexual minorities. This more nuanced concept distinguishes several undesirable effects of sexual prejudice against LGB individuals: enacted stigma, felt stigma, and internalized stigma. Anti-gay stigma continues to be frequently enacted through hostile comments, epithets, ostracism, discrimination, and even violence (Herek, 2009b). The sexual stigma felt or anticipated by gay men and lesbians can lead them to alter their behavior to avoid being the target of anti-gay comments or actions, thereby limiting their life choices, impairing their performance, and increasing psychological distress. When sexual stigma is internalized, gay and lesbian individuals incorporate derogatory societal attitudes toward homosexuality into their own self-concept, rejecting or negatively evaluating their same-sex sexual desires, sometimes with undesirable effects on their physical and mental health (Herek & Garnets, 2007).

In a society where openly gay and lesbian individuals appear on television and cross our paths every day on the street, the continued presence of homophobia and sexual stigma may be difficult for some to grasp. Only fifty years ago, open displays of same-sex sexuality were likely to land a person in jail. In the 1950s police raided gay bars routinely and arrested their customers; even a group meeting of gay men was illegal under the antivice statutes of the time. In 1953 President Eisenhower declared what he called sexual perversion (i.e., same-sex sexual behavior) to be a national security risk. Homosexuals were prohibited from holding government jobs and were banned from licensing for a wide variety of professions (including teaching, law, and medicine). By the 1960s, Americans rated homosexuals as more harmful to the country than any other group except Communists and atheists (Lewis & Rogers, 1999). Although the official policy of "don't ask don't tell" has been overturned, and LGB men and women are free to serve openly in the military, the culture in the military has been slow to change (Burks, 2011). In notes from the field 10.2 Andrew decides to come out in the military.

The climate has clearly changed in dramatic ways. Today, public expression of anti-gay intolerance is more likely to be condemned than sanctioned by the media and important social institutions. When a California teen sued his high school for the right to wear a t-shirt with an antigay biblical quotation, the school defended its ban on such displays as fulfilling the school's legal responsibility to

---

NOTES FROM THE FIELD 10.2
Being a Gay Man in the Military

Andrew joined the military right out of high school. He was not successful in school academically and felt he really did not have any other career options. His family could not afford to pay for college and he really wasn't that interested in attending college at that point. Andrew loved being in the Army. He liked the physical training, the sense of brotherhood, and the discipline. However, Andrew did not feel like he could be honest about his sexual orientation. Despite the fact that President Obama had ended the policy of "don't ask don't tell" in the military, the culture of the military clearly discouraged and stigmatized homosexuality. Andrew is tall, physically fit, strong, good with people, and a natural leader. He is not afraid to defy and fight against stereotypes about gay men; on the other hand, he fits many stereotypes of military men. Andrew kept his sexuality a secret for two years but finally the stress of worrying about getting caught became too much: while on leave he decided that he was going to come out in the military as much for himself as for every other gay man that felt silenced by the military culture. He came out to his sergeant first who was open and affirming but initially discouraged Andrew from telling the rest of his squad. Andrew respected his sergeant's decision and returned to regular duty. After discussing it with his superiors the sergeant decided that the squad should know. In a squad meeting Andrew was given the floor and he let his fellow soldiers know that he was gay. To his surprise, the announcement was uneventful with the squad; his buddies told him that they respected him as a soldier and that they were honored to serve with him.

protect all youths from a hostile environment, a defense that was upheld in federal court in 2006. A federal judge in Idaho ruled in 2004 that Hewlett-Packard was justified in firing an employee who posted antigay verses from the Bible at his desk in view of other employees, citing the company's need to attract a diverse workforce. In the ten years after Massachusetts became the first state to extend the right to legally marry to same-sex couples in 2003, more than a third of the states and the District of Columbia have legalized same-sex marriage. In a groundbreaking ruling in 2013, the Supreme Court struck down the Defense of Marriage Act (DOMA) as unconstitutional. DOMA had been passed by Congress in 1996 to restrict federal recognition of marriages to those between one man and one woman. By overturning DOMA, more than one thousand federal rules governing the rights of married people in pension, taxation, inheritance, health, education, immigration, and other matters will become applicable to same-sex couples who have been legally married. These cases show how much society has changed to extend basic rights, recognition, and protections to gays and lesbians; at the same time, the thirty-two states that have enacted constitutional bans on same-sex marriage also reveals how much prejudice against LGB people continues to be openly expressed by some segments of the population.

Although U.S. public opinion has evolved to the point where the majority no longer supports antigay discrimination in politics, housing, and jobs, there is still widespread significant opposition on moral grounds to full acceptance of same-sex sexuality in our culture (Loftus, 2001). Nearly half of U.S. survey respondents continue to express the opinion that homosexual sex "is just plain wrong" or "disgusting" (Herek, 2002). Although the proportion of U.S. adults who think same-sex sexual relations are "not wrong at all" has increased dramatically in two decades, from 12 percent in 1990 to 41 percent in 2010, an even larger proportion—44 percent—of adults in 2010 still felt that same-sex sex was "always wrong" (Smith, 2011). These negative attitudes are more widely held toward gay men than toward lesbians, and such disapproval is more often voiced by heterosexual men than heterosexual women, and by older people and those individuals with less education (Garnets & Kimmel, 2003; Herek & Glunt, 1993; Loftus, 2001). Anti-LGB prejudices are manifested in behavior as well as in attitudes. Over half of a national probability sample of LGB adults reported experiencing verbal harassment, and one in ten reported employment or housing discrimination based on their sexual orientation (Herek, 2009b).

Anti-LGB prejudice is rooted in the persisting view that same-sex sexuality is abnormal, an empirically unsound view that has seriously negative consequences for gays and lesbians. Society's view of same-sex sexuality has been influenced by dichotomies defining what is natural and unnatural, and what is moral and immoral, based primarily on fundamentalist religious beliefs. Some mainstream Christian denominations, for example, continue to treat gays and lesbians as errant sinners who can remain in the church only if they refrain from the "intrinsic moral evil" of same-sex sexual behavior. Such sentiments are conveyed in religious sayings such as, "The church loves the sinner but not the sin." Religious gays and lesbians face challenges due to biases against religion that can emerge within some segments of the LGB community in reaction to experiences of oppression in a religious context or in the name of religion. This conflict makes it difficult for some to reconcile their religious selves with their sexual orientation. A Jewish lesbian reported feeling rejected in her religious community because of her sexual orientation and rejected in her LGB community because she practiced Judaism (Abes, 2011). Some Christian denominations and most branches of non-Orthodox Judaism are, however, fully welcoming and affirming communities that provide deep reservoirs of solace and social support to their gay and lesbian members. The same Jewish woman who reported feeling rejected by some members of her community due to her lesbian identity also reported feeling a deep sense of belonging in the Jewish community and the ability to find the space for her two identities to coexist.

Societal rejection of same-sex sexuality facilitates the privileging of the members of another group—heterosexuals. Heterosexism pervades our society at all institutional levels and conveys the message that there is a hierarchy of sexuality in which heterosexuality is the ideal, and same-sex sexuality a poor, if not unacceptable, second choice. Heterosexuals are assumed to have an automatic right to live their lives openly in all public spaces, while LGB individuals are expected to live in silence and obscurity. This expectation is reflected in commonly held opinions like, "I don't have a problem with gays and lesbians as long as they don't flaunt it." In practice, these opinions often mean simply that people should not be openly gay. In light of such prejudices, gay rights organizations sometimes attempt to use straight-appearing spokespeople, which has led to observations that gays have won the right to be gay, but only as long as they don't look or act gay (Clarkson, 2005).

Some scholars have argued that homophobia has its roots in sexism (see Appleby, 2001) and others have asserted that homophobia is the driving force behind sexism, heterosexism, and racism (see Connell, 1990). Clearly, these claims are connected on many levels. Like other forms of oppression, homophobia is used to impose control over others through an existing or perceived power differential. Being a "real" man is often defined as the opposite of being feminine, or as not being gay or weak (Falomir-Pichastor & Mugny, 2009). Boys are taught that exaggerated masculinity can dispel perceptions that they are unmanly or, worse, gay. One way of preventing such perceptions is to engage in sexist behavior by putting women down, attempting to exclude them from public and occupational spheres, and treating them as objects for sexual predation. In addition, exaggerated masculinity is often expressed through the perpetration of violence against members of ethnic and racial minority groups and sexual minorities.

Gay men are thus defined as the cultural embodiment of what some call non-men, un-masculine sissies, and unnatural sexual inverts. Same-sex sexuality represents a major detour from the path to culturally ideal masculinity and is associated with many aspects of femininity that are often viewed as inferior or undesirable. Just as women are often stereotyped as sex objects, gay men and lesbians are often perceived almost exclusively in terms of their sexuality. As was suggested in the previous chapter, LGB individuals lead the cast of characters whose denigration has helped support heterosexual men's claim to a privileged place in the system of hegemonic masculinity. This may explain why heterosexual men condemn same-sex sexuality more strongly than heterosexual women do, and why they are often especially disapproving of sex between men. Straight men may feel threatened because they view gay men as representing sexual inverts whose behavior models that expected of women; they may also feel the need to distance themselves from the same-sex sexual desires they themselves experience but fear will stigmatize them. Even within the LGB community, traditional gender roles can emerge. Lesbian women have reported feeling isolated in male-dominated LGB activist organizations, observing that remnants of patriarchy persist in those environments and operate to silence women' voices (Shapiro, Rios, & Stewart, 2010).

Unfortunately, homophobic views start forming early in life, in elementary school. By the fourth grade, children have begun using homophobic labels such as "fag" and "queer" as insults for boys they see as not conforming to gender stereotypes (Barrie & Luria, 2004). One study in a school in New York found that 94 percent of the students surveyed reported hearing antigay epithets in school either "frequently" or "sometimes," and that sexual harassment was rarely confronted by school officials (Peters, 2003). Because of such harassment, the targeted students learn to internalize this homophobia, which places them at high risk for suicide, substance abuse, and sexual risk taking (Savin-Williams & Ream, 2003). Homophobia also results in violent attacks against gay men and lesbians (Chapell et al., 2004). The hostility toward same-sex sexuality that exists in our society also serves to keep a lid of secrecy on experimentation with same-sex sexual behavior, which is quite common among all youths, including those who eventually become exclusively heterosexual (Barrie & Luria, 2004). Moreover, the view that same-sex sexuality is abnormal is perpetuated by sex education programs in schools, in which LGB identity and behavior are either omitted or talked about in a negative manner (Sears, 2005).

Because everyone deserves to belong—to be seen as normal—the privileges that are granted to heterosexuals should be given to everyone. Yet lesbians and gays in many parts of the country continue to be denied the fundamental right to marry and bring up or adopt children. Many people believe that members of these groups are unable to raise children without causing them irreparable damage. However, studies of children raised by gay single parents and gay couples have shown that the children are no more or less likely to be gay themselves, nor do they have unusual gender identity or sexual orientation issues (Patterson, 2009). Moreover, studies using large representative samples have failed to detect any significant differences between teens living with gay parents and those living with straight parents on measures of psychological well-being, academic achievement, parent-child closeness, peer support, peer victimization, involvement in romantic relationships, initiation of sexual intercourse, substance use, and delinquency (Wainright, Russell, & Patterson, 2004; Wainright & Patterson, 2006, 2008). Similarly, studies of the younger children of gay and lesbian parents have found their psychological, social, and academic adjustment is comparable to children raised by heterosexual parents (Bos, Gartrell, & Van Gelderen, 2013).

However, there are times when social workers may need to help gay and lesbian parents and their children contend with the particular stressors they face due to homophobia, sexual prejudice, and stigma. Close to half of the children of lesbian couples report exposure to homophobic or discriminatory experiences from peers or teachers because of their parents' sexual orientation (Gartrell, Deck, Rodas, Peyser, & Banks, 2005). At more severe levels, these stigmatizing experiences of being excluded by peers or a target of gossip may increase hyperactivity in boys and lower self-esteem in the girls (Bos & Van Balen, 2008). In addition, social stigma can lead the children of gay and lesbian parents to fear rejection, and avoid discussing their families or bringing their friends home (Robitaille & Saint-Jacques, 2009). If their parents are experiencing internalized homophobia, the children may face intense conflicting pressures—to keep the parents' sexual orientation a secret and protect their parents from knowing about the homophobic incidents they may be exposed to (Fairtlough, 2008). One way of addressing these family dynamics is to ensure the children have greater contact with other children of gay and lesbian parents; by so doing, the negative effects of stigmatization appear to be reduced (Bos & Van Balen, 2008).

GAY AND LESBIAN RIGHTS MOVEMENTS

Throughout history, gay men and lesbians have struggled to gain societal, legal, cultural, and religious acceptance; have challenged antigay prejudice and discrimination; and have worked to gain legal rights and protections. In the twentieth century, these efforts began to take the form of organized large-scale social movements, starting after World War II with the Homophile movement, which emphasized love as the basis for same-sex sexuality; the gay liberation and gay and lesbian rights movements of the 1960s and 1970s; and the more recent lesbian feminist, queer, and transgender movements. These movements have varied in their specific aims and tactics, but they have all pursued the ultimate goal of achieving social equality for LGB individuals.

The impetus for these movements has been the humiliation, discrimination, and violence that gays and lesbians suffer because of their sexual orientation. This population has historically been afforded little protection under the law and has even suffered persecution and harassment from those whose job it is to protect them. Throughout much of the early twentieth century, gay bars and clubs were typically denied liquor licenses, so that they were forced to sell liquor illegally. This made them vulnerable to sometimes violent raids by police, after which the names of their patrons were often published in community newspapers. Although the gay liberation movement was already under way in 1969, it is often dated as starting with protests that broke out that year after police raids at the Stonewall Inn in New York City's Greenwich Village, when gay, lesbian, and transgender patrons decided that they were no longer willing to tolerate police harassment.

Following Stonewall, many local, and a handful of national, gay and lesbian liberation groups were formed; these often adopted the word "gay" to signify both members' positive view of their nonheterosexual sexualities and their desire to transcend fixed heterosexual and homosexual dichotomies. These movements were contemporary with other movements of the 1960s and early 1970s, including the black, Chicano, and women's liberation movements and sometimes pursued alliances with them, with limited success. They utilized some of the same ideology and tactics of these other movements; for example, the emphasis on "gay pride" was modeled on the "Black is beautiful" movement. By the mid-1970s, gay and lesbian movements had refocused on the goal of gaining recognition for gays and lesbians as a minority group and obtaining civil rights similar to those being sought by women and ethnic and racial minorities, and had established the rainbow flag as the symbol of the ideal of equal rights for people of all sexual orientations.

From the beginning, gay and lesbian groups faced internal challenges that shaped their future, questions about membership, goals, and tactics and spurred the creation of separate groups. Distinctive groups promoting lesbian feminism and challenging the dominance of men in the gay liberation movement emerged in the mid-1970s; these groups focused on the logical implications of feminism for lesbians and for all women rather than focusing exclusively on rights for sexual minorities. The gay rights movement was (and still is) criticized for being predominantly male, white, and middle class, and as such lacking adequate representation of ethnic minorities, women, and the working class. For example, the concept of coming out of the closet is based on a white middle-class viewpoint that emphasizes the importance of establishing an autonomous individual gay identity and often does not appeal to members of collectivistic ethnic cultures.

External challenges, most notably the arrival of AIDS in the early 1980s, led to the emergence of gay and lesbian groups that employed militant activism to respond to the health crisis, such as ACT-UP and Queer Nation. Transgender movements of the 1990s presented additional challenges for gay rights groups concerning their identity and membership, because these movements refocused attention on discrimination based on gender nonconformity rather than sexual orientation. By the end of the 1990s, however, renewed efforts by gay rights groups to build alliances and promote awareness of common concerns found expression in the adoption of acronyms like LGBT, LGBTQ, and LGBTI (lesbian, gay, bisexual, transgender, and intersex) that are inclusive of transgender, questioning, and intersex individuals.

As organizations striving for gay and lesbian liberation have matured over the years, differences in goals and tactics have emerged. There is neither consensus on the key items on the agenda for change nor agreement on priorities and the best strategies to attain them. For example, while initiatives at the state and federal levels to both ban and legalize gay marriage have captured the political and media spotlights, the legitimization of gay marriage is not the primary objective of many gay and lesbian organizations. Indeed, some criticize the pursuit of gay marriage as an inappropriate attempt to imitate heterosexual models defining relationships and families (Josephson, 2005). Others argue that the most important objective of these legalization efforts is to gain the same rights that heterosexuals have regarding inheritance, adoption, medical decisions, Social Security, and spousal benefits, not to mimic a heterosexual (patriarchal) way of organizing the relationship of two people who love each other.

Unfortunately, there remains widespread misunderstanding about the meaning and goals of the gay liberation movement. When gays talk about gay rights, heterosexuals often hear talk about sex, not personal freedom. Furthermore, many people believe that gays and lesbians want special rights, but in fact, gay rights are an issue of individual liberty, and many LGB rights organizations are at work today to secure for their constituencies the liberties that are protected by the U.S. Constitution.

SOCIAL WORK PRACTICE WITH LESBIAN, GAY, AND BISEXUAL CLIENTS

In working with lesbian, gay and bisexual clients, social workers must check their own attitudes toward LGB individuals and the extent to which they subscribe to stereotypes or long-discarded professional models, such as those attributing same-sex sexual orientations to psychopathology, developmental arrest, or some psychological disorder. Perhaps the most important lesson is that social workers cannot make assumptions about the sexual orientation of a client; the client deserves to have his or her presented identity be accepted, not discounted or questioned. Intake and assessment tools can be heterosexist and as such may be biased against LGB clients. The assessment of family support needs also to be inclusive of gay and lesbian partnerships. Exclusive use of words such as "husband" and "wife" conveys the message that only heterosexual norms and behaviors count. In the growing number of states, such as Massachusetts, where gay marriage is now legal, the meaning of these words needs to be reassessed. From a culturally grounded perspective, families are defined by the role they play or by what they do for the client, not by what they look like. Families of choice often serve the needs of individuals much more effectively than families of origin. This concept is illustrated in notes from the field 10.3. In addition, using the wrong labels can obscure the support systems or stressors that play key roles in the lives of clients.

NOTES FROM THE FIELD 10.3

Planning for the Worst

Liz, Andrea's partner of twenty-five years, was diagnosed with cancer three years ago. They had been through three years of chemo, surgery, and aggressive treatment, but the cancer has not relented. Andrea is exhausted and devastated about losing the love of her life. She and Liz have started planning for the end of Liz's life—where she would like to spend her last days, her burial plans, and how her life insurance was going to be distributed to their three children. As they were planning they became increasingly aware that Andrea had no right to make decisions after Liz was gone. Liz had not been in touch with her own mother because her mom was never able to fully accept Liz and Andrea as a family. As they were working on all the end-of-life arrangements, it became evident that her Liz's mother was her legal next of kin and that she would need to be involved in the conversation. Andrea, Liz, and her mom sat down to discuss the plans; although her mom said that she understood and agreed with their decisions, both Andrea and Liz left the meeting feeling that Liz's mom would not follow through. She might, but she might not, which made them both feel very uncomfortable and added to the already very sad and stressful situation. Because same-sex marriage is not allowed in their home state, they are not sure how valid an out-of-state marriage would be. The hospital social worker referred them to a lawyer who in turn has advised them to draw up a will, and for Liz to give custody of the children, legal survivorship rights, and power of attorney to Andrea. They liked the lawyer's advice; on the other hand, they continue to wish that their children would have the opportunity to reconnect with their grandmother after Liz's death. The social worker and the lawyer tell them that it is up to them to decide the course of action, but they are both concerned about custody issues.

Practitioners need to view their lesbian and gay clients as whole people, neither under- nor overestimating the role of sexual orientation in their lives. They should be alert both to overt and to more subtle forms of prejudice and discrimination that the client may be experiencing at home, school, and work, even those that the client has not fully recognized; practitioners can validate that these problems are real. Practitioners should monitor any signs of internalized homophobia that may manifest as depression and low self-esteem and disempower the client; they must also consider the adverse repercussions of these negative self-perceptions on the client's emotional and sexual development. At the same time, practitioners cannot assume that all of the client's issues and problems are connected to her or his sexual orientation or identity. They need to assess the role of the client's sexuality, along with all of her or his other defining identities, including the complex family and communal identity issues faced by ethnic minority clients. It is the practitioner's responsibility to become familiar with the diverse ways that lesbian and gay individuals develop sexual and gender identities, as well as the diverse forms and special challenges of their intimate and family relationships. By recognizing the diversity that exists within this population, practitioners will not presume that a particular arrangement is best for all clients.

Key Concepts

Sexual orientation: How people classify themselves and others sexually, based on feelings of attraction to other people, the gender categories of the objects of people's romantic and erotic desires, and the models of socially prescribed sexual behaviors that individuals follow

Stigma theory: The idea that sexual minorities are likely to avoid disclosure of their sexual identity when they expect to be viewed or treated unfavorably as a result

Machismo: The ideal of what it means to be a man in Latino culture, which views men as controlling, possessive, sexist, and domineering, as well as chivalrous and protective of kin

Marianismo: The ideal of what it means to be a woman in Latino culture, which views women as virtuous and self-sacrificing and implies a sense of powerlessness and resignation in the face of sexist oppression

Homophobia: Fear of and aversion or hostility toward same-sex sexual attraction, behavior and identity that results in prejudice and discrimination

Internalized homophobia: The acceptance of negative views of same-sex sexual attraction, behavior and identity that are incorporated into the self-concept of a gay or lesbian individual

Part IV

The Profession of Social Work Grounded in Culture

11

Cultural Norms and Social Work Practice

THE CULTURALLY GROUNDED PERSPECTIVE VIEWS SOCIAL WORK INTER-
ventions as products of unique cultural contexts. Interventions designed for and
tested in partnership with one community may not work with others unless there
is a systematic and comprehensive adaptation process. Lack of cultural specificity
can yield ineffective interventions or, even worse, can be more harmful than beneficial. Assessing a client's culture requires that the practitioner adopts a
researcher role and approaches the culture of the client as a client's asset and as
a learning tool for the practitioner. Sue (1998, 2006) has suggested three components for effective culturally competent practice:

1. Hypothesis testing: The use of cultural knowledge about groups in a tentative, exploratory fashion without arriving at any definitive or premature
   conclusions about clients or their cultures (the practitioner is mindful of
   the clients' social contexts and intersectionality)
2. Dynamic sizing: The ability to know when to generalize certain attitudes
   and behaviors exhibited by the client to other members of the same identity group (i.e., when certain norms or behaviors are culturally based and
   may be common to others in the identity group) and when to individualize
   (i.e., when they are a function of the client's personality and there is no
   cultural explanation for behaviors or attitudes)
3. Culturally specific expertise: The ability to work effectively with individuals from a particular culture and the possession of skills and abilities to
   develop rapport, to have a strong client-worker alliance, and to achieve the
   desired outcomes when working with members of that group (i.e., becoming a bicultural practitioner)

This chapter discusses the various factors that practitioners must consider in
order to choose an intervention that is culturally appropriate for the client, and
also discusses some ways that practitioners can incorporate aspects of clients'
cultures into the helping process as Sue recommends.

INDIVIDUALISM AND COLLECTIVISM

The United States, like other Western societies, can be described as having an individualistic orientation, meaning that the most common psychosocial unit of operation is the individual, not the group. Individualistic societies believe that the needs of the group are satisfied when the needs of the individual are satisfied, whereas collectivistic societies believe that individual needs are met when the group's needs are met. These orientations can have a profound impact on how clients describe their presenting problems. Clients from collectivistic societies may tell the social worker that they are anxious because they feel powerless to help a family or community member, while clients from an individualistic society may feel anxious because they are unable to solve problems alone.

American society fosters individualism, and its citizens expect the government to defend individual rights even at the expense of the collective well-being. Progressive and conservative social policy positions share a common heritage that places great stress on the individual and the individual's rights and well-being. Individualism has been part of the ideological core of many European Americans in the United States since their arrival. In contrast, indentured Europeans and African servants, enslaved Africans, colonized Native Americans, annexed residents of Mexico, Native Hawaiians, and many descendants of these groups, as well as women in general, have had less opportunity to share in the privileges enjoyed by white males. The more oppressed the group, the more its members have needed to rely on fellow members for survival. Strong community bonds have helped historically oppressed communities survive against difficult odds, and their members have relied on collective traditional helping systems. The collectivistic or communitarian approach rejects the individual-centered focus and favors the common good over individual concerns. At a global level, Jewish communities across many nations and throughout history have had to rely on their own religious and secular organizations to cope with persecution and exclusion. Many immigrant and refugee communities have developed grassroots organizations to welcome newcomers and serve their basic needs. In the United States, because of its rich ethnic and cultural diversity, collectivism is probably as much a part of the fabric of the nation as individualism, but it is not a prominent part of the American national myth, nor is it well represented in the laws of the nation.

Collectivistic cultures such as those of the Chinese and the Diné (Navajo) view mental and physical health as expressions of group harmony; the absence of health is regarded with shame and perceived to be the result of broken rules. These beliefs need to be taken into account by practitioners as they develop services for these populations. Research conducted with collectivistic populations has illuminated how groups' natural ways of helping are shaped by a collective orientation. For example, many Palestinians live in interdependence with others. Families are the main source of economic security and other forms of support.

Palestinian nuclear families live surrounded by an extended family of fifty to five hundred people (Saca-Hazboun & Glennon, 2011). Because of the societal context in which Palestinian families live, individuals rely on their families to survive, and the consequences of individual misconduct are shared by everyone within the larger extended family. A study conducted with Native American women from a Montana reservation investigated a related phenomenon called "communal mastery" (Hobfoll, Jackson, Hobfoll, Pierce, & Young, 2002). Communal mastery has been defined as the belief that individuals can attain their goals through their close interconnection with others (Hobfoll, Schröder, Wells, & Malek, 2002). Unlike the typical individualistic strategies of the mainstream culture, which rely on first-person statements and a sense of personal control, communal mastery relies on the individual's social attachment to others. Instead of "I" statements, individuals with high levels of communal mastery tend to use "we" statements. One of the main findings of the study was that women with high levels of communal mastery experienced less anger and fewer depressive moods than women with low levels of communal mastery (Hobfoll, Jackson, et al., 2002). Individuals from collectivistic cultures who are separated from their communities of origin as a result of migration or other reasons can experience high levels of stress resulting from the disappearance of their support systems. Such experiences can be traumatic for families and individuals who find themselves for the first time without a natural and culturally grounded support system.

It appears that individuals from groups that practice a more collectivist approach to family and group social organization bring with them unique sources of resiliency that may manifest in different ways in different cultural groups. The culturally grounded paradigm for practice both recognizes the risk of psychosocial imbalance and stress and integrates into the professional helping process the sources of resiliency embedded in the cultural backgrounds of individuals and communities, as well as their natural helping practices. Understanding and welcoming these culturally embedded collective approaches to helping and their corresponding forms of social organization is a prerequisite to effective social work practice. There is a risk that practitioners may oversimplify or generalize the impact of collectivism on ethnic minority groups or other identity groups. Across-national meta-analysis of dozens of studies on collectivism across the globe suggests that many developing societies that are assumed to be very collectivistic, such as those in Latin America and Asia, often use individualistic ways of seeking and giving help, while some developed societies in Europe have strong collectivistic features (Oyserman, Coon, & Kemmelmeier, 2002). Thus, while practitioners must take into account their knowledge of the client's culture, they must avoid pigeonholing clients based on that knowledge and must endeavor to learn about the community from which the client comes, as well as what kind of role the norms, values, and beliefs of the culture and the community play in the client's life.

Cultural norms are values and beliefs that influence the attitudes and behaviors of members of different cultural groups. Norms are learned from parents, teachers, peers, elders, and institutions such as organized religion and social clubs, and through traditional rituals and practices. Some norms are healthy and liberating, and some are unhealthy and oppressive. Cultural norms provide a consistent predisposition toward certain ideals, as well as a distaste for others, and prescribe standard behaviors as well as ritualistic practices. Norms are a summation of the typical activities and beliefs of a group of people. In the sense that they can be used by individuals to formulate expectations in interactions with others, cultural norms can be described as gentle stereotypes. Notes from the field 11.1 illustrates the fine line between cultural norms and stereotypes. When one approaches cultural norms as all-or-nothing dichotomies, disregarding middle ground and gray areas, they risk becoming stereotypes.

Table 11.1 points to several areas where culture and cultural differences may be highly salient as the practitioner works to understand the client's worldview and identify instances where differences with the worldviews of others (including the practitioner) may lead to misunderstandings that become problematic for clients. Culture can produce distinctive expectations about how people should identify themselves, interact and communicate with others, define their families, and prioritize family, religion, and work life. Culture even influences how people learn and approach problems. Although it is useful in that it provides a general set of normative themes that can help social workers understand cultural minority clients, workers must remember that it can be harmful to generalize these norms to all other cultures in a broad and all-encompassing manner. Such dichotomies,

---

NOTES FROM THE FIELD 11.1
Family Stereotypes

A group of high school students is producing an educational video for middle school students under the supervision of a professional video director. They were charged with the task of portraying Latino culture and its norms. The director, who is not Latino, suggests that the family in the story should have many children. Some of the students object; they perceive this to be a stereotype rather than a Latino cultural norm. The students from Latino backgrounds share stories about their parents' and grandparents' generations, among whom larger families were common, but note that their own older siblings and younger aunts and uncles who are married tend to have no more than two children. The script is rewritten to represent the modern Latino family more accurately, and a scene in which the question of the ideal family size comes up at a family birthday celebration is incorporated.

such as comparisons between Western and non-Western orientations or between whites and people of color, do not provide sufficient substantive information to identify culturally appropriate social work interventions (see table 11.1). Because of the fluidity of culture, in categorizing whole groups of people in such a manner, one runs the risk of oversimplifying the cultural journeys of many individuals and communities.

Despite the shortcomings of such typologies and categories, practitioners can be expected to look for some descriptive information regarding cultural norms as a guide or reference for their work with different cultural communities. Workers need to have some form of social address (i.e., a starting point or a tentative point of departure) for locating the client's culture (Bronfenbrenner, 1986). The desire to place the client somewhere in the cultural continuum often leads workers to assign the client an ethnic or other identity label. However, because identity is a personal choice, only the client can pick the right set of labels. The worker's role is to access all the available information about cultural attributes and use it as part of the assessment process. Cultural attributes identified through assessment are reviewed as part of clients' needs and strengths and are placed within the social context of the community.

THE CULTURAL PROFILES OF SEVERAL IDENTITY GROUPS

The following review of cultural attributes and natural helping styles of selected groups is offered as an initial introduction to possible attributes that can serve as the foundation upon which culturally relevant interventions are implemented and evaluated. Because of the ever-present risk of overgeneralization, this information needs to be used with caution.

Native Americans

Native Americans' traditional holistic approaches to helping rests on a cultural belief that humans are an integral part of their environment and that their physical, mental, spiritual, and community dimensions cannot be separated; this approach is typically depicted using the symbol of the medicine wheel (see figure 11.1) (Hodge, Limb, & Cross, 2009). This cultural approach to wellness has been used by healers and other medical personnel to address the difficult living conditions experienced by members of many Native American communities. Native Americans face persistent health disparities such as high rates of diabetes, substance abuse, and infectious diseases, in addition to high rates of violence. Practices that have helped Native people overcome challenges need to be examined and integrated whenever possible into the social service delivery system with this population.

Table 11.1 Comparison of Cultural Norms and Values

Aspect of culture	Mainstream American culture	Other cultures
Greetings	Informal, handshake	Formal embrace, bow, handshake.
Communication and language	Explicit, direct communication; emphasis on content (meaning found in words)	Implicit, indirect communication; emphasis on context (meaning found around words).
Dress and appearance	Dress-for-success ideal; wide range in accepted dress	Dress is seen as a sign of one's position, wealth, and prestige (religious rules may apply).
Food and eating habits	Eating as a necessity (e.g., eating fast food)	Dining as a social experience (religious rules may apply).
Time and time consciousness	Linear and exact time consciousness; value on promptness (time = money)	Elastic and relative time consciousness; time spent enjoying relationships.
Relationships, family, friends	Focus on nuclear family; responsibility for self; value placed on youth; age seen as handicap	Focus on extended family; loyalty and responsibility to family; age given status and respect
Values and norms	Individual orientation; independence; preference for direct confrontation of conflict	Group orientation; conformity; preference for harmony
Beliefs and attitudes	Egalitarian; challenging of authority; individuals control their destiny; gender equity	Respect for authority, social hierarchies, and social order; individuals accept their destiny; different roles for men and women
Mental processes and learning style	Linear, logical, sequential; problem-solving focus	Lateral, holistic, simultaneous; acceptance of life's difficulties
Work habits and practices	Emphasis on task; rewards based on individual achievement; work has intrinsic value	Emphasis on relationships; rewards based on seniority, relationships; work is a necessity of life

Source: Adapted from Gardenswartz & Rowe, A. (2006).

Figure 11.1   Medicine Wheel

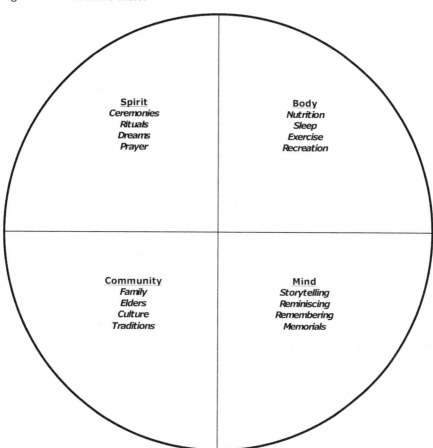

Native Americans often have social service needs that are different from those of other people in the United States, and their needs deserve special attention. Lack of transportation may be an insurmountable barrier for families living in remote areas of their reservations and far from social and health service providers. Native Americans often do not receive preventive and early care as a result of their fear of hospitals and the fear that they will become guinea pigs for experiments and research projects, as well as the knowledge that many Native Americans received poor treatment from these institutions in the past (Jones, 2006).

Although most Native Americans reside in cities, most Native American–specific social and health services are located on tribal lands. Urban Native Americans are often reluctant to seek health services in town because they feel like outsiders at doctor's offices, mental health clinics, and hospitals that do not observe Native American customs. For example, health-care and social service professionals often fail to introduce themselves or do not inquire about the patient's extended family, courtesies that the Native patient may consider very important. Lack of cultural competence becomes an obstacle when doctors, nurses, and social workers ask direct or very personal questions, indicate that they have little time to spend with the patient, or make the Native patient wait for long periods of time in an unfamiliar environment without any personal contact.

The social and emotional challenges experienced by Native American clients can often be linked to their unresolved grief and historical trauma (Campbell & Evans-Campbell, 2011). For example, Native youths who were taken away to boarding schools suffered not only the trauma of separation from their families at a very early age, but also frequent abuse in these institutions. For some, the lack of healthy role models has initiated a cycle of poor parenting (Campbell & Evans-Campbell, 2011). Family and multigenerational interventions can provide the support the client needs to heal.

The legacy of genocide gives Native Americans little reason to trust professionals outside the community or clan. Non-Native social workers need to use perseverance and work around client resistance in order to establish trust. In order to work effectively with Native American clients, the practitioner needs general and containment skills. General skills include communication and problem-solving skills based on a definition of the problem and arrival at a solution from a Native American perspective. Containment skills refer to the ability to listen, tolerate long periods of silence, and be patient (Weaver, 1999). As the tempo of communication is generally slower in traditional communities, Native social workers that are more assimilated and non-Native social workers often need to slow down their natural tempo in order to communicate effectively.

As the example in notes from the field 11.2 demonstrates, social work practitioners working with Native Americans may need to assess their clients' level of traditionalism. In this case, the worker assessed the group's communication style and concluded that the group members would not be comfortable with verbal and direct communication about their feelings. Although it may be appropriate to relate to a nontraditional client much as one would relate to a non–Native American individual, Native clients that are more traditional may respond better to culturally specific interventions (Thomason, 2000). Selected elements of traditional culture can be integrated into practice with respect and care. For example, The Red Road to Wellbriety incorporates Native American traditions and beliefs into the classic Alcoholics Anonymous structure, making the program more relevant and meaningful to traditional Native American participants (White, 2009). This integration is based on the recognition that culture and rituals are connected to a spiritual dimension of clients' lives. To attempt to appropriate those traditional and sacred practices—for example, by assuming the role of a traditional

> ## NOTES FROM THE FIELD 11.2
> ### Speaking with Our Hands
>
> Janet is a Native social worker who has been assigned to a pediatric oncology clinic operated by the American Indian Health Services, where she is to run a youth support group for cancer survivors. There are six people in the group: three boys and three girls ranging in age from nine to fourteen years old. They have been meeting for three weeks now, and the group members do not talk much. They mostly listen to the social worker. Janet has tried different techniques to help them externalize their feelings about their diagnoses and the fact that their cancer is in remission. This week she proposes that they paint vases. She explains the meaning of vase painting in their cultures and shows examples to the group. Pottery makers in their communities paint vases as a way of communicating their dreams and wishes for the future. The group members like the idea, and each one portrays her or his individual experiences, feelings, and hopes for the future on her or his own vase. Once finished, they share their work and everyone comments on the others' vases and the messages they convey. Janet summarizes the comments and proposes to the group that they exhibit their vases in the waiting room of the clinic for other children and their families to see.

healer and attempting to perform traditional rituals—would be a form of colonialism. However, the respectful integration of culturally based knowledge, beliefs, and rituals can be conducted effectively in partnership with the recognized holy person in the community. The shaman or her or his equivalent can help introduce the traditional content in an authentic manner and let the practitioner know of boundaries that he or she must respect.

African Americans

African Americans constitute a very diverse cultural group, and the intersectionality of many factors such as social class and gender creates many within-group differences. There is, however, some agreement that African Americans constitute a distinct ethnocultural community whose existence is valued for its own sake (Blum, 2006). An important first task for the social worker is recognizing the importance that clients place on maintaining connections to the African American community and its many sources of identity. African Americans have developed cultural products (e.g., music, literature, and science) that have enriched their community, U.S. society, and the whole world. Those cultural gifts are the product of enormous resiliency and are often expressions of cultural norms within African

American culture, such as connectedness, equality, emotional vitality, collective survival, cooperation, sharing, interdependence, reconciliation, and respect (Brown et al., 2013; Holliday, 2009).

Spirituality is another important component of African American culture that has shaped family and individual relationships, fostered political mobilization, and served as a source of hope and resiliency. Congruent with African American values, spirituality supports interconnectedness with the community, the divine, and the ancestors. Organized religion (especially Christianity and Islam) has sustained and continues to sustain black identity, created institutional settings for pursuit of social and political goals, and nurtured religious values and dignity (Fulton, 2011). Although the majority of African Americans are Christian, Islam and other traditions connected to African spirituality (e.g., Yoruba and Candomblé) play important roles in many communities around the nation. African Americans are more likely to attend religious services and pray in private than are their white Christian counterparts (Sahgal & Smith, 2009). Because of its cultural relevance, the infusion of spirituality into interventions with African Americans appears to be a natural integration. The use of prayer, quotes from the Bible or other holy books, and spiritual metaphors can be appropriate in certain circumstances. However, role definition and role differentiation are of concern here and must be addressed in supervision when one chooses to integrate spirituality into an intervention. There is a fine but important line between helping clients explore and draw on salient aspects of their spirituality, and providing spiritual direction. The integration of spirituality into social work practice needs to be done with caution.

African Americans also place a high value on family and children. Families vary greatly in size and structure as well as in composition. Ritual kinship, where "uncles," "aunts," and "cousins" may not be related by blood but have a commitment to the family as if they were family in a biological sense, is common in many communities. The practitioner working with African American families must honor and support their historical resiliency and ability to adapt through the use of highly effective support systems such as ritual kinship. These values have been incorporated into culturally tailored interventions such as the highly successful second-hand smoke prevention intervention called "Not in mama's kitchen" (VanGeest & Welch, 2008). Trisha's story in notes from the field 11.3 illustrates the cultural tradition of informal adoption (Boyd-Franklin, 2003). It is an example of how family is defined in some African American communities—and in many other cultures—based on its function and the benefits an individual receives from belonging to the family rather than on blood ties between individuals. Trisha's case presents an opportunity to incorporate cultural practices into the social services system. Such incorporation, however, requires not only changes to be made by the individual worker, but also changes to agency policy made by the board of directors and broader child welfare policies enacted by legislators. The social

---

NOTES FROM THE FIELD 11.3
Who Is Family?

Mrs. Johnson's best friend, Phyllis, died recently after a short illness. Phyllis had a three-year-old child named Trisha. Although there is no blood relationship between them, Trisha calls Mrs. Johnson "Auntie." After the funeral, Trisha goes to Mrs. Johnson's home for a few days. A week later when her grandmother comes by to pick her up, Trisha refuses to pack her backpack and says that she wants to stay with her auntie. Her grandmother is surprised by Trisha's reaction, but after discussing the situation with Mrs. Johnson, she allows Trisha to stay for another week. Trisha hardly knows her grandmother because her mom and her grandmother stopped communicating after Trisha was born. The worker handling the case from child protective services questions the fact that Trisha is staying with a person who is not kin and starts an investigation.

---

worker can facilitate collaboration between the different parties in order to arrive at a decision that will benefit all.

African American grandmothers have historically served as the primary caretakers of the children in the family. During slavery, African Americans relied on extended family networks that made fewer clear distinctions between the roles of the mother and roles of the grandmother. The tradition continues to be practiced as grandmothers take care of their own grandchildren as well as their grandchildren's children, nephews, nieces, and other non-kin members of the extended family. Intergenerational African American families with grandmothers and great-grandmothers at their helm have grown exponentially in the past decades as a result of high rates of substance abuse and an increase in the number of incarcerated African American women. After biological mothers, African American grandmothers and biological fathers have been identified as providing the highest quality of parenting (Simons, Chen, Simons, Brody, & Cutrona, 2006). Although these findings are encouraging in terms of the well-being of children, they raise some concerns about the well-being of the grandmothers who are doing the caregiving. The caregiver role can bring much stress to older women, especially when the mother is absent. The stress can be physical, emotional, and financial, as many grandmothers are not recognized as caregivers in the foster care system.

African Americans have developed abilities and coping mechanisms to deal with racism, and they rely on social support systems that they have perfected over generations. Therefore, one of the roles of the social worker is to help clients tap these resources and strengths as they create better conditions for the community. The social worker plays a broker role by connecting clients to services and resources outside their family and community networks. Social workers can also facilitate a balance between the natural supports existing within the community and the more formal resources and services that can ease the burden of caregivers.

A culturally grounded approach to social work practice celebrates African American culture and its expressions of resiliency, and supports individuals in their efforts to resist racism and cultural assimilation while producing lasting changes leading to the development of a more inclusive and just society. The culturally competent social worker can be effective by adopting an Afrocentric perspective, one that focuses on collectivity and on spiritual and moral development (Asante, 2007). While working with families, for example, social workers can take into account how African American parents socialize their children to live in hostile environments in which their culture and race are not always valued. Parents may feel the need to have a family conversation or may wait until their child experiences her or his first racist incident. From a culturally grounded perspective, the professional's role is to provide a safe environment where these important decisions can be thought through and where the interests and well-being of the child and the family are paramount. Sensitive and emotionally charged topics require an environment where self-disclosure is possible and where empathy and trust prevail. To provide such an environment, social workers of all ethnic backgrounds need to examine their own beliefs, attitudes, and behaviors toward racism. Self-examination can foster increased empathy and greater cultural competence.

Mexican Americans and Other Latinos

Mexican Americans constitute the largest subgroup of a very diverse umbrella group generally called Latino or Hispanic. Latinos constitute the largest ethnic minority group in the nation; many of them are Spanish speakers, the second-most-commonly spoken language in the United States. Many Latinos trace their ancestry to the Southwest before the Treaty of Guadalupe Hidalgo was signed, whereas other Latino families have come to the United States more recently. Many others have ancestors who came from one or more of the twenty-one nations in which Spanish is a principle national language. The terms "Latino" and "Hispanic" describe a diverse multiracial and multinational group of people with a connection to Spain, Latin America, and the Commonwealth of Puerto Rico.

It is important to remember that not all Latinos speak Spanish. There are hundreds of languages spoken in Latin America. Spanish and Portuguese are the two most commonly spoken European languages, but there are hundreds of Mayan languages, as well as other languages such as Nahuatl Aymara, Guaraní, Quechua, and Creole. Those who speak languages other than Spanish in many of these countries are often members of indigenous communities that predate the arrival of the Europeans and continue to face prejudice and discrimination as well as the consequences of centuries of social, educational, economic, and political inequality. When these individuals come to the United States, their lack of proficiency in both English and Spanish complicates their adjustment to U.S. society. As migration streams into the United States continue to expand and diversify, many social service agencies encounter clients from Latin America whose needs go beyond the needs presented by the traditional Spanish-speaking client.

As notes from the field 11.4 illustrates, Latinos are a multiethnic and multiracial group with Amerindian, European, African, and even Asian ancestry. Many Latinos identify as *la raza*, or "the people," the product of centuries of *mestizaje*, or the mixing of Native people of the Americas with people of Spanish and other European backgrounds as well as with those of African and Asian ancestry. A shared Spanish colonial past and a strong connection to Roman Catholic traditions and beliefs provide a set of cultural norms that are shared by many different Latino groups. However, not all Latinos are Roman Catholic, and not all Latinos observe these norms. It is possible to discern a set of norms that appear to be a

---

NOTES FROM THE FIELD 11.4
Recognizing Latino Diversity

La Casa de la Solidaridad is a well-established Latino social services agency located in a large city in the Midwest. Casa received an urban renewal grant and has started to implement a community development plan. Twelve representatives from different community agencies, social clubs, and churches form the leadership team. The social worker assigned to staff the leadership team notices that one man who introduced himself as José Rocha did not speak at all during the first session, although the agency provides simultaneous Spanish-to-English and English-to-Spanish translation services. During the coffee break, the social worker introduces herself and learns that Mr. Rocha comes from the state of Oaxaca in Mexico and does not feel comfortable speaking English or Spanish in public. His first language is Huautla Mazatec, one of the many Mayan languages spoken in southern Mexico and in Guatemala. At the beginning of the next meeting, the social worker speaks with the elected chair of the group, Mario Guttmann, an Argentinean American of German ancestry who speaks fluent German, English, and Spanish. Mr. Guttmann thanks the social worker for the information and suggests that Mr. Rocha's organization find a substitute for him who is fluent in Spanish and/or English. Another board member calls a vote and the motion does not pass. The board members propose that they look for alternatives that will facilitate Mr. Rocha's full participation, such as finding an additional interpreter who is fluent in Huautla Mazatec.

common denominator across subgroups while remaining mindful of the richness and diversity of various Latino groups.

Familismo is commonly recognized as a core Latino value. *Familismo* involves strong identification with and attachment to a nuclear and extended family, and an obligation to provide both material and emotional support to one's family (Calzada, Tamis-LeMonda, & Yoshikawa, 2012). *Familismo* exerts influence on Latinos regardless of the length of time they have lived in the United States. *Familismo* involves rituals such as gathering on Sundays for meals, going to church together, celebrating the *quinceañera* (a girl's debut as a woman on her fifteenth birthday), and participating in making decisions that affect the family. *Familismo* is associated with protective factors like interconnectedness, loyalty, solidarity, reciprocity, pride, and respect among family members (Lugo Steidel & Contreras, 2003). It is also a protective factor against depression, alcohol abuse, and delinquency in Latino adolescents (Calzada et al., 2012; Gil, Wagner, & Vega, 2000; Horton & Gil, 2008). Some warn that *familismo* should not be romanticized, and that it can, along with protective elements, also be a potential risk factor. The interconnectedness of family that characterizes *familismo* may increase stress when there is conflict within the family (Hernandez, Ramirez Garcia, & Flynn, 2010). An important aspect of *familismo* is *compadrazgo* (godparenting), in which the *compadres* (godparents) are considered something akin to coparents and help raise the child, providing a culturally based form of social security and child welfare in the event that the biological parents are absent or unable to provide for the child's needs.

Other Latino cultural norms that have implications for social work practice include *personalismo* and *simpatía*. *Personalismo* is the valuing of interpersonal relationships (being friendly) while *simpatía* is a word used to describe the cultural expectation that individuals avoid conflict and act in a good-natured and pleasant way toward others regardless. A social worker who shows respect for Latino clients and treats them in a friendly manner while recognizing the family hierarchy will be judged to have *personalismo,* and the client will be more likely to become engaged in the helping process and return for future sessions.

Cultural values and norms often influence the communication style of traditional Latino clients. For example, clients may avoid saying "no" to the social worker because "no" is perceived to be a rude word. Clients may not be in agreement with practitioners but will express their disagreement without saying "no" out of respect for the authority of the worker. In such clients, agreement is expressed more enthusiastically and the clinician can tell that the client is engaged from her or his body language. The client's behavior following the session may not be consistent with the social worker's understanding of the discussion, but the client may see no contradiction. Body language indicating anxiety, silence, and other expressions of discomfort needs to be noted and recorded. In mainstream non-Latino U.S. culture, direct communication tends to be the norm.

One person directly asks a question, and the other directly answers. In Latino cultures, as in most traditional cultures, direct communication with direct questioning can be viewed as impolite. Latino clients prefer not to address sensitive or personal matters right away. Instead, traditional clients feel more comfortable when they are allowed to arrive at the topic at hand in a more roundabout way and to address the topic in their own time.

Latino children are often taught not to say "yes" in some situations or to delay giving an affirmative answer for as long as possible. If someone offers something that an individual wants or needs, it is considered polite to say, "No, thank you," and wait for the offer to be repeated a second or third time before accepting. Notes from the field 11.5 provides an illustration of the misunderstandings that can result from such differences in communication styles. For example, some cultures teach individuals to avoid direct communication and to wait for a second or third offer before accepting it. When Graciela initially declined the offer of lemonade, Mrs. Williams probably thought she meant she really did not want any. In clinical situations, similar misunderstandings can occur. For example, Latino clients may be very uncomfortable answering certain questions but will not

---

NOTES FROM THE FIELD the Field 11.5
"No, Thank You"

Graciela is a fourteen-year-old Latina seventh grader with a very active social life within the boundaries of her own neighborhood. She has not had many opportunities to interact with youths and families from different ethnic backgrounds. This summer she is participating in her school's Family-to-Family exchange program and she will be spending a week with a family in another town and of a different ethnicity. The Williams have a daughter her age named Tracy, who will go back with Graciela to her home once the week is over and complete the exchange. Graciela is dropped off at the home of her host family by her father, who leaves promptly after meeting the Williams. It is a very hot day and Graciela is invited to sit with the family on the front porch. Mrs. Williams brings a tray with a large pitcher of lemonade and glasses for everyone. When offered a glass of lemonade, Graciela responds, "No, thank you." Nobody asks Graciela again if she would like to have a glass. Graciela was behaving as would be expected in her family. Her mother always says, "When you are visiting another family and you are offered refreshments, you first say no and only accept the second time around. It is not polite to accept right away." Graciela is very thirsty but remains quiet, waiting for Mrs. Williams to ask her again, but she never does.

explain why. If asked directly, they will not let the worker know that they are uncomfortable. They may feel that they should respect the authority of the worker—"She knows, she is the professional. Who am I to tell her that the information she wants is too private?" This kind of misunderstanding, however, can lead clients to drop out of treatment if they do not feel respected by the practitioner. Body language can be an indication of such discomfort, and the worker needs to assess these cues continuously in order to foster the strongest therapeutic alliance possible. The verbalization of dissatisfaction with services or a practitioner's approach is rare, especially among less-acculturated Latinos. Ignoring this style of communication can undermine the development of a strong therapeutic alliance (Paris et al., 2005).

Immigrant and refugee Latino families often experience unique mental health needs. Many women and children are forced by their economic, political, or family situations to immigrate to the United States; as a result of their forced migration they may feel angry, detached from their natural support systems, and isolated. Couples may experience marital problems due to the disruptions and adjustments precipitated by the migration process. Regardless of whether migration is forced or voluntary, recent immigrants often experience feelings of loss, grief, homesickness, and sadness (Van Ecke, 2005). Latino immigrants may face additional stress when resettling in the United States due to their documentation status and the political climate in many communities. For example, after the passage of Arizona Senate Bill 1070, a law that allowed police officers to stop any person they suspected of being in the country illegally, Latinos reported restricting their mobility, being less willing to report crimes to law enforcement, and delaying access to health care (Hardy & Bohan, 2012). Although the Latino norm of relying on family provides great support to immigrants and refugees, it may also allow them to delay seeking social services; this explains in part the underutilization of services by Latinos. The costs and burdens of immigration can place tremendous strains on immigrant families and the kin they rely on for much of the assistance they need. Networks of mutual assistance can break down when both the newcomers and those who have come before them are poor and needy, sometimes leading to sharp conflicts and even fallings-out that make them even more dependent on help from social services (Menjivar, 2000).

A major challenge in social work practice is the shortage of bilingual and bicultural practitioners. Even when Latinos master English, they may prefer to use Spanish to communicate their feelings. They may use English effectively in the transactions of daily living (i.e., when speaking from the head) but feel that English is an unnatural means for conveying emotion (i.e., when speaking from the heart).

As Antonio's case in notes from the field 11.6 demonstrates, being culturally grounded may require the practitioner to go beyond language to attempt a cultural connection. It is often critical for practitioners to master another language

NOTES FROM THE FIELD 11.6
Saying *Adios*

Antonio is an engineering student at a large university in California. His mother suddenly passed away in Mexico six months ago. Although he was able to attend the funeral, he feels that he was not able to say goodbye to her properly. He feels depressed and starts to see a social worker at student health services. The death of Antonio's mother immediately surfaces as the presenting problem. After four sessions during which they talk about her death, it becomes clear that Antonio needs to say goodbye to his mother in a more meaningful and culturally significant way. The social worker is Japanese American and only speaks a few words of Spanish. Despite his limited Spanish-language skills, he suggests that Antonio use the session to express to his mother all the things he did not have a chance to say to her. Antonio tries in English but cannot do it because he never spoke to his mother in English. The worker suggests that he conduct the conversation in Spanish and requests permission to tape it. Antonio is able to say what he needed to say, and the session becomes a turning point in his grieving process. Later they listen to the tape and discuss its cultural meaning and personal significance. In some regards, the social worker gave up his power by switching to a language he did not understand to serve the needs of the client.

when working intensively with a community that has many members whose English is limited. However, being culturally competent with Latinos, as with many other ethnic groups, goes beyond language proficiency and requires a comprehensive bicultural approach to practice.

Asian Americans

Despite great differences among ethnic groups, people of different national origins described as Asian American appear to share some common cultural values. Some of these commonalities can be traced to Buddhism and Confucian philosophies. There are six cultural values that are shared to some degree by different Asian American groups: (1) collectivism, (2) conformity to cultural norms, (3) emotional self-control, and family recognition through (4) achievement, (5) filial piety, and (6) humility (Kim, Atkinson, & Yang, 1999).

Collectivism refers to a tendency among community members to think about the group first, and a strong sense of allegiance to the group. Achievements are not attained individually, but as a group. Family or group needs take precedence over individual needs. Community members have well-defined social roles and expectations, and a sense of communal responsibility and respect for authority (Dhooper, 2003).

Conformity to norms is inculcated in Asian American families, like many other traditional cultural groups, under a principle of interdependence. The social work practice of encouraging clients to explore their personal goals and desires, with the ultimate objective that clients will develop into independently functioning individuals, contradicts some Asian philosophies according to which parents' wishes are expected to influence children's decisions regarding friends, spouses, housing arrangements, and residential locations, even during adulthood (Brammer, 2004). As family members go through the acculturation process, intergenerational disagreements may emerge, but not in the form of direct or open conflict. Interpreting behavior within the appropriate family and cultural context requires a proactive approach to decoding communication patterns and may require some triangulation. If the social worker gathers information from different members of the family through different channels, such as individual, family, and couples' sessions, and carefully compares the information gathered about the same event, phenomenon, or topic, contradictions can be identified, interpreted, and addressed. Cultural differences in communication style may be misinterpreted as resistance by social workers who received a Western-style education. For example, discussing personal and family problems outside the family is considered taboo in some Asian American communities, which may prevent their members from seeking outside help (Dhooper, 2003). However, when clients of Asian heritage do seek help, they often view the practitioner as a healer and leader who will provide direction. Therefore, the practitioner needs to make the role of the social worker clear to the client and help her or him set realistic expectations (Brammer, 2004). The fact that many recent immigrant families are unfamiliar with the social service system and with Western theories of health and illness may prevent them from seeking assistance or lead them to misunderstand the purpose of the intervention. Often, respectfully integrating traditional values and practices into the intervention can increase service utilization rates and services quality (Wang & Kim, 2010).

Asian Americans are sometimes described as possessing great *emotional self-control* and restraint. They might not demonstrate expressions of extreme happiness or sadness, but the lack of expressivity does not mean that clients are not feeling these emotions at a very deep level (Tsai, Chentsova-Dutton, Freire-Bebeau, & Przymus, 2002). Being stoic and enduring suffering in silence are important expressions of self-control. Clients' body language and verbal communication may be disorienting for uninitiated social workers. For example, in many Asian cultures there is an implicit understanding of parental love, and as such it is felt that there is no need to express it verbally. Some parent-child bonding assessment scales would not be appropriate for clients from Asian backgrounds, as the scales may ask pointed questions such as, "How often do you tell your child you love him or her?" Some Asian American views and practices with respect to illness and health that are considered appropriate by the culture of origin may be seen as questionable in the United States. For example, a patient who takes a stoic approach to pain and believes that suffering is an inevitable part of life may share very little information with a physician or hospital social workers. Some Asian worldviews consider sadness a healthy or ultimately positive experience that helps people move along the path to a more enlightened life, rather than a sign of depressive symptoms that may indicate pathology (Putri, Prawitasari, Hakim, Yuniarti, & Kim, 2011). On the other hand, displaying emotion is considered pathological or shameful (Hwang, Wood, Lin, & Cheung, 2006). Social workers can play a role as cultural mediators in facilitating the best possible utilization of the care systems available for patients.

Family recognition through *achievement* (e.g., academic achievement or professional success) is related to the idea of honoring the family through one's actions. Families also work together to achieve economic and social advancement. This approach can be a source of conflict, because these cultures still tend to have different expectations for women and for men. For example, many Asian women in the United States work along with their husbands in family-owned businesses but are expected to remain subservient. This expectation can lead to marital conflict and sometimes abuse. Family harmony is also at risk when immigrant children become more receptive to ideas of individualism and independence than their parents are, and more receptive than their parents wish them to be (Dhooper, 1991; Juang, Syed, & Cookston, 2012).

Filial piety is veneration and respect for one's elders. Advanced age is equated with wisdom. Older family members are expected to offer advice, and younger people are expected to seek advice from their older relatives. Filial piety also implies taking care of older relatives as their health declines rather than placing them in nursing homes.

Humility relates to collectivistic values that frown on any behavior that calls attention to oneself or one's personal achievements. Being humble implies deflecting attention from oneself even when one is being praised for achievements or for possessing a commendable attribute or qualification. In mainstream American corporate culture, many forms of performance reviews are based on self-appraisals in which employees are expected to "blow their own horn." Such a practice would be unthinkable for a traditional Asian American employee. Similarly, clients from Asian backgrounds may have difficulty with the notion that one can enhance one's own self-esteem by focusing on one's positive qualities and achievements.

There are a number of factors that can weaken individuals' and communities' observance of these six cultural values. For example, acculturation is believed to weaken the centrality of traditional cultural values in the lives of second- and third-generation immigrants. This process appears to be slower for Asian Americans than for other immigrant groups, as they appear to retain a strong connection to traditional norms and values longer (often up to three generations). However, Asian Americans do appear to undergo behavior changes (behavioral acculturation) at a fast rate (Kim et al., 1999). The pace at which value acculturation and behavioral acculturation occurs may be an expression of biculturalism, which allows young people to maintain two separate sets of values—one at home and the other outside the home.

A study conducted by Kim, Yang, Atkinson, Wolfe, and Hong (2001) with American college students of Chinese, Japanese, Korean, and Filipino ancestry found that participants assigned similar meaning to the six value dimensions but their levels of adherence to them varied by national origin. For example, Filipino Americans indicated lower levels of adherence to the practice of emotional self-control than the other three Asian American groups. The legacy of the Spanish and American colonization of the Philippines may account for this difference. Japanese Americans reported the strongest adherence to traditional values, although as a group they were farthest removed from the immigration experience. These findings reinforce the cautionary note about avoiding generalizations when one is identifying similarities across subgroups. Southeast Asian communities, for example, present some unique needs.

Because many Southeast Asian clients are members of refugee families, social workers with working knowledge of the symptoms of posttraumatic stress can provide invaluable support. Members of these communities suffer the stresses associated with migration and acculturation, which often result in depression and anxiety problems. Having become used to relying on a large informal social system (family, friends, and community) in their countries of origin, immigrants who have lost that system can spend much time and energy dealing with economic survival, racism, cultural conflicts, and isolation. A successful intervention with members of this group, as with any group, needs to be congruent with the client's belief system.

Social workers and their Asian American clients can benefit from an exploration of the client's new life in comparison with the old life and the transition and adaptation processes. The PIE perspective can be most beneficial in work with Asian American refugees and other recent immigrants, because it considers all levels (interpersonal, intrapersonal, organizational, community, and policy) of adjustment and well-being. In work with older generations, a narrative approach can be very useful for validating lost status and happiness as a step toward creating new narratives centered around hope and the future.

GENDER AND SEXUAL ORIENTATION

Social work is a predominantly female profession. Not only are most social work professionals and students female, but also historically most of the people receiving social services have been female (Hudson, 2006; Shaw & Shaw, 1997). The predominance of female clients occurs for many reasons. Not only are men less familiar with social services and available interventions, but they are also more apprehensive than women about seeking help (Kosberg, 2002). The under-utilization of services by men raises the question whether there may be a norma-tive gendered approach to social service delivery that is unintentionally alienating men. For example, some of the female-centered social work literature shines a negative light on heterosexual men as abusers and absent fathers. These percep-tions can create an unwelcoming environment for the male client.

Men are often referred to programs and services that have been developed for and evaluated with predominantly female clients by predominantly female social workers. For example, agencies with a family focus tend to have a difficult time engaging fathers in family sessions. It would be easy to conclude that fathers are not interested, are not committed, or simply do not want to participate. However, an alternative analysis may suggest that men experience great discomfort in the agency, in the treatment modality, and in their interactions with almost exclu-sively female social workers and other agency personnel. That being said, men still maintain the majority of managerial positions in social work agencies and most practice theories were developed by men (i.e., psychoanalytic), leading some to argue that despite its female majority, the profession is still dominated by a masculine perspective (Pease, 2011). The gendered nature of social work practice has the potential to affect client engagement and retention and requires aware-ness by social work practitioners and administrators. One could argue that there is also a need for a sexual orientation match between clients and workers. Such a match is probably not necessary or feasible most of the time. More important is a high degree of awareness and competence. For example, when working with a lesbian client who has just broken up with her partner, a heterosexual social worker may feel the need to make her own sexual orientation explicit. Is such self-disclosure an attempt to avoid transference, or is the social worker just trying to be honest with her client? Here are three statements a practitioner might make in such a situation:

1. "I am straight, but I believe I can understand what you are going through. However, I may need your help sometimes in order to understand your feelings. I am here to help."
2. "I have a husband and three kids. I want to make it clear that I am not a lesbian and that I do not really understand lesbian love."
3. "Transitions like the one you are going through are really difficult. I know just how you must feel. I was dumped by my boyfriend two weeks ago, but I am seeing someone else already."

Each of these responses uses self-disclosure differently. In the first statement, the worker is trying her best to be honest, to share something about herself in order to establish trust and empathy. This statement may not be considered ideal, but it is certainly affirming of the client-worker relationship. The second statement discloses personal information but only out of fear or homophobia. The social worker stresses who she is and who she is not in order to establish a boundary. This statement clearly reflects a lower level of awareness. Instead of self-disclosing to assist with the process, she self-discloses to avoid having to cross the boundary of sexual orientation and in order to remain in her biased comfort zone. The third statement shows how, in an attempt to create immediate rapport, the worker makes explicit her heterosexual status, vents about her own experience, and makes light of the client's distress by drawing an inappropriate parallel between their personal experiences, all without much regard for the client. Most definitely, this use of self-disclosure is inappropriate: the worker shares personal information without connecting it to the client. Self-disclosure can be a professionally responsible strategy, but only if it helps the client move on or become more engaged with the helping process.

Practitioners become more competent in their work with lesbian, gay, and bisexual clients when they ask themselves and their staff how to incorporate the experience of LGB clients into their protocols and into the overall culture of their agencies. For example, social workers and clients can make decisions together about whether to chart information about the client's sexual orientation. Their partners and children should be considered emergency contacts, and should have the right to receive information and make health decisions about the client.

Working with the lesbian, gay, or bisexual client is not the only way in which social work practitioners can help reduce the stressors that result from prejudice and harassment. School social workers are in a position to help both teachers and students overcome homophobia, and to prevent the school bullying that often takes a tragic toll on gender-nonconforming youths. Often, school is the social context in which the young LGB student most needs an intervention to make it a welcoming place. Several national school programs such as the Gay, Lesbian and Straight Education Network, which has chapters at schools all around the nation, offer support to students and their teachers. For parents, Parents and Friends and Families of Lesbians and Gays is also a very good resource.

Sexual orientation may present the same challenges reviewed under the prior discussions of ethnicity and gender, raising again the question of whether it is necessary for the social worker to have the same sexual orientation as the client. In fact, gay and lesbian practitioners can be of help to heterosexual clients and vice versa, just as heterosexual practitioners can be effective allies to their lesbian and gay colleagues and clients. Nonetheless, displaying certain symbols and becoming familiar with the experiences specific of gay and lesbian clients make that alliance more real and advance professional competence. The rainbow flag, for example, has been adopted by the gay movement as a symbol of pride and identity. It is common to see stickers of a rainbow flag displayed at social workers' offices. The rainbow flag indicates that the office is a welcoming and safe zone regardless of the sexual orientation of the worker and client.

ETHICS AND CULTURE: CULTURAL VALUES AND PRACTICES ARE NOT ALL INHERENTLY GOOD

It has been argued throughout this book that social workers need to be aware of different cultures and their histories in order to identify the right interventions for clients and increase their professional competence. Historically, social work has proceeded along two paths, one focusing on helping individuals adapt to society—the approach of the Charity Organization Society—and the other focusing on changing society, for example, through social reform efforts, in order to help the individual. These two approaches can be seen as parallel paths for promoting the welfare of the most vulnerable sectors of society, but they may also come into conflict or introduce tensions.

People who come from more traditional cultures may find that some of their traditional practices are in conflict with the practices or expectations of mainstream society. Parents in the United States, for example, are advised to use methods such as time out and grounding to discipline their children, but some parents may come from cultures where spanking and other harsh methods of punishment are the disciplinary norm. If investigated by child protective services, these latter families face the possibility of becoming the object of certain corrective actions that can carry serious consequences for the whole family. What is the role of the social worker in such cases? Culturally matched child protective services workers in Australia reported that, as immigrants themselves, they had a hard time with this particular cultural clash and tended to judge what others see as excessive punishment as acceptable (Dugger, 1996; Sawrikar, 2012). On the other hand, a worker who is not familiar with the cultural background of certain parenting practices may be more likely to overreact, alienate the parents, and even harm the family by making recommendations before knowing all the facts.

It is important to remember that cultures are constantly changing and that not all culturally based attitudes and behaviors are inherently good. Most of the time, culture heals, or, as the traditional Spanish-language saying states, *la cultura cura*. There are times, however, when oppression takes place in the name of culture. Examples of oppressive behaviors that have cultural roots are many. In recent years, there has been growing press coverage of female circumcision—various forms of genital cutting—in Africa and among African immigrant communities in the United States, Canada, and Europe. Female circumcision, which is banned by law in the United States, is one example of a practice over which there is a sharp disagreement. The larger society, including both mainstream society and other cultural minority communities, strongly oppose such practices, because they view them as a form of genital mutilation with serious negative physical and psychological consequences for young girls. Nonetheless, because the practices are grounded in notions of ethnic culture and religion, one needs to be aware of the risk that cultural minority communities may perceive objections to female circumcision to be anti-African. Moreover, although many African women have denounced the practice of genital cutting, and some mothers have even sought asylum status for themselves and their daughters in the United States and other countries to avoid having the practice forced on their daughters, others have demanded the right to continue with the practice and in some cases have taken their daughters to other countries to be circumcised (see Abusharaf, 2007, for a variety of women's perspectives on female circumcision). The academic consensus is against the practice and some authors have identified the practice as a contemporary example of cultural relativism (Galotti, 2007). The debate has raised important questions about who has the right to impose values on whom, and how cultural relativism and the universal liberal values embraced by social work can somehow be part of a normative continuum. At the end, the debate can be addressed only from an ethical standpoint protecting the rights and well-being of the individual.

Ethical dilemmas emerge when cultural norms and practices promoted by some members of a group are in direct conflict with the code of ethics of the profession and the law of the land. The question members of many minority cultures ask is, "Who has the right to determine which cultural practices are acceptable or unacceptable?" The right to self-determination and to practice the traditions of one's culture appears to be limited by the law, but not all legal behaviors are ethical, and not all ethical behaviors are legal.

In such cases where cultural clashes emerge with recent immigrant families, a necessary first step is to inform and educate the community about the law and explain how the cultural practice conflicts with it. Punitive measures should be used only when there is a clear sense that the information was understood but the behavior has not changed accordingly. There will be gray areas where a behavior may not be illegal but is considered unethical. In such cases, consulting with elders or cultural experts in the community may help the worker have more of an impact and achieve the desired changes. These very difficult ethical dilemmas need to be brought up first at the agency level in supervision, and if necessary in consultation with the agency's legal counsel; the confidentiality of the client must always be protected. The next chapter delves more deeply into the question of how to apply specific social work methods in ways that recognize, honor, and capitalize on the cultural backgrounds of clients and how to address possible value-based conflicts.

Key Concepts

Individualistic societies: Societies that believe that the needs of the group or society are satisfied when the needs of the individual are satisfied

Collectivistic societies: Societies that believe that the needs of an individual are satisfied when the needs of the group or society are satisfied

Cultural norms: Values and beliefs that influence the attitudes and behaviors of different cultural groups and are learned from parents, teachers, peers, elders, religion, social clubs, and traditional rituals and practices

Hypothesis testing: The use of existing cultural knowledge about cultural groups in a cautious or exploratory manner without arriving at any conclusions about clients or their cultures until more information is available

Dynamic sizing: The ability to know when to generalize certain attitudes and behaviors exhibited by the client to other members of the same identity group (i.e., when certain norms or behaviors are culturally based and may be common to others in the identity group) and when to individualize (i.e., when they are a function of the client's personality and there is no cultural explanation for such behaviors or attitudes)

Culturally specific expertise: The skills and abilities necessary to work effectively with individuals and groups from a particular culture by developing rapport and a strong client-worker alliance and achieving the desired outcomes when working with clients from that culture

Mestizaje: The mixing between Native peoples of the Americas and people of Spanish, European, African, and Asian ancestry

Familismo: The strong identification with and attachment to a nuclear or extended family and a willingly accepted obligation to provide both material and emotional support to one's family

Personalismo: The valuing of interpersonal relationships

Simpatía: The cultural expectation among Latinos that individuals avoid conflict and act in a good-natured and pleasant way

12

Culturally Grounded Methods of Social Work Practice

PROFESSIONAL SOCIAL WORK IS A WESTERN INVENTION, BUT OFTEN IT IS taught as if its methods of interventions are culturally neutral. Because of this oversight, not only do practitioners run the risk of implementing interventions that are ineffective due a lack of cultural fit between the intervention and the targeted population, but they also miss opportunities to incorporate culturally grounded ways of helping. For example, agencies and providers often target language as a key aspect of cultural diversity. A child welfare agency may develop policies to place foster children in families by matching the primary language spoken by the child while deemphasizing assessments of other relevant cultural factors. Although the agency workers are following an important component of a culturally grounded approach, reliance on language-matching addresses just one dimension of a successful culturally grounded intervention. When the desired results are not attained, there is a tendency to blame the client rather than to assess the cultural relevance of the service delivery system. The assimilationist model perpetuates the myth that if clients were just a little more like the white middle class, everything would be fine. Social workers must remember that the ultimate goal of any social work intervention is to serve, not to colonize (Aponte, 1994; Razack, 2009). Workers who are culturally unaware can easily become instruments of assimilation, misinterpreting difference as deviance or deficiency, and failing to recognize the strengths coming from culture that keep individuals and their families healthy.

Since the inception of the profession of social work in nineteenth-century England, most social work practice and research have focused on one-on-one interventions. Such models may feel natural and comfortable to many white middle-class clients and clients from other backgrounds who are acculturated or assimilated to mainstream culture. However, this individualistic approach may feel foreign or uncomfortable to others. In addition, definitions of well-being and happiness may vary between communities, and the means and approaches to intervene in times of crisis may vary as well.

Although the profession is now practiced globally and with clients from different cultural backgrounds, the cultural relevance of this traditional intervention is limited. One-on-one interventions present challenges because the social worker often has more power than the client does. As a result, the worker may unconsciously place her- or himself at the cultural center of the relationship, forcing the client to adjust to the cultural framework and the resulting boundaries imposed by the worker. Practitioners can greatly influence their clients' lives; their actions in one-on-one interventions can affect their clients for better or for worse. Unlike family interventions, group work, and community interventions, which are naturally conducive to horizontal relationships and client participation and empowerment, one-on-one interventions require a conscious effort to place clients and their culture at the center of the worker-consumer relationship. Thus, when practitioners engage in one-on-one interventions with clients, it is important that culture play a central role in the design and choice of the intervention. The client's culture must be approached as a possible source of strength, and the worker must take into account and incorporate the cultural and spiritual beliefs and practices of the client from the beginning, at the intake and assessment points.

So-called culturally neutral services and methods tend to disregard the unique contributions and needs of different ethnic communities. These interventions often enforce the dominant narrative and reflect a view of the world that does not recognize or celebrate the client's cultural heritage. When working with clients from different cultural backgrounds, social workers need to ask themselves not only what the right type of intervention is for the presenting problem, but also what the right type of intervention is for the client. If a one-on-one intervention is the answer to both questions, practitioners who are working with members of strongly collectivistic communities must find ways to integrate this type of intervention with a more collectivistic way of helping through group or family interventions. Change does not occur in isolation; new behaviors need to be rehearsed in social contexts as similar as possible to the daily life of the client.

CULTURALLY GROUNDED SOCIAL WORK WITH INDIVIDUALS AND THEIR FAMILIES

One way of implementing the culturally grounded approach in many agency settings is through family interventions. These interventions tend to pay close attention to the practitioner's impact on family members, and vice versa, not only focusing on the needs of individuals, but also taking into account the whole family system. Family interventions emphasize connections between individuals and view interactions systematically and structurally, but they seldom see families as networks that extend beyond the nuclear family. Different ethnic and identity groups may view their extended family networks in ways that need close exploration and understanding. For example, traditional Chinese identity is heavily influenced by relatives, and any attempt to empower an individual of Chinese background needs to involve or at least acknowledge all of the client's family members. Because interpersonal family relationships and harmony are very important in Chinese culture, social workers can best achieve the empowerment of clients as individuals by advocating for their rights and responsibilities in the context of their family roles and social statuses. The following set of principles can guide a culturally grounded approach to working with families.

1. Practitioners and families work together in relationships based on equality and respect.
2. Family members are a vital resource.
3. Practitioners enhance families and their capacity to support the growth and development of all family members: adults of all ages, youths, and children.
4. Interventions affirm and strengthen families' cultural, racial, and linguistic identities and enhance their ability to function in a multicultural society.
5. Practitioners are embedded in their communities and contribute to the community-building process.
6. Practitioners work with families to advocate services and systems that are fair, responsive, and accountable to the families served.
7. Practitioners work with families to mobilize formal and informal resources to support family development.
8. Interventions are flexible and continually responsive to emerging family and community issues.
9. Principles of family support are modeled in all program activities, including planning, governance, and administration (Jepson et al., 1997).

Recognizing the key role of family is just the first step. The next step involves recognizing that families live in densely interconnected social networks. They are part of a neighborhood, a house of worship, a tribe, a clan, and/or an identity community such as the gay, transgender, or deaf communities. The connection to other institutions or informal networks is a key element to consider during the assessment and action plan phases. Ignoring these connections may lead to misinterpretations and mistaken assessments. Notes from the field 12.1 illustrates the strong connections between culture, mental health, spirituality, and religion, and how these links can affect assessment and family interventions. In this example, the social work intern effectively integrated the belief systems and spiritual dimensions of the presenting problem, which resulted in an appropriate course of action for the family. She might have chosen a behavioral approach instead, one that encouraged the client to replace her disturbing thoughts about her niece's suicide with happier memories of her. Such an approach would have been premature, as it neither identified nor addressed the crux of the family's dilemma. The

NOTES FROM THE FIELD 12.1
Let Her Soul Rest in Peace

Leticia is a bilingual (Spanish/English) advanced practice MSW intern at an elementary school situated on the outskirts of a large city in the Southwest. For several weeks, she has been working with a Mexican family who recently immigrated to the United States. In supervision, Leticia expresses concerns about her perceived lack of progress with the Rodriguez family. The two children continue to present symptoms of depression and anxiety. Their symptoms are very similar to those shown by their mother after a niece who lived with them committed suicide six months earlier. Mother and children have recurring dreams about the dead young woman. Leticia has been encouraged by her field supervisor to address this issue directly with the mother. A few minutes into their next meeting, the mother shares her concern that the lack of a proper burial prevents her niece from resting in peace and moving on to the other world. No funeral mass or blessing of any kind took place because, given her understanding of the Roman Catholic Church's stance on suicide, she believed that no priest would perform the ceremony. Leticia is encouraged by her supervisor to double-check this assumption with the local parish priest. The priest offers to visit the family, and together they agree to have a mass of remembrance and prayer for the deceased niece. The ritual provides closure, and the whole family is able to move on with their grieving process. Soon after, the family's depressive symptoms begin to dissipate.

acknowledgement of key cultural dimensions of family life (unresolved grief) and their connection to other key social systems (church) resulted in positive change.

Families, which are formed by individuals in committed relationships that may not involve biological ties, are one of the strongest institutions in the United States as well as the rest of the globe. However, American society is characterized by a high rate of divorce, out-of-marriage births, and little contact between members of divorced families. Not only does the United States have one of the highest rates of divorce in the world, with about half of all first marriages ending in divorce, but it also has a high rate of remarriage. Over three-fourths of those who divorce eventually remarry someone else. As a result, about one child in five under the age of eighteen is a stepchild (Mechoulan, 2006). Nonetheless, despite dramatic changes in family structures over the past few decades, mainstream American culture tends to attach negative definitions to any form of family that does not conform to the traditional family structure of breadwinner father, homemaker mother, and their biological children.

Such dated beliefs about family are sometimes reflected in U.S. family policies, such as prohibitions and limitations on adoptions of children by gay couples and unmarried individuals. How families are formed is sometimes seen as more important than how well they perform essential functions for their members. Various efforts have aimed at regulating how families form without considering the needs of children first.

Families' different cultural backgrounds provide different cultural environments in which children become socialized. As part of that socialization process, children develop a worldview and a culture and learn how to interact with an outside environment that makes them aware of their race and ethnicity, often through the lenses of racism, ethnocentrism, and acculturation. It is within this context that social workers best enact their roles as advocates and cultural mediators.

CULTURALLY GROUNDED SOCIAL WORK WITH GROUPS

Members of oppressed and disadvantaged communities face a host of barriers in their quest to advance socially, economically, and spiritually. Some of these difficulties emerge from misunderstandings concerning their cultural status, racial inequality, lack of support systems, and stereotypical media portrayals. These and other factors reinforce a master narrative of who these groups are, why they experience life as they do, and what change is possible for them. By employing a mutual aid approach, group work provides an effective counterforce to the devaluation of cultural identities that occurs when cultural minorities are cast as the other. In groups, individuals can deconstruct and challenge stereotypical messages from the majority culture and can become aware of their own internalized oppression. The group helps them normalize their feelings and perceptions. Culturally grounded social work with groups connects individuals with their cultural roots and then explores what the group members have in common in terms of the past, the present, and their dreams for the future. This approach maximizes the potential of the members' narrative legacies and allows their commonalities to emerge. This culturally grounded process follows the identity development approach by helping group members to become aware of their identity in the context of their cultural background and its connection to their experience of oppression. Resources from the culture can be used creatively and respectfully to support this process as group members gain or regain awareness of their norms, values, and traditions. Group members from ethnic minority communities can share and support each other in their own challenges as they navigate between the two worlds represented by minority and majority communities.

Social workers of different identity backgrounds are often challenged to become familiar with the unique cultures that group members represent and the issues their communities are facing. Such knowledge is crucial for the effective facilitation of group activities. Regardless of their own background, social workers can educate themselves about a community's historical traditions, cultural beliefs, and norms, and they can learn how to integrate appropriate styles of communication respectfully. They can also work to comprehend the magnitude and implications of the loss of culture and be conscious of the community members' level of assimilation into the dominant culture.

Most social work with groups takes place within agency settings, and agencies customarily adopt a traditional culturally neutral approach to group facilitation. Group members are generally expected to absorb new knowledge, store it, and use it when needed. Freire (1994) described pedagogy of this type as "the banking approach to teaching" (p. 10), in which it is assumed that the teacher (worker) possesses something the student (client) needs but lacks. This approach is problematic because it pays no attention to the differences between the worker and the group members, relies on and reinforces client passivity, and disregards the complex contextual factors that contribute to the formation of the client's attitudes and behaviors.

Workers and clients perceive and evaluate their worlds differently. Developmental life experiences—as well as gender, sexual orientation, ability status, social class, and ethnicity—all shape an individual's worldview. When there are substantial differences in developmental factors and experiences there are even greater gaps between what workers and clients perceive as valuable knowledge. Culturally grounded group work attempts to remedy this situation by rescuing and validating community-based narratives.

Clients who find their culture reflected in the substance and format of group interventions are more likely to be motivated to participate in and to benefit from the experience. Group interventions that are grounded in the culture of the targeted population reflect on and recognize norms of behavior and other cultural products of the group. Therefore, culturally grounded group work uses culture to inspire group members. The objective is to highlight the resiliency factors that are present in the evolving cultural narratives that emerge from the group members' communities.

One way to ground work in the culture of the group members is to utilize practices from ethnographic interviewing (see chapter 15). To develop empathy among all members of a therapeutic group, group sessions can begin with an ethnographic interview, during which group members are invited to identify important parts of their culture (Corey, 2011). The interview may include questions on how individuals think their culture will influence their participation in the group or what things each individual may see differently from the rest of the group because of a unique cultural background. If a taboo topic is identified by a group member, the group facilitator can help the group address the topic; the facilitator can also develop a culturally appropriate strategy to recognize when avoidance of a topic is resistance, and when it is indication that the subject is taboo.

Group composition plays an important role in group outcomes. For example, the gender composition of the group has salient implications for group functioning (Meyers et al., 2005). Therefore, it is possible for gender to operate like any other status characteristic during group work. If the practitioner or the other group members bring rigid expectations about appropriate male and female behavior to the group, those expectations may actually affect behaviors and perceptions. Notes from the field 12.2 describes a situation where a group with a homogenous gender and cultural composition was used to address the needs of a specific cultural group. The homogeneous group composition in this example provided a safe environment where the young Arabic women were able to discuss the situation without being afraid of being judged by others.

Culture must be integrated from the pregroup phase to the formation and termination phases. Different cultures deal with conflict in different ways, and

---

NOTES FROM THE FIELD 12.2
Missing School

Manuel Benitez is a school social worker assigned to the bilingual and multicultural program of a large urban Midwestern school district. One of his roles is to monitor the academic achievement of students enrolled in the program who speak different languages. In a quarterly report to his supervisor, he notes an alarming trend among Arabic-speaking female middle school students. Their academic achievement continues to be very high, but they also have very high levels of absenteeism. Manuel interviews the Arabic-speaking teaching aides and learns that most of these girls are Palestinian and they are missing school so that they can visit their families' villages and refugee camps in preparation for prearranged marriages. He suggests the formation of an Arabic girls' group as a means to explore the situation and look for possible alternatives. Because he is male and does not speak Arabic, his first reaction was not to get involved and to find an Arabic-speaking female social worker to facilitate the group. His supervisor did not agree and encouraged Manuel to cofacilitate the group. He recruited an Arabic-speaking female social worker to cofacilitate the group with him. The two of them went together to all of the families' homes and explained the purpose of the group and asked them to sign permission slips allowing their daughters to attend the group. All except one of the mothers agreed to allow their daughters to participate in the group. The group members spoke mostly in Arabic and the cofacilitator summarized the exchanges for Manuel. How can the group leaders facilitate the group without alienating the group members from their families and culture?

some individuals may not have a great need to express themselves verbally. Thus, culturally grounded group work takes into account not only the content of the group sessions, but also the process itself, such that the "how" is as important as the "what."

CULTURALLY GROUNDED SOCIAL WORK WITH COMMUNITIES

Oppressed ethnic communities in the United States often are located in the bottom strata of income and wealth. Sometimes racism and discrimination become additional barriers to community development, and social workers may need to understand that, in these ethnic communities, people often find themselves in powerless positions. Social work in such communities is rooted in the settlement house movement, during which social workers not only provided services to the community, but also worked to empower marginalized groups. They organized communities, improved services, and administrated health programs. Although settlement houses still exist today (often in the form of community centers), they are under threat (Fabricant & Fisher, 2002b), and social work with communities in general is jeopardized by government downsizing and the abdication of responsibility to meet human needs. As a result, the importance of advocacy and client mobilization has increased. When working with communities, social workers need to remember that they "do not hold the answers to problems, but that in the context of collaboration, community members will develop the insights, skills, and capacity to resolve their own situations" (Gutierrez & Lewis, 1998, p. 8). Social workers build capacity for change by recognizing that members of the community live in oppressive circumstances that inhibit their ability to act effectively. When people begin to exercise control over the direction of their lives and have opportunities to join together to set priorities for their communities, their capacity for meeting personal and community goals is enhanced. The role of the community-building practitioner is to facilitate and strengthen the development of social networks as the means to support the development of strong communities that are able to exercise change and improve their living conditions (Fabricant & Fisher, 2002a).

It has been argued that community organizing has lost its purpose and relevance in postindustrial societies. Social and economic transformations produced by neoliberal policies ended the democratic/redistributive phase of community development and resulted in new forms of purposive social action aimed at achieving social justice (Newman, 2006). These new types of community-organizing efforts tend to be at the grassroots level and are playing a significant role in the creation of a more just society for the most oppressed and vulnerable sectors of society (Fisher & Kling, 1994; Speer & Christens, 2012). Many contemporary community-based social movements are being organized by ethnic minority groups, women, youth groups, and other sectors of society that were not well represented in the old social movements that flourished between World War II and the 1970s. These new movements tend to be identity based (e.g., based on ethnicity, gender, sexual orientation). These community efforts toward change and transformation originate in a collective identity, or shared sense of self, and in the organizing efforts that are inspired by this collective identity, which in turn reinforce the group's sense of identity. In this way, individuals achieve a collective sense that their shared identity is a source of oppression; at the same time, their identity can become a source of power through organizing (Duyvendak & Nederland, 2007).

The challenge for social workers who are practicing from a culturally grounded perspective is to bring together diverse grassroots efforts inspired by collective identities that share a geographic space and have similar social and political goals to form coalitions that can create lasting social change. Coalitions could help identity-centered efforts aim at lasting structural and policy changes beyond their own more limited change agendas.

FORMING COALITIONS WITHIN DIFFERENT ETHNOCULTURAL COMMUNITIES

In recent years, given the increasing intensity and frequency of interethnic conflicts around the world, numerous forces have demonstrated the need for multiethnic coalitions. The Los Angeles riots in 1992 revived and refocused research on interethnic conflicts in the United States because they revealed the complexity of relationships between different ethnic groups. Political conflict between African American and Latino communities can reflect competition for scarce resources between these ethnic groups, overlaid by conflict between immigrant and resident populations. Nationalistic interests and the interests of different ethnic groups also contribute to inter- and intraracial and inter- and intraethnic group tensions. Many grassroots efforts are concerned about the lack of recognition of common interests across communities and a rise in competition among groups on issues like jobs, education, housing, health care, crime control, and the role of government. At the same time, there has been a decline in the role played by mediating institutions like religious organizations, unions, and political parties in addressing these community issues.

The creation of cross-cultural alliances and coalitions may very well be an important step in decreasing the level of cultural and ideological fragmentation that characterizes many urban centers around the globe. When members of communities focus exclusively on their cultural differences, the resulting fragmentation tends to obscure the problems that they have in common, such as power differentials, privilege, access to resources and services, and wealth. Coalitions are a way of organizing across group lines to address these inequalities. While differences in multiethnic and racial communities are important, coalitions can provide a mechanism to take action around common interests on issues such as employment, income, housing, and medical care. Whereas at the macro level these differences may be very difficult to reconcile, short-term and issue-oriented multiethnic coalitions that develop at the neighborhood level may be able to surmount these differences around issues that are more specific. One strategy available to less-powerful ethnic groups is the formation of partnerships with groups that are more established. Such coalitions are necessary to enhance the chances that less-influential groups will be incorporated in a dominant local coalition.

As coalitions addressing a variety of social and health problems become more common, research has begun to identify the factors associated with effective coalitions. Kegler and Swan (2011) found that greater coalition member participation and satisfaction increased the effectiveness of the coalition's leadership, their task focus, the level of overall cohesion, and the members' influence on decision making, communication, and board representation, which in turn increased the development of new skills, the coalition's sense of community, and social capital. These factors may not, however, directly influence the quality of the coalitions' plans or the primary outcomes of coalition activities (Butterfoss, Goodman, & Wandersman, 1996). A case study of two health promotion coalitions found that their effectiveness was related to a number of diverse factors. Most important were a grassroots rather than bureaucratic source of vision; more staff time devoted to coalition-organizing activities than to the daily maintenance of the organization; a backstage role for staff in carrying out coalition activities, which allows coalition leaders to have a more visible role; frequent and productive communication among staff and members; high levels of cohesiveness; a more complex coalition structure during the intervention phase; and intensive and ongoing training and technical assistance (Kumpfer, Turner, Hopkins, & Librett, 1993). More recently, a study of eighty-eight coalitions found that inclusive discussions at meetings and the amount of time members spent outside of structured meetings (especially in the absence of paid staff) contributed to the members' perception of effectiveness (Wells, Feinberg, Alexander, & Ward, 2009).

The theoretical and empirical literature on multiethnic coalition building is limited; many explanations for why people form coalitions point to the self-interest of individuals and groups, however, and the realization that cooperation can maximize the benefits of the participants. Carmichael and Hamilton (1967) presented four requirements for successful multiethnic coalitions: (1) recognition of the interests of each party, (2) a shared belief that each party in the coalition stands to benefit, (3) acceptance that each party has its own base of power and decision making, and (4) agreement that the coalition must deal with specific and identifiable goals and issues. Shared views and ideologies may also be a prerequisite for the development of effective alliances based on a set of common interests.

Before functional coalitions can be developed, divisive issues like nationalism and identity politics may need to be addressed. Multicultural change is a process that recognizes the difference between groups while increasing interaction and cooperation between them, and recognizing differences and building bridges at the community level. Issues that may compromise or limit the effectiveness of a coalition include nationalistic ideologies, intense ethnic solidarity, and cultural and class differences that create barriers between its members. In addition, differences in group size, economic status, and resources can interfere with the coalition-building process.

In sum, a shared minority status does not automatically facilitate the formation of social and political coalitions. Members of ethnocultural minority communities form coalitions as they recognize their differences and honor their intergroup heterogeneity. Ideally, on the long list of issues that different groups bring to the table, a shared set of concerns can be identified. It is around the short list of shared issues or grievances that the social worker supports the formation of community coalitions and facilitates the identification of the shared power the coalition members have.

FOSTERING CULTURAL COMPETENCE IN AGENCIES AND AMONG STAFF

It is important for agencies to make an effort to become culturally competent and to be welcoming to different ethnoracial communities. The agency space itself—the behavior of the receptionist, the decor of the waiting room, and the way in which the social workers' offices are organized—can determine whether clients feel welcome. A very small reception area and clinical offices with one desk and two chairs are often the norm in agencies, even though cultural minority clients tend to seek help as a family or arrive accompanied by members of their extended family, family of choice, or other members of their support network. When there is no physical space for them, the message, whether intentional or unintentional, is that people in the client's support network are not welcome.

There are generally two main avenues to attain cultural competence in work with different ethnocultural communities: culturally specific agencies and culturally specific outreach programs within existing culturally neutral service-delivery systems. Both of these avenues have advantages and shortcomings: unfortunately, culturally specific agencies tend to lack technology and have fewer resources, while larger mainstream agencies with outreach programs run the risk of treating outreach to minority cultures as an add-on to their regular agency services.

Culturally specific social service agencies were developed in response to Native American, immigrant, and religious groups' search for grassroots solutions to their problems. For example, as a response to a lack of bicultural and bilingual social workers, many Latino communities around the nation have started Latino-centered agencies. Social workers in these agencies often play a cultural mediation role as their clients navigate the acculturation process, helping them to access opportunities and advance economically and socially. To mediate effectively between these two worlds, workers need to be familiar with both cultures, ideally in both languages. However, the reality is that the availability of bilingual and bicultural social workers is limited, so social workers who are not bicultural are being trained by ethnic-specific agencies to provide culturally competent diagnostics and to develop treatment plans for ethnic minority clients.

Culturally specific outreach programs within existing culturally neutral service-delivery systems are also very common among established social service agencies. These agencies recognize the need to serve minority ethnocultural clients and are aware of their own lack of culturally grounded services and outreach programs. Thus, in order to address their lack of cultural specificity, these agencies establish outreach programs staffed by members of the targeted community. These outreach programs are created as appendixes to the main organizational and leadership structures, and the minority constituencies are often not well represented in governing board and executive positions. Starting an outreach program is certainly a commendable effort, but representation in the decision-making and supervisory roles is very important in order to ensure a horizontal rather than a subservient relationship with the main agency structure.

Regardless of the organizational pathway that an agency follows, staff must remember to avoid stereotyping the minority client and to keep in mind that every population is heterogeneous and every individual is unique. In order to avoid ethnocentrism, clients should be regarded as experts in the interpretation of their own symptoms, strengths, and treatment preferences.

While working with cultural minority communities, the worker must examine the insider-outsider role as part of any practice effectiveness assessment. Acceptance of the role of the outsider often allows the process of enculturation to begin. Enculturation into a different culture does not mean pretending to be someone else, but rather means gaining familiarity and respect for a different cosmology or worldview. It is a long process, and it requires patience, open minds, and open hearts. This process can be monitored in supervision, and contradictory feelings can be identified and sorted out.

Social workers may turn to supervisors for guidance, or they may turn to a colleague in a type of interaction called peer consultation. Peer consultation allows the social worker to receive critical yet supportive feedback within an egalitarian relationship in which neither party has official responsibility for evaluating the other's performance. In work with members of an unfamiliar community, consultation with a cultural expert (such as those discussed in chapter 13) is highly recommended. Notes from the field 12.3 illustrates a possible strategy for workers to follow when seeking entry into an unfamiliar community. These consultants should be paid and must adhere to the same professional standards as would be expected in any other form of consultation, such as confidentiality. Community-based cultural consultants are best identified through referrals.

Through supervision, consultation, or a combination of the two, practitioners can reach out when confronted by ethical dilemmas connected to cultural differences. Ethical dilemmas with a cultural basis often emerge when cultural practices and norms appear to be in conflict with the standards set by the Code of Ethics of the National Association of Social Workers (2008). For example, clients may express their appreciation for the social worker's assistance in traditional cultural ways that cross professional boundary lines. A family may ask the worker to become their child's godparent. In these cases, a combination of cultural expert and professional consultation may be advisable in order to arrive at the best ethical decision without alienating or offending community members.

The repertoire of social work methods and interventions utilized by a given agency may not meet culturally grounded standards. If a type of intervention does not feel right to a worker, the chances are very high that it will not feel right to her or his clients. Social workers should listen to their culturally grounded radar and explore possible reasons why such feelings of discomfort emerge. Social workers may think that they do not know how to work across cultural boundaries and may perceive themselves to be lacking the awareness and knowledge needed for competent practice. Not honoring their own knowledge and experiences makes them vulnerable to adopting simplistic solutions that may result in oppressive approaches to practice. Honoring knowledge and common sense can be a much

---

NOTES FROM THE FIELD 12.3

Doña Matilde's Stamp of Approval

During a family violence prevention campaign involving *curanderas* (Latina traditional healers), the social worker coordinating the campaign engages the help of Doña Matilde, a well-respected *curandera* in the community who is originally from the Dominican Republic, as the liaison with the other women. Doña Matilde helps develop the contact list, cosigns the invitations to the planning meeting, and cofacilitates the meeting, which is held in her own home. Her role and respected status in the community give the effort immediate credibility. The social worker also gains credibility because at the meeting, Doña Matilde introduces Ms. Adler as a good person who cares about the community's children and youths.

better starting point for professional growth and effective practice. An important question to ask is, "How can I be more in tune with and responsive to the values and norms of my clients?" Social workers need to ask how their practice is consistent with their own norms and values and those of the profession. The practitioner's own background and professional experience, however, may not be sufficient to reconcile contradictions and gaps in her or his practice. If she or he cannot interpret or understand certain value conflicts, the practitioner should probably seek the assistance of a cultural expert from the community. It is not up to the social worker to determine in isolation the best culturally grounded practice for her or his clients.

In order to ensure that they are practicing culturally grounded social work, workers must screen evidence-based practices for cultural specificity. Interventions can be culturally biased even after going through the most rigorous effectiveness tests such as randomized trials. Workers must consider sample composition and contextual factors before unconditionally embracing science-based interventions. Issues of fidelity (was the intervention carried out as designed?) and sustainability (how long lasting are the desired outcomes?) need to be considered as well. Very effective but short-lived interventions may not be the ideal vehicle for sustainable change in resource-poor communities. The blending of traditional helping systems (discussed in chapter 13) and practices with innovative science-based approaches is suggested as the next generation of intervention research.

When the assumptions or ideology behind social work interventions are not questioned, ethnocentric ideas can be perpetuated. Culturally grounded social work practice requires critical thinking and constant assessment of the needs of clients and the assets arising from their cultures, assets that can be tapped to propel transformative change. Identifying those assets and utilizing them effectively are part of an ongoing assessment of what is and is not essential in the client's culture.

Key Concepts

Culturally grounded interventions with individuals: Individualized ways of helping that approach culture as a possible source of strength for the individual, starting at the intake and assessment points

Culturally grounded family interventions: Interventions that emphasize connections between individuals and view interactions systematically and structurally, and in which the nuclear and extended family are approached as support networks

Culturally grounded social work with groups: Interventions that connect individuals with their cultural roots and explore what the group members have in common in terms of the past, the present, and their dreams for the future

13

Culturally Grounded Community-Based Helping

UNTIL RECENTLY, TRADITIONAL HEALTH SYSTEMS WITH NON-WESTERN worldviews served the therapeutic needs of virtually every human group. Although these are important systems for delivering care, professionals trained in the West generally have little understanding of and tolerance for them. A professional degree is always desirable, but it does not necessarily guarantee culturally appropriate or effective services. There is much knowledge and service effectiveness to be gained through partnerships with paraprofessionals and traditional community-based helpers. Knowledge and experience come in different forms and are passed on in different ways.

Paraprofessionals can play a vital role in supporting the delivery of effective high-quality services. For example, a study comparing the effectiveness of three types of counselors—(1) professional counselors with at least a bachelor's degree and no personal history of addiction, (2) paraprofessional counselors who are addicts in recovery, and (3) paraprofessional counselors who have no personal history of drug addiction—found no differences between the professional and paraprofessional counselors in their overall effectiveness (Aiken, LoSciuto, & Ansetto, 1984). A review of Cognitive Behavioral Therapy (CBT) interventions found that paraprofessionals were as effective as professional therapists when working with clients suffering from anxiety and depression (Montgomery, Kunik, Wilson, Stanley, & Weiss, 2010). Culturally and community-based helpers often bring life experiences and unique skills and knowledge of the community to professional teams; these experiences and skills compensate for the lack of a higher academic degree. Often, many of the needs of clients can be channeled through traditional practitioners, but other physical and mental health needs require access to mainstream care systems. The two systems can complement each other, and the culturally grounded social worker can play the role of cultural mediator between the two systems. This chapter will review some of the culturally based helpers and paraprofessionals used by social service agencies and different cultural groups, and the important roles they play in the lives of clients. Social workers are encouraged to incorporate these traditional folk healers and other paraprofessionals into the helping process and to view these individuals as professional colleagues, as they represent a source of therapeutic help and can make valuable contributions to the well-being of clients.

PARAPROFESSIONALS

Paraprofessionals are aides who are often hired by social service agencies because of their cultural familiarity with the community the agency serves. Paraprofessionals receive direct supervision from a professional regarding the planning, delivery, and processing of services.

Social services agencies often employ paraprofessionals who are familiar with the community the agency serves. Paraprofessionals have generally not completed a course of formal training leading to professional credentialing in the field, or, if they have completed such a course, it may not be recognized in this country.

One service that paraprofessionals often provide is interpretation. Many clients from cultural minority backgrounds, particularly refugees and other recent immigrants, may not speak English or may not feel comfortable communicating in English. Paraprofessionals are often used in social service agencies as interpreters of not only the language, but also clients' affect and tone, as well as other cultural aspects of communication. They can advise practitioners on whether a client's attitudes and behaviors are considered the norm and acceptable in the culture of origin. For example, refugees and other immigrants who have various mental health needs as they adjust to a new life in the United States are often unfamiliar with Western social services. Their English may be limited, and they may experience cultural prohibitions that act as barriers to their ability to access services. In such cases, agencies may engage paraprofessionals who are bilingual and bicultural to provide interpretation services to bridge the cultural and linguistic gap between services and clients. Thus, paraprofessionals who are indigenous to the community are an ideal source of support and make valuable team members. They are effective at establishing trusting relationships with the people they serve. Nonetheless, because of the close networks in many immigrant and ethnic minority communities, one primary concern is confidentiality. Once hired by a social service agency, a paraprofessional must be trained and oriented to the profession and its code of ethics. Paraprofessionals must practice the same ethical standards as the professionals in the agency in terms of confidentiality. Paraprofessionals may be unfamiliar with such concepts, and it may be inadequate merely to provide them with written material to review. A face-to-face orientation that offers opportunities for exchange and debriefing is needed.

294 The Profession of Social Work Grounded in Culture

Because most social workers in the United States are English monolingual, interpreters are often a key part of social services delivery teams. There are several guidelines that agencies and workers should observe in working with interpreters. First, use only certified interpreters. If they are not available in your community, recruit your own, but provide them with comprehensive training. Ask a native speaker to help you check candidates' fluency and familiarity with social service and mental health vocabulary. When meeting with clients,

1. Introduce yourself and introduce the interpreter. Explain to the client the role each one of you plays and how you work together so that she or he will receive the best services available.
2. Always look at the client when speaking to her or him, and look at the interpreter only when you are talking to her or him. When the client speaks, look at her or him and express empathy. Do not give her or him a blank look.
3. Avoid saying to the interpreter, "Ask him . . . " or "Tell her . . . " Speak in the first person; the interpreter will do the same.
4. Speak in short units of speech—do not use long, involved sentences. Interpreters often use the consecutive interpreting format. In this system, the worker and client take turns speaking, and the interpreter interprets at the end of each turn. The longer either party talks, the greater is the possibility of error.
5. Be patient. An interpreted interview takes longer. Careful interpretation often requires the interpreter to provide long explanations. Not all words and concepts exist in other languages; therefore, interpreting in another language may require more words to express the same meaning.
6. Expect that the interpreter may occasionally pause to ask you for an explanation or clarification of terms in order to provide an accurate interpretation.
7. Agree on some basic rules when interviewing a family. For example, ask the family to agree that only one person will speak at a time; otherwise it will be difficult for the interpreter to translate.
8. Avoid colloquialisms, abstractions, idiomatic expressions, slang, similes, and metaphors.
9. The interpreter will relay all that is said in the presence of the client, will not omit anything that is said, and will not make remarks to others in the room that the client does not understand.
10. Listen to the client and watch for nonverbal communication. Often you can learn a lot by observing facial expressions, voice intonations, and body language.
11. Repeat important information. Always give the reason or purpose for an intervention or referral, and engage the client in all decisions.

12. Check the accuracy of the interpretation by asking the client to repeat in her or his own words any important information or instructions that have been communicated, with the interpreter facilitating. (University of Michigan Health System Interpreter Services, 2007)

Third-party interpretation is ideally a temporary stage. The recommended path is for social workers working with a specific language group to learn that language. There is no substitute for direct communication between the worker and the client. Even the most efficient interpreter creates distance in the therapeutic relationship.

CULTURALLY BASED HELPERS AND HEALERS

In most cultures, informal community-based healers, traditional healing practices, and the health beliefs surrounding them have major roles in promoting health and well-being. These informal practices and beliefs appear in diverse forms among many ethnic communities in the United States and other developed multicultural societies. Social workers and allied professionals often need to recognize and understand how clients can draw productively from these informal resources while also receiving professional help. Lack of awareness or disdain for traditional healing practices and beliefs can undermine the professional's effectiveness. Whereas a practitioner might view a middle-class European American client with approval because she believes that this client is empowered to address health challenges in a self-reliant manner, the same practitioner may perceive a Latina client as possessing a fatalistic or passive attitude of *si Dios quiere* (God willing) that is not helpful. A Haitian Creole client may subscribe to a belief system in which good health is viewed as the ability to achieve equilibrium between *cho* (hot) and *frèt* (cold), and illness is attributed to spiritual imbalances. These beliefs lead to the expectation that illness should be treated through both natural practices (herbs and human touch) and practices that address supernatural forces.

Spirituality can be a strong component of the client's cosmology, and social workers are learning more and more about how to explore the spiritual aspects of their clients' lives. Culture shapes spiritual beliefs, especially during a crisis event such as bereavement, and affects how an individual processes and resolves the crisis. Because spirituality may liberate or oppress the client, spirituality may or may not contribute to the client's empowerment. For example, social workers may need to help a client reflect on or reframe deeply held religious beliefs if those beliefs are leading the client to blame himself or herself for being a victim of domestic violence. It is through an exploration of the client's narratives and the respectful empathy that the social worker provides in response that the strengths arising from spirituality can be separated from beliefs that may be harmful. As evidence that spiritual practices and beliefs can play a role in a client's recovery mounts, social workers are seeking to improve their understanding of their clients' spiritual resources through the assessment process and one-on-one interventions.

Organized religion is one source through which spirituality is channeled, and it serves to reinforce spiritual and cultural practices, norms, and values. Some religions foster a type of spirituality that provides consolation, inspiration, and guidance and may promote responsibility, identity, and community building. On the other hand, other forms of organized religion may lead followers to resist change, may implicitly promote self-blame, or may encourage a fatalistic or passive perspective on life problems. In these instances, the social worker can engage with the client in a process of reflection to distinguish between the prescribed norms and behaviors that are helpful and the ones that are harmful. Learning about the basic tenets of the client's religion will assist the social worker to understand the client's behavior better and to identify possible misunderstandings. Having good working relationships with pastors, shamans, priests, rabbis, and other clergy in the community can be beneficial in arranging the consultations that are often needed. Thus understanding clients' spirituality is helpful at least at two levels. First, it provides the social worker with an understanding of the client's perceived purpose in life that may help explain the rationale for many behaviors and family patterns. Second, it helps the social worker understand the subjectively perceived spiritual forces that may serve as cues or motivations for the client's behavioral changes (Pellebon & Anderson, 1999).

Native American Traditions

Social work practitioners may feel challenged when working with clients from cultures in which needs and crises are explained by supernatural factors and addressed by spiritual powers and influences. Practitioners cannot address the needs of traditional Native American clients in isolation as if the presenting problems were only psychosocial phenomena. Native American medicine men and women (sometimes called shamans) have traditionally performed the Western roles of physician, psychiatrist, and spiritual leader (Puchala, Paul, Kennedy, & Mehl-Madrona, 2010; Struthers, Eschiti, & Patchell, 2008). Working in partnership with shamans and other tribal healers is congruent with Saleebey's (2002) strengths perspective, and using traditional healing methods in addition to mainstream interventions may prove very valuable. As notes from the field 13.1 demonstrates, social workers can play an important role in assisting clients to connect traditional healing approaches with standard social work interventions.

Some Native American communities have medicine men and women who use rituals and herbs to cure ailments. Individuals who practice Native American religions believe that disease as well other forms of mental, spiritual, and physical

---

NOTES FROM THE FIELD 13.1

Ho'oponopono

Scott is a social worker in a family social service agency in Kona, Hawaii. The Waipa family is having a difficult time with eighteen-year-old Lana, who has applied to and been accepted to a college on the mainland. Her parents, grandparents, uncles, and aunts are upset, mostly because she did not say anything about it until she received her letter of acceptance from the university congratulating her on her admission. Scott suggests the use of *ho'oponopono*.

Ho'oponopono is a traditional mediation process that Native Hawaiian families use to settle arguments, resolve hurt feelings, and mediate family conflicts. It is rooted in the Hawaiian values of respect for extended families, an emphasis on maintaining harmony in relationships, and the fostering of goodwill. The process is designed to restore harmony in the family. When an important issue arises, a member of the family is chosen as the leader, who mediates the process. The discussion encompasses therapeutic aspects like identification of the problem, consideration of its effects on the family system, possible solutions, and ways to implement the chosen solution (Hurdle, 2002).

The session takes place at home and the grandmother is chosen to lead it. Scott attends to support the family in the process, but he does not speak during the session.

---

imbalance are produced by a disruption of intrapersonal and interpersonal connections between the physical self (the body), the mental self (the mind), and the spiritual self (the soul/spirit). The individual aims at nurturing a good relationship with other human beings, the forces of the universe, and divine forces bigger than the individual (Wills, 2007). Therefore, the medicine man's or medicine woman's most important task is to maintain and restore harmony and health in the world through magical manipulation of daily life that affects the relationship of the individual with the forces of the cosmos.

Integrating traditional ways of healing with social work interventions may increase success in work with members of traditional Native American communities. For example, the Cheyenne River Indian Reservation in South Dakota approved a delinquency prevention program and an alcohol treatment program using traditional methods such as sweat lodges, the pipe fast, and the Sun Dance (Voss, Douville, Soldier, & Twiss, 1999). Since the 1980s there has been a resurgence of traditional healing methods across the nation's Native American communities. This resurgence often has not been specific to tribe of origin, as many

individuals and communities have lost their connection with some of their traditional ways of healing. Enculturation efforts have been implemented by tribal
government councils and other leaders to balance the erosion of traditional healing practices resulting from acculturation. A study conducted among the Yupik
people in Alaska found that the more traditional tribal members as well as those
who had gone through a process of enculturation used traditional healing practices more often than other tribal members and were in better health than the
more acculturated members who used only Western medical services (Wolsko,
Lardon, Mohatt, & Orr, 2007). Social workers need to assess the availability and
quality of traditional healing services, assess levels of enculturation and acculturation, and develop connections with medicine men and medicine women and other
healers in order to make effective referrals when necessary.

African American–Centered Approaches

There is a long and rich history of African American indigenous healers and
folk healing; this healing blends some aspects of traditional African healing with
coping practices that emerged as a response to the experience of slavery. In African
American cultures, representatives of organized religion such as ordained minis-
ters and clerics play a very important role as helpers, especially in matters of
mental health or psychological distress (Harley, 2005). Many African American
cultures also make use of other healers who are not connected to organized religion, such as hoodoo priests. Hoodoo's magic healing is based on African folk
medicine, which evolved in the United States and is sometimes called conjure.
The American Southern hoodoo has much in common with Haitian voodoo, and
both traditions can be traced to specific regions in Africa such as the Congo Basin
and the regions inhabited by the Igbo, Yoruba, and Bambara (Mitchem, 2007). In
some areas of the American South, some of these practices are still common
among the elderly in general; this is especially true in rural communities. Many
communities in the South have a strong connection to the original African cultures brought to the country by enslaved Africans (Patterson, 2005). The historical
unavailability of institutional health care in many of the black communities made
the folk healer the preferred, most-reliable, and most cost-effective option for
many African Americans (Mitchem, 2007).

Folk healing in the African American community is as much about relationships as it is about responding to specific health needs and providing treatments
(Fett, 2002). Social work interventions with African Americans are increasingly
attempting to connect to traditional and informal helping systems that are present in communities in order to increase their effectiveness. African American–
centered family healing, for example, aims at integrating communal knowledge,
communal values, and existing mental health constructs as part of mental health
treatment interventions (Elijah, 2002). The focus of the intervention and the main

change-producing agent are the family and the healing powers connected to African American culture. The family is seen as an interdependent system whose members can all support one another to overcome stressors. A culturally grounded perspective views the family as the main source of healing, while social workers are encouraged to be social healers, meaning that they can work with the family in its effort to heal its relationship to the rest of society and to identify and address sources of oppression, such as racism, and their effects on the well-being of family members.

Afrocentric approaches rely on strengths from the culture, but those strengths may or may not be present in families and communities. Many of the healing and coping mechanisms that have been used historically by members of different African American communities have been quantified and standardized. For example, the Africultural Coping Systems Inventory is a thirty-item measure consisting of culturally grounded coping strategies based on an African American–centered framework (Utsey, Brown, & Bolden, 2004). The strategies are categorized along four dimensions: (1) cognitive/emotional debriefing, (2) spiritual-centered coping, (3) collective coping, and (4) ritual-centered coping. This measurement tool can be useful at the assessment stage and can provide the practitioner with information about the client's level of connection to her or his culture of origin. The absence of any of these dimensions can be explored, and actions can be taken to enhance and strengthen these connections when appropriate.

African American women in many communities around the nation provide informal support to each other through what has been called "kitchen talk," informal gatherings of friends around the kitchen table during which they eat and talk about whatever is in their hearts and on their minds (Robinson & Howard-Hamilton, 2000). In contrast to mainstream support groups, kitchen talk groups integrate individuals' communications with a variety of healing rituals (Harley, 2006). In notes from the field 13.2, these informal networks were utilized to increase knowledge and awareness of breast cancer screening.

African American healing practices and beliefs can be integrated into social work through a narrative approach. For example, Parks (2007) suggests several questions regarding coping strategies, spirituality, and the use of ritual that can be used as a point of departure to help the social worker integrate specific coping mechanisms and beliefs into social work practice.

1. Describe your most helpful coping and problem-solving strategies. How do you make sense of your problems and life difficulties?
2. How does spirituality play a role in your life? How do you benefit from spirituality in your life? How do you believe good and evil play a role in your life? What are your beliefs about death?
3. What activities do you feel strengthen your bonds with your family members? How do you honor your ancestors? What activities make you feel a connection to your community?

NOTES FROM THE FIELD 13.2

Save Our Sisters

In North Carolina, African American women are more likely to be diagnosed with breast cancer in the later stages of the disease, when it is far more challenging to fight. This health disparity has been attributed to infrequent screening among older, and rural, low-income black women. After a traditional approach to health promotion had been only marginally successful, Save Our Sisters, a lay health advisor intervention was implemented. This intervention empowered natural helpers by providing them with knowledge and asking them to use their preexisting informal social networks to spread that knowledge in their community. The use of lay health workers reached the women in a way that traditional health-care systems could not. Save our Sisters hired Ms. Johnson to coordinate the intervention. She is a retired elementary school teacher but very active in many institutions in the local African American community. The past professional role and her current involvement in community organizations gave her immediate entry and acceptance. The team then conducted informal focus groups to gain better insight into how African American women view breast cancer, the medical system, and the screening process. These conversations revealed that the women believed that their health was very private, that they felt disconnected from the formal health system, and that the system in general had "an attitude," which typically resulted in them going to their friends and family when they had a health issue. Based on this information, ninety female lay health workers were recruited; these women were successful at organizing the community and providing individual support and knowledge. After two years, the intervention had reached about half of the women in the study areas and rates of mammogram screenings had increased by 7 percent in all areas and 11 percent among low-income women.

Source: Earp et al. (2002).

4. Are there any folk beliefs or healing practices that are important to you? How comfortable do you feel talking about them with relatives and friends?
5. What meaning do you give to your dreams? Describe how your dreams provide insight into your life.
6. Do you have a family or community advisor or a spiritual advisor? If so, describe how she or he has played an important part in your life. What would she or he say about your problem or life's difficulties? Imagine and

then describe a positive image that you can use as a resource to draw on your strengths. (Parks, 2007)

Healers in the Latino Community

The folk healing tradition of the Spanish-speaking Caribbean is the product of a centuries-old process of spiritual and cultural syncretism between the pre-Columbian, African, and Spanish Roman Catholic traditions. This culturally blended form of spirituality is called *espiritismo* (spiritism) and is a valuable resource for assisting clients with their medical needs as well as with their psychosocial and emotional needs (Rivera, 2005). Owing to the underrepresentation of Latinos in higher education in general and in social work in particular, paraprofessionals are commonly found in Latino-centered agencies. In such agencies, paraprofessionals may include *promotoras* (health educators; this role is generally filled by women; men are called *promotores*), *curanderos* (healers), *herbolarios* (herbalists), and *parteras* (midwives). *Promotoras* have been employed for many years by agencies to conduct home visits, primarily for carrying out prevention interventions. Home visits by *promotoras* have proved to improve the health outcomes of families (Martin, Camargo, Ramos, Lauderdale, Krueger, & Lantos, 2005). *Promotoras* are trained bicultural and bilingual Latina lay community health advisors who can play important roles in increasing the Latino community's awareness of the risks of certain diseases. They distribute information and make appropriate referrals, educate the community, provide emotional support, build the community, and advocate for increased access to health-care services (May et al., 2003). In addition, they provide a link between the community and the health-care system. Lack of fluency in English and the lack of education, coupled with low SES, act as barriers to health-care access for some Latino families. In these cases, *promotoras* are a bridge between the community and needed services.

Curanderism is a form of natural and practical medicine that works well with the Mexican American population, as well as with other Latino subgroups (Tafur, Crowe, & Torres, 2009). These traditional healers are called on to perform curative rituals and are often thought to have more authority and power than mental health professionals do (Hoogasian & Lijtmaer, 2010). Some illnesses, such as *empacho* (indigestion), *mal de ojo* (evil eye), and *susto* (fright), are believed to come from supernatural sources and as such are much more effectively treated by *curanderos*. Since different Latino communities use *curanderos* and *curanderas* (female *curanderos*) in different ways, in work with Latinos it is essential for the social worker to take into account the folk beliefs of the particular community to which the clients belongs, and the community's possibly unique use of *curanderos*. *Curanderos* believe that human beings occupy a natural world that interacts with, and even infuses, various parts of the self. The restoration of good health requires that these parts of the self and their connections to the natural world be brought into harmony. *Curanderos* blend some aspects of the Catholic tradition with indigenous non-Western medicinal beliefs and practices. As notes from the field 13.3 illustrates, involving *curanderos* and other community-based paraprofessionals as partners in interventions may require special and creative forms of communication and outreach.

Parteras, or midwives, also play an important role among Latino women. Home visits by lay workers may be more acceptable to pregnant women than a visit to a nurse or a doctor, which may have an impact on health outcomes as well as social and environmental risk factors. It has been demonstrated that home visits increase the use of preventive services by pregnant women and encourage

---

NOTES FROM THE FIELD 13.3

More Condoms, Please!

At the beginning of the AIDS pandemic, a group of Latino social workers became involved with an HIV/AIDS service agency to address the prevention needs of the Latino community in a large Midwestern city. The agency already had an information hotline, and the committee agreed to staff a Spanish-language hotline. A number was secured, training was conducted, and bilingual volunteers took turns staffing the hotline. Days, weeks, and months went by, but community members were not calling. The committee reassessed their strategy and concluded that a hotline was not a culturally grounded approach to reaching out to the target population. After a long brainstorming session, they decided to try a completely different strategy. They invited all the *curanderas* they knew in the city and offered them training on "HIV/AIDS 101." A dozen *curanderas* accepted the invitation. They were receptive to the information but often had much better insight into the issues than that of the professional trainers. They agreed to include safer sex as part of their discussions with their visitors. Rosa, one of the trainers, was concerned about distributing condoms at the end of the session, a common practice in all agency-sponsored trainings. She decided to leave a basket full of condoms on the table and to say nothing because she did not want to offend the women. At the end of the training, the women in attendance opened their purses and filled them with as many condoms as they were able to carry. Doña Teresa commented that she had grandchildren and many of her neighbors had children and grandchildren and then asked, "Do you have any more condoms?" At the end of the session, the basket was empty.

healthier behaviors (Biermann, Dunlop, Brady, Dubin, & Brann, 2006). For women who have a strong cultural identity, home visits may even affect psychological functioning. Some *parteras* actually assist with the home delivery of babies, a practice that may align with the client's rural traditions and also provides an alternative for undocumented pregnant women who are unwilling or unable to receive care in a health center.

Herbolarios and *herbolarias* (female *herbolarios*) identify and categorize herbs according to their medicinal properties and look at clients' patterns of food intake in order to address ailments. Herbs are used to fight both physical and emotional ailments. One study in Mexico found that 83 percent of family physicians accept the therapeutic use of herbal medicines, 100 percent of nurses and other non-physician health workers accept them, and 90 percent of patients use herbs (Taddei-Bringas, Santillana-Macedo, Romero-Cancio, & Romero-Tellez, 1999). In the United States the rate of medical herbal usage among Hispanics varies from 4 percent to 100 percent, depending on the region, with an average of 30 percent across samples reporting that they used herbs for medical purposes (Gardiner et al., 2012). The help of herbalists is sought not only by Latinos, but also by traditional African Americans, Native Americans, and Chinese Americans, among other groups.

Asian Americans and Healing

Asian Americans have one of the highest use rates of complementary and alternative medicine (CAM) of all ethnic minority groups in the United States. A large California-based study found that three out of four Asian American respondents had used at least one type of CAM in the past twelve months, which is significantly higher than the national prevalence rate of four out of ten. Chinese Americans reported the highest prevalence of any CAM use (86%), while South Asians reported the lowest prevalence among those of Asian heritage (67%). In contrast with other ethnic groups, acculturation and access to conventional medical care was unrelated to any CAM use for most Asian American subgroups. The study found that spirituality was the strongest predictor of CAM use for most Asian American subgroups (Hsiao et al., 2006).

Traditional Chinese medicine is a rational healing system developed and perfected over five thousand years in China and used by the descendants of Chinese immigrants in the United States and all over the world (Ng, 2006). Traditional Chinese medicine is based on the ancient Taoist idea of unity of the opposites of yin and yang. Health is believed to emerge from the balance of the yin and yang of the body, mind, and spirit, while disease emerges in the absence of balance. The balance of yin and yang is achieved or restored through a combination of methods such as the use of herbs, acupuncture, corrective posture techniques, and exercise.

Many Asian Americans and clients of other ethnic backgrounds bring with them ideas about healing that can be traced to Buddhism. In many regards, Buddhism and other traditional philosophies such as traditional Chinese medicine are very well aligned with social work approaches to culturally grounded interventions. Buddhism looks for the relationship between the biological, physical, mental, and spiritual dimensions of healing. Social workers interacting with clients whose beliefs are influenced by Buddhism can emphasize their holistic approach and avoid separating the psychosocial aspects of a presenting problem from the overall aim of achieving balance. Buddhists understand good health to be the result of a balanced interaction between mind and body, as well as between life and its environment (Buddhism and Health, 1996; Wijesinghe & Mendelson, 2012).

Elderly Asian and Asian American clients may have a much deeper connection to traditional beliefs than do their children and grandchildren, as a result of the process of acculturation. However, the whole family system is probably affected by these beliefs, and as such they can be a good entry point for interventions. For example, mindfulness and meditation are often integrated into social work interventions. In Buddhism, mindfulness is a skill that allows the individual to be aware of what is happening in the moment and to be less reactive. *Sati,* the word for "mindfulness" in Pali, the language of the earliest Buddhist canon, connotes awareness, attention, and remembering (Germer, 2005). Mindfulness has been shown to have important clinical value in complementing treatment efforts to address stress, depression, eating disorders, and addictions (Ostafin et al., 2006). Chawla and Marlatt (2006) encourage clinicians to incorporate techniques for achieving mindfulness in their practice with Asian Americans and other clients, as well as to engage in the personal practice of meditation as a means to connect with the client.

ASSESSING CLIENTS' CONNECTIONS TO TRADITIONAL HEALING BELIEFS AND PRACTICES

David Haber (2005) offers a set of open-ended questions to assess the client's level of connection to traditional healing beliefs and practices that can be incorporated into the assessment phase of the culturally grounded approach with clients from different cultures:

1. What do you think causes your specific health problem?
2. What is your favorite home remedy or other treatment that you turn to when you are experiencing this health problem?
3. Do you know others who have had a similar health problem, and what they do to treat it?
4. Do you think there is a way to prevent this health problem? If so, how?

5. How is the tradition of health care in your heritage different from the type of help you receive at the hospitals or clinics in the United States?
6. Do you have problems getting the help you need from doctors and other American health-care professionals? If so, how?
7. Who else besides doctors and other American health-care professionals do you rely on for help with health problems?
8. Do you keep your doctors and other American health-care professionals informed about other sources of health care that you are receiving?
9. Are you active in a religious institution or religious or spiritual group? If so, are health services provided there?
10. Is there a religious healer or leader who can help support the management of your health problem?

When assessments reveal that clients have a strong connection with cultural healing beliefs and practices, it is important that social workers, in addition to implementing culturally competent interventions, make use of the expertise of community helpers and healers. The integration of indigenous and innovative approaches not only will advance science, but also will strengthen culturally grounded social work practice.

Key Concepts

Paraprofessionals: Aides who assist professionals; often are social service agency employees who are usually hired because of their cultural familiarity with the community the agency serves

Shamans: Native American medicine men and women who use spiritual rituals and herbs to cure ailments

Promotoras (promotores): Latino lay health educators (who are usually female) who provide prevention intervention services in the homes of clients

Curanderos (curanderas): Latino traditional healers who use a combination of spiritual rituals and prayers and touch to cure common ailments such as *empacho* (indigestion), *mal de ojo* (evil eye), and *susto* (fright)

Parteras: Traditional midwives in Latino communities who are often part of the support system of the mother before, during, and after she gives birth

Herbolarios (herbolarias): Latino healers who prescribe herbs to fight both physical and emotional ailments

14

Social Policy and Culturally Grounded Social Work

SOCIAL POLICY AND SOCIAL WORK PRACTICE GO HAND IN HAND. SOCIAL policies often affect funding for various social programs, which in turn affects what social programs individuals can access, as well as what types of services social work practitioners can provide. Since social policy is directly connected to the social work profession, social work practitioners have a key role as advocates for social policies that help meet the needs of communities in an effective and culturally grounded manner. This chapter introduces the concept of distributive justice and explains its relevance to culturally grounded social work. It describes some of the government policies and programs that have been implemented in an effort to ensure distributive justice, as well as some of the debates surrounding them, and discusses the ways in which policy affects social work practice and the policy advocacy role social workers can play.

Historically, social work in the United States has been involved in social policy development and social policy change as a means to effectively address the needs of individuals, families, and communities. For example, settlement houses and charity organizations emphasized their clients' relationships with larger systems in their social environments, such as labor unions and political parties. This focus continues to be of great importance in social work. Social policy is concerned with the decision-making process that takes place in the legislative arena, the implementation of social programs, and the fundamental question of where to allocate resources.

DISTRIBUTIVE JUSTICE

The Aristotelian concept of distributive justice is deeply rooted in social work and it comes alive through the policy analysis conducted by social workers. Distributive justice aims at ensuring that members of society have access to reasonable economic resources, education, social services, and other resources based on the ethical principles of equity and solidarity among the least privileged. These principles often must compete with other principles embedded in the national identity of the country. For example, the economic structure of the United States has been strongly influenced by the eighteenth-century writings of Adam Smith, whose thesis of the invisible hand of the market proposed that natural market forces should take care of the distribution of resources in the most efficient and effective manner without the intervention of the state (Smith, 2000). This perspective expects that not everyone will be equally successful and that social class differences are an inevitable, even welcome, condition for the healthy functioning of the overall society and economy.

On the other end of the spectrum from Smith's invisible hand is John Rawls's theory of justice, a perspective used in social work to operationalize the concept of distributive justice (Rawls, 2009). Through the application of the principle of distributive justice, Rawls aimed at ensuring that in cases of unequal distribution, the most disadvantaged individuals reap the greatest benefits. Rawls maintained that the redistribution of resources to benefit the disadvantaged should be guided by two main principles: equal liberty (meaning that no person or entity may compromise the freedom of the individual in order to access services or goods) and the fair distribution of social goods.

Distributive justice can also be understood as the fair distribution of benefits and burdens, which is achieved by way of the mechanisms and tools provided by procedural justice (i.e., the fair administration of justice). Thus distributive justice refers not only to economic goods, but also to the fair allocation of socially produced goods like opportunity, power, and self-respect. For an individual to pursue his or her life plan, each must possess a fair share of the available social resources. For example, although health is not a tangible good, the ability to access the health-care system is a social good, as a healthy individual is better equipped to compete for jobs, advance socially, and achieve an optimal quality of life than an individual who does not have access to health care. The concept of distributive justice is relevant to culturally grounded social work: in the United States individuals are often denied goods, benefits, and access to social resources based on their membership in various groups with whom social workers frequently come in contact. For example, even when agencies are able to offer the best services available to members of different cultural communities, their target populations may not always be able to access them. If only a few people can access the services, then it is not an issue of some individuals being hard to serve, but rather a sign that something is clearly wrong with the service delivery system. The social work tenets of self-determination and self-direction are consistent with current economic trends and realities; they need to be implemented with justice, empathy, and common sense, however. When providers design systems of services, they often neglect to focus on how clients will experience a system as they attempt to navigate it. That is, during system design there is a tendency to group services according to their function instead of focusing more on clients and the paths they must follow to receive services and achieve positive outcomes.

Residential segregation—which has been fueled by economic institutions like mortgage lenders, and protected by housing policies that reflect the political influence of the well-off—is the physical separation of ethnic or racial groups in a residential context. As a result, it restricts employment opportunities and leads to a higher concentration of poverty in certain areas. Political leaders are more likely to cut spending in poor neighborhoods than in more affluent areas because many residents of poor neighborhoods are ethnic minorities with less political clout than are residents in wealthy neighborhoods.

Transportation enables people to access basic needs such as work, education, and health care. Unfortunately, decision making about public transportation and transportation infrastructure is biased in favor of those with political power and resources and largely ignores accessibility differences by gender, physical ability, and ethnicity. As a result, it rarely brings about necessary changes. Another important aspect of the provision of social services is the societal practices and conditions that make some communities invisible. For example, as whites moved to the suburbs, public policies contributed to the development of suburbs through such measures as massive subsidies to build freeways while federally approved discriminatory practices in lending and sales helped the suburbs remain predominantly white. While some of the more egregious acts of discrimination have since been outlawed, disparities between whites and ethnic minority applicants still exist in their ability to obtain loans and home insurance. Because of such disparities, recipients of income replacement assistance (e.g., TANF) from many poor neighborhoods who want to move into the labor force face a challenge finding employment since social networks of employers and job seekers are often limited by location. Many recipients of financial assistance are at a disadvantage not only because they are members of an ethnic or racial minority and frequently have low skill levels, but also because they are restricted in where they can live and how easily they can travel to available educational and career opportunities. They often face situations in which the jobs have moved away from them but they cannot afford to move to the jobs.

To correct these inequities and address the lack of distributive justice, the government has intervened over the years in different ways, with varying degrees of success. Such organized efforts usually have both supporters and critics, which generates intense policy debate.

THE WELFARE STATE

Although the tax and regulatory structures of U.S. society create what has been called a corporate welfare system that gives more resources and privileges to corporations than to the most disadvantaged members of society, the word "welfare" is generally associated with the poor. Historically, the idea of promoting social welfare has been embraced by most religions (Hungerman, 2005), and in the past it was common for religious institutions to care for the less fortunate, such as widows and orphans. For example, in Christian societies it was the church that assigned the roles of providers and recipients within the community. Today a welfare society can be described as one that is devoted to the well-being of its members and that has social welfare institutions operating at the state level. For example, the Scandinavian states have traditionally been described as model welfare societies (Slothuus, 2007). Although the version of the social welfare state implemented in the United States after World War II cannot be considered a classic welfare state in the Scandinavian tradition, it follows what might be called a mixed or hybrid model that combines strong social welfare characteristics with a liberal economic model.

In the United States, the term "social welfare" is commonly understood to mean a payment in kind or in cash to a person who needs support because of age, disability, poverty, or mental illness. The term "entitlement" is frequently used in the social policy literature to describe programs in which these types of transactions between the state and individuals and families take place. For example, Social Security and Medicare are entitlement programs. Workers who contributed to the system during their working years are entitled after retirement to receive a monthly check and health-care benefits once they meet the established qualification criteria. Those qualifications may change over time. For instance, the minimum age for drawing full Social Security retirement benefits will increase gradually from sixty-five to sixty-seven, and the amount that seniors pay as copayments for Medicare can be increased every year through congressional action.

When social welfare and labor policies are in development, conflicts often arise among different groups. Sometimes the state tries to support a group that has been underprivileged for a long time, which often fosters resentment among the dominant group. One view is that the welfare state perpetuates unemployment by allowing workers to live in comfort while unemployed, which inhibits their motivation to look for work or accept work that is demanding. People who have not paid into the welfare system, such as children, some disabled people, and people with other disadvantages who have never been in the labor force, are often made to feel that they are not entitled to the benefits provided by the welfare state. For example, retirees on Social Security are not generally stigmatized in the way that single mothers on TANF are.

Public opposition to social welfare is caused in part by the misconception that recipients would rather sit at home than work, that they are undeserving of these benefits, and that they are predominantly ethnic minorities. In fact, the majority of entitlement benefits are not received by able-bodied individuals choosing not to work. In 2010, 91 percent of entitlements were paid to the elderly, seriously disabled, or working adults, and most of the remaining 9 percent went to medical care, unemployment benefits, social security survivor benefits, and early retirees (see figure 14.1). When all entitlement benefits are taken into consideration—Social Security, Medicare, Medicaid and the Children's Health Insurance Program, unemployment insurance, the Supplemental Nutrition Assistance Program, Supplemental Security Income, TANF, school lunch program, earned income tax credits, and the Child Tax Credit—it is not low-income but rather high-income families who benefit disproportionately. The top 20 percent of income earners in the United States receive 32 percent of these entitlements (Sherman, Greenstein, & Ruffing, 2012).

Societies often use outsider groups like recent immigrants and guest workers as scapegoats and question these groups' rights to receive benefits that are guaranteed to citizens. From a distributive justice perspective, it could be argued that if children born to undocumented immigrants have no right to education or health care, they will grow up to be uneducated (and therefore minimally employable) and in poor health, a hardship not only for them, but also for society as a whole. As a result, as adults they will not be able to contribute as much to the system and will depend more on services. Moreover, when they are barred from receiving publicly funded health care, their normal childhood development is threatened and they increase the risk that uncontrolled infectious disease will spread through the general population. This example illustrates the concept of the welfare state as a safety net not only for those in need of services, but also

Figure 14.1   Who Received Entitlement Benefits in 2010?

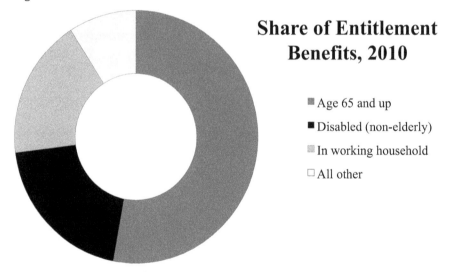

Share of Entitlement Benefits, 2010

- Age 65 and up
- Disabled (non-elderly)
- In working household
- All other

Source: Sherman, A., Greenstein, R., & Ruffing, K. (2012). *Contrary to 'entitlement society' rhetoric, over nine-tenths of entitlement benefits go to elderly, disabled, or working households*. Washington, DC: Center on Budget and Policy Priorities.

indirectly for all of society as an interconnected and interdependent living organism. The term "safety net" refers to the strategies society uses to respond to its members' unplanned needs. These individuals often make up a transitional group that people constantly enter and leave. A large proportion of the U.S. population, about two out of every five Americans, will use a social safety-net program for at least five years during their working lives (Rank & Hirschl, 2002). In the United States, the Supplemental Nutrition Assistance Program (SNAP, or food stamps) and Woman, Infants and Children) are examples of safety-net strategies used by a very diverse group of recipients.

In 1996 the U.S. Congress, with the support of President Bill Clinton, enacted sweeping welfare reform with strict work requirements for parents receiving TANF, and with lifetime limits on eligibility. Critics at the time charged that the changes were in large part motivated by the demonization of single mothers, who were often pejoratively called "welfare queens." Overlooked at the time was the inconvenient reality that the vast majority of TANF beneficiaries were dependent children. Unfortunately, these federal and state welfare policies have both directly and indirectly discriminated against racial minorities, in particular African Americans and recent immigrants. Many families were forced to rely on inadequate provisions for child care, and some became ineligible for health services provided through Medicaid. Almost two decades after the passage of the welfare reforms, 23 percent of all U.S. children are still living in families officially classified as poor (Bradshaw et al., 2012). The United States ranks twenty-fourth among twenty-five developed countries in terms of the percent of children not living in poverty, just slightly better than Romania (Bradshaw et al., 2012).

Antifamily social policies have forced families to depend on overburdened public and private services, as well as their own extended families. A study of ninety nonprofit organizations found that the 1996 welfare reforms had a substantial enough impact on these organizations—particularly on those serving a high proportion of minority clients—that they were unable to keep up with client demands (Reisch & Sommerfeld, 2002). The stated objective of these reforms was for poor parents to achieve full employment rather than to continue to rely on public assistance. Critics have charged that reforms were implemented in many states without adequate regard to the consequences for vulnerable families and children, and without recognition of the difficulties presented by labor market conditions. The reforms provided minimally for child care, forcing many single mothers to choose between placing their children in inadequate child-care facilities, burdening their extended family or friends with child-care requests, and leaving children unattended. The job training and employment counseling services that were supposed to create bridges from welfare to work were insufficient for many recipients who lacked educational credentials and job experience; for those trapped in economically depressed communities, jobs were not waiting on the other side of the bridge.

The Affordable Care Act, passed by the U.S. Congress in 2010, was one of the largest expansions of the welfare state since the war on poverty in the 1960s. The primary goal of the Affordable Care Act was to provide quality health care for all Americans and contain the rapidly increasing cost of health-care services. This bill was hotly contested in Washington. Individuals opposing the bill argued that it overextended the reach of the federal government and would hinder the efficiency of market forces. Despite continuing vocal opposition and attempts to overturn it provisions, the act has remained largely intact. In 2012 the U.S. Supreme Court upheld the portion of the act that legally requires every individual to purchase health insurance or pay an annual fine, but limited the state mandate to expand their Medicaid coverage (Larrat, Marcoux, & Vogenberg, 2013). Even with the limit on the state mandate to extend Medicaid, it is projected that 40 to 42 million uninsured or underinsured individuals will now have adequate health insurance, reducing the number of uninsured by 70 percent (Buettgens & Carroll, 2012; Schoen, Doty, Robertson, & Collins, 2011). The increase in eligible service users may place more demand on social work services. Social workers may also be asked to help their clients, particularly unemployed clients, navigate the new health-care exchange system or determine eligibility for Medicaid coverage. Another major provision of the act, the expansion of electronic health records, could provide opportunities for social workers to more successfully coordinate multiple systems of care and assess the social determinants that influence a client's health.

The Affordable Care Act is not limited to the provision of treatment for health issues. It includes laws that are intended to prevent disease and reduce health disparities (Kocher, Emanuel, & DeParle, 2010). Under the act, insurance plans are either required or given incentives to cover a range of preventive health services that are recommended by the U.S. Preventive Services Task Force (Koh & Sebelius, 2010). Some recommended prevention services include regular primary care visits, cancer screening, HIV screening, substance abuse counseling, and screening for depression. The bill also provides funding for programs that promote wellness in the workplace and in communities. In 2011, as part of the Affordable Care Act, the CDC awarded sixty-one Community Transformation Grants totaling $103 million to address nutrition, physical activity, and substance use including smoking, and to promote social and emotional wellness (CDC, 2012c). These initiatives provide optimal opportunities for social work practice and research and could have a major impact in increasing access to behavioral health services and to reduce and eventually eliminate health disparities.

Despite the passage of the act, the implementation of many of the provisions that address prevention are dependent on adequate budget appropriations, some of which were substantially cut in 2011 and 2012 (Larrat et al., 2013). In addition to providing services and ensuring that clients are able to navigate changes in the health-care system and receive care, social workers can also work to advocate for the full funding of programs that will work to reduce health disparities and improve that quality of life for their clients. Under provisions of the Affordable Care Act, social workers along with other helping professionals can also play a role in designing, implementing, and evaluating community-based prevention interventions that are culturally grounded.

Social work and allied professions are actively engaged in these efforts. For example, the National Association of Deans and Directors (2012) of Schools of Social Work has been actively engaged in these processes through their Behavioral Health Disparities Taskforce and research projects funded by the Office of Minority Health. The Taskforce recommendations include behavioral health practice competencies addressing health disparities within the framework of the Affordable Care Act.

The Tasksforce recommends that social workers will

- Have a commitment to the ongoing assessment of behavioral health needs and strengths of individuals, families, groups, communities, and organizations;
- Participate in the ongoing development and use of evidence-based and community-based strategies that promote behavioral health equity;
- Promote behavioral health equity across social, psychological, environmental, and economic contexts; and
- Actively engage health and mental health practitioners at all levels of practice with knowledge of multidimensional aspects of behavioral health disparities awareness. (National Association of Deans and Directors [NADD], 2012 p. 6).

AFFIRMATIVE ACTION

Affirmative action, discussed briefly in chapter 2, is defined as government policies that attempt to improve the educational and employment opportunities of historically oppressed populations in the United States. Similar efforts, under the same or different names, have also been conducted in other countries. In 1961 President John Kennedy established the President's Committee on Equal Employment Opportunity to end discrimination in employment and to ensure that race, religion, and national origin would not be factors in employers' consideration of job applicants. Later, President Lyndon Johnson transferred the committee's responsibilities to the Department of Labor. Johnson also prohibited discrimination in employment based on sex. In 1971, under President Nixon, all employers of five hundred or more workers were required to perform an annual analysis of areas in which they were deficient in the hiring of minority groups and women, file a report to the Office of Equal Employment Opportunity, and move to correct any deficiencies. However, the process for making these corrections, known as affirmative action, has been a controversial and contentious area of debate. Over time, affirmative action was extended to mean equal access not only to employment, but also to government contracts and higher education as well.

One of the arguments against affirmative action rests on the assumption that affirmative action undermines merit-based hiring and promotion practices, and that white men suffer reverse discrimination as a result. The charge that affirmative action undermines merit-based systems of employment misses an important point. As more of the skills needed for jobs are learned through on-the-job training rather than educational credentialing, those who are excluded from the bottom rungs of the job ladder remain at a permanent and ever-growing disadvantage. Rather than undermining merit-based systems for hiring and promotion, affirmative action may actually overcome some of this largely hidden bias by ensuring that recruitment and promotion practices do not exclude women and ethnic minorities. The issue here is not formal qualification, an automatic prerequisite for consideration, but the willingness of employers to train women and ethnic minorities to move up the ladder. There is no law that requires employers to explain why they have not trained someone when they say they have no qualified female or minority applicants for a job. Affirmative action reporting requirements are an important means of calling attention to these disparities.

Affirmative action programs in employment have been the focus of much controversy, but the thorniest issues concern questions regarding what is fair, and for whom. The charge that affirmative action leads to reverse discrimination against white men seems to strike a chord with many who view it as an unfair practice regardless of the benefits it might offer others. However, instances of proven reverse discrimination are few. In fact, research shows that despite affirmative action regulations, white men, not ethnic minorities, are most likely to receive preferential treatment in employment (Chao & Willaby, 2007; Giuliano, Levine, & Leonard, 2011). In truth, affirmative action can serve as a convenient scapegoat. That is, relatively few people are able to rise up the organizational pyramid to the top or choicest positions, but white men can attribute their failure to do so to imagined advantages that women and minorities are presumed to enjoy through affirmative action.

Affirmative action has also been an issue in education. Policies have been designed to provide greater parity in access to higher education, promoting the acquisition of the skills and credentials needed for success in the workplace. In our society, education is the main mechanism for social mobility, and a college degree is frequently a requirement for entering and remaining in the middle class. Schools in the United States are supposed to be environments in which young people of different SES can mingle, but in reality residential segregation by social class means that each school and school district tends to enroll students from a limited socioeconomic range. Even when schools are socioeconomically diverse, children from well-off families, a disproportionate number of whom are from white and Asian backgrounds, are more likely to do well on standardized aptitude tests and are tracked into more-advanced courses and college-preparatory programs (McDonough & Fann, 2007).

As residential segregation has increased in our society, economic disparities between school districts are also increasing. While policymakers work to reduce class disparities and address the problems associated with poverty (such as poor health, greater family instability, frequent moves, unsafe communities, environmental pollution, and so on), affirmative action can play a leveling role in ensuring access to higher education that is more equitable. Affirmative action in college and graduate school admissions helps counterbalance the disadvantages that children from less-well-off ethnic minority and white families experience as a result of large disparities in funding for elementary and secondary public education from one locality to another.

Affirmative action programs for college admissions are quite controversial, and the programs have narrowed their focus and reach over the past three decades in the face of a series of legal challenges. As a result, ethnic and racial quota systems are not permitted, and admissions policies permit consideration of an applicant's ethnicity or race as only one factor among many others. Admission of members of ethnic and racial minorities as a way to increase cultural diversity among students is still permissible. However, some states have moved away from affirmative action based on race and ethnicity toward a social class–based system. Some critics contend that all forms of affirmative action in college admissions are misguided or even harmful because they can create institutional mismatches that lead to high failure rates. After World War II there was a similar outcry regarding the benefits that returning soldiers received through the GI Bill, which granted millions of young men and women who otherwise would not have gone to college access to higher education. Such opposition failed to sway public policy, in large part because veterans were widely seen as deserving the help they received, a perception that seldom applies to today's beneficiaries of affirmative action. Some critics charge that academic standards are lowered when ethnic minority students are admitted to top schools for which they are unprepared academically (Hoffman & Lewitzki, 2005). However, these critics do not raise the same objections regarding legacy admissions, a widespread form of institutionalized discrimination in college admissions that favors applicants whose parents attended the college; these students generally come from the most privileged groups in society. In addition, such criticism disregards the role of other factors that may lead ethnic minority students to fail, such as tokenism, harassment, and an unsupportive campus climate.

Opposition to policies designed to compensate for unequal beginnings and provide the same opportunities to all individuals often reflects the belief that U.S. society is a meritocracy, and that differences in occupational and educational attainment are simply a result of individual differences in aptitude, motivation, and character. This thinking assumes members of different ethnic groups compete for advancement on a level playing field and downplays the fact that each group's history, circumstances, characteristics, and relative advantages vary at the start of the contest. Some may question the strategies or specific goals of affirmative action efforts. For example, proponents of partial inclusion may dismiss talk of societal parity as an elusive or impossible goal. Rather than setting parity in recruitment, promotion, and representation at the highest organizational levels as the benchmark for full inclusion of women and ethnic minorities, their less ambitious definition of successful inclusion might be to simply increase the visibility of target groups—such as having women achieve 5 percent representation among those in upper management rather than a percentage corresponding to their fraction of the labor pool, or showing evidence of incremental progress in increasing the representation of Latino college students.

AMERICANS WITH DISABILITIES ACT

Prior to the Industrial Revolution, people with disabilities faced many social obstacles to full participation in society and were considered a segment of the deserving poor. During the Industrial Revolution and the rise of individualistic norms and values, individuals with disabilities were frequently institutionalized (Rothmann, 1971). At the beginning of the twentieth century, substantial social stigma surrounded ability status (Thomson, 1996). This was exemplified in the 1927 Supreme Court ruling that upheld the constitutionality of the forced sterilization of women with developmental disabilities, mental illness, and epilepsy (Young, 2010). The Supreme Court decision argued that it was in the public's best interest to prevent proliferation of individuals with disabilities. As the twentieth century progressed, the status of individuals with disabilities gradually improved due in major part to a shift in the demographic makeup of those affected by disability statuses. Part of this shift was due to the increasing number of individuals who had been wounded in industrial plants or foreign wars. The shift could also be attributed to the rapid growth in medical technology that significantly extended people's lives, making it more likely that an individual would live with a disability (DeJong & Lifchez, 1983). In 1980, one in twelve individuals of working age was living with a disability; despite reductions in stigma, however, more than half of these people were unemployed (Bowe, 1985).

In the mid-1980s the disability community came together to advocate for the Americans with Disabilities Act (ADA), a law expanding the protections granted under the Civil Rights Act of 1964 to all individuals with disabilities. The campaign was framed as a civil rights issue and united disability organizations around the country (Young, 2010). The stated goal of the ADA was to "assure equality of opportunity, full participation, independent living, and economic self-sufficiency"

(Young, 2010, p. 27). Passed in 1991, the ADA sought to achieve this goal by requiring educational institutions and employers to provide reasonable accommodation to people with disabilities, and outlawed discrimination in wages, hiring, firing, and educational admissions (Thomas & Gostin, 2009). Employment protection not only had implications for wages, but also for health insurance, which in the United States is typically provided through employment. The passage of the law did not, however, result in increases in rates of employment among individuals living with disabilities and in some cases declines were observed (DeLeire, 2000). Some attribute this unexpected outcome to the reluctance of employers to hire individuals due to the cost of accommodations and the risk of litigation (Acemoglu & Angrist, 2001). Others argue that the decline in employment may be due to the way that the law was interpreted. In the years following the passage of the ADA, many cases were brought before the Supreme Court challenging the definition of disability and the line at which a person is "disabled enough" to warrant protection (Eichhorn, 1999). These lawsuits limited the number of people eligible for protection under the law, excluding individuals with AIDS, diabetes, cancer, epilepsy, and mental illness, and gave physicians responsibility for determining eligibility (Rush, 2012). The court rulings significantly limited the extent of protection and shifted the discussion away from equal rights and the prevention of discrimination.

In 2008, the ADA amendments act [ADAAA] was introduced and passed providing a broader definition of disability and focusing on discrimination in educational institutions (DeLisa, Silverstein, & Thomas, 2011). The definition of disability provided in this act included any impairment that substantially limits a person's ability to perform major life activities and provided a list of what constitutes major life activities (Thomas & Gostin, 2009). Despite attempts to clarify the definition of disability, the wide breadth of ability statuses covered has led to a lack of precision that remains one of the key challenges to a full implementation of the ADA. However, legal training sessions have improved the effectiveness of organizations in implementing these laws (Lee, Cayer, & Lan, 2006). Social workers can play a role in ensuring that the laws are followed both in their own agency and in firms where their clients are employed. Social workers can also become involved in coalitions actively working to ensure equal rights for individuals with disabilities.

SCHOOL RESEGREGATION

There is an important difference between racial desegregation and racial integration. The first refers to the ending of policies and practices that disallow or discourage contact between people of different races, while the second refers to the encouragement of interactions that occur between them. In the 1896 U.S.

Supreme Court decision *Plessy v. Ferguson*, the justices decided that according to the doctrine of "separate but equal," the state-sanctioned segregation of public facilities, including schools, did not violate the U.S. Constitution. This doctrine was challenged in 1954 in *Brown v. Board of Education of Topeka, Kansas,* when the Supreme Court ruled that the "separate but equal" clause was unconstitutional because it separated children based on skin color alone.

Today, more than fifty years after this pivotal Supreme Court decision spurred a decades-long struggle to desegregate public schools in the nation, there is still a wide achievement gap between African American, Latino, and white students, one that begins in elementary school and continues throughout high school (Wiggan, 2007). Although ethnic and racial minority children who attend racially integrated schools tend to perform better than their counterparts in segregated schools, progress toward desegregation has stalled or been reversed in some cases. Some argue that this is a distributive justice issue, not a race issue: all-white schools and schools with substantial white enrollments tend to have more resources and better-trained teachers, and poorly performing schools are often in lower-income African American and Latino neighborhoods. The flight of the wealthy to the more culturally and economically homogenous suburbs and the faltering political will in recent years to address educational inequities make it very difficult to improve the educational attainment of children from ethnic minority communities and to address resegregation.

Harvard University's Civil Rights Project examined the racial and ethnic composition of the nation's school districts between 1986 and 2000 and found that the segregation of white and black students remained the same or grew worse as the twentieth century came to a close (Sikkink & Emerson, 2008). As discussed in chapter 5, starting in the 1960s and 1970s some districts were ordered to promote desegregation. Because many of the cities were residentially segregated, busing was implemented to transport children across the city from their homes to schools located in different neighborhoods. Some parents were angry that their children had to attend schools outside their neighborhood, and minority students were harassed during bus rides as well as in school, where they were called derogatory names and teased, taunted, and intimidated. Moreover, students reported that many of the teachers lacked an understanding of African American culture and behavior, and their belief that black students had lower capacity for learning resulted in these students' placement in lower-ability groups (Harmon, 2002). In notes from the field 14.1, the school social worker addresses the impact of resegregation efforts on the student body.

Several policies have been introduced to narrow the achievement gap between white and minority students. The introduction of charter schools has shown promise when supplemented with wraparound services including early childhood education (Dobbie & Fryer, 2009). Magnet and charter schools allow parents to choose where to send their children, creating competition and increasing quality

NOTES FROM THE FIELD 14.1
Starting a Dialogue

Reshod had been working as a school social worker at Mountain High School for five years. The student body was primarily white and upper middle class. The city just introduced new legislation allowing any teenager in the city to attend any high school they chose, and creating specializations within high schools. The city was providing transportation and a stipend that could be applied to college for students who chose to participate in the magnet program. Mountain was slated to be the magnet school for the arts. When Reshod first heard about the new system he did not think it would really impact his school. In the fall he quickly realized that this was not the case. Many students that had been attending Mountain left to attend other magnet schools that fit their interests, and many students from outside the neighborhood began busing in. This significantly diversified the student body. Immediately Reshod noticed the cliques started to form based on neighborhoods and along racial lines. The first month went smoothly, but in October Reshod started to receive significantly more referrals for fights and verbal intimidation. He decided to go to the cafeteria at lunch and observe the dynamics. The second he walked in the room he felt the tension and observed that each group was staying strictly to themselves and behaving defensively if lines were crossed. Through discussion with the youths who were referred to him he was able to figure out who the leaders of the different cliques were and invited them into his office to have a discussion. At first the youths made it clear that they did not want to be in the same room together. The first meeting was not very productive and Reshod felt discouraged but resolved to continue to have this group meet. Before their next meeting a large fight took place after school on school grounds and twenty youths were suspended from school as a result. This incident provided an opening to start a dialogue about what was going on in their school, what the underlying issues were, and how they wanted it to be. After several months of meetings, these youths had developed a bond and were beginning to talk about what they could do to change the climate of their school. They were using their leadership to change the narrative in their groups and were strategizing ways to begin a schoolwide dialogue about race and conflict.

educational choices in neighborhoods with low-performing public schools (Henig, Holyoke, Brow, & Lacireno-Paquet, 2005; Zimmer & Bettinger, 2008). On the other hand, opponents argue that charter schools might exacerbate inequities in student outcomes. Charter schools reduce public school enrollment, resulting in funding cuts that affect the education of students who do not attend charter schools (Zimmer & Bettinger, 2008). There is also wide variation in the quality of education received at charter schools, with some showing excellent outcomes and others with subpar performance, in part because some charter schools have been established by people without backgrounds in education (Saltman, 2007; Sizer & Wood, 2008).

Immigration Policies

As a nation, the United States was founded by immigrants, and throughout its history it has relied on a fairly constant stream of immigration to fuel economic growth and development. However, U.S. immigration policies have not always been welcoming (Cornelius, 2006). The first anti-immigration law was passed in 1882, restricting the number of Chinese nationals who could enter the country legally and prohibiting their citizenship (Lee, 2003). The passage of this legislation was followed by a wave of violence and legal restriction of Chinese immigrants' civil rights (Johnson, 1996). Since that time there have been several peaks in anti-immigration sentiment and legislation in response to economic contractions or perceived threats to America's national security (Dinnerstein & Reimers, 1999; Massey & Pren, 2012). In 2008 the United States experienced a marked increase in anti-immigration sentiment fueled by the economic recession, culminating in the passage of some of the most restrictive anti-immigration policies in U.S. history. Although the U.S. Supreme Court eventually deemed many of these laws to be unconstitutional, the passage of aggressive laws aimed at undocumented immigrants and the anti-immigrant sentiment surrounding the debate affected many immigrant families and communities, including those who had immigrated legally.

In 2010, Arizona, Alabama, Georgia, Indiana, South Carolina, and Utah passed legislation restricting undocumented immigrants' access to services and increasing the ability of local and state police to enforce immigration laws (Hardy et al., 2012). Arizona's SB 1070, one of the most well-known anti-immigrant pieces of legislation in the group, authorized local law enforcement agents to stop anyone they suspected of being in the country illegally and to detain them if they did not provide the proper documentation. This law also made it illegal to transport undocumented individuals and for undocumented individuals to solicit work on the road. While the U.S. Supreme Court ruled most elements of SB 1070 unconstitutional in 2012, the passage of the law and the accompanying anti-immigration rhetoric in the state had an immediate impact on documented and undocumented Latinos (Hardy & Bohan, 2012). Four in ten Latinos in Arizona reported that they substantially decreased their involvement in the community as a result of the passage of the law (LatinoMetrics, 2010). The legislation also increased the level of fear among residents, restricted mobility, decreased their level of trust and willingness to partner with law enforcement to maintain safety in their neighborhoods, and decreased how frequently they accessed health care (Hardy & Bohan, 2012). Nationally the number of Latinos who reported that discrimination was a major problem increased 14 percent from 2002 to 2010 (Lopez, Morin, & Taylor, 2010). One social worker's response to the increase in anti-immigration legislation is discussed in notes from the field 14.2.

THE ROLE OF SOCIAL WORKERS IN POLICY

This chapter has provided several examples of policies that advanced the rights of certain populations and others that were enacted with the purpose of decreasing or eliminating such access by other groups. Social workers can play important roles as advocates in working to influence policy and change the allocation of resources to improve the quality of life of members of oppressed populations. Through its advocacy role, social work provides a strong voice in often-hostile policy environments. Although there has been some progress, advocacy efforts have not yet sufficiently influenced the legal and legislative systems to improve decisions and better serve the needs of cultural minorities.

Advocacy is possible when individuals and groups are empowered; when community members have a voice in making decisions that affect their lives, successful advocacy leads to higher levels of empowerment among the oppressed. Empowerment can be fostered through a variety of political activities, from individual resistance to oppression to mass political mobilization that challenges basic power relations in society. The empowerment process begins with the awareness that communities and individuals gain when they recognize the impact of inequalities related to religion, nationality, gender, SES, age, race, ability status, sexual orientation, and other factors on their lives. The reflection and action that follow can lead to policy analysis and policy change.

Social workers are in an ideal position to help individual clients and communities recognize the tools that can help them produce changes in policy. Practitioners hear their clients' complete stories rather than fragmented pieces of their lives, and the most effective advocacy occurs when individuals and communities are able to present themselves as whole people regardless of their circumstances. Society and its institutions tend not to see people with disabilities, poor people, and other oppressed people as whole people. For example, at the beginning of the AIDS epidemic, it was common to refer to a person with AIDS as an "AIDS

NOTES FROM THE FIELD 14.2

Keeping an Eye on the Legislature

Sara, a community outreach coordinator at a local agency serving Hispanic families, was becoming concerned about the anti-immigrant legislation that was being proposed at the legislature and the impact that it could have on the families and communities that she was serving. She heard about a coalition of Latino organizations that were working at the legislature to lobby against the passage of the proposed bills. At one of the meetings the coalition president announced that they were looking for someone to head the legislation tracking committee. Sara recalled briefly how a bill becomes a law but did not know anything about the infrastructure of her state's governing bodies. To her surprise someone nominated her for the role, it was seconded, and after a quick vote she was the new committee chair. Sara remembered that a friend of hers from the MSW program had gotten a job at a Domestic Violence Advocacy Coalition and used to tell her about going to the state capitol and talking to this senator or that representative. Sara called her and quickly got up to speed about the process and the resources available for tracking legislative bills. As she began her tracking, she was shocked at the number of bills that were being introduced that would have potentially harmful consequences for the communities that she served and that no one knew about—not her clients and not her colleagues at the agency. Convinced that awareness would move people to action, Sara asked the program director of the agency if she could conduct training for the employees and the consumers about the proposed legislation, how the bills could be tracked, and what could be done to influence the process. She was granted permission. The trainings were well received and at the end of each meeting she invited people to sign up to be on a Listserv so she could keep them up to date with recent developments. She announced that space would be provided at the agency every Saturday afternoon for anyone who wanted to meet to talk about action steps. On that first Saturday, twenty people showed up and the conversation began.

---

victim" instead of "a person living with AIDS." Referring to someone as a homeless person has the same essentializing effect that reduces the person to a single defining characteristic drained of her or his full humanity. Society in general and helping professionals in particular can easily fall into this trap of focusing narrowly on the characteristic that is seen as the presenting problem. One of the many ways in which social workers can play a role in culturally grounded policy development is by coaching their clients in how to present themselves as whole people in communicating with policymakers, as well as by educating those policy-makers. This type of communication informs a progressive policy agenda that benefits the community, and in turn the larger society.

Policy analysis is an essential step of advocacy that involves defining the problem, obtaining and interpreting the information needed to make sound decisions, developing and judging alternatives and considering ethical dilemmas, and deciding what the best choice is. From a culturally grounded perspective, clients' voices and narratives are a vital source of information for any policy analysis. Clients can inform policymakers not only about the problem, but also about the strengths and resources communities have to overcome the challenges they face, as well as their policy recommendations. Social workers in partnership with their clients often have opportunities to transform the policy-making process from one that rewards power and privilege to one that ensures distributive justice for all.

Culturally grounded policy development is a form of policy work that is informed by consumers. It bridges the gap that often exists between policymakers and the needs of cultural minority individuals and communities, and the effects that policy decisions have on them. Policy initiatives should be examined through the lenses of culture and social justice. For example, since the abolishment of apartheid, the South African government has led a process of participatory policy development that includes blacks and other people of color who were excluded from any policy development during the whites-only rule. During apartheid, social policy development was a top-down process that did not take into consideration any of the needs and assets of the black township residents. For ten years representatives of the excluded communities engaged in active policy development and planning activities, which led to the development of the idea of local economic development and institutionalized local participation in policy making and decision making as a key aspect of democratic South Africa.

Public policies at the local, state, and federal levels affect millions of people in significant and lasting ways. It is vital that policy decisions be made based on accurate information, informed analysis, and comprehensive interpretations, not on assumptions or half-truths. Uninformed policymakers run the risk of misinterpreting or manipulating the findings of research in social work and other social sciences, and relying on simplistic constructs or overgeneralizations about minority communities and oppressed groups. Overgeneralizations and stereotypes can misguide social policy formulation and social work practice, which can have the intended or unintended result of impeding the promotion of social justice. Notes from the field 14.3 provides an example of such risks.

Social justice was the impetus for the development of social work and has grown into the central mission of the profession. Social workers are not only practitioners, but also data gatherers and analysts who have direct access to clients and view them as expert informants. As experts, clients identify what system reforms are necessary. Historically, partnerships between oppressed groups and

---

NOTES FROM THE FIELD 14.3

Saturday Night's Not All Right for Fighting

The Los Alamos City Council has passed a resolution to forbid the Saturday evening low-riders *paseo* (drive) in order to increase the safety of the central city and enforce its gang prevention policy. Very few of the mostly Mexican American youths who enjoy fixing up their low-riders and driving them through the downtown area are gang members. Moreover, fixing their cars has become a very positive and creative leisure activity in the neighborhood, as well as a means of expressing ethnic pride. The report provided to the city council was clearly developed from an outsider's perspective and reflects stigma and prejudice about low-riders and their owners. There is no Mexican American representation on the city council.

---

social workers have played important roles in policy reform. For example, in the early 1990s low-income residents in Illinois successfully took part in the development and implementation of a welfare-to-work policy (O'Donnell, 1993). The professional social worker plays an important role as the facilitator of clients' examination of their own interests and in planning appropriate courses of action. Unfortunately, recipients of benefits are rarely engaged in the policy-making process.

Eradicating social inequalities and working with the oppressed to help them reach optimal functioning is part of the call of social work. Not only do social workers need to work to ensure that the voices of oppressed populations are heard, but they also must promote the development of policies that establish a pathway toward change and provide the needed resources that will bring more members of oppressed populations onto college campuses as students and into social service agencies in order to develop a new workforce that is representative of the diverse demographics of U.S. society.

Key Concepts

Empowerment: The ability to feel and act in control of one's destiny despite social and economic adversity

Distributive justice: A philosophy that aims at ensuring that all members of society have access to reasonable economic resources, education, social services, and other resources, based on the ethical principles of equity and solidarity

Social welfare: In the United States, a payment in kind or in cash to a person who needs support because of age, disability, poverty, unemployment, or mental illness; also a society that is devoted to the well-being of its members and that has social welfare institutions operating at the state level

Entitlement programs: Programs that provide payments to individuals who have paid into the program and have met other eligibility requirements, such as years of employment or age, and are therefore entitled to benefits

TANF (Temporary Aid to Needy Families): The major welfare program in the United States, which enforces strict work requirements and limits on lifetime eligibility

Safety net: The strategies a society uses to respond to its members' unplanned needs

Plessy v. Ferguson: 1896 Supreme Court decision that sanctioned the segregation of public facilities, including schools, by establishing the "separate but equal" doctrine

Brown v. Board of Education of Topeka, Kansas: 1954 Supreme Court decision that ruled that the "separate but equal" clause allowing racially segregated schools was unconstitutional

15

Culturally Grounded Evaluation and Research

RESEARCH IS A VITAL AND INTEGRAL PART OF SOCIAL WORK, EVEN FOR social workers who do not conduct research themselves. Effective social work requires social workers to be effective consumers of research. Research helps us understand the scope and severity of a problem, its trends over time, and its cost to individuals and communities. Research is concerned with building knowledge about the root causes of social problems and effective ways to address them. Social work informs many types of clinical, experimental, and survey research that develop from theory. Rigorous research either confirms or disconfirms theory, leading to improvements in concepts and how they are measured. Social workers engage in naturalistic research conducted in the field in order to observe behavior in its natural social and physical context. This more-qualitative research also builds theory. Unfortunately, too often practice and research are not well connected in social work, and researchers in universities and practitioners in the community are not always linked effectively through their professional organizations. However, culturally grounded social work practice cannot assume its proper place within the profession without culturally grounded research and evaluation to inform that practice.

Engaging in research is natural in social work because it is a profession that studies the interrelationships of individuals, communities, families, and social institutions and provides the empirical evidence that is needed to formulate effective social policies and improve service delivery. Because practitioners, unlike many researchers, work directly with members of the cultural groups they are studying, they have a critical role in identifying gaps in knowledge and in generating research ideas. The researcher, the outsider looking in through the lens of difference and privilege, often arrives at conclusions that do not reflect the experience of the group being studied. In contrast, social work practitioner-researchers are in a unique position that allows them to partner effectively with oppressed minority groups in generating knowledge.

Practitioners often are more closely involved with evaluation than with research. They may engage in evaluation to document the effectiveness of a program or amass evaluation results when seeking to defend or increase funding for that program. In today's increasingly multicultural society, evaluators are expected to be culturally competent and capable of adapting evaluation processes in a systematic way so that they are appropriate for the setting. The challenge for evaluators is to work effectively in different cultural settings in such a way that trust is maintained and partnerships are long lasting. Practitioners have an ethical responsibility to select interventions that can be evaluated for their effectiveness, and this requires them to be involved in conducting or making appropriate use of research. Unfortunately, clinicians are sometimes reluctant to assume the role of researcher because the time they can dedicate to research is limited, they often lack funds and training, and/or they do not have support from their agencies and their organizations do not offer incentives to conduct research. In addition, when consumed by the daily pressures of providing direct services, practitioners may see research as abstract, irrelevant, and disconnected from the needs of their clients. These views may foster the negative attitudes toward research held by many social workers. Practitioners sometimes believe research findings to be of limited clinical relevance because they regard their practice as rooted in the here and now, or in the specific needs of their clients. Research findings are sometimes viewed with suspicion by those who live in, work with, and advocate for communities. They may be considered irrelevant generalizations that do not apply to a particular case or community.

Although research and evaluation findings can have significant impacts on jobs, programs, and community investments, studies that have clear policy implications are often ignored. This occurs for many reasons. The findings and their policy implications may not be presented clearly for use by nonresearchers, or they may not be implemented because they run counter to deeply held values and beliefs or challenge entrenched interests. Sometimes practitioners are not reading the current research literature and lack the appropriate methodological background to interpret research results and apply the findings. However, increasing demands for accountability from governmental and private funders require social workers to demonstrate the efficacy of what they do, which provides new impetus to engage in research. A good way for practitioners to start contributing is by assessing the outcomes of their own practice.

OUTCOME ASSESSMENT AND ACCOUNTABILITY

The pressure for practitioners to engage in evaluation and research in general has significantly increased over the past two decades. Terms such as "outcome based," "evidence based," and" "best practices" have become part of the social work lexicon in the same way that they have been integrated into the professional jargon of other applied research fields. Social work, like these other fields, has been heavily influenced by what is commonly called the accountability movement.

Professional practitioners are being called on by government funding agencies, social service administrators, private foundations, and consumers to demonstrate that methods, practices, and interventions are achieving the desired outcomes and are being implemented in a cost-effective manner. Some believe that this movement has called into question the identity of social work as a profession because the only social service delivery systems that will survive are those that can demonstrate that they provide needed, useful, competent, and cost-effective services. Critics of the drive toward accountability propose an alternative benchmark for evaluating social work practice that emphasizes the inherent value of serving vulnerable communities even when results are difficult to document. There is also a risk that, taken to an extreme, outcome-based evaluation can hinder social work practice by prematurely concluding that an intervention should be stopped because of its lack of results. This risk is magnified in culturally grounded practice because it is essential to evaluate not only the outcomes, but also the appropriateness of the methods and practices being utilized in the evaluation process. Although evaluation and research are not neutral tools and can be manipulated to serve different ideologies, they are much needed. They are the best available means to ensure that innovation occurs, that the best existing science is used to design interventions, and that services achieve the intended outcomes in a culturally relevant manner.

Outcome assessment is a kind of evaluation that is used to decide whether a program is meeting its objectives—in other words, whether it is effective. In social work practice, there are two main outcomes: (1) the results of the practice, treatment, or intervention, or how the client's presenting problem was addressed; and (2) the outcome of the professional behavior, or what was done to change the nature of the problem. The first outcome has to do with the client's well-being, and the second with the quality of the treatment protocols (Unrau, Gabor, & Grinnell, 2007). Outcome assessments help determine whether practice innovations and interventions are useful.

The concept of accountability is central to the profession. For example, the *Code of Ethics* of the National Association of Social Workers (2008) stresses the importance of engaging in systematic evaluation of practice interventions and program implementation to guarantee that clients receive the best services possible. Practice evaluation provides a means to monitor the effectiveness of efforts to reach out to those in need. This type of evaluation is important because social workers work with clients who have serious real-life problems, and ineffectiveness can have serious implications for those we serve.

Effectiveness can be an elusive concept in work with cultural minority clients because interventions and practices often are not culturally grounded or appropriate. What does one do when an evaluation concludes that a standard intervention is not effectively reaching cultural minority clients? Rather than taking steps to terminate the intervention, it is important to bring innovation into play. Practitioners can design new interventions by involving community members, and the designs can be tested through rigorous research. Thus, research and evaluation are key tools for ensuring that cultural minority clients are able to access effective services.

EVALUATION AND RESEARCH

Evaluation and research are related but are not the same. An evaluation determines whether a practice or program is effective or ineffective, and requires that the practitioner judge its value based on empirical findings (Mertens, 2009). Evaluation identifies gaps in the applicability of existing models and methods of social work practice; research and innovation address those gaps. Once new treatments and interventions have been tested and the results carefully analyzed through research involving randomized trials or quasi-experimental methods, they can be implemented and evaluated in real-life settings. In social work, the word "evaluation" is typically used to mean program evaluation. In contrast, research addresses a wider range of questions about the behavior of clients, their families, and communities; the actions of social work practitioners and agencies; and the connections among helping professions, organizations, and larger societal institutions. The evaluation process helps social workers determine whether programs and interventions are effective and how they can make the appropriate changes. Evaluations are not free of bias: they are conducted by evaluators who bring their own cultural biases to their work. In addition, even when an evaluator has good intentions and very good methodological tools at her or his disposal, those evaluation tools or methodologies may be culturally biased.

Well-designed evaluation is client centered and confidential and targets specific issues and questions. As notes from the field 15.1 demonstrates, when evaluation is not culturally grounded and the cultural characteristics of providers and clients are disregarded, inaccurate assessments can lead to the wrong practice or policy recommendations. Because the findings of evaluations can be manipulated by a program's supporters as well as its opponents, the program evaluation process often involves intense political pressure. Politics may influence the way a research study is designed or how the findings are interpreted. Social workers conducting evaluations may feel pressure, both internally and externally, to find favorable outcomes, which can affect the evaluation methods they choose and how they interpret the data. Because their survival depends on their ability to demonstrate accountability through program evaluations based on concrete, measurable outcomes, it is not unusual for agencies to put technocrats in charge of program evaluation and to focus the evaluation on the most readily available numerical measures. Without a background in social science or social services,

---

NOTES FROM THE FIELD 15.1
Remembering Clients' Needs

An evaluator is ordered to assess the rates of utilization of a newly established county health clinic located in a largely traditional Muslim community. He evaluates the clinic's utilization rate by reviewing intake records.
He concludes that the services of the doctor assigned to the clinic are not
needed because he has the lowest patient-physician ratio in the county. The
patient-to-practitioner ratio for the nurse practitioner and social worker,
however, fall within the county's recommended range. He concludes that
the clinic is underutilized and recommends its closure. His rationale is that
it is not cost effective to maintain its expensive medical services with such
low patient utilization. Fortunately, the chair of the clinic's community
advisory board reviews the report before it is sent to the county health
authorities. She is perplexed by the fact that the report leaves out the gender
of the three key professionals who form the interdisciplinary team. She
insists that the evaluation fully consider the cultural implications of the
gender of the clinic's clients and practitioners. While most of the clients are
female, as are the nurse practitioner and the social worker, the physician is
male. The report is modified to recommend that the clinic engage the services of a female physician to serve the needs of the clientele, for whom any
intimate cross-gender physical contact is problematic.

---

they may be directed to rely on selective data and narrow methods that are most
likely to generate the desired conclusions. Such pressures may distort the process
of evaluating whether the program adequately serves the target population's
needs, and the distortion may be particularly acute when it involves cultural
minority populations because their perspective may not be taken into account in
the evaluation process.

Because members of oppressed communities tend to have less power and lack
representation, evaluations affecting their lives often do not take into account
their voices and perceptions. Evaluation reports often make recommendations
regarding the provision or interruption of services without consulting those who
are most affected by these recommendations. Due to the serious quality-of-life
implications of such decisions, program evaluations need to be guided by the best
empirical methods at the disposal of the evaluator. However, these tools are effective from a culturally grounded perspective only when they are embedded within
the social and cultural contexts in which the phenomenon being studied takes
place. Thus, culturally grounded evaluation is a participatory and reciprocal process where the professional evaluator contributes her or his technical expertise

and the community contributes its knowledge of the services or programs being evaluated.

CULTURALLY GROUNDED RESEARCH QUESTIONS, MEASURES, AND DESIGNS

Gaps in research on cultural minorities limit our understanding of how to engage these populations and how to tailor interventions for them. Critical social work focuses on challenging the oppression of marginalized groups by taking their voices and perspectives into consideration. To advance this key imperative of critical social work, new forms of research methods have been developed and other methods have been adapted from other fields as a means of taking into account the voices of oppressed populations and more accurately interpreting their perspectives regarding key social phenomena.

Much progress has been made, yet much remains to be done, especially regarding issues of cultural bias and nongeneralizability in the way that behaviors and attitudes are measured in research with cultural minority populations. There are potential problems with validity (i.e., whether or not measures gauge what they are intended to measure), and with reliability (i.e., the measures' internal consistency and stability over time). Researchers and practitioners alike cannot assume that an instrument measuring behavioral tendencies, attitudes, or mental health states that appears to be reliable and valid when tested with people from one culture will be reliable and valid when used with members of other cultural groups. However, the construction of culturally competent measures involves complex issues that go beyond resolving language difficulties to achieve linguistic or semantic equivalence. Effective intercultural communication requires knowledge of the other culture and its communication symbols. The process starts with immersion in the literature and the development of theory-based research questions or hypotheses and corresponding research designs with appropriate measures and analysis strategies.

Culturally grounded research requires not only a serious critique of measurement tools, but also fundamental reflection on how researchers frame their research questions and design studies. Asking the right question in research is very important, perhaps more important than the methods used to find an answer to the question. For example, studies of substance abuse etiology and treatment that compare different cultural groups may overlook important factors if they ask questions limited to whether there are differences in rates of use or different treatment outcomes among various groups. An approach more likely to generate culturally relevant findings might start by asking how substance use is defined in the culture and what social meaning it has to users and nonusers.

Because cultural specificity is a key concern of the culturally grounded approach, practitioners may wonder whether any form of cross-cultural generalizability is possible in measurement. This question requires consideration of the technical problems associated with cultural bias known as "metric and structural equivalence" (Byrne & van De Vijver, 2010). To achieve metric equivalence, the items comprising a scale should work together in exactly the same way across cultures and should reflect the same underlying construct. In designing a scale to measure quality of life, or life satisfaction, for example, researchers have to make choices about the various arenas of life that might be represented (self, spouse, children, friends, school, work, home, income, etc.) and the weight given in the scale to each one. It would be a mistake to assume that all cultures have the same priorities regarding different life arenas, or that the relative weight given to each is culturally universal.

Instruments are structurally equivalent across cultures when they have the same relationships with other key measures and outcomes. For example, an adolescent risk behavior scale that is used to screen youths for targeted prevention programs in schools might count the number of risky behaviors in which respondents have engaged in the last six months and develop cutoff scores to designate thresholds indicating high, moderate, low, and no risk. Questions of cultural bias can arise concerning whether the cutoffs should be the same for youths from all cultures, and whether engagement in different kinds of risk behaviors may be used to identify those in most need of targeted prevention from different ethnic and racial groups.

In addition to the problems that may be inherent to the assessment tools themselves, assessments are complicated by the fact that cultural minorities and members of the dominant culture may understand, interpret, and express answers to survey and interview questions differently. These potential problems regarding culturally biased assessment pose challenges for researchers and practitioners. How is it possible to have confidence in the reliability and validity of any of our assessment tools when we are working with members of cultural minorities? Until proved otherwise, shouldn't it be assumed that instruments are somehow culturally biased? There is no simple answer and no easy solution to these questions. The key issue is ensuring that social workers are educated and critical consumers of assessment tools. Even when practitioners lack the training, resources, or support necessary to engage in the work of developing and testing culturally unbiased assessment tools, they can still become educated and critically aware consumers of assessment tools.

A major challenge facing social work researchers is the need to generate knowledge that will enhance the relevance, effectiveness, and quality of social work practice for cultural minority groups. In order to do so, measures that capture the essence of culturally relevant and culturally sensitive variables must be developed. This is a very important task for researchers, just as the development of culturally competent interventions is important for practitioners. To make assessment tools culturally responsive, researchers need to become immersed in the culture before constructing the measures and must use community-based informants to identify and resolve any problems related to the cultural competence of the measures.

Single Case Designs

Evaluation methods and research methods in social work often use methods that examine an individual or small group of individuals; these are called single case designs, or case studies. In fact, most social workers are required to engage in ongoing evaluation of their practice by using single case designs. Progress notes and standardized assessment scales form the core of the data used in this type of evaluation. The problem with these data sources is that they are very vulnerable to cultural bias. Progress notes mostly reflect the client's spoken words and the worker's interpretation of those words. Assessment tools that are normed on samples that do not take into consideration a minority client's culture can generate a distorted and misleading client profile. Even if the assessment tools are culturally appropriate, the power differential between practitioners and their clients and a shortage of culturally competent supervision can undermine the effectiveness of the practice. The practitioner may then misinterpret the unsuccessful practice as a lack of engagement by the client, or she or he may exaggerate the client's deficiency or pathology.

In single subject evaluation, the risk of bias is heightened: it is only human to want to obtain findings that support the effectiveness of the intervention and indicate that the client's problems and suffering are being ameliorated. In single subject designs there is only one chance to demonstrate success, and success reflects positively on both the practitioner and the client. Clients may want to believe that practice interventions have yielded positive results for various reasons: to justify their decision to seek help, to have a sense of positive closure, to reassure themselves that they have responded in a way that is considered normal or expected, or simply to please the practitioner (Rubin & Babbie, 2008). The use of self-reporting and satisfaction surveys as the sole source of data is often not enough to arrive at any solid conclusions about the effectiveness of an intervention. Effectiveness needs to be assessed based on outcomes, and outcomes need to reflect the unique cultural characteristics of clients.

Another problem with single subject designs for evaluation and research in social work is that they often rely on client assessment instruments and methods that have been developed for the cultural majority. Even instruments that use the best methods to ensure reliability and validity can be inappropriate when used with populations for whom they were not intended. Biased assessment tools are of special concern in work with cultural minorities; for example, the instrument may take for granted certain assumptions related to mainstream culture that do not apply to cultural minority groups. It may be necessary for the practitioner to pay close attention to the language of the assessment instrument, and how it is translated and interpreted, in order to work with members of cultural minorities who are immigrants. Assessment scales may use words to describe moods and emotional states that do not translate exactly into other languages or mean the same thing in other cultures. Even when these ways of describing feelings can be translated accurately into other languages, cultural differences in emotional expression may affect one's willingness to express these feelings.

Research on the generalizability of a widely used screening instrument for depression, the Center for Epidemiologic Studies Depression scale (CES-D), illustrates several ways that assessment tools may be culturally biased. Among U.S. populations, scores on the CES-D vary according to nativity (U.S. born or not), country of origin, and level of acculturation. Latino immigrants to the United States, for example, are less willing to express positive emotional states than Latinos born in the United States (Iwata, Turner, & Lloyd, 2002). There are also substantial variations on the CES-D among Latinos from different generations; these differences show that perceptions of depressive mood are tied to the current level and nature of social support among Latinos (Liang, Van Tran, Krause, & Markides, 1989; Potochnick & Perreira, 2010). Not just overall scores but also the underlying structures of the CES-D have been shown to vary by culture. Research with different ethnic minority groups shows that their responses to the CES-D do not always cluster into distinctive subscales as they do for samples representing the cultural majority (Posner, Stewart, Marín, & Pérez-Stable, 2001). For example, in a comparison of twenty-eight studies using the CES-D, the measures of depressive affect (e.g., "You felt sad") and somatic symptoms ("You slept poorly") were comparable across cultural groups, but positive affect ("You felt happy") differed between Asian Americans and African Americans, and items measuring interpersonal problems ("People were not nice") among whites and Hispanics were not equivalent to other racial groups (Kim, DeCoster, Huang, & Chiriboga, 2011). Among Chinese Americans and Native Americans, the CES-D items reflecting somatic complaints (depressive effects on energy level, appetite, and sleep) were inseparable from items measuring general depressive affect (Dick, Beals, Keane, & Manson, 1994; Kuo, 1984; Ying, 1988). It is as if the physical and mental repercussions of depression are expressed inseparably for these groups but are separable realms for other ethnic groups.

Another example of cultural issues in assessment comes from a study of Chinese American families that showed that a widely used general assessment of family functioning—the Self-Report Family Inventory—required modification when used with this population. The scale was designed to assess several distinct areas of family life, such as competence, conflict, cohesion, expressiveness, and leadership. Only two stable factors out of the original six emerged from a factor analysis of responses from families of Chinese heritage: one general area concerned positive family behaviors and the absence of family problems, and the other focused on unhealthy family problems (Shek, 1998). The clustering of responses from the Chinese American families along fewer dimensions than those for the general population suggests that they have relatively undifferentiated attitudes toward their families, possibly because their culture does not encourage them to reveal their emotions in public. These findings suggest that the original Self-Report Family Inventory scale may be inappropriate for use with Chinese American populations, and that the revised subscales should be used instead.

Similarly, the Rosenberg Self-Esteem Scale, which is used frequently in social work practice, has been shown to be inconsistent across European American, Latino, Armenian and Iranian adolescents (Supple, Su, Plunkett, Peterson, & Bush, 2013), due to different interpretations of items like, "I wish I could have more respect for myself," "I am inclined to feel that I am a failure," and "I take a positive attitude toward myself." This suggests that the nuances of meaning that people may attach to words like "respect," "failure," and "positive attitude" may not resonate equally across all ethnic subcultures. Cultural norms that stress personal modesty (for example, some Asian cultural norms) can influence one's willingness to acknowledge personal achievement or admit failure.

Some of the problems relating to culturally biased assessment tools can be resolved through a back-translation process in which different groups of bilingual experts translate the instrument from English into another language and then another group translates the tool back to English. A comparison between the original and the translation reveals discrepancies in meanings, and those discrepancies can then be corrected (He & van de Vijver, 2012). Back-translation is an etic approach to research and assessment. Etic approaches use comparative tools to assess cultural appropriateness and cultural bias, often working backward to adapt mainstream tools for different cultural groups. Although back-translation ensures a high degree of linguistic or semantic equivalence in translated instruments, it does not eliminate the potential for serious problems of equivalence in content. Even when perfectly translated, phrases can resonate differently across cultures, and responses to them are influenced by cultural norms. For example, a scale developed for non-Latino whites to measure caregiver burden may pose questions that seem inappropriate to clients from communities that value filial obligations to elderly parents, because the questions assume that assistance to parents entails personal sacrifices, an assumption that may not be accurate in some cultures.

Several scales have been tested to ensure cultural equivalence. The Screen for Child Anxiety Related Emotional Disorders, a tool used to diagnose anxiety disorders in children, has five components. Four of those components have been found to be consistent across the populations of seven nations: Belgium, China,

Germany, Italy, the Netherlands, South Africa, and the United States (Hale, Crocetti, Raaijmakers, & Meeus, 2011). Similarly, the cultural relevance of a revised version of the Conflict Tactics Scale, a measure to assess dating violence, was tested in seventeen countries; findings indicated that the instrument was reliable and had good construct validity across sites (Straus, 2004).

Scales have also been developed with the goal of achieving cross-cultural equivalence from their inception. Ungar and Liedenberg (2011) worked cross nationally to develop a youth resilience measure, using a mixed methods methodology. The development began with focus groups in eleven different countries that explored ways that youths thrive when faced with adversity. Based on these findings, a scale with fifty-eight items was constructed; the scale was translated and then back-translated in each country's primary language, and then administered in a pilot test. Interviews were conducted with a subset of youths after they completed the survey, and the interviews were analyzed in conjunction with the survey data. The themes that emerged in the interviews were used to inform the construction of the final instrument. All of the original items had shown face validity—that is, they appeared to measure resilience. However, the pilot test revealed variation across countries in how the items were understood by the youths. The items were then cut to twenty-eight by retaining only questions that were consistent and relevant across cultures and congruent with qualitative findings. Although this method of measurement development requires considerably more time and resources than those restricted to one cultural group, the more elaborate process helps ensure that the tool is culturally grounded, relevant, and accurate across multiple cultural contexts. Despite efforts to ensure cultural equivalence by conducting cross-national validation studies, social workers may still need to be cautious when using these scales with clients. Findings may not be generalizable outside the context of their development. For example, a scale shown to be valid in China does not necessarily perform the same when used to assess Chinese Americans. Assessing how a measure is developed and how it performs across different groups is important for understanding research findings and conducting culturally grounded evaluation.

Qualitative and Mixed Methods

For many decades, quantitative research based on experimental or quasi-experimental methods, large probability samples, structured interviews or close-ended survey questions, hypothesis testing, and inferential statistics has been the accepted prototype for rigorous research. These quantitative research methods help us advance knowledge regarding the "what": What is happening? Who are the key players in the social phenomenon? Qualitative research is regaining legitimacy in social work research because it is more suitable for dealing with issues of social meaning and narratives, or the "how" and "why," issues that are especially important to consider in research with cultural minorities. To pursue the different kinds of questions that emerge in work with different cultural communities, researchers may need to use qualitative and mixed methods designs (combinations of qualitative and quantitative methods) rather than close-ended interviews, survey methods, or experimental approaches. Notes from the field 15.2 demonstrate how qualitative research can lead to the development of a culturally grounded intervention.

Qualitative methods encompass an array of research methodologies, including content analysis of documents and scripts, participant observation, open-ended and semistructured interviews, focus groups, and ethnography. Similar to survey and experimental methods that are more quantitative, qualitative research can be employed effectively in research with cultural minorities and can be utilized to address questions that are different from those that are typically addressed in quantitative research. In studies of cultural minority populations, a key advantage of most qualitative research tools is that the methods are emic in nature, meaning that they require the researcher to become intimately familiar with the

NOTES FROM THE FIELD 15.2
HIV Prevention

In a research project designing and evaluating an HIV intervention in Botswana, U.S.-based researchers proposed the use of the theory of planned behavior as a framework for the program. This theory proposes that individuals change their health behavior when they have more information and the self-efficacy to act on that information. The research partners in Botswana did not believe that this theory, developed in the West, adequately considered the context of their country and believed that an intervention that addressed only knowledge and self-efficacy would not be effective. The research team then decided to start the project by conducting in-depth individual interviews with youths and parents in order to gain a better understanding of the young people's experience with HIV. What they found was that the context of living in poverty was influencing the youths' HIV risk behaviors. Youths knew about HIV and how to prevent it, but they did not see much hope in the future and did not expect to live long, so practicing safer sex did not seem important to them. The researchers also found that sex was frequently being traded for material goods such as cell phones. The program that was developed as a result of the focus groups was called Own Your Future and incorporated several activities that focused on identifying strengths and setting goals for the future along with health education, job training and job placement, and assertiveness training.

culture from the perspective of its members, rather than using preconceived terms, typologies, or concepts to study and describe the group. The emic perspective is incorporated into several research methods, such as focus groups, intensive open-ended interviews, and systematic observation in natural settings. Each of these methods utilizes key informants from the community and allows them to characterize and assign meaning to their lives in their own terms (Merriam, 2009). The ethnographic method exemplifies the types of cultural processes and issues that qualitative research can address well. Ethnography is also an example of an approach that typically employs different research methodologies in combination.

Ethnography is the study of a particular culture or group, and an approach to studying ways of life that are different from our own. The ethnographer's approach is emic, allowing people from within a culture to provide a description or account of their experiences, beliefs, and behaviors. Ethnographers usually incorporate interviews with open-ended questions as part of the research to allow the interview subject's cultural ideas, categories, and themes to emerge; from these responses the ethnographer builds subsequent questions, analyses, and, in some cases, refined concepts and theories. Ethnographic research may draw on a selection of different qualitative and quantitative methodologies, including historical, demographic, economic, and geographic profiles of the group being studied; participant observation, where the researcher participates directly in the group's activities; intensive interviewing; and the use of key informants. Ethnographic research is distinctive in that it focuses on understanding cultural beliefs and culturally influenced behaviors, not from preexisting theory but from the perspective of members of the community. Ethnographers spend time in the field to become familiar with the language, norms, values, and experiences of those who are being studied and to acquire insight into their experiential world.

The broad applicability of ethnography for cultural grounded social work research is clear. Ethnography is an excellent tool for revealing similarities and differences in the way that people from different cultures view issues in their lives. For example, a study designed to improve the effectiveness of a peer education model for preventing HIV transmission among adolescents used one-on-one ethnographic interviews with adult staff, peer educators, and student participants (Ott, Evans, Halpern-Felshr, & Eyre, 2003). A form of content analysis was then used to transcribe and analyze the interviews in order to identify beliefs and ideas that were shared among, as well as unique to, each group of informants. The study found that although the three groups possessed similar beliefs and knowledge about HIV transmission and prevention, there were important differences in how they described their perceptions of HIV risk. While staff tended to describe HIV risks within a larger social developmental context, emphasizing the need to learn how to make healthy decisions about intimate relationships and sexual health, the student participants focused on HIV risks in sexual behaviors and demonstrated a good deal of anxiety about those risks. The peer educators held a variety of views similar to those of both the staff and student participants. The study showed that a focus on the content of the prevention message was not enough to address the program's effectiveness, and that evaluations needed to consider the different perceptions of HIV risk among adults, students, and peer educators.

In social work, ethnography can fill important gaps in knowledge about a community, such as information on their beliefs regarding risk behaviors, resiliencies for coping with adversity, and the operation of social services. The exploratory nature of ethnography allows the researcher to examine issues and problems that are not easy to study through traditional quantitative or experimental methods alone, such as how people learn about and access services, and how they behave as program participants. Ethnography is particularly valuable for gaining insight into people's perspectives. Federal agencies such as the National Park Service and the U.S. Census Bureau have used ethnographic studies to improve their understanding of the sociocultural life of groups whose beliefs and behavior are important to the missions of these programs. Even in clinical settings where there is an emphasis on the client's unique perspective and challenges, an ethnographic approach that considers the communities in which clients reside can help practitioners understand the cultural worlds that shape individual psychological and social lives, fill in the environmental context contributing to social and psychological disorder, and suggest culturally appropriate treatments.

While there is a century-old tradition in ethnography of combining different methods of data collection—such as observation, interviews, and documentary evidence—it is only in the past decade that researchers have begun to systemize the use of mixed methods designs that employ both qualitative and quantitative approaches in a single study (see Tashakkori & Teddlie, 2003). Several types of mixed methods designs have emerged; these differ in whether qualitative and quantitative methods are employed in tandem or in sequence, whether precedence is given to qualitative or quantitative approaches or they are given equal weight, and how data from the different methods are integrated in analysis. Regardless of the way that these approaches are combined, mixed methods designs have been shown to be powerful techniques for addressing issues in research with cultural minorities. For example, the initial qualitative phase of a mixed methods study of an African American community affected by HIV/AIDS used open-ended ethnographic interviewing techniques to find recurrent themes in the participants' language as they described living with the epidemic, such as struggles over blame and acceptance of both oneself and others (Hopson, Lucas, & Peterson, 2000). Analysis of the language used within the community to interpret the meaning and consequences of HIV/AIDS revealed the role of culture in risk behaviors and their prevention. Along with semistructured interviews that assessed community members' backgrounds and risk and protective behaviors, the researchers were able to design a subsequent quantitative instrument for a postintervention evaluation that contained questions that were phrased in ways that resonated with participants' understanding of their relationship to the epidemic. A similar mixed methods study explored Internet usage of men who have sex with men (Mustanski, Lyons, & Garcia, 2011). Because of the exploratory nature of the study, qualitative methods were used to elicit narratives about the men's use of the Internet. Themes and patterns in these narratives were treated as the primary data, but these data were then augmented with quantitative data about the rates and purposes of Internet use. The use of mixed methods strengthens the validity of both forms of data and gives a richer description of the phenomena under investigation.

The development of a culturally grounded assessment tool for urban Native American adolescents at risk of drug use provides an example of how culturally sensitive research can make effective use of mixed methods (Okamoto, 2006). The researchers combined qualitative focus group and quantitative survey methods to identify the most common and difficult situations in which Native youths were offered drugs. The focus groups were structured to allow small groups of youths to relate narratives of their daily lives and place their encounters with drugs within the social contexts that were meaningful to them. Qualitative analysis of the transcripts from the focus groups identified sixty-two distinctive situations of encounters with drugs, defined by the type of drug, the youths' relationship to the person offering the drug, the physical setting, and the presence of others from the youths' social network (Okamoto, LeCroy, Dustman, Hohmann-Marriott, & Kulis, 2004).

In the subsequent quantitative survey phase, another group of Native youths indicated how often they had encountered each of the situations and how difficult they were to navigate; researchers also gathered demographic and risk behavior information. Researchers then analyzed the data from those self-administered questionnaires to identify the most common sources of drugs used by each youth and placed his or her risk of and resiliency against drug use within the social context of specific drug offer situations (Kulis, Okamoto, Rayle, & Sen, 2006; Rayle et al., 2006).

While these examples of mixed methods involve a sequence where a qualitative approach preceded the quantitative phase, sometimes that order may be reversed with productive results. An example is the use of geographic information system (GIS) analysis. A GIS is a computer-based system that collects, stores, analyzes, and graphically displays data that can be mapped by geographic coordinates. Although this system is relatively new to the social sciences, GIS has quickly become a powerful tool for analyzing the physical, health, and social circumstances of geographically defined communities such as neighborhoods and schools, as well as any group that can be demarcated according to zip code, school district boundaries, census tracts, political boundaries, and any other geographic subdivision.

The mapping capabilities of GIS are frequently combined with information from the U.S. Census Bureau and government or industry reports. The merged information can be used to detail the demographic characteristics of geographical communities (e.g., population changes, ethnic and immigrant composition, and family structures), their health and behavioral risks (e.g., disease rates, exposure to environmental hazards, and crime and drug use rates), and their level of access to economic opportunities and needed services (e.g., location and density of employers, hospitals, clinics, and social service agencies). Using GIS, a researcher can compare the geographic concentrations of people at risk and in need of social services to the locations of the service providers, and then visualize transportation-related obstacles to service access. With GIS, variations in poverty levels can be assessed not at the neighborhood level, but block by block. In a study of elderly people living in South Carolina, GIS techniques provided information regarding elderly population characteristics for a particular county, located government and private sector resources, and identified gaps between the concentrations of elderly residents and the available resources, helping to target potentially unmet needs (Hirshorn & Stewart, 2003).

GIS can help identify social welfare issues that might go unnoticed when needs assessments rely primarily on those who come forward for services, as these individuals' needs may not represent the needs of cultural minorities. It can help social workers and service planners conceptualize and address issues at the community level and lead them to investigate distinctive cultural forces at work in these communities. GIS can be a springboard for effective mixed methods designs. It helps researchers formulate questions about the reasons for variations across geographic communities in health and welfare. These questions are best answered through subsequent qualitative methods such as focus groups, intensive interviews, and observational studies. GIS analysis is an important tool for administrators, because it allows them to visualize supply and demand and expand services where they are most needed; for community development plans that attempt to address a community's embedded political, social, and economic assets and liabilities; and for social service providers and agencies that want to compile and disseminate information about a community's service options to current and potential clients. It is also useful for gaining an understanding of community trends and changes.

BRIDGING THE GAP BETWEEN RESEARCH AND PRACTICE

There is a need for research with cultural minorities that can be translated into practical applications for policy and practice, a task that typically requires collaboration among practitioners, researchers, and policymakers. Advances in mixed methods hold great promise for improving the quality and relevance of research for social work practice, but it is more likely that practitioners will be educated consumers applying the published results of these methods than active participants in conducting the research. Social work practitioners seldom have the time or the support to conduct research and may see themselves as operating in a here-and-now world that is set apart from that of researchers. To bridge the research and practice divide, researchers and practitioners need to move beyond stereotypes that researchers are concerned only with the pursuit of abstract truths, while practitioners must rely only on their own practice experience to help their clients. To make research more relevant to practice, academics, practitioners, universities, and social service agencies have to collaborate to develop approaches for integrating practice and research that empower practitioners with useful information rather than scientific demonstrations of hypothetically effective but impractical practices. Two methods that have been proposed as means to bridge the gap between research and practice are community-based participatory action research (CBPR) and translational research.

Community-Based Participatory Action Research

Epstein (2009) advocates for an integration of practice-based research and research-informed practice by designing research to be relevant to practice rather than to establish effectiveness in the abstract. When social workers let research ideas develop from their clinical observations rather than basing them exclusively on past theories and findings, the chances are enhanced that findings that are relevant to practice will emerge. As long as social workers define themselves exclusively as either practitioners or researchers, there is little hope for meaningful advances in the development of practice knowledge development. If social workers were to define themselves as both practitioners and researchers, creative and productive knowledge-building efforts could occur.

The community-based participatory research (CBPR) model allows the necessary role integration between the practitioner and the researcher, but with a more manageable level of practitioner involvement than is often required by other methods. CBPR follows the key principles of Paulo Freire's work on effective pedagogy, which showed how researchers benefit from the experience and knowledge of local people. The difference between Freire's action research and CBPR is that action research is focused on stimulating a fundamental change process that empowers the community being studied, while CBPR is focused more narrowly on finding community solutions to concrete problems.

The W. K. Kellogg Foundation defines CBPR as "a collaborative approach to research that equitably involves all partners in the research process and recognizes the unique strengths that each brings. CBPR begins with a research topic of importance to the community and has the aim of combining knowledge with action and achieving social change to improve community health and eliminate health disparities." CBPR is used to consider the perspectives of all parties in the examination of problems with the goal of solving them. In traditional research settings, the researcher is thought to be the expert, the repository of knowledge who enlightens others; in contrast, CBPR gives communities the task of locating the needed knowledge. In CBPR, those who are affected are the ones who select the problem to be studied and collect the data used to address it. CBPR is similar to other participatory models such as action inquiry, action science, community-based research, and cooperative inquiry, all of which view the individuals under study as active participants in generating knowledge.

CBPR advocates a more egalitarian relationship between the researcher and the participants, and a more equitable distribution of tasks. The democratic philosophy of CBPR requires participants to be involved in all stages of the study as full stakeholders and to be treated as equals by the researchers. This means that the research methods are developed and applied in community settings and are based on collective community action, not on a design conceived in advance by university researchers. CBPR seeks to raise the consciousness of the oppressed and to encourage a collective response to social disadvantages. In CBPR, participants help develop research questions, design measures and instruments, collect information, and interpret, reflect, and act on the results. This engagement and reflection not only give the researcher a more valid and reliable interpretation of the data, but also transform the community's understanding of the nature of their problem. In terms of CBPR's applicability to culturally grounded social work, while traditional research may be conducted *on* cultural minorities, CBPR is research *with* and *by* minority group or community members. In traditional research, the project ends when the data are analyzed, but in CBPR action is the next logical stage once the analysis has been completed. CBPR may contribute to social progress for communities. Its main outcomes are not only findings, conclusions, and policy recommendations, but also increased social inclusion, participation by community members, and improved service user participation.

CBPR operates from an ecological perspective and consists of four processes—planning, action, observation, and reflection—all of which interact in a cycle until the research objectives are attained. The objective of CBPR is to promote health and social justice within the community and to help community members identify solutions to their problems. CBPR involves practitioners, community members, and researchers in a melding of research with education and action that takes advantage of the strengths, competencies, and potential promises in the research setting. Collaborations among researchers, community members, government agencies, and nonprofit organizations—all focused on collective action to address identified issues—are essential to both the CBPR process and its outcome.

With its emphasis on deliberate and concerted efforts to work with members of traditionally oppressed communities, CBPR is thus well aligned with social work's commitment to social justice. CBPR often takes place in communities that have been exploited or oppressed and addresses their concerns with the goal of achieving positive social change. The guiding principles of CBPR approach oppression as a problem rooted in macrosocial systems that require fundamental transformation of the social order, principles that are consistent with social work's progressive outlook.

For example, researchers used CBPR in a multiphase study of cultural and institutional obstacles that contribute to the reluctance of African Americans to use hospice services (Reese, Ahern, Nair, O'Faire, & Warren, 1999). The study used intensive open-ended interviews with African American pastors as well as questionnaires completed by hospice patients, churchgoers, and others from the community. The interviews helped the researchers identify a number of cultural beliefs and practices that were inconsistent with the hospice philosophy—such as opposition to accepting terminal disease, planning for death, and receiving care from strangers—sometimes for spiritual reasons. Pastors said that African American members of their congregations preferred to pursue vigorous medical treatment and rely on home remedies or prayer rather than accept palliative care from hospice, with its implicit acknowledgement of impending death. The wide-ranging research identified institutional barriers, such as the paucity of African American hospice staff and general distrust of the health-care system, and demonstrated that African Americans were more reluctant to consider hospice than European Americans. The study's foundation in CBPR guided its conclusions and recommendations; for example, the study called for culturally sensitive social work practice with African Americans that honors their spiritual beliefs and the adaptation of hospice services to the needs of African Americans and recommended that African American community and religious leaders be trained to present hospice options to their congregations in a realistic and sensitive way that recognizes culturally based concerns.

In addition to influencing the outcome of a study, CBPR also affects individuals who engage in the research process. In a CBPR project conducted with high school youths, the participants reported that the process helped them gain respect from teachers and administrators in the school, gave them the skills they need to make their voices heard, and shifted their perception of themselves from students to professionals (Ozer & Wright, 2012).

A CBPR model not only is inherently designed to benefit the community, but also enriches the research process. Compared to other research models, CBPR makes it easier to join together partners with diverse expertise to address complex public health problems. By increasing trust and bridging cultural gaps between partners, CBPR can enhance research by facilitating the recruitment, engagement, and retention of community members. By increasing the quality and validity of research, CBPR improves the relevance and expands the uses of the knowledge generated. CBPR also provides a bridge to ensure that research findings have the potential to be translated into workable community solutions.

Translational Research

Translational research was used first in the medical field, where it provided a model for addressing the gap between research and practice. The translational process involves overcoming all the obstacles that prevent the application of research findings beyond academic circles and professional journals, and identifying the best systems and incentives for rapidly incorporating proven findings into real-life practice. It is a form of technology transfer. In social work, practitioners can play a key role as partners in translational research and the testing of promising emerging practices.

Two forms of translational research have been distinguished (Woolf, 2008). The first to be developed, Type I translational research, focused on applying basic science on effective drugs and treatments to clinical health practice, a transfer of knowledge known as from "lab to bedside." Type II translational research investigates how to effectively transfer practice knowledge into community settings. Type II includes research on the best ways to design and implement health services and public health practices that are effective at closing health gaps by improving access, coordination, decision-making, and responsiveness to the community's real needs and resources. Type II translational research, for example, might involve a careful study of how to build a community's capacity and networks for assessing substance abuse needs and delivering culturally responsive prevention and treatment interventions (Hawkins et al., 2009; Pentz, Jasuja, Rohrbach, Sussman, & Bardo, 2006). Other examples of Type II translational research are studies of: multi-component interventions or practices that are employed in different combinations (e.g., antibullying programs that include one-on-one and small-group counseling, and schoolwide awareness components); programs targeting multiple health outcomes and comorbidities (e.g., substance use and mental health); extensions of proven interventions or practices into new settings (e.g., from schools to community centers) or using new formats (e.g., delivering them online); and methods for the widespread dissemination of effective programs or practices, or how to prepare to take them to scale for wider community impact.

Several practical strategies have been suggested to promote translational research in social work. A first step is for researchers to make their findings more accessible by providing clear summaries and explicating practice implications. A more difficult task is the creation of viable opportunities for researchers, academics, service providers, clients, and policymakers to come together and focus their attention on a given issue. Collaboratories have been suggested as one means to link these different groups technologically over distance. An example of a collaboratory is a virtual partnership created to promote evidence-based mental health practices in social work education and research (Lewis, Koston, Quartley, & Adsit, 2010). Collaboratories use the Internet to allow individuals to share information, enlarge their understanding of an issue, and identify solutions in a collaborative way. The objective of translational research is not only to design or recraft research findings so that they are more accessible to practitioners, but also to make it possible for social work researchers, practitioners, and policymakers to work together on issues of common concern.

DEVELOPING KNOWLEDGE ON DIFFERENT CULTURES

Both evaluation and research can be designed to enhance knowledge of cultural diversity through the recognition and incorporation of the different ways that knowledge can be generated. Research and evaluation that follow the principles and logic of the scientific method and that are empirically supported through careful observation are one of many ways of gaining knowledge. Although they may not receive the blessing of the scientific establishment, other forms of knowledge can also be of great use in the study of different cultural groups. This knowledge can be based on the personal experiences of members of the cultural groups, or it may be based on what people assume to be true because of what they have learned about the world through their families and communities.

Because of our society's preference for scientific knowledge, our knowledge of cultural groups tends to be generated not by them or with them, but rather for them by other so-called experts. Historically, oppressed groups such as women and cultural minorities have not played an equal role in the development of knowledge about themselves because they have had problems gaining entry into and acceptance as students and professors within the university circles where researchers are trained and where much research is conducted. In her or his position as outsider, the researcher may arrive at conclusions that do not reflect the experience of the group being studied. Much progress has been made in transforming academia into a more inclusive system where nontraditional perspectives are welcome. The ways that knowledge can be developed in partnership with members of oppressed communities discussed in this chapter need to be utilized more widely, and practitioners and researchers must continue to perfect them.

Key Concepts

Etic: A type of research approach that analyzes cultural phenomena from the perspective of one who is not a member of the culture being studied

Emic: A type of research approach that analyzes cultural phenomena from the perspective of a member of the culture being studied

Quantitative research: Typically an experimental or survey research method in social work that employs hypothesis testing and inferential statistics to study a group and is used to study the "what"

Qualitative research: Research methodologies that study the "why" and the "how," such as content analysis of documents and scripts, participant observation, open-ended and semistructured interviews, focus groups, and ethnography

Ethnography: A way of studying and describing a culture and an approach to gaining an understanding of a way of life different from one's own in which the researcher immerses her- or himself in the field to acquire insight into the experiential world of people; usually employs a variety of methods, such as intensive interviews and participant observation

Mixed methods research: The use of both qualitative and quantitative approaches in a single study

Community-based participatory research (CBPR): An orientation to research that uses a variety of research methods that actively engage representatives of the community being studied to help frame the research questions and methods and analyze and interpret findings

Translational research: Scientific research that is designed to make findings from basic science useful for practical applications that enhance health and well-being

16

Culturally Grounded Social Work and Globalization

AS INFORMATION, GOODS, AND PEOPLE CROSS NATIONAL BORDERS IN unprecedented numbers, globalization is affecting all aspects of society, including social work practice. The globalization process brings new opportunities and unfamiliar challenges to the profession. Globalization can be defined as the process by which the geographical, political, and cultural boundaries that separate individuals and societies weaken or dissipate. Globalization produces transculturation, which changes the way individuals perceive their world (Mastrogianni & Bhugra, 2003). Transculturalism may be experienced, for example, by a teenager residing in the Mexican city of Monterrey who sings along to American rap music without fully comprehending the lyrics. Transculturation allows him to experience an array of social processes simultaneously without leaving Mexico (Wagner, Diaz, Lopez, Collado, & Aldaz, 2002). The first process is an acculturation process into American culture that occurs as he integrates and adopts aspects of American culture such as its music and dress code but does not require him to cross the border with the United States. The second is a deculturalization process, which takes place as he lets go of aspects of his native Mexican culture, such as its traditional music. The third is the process of neoculturation, or the creation of new cultural artifacts incorporating elements of both the traditional and the new cultures, such as rap music with Spanish lyrics and Mexican cultural themes. The process of neoculturation includes two phases: (1) the loss or uprooting of a culture (deculturation) and the creation of a new culture that has elements of both but is still very different from both original cultures (Peña, 2004). For example, the interaction of European American and Hispanic cultures in the United States resulted in phenomena such as Spanglish (not English and not Spanish, but a new mixture of languages) and TexMex food. Transculturation creates a mosaic of all these cultural contributions. Those who live on the figurative and literal borders of countries and cultures may more easily embrace transculturalism because they exist in a bicultural or multicultural space, occupying two or more worlds simultaneously.

Although globalization is often seen as the opposite of nationalism or regionalism (Powell, 2007), societies that are very much involved in the globalization process have shown a parallel tendency to grow more regional and sectarian in outlook. In some ways, the stronger regional identity becomes possible as a result of the weakening of national governments and national identity, an outcome of globalization. As Spain, for example, has become increasingly integrated into the European Union, expressions of long-suppressed regional identities have become stronger. Spain's numerous autonomous regions have increased their demands for more social, cultural, and political autonomy, as well as recognition of regional languages and different political discourses. As communities become more global in their economic outlook and their national and regional identities are strengthened, the traditional concept of cultural identity is challenged. Globalization is connecting the economies and the cultures of the world in ways that make countries more dependent on each other.

Technology and transportation advances have compressed time and distance. The Internet places people around the globe in instant contact with the other, but it is not clear if this type of contact encourages understanding. Immigrant families may still arrive in the United States with an idealized and unrealistic view of what life in the United States is like, and migrants often develop a positive or idealized narrative of their experience in order to cope with the dislocation of being separated from their homeland. Technology allows for constant information flow for the narratives of recently arrived immigrants to the United States to be ever present in the lives of those who remain behind. With the proliferation of technology that allows for video communication, families both in the United States and in the sending country can connect regularly at minimal cost, and experience the others' environment in real time in ways never before possible.

Globalization is transforming the collective lives of societies through the accelerated movement of money, technology, goods, and people. People in the wealthy societies of the northern hemisphere and other developed nations enjoy comfortable incomes and shelter and marketable skills. They are in a position to choose where to live and where to work. On the other hand, people in developing nations in the southern hemisphere, the marginalized, the poor, and the disabled; refugees from war-ravaged areas; and immigrants escaping economic crises must rely on their blood ties, kin groups, and other support systems connected to their ethnic or religious affiliations to survive because the governments of their countries of origin have withdrawn much of their support under pressure from global forces. From a social justice and distributive justice perspective, globalization appears to distribute benefits to some people, but not others. When a job is outsourced to a developing country, the impact of globalization is experienced very differently by the now-unemployed worker, the CEO of the outsourcing corporation, its profit-earning shareholders, and the newly hired worker who receives low wages and no fringe benefits. One consequence of globalization is that many problems that certain societies experience can become globalized. Social and economic vulnerabilities and the problems they generate tend to merge and amplify across affected countries within the same region. The exportation of youth gangs from Los Angeles to cities in Central America—often spurred by U.S. deportation policies—has generated distressing social and legal challenges for communities in Tegucigalpa, Honduras, and Guatemala City, Guatemala (Arana, 2005). Globalization is not unidirectional, and works at many different levels. The AIDS pandemic, which affects communities and social work practice around the world, is perhaps the most widely publicized example of this unique multidirectional effect of globalization. The social work profession is being increasingly challenged to think globally: policymakers and service providers are no longer able to think about the psychosocial needs of their constituencies in isolation.

GLOBALIZATION AND SOCIAL WORK

Some may argue that globalization is producing a homogeneous culture based on consumerism at the expense of local cultures and other contextual differences, as well as the environment. This text adopts the viewpoint that social work practice promoting social justice needs to be grounded in the cultures of the communities being served. Perhaps recognizing and celebrating the centrality of culture is a means of resisting the homogeneity and oppression that people experience as part of a global consumer society, and a way of increasing participation and action in the pursuit of social justice. By strengthening their connections to their cultural identities, communities can begin to share and expand their collective power for social action, which in turn stimulates more social participation.

There are some concerns that globalization will lead to passivity and disengagement as groups outside the mainstream lose their cultural moorings. Although this is a valid concern, it does not have to be the case. However, communities cannot maintain their unique social identities and worldviews if their younger members are not aware of them. This is why interventions promoting social justice need to start at the cultural awareness level, or with Freire's conscientization efforts. It is from this perspective that a culturally grounded approach to social work practice is applicable in a globalizing world.

A global social work perspective has the potential to produce the desired outcomes at a broader level if practitioners use their understanding of the differences and similarities between countries to engage in international problem-solving activities. For example, human trafficking has become a global issue that affects members of many oppressed communities. To address human trafficking, social workers may need to become aware of the interconnectedness of social problems and how they are influenced by global economic and political forces. The social work profession is well qualified to deal with issues such as human trafficking and their consequences.

Schools of social work have been called to take the following steps as a way to foster a proactive response to globalization among social workers:

1. Embrace a global social and political justice agenda.
2. Develop a more direct role in solving issues of poverty at a global level within schools of social work.
3. Support the meaningful interaction of social workers with international bodies such as the World Bank and the United Nations, and with international social work organizations.
4. Facilitate the building of political solidarity among the poor (Seipel, 2003).

The same forces that allow businesses to operate as if national borders are irrelevant also allow social activists, labor organizers, journalists, academics, and many others to work on a global stage. The Internet is evolving into a global information infrastructure that transforms our sense of place and time, and opens the possibility of cultural, ideological, political, and religious exchange (Khiabany, 2003). Through social media and Internet news outlets, people are becoming increasingly aware of global issues. This technology also allows social movements to become global with unprecedented speed and ease. This was exemplified in 2011 when the Occupy Wall Street movement that started in New York City was replicated in over nine hundred cities around the world within a month of the original protest, with groups gathering in San José (Costa Rica), London, Tokyo, Rome, and Sydney, among others (Alessi, 2011). The spread of the protest not only reflected the rapid transfer of information, but also the universality of the complaints that were being brought in response to the global impact of the economic recession. The interconnectedness of the new global economy can have grave consequences but also unite people who are working for social justice. Globalization can have a positive effect on the lives of individuals and communities if there is some mechanism in place to fairly distribute the economic benefits that come from it, as well as the means to prevent or manage the negative consequences that globalization may produce, such as ecological degradation and violations of human and civil rights.

The *Code of Ethics* of the National Association of Social Workers (1999, p. 24; 2008, p. 24) states, "social workers should promote the general welfare of society, from local to global justice." Social workers tend to focus on local needs, and programs and services are designed to respond to those needs, but there is a need for social workers to become more active globally. In order to do so, social workers must be knowledgeable about the global environment because international economic and political forces have a direct impact on the well-being of local people.

Social workers increasingly confront international problems directly, for example through their work with refugees and vulnerable workers whose livelihoods are disrupted by the global economy. Lasting solutions will emerge as professionals increase their awareness and advocate for the creation of international institutional frameworks for problem solving across borders.

The profession of social work is going through its own process of globalization in order to respond to the needs of a transcultural client base. For example, a transnational and transcultural social work practice has been proposed as a means to intervene with the social and economic needs of immigrant communities (Lyons, 2006). Having a global perspective helps the practitioner understand the origin of problems as well as the complex relationships between the culture of origin and the emergence of transcultural identities within communities.

The globalization of social work can happen only if social work education is globalized. There is a need to broaden students' and faculty members' perspectives regarding their professional roles at the international level. There is no substitute for international educational experiences. Traveling to the country of origin of an immigrant community would greatly benefit the social worker in her or his understanding of the traditional culture as well as the possible tensions and contradictions that clients may be experiencing as they navigate the host culture.

The International Federation of Social Workers, for example, is an organization whose mission is to advance social justice and development through cooperation between social workers. Other social work organizations have an international focus; for example, the International Association for the Advancement of Social Work with Groups has chapters in several countries, and their members share their research and practice experiences at annual conferences. The National Association of Social Workers and the Council on Social Work Education have their own international offices and programs, which offer useful information and international exchange opportunities. Many schools of social work offer international summer immersion (language and culture) programs. Through these efforts and many others, the profession continues to become more international and globalized.

Another way the profession may address these issues is by recruiting social work students from within the communities being served. Globalization has made it increasingly important for practitioners, service providers, and even researchers to be truly bilingual and bicultural in order to reach members of many Latino and immigrant communities. A study of Head Start families found that mastery of the English language is the key that unlocks the door to the community for immigrant families, and bilingual social workers help overcome the barriers that prevent community members from accessing services and achieving their goals (Wall et al., 2000). In such situations, social workers often play a cultural mediation role as their clients navigate through the acculturation process, allowing them to access opportunities and advance economically and socially. To mediate effectively between these two worlds, workers need to be competent in both cultures. However, the reality is that the availability of bilingual and bicultural social workers is limited. Recruiting future social workers from these communities would allow the profession to address not only the growing need for bilingual practitioners and researchers, but also the them-versus-us mentality that is common among immigrants and other minority clients and often presents barriers to effective social work practice.

Globalization is challenging the one-on-one approach commonly used by practitioners and is making social workers recognize the importance of communities and groups as sources of transformation. Social workers from around the world are working together to design and test innovative interventions to ensure that oppressed communities benefit from globalization and to address the challenges of globalization. Many aspects of their research and practice innovation are applicable to communities in the United States; through professional exchange and collaboration, these communities can share and jointly research and evaluate the interventions.

THE RESEARCHER-PRACTITIONER AS THE INSIDER AND THE OUTSIDER

The culturally grounded approach to social work puts forward a horizontal relationship based on honest exchanges that position both the practitioner-researcher and the community as the experts. The ever-changing nature of culture and the rapid process of globalization make the development of a social work practitioner-researcher role imperative. The practitioner-researcher is always willing to ask another question and is ready to think outside the comfortable box of the familiar. Polarized conceptions of culture (i.e., old culture vs. new culture, culture of origin vs. host culture) are being questioned by transculturalism. The resurgence of qualitative methods in research involving cultural minorities, such as the use of ethnography and CBPR, helps practitioner-researchers understand how communities understand themselves and their own changing cultures (Somerville, 2006). A common question in practice and research with groups demarcated by race, ethnicity, gender, and sexual orientation is the extent to which the social worker needs to be a member of the group to conduct effective practice and meaningful research about it. As Robert Merton (1972) asked many decades ago in an article on the benefits and limitations of being an insider or an outsider, "Do you have to be one to understand one?" (p 23). It is important to consider the practitioner-researcher's stance as an insider or an outsider. Is it possible to speak of insiders and outsiders in a global and transcultural world? Do outsiders lack the insider's special insights into the group because they have not had the socialization and group experiences that are crucial for understanding the community's ever-changing culture, language, and behavior? Is awareness of the process of transculturation becoming more relevant to social workers than an awareness of the values and norms of the community's culture of origin? It appears that social workers need to both continue to be aware of and comfortable with the culture of origin and become familiar with the processes of cultural transformation (transculturation) and its impact on individuals, families, and communities.

The challenges faced by practitioner-researchers who are outsiders looking in seem more evident than the possible advantages. While insiders, by virtue of their social position, tend to share central interests with their communities, outsiders may intervene only after reflecting on conflicting interests and values between the host community and their own communities of origin. Insiders and outsiders may frame assessment and research questions differently. For outsiders, especially those who occupy privileged positions in the cultural and economic mainstream, the main challenge is being aware of how their positions may shape their conceptions of cultural minority communities and the kinds of questions and the frames of reference they bring to their practice with and research with these communities. They need to be conscious of their lack of understanding of the communities and find ways to incorporate the community members' perspectives in their approach to practice or research.

Practitioners also need to be aware of how privilege affects their access to the community. Inquiries into issues of cultural difference posed by outsiders may emphasize how the other is different, implicitly assuming and reinforcing the idea that the mainstream represents what is normal. This is the basis for the criticism that much practice and research conducted by outsiders presumes that only non-whites have racial and ethnic identities, that gender is significant only in the lives of women and transgender individuals, and that sexual orientation is only of interest to people sexually attracted to those of the same sex. White researchers run the risk of carrying what Peggy McIntosh (1990) calls the "knapsack of invisible privilege" (p 1) into the practice and research processes. Outsiders' social awkwardness and psychological discomfort—in addition to the potential for them to misunderstand or misrepresent cultural minorities—may compromise the effectiveness of the intervention; they may attempt to compensate with overzealousness but fail to devote sufficient attention to building trusting relationships within the community over time. Exploitation is also an issue, especially for practitioner-researchers whose approach is to drop—or parachute—into a vulnerable community briefly to try to fix the problem or extract data for their own research agenda and then leave.

Despite the difficult issues faced by those who are not members of the community under study, there are potential advantages to being an outsider. Outsiders may not be expected to screen their language and behavior in the same way as insiders and are less likely to face appeals to or questions about their loyalties to the group. Outsiders may elicit fuller and richer responses to certain questions than insiders because respondents may assume that insiders already know the answers, while outsiders require explanations that are more complete. This may be one reason that some practitioner-researchers find that working with clients who are dissimilar—for example, of a different ethnicity or gender—sometimes is easier than working with those who are similar (Gibson & Abrams, 2003). In addition, as the problems of cultural outsider status become more widely recognized, outsiders may develop a heightened awareness of the need to be clear and self-conscious about their practice and the methodological choices they make.

Insiders also face significant (though often more subtle) challenges in practicing and conducting research within their own communities. One challenge for insiders is avoiding equating their familiarity with their communities with effective practice. As a result of acculturation and transculturation, the ideas that practitioners and researchers have about their cultures of origin may be outdated or based on limited experience. Whereas outsiders run the risk of imposing their own cultural assumptions, categories, and meanings on the group being studied, insiders may struggle to gain some distance from their personal experience as a member of the community under study and may find it difficult to avoid judging a client's perspective on the culture as good or bad, correct or incorrect, or authentic or inauthentic. As members of the cultural minority group under study, insiders may have a history of deeply personal and emotional experiences of marginalization, experiences that, though similar, need to be kept distinct from those of the clients or research subjects (Kanuha, 2000).

Insiders have a special authenticity that is very useful in gaining access and the trust of the community but may compromise their objectivity. Insider status can also pose a problem by leading to the presumption of insider knowledge. Respondents may confide to insider practitioners through cultural code words and phrases and through nonverbal behaviors and gestures that reflect tacit understandings in the community. Respondents may feel comfortable making vague references or failing to clarify their ideas and expect the researcher to intuitively understand what they mean. Often these ideas may be communicated in a way that reinforces their common membership—"*You* would know what I mean," or "You know how *they* are." The problem here is twofold. The practitioner-researcher may not have knowledge of the person's experience of culture or of her or his local community, or of the effects of transculturation in the original culture, and may not understand various aspects of the culture in the same way as the respondent. In addition, any implicit cultural understandings have to be made explicit before they can be addressed or analyzed. Another set of problems for insiders is that the boundaries between practitioner and client or researcher and subject can easily blur.

Despite these different challenges, in a globalized world insiders and outsiders confront similar issues. Both groups need to reflect on their social position within a given community, the power differential between practitioners and their clients, and how they represent their own perspectives and those of their clients. Consciousness of social positions requires recognition of the tremendous variability that exists within cultural communities. Practitioners and researchers can be similar or different from those they work with in terms of education and social class background as well as in race, ethnicity, gender, sexual orientation, and age. The multiple ways that these social statuses may intersect and the effects of globalization and transculturation suggest that practitioners can only be partial insiders and seldom are complete outsiders. Those who grew up in the culture may change, such that even though they continue to be able to gain the trust of community members and understand their ways and values, they may or may not endorse all those practices and values.

Differences in power—across lines of ethnicity, class, gender, age, ability status, and sexual orientation—shape relationships between the researcher and the community under study regardless of whether the researcher is a relative insider or outsider. Social workers emphasize the importance of empowering the clients by both developing culturally appropriate interventions that take their perspective into consideration and negotiating with them their involvement and stake in the helping process. All practitioner-researchers face the difficult question of how they can represent the voices and perspectives of their clients while also presenting assessments as reflections of truth. Most choose a course between two extremes. Logical positivism, at one end, maintains that through careful observation, rigorous methods, and detached objectivity, practitioners can uncover facts and dynamics that independently exist in a social world. Postmodernism, on the other hand, maintains that all knowledge is socially constructed by individuals and by communities, such that any needs assessment reveals a multiplicity of perspectives rather than a single truth. Some postmodernists view attempts to seek truth not only as futile, but also as political acts that are designed to strengthen the powerful and privileged and silence the powerless. Regardless of where practitioners fall between these extremes, and whether they are relative insiders or outsiders to the cultural communities they are working with, they should consider how to represent the needs and desires of their clients and research subjects accurately and authentically. Eliot Liebow (1967), a sociologist who documented his groundbreaking qualitative research with African American men in *Talley's Corner*, described the challenge as always being aware of the distance between the perspectives of the researcher and the researched, but "walking the margins" (p. 250). What separated him from his research subjects was less a wall than a "chain-link fence, since despite the barriers we were able to look at each other, walk alongside each other, talk and occasionally touch fingers. When two people stand up close to the fence on either side, without touching it, they can look through the interstices and forget that they are looking through a fence" (pp. 250–251).

A culturally grounded perspective challenges the researcher-practitioner to be aware of the fence and at the same time to reach through it to hear the voices and capture the stories from the other side.

Key Concepts

Globalization: The process by which the geographical, political, and cultural boundaries that separate individuals and societies weaken or dissipate into a more universal set of norms and behaviors

Transculturation: An identity status produced by globalization that is not connected to one nation or one culture, but instead is a blend of multiple cultural sources from across the globe

Neoculturation: The creation of new cultural artifacts through the incorporation of elements of both the traditional and the new cultures that does not require the individual to leave her or his country of origin

References

Abalos, D. T. (2002). *The Latino male: A radical redefinition*. Boulder, CO: Lynne Rienner.

Abed, M. (2006). Clarifying the concept of genocide. *Metaphilosophy, 37*(3–4), 308–330.

Abes, E. S. (2011). Exploring the relationship between sexual orientation and religious identities for Jewish lesbian college students. *Journal of Lesbian Studies, 15*, 205–225.

Abram, F. Y., Slosar, J. A., & Walls, R. (2005). Reverse mission: A model for international social work education and transformative intra-national practice. *International Social Work, 48*(2), 161–176.

Abusharaf, R. M. (2007). *Female circumcision: Multicultural perspectives*. Philadelphia: University of Pennsylvania Press.

Acemoglu, D., & Angrist, J. D. (2001). Consequences of employment protection? The Case of the Americans with Disabilities Act. *Journal of Political Economy, 109*(5), 915–957.

Acevedo-Garcia, D., & Bates, L. M. (2007). Latino health paradoxes: Empirical evidence, explanations, future research, and implications. In H. Rodriguez, R. Saenz, C. Menjivar (Eds.), *Latino/as in the United States: Changing the face of America* (pp. 101–113). New York: Springer.

Acevedo-Garcia, D., Lochner, K. A., Osypuk, T. L., & Subramanian, S. V. (2003). Future directions in residential segregation and health research: A multilevel approach. *American Journal of Public Health, 93*, 215–221.

Acevedo-Garcia, D., Ospuk, T., McArdle, N., & Williams, D. R. (2008). Toward a policy relevant analysis of geographic and racial/ethnic health disparities. *Health Affairs, 27*, 321–333.

Adams, D. W. (1995). *Education for extinction: American Indians and the boarding school experience, 1875–1928*. Lawrence: University Press of Kansas.

Adler, N. E., & Stewart, J. (2010). Health disparities across the lifespan: Meaning, methods, and mechanisms. *Annals of the New York Academy of Sciences, 1186*, 5–23.

Adler, N. E., Boyce, T., Chesney, M. A., Cohen, S., & Folkman, S. (1994). Socioeconomic status and health: The challenge of the gradient. *American Psychologist, 49*, 15–24.

Ahmed, A. T., Mohammed, S. A., & Williams, D. R. (2007). Racial discrimination & health: Pathways & evidence. *Indian Journal of Medical Research, 126*, 318–327.

Ahmed, S. F., Morrison, S., & Hughes, I. A. (2004). Intersex and gender assignment: The third way? *Archives of Disease in Childhood, 89*, 847–850.

Aiken, L. S., LoSciuto, L. A., & Ansetto, M. A. (1984). Paraprofessional versus professional drug counselors: The progress of clients in treatment. *International Journal of the Addictions, 19*(4), 383–401.

Akresh, I. R. (2006). Occupational mobility among legal immigrants to the United States. *International Migration Review, 40*(4), 854–884.

Al Salmi, I., Hoy, W. E., Kondalsamy-Chennakesavan, S., Wang, Z., Gobe, G. C., Barr, E. L., & Shaw, J. E. (2008). Disorders of glucose regulation in adults and birth weight results from the Australian Diabetes, Obesity and Lifestyle (AusDiab) Study. *Diabetes Care, 31*, 159–164.

Alatar, M., Smith, M., & Umbreit, M. (2004). *National survey of Arab-Palestinian-Jewish dialogue groups*. St. Paul: University of Minnesota, School of Social Work, the Center for Restorative Justice and Peacemaking.

Alatas, S. F. (1993). On the indigenization of academic discourse. *Alternatives: Global, Local, Political, 18*, 307–338.

Alba, R., & Hee, V. (1997). Rethinking assimilation theory for a new era of immigration. *International Migration Review, 31*(4), 826–874.

Aldrich, R. (2003). *Colonialism and homosexuality*. London: Routledge.

Alegría, M., Mulvaney-Day, N., Torres, M., Polo, A., Cao, Z., & Canino, G. (2007). Prevalence of psychiatric disorders across Latino subgroups in the United States. *American Journal of Public Health, 97*, 68–75.

Alegría, M., Polo, A., Gao, S., Santana, L., Rothstein, D., Jimenez, A., . . . , & Normand, S. L. (2008). Evaluation of a patient activation and empowerment intervention in mental health care. *Medical Care, 46*, 247–256.

Alessi, C. (2011, October 18). Why is occupy Wall Street going global? *The Atlantic*. Retrieved from http://www.theatlantic.com/international/archive/2011/10/why-is-occupy-wall-street-going-global/246879/

Ali, T. S., Asad, N., Mogren, I., & Krantz, G. (2011). Intimate partner violence in urban Pakistan: Prevalence, frequency, and risk factors. *International Journal of Women's Health, 3*, 105–115.

Allport, G. W. (1954). *The nature of prejudice*. Garden City, NY: Anchor Books.

Alverez, L., & Buckley, C. (2013, July 13). Zimmerman is acquitted in Trayvon Martin Killing. Retrieved from http://www.nytimes.com/2013/07/14/us/george-zimmerman-verdict-trayvon-martin.html?pagewanted = all&_r = 0

American Indian Movement. (1972, October 31). Trail of broken treaties 20-point position paper. [Press release]. Retrieved from http://www.aimovement.org/ggc/trailofbrokentreaties.html

American Psychiatric Association. (2013). *Diagnostic and statistical manual of mental disorders*. (5th ed.). Arlington, VA: American Psychiatric Publishing.

Anbinder, T. (2006). Nativism and prejudice against immigrants. In R. Ueda (Ed.), *A companion to American immigration* (pp. 177–201). Malden, MA: Blackwell.

Anda, R. F., Croft, J. B., Felitti, V. J., Nordenberg, D., Giles, W. H., Williamson, D. F., & Giovino, G. A. (1999). Adverse childhood experiences and smoking during adolescence and adulthood. *Journal of the American Medical Association, 282*, 1652–1658.

Andall, J. (2002). Second-generation attitudes? African-Italians in Milan. *Journal of Ethnic and Migration Studies, 28*(3), 389–408.

Anderson, M. L., & Collins, P. H. (2004). *Race, class, and gender* (5th ed.). Belmont, CA: Thomson Wadsworth.

Aneshensel, C. S. (1992). Social stress: Theory and research. *Annual Review of Sociology, 18*, 15–38.

Angle, P. M. (Ed.). (1991). *The complete Lincoln-Douglas debates of 1858*. Chicago: University of Chicago Press.

Ansari, Z., Carson, N. J., Ackland, M. J., Vaughan, L., & Serraglio, A. (2003). A public health model of the social determinants of health. *Sozial-und Präventivmedizin, 48*, 242–251.

Anthis, K. (2002). The role of sexist discrimination in adult women's identity development. *Sex Roles, 47*(9/10), 477–484.

Aponte, H. J. (1994). *Bread and spirit: Therapy with the new poor: Diversity of race, culture, and values.* New York: W. W. Norton.

Appleby, G. (2001). Dynamics of oppression and discrimination. In G. Appleby, E. Colon, & J. Hamilton (Eds.), *Diversity, oppression, and social functioning* (pp. 36–52). Boston: Allyn and Bacon.

Arana, A. (2005, May/June). How the street gangs took Central America. *Foreign Affairs, 84*(3), 98–110.

Arizmendi, L. G., & Ortiz, L. (2004). Neighborhood and community organizing in Colonias: A case study in the development and use of Promotoras. *Journal of Community Practice, 12*, 23–35.

Aromaa, E., Tolvanen, A., Tuulari, J., & Wahlbeck, K. (2011). Personal stigma and use of mental health services among people with depression in a general population in Finland. *BMC* [BioMed Central] *Psychiatry, 11*, 52–58.

Arreola, D. D. (2012). Placemaking and Latino urbanism in a Phoenix Mexican immigrant community. *Journal of Urbanism: International Research on Placemaking and Urban Sustainability, 5*, 157–170.

Asante, M. (2007). *An Afrocentric manifesto.* London: Polity.

Asante, M. K. (Ed.). (2000). *Socio-cultural conflict between African American and Korean American.* Lanham, MD: University Press of America.

Ashcroft, B., Griffiths, G., & Tiffin, H. (2013). *Post-colonial studies: The key concepts.* (3rd ed.). London: Routledge.

Ashford, J. B., LeCroy, C. W., & Lortie, K. L. (2001). *Human behavior in the social environment* (2nd ed.). Belmont, CA: Wadsworth.

Ashford, J. B., LeCroy, C. W., & Lortie, K. L. (2006). *Human behavior in the social environment: A multidimensional perspective.* Pacific Grove, CA: Brooks/Cole.

Astone, N. M., Misra, D., & Lynch, C. (2007). The effect of maternal socio-economic status throughout the lifespan on infant birthweight. *Paediatric and Perinatal Epidemiology, 21*, 310–318.

Ayanian, J. Z., Weissman, J. S., Schneider, E. C., Ginsburg, J. A., & Zaslavsky, A. M. (2000). Unmet health needs of uninsured adults in the United States. *Journal of the American Medical Association, 284*, 2061–2069.

Aybars, A. I. (2007). Work-life balance in the EU and leave arrangements across welfare regimes. *Industrial Relations Journal, 38*(6), 569–590.

Ayers, S. L., Kulis, S., & Marsiglia, F. F. (2013). The impact of ethnoracial appearance on substance use in Mexican heritage adolescents in the Southwest United States. *Hispanic Journal of Behavioral Sciences, 35*, 227–240.

Ayón, C., Marsiglia, F. F., & Parsai, M. B. (2010). Latino family mental health: Exploring the role of discrimination and familismo. *Journal of Community Psychology, 38*, 742–756. PMCID: PMC2947026

Azpurua, A., & Long, C. (August 16, 2010). Attacks against Mexican immigrants in NYC's Staten Island inflame black-Hispanic tensions. Retrieved from http://www.foxnews.com/us/2010/08/16/attacks-mexican-immigrants-nycs-staten-island-inflame-black-hispanic-tensions/

Bacal, A. (1994). *Types of ethnic identity responses to ethnic discrimination: An experiential approach to Mexican American identity.* Gothenburg, Sweden: University of Gothenburg.

Bailey, J., & Pillard, R. (1991). A genetic study of male sexual orientation. *Archives of General Psychiatry, 48*, 1089–1096.

Bailey, J., Pillard, R., Neale, M., & Agyei, Y. (1993). Heritable factors influence sexual orientation in women. *Archives of General Psychiatry, 50,* 217–223.

Bailey, M. J., & Dynarski, S. M. (2011). Gains and gaps: Changing inequality in US college entry and completion. NBER Working Paper 17633. National Bureau of Economic Research, Cambridge, MA.

Baker, A. C., Jensen, P. J., & Kolb, D. A. (2005). Conversation as experiential learning. *Management Learning, 36*(4), 411–427.

Baker, D. K. (2005). Beyond women and economics: Rereading "women's work." *Journal of Women in Culture and Society, 30*(4), 2189–2209.

Bamshad, M. J., & Olson, S. E. (2003). Does race exist? *Scientific American, 289*(6), 78–85.

Bandura, A., & Bussey, K. (2002). On broadening the cognitive, motivational, and sociostructural scope of theorizing about gender development and functioning: Comment on Martin, Ruble, and Szkrybalo (2002). *Psychological Bulletin, 130,* 691–701.

Banks, J., Marmot, M., Oldfield, Z., & Smith, J. P. (2006). Disease and disadvantage in the United States and England. *Journal of the American Medical Association, 295,* 2037–2045.

Barinaga, M. (1991). Is homosexuality biological? *Science, 253*(5023), 956–958.

Barker, D. J. (2003). Editorial: The developmental origins of adult disease. *European Journal of Epidemiology, 18,* 733–736.

Barker, D. J., Eriksson, J. G., Forsen, T., & Osmond, C. (2002). Fetal origins of adult disease: Strength of effects and biological basis. *International Journal of Epidemiology, 31,* 1235–1239.

Barnett, E., Braham, V. E., Casper, M. L., Elmes, G. A., & Halverson, J. A. (2007). *Men and heart disease: An atlas of racial and ethnic disparities in mortality.* Retrieved from ftp://ftp .cdc.gov/pub/Publications/mens_atlas/00-atlas-all.pdf

Barnoya, J., & Glantz, S. A. (2005). Cardiovascular effects of secondhand smoke nearly as large as smoking. *Circulation, 111,* 2684–2698.

Barr, D. A., & Wanat, S. F. (2005). Listening to patients: Cultural and linguistic barriers to health care access. *Family Medicine, 37,* 199–204.

Barrie, T., & Luria, Z. (2004). Sexuality and gender in children's daily worlds. In M. S. Kimmel & R. F. Plante (Eds.), *Sexualities: Identities, behaviors, and society* (pp. 74–85). New York: Oxford University Press.

Bartley, M., & Plewis, I. (2002). Accumulated labour market disadvantage and limiting long-term illness: Data from the 1971–1991 Office for National Statistics' Longitudinal Study. *International Journal of Epidemiology, 31,* 336–341.

Basile, K. C., Chen, J., Black, M. C., & Saltzman, L. E. (2007). Prevalence and characteristics of sexual violence victimization among US adults, 2001–2003. *Violence and Victims, 22,* 437–448.

Baubôck, R. (2002). Political community beyond the sovereign state, supranational federalism, and transnational minorities. In S. Vertovec & R. Cohen (Eds.), *Conceiving cosmopolitanism: Theory, context and practice* (pp. 110–136). London: Oxford University Press.

Baum, A., Garofalo, J. P., & Yali, A. (1999). Socioeconomic status and chronic stress: Does stress account for SES effects on health? *Annals of the New York Academy of Sciences, 896,* 131–144.

Bayer, K. (2005). Cosmetic surgery and cosmetics: Redefining the appearance of age. *Generations, 29,* 13–18.

Becker, S. O., & Woessmann, L. (2009). Was Weber wrong? A human capital theory of Protestant economic history. *Quarterly Journal of Economics, 124,* 531–596.

Begard, L. (2007). *The comparative histories of slavery in Brazil, Cuba, and the United States.* London: Cambridge University Press.

Behrens, A., Uggen, C., & Manza, J. (2003). Ballot manipulation and the "menace of Negro domination": Racial threat and felon disenfranchisement in the United States, 1850–2002. *American Journal of Sociology, 109*(3), 559–605.

Bejel, E. (2001). *Gay Cuban nation.* Chicago: University of Chicago Press.

Belkin, A., & Bateman, G. (2003). *Don't ask, don't tell: Debating the gay ban in the military.* Boulder, CO: Lynne Rienner.

Bellamy, A. J. (2012). Mass killing and the politics of legitimacy: Empire and the ideology of selective extermination. *Australian Journal of Politics & History, 58,* 159–180.

Benard, B. (2002). Turnaround people and places: Moving from risk to resiliency. In D. Saleebey (Ed.), *The strengths perspective in social work practice* (3rd ed., pp. 213–227). Boston: Allyn and Bacon.

Berger, P. L., & Luckmann, T. (1966). *The social construction of reality: A treatise in the sociology of knowledge.* New York: Doubleday.

Berkhofer, R. F. (1978). *The white man's Indian: Images of the American Indian from Columbus to the present.* New York: Random House.

Berkman, L. F., & Glass, T. (2000). Social integration, social networks, and health. In L. F. Berkman & I. Kawachi (Eds.), *Social epidemiology* (pp. 137–173). New York: Oxford University Press.

Berliner, D. C. (2006). Our impoverished view of education reform. *College Teacher Record, 108*(6), 949–995.

Berry, J. W., Phinney, J. S., Sam, D. L., & Vedder, P. (2006). Immigrant youth: Acculturation, identity, and adaptation. *Applied Psychology, 55,* 303–332.

Bertocchi, G., & Dimico, A. (2012). The racial gap in education and the legacy of slavery. *Journal of Comparative Economics, 40,* 581–595.

Biblarz, T. J., & Savci, E. (2010). Lesbian, gay, bisexual, and transgender families. *Journal of Marriage and Family, 72,* 480–497.

Bielby, W., & Baron, J. (1984). A woman's place is with other women: Sex segregation within organizations. In B. F. Reskin (Ed.), *Sex segregation in the workplace: Trends, explanations, remedies* (pp. 27–55). Washington, DC: National Academy Press.

Bielby, W., & Baron, J. (1986). Men and women at work: Sex segregation and statistical discrimination. *American Journal of Sociology, 91*(4), 759–799.

Biermann, J., Dunlop, A., Brady, C., Dubin, C., & Brann, A. (2006). Promising practices in preconception care for women at risk for poor health and pregnancy outcomes. *Maternal and Child Health Journal, 10,* S21–S28.

Birzer, M. L., & Birzer, G. H. (2006). Race matters: A critical look at racial profiling: It's a matter of the courts. *Journal of Criminal Justice, 34*(6), 643–651.

Bishop, A. (2002). *Becoming an ally: Breaking the cycle of oppression in people.* New York: Zed Books.

Blackburn, E. H., Greider, C. W., & Szostak, J. W. (2006). Telomeres and telomerase: The path from maize, Tetrahymena and yeast to human cancer and aging. *Nature Medicine, 12,* 1133–1138.

Blas, E., & Kurup, A. S. (Eds.). (2010). *Equity, Social Determinants, and Public Health Programmes*. Geneva: World Health Organization.

Blauner, R. (1972). *Racial oppression in America*. New York: Harper and Row.

Blum, L. (2006). Comments on Eamonn Callan. *Symposia on Gender, Race, and Philosophy, 2*(2), 1–4.

Blumberg, R. L. (1984). *Civil rights: The 1960s freedom struggle*. Boston: Twayne.

Bluthenthal, R. N., Jacobson, J. O., & Robinson, P. L. (2007). Are racial disparities in alcohol treatment completion associated with racial differences in treatment modality entry? Comparison of outpatient treatment and residential treatment in Los Angeles County, 1998 to 2000. *Alcoholism: Clinical and Experimental Research, 31*, 1920–1926.

Bly, R. (1990). *Iron John: A book about men*. Cambridge, MA: Da Capo Books.

Boardman, J. D. (2004). Stress and physical health: The role of neighborhoods as mediating and moderating mechanisms. *Social Science & Medicine, 58*, 2473–2483.

Bobak, M., & Marmot, M. (1996). East-West mortality divide and its potential explanations: Proposed research agenda. *British Medical Journal, 312*, 421–425.

Bobo, L. D. (2011). Somewhere between Jim Crow & post-racialism: Reflections on the racial divide in America today. *Daedalus, 140*, 11–36.

Bobo, L., & Fox, C. (2003). Race, racism, and discrimination: Bridging problems, methods, and theory in social psychological research. *Social Psychology Quarterly, 66*(4), 319–332.

Bockting, W., & Coleman, E. (2007). Developmental stages of transgender coming-out process: Toward an integrated identity. In R. Ettner, S. Monstrey, & A. E. Eyler (Eds.), *Principles in transgender medicine and surgery* (pp. 185–208). New York: Hayworth Press.

Bodei, R. (2002). *Destini personali: L'età della colonizzazione delle coscienze*. Milan, Italy: Feltrinelli.

Boes, M., & Van Wormer, K. (1997). Social work with homeless women in emergency rooms: A strengths-feminist perspective. *Affilia: Journal of Women and Social Work, 12*(4), 408–427.

Bogenschneider, K. (1996). An ecological risk/protective theory for building prevention programs, policies, and community capacity to support youth. *Family Relations, 45*, 127–138.

Bohon, S. A., Johnson, M. K., & Gorman, B. K. (2006). College aspirations and expectations among Latino adolescents in the United States. *Social Problems, 53*, 207–225.

Bond, L., Wheeler, D. P., Millett, G. A., LaPollo, A. B., Carson, L. F., & Liau, A. (2009). Black men who have sex with men and the association of down-low identity with HIV risk behavior. *American Journal of Public Health, 99*, S92–S95.

Bonilla-Silva, E. (2006). *Racism without racists: Color-blind racism and the persistence of racial inequality in the United States* (2nd ed.). Lanham, MD: Rowman & Littlefield.

Bonvillain, N. (2001). *Women and men: Cultural constructs of gender* (3rd ed.). Upper Saddle River, NJ: Prentice Hall.

Borjas, G. J., & Katz, L. F. (2007). *Mexican immigration to the United Status*. Chicago: University of Chicago Press.

Bos, H., & Van Balen, F. (2008). Children in planned lesbian families: Stigmatization, psychological adjustment and protective factors. *Culture, Health, & Sexuality, 10*, 221–236.

Bos, H., Gartrell, N., & Van Gelderen, L. (2013) Adolescents in lesbian families: DSM-oriented scale scores and stigmatization. *Journal of Gay & Lesbian Social Services, 25*, 121–140.

Bowe, F. (1985). *Disabled adults in America*. Washington, DC: United States Government Printing Office.

Boyd-Franklin, N. (2003). *Black families in therapy: Understanding the African American experience*. New York: Guilford.

Boykin, K. (2005). *Beyond the down low: Sex, lies and denial in black America*. New York: Carroll & Graf.

Bradley, R. H., & Corwyn, R. F. (2002). Socioeconomic status and child development. *Annual Review of Psychology, 53*, 371–399.

Bradshaw, J., Chzhen, Y., Main, G., Martorano, B., Menchini, L., & De Neubourg, C. (2012). Relative income poverty among children in rich countries. Working Paper No. 2012–01, UNICEF Innocenti Research Centre, Florence, Italy.

Brady, D., & Burroway, R. (2012). Targeting, universalism, and single-mother poverty: A multilevel analysis across 18 affluent democracies. *Demography, 49*, 719–746.

Brammer, R. (2004). *Diversity in counseling*. Belmont, CA: Thomson.

Brannon, R. (1976). The male sex role—and what it's done for us lately. In R. Brannon & D. David (Eds.), *The forty-nine percent majority* (pp. 1–40). Reading, MA: Addison-Wesley.

Brault, M. W. (2012). *Americans with disabilities: 2010*. Washington, DC: U. S. Department of Commerce.

Braveman, P. A., Cubbin, C., Egerter, S., Chideya, S., Marchi, K. S., Metzler, M., & Posner, S. (2005). Socioeconomic status in health research. *Journal of the American Medical Association, 294*, 2879–2888.

Braveman, P. A., Cubbin, C., Egerter, S., Williams, D. R., & Pamuk, E. (2010). Socioeconomic disparities in health in the United States: What the patterns tell us. *American Journal of Public Health, 100*, S186–S196.

Braveman, P., & Barclay, C. (2009). Health disparities beginning in childhood: A life-course perspective. *Pediatrics, 124*, S163–S175

Braveman, P., & Gruskin, S. (2003). Poverty, equity, human rights and health. *Bulletin of the World Health Organization, 81*, 539–545.

Braveman, P., Egerter, S., & Williams, D. R. (2011). The social determinants of health: Coming of age. *Annual Review of Public Health, 32*, 381–98.

Breiding, M. J., Black, M. C., & Ryan, G. W. (2008). Prevalence and risk factors of intimate partner violence in eighteen US states/territories, 2005. *American Journal of Preventive Medicine, 34*, 112–118.

Bronfenbrenner, U. (1986). Ecology of the family as a context for human development. *Developmental Psychology, 22*, 723–742.

Brookey, R. A. (2002). *Reinventing the male homosexual: The rhetoric and power of the gay gene*. Bloomington: Indiana University Press.

Brooks, W., & Hampton, G. (2005). Safe discussions rather than first hand encounters: Adolescents examine racism through one historical fiction text. *Children's Literature in Education, 36*(1), 1573–1693.

Brophy-Baermann, M., & Bloeser, A. J. (2006). Stealthy wealth: The untold story of welfare privatization. *Harvard International Journal of Press/Politics, 11*, 89–112.

Brown, C. L., Love, K. M., Tyler, K. M., Garriot, P. O., Thomas, D., & Roan-Belle, C. (2013). Parental attachment, family communalism, and racial identity among African American college students. *Journal of Multicultural Counseling and Development, 41*, 108–122.

Brown, K. T., Ward, G. K., Lightbourn, T., & Jackson, J. S. (1999). Skin tone and racial identity among African Americans: A theoretical and research framework. In R. L. Jones (Ed.), *Advances in African American psychology: Theory, paradigms, and research* (pp. 191–215). Hampton, VA: Cobb & Henry.

Brown, S. C., Mason, C. A., Lombard, J. L., Martinez, F., Plater-Zyberk, E., Spokane, A. R., . . . , & Szapocznik, J. (2009). The relationship of built environment to perceived social support and psychological distress in Hispanic elders: The role of "eyes on the street." *Journals of Gerontology Series B: Psychological Sciences and Social Sciences, 64,* 234–246.

Brown-Dean, K. L. (2007). Permanent outsiders: Felon disenfranchisement and the breakdown of black politics. In G. A. Persons (Ed.), *The expanding boundaries of black politics* (pp. 103–120). Edison, NJ: Transaction.

Brunner, E., & Marmot, M. (2005). Social organization, stress, and health. In M. G. Marmot & R. G. Wilkinson (Eds.), *The social determinants of health* (2nd ed.) (pp.6–30). Oxford: Oxford University Press.

Buddhism and Health. (1996). Healing the ills of body and spirit. *Soka Gakkai International Quarterly.* Retrieved from http://www.purifymind.com/BuddhismHealth.htm

Buekens, P., Notzon, F., Kotelchuck, M., & Wilcox, A. (2000). Why do Mexican Americans give birth to few low-birth weight infants? *American Journal of Epidemiology, 152*(4), 347–351.

Buettgens, M., & Carroll, C. (2012). *Eliminating the individual mandate: Effects on premiums, coverage and uncompensated care.* Retrieved from http://www.urban.org/UploadedPDF/412480-Eliminating-the-Individual-Mandate.pdf?RSSFeed = Urban.xml

Buettner, R., & Glaberson, W. (2012, July 1) Courts putting stop-and-frisk policy on trial. *New York Times,* p. A1.

Burdge, B. J. (2007). Bending gender, ending gender: Theoretical foundations for social work practice with the transgender community. *Social Work, 52,* 243–250.

Bureau of Labor Statistics (BLS). (2010, December). Women in the labor force: A data book. BLS Report 1026. Author, Washington, DC.

Bureau of Labor Statistics (BLS). (2013, February). Women in the labor force: A data book. BLS Report 1040. Author, Washington, DC. Retrieved from http://www.bls.gov/cps/wlf-databook-2012.pdf

Burke, P. J. (2006). Identity change. *Social Psychology Quarterly, 69,* 81–96.

Burks, D. J. (2011). Lesbian, gay, and bisexual victimization in the military: An unintended consequence of "Don't ask, don't tell"? *American Psychologist, 66,* 604–613.

Burton, L. M., Lichter, D. T., Baker, R. S., & Eason, J. M. (2013, May 15). Inequality, family processes, and health in the "new" rural America. *American Behavioral Scientist.* Retrieved from http://abs.sagepub.com/content/early/2013/05/13/0002764213487348

Butterfoss, F. D., Goodman, R. M., & Wandersman, A. (1996). Community coalitions for prevention and health promotion: Factors predicting satisfaction, participation, and planning. *Health Education Quarterly, 23*(1), 65–79.

Byrne, B. M., & van De Vijver, F. J. (2010). Testing for measurement and structural equivalence in large-scale cross-cultural studies: Addressing the issue of nonequivalence. *International Journal of Testing, 10,* 107–132.

Caetano, R., & Medina-Mora, M. E. (1988). Acculturation and drinking among people of Mexican descent in Mexico and in the United States. *Journal of Studies on Alcohol, 49,* 462–471.

Calasanti, T. (2005). Ageism, gravity, and gender: Experiences of aging bodies. *Generations, 29,* 8–12.

Calasanti, T. M., & Slevin, K. F. (2001). *Gender, social inequalities, and aging.* Walnut Creek, CA: Alta Mira.

Caldas, S. J., Bankston, C. L., & Cain, J. S. (2007). A case study of teachers' perceptions of school desegregation and the distribution of social and academic capital. *Education and Urban Society, 39*(2), 194–222.

Calzada, E. J., Tamis-LeMonda, C. S., & Yoshikawa, H. (2012). Familismo in Mexican and Dominican families from low-income, urban communities. *Journal of Family Issues.* doi:10.1177/0192513X12460218

Campbell, C. D., & Evans-Campbell, T. (2011). Historical trauma and Native American child development and mental health: An overview. In M. C. Sarche, P. Spicer, P. Farrell, & H. E. Fitzgerald (Eds.), *American Indian children and mental health: Development, context, prevention and treatment* (pp. 1–26). Santa Barbara, CA: Praeger.

Campbell, C., & Jovchelovitch, S. (2000). Health, community and development: Towards a social psychology of participation. *Journal of Community & Applied Social Psychology, 10*(4), 255–270.

Campbell, G., Miers, S., & Miller, J. C. (2006). Children of European systems of slavery: Introduction. *Slavery & Abolition, 27*(2), 163–182.

Carmichael, S., & Hamilton, C. V. (1967). *Black power: The politics of liberation in America.* New York: Vintage.

Carver, P. R., Yunger, J. L., & Perry, D. G. (2003). Gender identity and adjustment in middle childhood. *Sex Roles, 49*(3/4), 95–109.

Casas, B. de las. (1992). *A short account of the destruction of the Indies.* New York: Penguin. (Original work published 1552)

Cassin, S. E., & von Ranson, K. A. (2005). Personality and eating disorders: A decade in review. *Clinical Psychology Review, 25*(7), 895–916.

Castelli, L., De Amicis, L., & Sherman, S. J. (2007). The loyal member effect: On the preference for ingroup members who engage in exclusive relations with the ingroup. *Developmental Psychology, 43,* 1347–1359.

Castro, F. G. (2005, March). *Acculturation and drug use: New findings and future directions.* Paper presented at the Southwest Interdisciplinary Research Consortium, Tempe, AZ.

Catalano, S. (2005). *Criminal victimization, 2004.* Washington, DC: U.S. Department of Justice, Bureau of Justice Statistics.

Catalyst. (2013). *Catalyst pyramid: U.S. women in business.* New York: Catalyst.

Catterall, H. T. (Ed.). (1968). *Judicial cases concerning American slavery and the Negro* (Vol. 1). New York: Octagon Books. (Original work published 1926)

Caughy, M. O. B., O'Campo, P. J., & Muntaner, C. (2003). When being alone might be better: Neighborhood poverty, social capital, and child mental health. *Social Science & Medicine, 57,* 227–237.

Cawthon, R. M., Smith, K. R., O'Brien, E., Sivatchenko, A., & Kerber, R. A. (2003). Association between telomere length in blood and mortality in people aged 60 years or older. *The Lancet, 361,* 393–395.

Center for Advanced Studies in Child Welfare (CASCW). (2001). *The contribution of ethnographic interviewing to culturally competent practice. (*CASCW Practice Notes, 10, 1–5). CASCW, St. Paul, MN. Retrieved from http://cascw.umn.edu/wp-content/uploads/2014/01/Practice-Notes-10.pdf

Center for American Women in Politics (2013). Women in elective office 2013: Fact sheet. Retrieved from http://www.cawp.rutgers.edu/fast_facts/levels_of_office/documents/elective.pdf

Centers for Disease Control and Prevention (CDC). (2003). HIV/STD risk in young men who have sex with men who do not disclose their sexual orientation—six U.S. cities, 1994–2000. *Morbidity and Mortality Weekly Report, 52*, 82–86.

Centers for Disease Control and Prevention (CDC). (2007). *National health interview survey on disability.* Retrieved from http://www.cdc.gov/nchs/nhis/nhis_disability.htm

Centers for Disease Control and Prevention (CDC). (2008). Smoking-attributable mortality, years of potential life lost, and productivity losses—United States, 2000–2004. Retrieved from http://www.cdc.gov/tobacco/data_statistics/mmwrs/byyear/2008/mm5745a3/highlights.htm

Centers for Disease Control and Prevention (CDC). (2012a). Coccidioidomycosis (Valley Fever). Retrieved from http://www.cdc.gov/fungal/diseases/coccidioidomycosis/

Centers for Disease Control and Prevention (CDC). (2012b). Community Transformation Grant Program Fact Sheet. Retrieved from http://www.cdc.gov/communitytransformation/funds/index.htm

Centers for Disease Control and Prevention (CDC). (2012c). Fact sheets: Alcohol use and health. Retrieved from http://www.cdc.gov/alcohol/fact-sheets/alcohol-use.htm

Centers for Disease Control and Prevention (CDC). (2014). Current cigarette smoking among adults: United States 2005–2012. *Morbidity and Mortality Weekly Report, 63*, 29–34.

Chanbonpin, K. (2005). How the border crossed us: Filling the gap between *Plume v. Seward* and the dispossession of Mexican landowners in California after 1848. *Cleveland State Law Review, 52*, 297–319.

Chandra, A., Mosher, W. D., Copen, C., & Sionean, C. (2011). Sexual behavior, sexual attraction, and sexual identity in the United States: Data from the 2006–2008 national survey of family growth. *National Health Statistics Report* (Centers for Disease Control and Prevention), *36,* 1–36.

Chao, G. T., & Willaby, H. W. (2007). International employment discrimination and implicit social cognition: New directions for theory and research. *Applied Psychology, 56*(4), 678–688.

Chapell, M., Casey, D., De la Cruz, C., Ferrell, J., Forman, J., Lipkin, R., . . . , & Whittaker, S. (2004). Bullying in college by students and teachers. *Adolescence San Diego, 39*, 53–64.

Charles, M., & Grusky, D. B. (2004) *Occupational ghettos: The worldwide segregation of women and men.* Palo Alto, CA: Stanford University Press.

Chartier, K., & Caetano, R. (2010). Ethnicity and health disparities in alcohol research. *Alcohol Research & Health: The Journal of the National Institute on Alcohol Abuse and Alcoholism, 33*, 152–160.

Chatterjee, P. (1998). The gold rush legacy: Greed, pollution, and genocide. *Earth Island Journal, 3*(2), 26–27.

Chávez, E. (2002). *My people first! "Mi raza primero!" Nationalism, identity, and insurgency in the Chicano movement in Los Angeles, 1966–1978.* Berkeley and Los Angeles: University of California Press.

Chawla, N., & Marlatt, G. (2006). The varieties of Buddhism. In E. T. Dowd & S. L. Nielsen (Eds.), *The psychologies of religion* (pp. 271–286). New York: Springer.

Chen, E., Langer, D. A., Raphaelson, Y. E., & Matthews, K. A. (2004). Socioeconomic status and health in adolescents: The role of stress interpretations. *Child Development, 75,* 1039–1052.

Cherkas, L. F., Aviv, A., Valdes, A. M., Hunkin, J. L., Gardner, J. P., Surdulescu, G. L., . . . , & Spector, T. D. (2006). The effects of social status on biological aging as measured by white blood cell telomere length. *Aging Cell, 5*, 361–365.

Chin, G., & Karthikeyan, H. (2002). Preserving racial identity: Population patterns and the application of anti-miscegenation statutes to Asian Americans, 1910–1950. *Berkeley Asian Law Journal, 9*, 1–213.

Chodorow, N. (1978). *The reproduction of mothering.* Berkeley and Los Angeles: University of California Press.

Choi, Y., & Lahey, B. B. (2006). Testing the model minority stereotype: Youth behaviors across racial and ethnic groups. *Social Service Review, 80*(3), 419–452.

Chuang, Y. C., Cubbin, C., Ahn, D., & Winkleby, M. A. (2005). Effects of neighbourhood socioeconomic status and convenience store concentration on individual level smoking. *Journal of Epidemiology and Community Health, 59*, 568–573.

Clair, J. A., Beatty, J. E., & MacLean, T. L. (2005). Out of sight but not out of mind: Managing invisible social identities in the workplace. *Academy of Management Review, 30*(1), 78–95.

Clark, C., Ryan, L., Kawachi, I., Canner, M. J., Berkman, L., & Wright, R. J. (2008). Witnessing community violence in residential neighborhoods: A mental health hazard for urban women. *Journal of Urban Health, 85*, 22–38.

Clark, N. (2004). Mirror, mirror on the wall . . . are muscular men the best of all? The hidden turmoil of muscle dysmorphia. *American Fitness, 22*(1), 52–55.

Clark, R., Anderson, N. B., Clark, V. R., & Williams, D. R. (1999). Racism as a stressor for African Americans: A biopsychosocial model. *American Psychologist, 54*, 805.

Clarke, L. H. (2002). Older women's perceptions of ideal body weights: The tensions between health and appearance motivations for weight loss. *Ageing and Society, 22*, 751–773.

Clarkson, J. (2005). Contesting masculinity's makeover: Queer eye, consumer masculinity, and "straight-acting" gays. *Journal of Communication Inquiry, 29*(3), 235–255.

Clement, R. W., & Krueger, J. (2002). Social categorization moderates social projection. *Journal of Experimental Social Psychology, 38*(3), 219–231.

Clements-Nolle, K., Marx, R., & Katz, M. (2006). Attempted suicide among transgender persons: The influence of gender-based discrimination and victimization. *Journal of Homosexuality, 51*, 53–69.

Cockerham, W. C. (2000). The sociology of health behavior and health lifestyles. *Handbook of Medical Sociology, 5*, 159–172.

Cohen, J. A., Mannarino, A. P., & Deblinger, E. (2006). *Treating trauma and traumatic grief in children and adolescents.* New York: Guilford.

Cohen, J. A., Mannarino, A. P., & Knudsen, K. (2004). Treating childhood traumatic grief: A pilot study. *Journal of the American Academy of Child & Adolescent Psychiatry, 43*, 1225–1233.

Cohen, J. H., Tiesman, H. M., Bossarte, R. M., & Furbee, P. M. (2009). Rural-urban differences in injury hospitalizations in the U.S., 2004. *American Journal of Preventive Medicine, 36*, 49–55.

Cohen, P. N. (2004). The gender division of labor: "Keeping house" and occupational segregation in the United States. *Gender & Society, 18*, 239–252

Cohen, S., Janicki-Deverts, D., Chen, E., & Matthews, K. A. (2010). Childhood socioeconomic status and adult health. *Annals of the New York Academy of Sciences, 1186*, 37–55.

Cohn, S. (1985). *The process of occupational sex-typing: The feminization of clerical labor in Great Britain.* Philadelphia: Temple University Press.

Coimbra, C. E. A., Santos, R. V., Welch, J. R., Cardoso, A M., Carvalho de Souza, M., Garnelo, L., . . . , & Horta, B. L. (2013). The first national survey of indigenous people's health and nutrition in Brazil: Rationale, methodology, and overview of results. *BMC Public Health., 13*(52). Retrieved from http://biomedcentral.com/1471–2458/13/52

Colen, C. G., Geronimus, A. T., Bound, J., & James, S. A. (2006). Maternal upward socioeconomic mobility and black-white disparities in infant birthweight. *American Journal of Public Health, 96*, 2032–2039.

Collins, B. A., Toppelberg, C. O., Suárez-Orozco, C., O'Connor, E., & Nieto-Castañon, A. (2011). Cross-sectional associations of Spanish and English competence and well-being in Latino children of immigrants in kindergarten. *International Journal of the Sociology of Language, 2011*, 5–23.

Collins, P. H. (1998). *Fighting words: Black women and the search for justice.* Minneapolis: University of Minnesota Press.

Commission on Social Determinants of Health (2008). *CSDH Final Report: Closing the gap in a generation: Health Equity through action on the social determinants of health.* Geneva: World Health Organization.

Communities for a Better Enviroment (2010). *East Oakland Particulate matter 2.5 community-based air monitoring research report.* Retrieved from http://www.cbecal.org/organizing/northern-california/oakland/

Community Policing Consortium. (2004). *To protect and serve: An overview of community policing on Indian reservations.* Retrieved from https://web.archive.org/web/20010627040336/http:/www.communitypolicing.org/pf/am_ind/ch2.html

Connell, R. W. (1987). *Gender and power.* Stanford, CA: Stanford University Press.

Connell, R. W. (1990). An iron man: The body and some contradictions of hegemonic masculinity. In M. A. Messner & D. F. Sabo (Eds.), *Sport, men and the gender order: Critical feminist perspectives* (pp. 83–95). Champaign, IL: Human Kinetics Books.

Connell, R. W., & Messerschmidt, J. W. (2005). Hegemonic masculinity: Rethinking the concept. *Gender & Society, 19*, 829–859.

Constantinople, A. (2005). Masculinity-femininity: An exception to a famous dictum? *Feminism & Psychology, 15*(4), 385–407.

Cook, D. G., & Strachan, D. P. (1997). Health effects of passive smoking. 3. Parental smoking and prevalence of respiratory symptoms and asthma in school age children. *Thorax, 52*, 1081–1094.

Cooley, C. H. (1918). *Social process.* New York: Scriber's Sons.

Cooper, K. (2009). Social work practice with transgender and gender variant youth and their families. In G. Mallon (Ed.) *Social work practice with transgender and gender-variant youth* (pp. 122–139). New York: Routledge.

Cooper, R. S., Kaufman, J. S., & Ward, R. (2003). Race and genomics. *New England Journal of Medicine, 348*, 1166–1170.

Corey, G. (2011). *Theory & practice of group counseling.* Belmont, CA: Cengage Books.

Cornelius, W. A. (2006). Impacts of border enforcement on unauthorized Mexican migration to the United States. Retrieved from http://borderbattles.ssrc.org/Cornelius/

Cosby, A., Aanstoos, K., Matta, M., Porter, J., & James, W. (2013). Public support for Hispanic deportation in the United States: The effects of ethnic prejudice and perceptions of economic competition in a period of economic distress. *Journal of Population Research, 30*, 87–96.

Cotterill, R. W., & Franklin, A. W. (1995). *The urban grocery store gap* (No. 08). University of Connecticut, Department of Agricultural and Resource Economics, Charles J. Zwick Center for Food and Resource Policy, Storrs, CT.

Crawford, I., Allison, K. W., Zamboni, B. D., & Soto, T. (2002). The influence of dual-identity development on the psychosocial functioning of African American gay and bisexual men. *Journal of Sex Research, 39*(3), 179–189.

Creedon, P. J., & Cramer, J. (2006). *Women in mass communication.* Thousand Oaks, CA: Sage.

Crichlow, W. (2004). *Buller men and batty boys: Hidden men in Toronto and Halifax black communities.* Toronto, ON: University of Toronto Press.

Crimmins, E. M., Soldo, B. J., Kim, J. K., Alley, D. E. (2005). Using anthropometric indicators for Mexicans in the United States and Mexico to understand the selection of migrants and the "Hispanic paradox." *Biodemography and Social Biology, 52,* 164–177.

Cristia, J. P. (2009). Rising mortality and life expectancy differentials by lifetime earnings in the United States. *Journal of Health Economics, 28,* 984–995.

Crocker, J., & Knight, K. M. (2005). Contingencies of self-worth. *Current Directions in Psychological Science, 14*(4), 200–203.

Cross, T. A., Earle, K. A., & Simmons, D. (2000). Child abuse and neglect in Indian county: Policy issues. *Families in Society: Journal of Contemporary Human Services, 81*(1), 49–65.

Cummins, S., & Macintyre, S. (2002). "Food deserts": Evidence and assumption in health policy making. *British Medical Journal, 325,* 436.

Dancey, C. P. (1990). Sexual orientation in women: An investigation of hormonal and personality variables. *Biological Psychology, 30*(3), 251–264.

Davis, J. R. (2007). Making a difference: How teachers can positively affect racial identity and acceptance in America. *Social Studies, 95*(5), 209–216.

Dawkins, M. (2010). Mixed messages: Barack Obama and post-racial politics. *Post Identity, 30,* 9–17.

Dawson, D. A., Grant, B. F., Stinson, F. S., Chou, P. S., Huang, B., & Ruan, W. (2005). Recovery from DSM-IV alcohol dependence: United States, 2001–2002. *Addiction, 100,* 281–292.

De Jonge, J., Bosma, H., Peter, R., & Siegrist, J. (2000). Job strain, effort-reward imbalance and employee well-being: A large-scale cross-sectional study. *Social Science & Medicine, 50,* 1317–1327.

de-Graft Aikins, A., Boynton, P., & Atanga, L. (2010). Developing effective chronic disease interventions in Africa: Insights from Ghana and Cameroon. *Globalization and Health, 6:6,* 1–15. doi:10.1186/1744-8603-6-6

Deichmann, U. (1999). Geographic aspects of inequality and poverty. Retrieved from http://www-wds.worldbank.org/external/default/WDSContentServer/WDSP/IB/2013/04/10/000445729_20130410160023/Rendered/PDF/765100WP0Geogr00Box374382B00PUBLIC0.pdf/

DeJong, G., & Lifchez, R. (1983). Physical disability and public policy. *Scientific American, 248,* 40–49.

DeLeire, T. (2000). The wage and employment effects of the Americans with Disabilities Act. *Journal of Human Resources, 35,* 693–715.

Delgado, M. Y., Updegraff, K. A., Roosa, M. W., & Umaña-Taylor, A. J. (2011). Perceived discrimination and Mexican-origin youth adjustment: The moderating roles of mothers' and fathers' cultural orientations and values. *Journal of Youth & Adolescence, 40,* 125–139.

DeLisa, J., Silverstein, R., & Thomas, P. (2011). Commentary: More implications of the 2008 amendments to the Americans with Disabilities Act: Influencing institutional policies, practices, and procedures. *Academic Medicine, 86,* 677–679.

DeNavas-Walt, C., Proctor, B. D., Smith, J. C. (2013). Income, poverty, and health insurance coverage in the United States; 2009. In C. Estes, S. Chapman, C. Dodd, B. Hollister & C. Harrington (Eds.), *Health policy: Crisis and reform* (pp. 267–312). Burlington, MA: Jones & Barlett.

Denner, J., Kirby, D., Coyle, K., & Brindis, C. (2001). The protective role of social capital and cultural norms in Latino communities: A study of adolescent births. *Hispanic Journal of Behavioral Sciences, 23*, 3–21.

Derose, K. P., Escarce, J. J., & Lurie, N. (2007). Immigrants and health care: sources of vulnerability. *Health Affairs, 26*, 1258–1268.

Derrida, J. (1982). *Margins of philosophy*. Chicago: University of Chicago Press.

Dessel, A., Rogge, M. E., & Garlington, S. B. (2006). Using intergroup dialogue to promote social justice and change. *Social Work, 51*, 303–315.

DeVoe, J. F., Darling-Churchill, K. E., & Snyder, T. D. (2008). Status and trends in the education of American Indians and Alaska Natives, 2008. NCES 2008–084. U.S. Department of Education, Washington, DC. Retrieved from http://nces.ed.gov/pubs2008/2008084.pdf

Dhooper, S. S. (1991). Toward and effective response to the needs of Asian-Americans. *Journal of Multicultural Social Work, 1*(2), 65–81.

Dhooper, S. S. (2003). Health care needs of foreign-born Asian Americans: An overview. *Health and Social Work, 28*(1), 63–74.

Di Palma, S. L., & Topper, G. G. (2001). Social work academia: Is the glass ceiling beginning to crack? *Affilia: Journal of Women and Social Work, 16*(1), 31–45.

Diamond, L., & Savin-Williams, R. (2000). Explaining diversity in the development of same-sex sexuality among young women. *Journal of Social Issues, 56*(2), 297–313.

Diaz, R. F. (1997). Macho, Latino, HIV+ (AIDS prevention among Latinos). *Advocate, 747*, 9–10.

Dick, R. W., Beals, J., Keane, E. M., & Manson, S. M. (1994). Factoral structure of the CES-D among American Indian adolescents. *Journal of Adolescence, 17*, 73–79.

Dickinson, J., & Young, B. (2003). *A short history of Quebec*. Montreal: McGill-Queen's University Press.

Diez-Roux, A. V. D., Merkin, S. S., Arnett, D., Chambless, L., Massing, M., Nieto, F. J., . . . , & Watson, R. L. (2001). Neighborhood of residence and incidence of coronary heart disease. *New England Journal of Medicine, 345*, 99–106.

Diez-Roux, A. V., Nieto, F. J., Muntaner, C., Tyroler, H. A., Comstock, G. W., Shahar, E., . . . , & Szklo, M. (1997). Neighborhood environments and coronary heart disease: A multilevel analysis. *American Journal of Epidemiology, 146*, 48–63.

Dinnerstein, L., & Reimers, D. M. (1999). *Ethnic Americans: A history of immigration*. New York: Columbia University Press.

DiPiero, T. (2002). *White men aren't*. Durham, NC: Duke University Press.

Diversi, M., & Finley, S. (2010). Poverty pimps in the academy: A dialogue about subjectivity, reflexivity, and power in decolonizing production of knowledge. *Cultural Studies Critical Methodologies, 10*, 14–17.

Dobbie, W., & Fryer Jr, R. G. (2009). Are high quality schools enough to close the achievement gap? Evidence from a social experiment in Harlem. NBER Working Paper w15473. National Bureau of Economic Research, Cambridge, MA.

Doble, J., & Yarrow, A. L. (2007). *Walking a mile: A first step toward mutual understanding*. Retrieved from http://www.publicagenda.org/files/walkingamile.pdf

Dode, L. (2004). *A history of homosexuality.* Victoria, BC: Trafford.

Dominelli, L. (1998). Anti-oppressive practice in context. In R. Adams, L. Dominelli, & M. Payne (Eds.), *Social work, themes, issues and critical debates* (pp. 3–22). London, MacMillan.

Dominguez, T. P. (2008). Race, racism, and racial disparities in adverse birth outcomes. *Clinical Obstetrics and Gynecology, 51*, 360–370.

Dorling, D. (2011). *Injustice: Why social inequality persists.* Bristol, UK: The Policy Press.

Downey, J., Ehrhardt, A. A., Schiffman, M., Dyrenfurth, I., & Becker, J. (1987). Sex hormones in lesbian and heterosexual women. *Hormones and Behavior, 21*(3), 347–357.

Dreher, M., & MacNaughton, N. (2002). Cultural competence in nursing: Foundation or fallacy? *Nursing Outlook, 50*, 181–186.

Drewnowski, A., & Specter, S. E. (2004). Poverty and obesity: The role of energy density and energy costs. *American Journal of Clinical Nutrition, 79*, 6–16.

Drijber, B. C., Reijnders, U. J., & Ceelen, M. (2013). Male victims of domestic violence. *Journal of Family Violence, 28*, 173–178.

Droogsma, R. A. (2007). Redefining hijab: American Muslim women's standpoints on veiling. *Journal of Applied Communication Research, 35*(3), 294–319.

DryWater-Whitekiller, V. (2006). What the dominant society can't give me: Perceptions of Native American elders teaching Native traditions. *Journal of Baccalaureate Social Work, 12*, 71–86.

Du Bois, W. E. B. (1969). The souls of black folk. New York: Signet. (Original work published 1903)

DuBois, E. C. (1999). *Feminism and suffrage: The emergence of an independent women's movement in America, 1848–1869.* Ithaca, NY: Cornell University Press.

Duffy, E. (1995). Horizontal violence: A conundrum for nursing. *Collegian: The Australian Journal of Nursing Practice, Scholarship & Research, 2*, 5–17.

Dugger, W. (1996). *Inequality: Radical institutionalist views on race, gender, class, and nation.* Westport, CT: Greenwood Press.

Duran, B. M. (2005). American Indian/Alaska Native health policy. *American Journal of Public Health, 95*(5), 758.

Duran, B., & Walters, K. L. (2004). HIV/AIDS prevention in "Indian country": Current practice, indigenist etiology models, and postcolonial approaches to change. *AIDS Education and Prevention, 16*, 187–201.

Durkheim, E. (1965). *The elementary forms of religious life.* Glencoe, IL: Free Press. (Original work published 1912)

Durkheim, E. (2004). *The division of labor.* New York: Free Press. (Original work published 1933)

Durose, M. R., Harlow, C. W., Langan, P. A., Motivans, M., Rantala, R. R., & Smith, E. L. (2005). *Family violence statistics: Including statistics on strangers and acquaintances.* Retrieved from http://www.bjs.gov/index.cfm?ty = pbdetail&iid = 828

Duyvendak, J. W., & Nederland, T. (2007). New frontiers for identity politics? The potential pitfalls of patient and civic identity in the Dutch patient's health movement. In P. G. Coy (Ed.), *Research in social movements, conflict and change* (pp. 261–282). St. Louis, MO: Elsevier.

Dwairy, M. A. (2006). *Counseling and psychotherapy with Arabs and Muslims: A culturally sensitive approach.* New York: Teachers College Press.

Earp, J. A., Eng, E., O'Malley, M. S., Altpeter, M., Rauscher, G., Mayne, L., . . . & Qaqish, B. (2002). Increasing use of mammography among older, rural African American women: Results from a community trial. *American Journal of Public Health*, *92*, 646–654.

Edelsky, C. (1981). Who's got the floor? *Language in Society, 10,* 383–421.

Edelstein, D. M. (2004). Occupational hazards: Why military occupations succeed or fail. *International Security*, *29*, 49–91.

Eichhorn, L. (1999). Major litigation activities regarding major life activities: The failure of the "disability" definition in the Americans with Disabilities Act of 1990. *North Carolina Law Review*, *77*, 1405.

el-Ghobashy, T., & Saul, M. H. (2013, May 6). New York police use of stop-and-frisk drops: Plummet in disputed tactic tracks overall decrease in crime. *Wall Street Journal.* Retrieved from http://online.wsj.com/news/articles/SB1000142412788732337250457846736150799 7492

Elijah, M. (2002). African centered family healing: An alternative paradigm. *Journal of Health & Social Policy, 16*(1–2), 185–193.

Ellen, I. G., Cutler, D. M., & Dickens, W. (2000). Is segregation bad for your health? The case of low birth weight [with comments]. *Brookings-Wharton papers on urban affairs*, 203–238.

Elliott, M. (2000). The stress process in neighborhood context. *Health & Place*, *6*, 287–299.

Ellison, C. G., Musick, M. A., & Henderson, A. K. (2008). Balm in Gilead: Racism, religious involvement, and psychological distress among African-American adults. *Journal for the Scientific Study of Religion*, *47*, 291–309.

Eltis, D. (2000). *The rise of African slavery in the Americas.* London: Cambridge University Press.

England, P. (1992). *Comparable worth: Theories and evidence.* New York: Aldine de Gruyter.

England, P. (2010). The gender revolution uneven and stalled. *Gender & Society*, *24*, 149–166.

Epel, E. S., Blackburn, E. H., Lin, J., Dhabhar, F. S., Adler, N. E., Morrow, J. D., & Cawthon, R. M. (2004). Accelerated telomere shortening in response to life stress. *Proceedings of the National Academy of Sciences of the United States of America*, *101*, 17312–17315.

Epstein, I. (2009). Promoting harmony where there is commonly conflict: Evidence-informed practice as an integrative strategy. *Social Work in Health Care*, *48*, 216–231.

Espenshade, T. J., Baraka, J. L., & Huber, G. A. (1997). Implications of the 1996 welfare and immigration reform acts for US immigration. *Population and Development Review*, 23, 769–801.

Espiritu, Y. L. (1996). *Asian American women and men: Labor, laws and love.* Thousand Oaks, CA: Sage.

Esposito, L., & Murphy, J. (2000). Another step in the study of race relations. *Sociological Quarterly, 41*(2), 171–187.

Estes, R. J. (2009). *United States-Based Conceptualization of International Social Work Education.* Report for the Global Commission of the Council on Social Work Education (CSWE). Accessed from http://www.cswe.org/File.aspx?id=31429

Evans, G. W. (2004). The environment of childhood poverty. *American Psychologist, 59*, 77–92.

Evans, G. W., & Kantrowitz, E. (2002). Socioeconomic status and health: the potential role of environmental risk exposure. *Annual Review of Public Health*, *23*, 303–331.

Eyerman, R. (2002). *Cultural trauma: Slavery and the formation of African-American identity.* New York: Cambridge University Press.

..

Fabricant, M., & Fisher, R. (2002a). Agency based community building in low income neighborhoods: A praxis framework. *Journal of Community Practice, 10*(2), 1–22.

Fabricant, M., & Fisher, R. (2002b). *Settlement houses under siege: The struggle to sustain community.* New York: Columbia University Press.

Fagan, P., Moolchan, E. T., Lawrence, D., Fernander, A., & Ponder, P. K. (2007). Identifying health disparities across the tobacco continuum. *Addiction, 102*, 5–29.

Fairlie, R. W., Kapur, K., & Gates, S. (2011). Is employer-based health insurance a barrier to entrepreneurship? *Journal of Health Economics, 30*, 146–162.

Fairtlough, A. (2008). Growing up with a lesbian or gay parent: Young people's perspectives. *Health and Social Care in the Community, 16*, 521–528.

Falomir-Pichastor, J. M., & Mugny, G. (2009). "I'm not gay . . . I'm a real man!": Heterosexual men's gender self-esteem and sexual prejudice. *Personality and Social Psychology Bulletin, 35*, 1233–1243.

Farley, J. E. (2000). *Majority-minority relations* (4th ed.). Upper Saddle River, NJ: Prentice Hall.

Farrell, W. (2005). *Why men earn more: The startling truth behind the pay gap—and what women can do about it.* New York: American Management Association.

Fasching, D. J. (1992). *Narrative theology after Auschwitz: From alienation to ethics.* Minneapolis, MN: Augsburg Fortress Press.

Fausto-Sterling, A. (1993). The five sexes: Why male and female are not enough. *Sciences, 33*, 20–25.

Fay, R. E., Turner, C. F., Klassen, A. D., & Gagnon, J. H. (1989). Prevalence and patterns of same-gender sexual contact among men. *Science, 243*, 338–348.

Feagin, J. (2000). *Racist America: Roots, current realities, and future reparations.* New York: Routledge.

Feagin, J., Johnson, J., & Rush, S. (2000). Doing anti-racism toward an egalitarian American society. *Contemporary Sociology, 29*(1), 95–110.

Feher, M. (1994). The schism of '67: On certain restructurings of the American Left from the civil rights movement to the multicultural constellation. In P. Berman (Ed.), *Blacks and Jews: Alliances and agreements* (pp. 263–285). New York: Delacorte Press.

Feijten, P., & Mulder, C. H. (2010). Gender, divorce and housing—a life course perspective. In D. Reuschke (Ed.), *Wohnen und Gender. Theoretische, politische, soziale und räumliche Aspekte* (pp. 175–193). Wiesbaden, Germany: VS Verlag für

Fein, H. (2002). Genocide: A sociological perspective. In A. L. Hinton (Ed.), *Genocide: An anthropological reader* (pp. 74–90). Oxford: Blackwell.

Feinberg, M. E., Rindenour, T. A., & Greenberg, M. T. (2007). Aggregating indices of risk and protection for adolescent behavior problems: The Communities That Care Youth Survey. *Journal of Adolescent Health, 40*(6), 506–513.

Fenzsch, N. (2005). "It is scarcely possible to conceive that human beings could be so hideous and loathsome": Discourses of genocide in eighteenth- and nineteenth-century American and Australia. *Patterns of Prejudice, 39*(2), 97–115.

Ferguson, I., & Woodward, R. (2009). *Radical social work in practice: Making a difference.* Bristol, UK: Policy Press.

Ferguson, I., Lavalette, M., & Whitmore, E. (2005). *Globalization, global justice and social work.* London: Routedge.

Fernandez, R. M. (2004). Space in the study of labor markets. *Annual Review of Sociology, 30*, 545–569.

Ferrie, J. E., Shipley, M. J., Stansfeld, S. A., & Marmot, M. G. (2002). Effects of chronic job insecurity and change in job security on self reported health, minor psychiatric morbidity, physiological measures, and health related behaviours in British civil servants: The Whitehall II study. *Journal of Epidemiology and Community Health, 56*, 450–454.

Fett, S. M. (2002). *Working cure: Healing, health, and power on southern slave plantations.* Chapel Hill: University of North Carolina Press.

Field, C. A., & Caetano, R. (2005). Intimate partner violence in the U. S. general population: progress and future directions. *Journal of Interpersonal Violence, 20*(4), 463–469.

Field, N. P., Om, C., Kim, T., & Vorn, S. (2011). Parental styles in second generation effects of genocide stemming from the Khmer Rouge regime in Cambodia. *Attachment & Human Development, 13*, 611–628.

Finch, B. K., Frank, R., & Vega, W. A. (2004). Acculturation and acculturation stress: A social-epidemiological approach to Mexican Migrant farmworkers' Health. *International Migration Review, 38*, 236–262.

Finnigan, D. (1995). Our cheap clothes and their horror stories: Thais, other minorities abused in sweatshops that keep prices down. *National Catholic Reporter, 32*(6), 10–11.

Fisher, A., & Sonn, C. (2003). Identity and oppression: Differential responses to an in-between status. *American Journal of Community Psychology, 31*(1–2), 117–129.

Fisher, R., & Kling, J. (1994). Community organization and new social movement's theory. *Journal of Progressive Human Services, 5*(2), 5–23.

Flores, Y. N., Yee, H. F., Leng, M., Escarce, J. J., Bastani, R., Salmerón, J., & Morales, L. S. (2008). Risk factors for chronic liver disease in Blacks, Mexican Americans, and Whites in the United States: Results from NHANES IV, 1999–2004. *American Journal of Gastroenterology, 103*, 2231–2238.

Foster, H. W., Wu, L., Bracken, M. B., Semenya, K., & Thomas, J. (2000). Intergenerational effects of high socioeconomic status on low birth weight and preterm birth in African Americans. *Journal of the National Medical Association, 92*, 213–221.

Foucault, M. (1978). *The history of sexuality.* New York: Pantheon.

Foucault, M. (1980). *Power/knowledge: Selected interviews and other writings.* New York: Pantheon.

Franklin, J. H., & Moss, A. A. (1994). *From slavery to freedom: A history of African Americans* (7th ed.). New York: Knopf.

Frederick, T. J., McCarthy, B., & Hagan, J. (2013). Perceived danger and offending: Exploring the links between violent victimization and street crime. *Violence and Victims, 28*, 16–35.

Freire, P. (1970). *Pedagogy of the oppressed.* New York: Seabury Press.

Freire, P. (1994). *Pedagogy of hope: Reliving pedagogy of the oppressed.* New York: Continuum.

Friedan, B. (2001). *The feminine mystique* New York: W. W. Norton. (Original work published 1963)

Friedberg, L. (2000). Dare to compare. *American Indian Quarterly, 24*(3), 353.

Frieden, T. R. (2011). Foreword: CDC health disparities and inequalities report. *Morbidity and Mortality Weekly Report, 60*, 1–1.

Frith-Smith, H., & Singleton, H. (2000). *Urban American Indian children in Los Angeles County: An investigation of available data.* Prepared for the Los Angeles County American Indian Children's Council, UCLA, American Indian Studies Center, Los Angeles. Retrieved from http://www.standupca.org/reports/ Heather%20Singelton%20Study%20on%20Urban%20Indians.pdf

Frye, M. (2003). Oppression. In M. L. Andersen & P. H. Collins (Eds.), *Race, class, and gender* (5th ed., pp. 49–51). Belmont, CA: Wadsworth Press.

Fulton, B. R. (2011). Black churches and HIV/AIDS: Factors influencing congregations' responsiveness to social issues. *Journal for the Scientific Study of Religion, 50*, 617–630.

Galotti, A. E. (2007). Relativism, universalism, and applied ethics: The case of female circumcision. *Constellations, 14*(1), 91–111.

Gamst, G., Dana, R. H., Der-Karabetian, A., Aragón, M., Arellano, L. M., & Kramer, T. (2002). Effects of Latino acculturation and ethnic identity on mental health outcomes. *Hispanic Journal of Behavioral Sciences, 24*, 479–504

Garces, E., Thomas, D., & Currie, J. (2002). Longer-term effects of Head Start. *American Economist, 92*, 999–1012.

Gardenswartz, L., & Rowe, A. (2006). *Managing diversity survival guide: A complete collection of checklists, activities, and tips*. Burr Ridge, IL: Irwin Professional.

Garcia-Moreno, C., Jansen, H. A., Ellsberg, M., Heise, L., & Watts, C. H. (2006). Prevalence of intimate partner violence: Findings from the WHO [World Health Organization] multi-country study on women's health and domestic violence. *The Lancet, 368*, 1260–1269.

Gardiner, P., Whelan, J., White, L. F., Filippelli, A. C., Bharmal, N., & Kaptchuk, T. J. (2012). A systematic review of the prevalence of herb usage among racial/ethnic minorities in the United States. *Journal of Immigrant and Minority Health, 15*, 1–12.

Garnets, L., & Kimmel, D. C. (2003). *Psychological perspectives on lesbian, gay, and bisexual experiences*. New York: Columbia University Press.

Gartrell, N., Deck, A., Rodas, C., Peyser, H., & Banks, A. (2005). The national lesbian family study 4: Interviews with the 10-year-old children. *American Journal of Orthopsychiatry, 75*, 518–524.

Gartzia, L. (2011, January). The gendered nature of (male) leadership: Expressive identity salience and cooperation. *Academy of Management Proceedings, 2011*(1), 1–6.

Gates, G. (2011). *How many people are lesbian, gay, bisexual, and transgender?* Retrieved from http://williamsinstitute.law.ucla.edu/wp-content/uploads/Gates-How-Many-People-LGBT-Apr-2011.pdf

Gates, G. G. (2013) *LGBT parenting in the U. S.* Retrieved from http://williamsinstitute.law.ucla.edu/research/census-lgbt-demographics-studies/lgbt-parenting-in-the-united-states/

Gates, G. G., & Newport, F. (2012) *Gallup special report: The U. S. adult LGBT population.* Retrieved from http://williamsinstitute.law.ucla.edu/research/census-lgbt-demographics-studies/gallup-lgbt-pop-feb-2013/

Gates, G. G., & Newport, F. (2013). *Gallup special report: New estimates of the LGBT population in the United States.* Retrieved from http://williamsinstitute.law.ucla.edu/?s = Gallup + special + report%3A + New + estimates + of + the + LGBT + population + in + the + United + States&cat = 3

Gecková, A., Van Dijk, J. P., Stewart, R., Groothoff, J. W., & Post, D. (2003). Influence of social support on health among gender and socio-economic groups of adolescents. *European Journal of Public Health, 13*, 44–50.

Gellately, R., & Kiernan, B. (2003). *The specter of genocide: Mass murder in historical perspective*. Cambridge, UK: Cambridge University Press.

Germer, C. K. (2005). *Mindfulness and psychotherapy*. New York: Guilford.

Gianaros, P. J., Jennings, J. R., Sheu, L. K., Greer, P. J., Kuller, L. H., & Matthews, K. A. (2007). Prospective reports of chronic life stress predict decreased grey matter volume in the hippocampus. *Neuroimage, 35,* 795–803.

Gibson, P., & Abrams, L. (2003). Racial difference in engaging, recruiting, and interviewing African American women in qualitative research. *Qualitative Social Work, 2,* 457–476.

Giddens, A. (2006). *Sociology* (5th ed.). Malden, MA: Polity.

Gil, A., Wagner, E., & Vega, W. (2000). Acculturation, familism and alcohol use among Latino adolescent males: Longitudinal relations. *Journal of Community Psychology, 28,* 443–458.

Gil, D. (1998). *Confronting injustice and oppression: Concepts and strategies for social workers.* New York: Columbia University Press.

Gilroy, P. (2005). *Postcolonial melancholia.* New York: Columbia University Press.

Girves, J. E., Zepeda, Y., & Gwathmey, J. K. (2005). Mentoring in a post-affirmative action world. *Journal of Social Issues, 61*(3), 449–479.

Giuliano, L., Levine, D. I., & Leonard, J. (2011). Racial bias in the manager-employee relationship: An analysis of quits, dismissals, and promotions at a large retail firm. *Journal of Human Resources, 46,* 26–52.

Givens, S. M. B., & Monahan, J. L. (2005). Priming mammies, Jezebels, and other controlling images: An examination of the influence of mediated stereotypes on perceptions of an African American woman. *Media Psychology, 7*(1), 87–106.

Glassgold, J. M. (2009). The case of Felix: An example of gay-affirmative, cognitive-behavioral therapy. *Pragmatic Case Studies in Psychotherapy, 5,* 1–21.

Glick, J. E., & White, M. J. (2004). Post-secondary school participation of immigrant and native youth: The role of familial resources and educational expectations. *Social Science Research, 33,* 272–299.

Goffman, E. (1963). *Stigma.* Englewood Cliffs, NJ: Prentice Hall.

Golash-Boza, T. (2006). Dropping the hyphen? Becoming Latino(a)-American through racialized assimilation. *Social Forces, 85*(1), 27–55.

Golnaraghi, G., & Mills, A. J. (2013). Unveiling the myth of the Muslim woman: A postcolonial critique. *Equality, Diversity and Inclusion: An International Journal, 32,* 157–172.

Gonçalves, M. M., Matos, M., & Santos, A. (2009). Narrative therapy and the nature of "innovative moments" in the construction of change. *Journal of Constructivist Psychology, 22,* 1–23.

Goñi-Legaz, S., Ollo-López, A., & Bayo-Moriones, A. (2010). The division of household labor in Spanish dual earner couples: Testing three theories. *Sex Roles, 63,* 515–529.

Gordon, C. (1996). Adolescent decision making: A broadly based theory and its application to the prevention of early pregnancy. *Adolescence, 31*(123), 561–584.

Gordon, M. (1964). *Assimilation in American life.* New York: Oxford University Press.

Gordon-Larsen, P., Nelson, M. C., Page, P., & Popkin, B. M. (2006). Inequality in the built environment underlies key health disparities in physical activity and obesity. *Pediatrics, 117,* 417–424.

Gorman, B. K., & Sivaganesan, A. (2007). The role of social support and integration for understanding socioeconomic disparities in self-rated health and hypertension. *Social Science & Medicine, 65,* 958–975.

Gorman, E. H. (2005). Gender stereotypes, same-gender preferences, and organizational variation in the hiring of women: Evidence from law firms. *American Sociological Review, 70,* 702–728.

Gough, B., Weyman, N., Alderson, J., Butler, G., & Stoner, M. (2008). "They did not have a word": The parental quest to locate a "true sex" for their intersex children. *Psychology and Health, 23*, 493–507.

Graham, J. R., Shier, M. L., & Brownlee, K. (2012). Contexts and their impact on social work: A comparative analysis of the context of geography and culture. *Journal of Ethnic and Cultural Diversity in Social Work, 21*, 111–128.

Gray, J. A., Stone, J. A., & Stockard, J. (2006). *Childbearing, marriage and human capital investment.* University of Oregon, Portland. Retrieved from http://hdl.handle.net/1794/2463

Gray, M., & Heinsch, M. (2009). Ageing in Australia and the increased need for care. *Ageing International, 34*, 102–118.

Gray, M., & Heinsch, M. (2010, February 3). *Mapping the human services in Australia: The context of social work practice.* Paper presented to the Australian Council of Heads of Schools of Social Work, Launceston, Tasmania.

Greenhouse, S. (2012, July 25). C. J.'s Seafood fined for labor abuses. *New York Times*, p. B6.

Greer, K. (2002). Walking an emotional tightrope: Managing emotions in a women's prison. *Symbolic Interaction, 25*(1), 117–139.

Gregg, G. S. (1991). *Self-representation: Life narrative studies in identity and ideology.* New York: Greenwood Press.

Grewal, I., & Kaplan, C. (2001). Global identities: Theorizing transnational studies of sexuality. *GLQ: A Journal of Lesbian and Gay Studies, 7*, 663–679.

Griffin, H. (2000). Their own received them not: African American lesbians and gays in black churches. In D. Constantine-Simms (Ed.), *The greatest taboo: Homosexuality in black communities* (pp. 110–121). Los Angeles: Alyson.

Griffith, R. M., & Savage, B. D. (2006). *Women and religion in the African diaspora: Knowledge, power and performance.* Baltimore: Johns Hopkins University Press.

Grippo, A. J., Gerena, D., Huang, J., Kumar, N., Shah, M., Ughreja, R., & Carter, C. S. (2007). Social isolation induces behavioral and neuroendocrine disturbances relevant to depression in female and male prairie voles. *Psychoneuroendocrinology, 32*, 966–980.

Gruenewald, P. J., Freisthler, B., Remer, L., LaScala, E. A., & Treno, A. (2006). Ecological models of alcohol outlets and violent assaults: Crime potentials and geospatial analysis. *Addiction, 101*, 666–677.

Grzybowski, S., Stoll, K., & Kornelsen, J. (2011). Distance matters: A population based study examining access to maternity services for rural women. *BMC* [BioMed Central] *Health Services Research, 11*, 147–155.

Guelzo, A. C. (2006). Restoring the proclamation: Abraham Lincoln, confiscation, and emancipation in the Civil War Era. *Howard Law Journal, 50*, 397–899.

Guo, G., & Harris, K. M. (2000). The mechanisms mediating the effects of poverty on children's intellectual development. *Demography, 37*, 431–447.

Gurman, A., & Fraenkel, P. (2002). The history of couple therapy: A millennial review. *Family Process, 41*(2), 199–260.

Gutierrez, L., & Lewis, E. A. (1998). Strengthening communities through groups: A multicultural perspective. In H. Bertcher, I. F. Kurtz, & A. Lamont (Eds.), *Rebuilding communities: Challenges for group work* (pp. 5–16). New York: Haworth Press.

Gutierrez, L., Ortega, R., & Yeakley, A. (2000). Educating students for social work with Latinos: Issues for the new millennium. *Journal of Social Work Education, 36*(3), 541.

Gutiérrez, R. A. (2013). Reactive ethnic formations and panethnic identities: The creation of Latinos in the United States. *Revue LISA/LISA e-journal*, 11 doi:10.4000/lisa.5279

Haber, D. (2005). Cultural diversity among older adults: Addressing health education. *Educational Gerontology, 31*(9), 683–697.

Haidt, J., Graham, J., & Joseph, C. (2009). Above and below left–right: Ideological narratives and moral foundations. *Psychological Inquiry, 20*, 110–119.

Halberstam, J. (2005). *In a queer time and place: Transgender bodies, subcultural lives*. New York: New York University Press.

Hale, W. W., Crocetti, E., Raaijmakers, Q. A., & Meeus, W. H. (2011). A meta-analysis of the cross-cultural psychometric properties of the Screen for Child Anxiety Related Emotional Disorders (SCARED). *Journal of Child Psychology and Psychiatry, 52*, 80–90.

Hancock, A.-M. (2005). W. E. B. Du Bois: Intellectual forefather of intersectionality? *Souls, 7*(3–4), 74–84.

Hancock, A.-M. (2007a). Intersectionality as a normative and empirical paradigm. *Politics & Gender, 3*(2), 248–254.

Hancock, A.-M. (2007b). When multiplication doesn't equal quick addition: Examining intersectionality as a research paradigm. *Perspectives on Politics, 5*(1), 63–79.

Hand, C. A. (2006). An Ojibwe perspective on the welfare of children: Lessons and visions for the future. *Children and Youth Services Review, 28*(1), 20–46.

Haney-Lopez, I. (2006). *White by law: The legal construction of race*. New York: New York University Press.

Hanley, J. A., Turner, E., Bellera, C., & Telsch, D. (2003). How long did their hearts go on? A *Titanic* study. *British Medical Journal, 327*, 1457–1458.

Hardy, L. J., & Bohan, K. (2012). *A Beautiful Life-Hermosa Vida-Nizhóní Liná: Community engaged assessment and strategy report*. Flagstaff, AZ: North County Health Care.

Hardy, L. J., Getrich, C. M., Quezada, J. C., Guay, A., Michalowski, R. J., & Henley, E. (2012). A call for further research on the impact of state-level immigration policies on public health. *American Journal of Public Health, 102*, 1250–1253.

Harley, D. A. (2005). The black church: A strength-based approach in mental health. In D. A. Harley & K. J. M. Dillard (Eds.), *Contemporary mental health issues among African Americans* (pp. 293–306). Alexandria, VA: American Counseling Association.

Harley, D. A. (2006). Indigenous healing practices among rural elderly African Americans. *International Journal of Disability, Development and Education, 53*(4), 433–452.

Harmon, D. (2002). They won't teach me: The voices of gifted African American inner-city students. *Roeper Review, 24*(2), 68–75.

Harris, A. (2012). Critical race theory. In N. J. Smelser & P. B. Baltes (Eds.), *International Encylocpedia of Social and Behavioral Sciences*. Retrieved from http://works.bepress.com/angela_harris/17

Harris, R., Tobias, M., Jeffreys, M., Waldegrave, K., Karlsen, S., & Nazroo, J. (2006). Racism and health: The relationship between experience of racial discrimination and health in New Zealand. *Social Science & Medicine, 63*, 1428–1441.

Hasin, D. S., Stinson, F. S., Ogburn, E., & Grant, B. F. (2007). Prevalence, correlates, disability, and comorbidity of DSM-IV alcohol abuse and dependence in the United States: Results from the national epidemiologic survey on alcohol and related conditions. *Archives of General Psychiatry, 64*, 830–842

Hassan, I. (2003). Beyond postmodernism: Toward an aesthetic of trust. *Journal of Theoretical Humanities, 8*(1), 3–11.

Hatch, L. R. (2005). Gender and ageism. *Generations, 29*, 19–24.

Hawkins, J. D., Oesterle, S., Brown, E. C., Arthur, M. W., Abbott, R. D., Fagan, A. A., & Catalano, R. F. (2009). Results of a Type 2 translational research trial to prevent adolescent drug use and delinquency: A test of Communities That Care. *Archives of Pediatric and Adolescent Medicine, 163*, 789–798.

Hayek, F. A. (1963). *The sensory order: An inquiry into the foundations of theoretical psychology.* Chicago: University of Chicago Press.

Hayes-Bautista, D. E. (2002). The Latino health research agenda for the twenty-first century. *Latinos: Remaking America, 1.2*, 215–235.

He, J., & van de Vijver, F. (2012). Bias and equivalence in cross-cultural research. Online readings in psychology and culture. Retrieved from http://scholarworks.gvsu.edu/orpc/vol2/iss2/8/

Healey, J. F. (2011). *Diversity and society: Race, ethnicity, and gender, 2011/2012 update.* Thousand Oaks, CA: Pine Forge Press.

Heart, M. Y. H. B. (2003). The historical trauma response among natives and its relationship with substance abuse: A Lakota illustration. *Journal of Psychoactive Drugs, 35*, 7–13.

Heatherington, L., & Lavner, J. A. (2008). Coming to terms with coming out: Review and recommendations for family systems-focused research. *Journal of Family Psychology, 22*, 329–343.

HeavyRunner, I., & Marshall, K. (2003). Miracle survivors: Promoting resilience in Indian students. *Tribal College Journal, 14*, 14–18.

Hegar, R. L. (2012). Paulo Freire: Neglected mentor for social work. *Journal of Progressive Human Services, 23*, 159–177.

Henig, J. R., Holyoke, T. T., Brown, H., & Lacireno-Paquet, N. (2005). The influence of founder type on charter school structures and operations. *American Journal of Education, 111*, 487–588.

Herek, G. M. (2002). Gender gaps in public opinion about lesbians and gay men. *Public Opinion Quarterly, 66*(1), 40–66.

Herek, G. M. (2009a). Sexual stigma and sexual prejudice in the United States: A conceptual framework. *Contemporary Perspectives on Lesbian, Gay, and Bisexual Identities.* doi:10.1007/978–0–387–09556–1

Herek, G. M. (2009b). Hate crimes and stigma-related experiences among sexual minority adults in the United States: Prevalence estimates from a national probability sample. *Journal of Interpersonal Violence, 24*, 54–74.

Herek, G. M., & Garnets, L. D. (2007). Sexual orientation and mental health. *Annual Review of Clinical Psychology, 3*, 353–375.

Herek, G. M., & Glunt, E. K. (1993). Interpersonal contact and heterosexuals' attitudes toward gay men: Results from a national survey. *Journal of Sex Research, 30*, 239–244.

Herek, G. M., Cogan, J., & Gillis, R. (2002). Victims experiences in hate crimes based on sexual orientation. *Journal of Social Issues, 58*(2), 319–339.

Hernandez, B., Ramirez Garcia, J., & Flynn, M. (2010). The role of familism in the relation between parent-child discord and psychological distress among emerging adults of Mexican descent. *Journal of Family Psychology, 24*, 105–114.

Hernández, J. A. (2012). *Mexican American colonization during the nineteenth century: A history of the US-Mexico borderlands.* New York: Cambridge University Press.

Heron, M. (2007). Deaths: Leading causes for 2004. *Centers for Disease Control, National Vital Statistics Reports, 56*(5), 1–96.

Herring, C., Keith, V. M., & Horton, H. D. (2004). *Skin deep: How race and complexion matter in the "color blind" era.* Urbana: University of Illinois Press.

Hertzman C. (1999). The biological embedding of early experience and its effects on health in adulthood. *Annals of the New York Academy of Sciences, 896,* 85–95.

Hewstone, M. (2003). Panacea for prejudice? *Psychologist, 16,* 352–355.

Hibel, L. C., Mercado, E., & Trumbell, J. M. (2012). Parenting stressors and morning cortisol in a sample of working mothers. *Journal of Family Psychology, 26,* 738–746.

Hill, D. B., & Willoughby, B. L. B. (2005). The development and validation of the genderism and transphobia scale. *Sex Roles, 53,* 531

Hill, M. J. (2013). Is the black community more homophobic?: Reflections on the intersectionality of race, class, gender, culture and religiosity of the perception of homophobia in the black community. *Journal of Gay & Lesbian Mental Health, 17,* 208–214.

Hill, M., & Ballou, M. (2013). *The foundation and future of feminist therapy.* New York: Routledge.

Hilton, J. L., & von Hippel, W. (1996). Stereotypes. *Annual Review of Psychology, 47,* 237–272.

Himmelstein, D. U., Thorne, D., Warren, E., & Woolhandler, S. (2009). Medical bankruptcy in the United States, 2007: Results of a national study. *American Journal of Medicine, 122,* 741–746.

Hines, J. M. (2012). Using an anti-oppressive framework in social work practice with lesbians. *Journal of Gay & Lesbian Social Services, 24,* 23–39.

Hinrichs, P. (2010). The effects of the national school lunch program on education and health. *Journal of Policy Analysis and Management, 29,* 479–505.

Hirshorn, B., & Stewart, J. (2003). Geographic information systems in community-based gerontological research and practice. *Journal of Applied Gerontology, 22*(1), 134–151.

Hobfoll, S. E., Jackson, A., Hobfoll, I., Pierce, C., & Young, S. (2002). The impact of communal-mastery versus self-mastery on emotional outcomes during stressful conditions: a prospective study of Native American women. *American Journal of Community Psychology, 30*(6), 853–872.

Hobfoll, S. E., Schröder, K. E. E., Wells, M., & Malek, M. (2002). Communal versus individualistic construction of sense of mastery in facing life changes. *Journal of Social and Clinical Psychology, 21*(4), 362–399.

Hochschild, A. (1998). *King Leopold's ghost: A story of greed, terror, and heroism in colonial Africa.* Boston: Houghton Mifflin.

Hochschild, A., & Machung, A. (1989). *The second shift: Working parents and the revolution at home.* New York: Viking.

Hodge, D. R., Limb, G. E., & Cross, T. L. (2009). Moving from colonization toward balance and harmony: a Native American perspective on wellness. *Social Work, 54,* 211–219.

Hoff, E. (2003). The specificity of environmental influence: Socioeconomic status affects early vocabulary development via maternal speech. *Child Development, 74,* 1368–1378.

Hoffman, J. L., & Lewitzki, K. E. (2005). Predicting college success with high school grades and test scores: Limitations for minority students. *Review of Higher Education, 28*(4), 455–474.

Hogg, M. A. (2006). Social identity theory. In P. J. Burke (Ed.), *Contemporary social psychological theories* (pp. 111–136). Palo Alto, CA: Stanford University Press.

Holliday, B. G. (2009). The history and visions of African American psychology: Multiple pathways to place, space, and authority. *Cultural Diversity and Ethnic Minority Psychology, 15*, 317–337.

Holzman, C., Jetton, J., Siler-Khodr, T., Fisher, R., & Rip, T. (2001). Second trimester corticotropin-releasing hormone levels in relation to preterm delivery and ethnicity. *Obstetrics & Gynecology, 97*, 657–663.

Hondagneu-Sotelo, P. (2001). *Domestica: Immigrant workers caring and cleaning in America.* Berkeley and Los Angeles: University of California Press.

Hoogasian, R., & Lijtmaer, R. (2010). Integrating Curanderismo into counselling and psychotherapy. *Counselling Psychology Quarterly, 23*, 297–307.

hooks, b. (1981). *Ain't I a woman? Black women and feminism.* Boston: South End Press.

hooks, b. (1984). *Feminist theory from the margin to the center.* Boston: South End Press.

hooks, b. (1990). *Yearning: Race, gender, and cultural politics.* Boston: South End Press.

Hopson, R. K., Lucas, K. J., & Peterson, J. A. (2000). HIV/AIDS talk: Implications for prevention, intervention and evaluation. *New Directions for Evaluation, 86*, 29–42.

House, J. S., & Williams, D. R. (2000). Understanding and reducing socioeconomic and racial/ethnic disparities in health. In *Promoting health: Intervention strategies from social and behavioral research* (81–124). Washington, DC: National Academy Press.

Howard-Bobiwash, H., & Krouse, S. A (2009). *Keeping the campfires going: Native women's activism in urban communities.* Lincoln; University of Nebraska Press.

Howe, D. (2005). Modernity, postmodernity and social work. *British Journal of Social Work, 24*(5), 513–532.

Hoxby, C. M., & Avery, C. (2013). Missing one-offs: The hidden supply of high-achieving, low-income students. *Brookings Papers on Economic Activity, 1*, 1–46.

Hsiao, A., Wong, M. D., Goldstein, M. S., Becerra, L. S., Cheng, E. M., & Wegner, N. S. (2006). Complementary and alternative medicine among Asian American subgroups: Prevalence, predictors, and lack of relationship with acculturation and access to conventional health care. *Journal of Alternative and Complementary Medicine, 12*(10), 1003–1010.

Hudson, A. (2006). Feminism and social work: Resistance or dialogue? *British Journal of Social Work, 15*(6), 635–655.

Hudson, W. W., & Ricketts, W. A. (1980). A strategy for the measurement of homophobia. *Journal of Homosexuality, 5*, 357–372.

Huffman, M. L., & Cohen, P. N. (2004). Occupational segregation and the gender gap in workplace authority: National vs. local labor markets. *Sociological Forum, 19*, 121–147.

Huffman, M. L., Cohen, P. N., & Pearlman, J. (2010). Engendering change: Organizational dynamics and workplace gender desegregation, 1975–2005. *Administrative Science Quarterly, 55*, 255–277.

Human Rights and Equal Opportunities Commission. (1997). *Report of the national inquiry into the separation of Aboriginal and Torres Strait Islander children from their family.* Sydney, Australia: Author.

Hungerman, D. M. (2005). Are church and state substitutes? Evidence from the 1996 welfare reform. *Journal of Public Economics, 89*(11/12), 2245–2267.

Hunnicutt, G. (2009). Varieties of patriarchy and violence against women resurrecting "Patriarchy" as a theoretical tool. *Violence against Women, 15*, 553–573.

Huo, Y. J., Molina, L. E., Binning, K. R., & Funge, S. P. (2010). Subgroup respect, social engagement, and well-being: A field study of an ethnically diverse high school. *Cultural Diversity and Ethnic Minority Psychology, 16*, 427–437.

Hurdle, D. (2002). Native Hawaiian traditional healing: Culturally based interventions for social work practice. *Social Work, 47*(2), 183–193.

Hwang, W. C., Wood, J. J., Lin, K. M., & Cheung, F. (2006). Cognitive-behavioral therapy with Chinese Americans: Research, theory, and clinical practice. *Cognitive and Behavioral Practice, 13*, 293–303.

Hyde, C. A., & Deal, K. H. (2003). Does gender matter? Male and female participation in social work classrooms. *Affilia, 18*, 192–209.

Hyde, J. S. (2005). The genetics of sexual orientation. In J. S. Hyde (Ed.), *Biological substrates of human sexuality* (pp. 9–20). Washington, DC: American Psychological Association.

Hyde, J. S., & Kling, K. C. (2001). Women, motivation, and achievement. *Psychology of Women Quarterly, 25*, 364–378.

Igartua, K. J., Gill, K., & Montoro, R. (2003). Internalized homophobia: A factor in depression, anxiety, and suicide in the gay and lesbian population. *Canadian Journal of Community Mental Health, 22*, 15–30.

Ignatiev, N. (1995). *How the Irish became white*. New York: Routledge.

International Forum on Globalization. (2002, Spring). *Report summary: A better world is possible: Alternatives to economic globalization*. San Francisco: Author.

Iwata, N., Turner, R. J., & Lloyd, D. A. (2002). Race/ethnicity and depressive symptoms in community-dwelling adults: A differential item functioning analysis. *Psychiatry Research, 110*(3), 281–289.

James, J. (2001). Radicalizing feminism. In J. James & T. D. Sharpley-Whiting (Eds.), *The black feminist reader* (pp. 239–258). Malden, MA: Basil Blackwell.

James, R. K., & Gilliland, B. E. (2008). *Crisis intervention strategies*. Pacific Groves, CA: Brooks.

Jandt, F., & Hundley, H. (2007). Intercultural dimensions of communicating masculinities. *Journal of Men's Studies, 15*(2), 216–231

Jarama, S. L., Kennamer, J. D., Poppen, P. J., Hendricks, M., & Bradford, J. (2005). Psychosocial, behavioral, and cultural predictors of sexual risk for HIV infection among Latino men who have sex with men. *AIDS and Behavior, 9*, 513–523.

Jennings, M. K. (2006). The gender gap in attitudes and beliefs about the place of women in American political life: A longitudinal, cross-generational analysis. *Politics & Gender, 2*(2), 193–219.

Jepson, E. S., Thomas, J., Markward, A., Kelly, J. A., Koser, G., & Diehl, D. (1997). *Making room at the table: Fostering involvement in the planning and governance of formal support systems*. Chicago: Family Resource Coalition of America.

Johnson, H. P. (1996). *Undocumented immigration to California: 1980–1993*. Retrieved from Public Policy Institute of California, San Francisco, CA: http://www.ppic.org/content/pubs/report/R_996HJR.pdf

Jones, D. S. (2006). The persistence of American Indian health disparities. *American Journal of Public Health, 96*(12), 2122–2134.

Josephson, J. (2005). Citizenship, same-sex marriage, and feminist critiques of marriage. *Perspectives on Politics, 3*(2), 269–284.

Juang, L. P., Syed, M., & Cookston, J. T. (2012). Acculturation-based and everyday parent–adolescent conflict among Chinese American adolescents: Longitudinal trajectories and implications for mental health. *Journal of Family Psychology, 26*, 916–926.

Kagawa-Singer, M., Dadia, A. V., Yu, M. C., & Surbone, A. (2010). Cancer, culture, and health disparities: Time to chart a new course? *California Cancer Journal for Clinicians, 60,* 12–39.

Kalman, B. (2009). *Canada: The culture.* Toronto, ON: Crabtree Publishing Company.

Kane, E. W. (2006). "No way my boys are going to be like that!": Parents' responses to children's gender nonconformity. *Gender and Society, 20,* 149–176.

Kanter, R. M. (1977). *Men and women of the corporation.* New York: Basic Books.

Kanuha, V. K. (2000). "Being" native versus "going" native: Conducting social work research as an insider. *Social Work, 45*(5), 439–447.

Kaplan, G. A., Pamuk, E. R., Lynch, J. W., Cohen, R. D., & Balfour, J. L. (1996). Inequality in income and mortality in the United States: Analysis of mortality and potential pathways. *British Medical Journal, 312,* 999–1003.

Karp, A. J. (1976). *Golden door to America: The Jewish immigrant experience.* New York: Viking Press.

Kawai, T. (2006). Postmodern consciousness in psychotherapy. *Journal of Analytical Psychology, 51*(3), 437–450.

Kaya, Y., & Cook, K. J. (2010). A cross-national analysis of physical intimate partner violence against women. *International Journal of Comparative Sociology, 51,* 423–444.

Kegler, M. C., & Swan, D. W. (2011). Advancing coalition theory: The effect of coalition factors on community capacity mediated by member engagement. *Health Education Research, 27*(4), 572–584.

Keithly, D. C., & Rombough, S. (2007). The differential social impact of Hurricane Katrina on the African American population of New Orleans. *Race, Gender & Class, 14,* 142–153.

Keleher, T., & Johnson, T. (2001). Confronting institutional racism. *Leadership, 30*(4), 24–30.

Kenagy, G. P. (2005). Transgender health findings from two needs assessment studies in Philadelphia. *Health and Social Work, 30,* 19–26.

Kennedy, R. (2003). *Interracial intimacies: Sex, marriage, identity, and adoption.* New York: Pantheon.

Kenney, K. (2002). Counseling interracial couples and multiracial individuals: Applying a multicultural counseling competency framework. *Counseling and Human Development, 35*(4), 1–13.

Kesler, C., & Hout, M. (2010). Entrepreneurship and immigrant wages in US labor markets: A multi-level approach. *Social Science Research, 39,* 187–201.

Kessler, R. C., Mickelson, K. D., & Williams, D. R. (1999). The prevalence, distribution, and mental health correlates of perceived discrimination in the United States. *Journal of Health and Social Behavior,* 208–230.

Khiabany, G. (2003). Globalization and the Internet: Myths and realities. *Trends in Communication, 11,* 137–153.

Kidder, D. L. (2002). The influence of gender on the performance of organizational citizenship behaviors. *Journal of Management, 28,* 629–648.

Kim, B. S. K., Atkinson, D. R., & Yang, P. H. (1999). The Asian values scale: Development, factor analysis, validation, and reliability. *Journal of Counseling Psychology, 46*(3), 342–352.

Kim, B. S. K., Yang, P. H., Atkinson, D. R., Wolfe, M. M., & Hong, S. (2001). Cultural value similarities and differences among Asian American ethnic groups. *Cultural Diversity and Ethnic Minority Psychology, 7*(4), 343–361.

Kim, G., DeCoster, J., Huang, C. H., & Chiriboga, D. A. (2011). Race/ethnicity and the factor structure of the Center for Epidemiologic Studies Depression Scale: A meta-analysis. *Cultural Diversity and Ethnic Minority Psychology, 17*, 381–396.

Kim, S. (2013). Former Silicon Valley venture capital partner wants "justice" in sex discrimination suit. Retrieved from http://abcnews.go.com/Business/venture-capital-partner-justice-silicon-valley-sexual-discrimination/story?id = 19450094

Kimmel, M. (1996). *Manhood in America: A cultural history.* New York: Free Press.

Kimmel, M. S. (2000). *The gendered society.* New York: Oxford University Press.

King, R. D., Massoglia, M., & Uggen, C. (2012). Employment and exile: US criminal deportations, 1908–2005. *American Journal of Sociology, 117*, 1786–1825.

Kinsey, A. C., Pomeroy, W. B., & Martin, C. E. (1949). *Sexual behavior in the human male.* Philadelphia: W. B. Saunders.

Kisthardt, W. E. (2002). The strengths perspective in interpersonal helping: Purpose, principles, and functions. In D. Saleebey (Ed.), *The strengths perspective in social work practice*(3rd ed., pp. 163–185). Boston: Allyn and Bacon.

Kite, M. E., Stockdale, G. D., Whitley, B. E., & Johnson, B. T. (2005). Attitudes toward younger and older adults: An updated meta-analytic review. *Journal of Social Issues, 61*, 241–266.

Klonoff, E., & Landrine, H. (2000). Is skin color a marker for racial discrimination?: Explaining the skin color-hypertension relationship. *Journal of Behavioral Medicine, 23*, 329–338.

Klumb, P. L., & Lampert, T. (2004). Women, work, and well-being 1950–2000: a review and methodological critique. *Social Science & Medicine, 58*, 1007–1024.

Knudsen, E. I., Heckman, J. J., Cameron, J. L., & Shonkoff, J. P. (2006). Economic, neurobiological, and behavioral perspectives on building America's future workforce. *Proceedings of the National Academy of Sciences, 103*, 10155–10162.

Kocher, R., Emanuel, E. J., & DeParle, N. A. M. (2010). The Affordable Care Act and the future of clinical medicine: The opportunities and challenges. *Annals of Internal Medicine, 153*, 536–539.

Koeske, G. F., & Krowinski, W. J. (2004). Gender-based salary inequality in social work: Mediators of gender's effect on salary. *Social Work, 49,* 309–317.

Koettl, J. (2009). Human trafficking, modern day slavery, and economic exploitation. Social Protection Discussion Paper no. 0911. World Bank, Washington, DC.

Koh, C. (2006). Reviewing the link between creativity and madness: A postmodern perspective. *Educational Research and Reviews, 1*(7), 213–221.

Koh, H. K., & Nowinski, J. M. (2010). Health equity and public health leadership. *American Journal of Public Health, 100*, S1, S9–S11.

Koh, H. K., & Sebelius, K. G. (2010). Promoting prevention through the affordable care act. *New England Journal of Medicine, 363*, 1296–1299.

Koh, H. K., & Sebelius, K. G. (2012). Ending the tobacco epidemic. *Journal of the American Medical Association, 308*(8), 767–768.

Koh, H. K., Massin-Short, S., & Elqura, L. (2009). Disparities tobacco use and lung cancer. In H. K. Koh (Ed.), *Toward the elimination of cancer disparities* (pp. 109–135). New York: Springer.

Koh, H. K., Nowinski, J. M, & Piotrowski, J. J. (2011). A 2020 vision for educating the next generation of public health leaders. *American Journal of Preventative Medicine, 40*(2), 199–202.

Koh, H. K., Oppenheimer, S. C., Massin-Short, S. B., Emmons, K. M., Geller, A. C., & Viswanath, K. (2010). Translating research evidence into practice to reduce health disparities: A social determinants approach. *American Journal of Public Health, 100,* S72.

Kosberg, J. (2002). Heterosexual male: A group forgotten by the profession of social work. *Journal of Sociology and Social Welfare, 29*(3), 51–71.

Kowalski, K. (2003). The emergence of ethnic and racial attitudes in preschool-aged children. *Journal of Social Psychology, 143*(6), 677–691.

Krieger, N. (1987). Shades of difference: Theoretical underpinnings of the medical controversy on black/white differences in the United States, 1830–1870. *International Journal of Health Services, 17,* 259–278.

Krieger, N., Rehkopf, D. H., Chen, J. T., Waterman, P. D., Marcelli, E., & Kennedy, M. (2008). The fall and rise of US inequities in premature mortality: 1960–2002. *PLoS Medicine, 5,* e46–e76.

Ku, L. (2009). Health insurance coverage and medical expenditures of immigrants and native-born citizens in the United States. *American Journal of Public Health, 99,* 1322–1328.

Ku, L., & Matani, S. (2001). Left out: Immigrants' access to health care and insurance. *Health Affairs, 20,* 247–256.

Kuhn, A. (2013). Structures of patriarchy and capital in the family. In A. Kuhn & A. Wolpe (Eds.), *Feminism and materialism (RLE feminist theory): Women and modes of production* (pp. 59–85). New York: Routledge.

Kulis, S., Marsiglia, F. F., & Hurdle, D. (2003). Gender identity, ethnicity, acculturation and drug use: Exploring differences among adolescents in the Southwest. *Journal of Community Psychology, 31,* 1–22.

Kulis, S., Marsiglia, F. F., & Nieri, T. (2009). Perceived ethnic discrimination versus acculturation stress: Influences on substance use among Latino youth in the Southwest. *Journal of Health and Social Behavior, 50,* 443–459.

Kulis, S., Marsiglia, F. F., Yabiku, S. T., & Kopak, A. M. (2010, June). Acculturative stress and substance use among Mexican-heritage early adolescents: Differentiating experimentation and heavy use using two-part latent growth curve models. Poster presentation at the Society for Prevention Research annual meeting, Denver, CO.

Kulis, S., Napoli, M., & Marsiglia, F. F. (2002). Ethnic pride, biculturalism, and drug use norms of urban American Indian adolescents. *Social Work Research, 26,* 2, 101–112.

Kulis, S., Okamoto, S. K., Rayle, A. D., & Sen, S. (2006). Social contexts of drug offers among American Indian youth and their relationship to substance use: An exploratory study. *Journal of Cultural Diversity and Ethnic Minority Psychology, 12*(1), 30–44.

Kulwicki, A. D., & Miller, J. (1999). Domestic violence in the Arab American population: Transforming environmental conditions through community education. *Issues in Mental Health Nursing, 20,* 199–215.

Kumpfer, K., Turner, C., Hopkins, R., & Librett, J. (1993). Leadership and team effectiveness in community coalitions for the prevention of alcohol and other drug abuse. *Health Education Research, 8*(3), 359–374.

Kuo, W. (1984). Prevalence of depression among Asian Americans. *Journal of Nervous and Mental Disease, 172,* 449–457.

Kuper, H., Singh-Manoux, A., Siegrist, J., & Marmot, M. (2002). When reciprocity fails: Effort–reward imbalance in relation to coronary heart disease and health functioning within the Whitehall II study. *Occupational and Environmental Medicine, 59,* 777–784.

Kuzawa, C. W., & Sweet, E. (2009) Epigenetics and the embodiment of race: Developmental origins of US racial disparities in cardiovascular health. *American Journal of Human Biology, 21,* 2–15.

Lake, A., & Townshend, T. (2006). Obesogenic environments: exploring the built and food environments. *Journal of the Royal Society for the Promotion of Health, 126,* 262–267.

Landrine, H., & Klonoff, E. A. (2000). Racial segregation and cigarette smoking among blacks: findings at the individual level. *Journal of Health Psychology, 5,* 211–219.

Landrine, H., Klonoff, E. A., Gibbs, J., Manning, V., & Lund, M. (1995). Physical and psychiatric correlates of gender discrimination. *Psychology of Women Quarterly, 19,* 473–492.

Långström, N., Rahman, Q., Carlström, E., & Lichtenstein, P. (2010). Genetic and environmental effects on same-sex sexual behavior: A population study of twins in Sweden. *Archives of Sexual Behavior, 39,* 75–80.

Larrat, E. P., Marcoux, R. M., & Vogenberg, F. R. (2013). The Affordable Care Act: New features in 2013. *Pharmacy and Therapeutics, 38,* 164–165.

Larsen, B. W., & Jesch, G. W. (1980). Students training in an American Indian setting. *Social Casework, 61*(8), 512–518.

Larson, A., Gillies, M., Howard, P. J., & Coffin, J. (2007). It's enough to make you sick: The impact of racism on the health of Aboriginal Australians. *Australian and New Zealand Journal of Public Health, 31,* 322–329.

Larson, K., & Halfon, N. (2010). Family income gradients in the health and health care access of US children. *Maternal and Child Health Journal, 14,* 332–342.

Larsson, B., Seidell, J., Svärdsudd, K., Welin, L., Tibblin, G., Wilhelmsen, L., & Björntorp, P. (1989). Obesity, adipose tissue distribution and health in men: The study of men born in 1913. *Appetite, 13,* 37–44.

LatinoMetrics (2010). *US Latinos' perceptions & actions around immigration debate: Law enforcement, lifestyle and voting impact.* Retrieved from http://lulac.org/assets/pdfs/HF-LatinoMetrics-Immigration-BriefStudy.pdf

Latkin, C. A., & Curry, A. D. (2003). Stressful neighborhoods and depression: A prospective study of the impact of neighborhood disorder. *Journal of Health and Social Behavior, 44,* 34–44.

Laumann, E. O., Gagnon, J. H, Michael, J. T., & Michaels, S. (1994). *The social organization of sexuality: Sexual practices in the United States.* Chicago: University of Chicago Press.

Lawson, J. (2003). The wounds we hide: The silent scars of racism are not limited to communities of color. Until we confront how racism shapes the lives of whites, we will not be healed. *Other Side, 39*(9), 10–17.

Lazarsfeld, P., & Merton, R. K. (1954). Friendship as a social process: A substantive and methodological analysis. In M. Berger, T. Abel, & C. H. Page (Eds.), *Freedom and control in modern society* (pp. 18–66). New York: Van Nostrand.

Lazarus, R. S., & Folkman, S. (1984). *Stress, appraisal, and coping.* New York: Springer.

Leaper, C., & Robnett, R. D. (2011). Women are more likely than men to use tentative language, aren't they? A meta-analysis testing for gender differences and moderators. *Psychology of Women Quarterly, 35,* 129–142.

Leavelle, T. N. (1998). "We will make it our own place." *American Indian Quarterly, 22*(4), 435–457.

Lee, E. (2003). At America's gates: Chinese immigration during the exclusion era, 1882–1943. Chapel Hill, NC: University of North Carolina Press.

Lee, H. K., Chou, S. P., Cho, M. J., Park, J. I., Dawson, D. A., & Grant, B. F. (2010). The prevalence and correlates of alcohol use disorders in the United States and Korea: A cross-national comparative study. *Alcohol, 44,* 297–306.

Lee, H., Cayer, N. J., & Lan, G. Z. (2006). Changing federal government employee attitudes since the Civil Service Reform Act of 1978. *Review of Public Personnel Administration, 26,* 21–51.

Lee, J. A. B. (2001). *The empowerment approach to social work practice* (2nd ed.). New York: Columbia University Press.

Lee, S. J., Wong, N. W. A., & Alvarez, A. N. (2008). The model minority and the perpetual foreigner: Stereotypes of Asian Americans. In N. Tewari & A. N. Alvarez (Eds.), *Asian American Psychology: Current Perspectives* (pp. 69–84). New York: Routledge.

Leinsalu, M., Vågerö, D., & Kunst, A. E. (2003). Estonia 1989–2000: Enormous increase in mortality differences by education. *International Journal of Epidemiology, 32,* 1081–1087.

Lemelle, A. J., & Battle, J. (2004). Black masculinity matters in attitudes toward gay males. *Journal of Homosexuality, 47,* 39–41.

Leppel, K. (2007). Home-ownership among opposite and same sex couples in the US. *Feminist Economics, 13*(1), 1–30.

Lev, A. I., & Moore, B. (2000). Social work embraces transgender. *American Psychological Association, division 44 newsletter, 16*(1), 16.

Levant, R. F. (2011). Research in the psychology of men and masculinity using the gender role strain paradigm as a framework. *American Psychologist, 66,* 765–776.

Levin, J., & Levin, W. (1982). *The functions of discrimination and prejudice* (2nd ed.). New York: Harper and Row.

Levinson, J., & Young, D. (2010). Implicit gender bias in the legal profession: An empirical study. *Duke Journal of Gender Law & Policy, 18,* 1–44.

Levy, D. L. (2009). Gay and lesbian identity development: An overview for social workers. *Journal of Human Behavior in the Social Environment, 19,* 978–993.

Lewis, G., & Rogers, M. (1999). Does the public support equal employment rights for gays and lesbians? In D. B. Riggle & B. Tadlock (Eds.), *Gays and lesbians in the democratic process* (pp. 118–145). New York: Columbia University Press.

Lewis, L. A., Koston, Z., Quartley, M., & Adsit, J. (2010). Virtual communities of practice: Bridging research and practice using Web 2. 0. *Journal of Educational Technology Systems, 39,* 155–161.

Lewis, O. (1966). The culture of poverty. *Scientific American, 215*(4), 19–25.

Li, Z., Page, A., Martin, G., & Taylor, R. (2011). Attributable risk of psychiatric and socio-economic factors for suicide from individual-level, population-based studies: A systematic review. *Social Science & Medicine, 72,* 608–616.

Liang, J., Van Tran, T., Krause, N., & Markides, K. S. (1989). Generational differences in the structure of the CES-D scale in Mexican Americans. *Journal of Gerontology, 44,* 110–120.

Lichter, D. (2013). Integration or fragmentation? Racial diversity and the American future. *Demography, 50,* 359–391.

Liebow, E. (1967). *Tally's corner.* Boston: Little, Brown.

Lin, C. C., Rogot, E., Johnson, N. J., Sorlie, P. D., & Arias, E. (2003). A further study of life expectancy by socioeconomic factors in the National Longitudinal Mortality. *Ethnicity and Disease, 13,* 240–247.

Link, B. G., & Phelan, J. (1995). Social conditions as fundamental causes of disease. *Journal of Health and Social Behavior, 35,* 80–94.

Link, B., & Phelan, J. (2000). Evaluating the fundamental cause explanation for social disparities in health. In C. E. Bird, P. Conrad, & A. M. Fremont (Eds.), *Handbook of medical sociology* (5th ed., pp. 33–46). Upper Saddle River, NJ: Prentice-Hall.

Liu-Mares, W., MacKinnon, J. A., Sherman, R., Fleming, L. E., Rocha-Lima, C., Hu, J. J., & Lee, D. J. (2013). Pancreatic cancer clusters and arsenic-contaminated drinking water wells in Florida. *BMC* [BioMed Central] *Cancer, 13,* 111–119.

Lo, S. C., Reisen, C. A., Poppen, P. J., Bianchi, F. T., & Zea, M. C. (2011). Cultural beliefs, partner characteristics, communication, and sexual risk among Latino MSM. *AIDS and Behavior, 15,* 613–620.

Lobo, S. (2002). Census-taking and the invisibility of urban American Indians. Retrieved from http://www.prb.org/Articles/2002/CensusTakingandtheInvisibilityofUrbanAmerican Indians.aspx

Loch, D. (2009). Immigrant youth and urban riots: A comparison of France and Germany. *Journal of Ethnic and Migration Studies, 35,* 791–814.

Lofquist, D. (2012, May). *Same sex couples consistency reporting marital status.* Paper presented at the meeting of Annual Meeting of the Population Association of America, San Francisco. Retrieved from http://www.census.gov/hhes/samesex/

Loftus, J. (2001). America's liberalization in attitudes toward homosexuality, 1973 to 1998. *American Sociological Review, 66*(5), 762–782.

Lone-Knapp, F. (2000). Rez talk. *American Indian Quarterly, 24*(4), 635–641.

Longres, J. F. (2000). *Human behavior in the social environment* (3rd ed.). Itasca, IL: F. E. Peacock.

Lopez, M. H., Morin, R., & Taylor, P. (2010). *Illegal immigration backlash worries, divides Latinos.* Pew Research Center: Washington, DC.

Lopez, S. R., Nelson, K. A., Polo, J. A., Jenkins, J., Karno, M., & Snyder, K. (1998, August). *Family warmth and the course of schizophrenia of Mexican Americans and Anglo Americans.* Paper presented at the International Congress of Applied Psychology, San Francisco.

Loury, S., & Kulbok, P. (2007). Correlates of alcohol and tobacco use among Mexican immigrants in rural North Carolina. *Family Community Health, 30,* 247–256.

Louw, P. E. (2004). *The rise, fall and legacy of apartheid.* New York: Praeger.

Lovaas, K. E., & Jenkins, M. M. (Eds.). (2007). *Sexualities and communication in everyday life: A reader.* Thousand Oaks, CA: Sage Publications.

Lu, A., & Wong, Y. J. (2013). Stressful experiences of masculinity among US-born and immigrant Asian American men. *Gender & Society, 27,* 345–371.

Lugo Steidel, A., & Contreras, J. (2003). A new familism scale for use with Latino populations. *Hispanic Journal of Behavioral Sciences, 25,* 312–330.

Lyons, K. (2006). Globalization and social work: International and local implications. *British Journal of Social Work, 36*(1), 365–380.

Maccio, E. M. (2011). Self-reported sexual orientation and identity before and after sexual reorientation therapy. *Journal of Gay & Lesbian Mental Health, 15,* 242–259.

Macionis, J., & Gerber, L. (2010). Culture. *Sociology* (7th ed.). Toronto, ON: Pearson Canada.

Mackenbach, J. P., Stirbu, I., Roskam, A. J. R., Schaap, M. M., Menvielle, G., Leinsalu, M., & Kunst, A. E. (2008). Socioeconomic inequalities in health in 22 European countries. *New England Journal of Medicine, 358,* 2468–2481.

Macklem, P. (2001). *Indigenous difference and the constitution of Canada*. Toronto, ON: University of Toronto Press.

Madrian, B. C. (1994). Employment-based health insurance and job mobility: Is there evidence of job-lock? *Quarterly Journal of Economics, 109,* 27–54.

Magana, L., & Short, R. (2002). Political rhetoric, immigration attitudes, and contemporary prejudice: A Mexican American dilemma. *Journal of Social Psychology, 142*(6), 701–712.

Mair, C., Roux, A. D., & Galea, S. (2008). Are neighbourhood characteristics associated with depressive symptoms? A review of evidence. *Journal of Epidemiology and Community Health, 62,* 940–946.

Manion, J. C. (2003). Girls blush, sometimes: Gender, moral agency, and the problem of shame. *Hypatia, 18,* 21–41.

Marcellin, R. L., Bauer, G. R., & Scheim, A. I. (2013). Intersecting impacts of transphobia and racism on HIV risk among trans persons of colour in Ontario, Canada. *Ethnicity and Inequalities in Health and Social Care, 6,* 97–107.

Marmot, M., & Wilkinson, R. (2006). *Social determinants of health* (2nd ed.) Oxford, UK: Oxford University Press.

Marmot, M. (2003). Understanding social inequalities in health. *Perspectives in Biology and Medicine, 46*(3), S9–S23.

Marmot, M. G., & Bell, R. (2009). Action on health disparities in the United States: Commission on Social Determinants of Health. *Journal of the American Medical Association, 301,* 1169–1171. doi:10.1001/jama.2009.363

Marmot, M. G., Bosma, H., Hemingway, H., Brunner, E., & Stansfeld, S. (1997). Contribution of job control and other risk factors to social variations in coronary heart disease incidence. *The Lancet, 350,* 235–239.

Marsiglia, F. F., & Navarro, R. (1999). Acculturation and HIV/AIDS knowledge and perception of risk among a group of Mexican American middle school students. *Journal of HIV/AIDS Prevention and Education for Adolescents and Children, 3,* 43–61.

Marsiglia, F. F., & Waller, M. (2002). Language preference and drug use among Southwestern Mexican American middle school students. *Children & Schools, 25,* 145–158.

Marsiglia, F. F., Bermudez-Parsai, M., & Coonrod, D. (2010). Familias Sanas: An intervention designed to increase rates of postpartum visits among Latinas. *Journal of Health Care for the Poor and Underserved, 21,* 119–131.

Marsiglia, F. F., Kulis, S., & Hecht, M. L. (2001). Ethnic labels and ethnic identity as predictors of drug use and drug exposure among middle school students in the Southwest. *Journal of Research on Adolescence, 11,* 21–48.

Marsiglia, F. F., Kulis, S., Fitzharris, B., & Becerra, D. (2010). Acculturation gaps and externalizing youth problem behaviors: Assets and challenges of Southwestern Mexican immigrant families. *Social Work Forum, 42/43,* 6–26.

Marsiglia, F. F., Kulis, S., Hecht, M. L., & Sills, S. (2004). Ethnic self-identification and ethnic identity as predictors of drug norms and drug use among pre-adolescents in the Southwest. *Substance Use and Misuse, 39,* 7, 1061–1094.

Marsiglia, F. F., Kulis, S., Wagstaff, D. A., Elek, E., & Dran, D. (2005). Acculturation status and substance use prevention with Mexican and Mexican American youth. *Journal of Social Work Practice in the Addictions, 5,* 85–111.

Martin, M., Camargo, M., Ramos, L., Lauderdale, D., Krueger, K., & Lantos, J. (2005). The evaluation of a Latino community health worker HIV prevention program. *Hispanic Journal of Behavioral Sciences, 27*(3), 371–384.

Marx, K. (1970). *Critique of Hegel's philosophy of right*. Cambridge, UK: Cambridge University Press. (Original work published 1843)

Mason, P. L. (2011). Moments of disparate peaks: Race-gender wage gaps among mature persons, 1965–2007. *Review of Black Political Economy, 38*, 1–25.

Massey, D. S. (2004). Segregation and Stratification: A Biosocial Perspective. *Du Bois Review, 1*, 7–25.

Massey, D. S. (2009). Racial formation in theory and practice: The case of Mexicans in the United States. *Race and Social Problems, 1*, 12–26.

Massey, D. S., & Pren, K. A. (2012). Unintended consequences of US immigration policy: Explaining the Post 1965 surge from Latin America. *Population and Development Review, 38*, 1–29.

Mastrogianni, A., & Bhugra, D. (2003). Globalization, cultural psychiatry and mental distress. *International Journal of Social Psychology, 49*(3), 163–165.

Mather, M., & Rivers, K. L. (2006). City Profiles of Child Well-Being: Results from the American Community Survey. Washington, DC: Annie E. Casey Foundation.

Mathers, C. D., & Loncar, D. (2006). Projections of global mortality and burden of disease from 2002 to 2030. *PLoS Medicine, 3*, e442.

Matthews, K. A., Sowers, M. F., Derby, C. A., Stein, E., Miracle-McMahill, H., Crawford, S. L., & Pasternak, R. C. (2005). Ethnic differences in cardiovascular risk factor burden among middle-aged women: Study of Women's Health Across the Nation (SWAN). *American Heart Journal, 149*, 1066–1073.

Mattingly, M. J., Johnson, K. M., & Schaefer, A. (2011). More poor kids in more poor places: Children increasingly live where poverty persists (Paper 150). Carsey Institute, Durnham, NH.

Mauer, M. (2011). Addressing racial disparities in incarceration. *Prison Journal, 91*, 87S–101S.

May, M. L., Bowman, G. J., Ramos, K. S., Rincones, L., Rebollar, M. G., Rosa, M. L. . . . Ramos, I. M. (2003). Embracing the local: Enriching scientific research, education, and outreach on the Texas-Mexico border through a participatory action research partnership. *Environmental Health Perspectives, 111*(13), 1571–1577.

Mays, V. M., Cochran, S. D., & Barnes, N. W. (2007). Race, race-based discrimination, and health outcomes among African Americans. *Annual Review Psychology, 58*, 201–225.

McBride, S. (2013). Ex-Kleiner partner Ellen Pao wants her day in court. Retrieved from http://www.mercurynews.com/business/ci_23496686/ex-kleiner-partner-ellen-pao-wants-her-day

McCall, L. (2005). The complexity of intersectionality. *Signs, 30*(3), 1771–1800.

McCollom, S. (1996, August). *Hispanic immigrant attitude towards African Americans: A study of intergroup contact*. Paper presented at the Annual Meeting of the American Sociological Association, New York.

McCreary, D. R., Saucier, D. M., & Courtenay, W. H. (2005). The drive for muscularity and masculinity: Testing the associations among gender-role traits, behaviors, attitudes, and conflict. *Psychology of Men & Masculinity, 6*, 83–94.

McDonough, P., & Fann, A. J. (2007). The study of inequality. In P. J. Gumport (Ed.), *Sociology of higher education: Contributions and their contexts* (pp. 53–92). Baltimore: Johns Hopkins University Press.

McEwen, B. S. (1998). Protective and damaging effects of stress mediators. *New England Journal of Medicine, 338*, 171–179.

McEwen, B. S. (2008). Central effects of stress hormones in health and disease: Understanding the protective and damaging effects of stress and stress mediators. *European Journal of Pharmacology, 583*, 174–185.

McEwen, B. S., & Gianaros, P. J. (2010). Central role of the brain in stress and adaptation: Links to socioeconomic status, health, and disease. *Annals of the New York Academy of Sciences, 1186*, 190–222.

McGinnis, J. M., Williams-Russo, P., & Knickman, J. R. (2002). The case for more active policy attention to health promotion. *Health Affairs, 21*, 78–93.

McIntosh, P. (1990). White privilege: Unpacking the invisible knapsack. *Independent School, 49*(2), 31–36.

McKeever, M., & Wolfinger, N. H. (2006). Shifting fortunes in a changing economy: Trends in the economic well-being of divorced women. In L. Kowaleski-Jones & N. H. Wolfinger (Eds.), *Fragile families and the marriage agenda* (pp. 127–157). New York: Springer.

McKenna, M. T., Michaud, C. M., Murray, C. J. L., & Marks, J. S. (2005). Assessing the burden of disease in the United States using disability-adjusted life years. *American Journal of Preventive Medicine, 28*(5), 415–423.

McKeown, E., Nelson, S., Anderson, J., Low, N., & Elford, J. (2010). Disclosure, discrimination and desire: Experiences of Black and South Asian gay men in Britain. *Culture, Health & Sexuality, 12*, 843–856.

McKerl, M. (2007). Multiculturalism, gender and violence: Multiculturalism: Is it bad for women? *Culture and Religion, 8*(2), 187–217.

McKernan, S.-M., & Ratcliffe, C. (2005). Events that trigger poverty entries and exit. *Social Science Quarterly, 86*(1), 1146–1169.

McKinney, C. M., Caetano, R., Harris, T. R., & Ebama, M. S. (2009). Alcohol availability and intimate partner violence among US couples. *Alcoholism: Clinical and Experimental Research, 33*, 169–176.

McManus, P., & DiPrete, T. (2001). Losers and winners: The financial consequences of separation and divorce for men. *American Sociological Review, 66*, 246–268.

McPhail, B. A. (2004). Setting the record straight: Social work is not a female-dominated profession. *Social Work, 49*, 323–326.

McPherson, M., Smith-Lovin, L., & Cook, J. (2001). Birds of a feather: Homophily in social networks. *Annual Review of Sociology, 27*, 415–444.

Mead, G. H. (1934). *Mind, self and society.* Chicago: University of Chicago Press.

Mechoulan, S. (2006). Divorce laws and the structure of the American family. *Journal of Legal Studies, 35*, 143–174.

Menéndez, M., Benach, J., Muntaner, C., Amable, M., & O'Campo, P. (2007). Is precarious employment more demanding to women's health than men's? *Social Science & Medicine, 64*(4), 776–781.

Menjivar, C. (2000). *Fragmented ties: Salvadoran immigrant networks in America.* Berkeley and Los Angeles: University of California Press.

Merriam, S. B. (2009). *Qualitative research: A guide to design and implementation.* San Francisco: Jossey-Bass.

Mertens, D. M. (2009*). Research and evaluation in education and psychology: Integrating diversity with quantitative, qualitative, and mixed methods.* Thousand Oaks, CA: Sage.

Merton, R. K. (1972). Insiders and outsiders: A chapter in the sociology of knowledge. *American Journal of Sociology, 78*(1), 9–47.

Meyer, J. D., Nichols, G. H., Warren, N., & Reisine, S. (2008). Maternal occupation and risk for low birth weight delivery: Assessment using state birth registry data. *Journal of Occupational & Environmental Medicine, 50*(3), 306–315.

Meyers, R. A., Berdahl, J. L., Brashers, D., Considine, J. R., Kelly, J. R., Moore, C., . . . , & Spoor, J. R. (2005). Understanding groups from a feminist perspective. In M. S. Poole, & A. B. Hollingshead (Eds.), *Theories of small groups: Interdisciplinary perspectives.* (pp. 241–276). Thousand Oaks, CA: Sage.

Michael, R., Gagnon, J., Laumann, E., & Kolata, G. (1994). *Sex in America: A definitive survey.* New York: Warner Books.

Middleton, V. A., Anderson, S. K., & Banning, J. H. (2009). The journey to understanding privilege: A meta-narrative approach. *Journal of Transformative Education, 7*(4), 294–311.

Mihesuah, D. (1996). *American Indians: Stereotypes and realities.* Atlanta, GA: Clarity.

Miller, M. (2013). Sex discrimination led to firing, ex-DEP administrator claims. *The Patriot News.* Retrieved from http://www.pennlive.com/midstate/index.ssf/2013/07/sex_discrimination_led_to_firi.html

Mirowsky, J., & Ross, C. E. (2003). *Education, social status, and health.* New York: Transaction Books.

Mishel, L. R., Bernstein, J., & Allegretto, S. (2007). *The state of working America 2006/2007,* (10th ed.). Ithaca, NY: ILR.

Mitchell, C. M., Kaufman, C. E., & the Pathways of Choice and Healthy Ways Project Team. (2002). Structure of HIV knowledge, attitudes, and behaviors among American Indian young adults. *AIDS Education and Prevention, 14,* 401–418.

Mitchem, S. (2007). *African American folk healing.* New York: New York University Press

Moane, G. (1999). *Gender and colonialism: A psychological analysis of oppression and liberation.* New York: St. Martin's Press.

Moen, P., & Roehling, P. (2005). *The career mystique: Cracks in the American dream.* New York: Rowman & Littlefield.

Mohanty, C. T. (1988). Under Western eyes: Feminist scholarship and colonial discourses. *Feminist Review, 30,* 61–88.

Mokdad, A. H., Marks, J. S., Stroup, D. F., & Gerberding, J. L. (2004). Actual causes of death in the United States, 2000. *Journal of the American Medical Association, 291,* 1238–1245.

Montez, J. K., Angel, J. L., & Angel, R. J. (2009). Employment, marriage, and inequality in health insurance for Mexican-origin women. *Journal of Health and Social Behavior, 50,* 132–148.

Montgomery, E. C., Kunik, M. E., Wilson, N., Stanley, M. A., & Weiss, B. (2010). Can paraprofessionals deliver cognitive-behavioral therapy to treat anxiety and depressive symptoms? *Bulletin of the Menninger Clinic, 74,* 45–62.

Moraga, C. (2004). La Güera. In M. L. Andersen & P. H. Collins (Eds.), *Race, class, and gender* (pp. 28–35). Belmont, CA: Wadsworth Press.

Moran, J. R., Fleming, C. M., Somervall, P., & Manson, S. M. (1999). Measuring bicultural ethnic identity among American Indian adolescents: A factor analytic study. *Journal of Adolescent Research, 14,* 405–426.

Morash, M., Bui, M., & Santiago, A. (2000). Gender specific ideology of domestic violence in Mexican origin families. *International Review of Victimology, 1,* 67–91.

Moreau, M., Osgood, J., & Halsall, A. (2007). Making sense of the glass ceiling in schools: An exploration of women teachers' discourses. *Gender & Education, 19,* 237–253. doi:10.1080/09540250601166092

Morenoff, J. D., Sampson, R. J., & Raudenbush, S. W. (2001). Neighborhood inequality, collective efficacy, and the spatial dynamics of urban violence. *Criminology, 39*, 517–558.

Morland, K., Diez-Roux, A. V., & Wing, S. (2006). Supermarkets, other food stores, and obesity: The Atherosclerosis Risk in Communities Study. *American Journal of Preventive Medicine, 30*, 333–339.

Morland, K., Wing, S., & Roux, A. D. (2002). The contextual effect of the local food environment on residents' diets: The Atherosclerosis Risk in Communities Study. *Journal Information, 92*, 1761–1767.

Morris, J. K., Cook, D. G., & Shaper, A. G. (1994). Loss of employment and mortality. *British Medical Journal, 308*, 1135–1139.

Morrow, D. F. (2004). Social work practice with gay, lesbian, bisexual, and transgender adolescents. *Families in Society: Journal of Contemporary Social Services, 85*, 91–99.

Mosher, W. D., Copen, C., & Sionean, C. (2011). *Sexual behavior, sexual attraction, and sexual identity in the United States: Data from the 2006–2008 National Survey of Family Growth.* U.S. Department of Health and Human Services, Centers for Disease Control and Prevention, National Center for Health Statistics.

Mullaly, B. (2002) *Challenging oppression: A critical social work approach.* Toronto, ON: Oxford University Press.

Mullaly, B. (2007). *The new structural social work: Ideology, theory, and practice.* Toronto, ON: Oxford University Press.

Murguia, E., & Telles, E. E. (1996). Phenotype and schooling among Mexican Americans. *Sociology of Education, 69*(4), 276–289.

Murray, L. R. (2003). Sick and tired of being sick and tired: Scientific evidence, methods, and research implications for racial and ethnic disparities in occupational health. *American Journal of Public Health, 93*, 221–226.

Mustanski, B., Lyons, T., & Garcia, S. C. (2011). Internet use and sexual health of young men who have sex with men: A mixed-methods study. *Archives of Sexual Behavior, 40*, 289–300.

Naphy, W. (2006). *Born to be gay: A history of homosexuality.* Gloucestershire, UK: Tempus.

National Association of Deans and Directors [NADD] 2012. A behavioral health disparities curriculum infusion initiative: Eliminating behavioral health disparities for racial and ethnic minority populations. Retrieved from http://www.naddssw.org/pages/wp-content/uploads/2010/10/Behavioral-Health-Disparities-Literature-Review_Final.pdf

National Center for Health Statistics. (2006). *National hospital ambulatory medical care survey: 2004 emergency department summary.* Hyattsville, MD: Author.

National Center for Health Statistics. (2012). *Health, United States, 2011: With special feature on socioeconomic status and health.* Hyattsville, MD: US Department of Health and Human Services.

National Institutes of Health (NIH). (2002). Strategic research plan and budget to reduce and ultimately eliminate health disparities. *Volume I–Fiscal Years, 2006.* U.S. Department of Health and Human Services, Washington, DC.

National Institutes of Health (NIH). (2006). *National Kidney Disease Education Program fact sheet: African Americans & kidney disease.* National Institutes of Health Publication No. 04–5577 (Rev. April 2006). National Institutes of Health, Washington, DC.

Nayar, K. R. (2007). Social exclusion, caste & health: A review based on the social determinants framework. *Indian Journal of Medical Research, 126*, 355–363.

Nayga Jr., R. M., & Weinberg, Z. (1999). Supermarket access in the inner cities. *Journal of Retailing and Consumer Services, 6,* 141–145.

Naylor, L. L. (Ed.). (1997). *Cultural diversity in the United States.* Westport, CT: Bergin & Garvey.

Neumark, D., & Button, P. (2013). Did age discrimination protections help older workers weather the great recession? NBER Working Paper w19216. National Bureau of Economic Research, Cambridge, MA.

Newman, K. (2006). Democracy, bureaucracy and difference in US development politics since 1968. *Progress in Human Geography, 30*(1), 44–61.

Newman, W. M. (1973). *American pluralism: A study of minority groups and social theory.* New York: Harper and Row

Ng, R. (2006). Exploring healing and the body through indigenous Chinese medicine. In J. F. Kunnie & N. I. Goduka (Eds.), *Indigenous people's wisdom and power* (pp. 95–116). London: Ashgate.

Nolen-Hoeksema, S. (2004). Gender differences in risk factors and consequences for alcohol use and problems. *Clinical Psychology Review, 24,* 981–1010.

Norris, T., Vines, P. L., & Hoeffel, E. M. (2012). *The American Indian and Alaska Native population: 2010.* US Department of Commerce, Economics and Statistics Administration, US Census Bureau, Washington, DC.

Northridge, J., Ramirez, O. F., & Stingone, J. A. (2010). The role of housing type and housing quality in urban children with asthma. *Journal of Urban Health, 87,* 211–224.

O'Brien, M., Peyton, V., Mistry, R., Hruda, L., Jacobs, A., Caldera, Y., . . . Roy, C. (2000). Gender-role cognition in three-year-old boys and girls. *Sex Roles, 42*(11/12), 1007–1025.

O'Connell, M., & Feliz, S. (2011, September 27). *Same-sex couple household statistics from the 2010 census.* US Census Bureau. SEHSD Working Paper 2011–26. U.S. Bureau of the Census, Washington, DC.

O'Donnell, S. (1993). Involving clients in welfare policy-making. *Social Work, 38*(5), 629–635.

O'Neil, B. A., Forsythe, M. E., & Stanish, W. D. (2001). Chronic occupational repetitive strain injury. *Canadian Family Physician, 47,* 311–316.

O'Riordan, K. (2012). The life of the gay gene: From hypothetical genetic marker to social reality. *Journal of Sex Research, 49,* 362–368.

Office of Applied Studies. (2008). Results from the 2007 National Survey on Drug Use and Health: National findings (DHHS Publication No. SMA 08–4343, NSDUH Series H–34). Rockville, MD: Substance Abuse and Mental Health Services Administration. Also available from http://oas.samhsa.gov

Office of Minority Health (2013). The National CLAS Standards. Retrieved from http://minorityhealth.hhs.gov/templates/browse.aspx?lvl = 2&lvlID = 15

Ogletree, S. M., Figueroa, P., & Pena, D. (2005). A double standard in death? Gender differences in obituaries. *OMEGA—Journal of Death and Dying, 51(4),* 337–342.

Okamoto, S. K., LeCroy, C. W., Dustman, P., Hohmann-Marriott, B., & Kulis, S. (2004). An ecological assessment of drug related problem situations for American Indian adolescents of the Southwest. *Journal of Social Work Practice in the Addictions, 4*(3), 47–63.

Okamoto, S. K., LeCroy, C. W., Tann, S. S., Rayle, A. D., Kulis, S., Dustman, P., & Berceli, D. (2006). The implications of ecologically based assessment for primary prevention with indigenous youth populations. *Journal of Primary Prevention, 27*(2), 155–170.

Olaniyan, D. A., & Okemakinde, T. (2008). Human capital theory: Implications for educational development. *Pakistan Journal of Social Sciences, 5*, 479–483.

Olneck, M. R. (2009). What have immigrants wanted from American schools? What do they want now? Historical and contemporary perspectives on immigrants, language, and American schooling. *American Journal of Education, 115*, 379–406.

Omi, M., & Winant, H. (1998). Racial formations. In P. S. Rothenberg (Ed.), *The social construction of race, class, gender, and sexuality* (4th ed.; pp. 13–22). New York: St. Martin's Press.

Organisation for Economic Co-operation and Development (OECD). (2008). *Growing unequal? Income distribution and poverty in OECD countries.* Paris: Author.

Organisation for Economic Co-operation and Development (OECD). (2011). *Divided We Stand: Why inequality keeps rising.* Paris: Author. Retrieved from http://www.oecd.org/els/social/inequality

Ortíz Hendricks, C. (2005). The multicultural triangle of the child, the family and the school: Culturally competent approaches. In E. P. Congress & M. J. Gonzalez (Eds.), *Multicultural perspectives in working with families* (pp. 71–92). New York: Springer.

Ortiz, S. Y., & Roscigno, V. J. (2009). Discrimination, women, and work: Processes and variations by race and class. *Sociological Quarterly, 50*, 336–359. doi:10.1111/j.1533–8525.2009.01143

Ostafin, B. D., Chawla, N., Bowen, S., Dillworth, T. M., Witkiewitz, K., & Marlatt, G. A. (2006). Intensive mindfulness training and the reduction of psychological distress: A preliminary study. *Cognitive and Behavioral Practice, 13*(3), 191–197.

Ostrove, J. M., Cole, E. R., & Oliva, G. A. (2009). Toward a feminist liberation psychology of alliances. *Feminism & Psychology, 19*, 381–386.

Osypuk, T. L., & Acevedo-Garcia, D. (2008). Are racial disparities in preterm birth larger in hypersegregated areas? *American Journal of Epidemiology, 167*, 1295–1304.

Ott, M. A., Evans, N. L., Halpern-Felshr, B. L., & Eyre, S. L. (2003). Differences in altruistic roles and HIV risk perception among staff, peer educators, and students in an adolescent peer education program. *AIDS Education and Prevention, 15*(2), 159–171.

Ouellette-Kuntz, H., Burge, P., Brown, H. K., & Arsenault, E. (2010). Public attitudes towards individuals with intellectual disabilities as measured by the concept of social distance. *Journal of Applied Research in Intellectual Disabilities, 23*, 132–142.

Outshoorn, J. (2012). Assessing the impact of women's movements. *Women's Studies International Forum, 35*, 147–149.

Outwin, C. P. M. (1996). Securing the leg irons: Restriction of legal rights for slaves in Virginia and Maryland, 1625–1791. *Early America Review, 1*(3). Retrieved from http://www3.gettysburg.edu/~tshannon/hist106web/Slave%20Communities/atlantic_world/slavery.htm

Owens, L. H. (1976). *This species of property: Slave life and culture in the Old South.* Oxford: Oxford University Press.

Oyserman, D., Coon, H., & Kemmelmeier, M. (2002). Rethinking individualism and collectivism: Evaluation of theoretical assumptions and meta-analyses. *Psychological Bulletin, 128*, 3–73.

Ozer, E. J., & Wright, D. (2012). Beyond school spirit: The effects of youth-led participatory action research in two urban High Schools. *Journal of Research on Adolescence, 22*, 267–283.

Padavic, I., & Reskin, B. F. (2002). *Women and men at work*. Thousand Oaks, CA: Pine Forge Press.

Padilla, A. M., & Perez, W. (2003). Acculturation, social identity, and social cognition: A new perspective. *Hispanic Journal of Behavioral Sciences, 25*, 35–55.

Pagden, A. R. (1975). *The Maya: Diego de Landa's account of the affairs of Yucatán*. Chicago: J. Philip O'Hara.

Paradies, Y. (2006). A systematic review of empirical research on self-reported racism and health. *International Journal of Epidemiology, 35*(4), 888–901.

Pardo, M. (1998). Mexican American women grassroots activists: Mothers of East Los Angeles *(pg. 251-262)*. In K. V. Hansen & A. I. Garey, *Families in the U.S.: Kinship and domestic politics (Women in political economy)*. Philadelphia: Temple University Press.

Paris, M., Añez, L. M., Bedregal, L. E., Andrés-Hyman, R. C., & Davidson, L. (2005). Help seeking and satisfaction among Latinas: The roles of setting, ethnic identity, and therapeutic alliance. *Journal of Community Psychology, 33*(3), 299–312.

Park, R. E. (1930). Assimilation, social. In E. Seligman & A. Johnson (Eds.), *Encyclopedia of the social sciences* (pp. 281–283). New York: Macmillan.

Parks, F. M. (2007). Working with narratives: Coping strategies in African American folk beliefs and traditional healing practices. *Journal of Human Behavior in the Social Environment, 15*(1), 135–147.

Parsons, T. (1961). *Theories of society*. Glencoe, IL: Free Press.

Pascall, G., & Lewis, J. (2004). Emerging gender regimes and policies for gender equality in a wider Europe. *Journal of Social Policy, 33*, 373–394.

Pastor, M. (2001). Geography and opportunity. In N. Smelser, W. J. Wilson, & F. Mitchell (Eds.), *America becoming: Racial trends and their consequences* (pp. 435–468). Washington, DC: National Academy Press.

Patterson, C. J. (2009). Children of lesbian and gay parents: Psychology, law, and policy. *American Psychologist, 64*, 727–736.

Patterson, J. M. (2002). Integrating family resiliency and family stress theory. *Journal of Marriage and Family, 64*(2), 349–360.

Patterson, O. (2003, June 22). Affirmative action: The sequel. *New York Times*, Sec. 4, p. 11.

Patterson, T. R. (2005). *Zora Neale Hurston and a history of southern life*. Philadelphia: Temple University Press.

Paul, K. I., & Moser, K. (2009). Unemployment impairs mental health: Meta-analyses. *Journal of Vocational Behavior, 74*, 264–282.

Paxton, P., & Mughan, A. (2006). What's to fear from immigrants? Creating an assimilationist threat scale. *Political Psychology, 27*(4), 549–568.

Pear, R. (2012, May 16). House vote sets up battle on domestic violence bill. *New York Times*, p. A19.

Pease, B. (2011). Men in social work challenging or reproducing an unequal gender regime? *Affilia, 26*, 406–418.

Pellebon, D. A., & Anderson, S. C. (1999). Understanding the life issues of spiritually based clients. *Families in Society: The Journal of Contemporary Human Services, 80*(3), 229–238.

Peña, S. (2004). Pájaration and transculturation: Language and meaning in Miami's Cuban's American gay worlds. In W. Leap & T. Boellstorff (Eds.), *Speaking in queer tongues: Globalization and gay language* (pp. 231–249). Urbana: University of Illinois Press

Pentz, M. A., Jasuja, G. K., Rohrbach, L. A., Sussman, S., & Bardo, M. T. (2006). Translation in tobacco and drug abuse prevention research. *Evaluation and Health Professions, 29,* 246–271.

Perreira, K., Crosnoe, R., Fortuny, K., Pedroza, J., Ulvestad, K., Weiland, C., & Yoshikawa, H. (2012). *Barriers to immigrants' access to health and human services programs.* Washington, DC: US Department of Health and Human Services.

Perrone, K. M., Wright, S. L., & Jackson, Z. V. (2009). Traditional and nontraditional gender roles and work: Family interface for men and women. *Journal of Career Development, 36,* 8–24.

Perry, B. L., Stevens-Watkins, D., & Oser, C. B. (2013). The moderating effects of skin color and ethnic identity affirmation on suicide risk among low-SES African American women. *Race and Social Problems, 5,* 1–14.

Peters, A. J. (2003). Isolation or inclusion: Creating safe spaces for lesbian and gay youth. *Families in Society: Journal of Contemporary Human Services, 84*(3), 331–340.

Phelan, J. C., & Link, B. G. (2005). Controlling disease and creating disparities: A fundamental cause perspective. *Journals of Gerontology Series B: Psychological Sciences and Social Sciences, 60,* S27–S33.

Phelan, J. C., Link, B. G., Diez-Roux, A., Kawachi, I., & Levin, B. (2004). "Fundamental causes" of social inequalities in mortality: A test of the theory. *Journal of Health of Social Behavior, 45,* 265–285.

Phinney, J. S. (2003). Ethnic identity and acculturation. In K. M. Chun, P. B. Organista, & G. Marín (Eds.), *Acculturation: Advances in theory, measurement, and applied research* (pp. 63–82). Washington, DC: American Psychological Association.

Piketty, T., & Saez, E. (2012, October). Top incomes and the Great Recession: Recent evolutions and policy implications. In *13th Jacques Polak Annual Research Conference, Washington, DC, November* (pp. 8–9). Washington, DC: International Monetary Fund.

Pomerantz, S., Ruby, R., & Stefanik, A. (2013). Girls run the world? Caught between sexism and postfeminism in school. *Gender & Society, 27,* 185–207.

Poole, G. E., & Galpin, G. (2011). Prevalence of victims of torture in the health screening of quota refugees in New Zealand during 2007–2008 and implications for follow-up care. *New Zealand Medical Journal, 124,* 18–24.

Pope, M. (1995). The "salad bowl" is big enough for us all: An argument for the inclusion of lesbians and gay men in any definition of multiculturalism. *Journal of Counseling and Development, 73,* 301–304.

Popkin, B. M., Duffey, K., & Gordon-Larsen, P. (2005). Environmental influences on food choice, physical activity and energy balance. *Physiology & Behavior, 86,* 603–613.

Portes, A., & Rivas, A. (2011). The adaptation of migrant children. *The Future of Children, 21,* 219–246.

Posner, S. F., Stewart, A. L., Marín, G., & Pérez-Stable, E. J. (2001). Factor variability of the Center for Epidemiological Studies Depression scale (CES-D) among urban Latinos. *Ethnicity and Health, 6*(2), 137–144.

Potochnick, S. R., & Perreira, K. M. (2010). Depression and anxiety among first-generation immigrant Latino youth: Key correlates and implications for future research. *Journal of Nervous and Mental Disease, 198,* 470–477.

Powell, D. R. (2007). *Critical regionalism: Connecting politics and culture in the American landscape.* Chapel Hill: University of North Carolina Press.

Powell, L. M., Slater, S., Mirtcheva, D., Bao, Y., & Chaloupka, F. J. (2007). Food store availability and neighborhood characteristics in the United States. *Preventive Medicine, 44*, 189–195.

Powers, K. M. (2006). An exploratory study of cultural identity and culture-based education programs for urban American Indian students. *Urban Education, 41*(1), 20–49.

Preece, J. J. (2006). *Minority rights.* London: Polity.

Presser, H. B. (2000). Nonstandard work schedules and marital instability. *Journal of Marriage and Family, 62*, 93–110.

Pressman, D. L., & Bonanno, G. (2007). With whom do we grieve? Social and cultural determinants of grief processing in the United States and China. *Journal of Social and Personal Relations, 24*(5), 729–746.

Prewitt-Freilino, J. L., Caswell, T. A., & Laakso, E. K. (2012). The gendering of language: A comparison of gender equality in countries with gendered, natural gender, and genderless languages. *Sex Roles, 66*, 268–281.

Price, D. V. (2004). *Borrowing inequality: Race, class, and student loans.* Boulder, CO: Lynne Rienner.

Probert, B. (2005). "I just couldn't fit it in": Gender and unequal outcomes in academic careers. *Gender, Work and Organization, 12*(1), 50–72.

Puchala, C., Paul, S., Kennedy, C., & Mehl-Madrona, L. (2010). Using traditional spirituality to reduce domestic violence within aboriginal communities. *Journal of Alternative and Complementary Medicine, 16*, 89–96.

Purdie-Vaughns, V., & Eibach, R. P. (2008). Intersectional invisibility: The distinctive advantages and disadvantages of multiple subordinate-group identities. *Sex Roles, 59*, 377–391.

Putri, A. K., Prawitasari, J. E., Hakim, M. A., Yuniarti, K. W., & Kim, U. (2011). Sadness as perceived by Indonesian male and female adolescents. *International Journal of Research Studies in Psychology, 1*, 27–36.

Pyke, K. D. (2010). What is internalized racial oppression and why don't we study it? Acknowledging racism's hidden injuries. *Sociological Perspectives, 53*, 551–572.

Qadeer, M., Agrawal, S. K., & Lovell, A. (2010). Evolution of ethnic enclaves in the Toronto metropolitan area, 2001–2006. *Journal of International Migration and Integration/Revue de L'integration et de la Migration Internationale, 11*, 315–339.

Raj, A., & Silverman, J. (2002). Violence against immigrant women: The roles of culture, context, and legal immigrant status on intimate partner violence. *Violence against Women, 8*(3), 367–398.

Ramirez-Valles, J., Fergus, S., Reisen, C. A., Poppen, P. J., & Zea, M. C. (2005). Confronting stigma: Community involvement and psychological well-being among Latino lesbians and gay men. *Hispanic Journal of Behavioral Sciences, 27*, 101–119.

Rank, M. R., & Hirschl, T. A. (2002). Welfare use as a life course event: Toward a new understanding of the U. S. safety net. *Social Work, 47*(3), 237–249.

Rawley, J. A., & Behrendt, S. D. (2005). *The transatlantic slave trade: A history.* Lincoln: University of Nebraska Press.

Rawls, J. (2009). *A theory of justice.* Cambridge, MA: Harvard University Press.

Rayle, A. D., Kulis, S., Okamoto, S. K., Tann, S. S., LeCroy, C. W., Dustman, P. A., & Burke, A. (2006). Who is offering and how often? Gender differences in drug offers among American Indian adolescents of the Southwest. *Journal of Early Adolescence, 26*(3), 1–22.

Razack, N. (2009). Decolonizing the pedagogy and practice of international social work. *International Social Work, 52*, 9–21.

Reamer, F. G. (2006). *Ethical standards in social work: A critical review of the NASW Code of Ethics*. Washington, DC: National Association of Social Workers Press.

Rees, S., Silove, D., Chey, T., Ivancic, L., Steel, Z., Creamer, M., . . . , & Forbes, D. (2011). Lifetime prevalence of gender-based violence in women and the relationship with mental disorders and psychosocial function. *Journal of the American Medical Association, 306,* 513–521.

Reese, D. J., Ahern, R. E., Nair, S., O'Faire, J. D., & Warren, C. (1999). Hospice access and use by African Americans: Addressing cultural and institutional barriers through participatory action research. *Social Work, 44*(6), 549–559.

Reisch, M., & Sommerfeld, D. (2002). Race, welfare reform, and nonprofit organizations. *Journal of Sociology and Social Welfare, 29*(1), 155–177.

Repetti, R. L., Matthews, K. A., & Waldron, I. (1989). Employment and women's health: Effects of paid employment on women's mental and physical health. *American Psychologist, 44,* 1394.

Repetti, R. L., Taylor, S. E., & Seeman, T. E. (2002). Risky families: family social environments and the mental and physical health of offspring. *Psychological Bulletin, 128,* 330–366.

Rice, J. (2001). Poverty, welfare, and patriarchy: How macro-level changes in social policy can help low-income women. *Journal of Social Issues, 57*(2), 355–374.

Rich-Edwards, J. W., Kleinman, K., Michels, K. B., Stampfer, M. J., Manson, J. E., Rexrode, K. M., . . . , & Willett, W. C. (2005). Longitudinal study of birth weight and adult body mass index in predicting risk of coronary heart disease and stroke in women. *British Medical Journal, 330,* 1115–1121.

Rich-Edwards, J., Krieger, N., Majzoub, J., Zierler, S., Lieberman, E., & Gillman, M. (2001). Maternal experiences of racism and violence as predictors of preterm birth: Rationale and study design. *Paediatric and Perinatal Epidemiology, 15,* 124–135.

Richie, B. (2000). A black feminist reflection on the antiviolence movement. *Signs, 25,* 1133–1137.

Riggs, C. (2000). American Indians, economic development, and self-determination in the 1960s. *Pacific Historical Review, 69*(3), 431.

Rinderle, S. (2005). The Mexican diaspora: A critical examination of signifiers. *Journal of Communication Inquiry, 29*(4), 294–316.

Ring, P. E. (2001). Invisible no more: Native Americans of the Northeast have eluded extinction. *The World and I Online, 16*(10), 179–184.

Rios, R., Aiken, L. S., & Zautra, A. J. (2012). Neighborhood contexts and the mediating role of neighborhood social cohesion on health and psychological distress among Hispanic and non-Hispanic residents. *Annals of Behavioral Medicine, 43,* 50–61.

Ritter, G. (1997). Silver slippers and a golden cap: L. Frank Baum's *The Wonderful Wizard of Oz* and historical memory in American politics. *Journal of American Studies, 31*(2), 171–202.

Rivera, E. T. (2005). Espiritismo: The flywheel of the Puerto Rican spiritual traditions. *Revista Interamericana de Psicología/Interamerican Journal of Psychology, 39*(2), 295–300.

Roberts, E. M. (1997). Neighborhood social environments and the distribution of low birth weight in Chicago. *American Journal of Public Health, 87,* 597–603.

Robinson, T. L., & Howard-Hamilton, M. F. (2000). *The convergence of race, ethnicity, and gender: Multiple identities in counseling*. Upper Saddle River, NJ: Prentice Hall.

Robitaille, C., & Saint-Jacques, M. C. (2009). Social stigma and the situation of young people in lesbian and gay stepfamilies. *Journal of Homosexuality, 56,* 421–442.

Rochlin, M. (1992). Heterosexual questionnaire. In W. Blumenfeld (Ed.), *Homophobia: How we all pay the price* (pp. 203–204). Boston: Beacon Press.

Rodriguez, M. S. (2005). Labor rights are civil rights: Mexican American workers in twentieth-century America. *Labor, 2*(4), 106–108.

Romley, J. A., Cohen, D., Ringel, J., & Sturm, R. (2007). Alcohol and environmental justice: The density of liquor stores and bars in urban neighborhoods in the United States. *Journal of Studies on Alcohol and Drugs, 68*, 48–55.

Rosales, F. A. (1996). *Chicano! The history of the Mexican American civil rights movement*. Houston, TX: Arte Publico Press.

Rosales, F. A. (2000). *Testimonio: A documentary history of the Mexican American struggle for civil rights*. Houston, TX: Arte Publico.

Rosas, G. (2006). The thickening borderlands. *Cultural Dynamics, 18*(3), 335–349.

Roth, L. M. (2006). *Selling women short: Gender and money on Wall Street*. Princeton, NJ: Princeton University Press.

Rothmann, D. J. (1971). *The discovery of the asylum: Social order and disorder in the new republic*. Piscataway, NJ: Transaction Publishers.

Rousseau, C., & Tate, W. F. (2003). No time like the present: Reflecting on equity in school mathematics. *Theory into Practice, 42*, 210–216.

Rubin, A., & Babbie, E. R. (2008). *Research methods for social work*. Belmont, CA: Cengage Learning.

Rumbaut, R., & Portes, A. (2001). *Ethnicities: Children of immigrants in America*. Berkeley and Los Angeles: University of California Press.

Rush, C. L. (2012). Amending the Americans with Disabilities Act: Shifting equal employment opportunity obligations in public human resource management. *Review of Public Personnel Administration, 32*, 75–86.

Rush, M., & Keenan, M. (2013). The social politics of social work: Anti-oppressive social work dilemmas in twenty-first-century welfare regimes. *British Journal of Social Work*, 1–18. doi:10.1093/bjsw/bct014. Retrieved from http://bjsw.oxfordjournals.org/

Ryan, R. M., Fauth, R. C., & Brooks-Gunn, J. (2006). Childhood poverty: Implications for school readiness and early childhood education. In B. Spodek, & O. N. Saracho (Eds.), *Handbook of research on the education of children* (2nd ed., pp. 323–346). Mahwah, NJ: Erlbaum Associates.

Saca-Hazboun, H., & Glennon, C. A. (2011). Cultural influences on health care in Palestine. *Clinical Journal of Oncology Nursing, 15*, 281–286.

Saewyc, E., Wang, N., Chittenden, M., & Murphy, A. (2006). *Building resilience in vulnerable youth*. Vancouver, BC: The McCreary Centre Society.

Sahgal, N., & Smith, G. (2009). A religious portrait of African Americans. Report No. 389. The Pew Forum on Religion and Public Life, The Pew Research Center, Washington, DC. Retrieved from http://www.pewforum.org/2009/01/30/a-religious-portrait-of-african-americans/

Sakamoto, A., & Woo, H. (2007). The socioeconomic attainments of second-generation Cambodian, Hmong, Laotian, and Vietnamese Americans. *Sociological Inquiry, 77*(1), 44–75.

Sakamoto, I., & Pitner, R. O. (2005). Use of critical consciousness in anti-oppressive social work practice: Disentangling power dynamics at personal and structural levels. *British Journal of Social Work, 35*(4), 435–452.

Saleebey, D. (Ed.). (2002). *The strengths perspective in social work practice* (3rd ed.). Boston: Allyn and Bacon.

Saltman, K. J. (2007). *Capitalizing on disaster: Taking and breaking public schools*. Herndon, VA: Paradigm.

Sam, D. L., & Berry, J. W. (2010). Acculturation when individuals and groups of different cultural backgrounds meet. *Perspectives on Psychological Science, 5*, 472–481.

Sameroff, A. (2010). A unified theory of development: A dialectic integration of nature and nurture. *Child Development, 81*, 6–22.

Sandstrom, K. L., Martin, D. D., & Fine, G. A. (2001). Symbolic interactionism at the end of the century. In G. Ritzer & B. Smart (Eds.), *Handbook of social theory* (pp. 217–231). London: Sage.

Sano, Y., & Richards, L. N. (2011). Physical health, food security, and economic well-being: The rural perspective. In J. W. Bauer & E. M. Dolan (Eds.), *Rural families and work: Context and problems* (pp. 77–98). New York: Springer.

Sarbin, T. R. (1986). The narrative as a root metaphor for psychology. In T. R. Sarbin (Ed.), *Narrative psychology: The storied nature of human conduct* (pp. 3–21). New York: Praeger.

Saucedo, L. M., & Morales, M. C. (2010). Masculinities narratives and Latino immigrant workers: A case study of the Las Vegas residential construction trades. *Harvard Journal of Law & Gender, 33*, 625–659.

Savin-Williams, R. C. (2005). *The new gay teenager*. Cambridge, MA: Harvard University Press.

Savin-Williams, R. C., & Ream, G. L. (2003). Suicide attempts among sexual-minority male youth. *Journal of Clinical Child & Adolescent Psychology, 32*(4), 509–522.

Sawrikar, P. (2012). A qualitative study on the pros and cons of ethnically matching culturally and linguistically diverse (CALD) client families and child protection caseworkers. *Children and Youth Services Review, 35*, 321–331.

Schiele, J. H. (1997). The contour and meaning of Afrocentric social work. *Journal of Black Studies, 27*(6), 800–826.

Schiele, J. H. (2007). Implications of the equality-of-oppressions paradigm for curriculum content on people of color. *Journal of Social Work Education, 43*, 83–100.

Schnittker, J. (2004). Education and the changing shape of the income gradient in health. *Journal of Health and Social Behavior, 45*, 286–305.

Schoen, C., Doty, M. M., Robertson, R. H., & Collins, S. R. (2011). Affordable Care Act reforms could reduce the number of underinsured US adults by 70 percent. *Health Affairs, 30*, 1762–1771.

Schwalbe, M., Godwin, S., Holden, D., Schrock, D., Thompson, S., & Wolkomir, M. (2000). Generic processes in the reproduction of inequality: An interactionist analysis. *Social Forces, 79*(2), 419–453.

Schwartz, S. J., Pantin, H., Coatsworth, D., & Szapocznik, J. (2007). Addressing the challenges and opportunities for today's youth: Toward an integrative model and its implications for research and intervention. *Journal of Primary Prevention, 28*(2), 117–144.

Sears, J. T. (2005). *Gay, lesbian and transgender issues in education: Programs, policies, and practice*. Binghamton, NY: Harrington Park Press.

Seed, P. (2011). Three treaty nations compared: Economic and political Consequences for indigenous peoples in Canada, the United States, and New Zealand. In P. W. DePasquale (Eds.) *Natives and settlers, now and then: Historical issues and current perspectives on treaties and land claims in Canada* (pp. 17–32). Edmonton, ALB: University of Alberta Press.

Seeman, T. E., Crimmins, E., Huang, M. H., Singer, B., Bucur, A., Gruenewald, T., . . . , & Reuben, D. B. (2004). Cumulative biological risk and socio-economic differences in mortality: MacArthur studies of successful aging. *Social Science & Medicine, 58*, 1985–1997.

Segerstrom, S. C., & Miller, G. E. (2004). Psychological stress and the human immune system: A meta-analytic study of 30 years of inquiry. *Psychological Bulletin*, 130, 601–630.

Seipel, M. M. O. (2003). Global poverty: No longer an untouchable problem. *International Social Work, 46*, 191–207.

Shapiro, D. N., Rios, D., & Stewart, A. J. (2010). Conceptualizing lesbian sexual identity development: Narrative accounts of socializing structures and individual decisions and actions. *Feminism & Psychology, 20*, 491–510.

Sharlin, S. A., & Moin, V. (2001). New immigrant's perceptions of family life in origin and host cultures: In-group and out-group favoritism effect. *Journal of Comparative Family Studies, 32*(3), 405–420.

Shaw, I., & Shaw, A. (1997). Keeping social work honest: Evaluating as profession and practice. *British Journal of Social Work, 27*(6), 847–869.

Shaw, L. A., & Wainryb, C. (1999). The outsider's perspective: Young adults' judgments of social practices of other cultures. *British Journal of Developmental Psychology, 17*, 451–471.

Shek, D. T. L. (1998). The Chinese version of the self-report family inventory: Does culture make a difference? *Research on Social Work Practice, 8*(3), 315–329.

Sherman, A., Greenstein, R., & Ruffing, K. (2012). *Contrary to 'entitlement society' rhetoric, over nine-tenths of entitlement benefits go to elderly, disabled, or working households.* Washington, DC: Center on Budget and Policy Priorities.

Sherr, M. E. (2006). The Afrocentric paradigm: A programmatic discourse about social work practice with African Americans. *Journal of Human Behavior in the Social Environment, 13*(3), 1–17.

Shippee, T. P., Rinaldo, L., & Ferraro, K. F. (2012). Mortality risk among black and white working women: The role of perceived work trajectories. *Journal of Aging and Health, 24*, 141–167.

Shively, C. A., & Clarkson, T. B. (1994). Social status and coronary artery atherosclerosis in female monkeys. *Arteriosclerosis, Thrombosis, and Vascular Biology, 14*, 721–726.

Shonkoff, J. P., Boyce, W. T., & McEwen, B. S. (2009). Neuroscience, molecular biology, and the childhood roots of health disparities: Building a new framework for health promotion and disease prevention. *Journal of the American Medical Association, 301*, 2252–2259.

Shrake, E. K., & Rhee, S. (2004). Ethnic identity as a predictor of problem behaviors among Korean American adolescents. *Adolescence, 39*, 601–622.

Siddiqi, A., Zuberi, D., & Nguyen, Q. C. (2009). The role of health insurance in explaining immigrant versus non-immigrant disparities in access to health care: Comparing the United States to Canada. *Social Science & Medicine, 69*, 1452–1459.

Sikkink, D., & Emerson, M. O. (2008). School choice and racial segregation in US schools: The role of parents' education. *Ethnic and Racial Studies, 31*, 267–293.

Silliman, J. (2011). "Progressive masculinities": Oxymoron or achievable? In D. Jain & D. Elson (Eds.). *Harvesting feminist knowledge for public policy* (pp. 307–330). Thousand Oaks, CA: Sage.

Simons, L. G., Chen, Y., Simons, R. L., Brody, G., & Cutrona, C. (2006). Parenting practices and child adjustment in different types of households: A study of African American families. *Journal of Family Issues, 27*(6), 803–825.

Sizer, T., & Wood, G. (2008). Charter schools and the values of public education. In L. Dingerson, B. Miner, B. Peterson, & S. Walters (Eds.), *Keeping the promise? The debate over charter schools* (pp. 3–16). Milwaukee, WI: A Rethinking Schools Publication.

Skrbis, Z., Kendall, G., & Woodward, I. (2004). Locating cosmopolitanism: Between humanist ideal and grounded social category. *Theory, Culture & Society, 21*(6), 115–136.

Slattery, J. (2004). *Counseling diverse clients: Bringing context into therapy.* Pacific Grove, CA: Thomson Brooks/Cole.

Slevin, P. (2010, July 26). Deportation of illegal immigrants increases under Obama administration. *Washington Post.* Retrieved from http://www.washingtonpost.com/wp-dyn/content/article/2010/07/25/AR2010072501790_3.html?sid = ST2010082704452

Slothuus, R. (2007). Framing deservingness to win support for welfare state retrenchment. *Scandinavian Political Studies, 30*(3), 323–344.

Smedley, A., & Smedley, B. D. (2005). Race as biology is fiction, racism as a social problem is real. *American Psychologist, 60*(1), 16–26.

Smith, A. (2000). *The wealth of nations.* New York: Random House. (Original work published 1776)

Smith, D. E. (1988). *The everyday world as problematic: A feminist sociology.* Toronto, ON: University of Toronto Press.

Smith, J. R., Terry, D. J., & Hogg, M. A. (2006). Who will see me? The impact of type of audience on willingness to display group-mediated attitude–intention consistency. *Journal of Applied Social Psychology, 36*, 1173–1197.

Smith, T. W. (2011). *Public attitudes toward homosexuality.* Retrieved from http://www.norc.org/PDFs/2011%20GSS%20Reports/GSS_Public%20Attitudes%20Toward%20Homosexuality_Sept2011.pdf

Smokowski, P. R., & Bacallao, M. L. (2007). Acculturation, internalizing mental health symptoms, and self-esteem: Cultural experiences of Latino adolescents in North Carolina. *Child Psychiatry and Human Development, 37*, 273–292.

Sokoloff, N. J., & Dupont, I. (2005). Domestic violence at the intersections of race, class, and gender. *Violence against Women, 11*(1), 38–64.

Soltero, C. R. (2006). *Latinos and American law: Landmark Supreme Court cases.* Austin: University of Texas Press.

Somerville, M. (2006). Postmodern emergence. *International Journal of Qualitative Studies in Education, 20*(2), 225–243.

Sowards, S. K., & Pineda, R. D. (2013). Immigrant narratives and popular culture in the United States: Border spectacle, unmotivated sympathies, and individualized responsibilities. *Western Journal of Communication, 77*, 72–91.

Speer, P. W., & Christens, B. D. (2012). Local community organizing and change: Altering policy in the housing and community development system in Kansas City. *Journal of Community & Applied Social Psychology, 22*, 414–427.

Stannard, D. E. (1993). *The American holocaust: The conquest of the New World.* New York: Oxford University Press.

Staum, M. (2003). *Labeling people: French scholars on society, race, and empire, 1815–1848.* Montreal, Canada: McGill-Queen's University Press.

Steinberg, S. (1981). *The ethnic myth: Race, ethnicity, and class in America*. Boston: Beacon Press.

Steinbugler, A. C., Press, J. E., & Johnson Dias, J. (2006). Gender, race, and affirmative action: Operationalizing intersectionality in survey research. *Gender & Society, 20*(6), 805–825.

Steptoe, A., & Marmot, M. (2002). The role of psychobiological pathways in socio-economic inequalities in cardiovascular disease risk. *Europe Heart Journal*, 23, 13–25

Stets, J. E. (2005). Examining emotions in identity theory. *Social Psychology Quarterly, 68*, 39–56.

Stets, J. E. (2006). Identity theory. In P. J. Burke (Ed.), *Contemporary social psychological theories* (pp. 88–110). Stanford, CA: Stanford University Press.

Stets, J. E., & Burke, P. J. (2000). Identity theory and social identity theory. *Social Psychology Quarterly, 67*, 224–237.

Stewart, A. (2005). Choosing care: Dilemmas of a social market. *Journal of Social Welfare and Family Law, 27*(3), 299–314.

Stewart, A. L., Dean, M. L., & Gregorich, S. E. (2007). Race/ethnicity, socioeconomic status and the health of pregnant women. *Journal of Health Psychology, 12*, 285–300.

Stiffman, A. R., Freedenthal, S., Dore, P., Ostmann, E., Osborne, V., & Silmere, H. (2006). The role of providers in mental health services offered to American-Indian youths. *Psychiatric Services, 57*, 1185–1191.

Stotzer, R. L. (2009). Violence against transgender people: A review of United States data. *Aggression and Violent Behavior, 14*, 170–179.

Straus, M. A. (2004). Cross-cultural reliability and validity of the Revised Conflict Tactics Scales: A study of university student dating couples in 17 nations. *Cross-Cultural Research, 38*, 407–432.

Strogatz, D. S., Croft, J. B., James, S. A., Keenan, N. L., Browning, S. R., Garrett, J. M., & Curtis, A. B. (1997). Social support, stress, and blood pressure in black adults. *Epidemiology, 8*, 482–487.

Struthers, R., Eschiti, V. S., & Patchell, B. (2008). The experience of being an Anishinabe man healer: Ancient healing in a modern world. *Journal of Cultural Diversity, 15*, 70–75.

Stryker, S., & Burke, P. J. (2000). The past, present, and future of an identity theory. *Social Psychology Quarterly, 63*, 284–297.

Stryker, S., & Whittle, S. (2006). *The transgender studies reader*. New York: Routledge.

Substance Abuse and Mental Health Services Administration, Center for Behavioral Health Statistics and Quality. (2011, December 1). The TEDS Report: Injection Drug Abuse Rockville, MD: Admissions to Substance Abuse Treatment.

Sue, S. (1998). In search of cultural competence in psychotherapy and counseling. *American Psychologist, 53*, 440–448.

Sue, S. (2006). Cultural competency: From philosophy to research and practice. *Journal of Community Psychology, 34*, 237–245.

Sundquist, E. (2005). *Strangers in the land: Blacks, Jews, post-Holocaust America*. Cambridge, MA: Harvard University Press.

Supple, A. J., Su, J., Plunkett, S. W., Peterson, G. W., & Bush, K. R. (2013). Factor structure of the Rosenberg Self-Esteem Scale. *Journal of Cross-Cultural Psychology, 44*, 748–764.

Suter, E. A., & Toller, P. W. (2006). Gender role and feminism revisited: A follow-up study. *Sex Roles, 55*, 135–146.

Sweeney, F. (2006). The black Atlantic American studies and the politics of the postcolonial. *Comparative American Studies, 4*(2), 115–133.

Swim, J. K., Aikin, K. J., Hall, W. S., & Hunter, B. A. (1995). Sexism and racism: Old-fashioned and modern prejudices. *Journal of Personality and Social Psychology, 68*(2), 199–214.

Swim, J. K., Hyers, L. L., Cohen, L. L., & Ferguson, M. J. (2001). Everyday sexism: Evidence for its incidence, nature, and psychological impact from three daily diary studies. *Journal of Social Issues, 57*, 31–53.

Symington, A. (2004). Intersectionality: A tool for gender and economic justice. *Women's Rights and Economic Change, 9*, 1–8.

Szapocznik, J., & Coatsworth, J. D. (1999). An ecodevelopmental frame-work for organizing the influences on drug abuse: A developmental model of risk and protection. In M. D. Glantz & C. R. Hartel (Eds.), *Drug abuse: Origins and interventions* (pp. 331–366). Washington, DC: American Psychological Association.

Szasz, T. S. (1970). *The manufacture of madness: A comparative study of the Inquisition and the mental health movement.* New York: Harper and Row.

Taddei-Bringas, G. A., Santillana-Macedo, M. A., Romero-Cancio, J. A., & Romero-Tellez, M. B. (1999). Aceptación y uso de herbolería en medicina familiar. *Salud Publica Mexicana, 41*, 216–220.

Tafur, M. M., Crowe, T. K., & Torres, E. (2009). A review of curanderismo and healing practices among Mexicans and Mexican Americans. *Occupational Therapy International, 16*, 82–88.

Tajfel, H., & Turner, J. C. (2004) The social identity theory of intergroup behavior. In J. T. Jost & J. Sidanius (Eds.), *Political psychology: Key readings* (pp. 276–293). New York: Psychology Press.

Takaki, R. (1993). *A different mirror.* Boston: Little, Brown.

Takaki, R. (1998). *Strangers from a different shore.* Boston: Back Bay Books.

Tartakovsky, E. (2012). Factors affecting immigrants' acculturation intentions: A theoretical model and its assessment among adolescent immigrants from Russia and Ukraine in Israel. *International Journal of Intercultural Relations, 36*, 83–99.

Tashakkori, A., & Teddlie, C. (Eds.). (2003). *Handbook of mixed methods in social and behavioral research.* Thousand Oaks, CA: Sage.

Taylor, P. S. (1972). *An American-Mexican frontier.* Chapel Hill: University of North Carolina Press.

Taylor, S. E., Lerner, J. S., Sage, R. M., Lehman, B. J., & Seeman, T. E. (2004). Early environment, emotions, responses to stress, and health. *Journal of Personality, 72*, 1365–1394.

Taylor-Brown, S., Garcia, A., & Kingson, E. (2001). Cultural competence versus cultural chauvinism: Implications for social work. *Health and Social Work, 26*(3), 185–188.

Tazi, N. (2007). Is it possible to be both a cosmopolitan and a Muslim? In S. Ossman (Ed.), *The places we share* (pp. 65–76). Lanham, MD: Lexington Books.

Telles, E. E., & Murguia, E. (1990). Phenotypic discrimination and income differences among Mexican Americans. *Social Science Quarterly, 73*(1), 114–119.

Theurl, E., & Winner, H. (2011). The male–female gap in physician earnings: Evidence from a public health insurance system. *Health Economics, 20*, 1184–1200.

Thoits, P. A. (1983). Multiple identities and psychological well-being: A reformulation and test of the social isolation hypothesis. *American Sociological Review, 48*, 174–187.

Thomas, J., Thomas, D. J., Pearson, T., Klag, M., & Mead, L. (1997). Cardiovascular disease in African American and white physicians: the Meharry cohort and Meharry-Hopkins cohort studies. *Journal of Health Care for the Poor and Underserved, 8*, 270–283.

Thomas, N. M. (2005). On headscarves and heterogeneity: Reflections on the French Foulard affair. *Dialectical Anthropology, 29*(3/4), 373–386.

Thomas, V. L., & Gostin, L. O. (2009). The Americans with Disabilities Act. *Journal of the American Medical Association, 301*, 95–97.

Thomason, T. C. (2000). Issues in the treatment of Native Americans with alcohol problems. *Journal of Multicultural Counseling and Development, 78*, 243–252.

Thompson, M., & Sekaquaptewa, D. (2002). When being different is detrimental: Solo status and the performance of women and racial minorities. *Analyses of Social Issues and Public Policy, 2*, 183–203.

Thompson, N. (2006). *Anti-discriminatory practice.* Basingstoke, UK: Palgrave Macmillan.

Thomson, R. G. (1996). *Freakery: Cultural spectacles of the extraordinary body.* New York: New York University Press.

Thorton, R. (2000). Population history of Native North Americans. In M. R. Haines & R. H. Steckel (Eds.), *A population history of North America* (pp. 9–59). London: Cambridge University Press.

Thrupkaew, N. (2002). The myth of the model minority. *American Prospect, 13*(7), 38–44.

Tjaden, P., & Thoennes, N. (2000). Full report of the prevalence, incidence, and consequences of violence against women. Retrieved from https://www.ncjrs.gov/pdffiles1/nij/183781.pdf

Tomaskovic-Devey, D., & Skaggs, S. (2002). Sex segregation, labour process organisation, and gender earnings inequality. *American Journal of Sociology 108*, 102–128.

Tonigan, J. S. (2003). Project match treatment participation and outcome by self-reported ethnicity. *Alcoholism: Clinical and Experimental Research, 27*, 1340–1344.

Torres Stone, R. A., & Meyler, D. (2007). Identifying potential risk and protective factors among non-metropolitan Latino youth: Cultural implications for substance use research. *Journal of Immigrant and Minority Health, 9*(2), 95–107.

Torres-Saillant, S. (2006). Political roots of Chicano discourse. *Latino Studies, 4*(4), 452–464.

Tran, C. G., & Des Jardins, K. (2000). Domestic violence in Vietnamese refugee and Korean immigrant communities. In J. L. Chin (Ed.), *Relationships among Asian American women* (pp. 71–96). Washington, DC: American Psychological Association.

Truett, S. (2006). *Fugitive landscapes: The forgotten history of the U.S.-Mexico borderlands.* New Haven, CT: Yale University Press.

Tsai, J. L., Chentsova-Dutton, Y., Freire-Bebeau, L., & Przymus, D. E. (2002). Emotional expression and physiology in European Americans and Hmong Americans. *Emotion, 2*, 380–397.

Tsang, A. K. T. (2001). Representation of ethnic identity in North American social work literature: A dossier of the Chinese people. *Social Work, 46*(3), 229–254.

Tse, L. (1999). Finding a place to be: Ethnic identity exploration of Asian Americans. *Adolescence, 34*(133), 121–130.

Turquet, L., Seck, P., & Azcona, G. (2011). *Progress of the world's women 2011–2012: In pursuit of justice.* New York: UN Women.

U. S. Census Bureau. (2006). *Nation's population one-third minority.* Washington, DC: U. S. Department of Commerce.

U. S. Census Bureau. (2010). *American FactFinder fact sheet: Households and families.* Retrieved from http://factfinder2.census.gov/faces/tableservices/jsf/pages/productview.xhtml?pid=ACS_11_5YR_S1101&prodType=table

U. S. Census Bureau. (2013). Median earnings in the past 12 months (in 2010 inflation-adjusted dollars) by sex by educational attainment for the population 25 years and over. Retrieved from http://factfinder2.census.gov/faces/tableservices/jsf/pages/productview.xhtml?pid=ACS_10_1YR_B20004&prodType=table

U.S. Census Bureau. (2011). Same-sex couple households. American Community Survey Briefs, ACSBR/10–03. U.S. Department of Commerce, Washington, DC.

U.S. Criminal Code. (2012). Retrieved from http://uscode.house.gov/download/download.shtml

U.S. Department of Health and Human Services (DHHS). (2001). *Mental health: Culture, race, ethnicity–a supplement to mental health: Report of the surgeon general.* Rockville, MD: U. S. Dept. of Health and Human Services, Substance Abuse and Mental Health Services Administration, Center for Mental Health Services.

U.S. Department of Health and Human Services (DHHS). (2004). *2004 National Healthcare Disparities Report.* Rockville, MD: Agency for Healthcare Research and Quality.

U.S. Department of Justice. (2013). Justice Department settles sex discrimination lawsuit against the town of Griffith, Indiana. Retrieved from http://www.justice.gov/opa/pr/2013/June/13-crt-665.html

Uchino, B. N. (2006). Social support and health: A review of physiological processes potentially underlying links to disease outcomes. *Journal of Behavioral Medicine, 29*, 377–387.

Uchino, B. N., Cacioppo, J. T., & Kiecolt-Glaser, J. K. (1996). The relationship between social support and physiological processes: A review with emphasis on underlying mechanisms and implications for health. *Psychological Bulletin, 119*, 488–531.

Umaña-Taylor, A. J., & Guimond, A. (2010). A longitudinal examination of parenting behaviors and perceived discrimination predicting Latino adolescents' ethnic identity. *Developmental Psychology, 46*, 636–650. doi:10.1037/a0019376

Umaña-Taylor, A. J., & Updegraff, K. (2007). Latino adolescents' mental health: Exploring the role of discrimination, ethnic identity, acculturation, and self-esteem. *Journal of Adolescence, 30*, 549–567. doi:10.1016/j.adolescence.2006.08.002

Ungar, M., & Liebenberg, L. (2011). Assessing resilience across cultures using mixed methods: Construction of the child and youth resilience measure. *Journal of Mixed Methods Research, 5*, 126–149.

United Nations. (1951). *Convention on the prevention and punishment of the crime of genocide.* Geneva: Author.

University of Michigan Health System Interpreter Services. (2007). *Provider guidelines: Tips for working with an interpreter.* Retrieved from http://www.med.umich.edu/interpreter/

Unrau, Y. A., Gabor, P. A., & Grinnell, R. M. (2007). *Evaluation in social work: The art and science of practice.* New York: Oxford University Press.

Utsey, S. O., Brown, C., & Bolden, M. A. (2004). Testing the structural invariance of the Africultural Coping Systems Inventory across three samples of African descent populations. *Educational and Psychological Measurement, 64*, 185–195.

Valencia, R. R. (2005). The Mexican American struggle for equal educational opportunities in *Mendez v. Westminster*: Helping to pave the way for *Brown v. Board of Education. Teachers College Record, 107*(3), 389–423.

Van Ecke, Y. (2005). Immigration from an attachment perspective. *Social Behavior and Personality, 33*(5), 467–476.

Van Herk, K. A., Smith, D., & Andrew, C. (2011). Examining our privileges and oppressions: incorporating an intersectionality paradigm into nursing. *Nursing Inquiry, 18,* 29–39.

Van Oudenhoven, J. P., Judd, C., & Ward, C. (2008). Social psychology and immigration: Relations between immigrants and host societies. In L. Steg, B. Buunk, & T. Rothengatter (Eds.). *Applied social psychology: Understanding and managing social problems* (pp. 141–161). Cambridge, UK: Cambridge University Press.

Van Wormer, K. (1984). Becoming homosexual in prison: A socialization process. *Criminal Justice Review, 9,* 22–27.

VanGeest, J. B., & Welch, V. L. (2008). Evaluating "Not in Mama's kitchen": Second-hand smoke campaign in Georgia. *Journal of Health Disparities Research and Practice, 2,* 73–87.

Vega, W. A., Rodrigues, M. A., Gruskin, E. (2009). Health disparities in the Latino population. *Epidemiology Review., 31,* 99–112.

Verloo, M. (2006). Multiple inequalities, intersectionality and the European Union. *European Journal of Women's Studies, 13*(3), 211–228.

Vertovec, S., & Cohen, R. (Eds.). (2002). *Conceiving cosmopolitanism: Theory, context and practice*. London: Oxford University Press.

Victoroff, M. S. (2006). When should bad behavior become a covered disease? *Managed Care, 15*(3), 24–26.

Vidales, G. T. (2010). Arrested justice: The multifaceted plight of immigrant Latinas who faced domestic violence. *Journal of Family Violence, 25,* 533–544.

Virtanen, M., Kivimäki, M., Joensuu, M., Virtanen, P., Elovainio, M., & Vahtera, J. (2005). Temporary employment and health: A review. *International Journal of Epidemiology, 34,* 610–622.

Vodde, R., & Gallant, J. P. (2002). Bridging the gap between micro and macro practice: Large scale change and a unified model of narrative-deconstructive practice. *Journal of Social Work Education, 38*(3), 439–459.

Voss, R. W., Douville, V., Soldier, A. L., & Twiss, G. (1999). Tribal and shamanic-based social work practice: A Lakota perspective. *Social Work, 44*(3), 228–241.

Votruba-Drzal, E. (2003). Income changes and cognitive stimulation in young children's home learning environments. *Journal of Marriage and Family, 65,* 341–355.

Vygotsky, L. (1979). *Mind in society: The development of higher psychological processes.* Cambridge, MA: Harvard University Press.

Wagner, F., Diaz, D. B., Lopez, A. L., Collado, M. E., & Aldaz, E. (2002). Social cohesion, cultural identity, and drug use in Mexican rural communities. *Substance Use and Misuse, 37*(5–7), 715–747.

Wainright, J. L., & Patterson, C. J. (2006). Delinquency, victimization, and substance use among adolescents with female same-sex parents. *Journal of Family Psychology, 20,* 526–530.

Wainright, J. L., & Patterson, C. J. (2008). Peer relations among adolescents with female same-sex parents. *Developmental Psychology, 44,* 117–126. doi:10.1037/0012-1649.44.1.117

Wainright, J. L., Russell, S. T., & Patterson, C. J. (2004). Psychosocial adjustment and school outcomes of adolescents with same-sex parents. *Child Development, 75,* 1886–1898.

Wald, K. D., & Calhoun-Brown, A. (2006). *Religion and politics in the United States* (5th ed.). Lanham, MD: Rowman & Littlefield.

Walker, R. E., Keane, C. R., & Burke, J. G. (2010). Disparities and access to healthy food in the United States: A review of food deserts literature. *Health & Place, 16*, 876–884.

Walker, S. (2001). Tracing the contours of postmodern social work. *British Journal of Social Work, 31*(1), 29–39.

Wall, S. M., Timberlake, E. M., Farber, M. Z., Sabatino, C. A., Liebow, H., Smith, N. M., & Taylor, N. E. (2000). Needs and aspirations of the working poor: Early Head Start program applicants. *Families in Society: Journal of Contemporary Human Services, 81*(4), 412–422.

Wallerstein, I. (1974). *The modern world system.* New York: Academic Press.

Wang, S., & Kim, B. S. (2010). Therapist multicultural competence, Asian American participants' cultural values, and counseling process. *Journal of counseling psychology, 57*, 394–401.

Warburton, D. E., Nicol, C. W., & Bredin, S. S. (2006). Health benefits of physical activity: The evidence. *Canadian Medical Association Journal, 174*, 801–809.

Ward, E. G. (2005). Homophobia, hypermasculinity and the US black church. *Culture, Health & Sexuality, 7*(5), 493–504.

Warfa, N., Curtis, S., Watters, C., Carswell, K., Ingleby, D., & Bhui, K. (2012). Migration experiences, employment status and psychological distress among Somali immigrants: A mixed-method international study. *BMC* [BioMed Central] *Public Health, 12*, 749–761.

Warren, P. Y. (2011). Perceptions of police disrespect during vehicle stops: A race-based analysis. *Crime & Delinquency, 57*, 356–376.

Wasserman, B. D., & Weseley, A. J. (2009). ¿Qué? Quoi? Do languages with grammatical gender promote sexist attitudes? *Sex Roles, 61*, 634–643.

Waters, M. (1994). Ethnic and racial identities of second generation black immigrants in New York City. *International Migration Review, 28*(4), 795–826.

Watkins-Hayes, C., Pittman-Gay, L., & Beaman, J. (2012). "Dying from" to "living with": Framing institutions and the coping processes of African American women living with HIV/ AIDS. *Social Science & Medicine, 74*, 2028–2036.

Watson, R. L. (2006). Abolition, violence and rape: Thoughts on the post-emancipation experiences of the United Sates and the Cape colony. *Safundi, 7*(2), 1–14.

Weaver, H. (1999). Indigenous people and the social work profession: Defining culturally competent services. *Social Work, 4*(3), 217–225.

Weaver, H. N. (2000). Culture and professional education: The experiences of Native American social workers. *Journal of Social Work Education, 36*, 415–428.

Weber, D. (1973). *Foreigners in their native land.* Albuquerque: University of New Mexico.

Weber, M. (1968). *Economy and society: An outline of interpretive sociology.* New York: Bedminster Press. (Original work published 1928)

Welch, D., Welch, L., & Piekkari, R. (2005). Speaking in tongues: The importance of language in international management processes. *International Studies of Management and Organization, 35*(1), 10–27.

Wells, R., Feinberg, M., Alexander, J. A., & Ward, A. J. (2009). Factors affecting member perceptions of coalition impact. *Nonprofit Management and Leadership, 19*, 327–348.

Wen, M., Cagney, K. A., & Christakis, N. A. (2005). Effect of specific aspects of community social environment on the mortality of individuals diagnosed with serious illness. *Social Science & Medicine, 61*, 1119–1134.

Werbner, P. (2005). The translocation of culture: "Community cohesion" and the force of multiculturalism in history. *Sociological Review, 53*(4), 754–768.

Werner, E. E. (2005). Resilience research: Past, present, and future. In R. D. V. Peters, B. Leadbeater, & R. J. McMahon (Eds.), *Resilience in children, families, and communities* (pp. 3–11). New York: Plenum.

West, C., & Zimmerman, D. H. (1983). Small insults: A study of interruptions in cross-sex conversations between unacquainted persons. In B. Thorne, C. Kramarae, & N. Henley (Eds.), *Language, gender, and society* (pp. 103–117). Rowley, MA: Newbury.

Whitaker, T., Weismiller, T., & Clark, E. (2006). *Assuring the sufficiency of a frontline workforce: A national study of licensed social workers. Executive summary.* Washington, DC: National Association of Social Workers.

Whitam, F., Diamond, M., & Martin, J. (1993). Homosexual orientation in twins: A report on sixty-one pairs and three triplet sets. *Archives of Sexual Behavior, 22,* 187–206.

White, A. M. (2006). "You've got a friend": African American men's cross-sex feminist friendships and their influence on perceptions of masculinity and women. *Journal of Social and Personal Relationships, 23*(4), 523–542.

White, W. L. (2009). The mobilization of community resources to support long-term addiction recovery. *Journal of Substance Abuse Treatment, 36,* 146–158.

Whitehead, M., & Dahlgren, G. (2006). *Concepts and principles for tackling social inequities in health: Levelling up Part 1.* World Health Organization: Studies on social and economic determinants of population health. World Health Organization, Copenhagen, Denmark.

Whitehead, M., Dahlgren, G., & Evans, T. (2001). Equity and health sector reforms: can low-income countries escape the medical poverty trap? *The Lancet, 358,* 833–836.

Whitley, B. E., & Kite, M. E. (2006). *The psychology of prejudice and discrimination.* Belmont, CA: Thomson & Wadsworth.

Wiggan, G. (2007). Race, school achievement, and educational inequality: Toward a student-based inquiry perspective. *Review of Educational Research, 77*(93), 310–333.

Wijesinghe, S., & Mendelson, C. (2012). The health behavior of Sri Lankan Buddhist nuns with Type 2 diabetes: Duty, devotion, and detachment. *Journal of Religion and Health,* doi:10.1007/s10943-012-9592-y

Wilchins, R. (2004). *Queer theory, gender theory.* Los Angeles: Alyson Books.

Wilcox, M. M. (2014). "Lgbttsqqiaa . . ." *Contexts, 13,* 12–14. doi:10.1177/1536504214522003

Wilkinson, R. G. (1992). National mortality rates: The impact of inequality? *American Journal of Public Health, 82,* 1082–1084.

Wilkinson, R. G. (2006). The impact of inequality. *Social Research: An International Quarterly, 73,* 711–732.

Wilkinson, R. G., & Marmot, M. G. (2003). *Social determinants of health: The solid facts.* Geneva: World Health Organization.

Wilkinson, R. G., & Pickett, K. E. (2006). Income inequality and population health: A review and explanation of the evidence. *Social Science & Medicine, 62,* 1768–1784.

Wilkinson, R. G., & Pickett, K. E. (2007). The problems of relative deprivation: Why some societies do better than others. *Social Science & Medicine, 65,* 1965–1978.

Wilkinson, R. G., & Pickett, K. E. (2009). Income inequality and social dysfunction. *Annual Review of Sociology, 35,* 493–511.

Williams, D. R., & Collins, C. (2001). Racial residential segregation: A fundamental cause of racial disparities in health. *Public Health Reports, 116,* 404–416.

Williams, D. R., & Jackson, P. B. (2005). Social sources of racial disparities in health. *Health Affairs, 24,* 325–334.

Williams, D. R., & Mohammed, S. A. (2008) Poverty, migration, and health. In A. C. Lin & D. R. Harris (Eds.), *The colors of poverty* (pp. 135–169). New York: Russell Sage Foundation.

Williams, D. R., & Mohammed, S. A. (2009). Discrimination and racial disparities in health: Evidence and needed research. *Journal of Behavioral Medicine, 32*, 20–47.

Williams, D. R., Mohammed, S. A., Leavell, J., & Collins, C. (2010). Race, socioeconomic status, and health: Complexities, ongoing challenges, and research opportunities. *Annals of the New York Academy of Sciences, 1186*, 69–101.

Williams, D. R., Neighbors, H. W., & Jackson, J. S. (2003). Racial/ethnic discrimination and health: Findings from community studies. *American Journal of Public Health, 93*, 200–208.

Williams, D. R., Sternthal, M., & Wright, R. J. (2009). Social determinants: Taking the social context of asthma seriously. *Pediatrics, 123*, S174–S184.

Williams, R. M., & Peterson, C. L. (1998). The color of memory: Interpreting twentieth-century U. S. social policy from a nineteenth-century perspective. *Feminist Studies, 24*, 7–25.

Wills, M. (2007). Connection, action, and hope: An invitation to reclaim the "spiritual" in health care. *Journal of Religion and Health, 46*(3), 423–436.

Winter, E. (2007). Neither "America" nor "Quebec": Constructing the Canadian multicultural nation. *Nations and Nationalism, 13*(3), 481–503.

Winters, K. (2005). Gender dissonance: Diagnostic reform of gender identity disorder for adults. *Journal of Psychology & Human Sexuality, 17*, 71–89.

Wiseman, H., Metzl, E., & Barber, J. P. (2006). Anger, guilt, and intergenerational communication of trauma in the interpersonal narratives of second generation Holocaust survivors. *American Journal of Orthopsychiatry, 76*, 176–184.

Wissler, C. (2005). *The American Indian: An introduction to the anthropology of the New World* (2nd ed.). London: Oxford University Press.

Wolsko, C., Lardon, C., Mohatt, G. V., & Orr, E. (2007). Stress coping and well-being among the Yup'ik of the Yukon-Kuskokwim delta: The role of enculturation and acculturation. *International Journal of Circumpolar Health, 66*(1), 51–61.

Wong, Y. J., Owen, J., Tran, K. K., Collins, D. L., & Higgins, C. E. (2012). Asian American male college students' perceptions of people's stereotypes about Asian American men. *Psychology of Men & Masculinity, 13*, 75–88.

Wood, J. (1994). *Gender lives: Communication, gender, and culture.* Belmont, CA: Wadsworth.

Woolf, S. H. (2008). The meaning of translational research and why it matters. *Journal of the American Medical Association, 299*, 211–213.

Woolf, S. H., Johnson, R. E., Fryer Jr., G. E., Rust, G., & Satcher, D. (2004). The health impact of resolving racial disparities: An analysis of US mortality data. *American Journal of Public Health, 94*, 2078–2081.

World Health Organization (WHO). (2010). *Hidden cities: Unmasking and overcoming health inequities in urban settings.* Geneva: Author.

World Health Organization (WHO). (2012). *World health statistics 2012.* Geneva: Author.

World Health Organization (WHO). (2013). *Life expectancy at birth: 2011.* Retrieved from http://gamapserver.who.int/gho/interactive_charts/mbd/life_expectancy/atlas.html

Wright, G. (2006). *Slavery and American economic development.* Baton Rouge: Louisiana State University Press.

Xu, K., Evans, D. B., Kawabata, K., Zeramdini, R., Klavus, J., & Murray, C. J. (2003). Household catastrophic health expenditure: A multicountry analysis. *The Lancet, 362*, 111–117.

Yan, M. C. (2008). Exploring cultural tensions in cross-cultural social work practice. *Social Work, 53*, 317–328.

Yan, M. C., & Wong, Y. L. R. (2005). Rethinking self-awareness in cultural competence: Toward a dialogic self in cross-cultural social work. *Families in Society: The Journal of Contemporary Social Services, 86*, 181–188.

Yen, I. H., & Syme, S. L. (1999). The social environment and health: A discussion of the epidemiologic literature. *Annual Review of Public Health, 20*, 287–308.

Ying, Y. (1988). Depressive symptomatology among Chinese-Americans as measured by the CES-D. *Journal of Clinical Psychology, 44*, 739–746.

Yoon, E., Hacker, J., Hewitt, A., Abrams, M., & Cleary, S. (2012). Social connectedness, discrimination, and social status as mediators of acculturation/enculturation and well-being. *Journal of Counseling Psychology, 59*, 86–96.

Yoon, Y., & Yi, H. (2012). *Liver cirrhosis mortality in the United States, 1970–2009* (Surveillance Report #93). Retrieved from http://pubs.niaaa.nih.gov/publications/Surveillance93/Cirr09.pdf

Yoshimasu, K., Kiyohara, C., & Miyashita, K. (2008). Suicidal risk factors and completed suicide: Meta-analyses based on psychological autopsy studies. *Environmental Health and Preventive Medicine, 13*, 243–256.

Young, J. M. (2010). *Equality of opportunity: The making of the Americans with Disabilities Act*. Washington, DC: National Council on Disability.

Yuan, Y. C., & Gay, G. (2006). Homophily of network ties and bonding and bridging social capital in computer-mediated distributed teams. *Journal of Computer-Mediated Communication, 11*, 1062–1084.

Zawadzki, M. J., Shields, S. A., Danube, C. L., & Swim, J. K. (2013). Reducing the endorsement of sexism using experiential learning: The workshop activity for gender equity simulation (WAGES). *Psychology of Women Quarterly, 38.1*, 74–92.

Zhou, M. (2004). Are Asian Americans becoming white? *Context, 3*(1), 29–37.

Zigler, E., Marsland, K. W., & Lord, H. (2009). *Tragedy of child care in America*. New Haven, CT: Yale University Press.

Zimbardo, P. G. (1971). *Politics of persuasion*. Unpublished manuscript, Stanford University, Stanford, CA.

Zimmer, R., & Bettinger, E. P. (2008). Beyond the rhetoric: Surveying the evidence on vouchers and tax credits. In H. F. Ladd & E. B. Fiske (Eds.), *Handbook of research in education finance and policy* (447–466). New York, NY: Routledge.

Zunzunegui, M. V., Alvarado, B. E., Del Ser, T., & Otero, A. (2003). Social networks, social integration, and social engagement determine cognitive decline in community-dwelling Spanish older adults. *The Journals of Gerontology Series B: Psychological Sciences and Social Sciences, 58*, S93–S100.

Index

About the Authors

FLAVIO FRANCISCO MARSIGLIA (PhD, Case Western Reserve University; MSW, Universidad de la República, Uruguay) is the Distinguished Foundation Professor of Cultural Diversity and Health in the School of Social Work at Arizona State University. He is the lead instructor of the Diversity and Oppression course sequence in the BSW and MSW programs, as well as the director and principal investigator of the Southwest Interdisciplinary Research Center, which is a Center of Excellence funded by the National Institute on Minority Health and Health Disparities (NIMHD) at the National Institutes of Health (NIH). He has conducted research on culturally grounded interventions in connection with a variety of topics such as substance abuse prevention, HIV/AIDS prevention, and culturally specific social and health services. He has published more than one hundred peer-reviewed articles, and has presented at numerous national and international research conferences. Professor Marsiglia has received many awards and recognitions, including the 2006 National Award of Excellence in Mentorship from the National Hispanic Science Network on Drug Abuse and the 2012 Community, Culture, and Prevention Science Award from the Society for Prevention Research. In 2012 he was inducted into the American Academy of Social Work and Social Welfare.

STEPHEN KULIS (PhD, MA, Columbia University) is professor of sociology in the T. Denny Sanford School of Social and Family Dynamics at Arizona State University and an affiliated faculty member in the School of Social Work, the Justice and Social Inquiry program, and the Women and Gender Studies program. He is the director of research at the Southwest Interdisciplinary Research Center, a Center of Excellence funded by the National Center on Minority Health and Health Disparities at the National Institutes of Health. His research has focused on cultural processes in health disparities, such as the role of gender and ethnic identity in youth drug use and prevention interventions, cultural adaptation of prevention programs for ethnic minority youths and their parents, contextual neighborhood and school-level influences on individual-level risk and protective behaviors, gender and racial inequities in professions, and the organizational sources of ethnic and gender discrimination. His articles have been published in such periodicals as *Prevention Science, Cultural Diversity and Ethnic Minority Psychology, Journal of Early Adolescence,* and *Substance Use and Misuse.*